RAJASTHAN
DEVELOPMENT REPORT

सत्यमेव जयते

PLANNING COMMISSION
GOVERNMENT OF INDIA

Rajasthan Development Report

सत्यमेव जयते

PLANNING COMMISSION
GOVERNMENT OF INDIA
NEW DELHI

Published by

ACADEMIC FOUNDATION
NEW DELHI

Photographs on the front cover:
Courtesy, State Government of Rajasthan

- The Bundi painting depicts a queen with her maidens. It is one of the many master pieces that adorn the walls of the Chitrashala at Taragarh Fort, Bundi.
- An oil well named Mangala I, discovered by Cairn Energy, was dedicated to Nation in February, 2004. The oil well, located 35 kms. from Barmer District is estimated to have 45 crore to 110 crore barrels of oil.
- The undulating sands of the desert against the setting sun provide a panoramic view of the camel and its human companion.

Photograph on the back cover:
Copyright © WHO / P. Virot

- The barren landscape motivates the people of the desert to acquire most colourful costumes and ornaments. The woman is dressed up in traditional attire and jewellery.

First Published in 2006 by
Academic Foundation
4772-73 / 23 Bharat Ram Road, (23 Ansari Road), Darya Ganj, New Delhi - 110 002 (India).
Phones : 23245001 / 02 / 03 / 04. Fax : +91-11-23245005. E-mail : academic@vsnl.com
www.academicfoundation.com

Published under arrangement with :
Planning Commission,
Government of India,
New Delhi.

Rajasthan Development Report
ISBN 81-7188-464-4

Designed and typeset by Italics India, New Delhi
Printed and bound in India.

Contents

...CONTD. ...

...CONTD. ...

The Core Group

1. **Dr. Syeda Hameed** — **Chairperson**
   Member, Planning Commission
   New Delhi

2. **Shri Siya Ram Meena** — **Member**
   Secretary, Planning, Government of Rajasthan

3. **Dr. Sudhir Varma** — **Member**
   Director, Social Policy Research Institute (SPRI), Jaipur

4. **Ms. Sushma Choudhary** — **Member-Secretary**
   Principal Adviser (SP–W), Planning Commission

Shri Sompal, former Member, Planning Commission served as chairman of the Core Group during 2002-04. Shri Pradeep Sen, former Secretary, Planning, Government of Rajasthan, Dr. C.S. Barla, former Director (Research), SPRI, Jaipur, Shri P.S.S Thomas and Shri Surendranath, former Advisers, Planning Commission served as members of the Core Group for various periods during 2002-04.

Preface and Acknowledgement

Rajasthan is projected as a drought-prone and backward state in India. More than 61 per cent of the state's total area is arid or semi-arid and experiences frequent spells of drought.

Yet, the state has recorded a steady growth in agriculture, industry, infrastructure and human resource development. It is claimed that five decades of planning in Rajasthan has brought a miraculous change in the potential of development across the state. This is evident from the fact that over the past one decade, notwithstanding a slow down at the national level, Rajasthan's net state domestic product (NSDP) has registered a positive growth rate.

In 2001, the Planning Commission decided to get a State Development Report (SDR) prepared showing an evaluation of the performance of State's economy through the past five decades. This task was assigned to Social Policy Research Institute (SPRI), Jaipur. A comprehensive TOR was prepared for this purpose and Draft SDR was submitted by SPRI to Planning Commission in March 2002. An attempt was made to analyse the development in various sectors of the state's economy and identify constraints to development for each sector. The Report was formally presented to Planning Commission in November 2003, incorporating the observations of Planning Commission advisers. In the meantime we also received detailed observations and comments from Ms. S. Choudhary, Principal Adviser, (State Plans-W), Planning Commission as also from the various departments of the Government of Rajasthan.

We were fortunate indeed to receive observations of Shri Sompal, Former Member Planning Commission on our report. He, inspite of his busy schedule read the entire report and sent his comments to us in February 2004. On March 4, 2004, he took the trouble of coming to Jaipur and discussing various sections of the Report with our experts. The present form of the SDR is a culmination of his written comments, and their elaboration at the meeting. We have endeavoured to incorporate most of the observations made so far by Shri Sompal, Ms. Choudhary, Department of Planning, GoR and others.

On behalf of the SPRI, I must express our deep sense of gratitude to Planning Commission for providing financial support for this assignment. Comments and cooperation received from Shri Sompal, Former Member, Planning Commission; Ms. S. Choudhary, Principal Adviser (SP-W), Planning Commission; Dr. N.J. Kurian, Former Adviser, Planning Commission; Shri N.D. George, Director (SP-W), Planning Commission; Shri Vijay Kumar, Former Director (SP-W); Planning Commission and Dr. M.V. Rao, PS to Shri Sompal and others are gratefully acknowledged.

Our efforts could not succeed without the support of Hon'ble Chairman of SPRI, Shri Shiv Charan Mathur. The Consultants who worked hard for preparing this report included eminent scholars such as, Prof. L.N. Nathuramka, Dr. M.K. Mathur, Shri C.B. Mathur, Shri P.N. Bhandari, Shri L.C. Gupta, Dr. Razia Pendse, Prof. H.S. Sharma, Shri G.P. Mathur, Prof. R.C. Swarnkar, and Ms. Kirti Vyas. They deserve our heart-felt gratitude. Last, but not the least, my colleagues in the research team, namely, Shri Manish Tiwari, Dr. Shuchi Mathur, Dr. Kusum Bhatt, Dr. Anju Pareek, Ms. Nandita Mathur, and Shri Vinod Kewalramani must be thanked for the active cooperation and support extended in completing this report.

(C.S. BARLA)
Director (Research)
Social Policy Research Institute

एम. एस. आहलुवालिया
MONTEK SINGH AHLUWALIA

उपाध्यक्ष
योजना आयोग
भारत
DEPUTY CHAIRMAN
PLANNING COMMISSION
INDIA

FOREWORD

One of the important Tenth Plan initiatives of the Planning Commission was to sponsor the preparation of State Development Reports with much of the work being done by reputed national level institutes. This exercise was undertaken in recognition of the fact that economic circumstances and performance in individual States varied considerably and it was necessary to examine development challenges for individual States in the light of State specific constraints and circumstances. The basic idea is to produce quality reference documents on development profile of individual States and the possible strategies for accelerating growth, and reducing poverty and inequality.

The Rajasthan State Development Report reviews Rajasthan's experience and highlights issues critical for the State's development in the years ahead. I hope its publication will stimulate debate on growth strategies appropriate for Rajasthan. I am sure the road map indicated in the Report will stimulate a broader awareness of the critical policy issues facing the State and will assist the State to move to a higher growth path and to achieve all round human and economic development.

Montek S Ahluwalia

(M.S. AHLUWALIA)

योजना भवन, संसद मार्ग, नई दिल्ली – 110001 दूरभाष : 23096677, 23096688 फैक्स : 23096699
Yojna Bhawan, Parliament Street, New Delhi : 110001 Phones: 23096677, 23096688 Fax : 23096699, E-mail : dch@yojana.nic.in

सत्यमेव जयते

VASUNDHARA RAJE

CHIEF MINISTER RAJASTHAN

MESSAGE

Rajasthan is the country's largest State. Centuries of social inequality and hyper-aridity have given Rajasthan the unenviable position of being known as a State poor in resources, education and development. It is thus a challenge to deliver to the people of the State a set of welfare services which are sustainable environmentally, viable economically, and equitable socially. Abject poverty, dependence on rain-fed bio-mass production and high levels of illiteracy are issues which need to be attended to on a priority basis. Being a predominantly rural, agrestic economy, the focus has to be village centric. At the same time, creation of economic infrastructure is also essential to further growth with equality and employment.

The State Development Report is an important document aimed to take stock of the State of affairs in each sector, identify critical gaps and suggest ways and means to plug them. It is expected that this document shall prove to be an important tool for Policy Planners and Development Managers.

(Vasundhara Raje)

डॉ. सईदा हमीद
Dr. Syeda Hameed

सत्यमेव जयते

सदस्य
योजना आयोग
योजना भवन
नई दिल्ली–110 001
MEMBER
PLANNING COMMISSION
YOJNA BHAWAN
NEW DELHI-110 001

INTRODUCTION

The Rajasthan State Development Report (SDR) is one of a series of such studies being sponsored by the Planning Commission in collaboration with various state governments and reputed research institutions. The main purpose of this initiative of the Planning Commission is to make available to all concerned, well-researched and credible documents which independently analyse state level development issues and identify critical areas which require the attention of the policymakers.

A core committee under the Chairmanship of Shri Sompal, former Member, Planning Commission worked out modalities for preparing the Rajasthan State Development Report and availed of the expertise of the Social Policy Research Institute (SPRI), Jaipur. The Government of Rajasthan also closely collaborated with the project.

The Rajasthan SDR is a well-researched document which analyses the entire gamut of development issues concerning the state, covering all the important sectors of the state's economy. The Report also contains a large amount of useful state and sub-state level data on various sectors and issues. I am sure the Report will be useful to planners, decision makers and all those who are concerned with the development of the state.

I would like to place on record Planning Commission's appreciation to all those who have worked hard in preparing the Report, especially the Chairman of the Social Policy Research Institute (SPRI), Jaipur, Shri Shiv Charan Mathur and other experts of his Institute. Our thanks are also due to the Government of Rajasthan for collaborating in the preparation of the Report.

(SYEDA HAMEED)

दूरभाष : 23096570 फैक्स : 23096571
Telephone: 23096570 Fax : 23096571, email: s.hameed@yojana.nic.in

SOMPAL
Former Member
Planning Commission

L-502 Ambience Island
NH-8 Gurgaon – 122 002
Haryana

MESSAGE

I am delighted to note that the State Development Report on Rajasthan has come out. I congratulate the Planning Commission and the Social Policy Research Institute, Jaipur on bringing out this excellent and comprehensive document.

During 2002-03 as Member, Planning Commission, I had the privilege of chairing the Core Group responsible for preparing the Report, and had occasion to go through the initial draft and make several suggestions, which have since been incorporated.

The Report contains valuable data and analyses on various developmental issues concerning the State of Rajasthan. I hope it will serve as useful reference material and stimulate informed debate on core policy issues. I also fervently hope that the State Government will give due consideration to the suggestions made in the Report for initiating necessary reforms and improving governance, which are unanimously considered essential for enhancing the pace of development and making it more participatory and equitable.

Sompal

(SOMPAL)

List of Tables, Figures and Boxes

Tables

Appendices

Figures

Boxes

Abbreviations

ACA	Additional Central Assistance
ADB	Asian Development Bank
ADT	Average Daily Traffic
ANM	Auxiliary Nurse Midwife
ARV	Annual Rental Value
ASI	Annual Survey of Industries
BCR	Balance from Current Revenues
BOLT	Build-Operate-Lease-Transfer
BOO	Build-Own-Operate
BOT	Build-Operate-Transfer
BPL	Below Poverty Line
BWSSB	Bangalore Water Supply and Sewerage Board
CAZRI	Central Arid Zone Research Institute
CDS	Centre for Development Studies
CECOEDECON	Centre for Community Economics and Development Consultant Society
CHC	Community Health Centre
CIDA	Canadian International Development Agency
CIGs	Common Interest Groups
CII	Confederation of Indian Industry
COPP	Committee on Plan Projects
CSS	Centrally Sponsored Schemes
CSWB	Central Social Welfare Board
DDP	Desert Development Programme
DLB	Directorate of Local Bodies
DPAP	Drought Prone Area Programme
DPIP	District Poverty Initiatives Project
DRDA	District Rural Development Agency
DWACRA	Development of Women and Children in Rural Areas
DWDSC	Department of Watershed Development and Soil Conservation
EAPs	Externally Assisted Projects
EAS	Employment Assurance Scheme
EPIPs	Export Promotion Industrial Parks
FFW	Food for Work Programme
FIRE	Financial Institution Reform and Expansion
GAIL	Gas Authority of India Ltd.
GEF	Global Environment Facility
GFCF	Gross Fixed Capital Formation
GSDP	Gross State Domestic Product
HUDCO	Housing and Urban Development Corporation
IADP	Intensive Agriculture District Programme
IAY	Indira Awas Yojana
ICAR	Indian Council of Agricultural Research
ICDS	Integrated Child Development Scheme
ICOR	Incremental Capital Output Ratio
IEM	Industrial Entrepreneur Memorandum
IGNP	Indira Gandhi Nahar Project

IIRM	Indian Institute of Rural Management
IMR	Infant Mortality Rate
IRDP	Integrated Rural Development Programme
IT	Information Technology
ITDC	India Tourism Development Corporation
ITIs	Industrial Training Institutes
JDA	Jaipur Development Authority
JGSY	Jawahar Gram Samridhi Yojana
JMC	Jaipur Municipal Corporation
JRY	Jawahar Rozgar Yojana
KVIB	Khadi and Village Industries Board
KVKs	Krishi Vigyan Kendras
kWh	Kilowatt Hour
LDWP	Local Development Works Programme
LoI	Letters of Intent
Mcm	Million Cubic Metres
MES	Manufacturing Engineering Section
MFC	Municipal Financial Corporation
MNCs	Multinational Corporations
MoRTH	Ministry of Road Transport and Highways
MoU	Memorandum of Understanding
MSP	Minimum Support Price
Mt	Million Tonnes
Mu	Million Units
MWS	Million Well Scheme
NAPS	Narora Atomic Power Station
NARP	National Agriculture Research Project
NCCF	National Contingency Calamity Fund
NCR	National Capital Region
NDC	National Development Council
NES	National Extension Service
NGO	Non Government Organisation
NHDC	National Handloom Development Corporation
NHDP	National Highways Development Programme
NIPFP	National Institute of Public Finance and Policy
NLCB	National Land Use & Conservation Board
NORAD	Norwegian Agency for Development Cooperation
NPAs	Non Performing Assets
NREP	National Rural Employment Programme
NRIs	Non-resident Indians
NSC	National Seeds Corporation
NSDP	Net State Domestic Product
NWDB	National Wasteland Development Board
NWDPRA	National Watershed Development Programme for Rainfed Agriculture
O&M	Operation and Maintenance
OCBs	Overseas Corporate Bodies
OIL	Oil India Ltd
ONGC	Oil and Natural Gas Commission
PHC	Primary Health Centre
PLF	Plant Load Factor
PMGSY	Pradhan Mantri Gram Sadak Yojana
PRIs	Panchayati Raj Institutions
PWD	Public Works Department
RAJCOMP	Rajasthan State Agency for Computer Services
RAJFED	Rajasthan State Cooperative Federation
RAJSICO	Rajasthan Small Industries Corporation Ltd.
RAPP	Rajasthan Atomic Power Project
RBI	Reserve Bank of India
RCDF	Rajasthan Cooperative Dairy Federation
REDA	Rajasthan Energy Development Agency
RFC	Rajasthan Finance Corporation
RHDC	Rajasthan Handloom Development Corporation
RIDF	Rural Infrastructure Development Fund
RIICO	Rajasthan State Industrial Development & Investment Corporation
RLEGP	Rural Landless Employment Guarantee Programme
RMK	Rashtriya Mahila Kosh
ROI	Return on Investment

RRBs	Regional Rural Banks
RSAMB	Rajasthan State Agriculture and Marketing Board
RSBCC	Rajasthan State Bridge and Construction Corporation
RSBCS	Rajasthan State Bunkar Cooperative Sangh
RSEB	Rajasthan State Electricity Board
RSERC	Rajasthan State Electricity Regulatory Commission
RSIC	Rajasthan Small Industrial Corporation
RSMM	Rajasthan State Minerals and Metals
RSRDCC	Rajasthan State Road Development and Construction Corporation
RSRTC	Rajasthan State Road Transport Corporation
RSSC	Rajasthan State Seed Corporation
RSWC	Rajasthan State Women's Cooperatives
RTDC	Rajasthan Tourism Development Corporation
RUDA	Rajasthan Non-Farm Development Agency
RUIDP	Rajasthan Urban Infrastructure Development Project
SAIL	Steel Authority of India Ltd
SDP	State Domestic Product
SEZs	Special Economic Zones
SFC	State Finance Commission
SFCI	State Farm Corporation of India
SGSY	Swarnajayanti Gram Swarozgar Yojana
SLPEs	State-Level Public Sector Enterprises
SSI	Small-Scale Industry
STEP	Science and Technology Entrepreneur Park
TAF	Tourist Assistance Force
TBA	Traditional Birth Attendant
TDP	Tribal Development Programme
TFR	Total Fertility Rate
TIB	Tourist Information Bureaus
TRYSEM	Training of Rural Youth for Self-Employment
TSS/JLY	Traditional Source Scheme/Janta Jal Yojana
UAs	Urban Agglomerations
UITs	Urban Improvement Trusts
ULBs	Urban Local Bodies
VAN	Value-Added Network
WPR	Work Participation Rate

Executive Summary

Agriculture

Agriculture and animal husbandry are the main occupations of a majority of people in Rajasthan. The western region depends mainly on animal husbandry and is widely known for local animal breeds, both for milk and draught.

Agriculture in Rajasthan is mostly dependent on the monsoon, which is not only erratic and uncertain but also has a short span. In terms of agro-climatic characteristics, the state ranges from arid to semi-arid. Rivers in Rajasthan are non-perennial except for the Chambal and Mahi. The state has been categorised into ten agro-climatic zones for development.

The major *kharif* crops of the state are *bajra, jowar,* maize, pulses, *guar,* cotton and soyabean and the *rabi* corps are wheat, gram, rapeseed and mustard. Rajasthan has made substantial improvement in crop production, especially after the Green Revolution. The area and production of crops like wheat, rapeseed and mustard, *rabi* pulses, and cotton have increased. There has been negative growth in coarse cereals and *kharif* pulses whereas *rabi* crops like wheat, rapeseed and mustard have recorded positive growth. Although the total quantity of seeds distributed has increased, crop-wise figures of seeds distributed show some distortions. The consumption of fertilisers (N+P+K) is nearly half of the national average. The indiscriminate use of fertilisers and that too in wrong proportions is a cause of concern. The use of organic manure is very poor.

Horticulture development and agro-processing in the state are very weak and reliable information on the production of fruits and vegetables is also not available.

Nearly 70 per cent of the area in Rajasthan is rainfed. As the rainfall is meagre and erratic, agriculture is full of risks and uncertainties. The subsistence type of agriculture prevalent in the state puts extra burden on natural resources like land, water and vegetation. It has been observed that since 1974-75, 22 lakh hectares (ha) area has been treated under watershed development programmes of Drought-Prone Area Programme (DPAP), Desert Development Programme (DDP), National Watershed Development Programme for Rainfed Agriculture (NWDPRA), externally aided watershed projects etc. However, the sustainability of work done is an issue. Agricultural mechanisation, which can benefit both rainfed and irrigated areas, is also a neglected area.

For irrigated areas, 'on-farm' water management is an area of great concern and needs to be given attention to improve water use efficiency. Ground water is mainly used for irrigation purposes and this results in over exploitation of this resource, the regeneration of which is dependent on rains. There are large areas in the state where water has been seriously over exploited.

Rajasthan is rich in animal wealth and has the distinction of having the largest population of cattle, sheep and camels. The state produces 10 per cent of the country's milk, 30 per cent meat and has the highest share of wool production.

Industries and Minerals

Five industrial policies have been promulgated in Rajasthan since 1951. All the major industries have been categorised as thrust sectors. In the industrial policies of 1994 and 1998, the Single Window Clearance Scheme was initiated, under which new industries were assured prompt clearance of their investment proposals. However, bureaucratic delays have persisted.

Industrial development in Rajasthan has suffered from a number of flaws:

- heavy concentration in only eight districts;
- predominance of small-scale units;
- high proportion of sick units;
- low value addition per worker;
- comparatively small scale of operations, which affects the competitiveness of industrial units in the national and international markets; and
- overall indifference of bureaucrats towards encouraging new entrepreneurs.

Mineral development in Rajasthan has also remained confined to only few districts, although the state has virtual monopoly in respect of some minerals such as felspar, limestone, marble, gypsum, marble and granite.

Agro-processing industries have not received the warranted attention in Rajasthan. Inspite of Rajasthan being a milk-surplus state, the processing of milk is still accorded low priority.

Handloom, Khadi and Handicrafts

The handloom and *khadi* units in Rajasthan are very small in size. Further, more than 34 per cent of handloom and *khadi* production is concentrated only in three districts. At the same time, it would be difficult for these units to survive if subsidies are withdrawn. Further, even though handicrafts of Rajasthan, especially gems and jewellery are good foreign exchange earners, a major part of value added in this sector is appropriated by middlemen.

Roads

The total length of roads across the state has increased from 37,000 km to over 1.5 lakh km over the past five decades. However, the proportion of fair weather roads continues to remain high. Secondly, almost 50 per cent of villages in Rajasthan still do not have any connectivity, although in quite a few districts not only are road conditions good, but the average length of roads is very high. Against the all-India average of 67 km. of roads per 100 km^2, the corresponding road length in Rajasthan is less than 27 km. Further, the state government does not have adequate resources for the maintenance of roads, and such work is done only on *ad hoc* basis.

The state has very low capacity of high density corridors. The ratio of four lane national highways (NH) and two lane state highways (SH) to total road length continues to be extremely low, though 90 per cent of road traffic moves on these roads.

Power

Against a bare 13 MW of power generation in 1951, the present generation capacity in the state has reached 3900 MW. However, there are wide inter-district variations in the consumption of power. Most of the power generated in Rajasthan is based on coal and the cost of generation is high because of the low calorific value of coal from the Jharia coalfields. Yet, the vast lignite reserves available in western districts continue to remain unused for power generation.

Since 1998, the transmission and distribution (T & D) losses have risen from 35 per cent to 42 per cent. It is ironical that in spite of power sector reforms, no private investment has been made in power sector.

Demography and Urban Development

The growth rate of population in the state has been higher than the national average. Further, the pace of urbanisation has also been high which resulted in the mushrooming growth of *kutchi bastis* (shanty towns), problems related to sanitation and sewerage, and stress on ground water resources due to spurt in the demand for water.

Since 1993, the annual demand for water for various purposes has increased from 621.4 cubic mm to 1017.5 cubic mm. The ground water levels in 200 out of the 247 blocks in the state have become very critical. This problem is likely to assume more serious dimensions in the coming decades.

Sewerage, sanitation, wastewater disposal and management of solid waste in Rajasthan's cities are dismal. Hopefully these problems will be solved through the Rajasthan Urban Infrastructure Development Project, at least in six largest cities. However, due to lack of resources, other cities and towns will continue to face these problems.

Tourism

In spite of numerous forts, fortresses, monuments and heritage sites dotting Rajasthan, tourist arrivals in the state have not increased significantly. Programmes and policies framed to woo domestic and international tourists were not demand oriented. Foreign tourists have experienced harassment and a sense of insecurity, and thus hesitate to visit Rajasthan for the second time.

Finances

The state has been under a great fiscal stress. Over 75 per cent of revenue receipts are absorbed in payment of salaries, wages and interest on loans. Public debt has increased from Rs. 22,000 crore to Rs. 45,000 crore between 1998 and 2002. Overstaffing in government offices and stagnant tax and non-tax revenues are some other factors causing financial stress. Tax buoyancy in the state is far lower than many other states.

The implementation of the Fifth Pay Commission Recommendations has led to a phenomenal increase in the public expenditure on salaries, wages and pensions. Between 1987 and 2002, the number of government employees - including the gazetted officers - has also increased. Besides, due to mounting debt, there has been a significant rise in interest payment.

Owing to low tax buoyancy, tax receipts in Rajasthan are approaching a saturation level, while the state government has not been able to increase non-tax revenues. When these trends are juxtaposed with revenue expenditure, it presents a very dismal picture of mounting revenue and fiscal deficits. However, the capital account has persistently shown a surplus.

The state-level public sector undertakings have not been able to earn profit. As a result, they are not able to contribute to the state's development plans. Yet, there is no disinvestment policy even for units whose net worth has turned negative. The state had to rely on public borrowings to finance its Eighth Plan. The percentage of public borrowings to Plan expenditure was more than 161 per cent during the Ninth Five Year Plan.

Governance

After independence, a uniform system of tenancy, land revenue and settlement was introduced. With the state taking on developmental tasks, the size of the government as well as the number of channels for processing official files registered an increase, which resulted in a phenomenal increase in public expenditure on salaries and inordinate delay in taking even important decisions.

The state government has set up four Rajiv Gandhi Missions to address major problems confronting the state and has given more powers to panchayati raj institutions (PRIs). It also has enacted the Right to Information Act. Besides, numerous campaigns to solve various problems of urban and rural people have been held, although with very little success. To promote grassroot planning, District Planning Committees have been constituted in all districts. Yet, the long pending revenue and settlement disputes warrant an early disposal.

Women

Rajasthan ranks low on the Gender Development Index and Gender Empowerment Index. Women continue to have a lower status than men, resulting in frequent atrocities against them. Female work participation rate in Rajasthan is low in both rural as well as urban areas. The level of female literacy and also enrolment of girls in primary and upper primary schools is very low and dropout rates are high. The average age at marriage in Rajasthan is around 15 years.

Environment

The major environmental problems confronting the state are related to growing soil salinity and alkalinity and mixture of fluoride and other hazardous toxic chemicals in water. In some areas mining activities have created serious ecological hazards. All major cities have developed a problem of mounting solid waste. Traditional methods of conservation of rainwater have been neglected in the state, in spite of the water scarcity.

Human Development

Rajasthan also ranks lower on the Human Development Index than many other states. Inspite of an impressive increase in level of literacy and number of hospitals and educational institutions both in the public and private sector, a sizeable section of the population remains deprived of these facilities. Paradoxically, in recent years, institutions providing higher (general) and technical education have registered a huge increase without assessing the present and future demand. Further, the increasing strain on public finances has jeopardised the programme for improvement in the quality of education and health.

Recommendations

Agriculture

A holistic development strategy for agriculture warrants the implementation of the following suggestions:

- **State Land Use Policy**: The state should formulate a State Land Use Policy in line with the National Land Use Policy. A land use policy will take care of land use as per land classification, tenancy law, ceiling laws, mortgage of land, and many legal aspects suggested in the report. This also includes allotment of cultivable wasteland to rural people for development, with logistic support.

- **State Water Policy**: The state framed a Water Policy in 1999. The provisions under this should be implemented with all seriousness. Water tariffs need to be rationalised and water use efficiency needs to be improved by strengthening the Water Users Associations.
- **Planning Approach**: The Agro-Climatic Regional Planning approach has been suggested for planning for natural resources. Dove-tailing the activities of agriculture, horticulture, animal husbandry, watershed, rural development, etc., is required to get optimum results.
- **Perspective Plan for 25 Years**: The Planning Commission has prepared a '25 Years Perspective Plan for the Development of Rain-fed Areas of India'. The state government should also attempt something similar to cover all rainfed areas for implementation in a specific time frame. Such a plan may be prepared as per agro-climatic zones of the state, taking each district as a major unit. The watershed approach should be adopted for all investment proposals. Pooling of funds of all concerned departments should form the basis for implementation of all programmes.
- There is a gap in the transfer of production technology to farmers and the extension system needs to be revamped to address this issue. There is hardly any extension and education programme on soil and water conservation technologies, horticulture development and animal husbandry sectors.
- Research efforts on *bajra*, pulses, date palm, animal breeding, fruits, vegetables, spices, aromatic and medicinal plants, etc. need to be strengthened. The research on farming system approach for different agro-climatic zones needs to be accelerated. An organic linkage is warranted between State Agriculture Universities, the Central Arid Zone Research Institute (CAZRI) of the Indian Council of Agricultural Research (ICAR) and the state government to jointly identify and implement the transfer of technologies to rural areas.
- All watershed development programmes should have a common implementing agency and norms for works should be the same for different projects.
- Providing minimum support price (MSP) and procurement of foodgrains (mainly *bajra*), should be a priority to avoid hardship to farmers. Higher MSP on durum wheat to encourage its cultivation would also be required.
- Given the size of the agricultural sector, and hostile agro-climatic conditions, higher Plan allocations (between 10 and 11 per cent) should be made for the agriculture sector to revive and strengthen the state's economy.
- A task force for the development of horticulture and agro-processing should be constituted.
- A holistic approach covering breeding, feeding and health management in the livestock sector is needed. Emphasis needs to be given to conserving local breeds of Rajasthan.

Industries, Handlooms, Village Industries, Minerals

- A task force must be appointed to study the roadblocks to new investment in industries in Rajasthan in relation to the neighbouring states.
- Bureaucratic hassles prevalent in the implementation of the Single Window Clearance Scheme must be removed.
- Processing of agricultural products like coriander, mustard, vegetables, fruits and spices etc. within the state must be given top priority to provide additional employment and retention of value added within Rajasthan.
- In order to meet the challenges of globalisation, a task force needs to be appointed to study the competitive strength of industries and suggest measures to improve their efficiency.
- The state government must try to establish coordination between the departments of forests and mining to evolve an environment-friendly mining policy.
- Coordination among different state government agencies responsible for the development of industries must be ensured via the Bureau of Industrial Promotion to promote industrial investment.
- Market friendly strategies must be adopted for handloom, khadi and village industries so as to enable these units to improve their efficiency and develop with minimum support in terms of subsidies etc.
- For reducing inter-regional imbalances in industrial development, limestone and ceramic-

based industries may be set up in the western and southern districts, while agro-processing units may be set up in the eastern districts.

- Chronic loss-making PSUs, must be closed without any further delay.

Roads

- In view of the poor connectivity in districts like Jhalawar, Ganganagar, Bundi, Chittorgarh, Sirohi, Dungarpur, Banswara, Karauli etc., top priority needs to be given to building new roads in these districts. Upgradation of roads in other districts is also required.
- To ensure better quality of roads, and minimise corruption, the system of awarding construction contract to the lowest bidder must be done away with.
- Adequate funds must be made available for maintenance of roads. A long-term policy needs to be formulated for this purpose.
- The build-operate-transfer (BOT) model must be extended for upgrading of village roads as also for widening the major district roads and other district roads.

Power

- Vigilance committees constituted to check theft of power must be given more powers. Participatory management of power stations may be helpful in areas outside the jurisdiction of vigilance committees.
- Techno-economic feasibility of lignite and gas power generation in Jaiselmer and Barmer districts must be studied on a priority basis. This would enable the state government to generate power at a low cost, and save money spent on purchasing power from other states.
- Downsizing the five power corporations has to be initiated to reduce the cost of generating, transmitting and distributing power.
- A strategy must be prepared to woo large Indian companies to study the prospects of power generation in Rajasthan, and provide them incentives to invest in this sector.
- The potential of wind energy and solar power, especially in the western districts, must be studied.
- All PSEs must be run on commercial lines with minimum room for losses.

Tourism

- Forts, fortresses and ancient monuments located in different parts of Rajasthan need a facelift. Financial institutions must be approached to provide resources for this purpose.
- Domestic tourists need to be given due attention at all centres of pilgrimage.
- Effective measures must be taken to provide security to international tourists.
- A task force must be constituted to assess the needs of both the domestic and international tourists, and appropriate strategies designed to promote tourism accordingly.

State Finances

A high power committee needs to be constituted with the following tasks:

- determine the right size of the government,
- make recommendations on expenditure compression, especially on the revenue account, and advise the state government on the productive uses of public debt.
- High interest bearing debt must be converted into low interest bearing securities.
- A task force should be set up to study the potential of raising non-tax revenue as well as rationalising the rates presently in vogue for various taxes.
- The state government must ensure timely completion of all projects. This would help check cost escalation and, at the same time, ensure early accrual of benefits.

Demography and Urban Development

- The Couple Protection Rate must be raised in order to check population growth.
- Besides, for creating awareness about family planning in rural areas, groups of women may be organised under the leadership of female ward *panchas* and *sarpanchs* for motivating people to adopt birth control measures.
- Urban local bodies may be given adequate powers to raise revenues. They may be involved in supplying drinking water in towns and cities.

- Immediate action must be taken for redressing the problem of fluoride content in water. Mobile laboratories may be constituted to test the quality of water being supplied in cities and towns.
- Urban local bodies must be given adequate support for providing sanitation, drainage and solid waste management, particularly in fast growing cities such as Jaipur, Jodhpur, Kota, Ajmer and Alwar.

Environment

The State Pollution Control Board must be given more powers to take action against polluters in different sectors, such as agriculture, industry and transport.

Human Development

- The state urgently needs a Manpower Plan for ensuring a balance between demand and supply of various types of professionals.
- A holistic approach is required for educational programmes covering enrolment and retention rates of children in primary and upper primary schools.
- Subsidy on higher education and specialised health services must be drastically reduced, while the quality of teaching at lower levels must be improved.
- Non-resident Indians must be motivated to invest in the health and education sectors.

District Map of Rajasthan

Chapter 1

Economic Profile

Introduction

Situated in the north-west of India, Rajasthan has immense development potential, which, unfortunately, has not been adequately leveraged and the state has remained an under-developed region. The state came into existence on November 1, 1956 by the reorganisation of 19 princely states and three chiefships, which varied in size, administrative efficiency and socio-economic development. The state now has 32 districts, 241 *tehsils* and 237 development blocks.[1] It is known as India's desert state since 61 per cent of its area, covering 11 districts inhabited by 40 per cent of the population, is either desert or semi-desert – the Thar – which has made the state vulnerable to droughts and famines.

Physiography

Rajasthan is the largest state in the country, spread over 3.42 lakh sq km. The state can be broadly classified into plains in the north and northeast, hills and plateau in the eastern part and desert in the western region. The 550-km long Aravalli hills range, running from the north-east to the south-west of the state, divide the state diagonally into two parts – the western arid region and the eastern semi-arid regions.

Though Rajasthan accounts for 10.4 per cent of the country's total geographical area, it has only 1.2 per cent of India's total water resources. Barring the Chambal and Mahi, the 11 rivers of the state are non-perennial. Most of them do not join any defined drainage system, and get lost in the sands or drain into inland pondage like Sambhar salt lake. Rajasthan is a rainfed state, precipitation being the only source of annually renewable water supply, whether it is rivers or wells or ponds etc. Rajasthan gets 29 days of rain annually, with average rainfall of 58 cm, ranging between 310 mm in the western region and 700 mm in the eastern region. The south-west monsoon (June to September) accounts for nearly 90 per cent of rainfall in the state.

Thus ground water is the major source of water both for irrigation as well as consumption. Out of the state's 237 blocks, ground water has been over exploited in 74, while 20 are in the dark zone (an area where the average rate of depletion is more than 0.40 m/year). This has significant consequences for agricultural development as well as the availability of water for industries and human consumption.

Rajasthan has a variety of soils, reflecting different parent material and physiographic land features. These are categorised under five heads: aridisols, alfisols, entisols, inceptisols and vertisols. The state has a forest cover of only 9.32 per cent, most of it confined to the hilly areas in the eastern and southern regions.

Structure of the Economy

Rajasthan's economy is predominantly agricultural and rural in nature and there are wide fluctuations in the growth rate of the net state domestic product (NSDP) due to uncertainties in agricultural production, which is almost entirely dependent on rainfall.

As Table 1.2 shows, there has been a drastic decline in the share of the primary sector from 47.77 per cent in 1980-81 to 29.7 per cent in 2000-2001. The share of the secondary sector increased moderately from 19.49 per cent to 26.34 per cent during this period, while the share of the tertiary sector increased significantly from about 32.74 per cent to 43.9 per cent. The fastest growing segment of the tertiary sector has been trade, hotels and restaurants, which alone accounts for 15 per cent of the NSDP.

1. As in many other states, in Rajasthan too administrative units (tehsils) are different from the development blocks.

TABLE 1.1

Net State Domestic Product of Rajasthan at 1993-94 prices

(Rs. Crore)

Year	*NSDP*
1980-81	12738.23
1990-91	28857.16
1991-92	27252.07
1992-93	30726.25
1993-94	28976.90
1994-95	34268.92
1995-96	3553.035
1996-97	39681.79
1997-98	44509.34
1998-99	46178.96
1999-00	45121.53
2000-01	44335.02
2001-02	48940.47

Source: Net State Domestic Product of Rajasthan (2002), Directorate of Economics and Statistics, Jaipur.

TABLE 1.2

Components of NSDP in Rajasthan (%)

Year	*Primary Sector*	*Secondary Sector*	*Tertiary Sector*
1980-81	47.77	19.49	32.74
1990-91	43 52	20.78	35.70
1993-94	37.12	23.35	39.53
1996-97	39.86	22.20	37.94
1999-00	32.33	25.70	42.07
2000-01	29.73	26.34	43.93

The share of the manufacturing sector in NSDP (currently at 16 per cent at 1993-94 prices) is projected to increase to 26 per cent in the next few years through accelerated industrial growth for which there is ample scope in the state. The high growth of income originating from the service sector is a global phenomenon, and it has wider repercussions on the state's economy, particularly in the field of public finance Post 1997-98, largely due to the implementation of the Fifth Pay Commission recommendations, the burden of salaries, wages and pension on the state exchequer rose from Rs. 4,015 crore in 1997-98 to Rs. 7,412 crore in 2001-02. As a percentage to total NSDP, this ratio has shot up from 7.0 per cent to 9.8 per cent in this period. But the sluggish growth of the manufacturing sector is a cause of real worry, because the growth of agriculture and industry is essential for sustained growth of the entire economy.

Growth in Per Capita Income

The per capita NSDP of Rajasthan (measured at 1993-94 prices) was Rs. 12,557 in 2000-2001, placing it in the eleventh rank among all states. In that year, the per capita NSDP at the all-India level was Rs. 16703. The per capita income of the state, however, has shown erratic growth partly on account of frequent droughts, but largely due to high growth rate of population.

Social Indicators

Education, health, family welfare, nutrition, sanitation, water supply, roads and social security are the basic social infrastructure that people require. Unfortunately Rajasthan has been lagging behind in social development due to the slow growth of the economy and low per capita income. Although there has been an improvement in various social indicators (Table 1.3), the state needs to make far more progress in its social indicators to abandon the BIMARU label.[2]

TABLE 1.3

Changes in Prominent Social Indicators (1981 to 2001)

Literacy Rate (Persons) (aged 7 years & above)	*Enrolment at Primary Stage (I-V) (in lakh) (Total)*	*Enrolment at upper Primary Stage (VI-VIII) (in lakh) (Total)*	*Life Expectancy at Birth (years) (1993-97)[3]*	*Primary Health Centres (number)*
30.1 (1981)	29.1 (1980-81)	7.7 (1980-81)		232 (1979-80)
38.6 (1991)	46.4 (1990-91)	13.7 (1990-91)	60.1	1059 (1989-90)
61.0 (2001)	69.0 (1997-98)	19.8 (1997-98)	62.2 (2001-06)	1674 (1999-2000)
	81.04 (2001-02)	25.09 (2001-02)		1703 (2000-01)

Note: Numbers in parenthesis indicate year of data

Source: Some Development Facts of Rajasthan 1956-1999, August 2000 & Statistical Abstract of Rajasthan 2000.

2. BIMARU means sickly and is an acronym derived from the names of Bihar, Madhya Pradesh, Rajasthan and Uttar Pradesh, four of India's most underdeveloped states.
3. Life expectancy in India is estimated at birth.

Employment and Unemployment

Work Participation Rate

According to the provisional population figures of Census 2001, Rajasthan has 2.38 crore main and marginal workers, who account for 42.11 per cent of the state's total population. The work participation rate (WPR) increased from 36.61 per cent in 1981 to 38.87 per cent in 1991 and to 42.11 per cent in 2001. In 2001, WPR was 39.26 per cent in India, while it was 42.75 per cent in Madhya Pradesh, 42.10 per cent in Gujarat, and 32.60 per cent in Uttar Pradesh.

There are interesting rural-urban and male-female differentials in the WPR. The WPR among males was 50.07 per cent, as compared to a mere 33.48 per cent among females. In rural areas, the WPR was 45.94 per cent, while it was 29.56 per cent in the urban areas. The WPR among rural males was 50.82 per cent and 47.64 per cent among urban males. Interestingly, the WPR among urban females was extremely low at 9.24 per cent as compared to 40.70 per cent among rural females.[4]

Distribution of Workers

Table 1.4 shows the distribution of workers (main and marginal) in Rajasthan as per Census 2001.[5] In line with the dominance of agriculture in the state's economy, 66 per cent workers were engaged in agricultural activities, 55.37 per cent as cultivators and 10.63 per cent as agricultural labourers. One out of every ten workers is an agricultural labourer in Rajasthan. Moreover, at 83.46 per cent, the female WPR in the agricultural sector is much higher than male participation rate of 55.23 per cent. Thus, the female participation in the agricultural sector is very high as compared to the male participation. Workers in the household industry constitute only 2.7 per cent of total workers, but males have a higher share of 42 per cent, as against 14 per cent in the case of females.

Unemployment Situation

Unemployment data are collected once in five years by the National Sample Survey Organisation (NSSO) in its successive rounds. Table 1.5 shows the unemployment rates for 1999-2000 on the basis of usual status, weekly status and current daily status (CDS) for rural and urban and male and female categories.[6]

TABLE 1.4

Distribution of Workers (Main and Marginal) in Rajasthan

(Per cent)

		Cultivator Labourers	*Agricultural Household*	*Workers in Industry*	*Other Workers*	*Total*
Total	Persons	55.37	10.63	2.74	31.26	100
	Male	48.17	7.06	2.73	42.04	100
	Female	67.02	16.44	2.76	13.78	100

Source: Provisional Population Totals, Paper-3 of 2001, Distribution of workers and non-workers, May, 2002.

TABLE 1.5

Unemployment Rates in India (1999-2000)

% of labour-force

	Rural			*Urban*		
	Usual Status (adjusted)	*Current Weekly Status*	*Current Daily Status*	*Usual Status (adjusted)*	*Current Weekly Status*	*Current Daily Status*
Male	0.6	2.6	3.3	2.6	4.0	4.7
Female	0.1	1.5	1.9	2.1	2.7	3.5
Persons	0.4	2.2	2.8	2.5	3.8	4.5

Source: Employment and Unemployment in India 1999-2000, NSS, 55th Round (July 1999-June 2000), Report No. 458, May 2001 (Part I).

The Special Group on Targeting Ten Million Employment Opportunities Per Year, headed by Planning Commission member Dr. S.P. Gupta, has used the CDS concept for estimating the incidence of unemployment in India and various states. According to this, the unemployment rate was higher in urban areas (4.5 per cent) than in rural areas (2.8 per cent). It was highest among urban male (4.7 per cent) and lowest among rural female (1.9 per cent). DES, Rajasthan has also published data on employment and unemployment in Rajasthan in December 2001, based on the state sample for the NSSO's 55th Round (1999-2000) but there is a slight difference in the Central sample of the NSSO and the state sample results. For the sake of uniformity in the presentation, this study has used the Central sample results only, as they bring out the trend quite adequately for our purpose.

The Task Force on Employment Opportunities, headed by Shri Montek Singh Ahluwalia, in its report of June 2001, had used Usual Principal and Subsidiary Status basis (UPSS) for estimation of employment and unemployment in India. But the Special Group, in its May 2002 report, has considered CDS as a better measure to capture unemployment. For this a special tabulation has been done by NSSO.

4. Provisional Population Totals, Paper-3 of 2001, Distribution of Workers and Non-workers, May, 2002, Chapter 2. Director of Census Operations, Rajasthan
5. *ibid*, p. 24
6. Employment and Unemployment in India 1999-2000, NSS, 55th Round (July 1999-June 2000), Report No.458, May 2001 (Part I), pp.139-142.

According to the Special Group's report, against the national rural unemployment rate of 7.1 per cent in 1999-2000, rural unemployment in Rajasthan was only 2.8 per cent. In urban areas, only 4.5 per cent persons were unemployed in Rajasthan against the national average of 7.7 per cent.

Underemployment

Underemployment is more prevalent in Rajasthan than open unemployment. Seasonal unemployment is a form of underemployment and this is common in Rajasthan. Since agriculture is rainfed, it does not provide employment throughout the year. Rural artisans also do not get work for the whole year. Thus, people in both rural and urban areas are available for additional work in some seasons. Table 1.6 shows the proportion of people in Rajasthan demanding additional work in 1993-94.[7]

TABLE 1.6

Proportion of People Demanding Additional Work

(Per cent)

Location	*Male*	*Female*
Rural	6.2	3.6
Urban	2.8	2.0

It is evident that the incidence of underemployment is quite high in rural areas as compared to urban areas, both for male as well as female. People have to be assisted through relief works during droughts and famines in the state.

Ironically, while the S.P. Gupta Committee estimated employment elasticity at the national level at 0.165 for 1999-2000, and also measured the change in such elasticity over one decade, no such exercise has been attempted for Rajasthan. The state government must constitute a special group of experts to estimate employment elasticity for different sectors and changes taking place therein from time to time.

Availability of Infrastructure

Electricity

The installed power generation capacity in the state at the end of 2000-2001 was 3997.97 MW, only half of which is procured from within the state. Per capita consumption of power in the state was estimated at 329 KWh in 1998-99, placing Rajasthan tenth among 17 states while the demand was estimated at 422 KWh. There was power shortage to the extent of 9.6 per cent in 1980-81; which has increased in later years to 22 per cent. Measures are being taken to increase installed capacity in the next few years so that the state can become self-sufficient. The state has the potential to increase power supply from different sources – thermal, hydel (procured from Madhya Pradesh), nuclear, solar, wind, etc. Out of the state's 39,789 villages, 37,276 (93.7 per cent) had been electrified till 2001.

7. Employment and Unemployment in India 1993-94, NSS, 50th Round, Report No. 409 of NSSO, March 1997, p.158.

Road Development

The total road length was 1,52,880 km on March 31, 2003, with an additional 4298 km road length to be added in 2003-04. The state has a very low road density of 46 km per 100 sq. km at the end of March 2004 against the national average of 75 km per 100 sq. km. As of 31 March 2004, 48 per cent of the state's villages were not connected with bitumen treated (BT) or any other type of good road.

Railway Development

Rajasthan lags behind in railway development. Even as late as 1992-93, the total length of rail tracks per 100 km in Rajasthan was 16.77 km, which increased to 28 km in 1999. At the end of March 2001, the total length of railway routes was 5926 km, which was 9.4 per cent of the total route in the country. The national average length per 1000 km^2 was 19.2 km against 17.3 km in Rajasthan. Further, only about 51 per cent of total railway track in the state was under broad gauge. The 2002-03 budget makes provision for further extending railway facilities.

Poverty in the State

Table 1.7 shows that the poverty ratio in Rajasthan has gone down considerably from 34.46 per cent in 1983 to 15.28 per cent in 1999-2000. This has been possible because of the poverty reduction programmes initiated during this period. As poverty is measured on the basis of calorie consumption, there is a growing feeling it would be more meaningful to estimate poverty ratio on the basis of minimum level of living (food, clothing and housing). Rapid economic growth is necessary for reducing the incidence of poverty in the state.

The state government is implementing various rural development programmes, with the primary objective of poverty alleviation and creation of employment opportunities in rural areas.

TABLE 1.7

Percentage of Population in Poverty

	1983	1987-88	1993-94	1999-2000
Rajasthan	**34.46**	**35.15**	**27.41**	**15.28**
All India	44.48	38.86	35.97	26.10

Source: Planning Commission

Seven districts (Baran, Churu, Dausa, Dholpur, Jhalawar, Rajsamand, and Tonk) have been selected for poverty alleviation within a time span of five years under the World Bank-assisted District Poverty Initiatives Project (DPIP). The project will cover nearly 7000 villages in these selected districts and is likely to be completed by December 2005. Under these projects, rural poor are empowered to mobilise themselves into Common Interest Groups (CIGs), identify and undertake activities that will help them overcome poverty and maintain the created assets. A separate bank account will be opened for this in which each beneficiary will deposit his share for the maintenance of the asset. The activities taken up under DPIP would relate to agriculture, rural infrastructure, social services and micro enterprises.

Table 1.8 shows some inter-state comparisons in terms of poverty.

TABLE 1.8

Poverty Ratio in 1993-94 and 1999-2000

(Per cent)

	Rural			Urban		
	1993-94	1999-00	Change in Proportion of Poor (percentage points)	1993-94	1999-00	Change in Proportion of Poor (percentage points)
1	2	3	4 (3-2)	5	6	7 (6-5)
All-India	39.36	36.35	-3.01	30.37	28.76	-1.61
Bihar	64.41	58.85	-5.56	45.03	45.10	0.07
Madhya Pradesh	36.93	39.35	2.43	46.02	46.29	0.27
Uttar Pradesh	39.08	29.87	-9.21	34.23	36.39	2.16
Rajasthan	**25.92**	**15.01**	**-10.91**	**30.60**	**24.36**	**-6.24**
Punjab	17.61	14.24	-3.37	6.79	6.74	-0.05
West Bengal	54.15	56.16	2.01	20.97	16.74	-4.23
Maharashtra	50.21	50.00	-0.21	33.52	32.16	-1.36

Source: K. Sundaresan's Working Paper No. 95, Centre for Development Economics, July 2001, Table 12, p.35.

At 10.9 percentage points, the fall in rural poverty levels in Rajasthan between 1993-94 and 1999-2000 appears to be quite satisfactory. The fall in urban poverty (6.24 percentage points) was also significant. But the fall in rural poverty in Rajasthan in 1999-2000 can be calculated in relation to the poverty level in 1993-94 also. It was then 42 per cent, which was pretty high. Thus, the rural poverty ratio in Rajasthan declined very significantly in 1999-2000 (as per 55th round of NSS) as compared to the period 1993-94 (50th round).

The problem is that in India poverty is calculated on the basis of calorie intake. In Rajasthan, a majority of the people consume millets (*bajra*) which are cheaper. When the price of wheat rises, many wheat-consuming households also switch over to *bajra*, thus reducing the cost of buying the required calories. This phenomenon explains the reasons for a sharp decline in rural poverty in Rajasthan.

Fiscal Situation[8]

As in the case of most states, the fiscal situation in Rajasthan is also under tremendous stress. The revenue deficit in 2000-01 was Rs. 2634.6 crore and rose to Rs. 3924 crore in 2003-04. Interest liability has reached a level of 32 per cent of revenue receipts for 2002-2003 (BE).

Capital outlay (which is used for asset-creation in the economy) was Rs. 1,384 crore in 2000-2001, which was only 2 per cent of gross state domestic product (GSDP), a fall from 3.9 per cent in 1997-98. This sharp decline in capital outlay as a ratio of GSDP is not a happy augury for the growth of the economy. Moreover, in 2000-2001, the gross fiscal deficit was Rs. 4,313 crore. Thus, capital outlay as a ratio of gross fiscal deficit was only 32 per cent, which means that only about one-third of the net borrowings of the government were being used for asset-creation or investment purposes. This ratio must be quite high to accelerate economic growth.

Outstanding debt and other liabilities of the state at the end of March 2003 (BE) were estimated to be Rs. 44,380 crore, which is about 46 per cent of GSDP. If debt increases at a faster rate than GSDP in the next few years, the debt-GSDP ratio may cross the 50 per cent mark.

The state will have to take steps to accelerate the growth rate of GSDP at current prices, raise revenue and compress expenditure. Introduction of zero based

8. Details of State Finances are given in Chapter 8.

budgeting in each government department is necessary. Private investment will help the state economy grow and increase revenues and necessary incentives must be given for this.

Fiscal Situation in Relation to Rest of India

Table 1.9 presents leading fiscal indicators for some states. There have been changes in these ratios in recent years. In some cases, the situation has worsened, while in others, there may have been some improvement. This study uses the actual positions (not BE or RE) to derive meaningful results from the given data.

TABLE 1.9

Major Fiscal Indicators

(Percentage)

State	*Total Debt/ GSDP*	*Total Liabilities/ Revenue Receipts*		*Interest Payments/ Revenue Receipts*		*RD/GFD*
	2000-01	1990-91	2000-01	1990-91	2000-01	2000-01
Rajasthan	**38.6**	**157.2**	**247**	**14.4**	**26.9**	**61.1**
Gujarat	27.0	184.4	189	14.1	19.9	78.9
U.P.	38.2	170.8	268	16.4	34.9	61.8
Punjab	42.1	347.1	297	17.9	25.0	59.8
Kerala	34.6	184.8	274	14.5	25.9	81.2
West Bengal	33.8	191.5	325	15.5	36.8	69.4

Note: GSDP = Gross State Domestic Product
RD = Revenue Deficit
GFD = Gross Fiscal Deficit

Source: State Finances: A Study of Budgets of 2002-03, RBI, February 2003, Various Tables for 2001-02.

Inferences

In 1997-98, total debt/GSDP ratio for Rajasthan was 28 per cent, which increased to 44.37 per cent in 2000-2001 and further to 52.5 per cent in 2003-04 (RE). Total liabilities as a ratio of revenue receipts in Rajasthan increased from 157 per cent in 1990-91 to 246 per cent in 1998-99 in Rajasthan, while it declined in Gujarat. The increases for Uttar Pradesh and West Bengal have been quite significant. Interest liabilities as a ratio of revenue receipts have been increasing rapidly, from 14 per cent in 1990-91 to 27 per cent in 1998-99 for Rajasthan and are likely to touch 31 per cent in 2002-2003 (BE). Punjab is in a worse position, with interest liabilities as a ratio of revenue receipts having crossed 37 per cent in 1998-99. Revenue deficit as percentage of GFD was 61 per cent in Rajasthan in 2000-2001, which means that 61 per cent of the state government's borrowings were utilised for financing current expenditure, implying a very low sustainability of state finances. But the same ratio was more than 85 per cent in Punjab and nearly 80 per cent in the case of Kerala and West Bengal. Thus, most state governments seem to be spending huge amount of their borrowings for meeting their revenue deficits, and this situation needs to be corrected immediately.

Hard options are needed to restore the state's fiscal balance. For this, a Fiscal Responsibility and Budget Management law must be passed at the state level too, and necessary changes in the economic parameters like GSDP should be introduced, so as to achieve the target of reducing the revenue deficit by half per cent a year to a zero-level at some future date. The state will also need to adopt vigorous measures to accelerate the growth rate of GSDP at current prices and take steps for resource mobilisation and expenditure compression. Introducing zero based budgeting in each department for expenditure management and compression is an imperative. Apart from a roadmap for zero based budgeting for each department, delineating the job description for each functionary in every department and eliminating duplication of work is also necessary. Two or more departments may be merged, wherever warranted. This would serve the twin goals of reducing unproductive and unnecessary public expenditure as well as streamlining the tax procedures and *making them friendly for tax payers*. A task force must be constituted for this purpose.

An increase in private investment (both domestic and foreign) would go a long way in strengthening the state's economy, and, thereby, improving its revenue-raising potential and a package of incentives needs to be designed for this. The components of this package could include tax holiday, wherever desirable, allotting industrial sites at concessional rates, prompt power and water connections, availability of credit on reasonable terms, and improved road connectivity so as to ensure proximity with market.

Apart from this, the following steps may also need to be taken: strict penalties for tax evasion; increasing user charges for power, water, higher education etc. so as to minimise the burden of non-merit subsidies; involving the private sector in the provision of these services and supporting them in recovering the cost. In order to sanction credit via financial institutions such as banks and the Rajasthan Finance Corporation (RFC) and guarding against non-performing assets (NPAs), the project proposals must be subjected to thorough

TABLE 1.10

Investment Data for India and Rajasthan

(Rs. crore)

	Proposed Investment Under IEMs + LoIs from August 1991 to December 2000	*Cumulative Financial Assistance Disbursed by All-India Financial Institutions till March 2000*	*Cumulative Financial Assistance Disbursed by SFC till March 2000 (i.e. RFC)*	*Cumulative Financial Assistance Disbursed by SIDC, i.e. RIICO till March 2000*
Rajasthan	**36794 (3.8)**	**140227 (3.5)**	**16290 (6.1)**	**554 (3.3)**
All-India	960423	3941705	26595	16800

Note: Figures in parenthesis are percentage to national total

Source: 'Saga of Paradigm Shifts' (C. Rangarajan), *p.16*, Survey of Indian Industry 2001, *(The Hindu), & Report of Development Banking In India 1999-2000, various tables.*

financial and economic appraisal. However, if loan arrears are outstanding against weaker sections, recovery of a part of such arrears may be waived.

Investment Activity in the State

The role of private investment has acquired special significance in the wake of economic reforms initiated in 1991. Data on private investments are not available in a compact, detailed and systematic form. But a broad idea of industrial investment proposals can be formed on the basis of proposed investment in the state from August 1991 to December 2000 under industrial entrepreneurial memoranda (IEMs)[9] and letters of intent (LoIs), issued in respect of items under licensing, cumulative share of financial assistance disbursed by all-India financial institutions (Industrial Development Bank of India, Industrial Finance Corporation of India, ICICI, Small Industries Development Board of India (IIBI), Life Insurance Corporation, Unit Trust of India and General Insurance Corporation) to Rajasthan and cumulative assistance disbursed by RFC and Rajasthan State Industrial Development & Investment Corporation (RIICO). Table 1.10 has data on this along with the percentage share of Rajasthan in the national total.

Clearly, Rajasthan's share in total national investments and credit disbursements is rather low, which is in line with indicators like the number of factories, employment, fixed capital and value-added by manufacture in the all India totals.

Industrial licensing is mandatory in the following five sectors:

- Distillation and brewing of alcoholic drinks;
- Cigars and cigarettes made of tobacco and manufactured tobacco substitutes;
- Electronics, aerospace and defence equipment;
- Industrial explosives, including detonating fuse, safety fuse, gun powder, nitrocellulose and matches; and
- Hazardous chemicals.

The progress of proposed investments under IEMs and LoIs and financial assistance disbursed by all-India financial institutions, RFC and RIICO indicates the slow pace of industrial development in Rajasthan. With faster growth of infrastructural facilities and the formulation of viable industrial projects in the state, the state's share in investment activity may be raised.

Since RFC and RIICO are state-level financial institutions, their role in facilitating industrial development in the state is extremely important. While RIICO develops industrial areas and provides infrastructure such as land, electricity, water connections and roads, the RFC finances the construction of buildings, purchase of machinery and equipment etc. They also have an important role in socio-economic development as they, *inter alia*, support women entrepreneurs, weaker sections of the community etc. They also supplement the role of the national level industrial development and financial institutions. There are suggestions that RFC and RIICO be converted into commercial banking institutions to enable them to contribute better to industrial development.

Direct intervention by RFC and RIICO has, to some extent, been instrumental in promoting industrial development in Rajasthan. Now that the infrastructure has come up through planned development, increased

9. In an industrially backward state like Rajasthan, Industrial Entrepreneurial Memoranda (IEMs) have an important role, since they are based on the information available to entrepreneurs about the potential of developing certain types of industry. Under the given environment, an entrepreneur is able to show his interest in setting up some industry in a specified area. Thus, IEMs are important, in spite of liberalised regime.

TABLE 1.11

Investment Position of Different States

(Rs. crore)

	Proposed Investment Under IEMs + LoIs from August 1991 to December 2000	*Cumulative Financial Assistance Disbursed by All-India Financial Institutions till March 2000*	*Cumulative Financial Assistance Disbursed by Respective SFCs till March 2000*	*Cumulative Financial Assistance Disbursed by respective SIDCs till March 2000*
All-India	960423	3941705	26595	16800
Rajasthan	**36794** **(3.8)**	**140227** **(3.5)**	**1629** **(6.1)**	**554** **(3.3)**
Gujarat	66606 (6.9)	561524 (14.2)	2454 (9.2)	1589 (9.4)
Madhya Pradesh	67522 (7.0)	161153 (4.1)	849 (3.2)	364 (2.2)
Maharashtra	200224 (20.8)	918066 (23.3)	2655 (10.0)	5186 (30.9)
Uttar Pradesh	78659 (8.2)	242209 (6.1)	2787 (10.5)	2121 (12.6)
West Bengal	34053 (3.5)	173175 (4.4)	701 (2.6)	640 (3.8)

Note: Figures in parentheses are percentage of national investment figures

Source: 'Saga of Paradigm Shifts' (C. Rangarajan), *p.16*, Survey of Indian Industry 2001, *(The Hindu), & Report of Development Banking In India 1999-2000, various tables.*

private investment will further accelerate the process of economic development in general. An enabling environment created by the state government, and direct intervention by RFC and RIICO can reinforce each other in the process of development.

Inter-state Comparison of Investment Activity

It would be interesting to evaluate the investment growth in Rajasthan with that in some selected states. Table 1.11 indicates the relative position of different states in national investment activity.

Significantly, Maharashtra's share in IEMs and LoIs, taken together, till December 2000, was about 21 per cent of national investment. Assistance from all-India financial institutions was 23.3 per cent of the national average; from the Maharashtra State Finance Corporation (SFC) 10 per cent and from the Maharashtra State Industrial Development Corporation (SIDC) 30.9 per cent.

West Bengal's investment position is broadly similar to that of Rajasthan, except in the case of assistance from the SFC where Rajasthan performed much better. Maharashtra and Gujarat are the two major states which have attracted higher industrial investments from domestic and foreign investors because of better investment climate and infrastructure facilities. Rajasthan also needs to create a more investment-friendly environment by cutting down on lengthy procedures and providing proper infrastructure facilities.

Rajasthan vis-à-vis Other States

How does Rajasthan compare with other states with regard to overall economic growth and social progress?

GSDP Growth Rates

Table 1.12 shows wide variation in growth performance across states in the pre-reform period (1980-81 to 1990-91), and the post-reform period (1991-92 to 1998-99).

TABLE 1.12

Rate of Growth of GSDP (1980-81 prices)

(% per annum)

States	*1980-81 to 1990-91*	*1991-92 to 1998-99*
Bihar	4.66	2.88
Uttar Pradesh	4.95	3.58
Madhya Pradesh	4.56	5.89
Rajasthan	**6.60**	**5.85**
Gujarat	5.08	8.15
Maharashtra	6.02	8.01
Punjab	5.32	4.77
Orissa	4.29	3.56
GDP (National Accounts) (country as a whole)	5.47	6.50

Source: "States Under Reforms: Uneven Growth Momentum" (Montek S. Ahluwalia), p.27, Survey of Indian Industry 2001.

It is evident that Rajasthan has performed fairly well in relation to GSDP. Between 1980-81 and 1990-91, its growth rate was 6.60 per cent per annum, which was the highest amongst 14 states studied for the purpose. It was also higher than the national average of 5.47 per cent. Kerala achieved the lowest growth rate of 3.57 per cent during this period. But during the reforms period (1991-92 to 1998-99), Rajasthan's growth rate declined to 5.85 per cent, which was lower than the national average of 6.50 per cent. However, it was still higher than states like Bihar, Uttar Pradesh, Orissa, Kerala and Punjab. In the 1990s, Gujarat achieved the highest growth rate of 8.15 per cent, followed by Maharashtra with 8 per cent. Kerala, despite its commendable achievements in human development indices, performed poorly on the economic front, while Rajasthan demonstrated poor human development indices but creditable economic performance. This shortcoming needs to be rectified in the Tenth Plan period by streamlining and strengthening the administration of the social sector.[10]

The growth rate of per capita GSDP in Rajasthan was 3.96 per cent per year in the 1980s and 3.48 per cent in the 1990s, the reduction being attributed to population increase. Interestingly, Rajasthan had the highest growth rate of per capita GSDP among 14 states during 1981-91 and it was also higher than the combined average for 14 states. In the 1990s, Gujarat recorded the highest growth rate in per capita terms of 6.73 per cent, followed by Maharashtra with 6.19 per cent. Rajasthan's per capita GSDP growth was about half of that of Gujarat in the 1990s and the gap needs to reduced by accelerating the overall growth rate and decelerating population growth rate.

Demographic Indicators

Rajasthan's population increased from 34.3 million in 1981 to 56.5 million in 2001. The decadal growth of population has come down from 32.44 in 1971-81 to 28.33 in 1991-2001. The inter-district decadal variation (1991-2001) ranged from 19.88 in Rajsamand to 47 in Jaisalmer. According to the 2001 Census figures (provisional), Rajasthan has a population density of 165, against 129 in 1991. The population density ranged from 13 in Jaisalmer to 471 in Jaipur.

Rajasthan, along with few other states in north India has poor human development indicators. The backwardness of these states has to do with various factors relating to historical legacy, geography, literacy levels access to modern media etc. It would be unfair to compare Rajasthan with Kerala because the latter's success in human development has a long history of social progress.

Infrastructure, Agriculture and Industry

Rajasthan has lagged behind many other states in several economic indicators. The following weights have been assigned for preparing socio-economic infrastructure indices: power (20 per cent), irrigation (20 per cent), roads (15 per cent), railways (20 per cent), post offices (5 per cent), education (10 per cent), health (4 per cent) and banking (6 per cent). Table 1.13 presents the socio-economic infrastructure indices for 1999.

TABLE 1.13

Socio-Economic Infrastructure Indices for Selected States (1999)

States	*Socio-economic Infrastructure Index (1999)*	*Per Hectare Fertiliser Consumption on Gross cropped area (plant nutrient kg/ha) (1999-2000)*	*NVA in Factory Sector (% share in all-India total) (1996-97)*
Bihar	81.3	98.4	4.9
Gujarat	124.3	91.0	12.3
Madhya Pradesh	76.8	46.1	5.6
Uttar Pradesh	101.2	123.5	9.6
Punjab	187.6 (H)	180.0	3.6 (L)
West Bengal	111.2	133.8	5.5
Maharashtra	112.8	88.8	21.2 (H)
Rajasthan	**75.9 (L)**	**36.0**	**3.5 (1997-98) (L)**
All-India	100	94.7	100.0

Note: H = highest; L = lowest

Source: For Infrastructure, T.C.A. Anant, K.L. Krishna & Uma Datta Roy Choudhry (1999), Measuring Inter-State Differentials in Infrastructure in EFC Report, June 2000, p. 218, Annexure VI.5., for columns (3) and (4), Statistical Outline of India 2001-2001, p.133 & p.146 respectively.

Rajasthan is at the lowest level in all the three indicators and is, therefore, considered backward in terms of agricultural and industrial development. Even in 1998-99, the net value added in the factory-sector in Rajasthan was a mere 2.5 per cent compared to 21.5 per cent in Maharashtra, 13 per cent in Gujarat and 7.2 per cent in Uttar Pradesh.[11] Rajasthan has to take big strides in improving its industrial position in future.

10. Measured at constant (1993-94) prices, growth rate of per capita income is conventionally regarded as an index of real growth. However, policy makers have started using a much broader concept for measuring the growth or development in a given state. Now, besides growth rate of per capita income at constant prices, reduction in inequalities of income, creation of additional employment opportunities, and improvement in human development parameters such as literacy, health, gender empowerment social security etc. are also taken into account when assessing levels of development.

11. Annual Survey of Industries 1998-99-Vol. I, CSO, March 2001. This is largely due to an extremely small size of most industrial units all over the state, and very high share of inputs coupled with low value added in industrial units.

Its infrastructure index is three-fourths of the average national level and per hectare consumption of fertilisers is one-fifth the level attained in Punjab. Fertiliser consumption, coverage under high-yielding variety seeds, percentage of area under irrigation etc. are some indicators which determine the levels of productivity and income of farmers. All these inputs also show a stress on the available water resources. In fact, for a water-scarce state like Rajasthan low consumption of chemical fertilisers per ha. may not serve as an indicator of low agricultural development.

District-wise Economic Profile

Major Demographic Indicators

The districts with a high percentage decadal growth rate in population in 1991-2001 were Jaisalmer (47.45 per cent), followed by Bikaner (38.18 per cent) and Barmer (36.83 per cent). The districts with a low percentage decadal growth rate during this period were Rajsamand (19.88 per cent) followed by Jhunjhunu (20.90 per cent) and Chittorgarh (21.46 per cent). The decadal growth for the state as a whole was 28.33 per cent. Unlike Kerala, there is no explicit correlation between the literacy rate and decadal growth of population. After a careful study of the impact of immigration on the population of the high growth districts, measures towards population control and family planning should be concentrated more vigorously in these districts.

Kota district had the highest literacy rate of 74.45 per cent, followed by Jhunjhunu (73.61 per cent) and Sikar (71.19 per cent). The districts with low literacy rate were Banswara (44.22 per cent), Jalore (46.51 per cent) and Dungarpur (48.32 per cent) while the state average was 61.03 per cent. The literacy campaign should be intensified, especially in districts with literacy rates below 50 per cent. But literacy programmes should be continued with greater vigour in other districts also.

As population growth rates and literacy rates have a direct impact on economic growth of a region, these need to be given a very high priority in the population planning agenda.

Agriculture and Allied Sectors

Animal Husbandry[12]

Animal husbandry is a significant source of supplementary income (in some cases, main source) in Rajasthan. The total livestock in the state in 1997 has been estimated at 5.47 crore, out of which the number of cattle was 1.21 crore, buffaloes 97.7 lakh, sheep 1.46 crore, goats 1.70 crore, and the rest were other livestock such as horses and camels etc. Udaipur had the highest number of cattle (9.69 lakh) while Barmer had the highest sheep population (15.3 lakh). Droughts and famines take a heavy toll of livestock and necessary steps should be taken to preserve and promote the state's cattle wealth.

Cooperatives[13]

The total number of cooperative societies in Rajasthan in 1999-2000 was 19909. The number of cooperatives exceeded 1000 in five districts: Ajmer (1004), Alwar (1158), Bikaner (1046), Jaipur (2428) and Jodhpur (1330). Cooperative credit and non-credit institutions can play an important role in improving the economic conditions of the weaker sections of society, provided they function efficiently and effectively. The point needs to be made that the state's Cooperative Department has grown enormously and is hamstrung by multiple laws. A review of the Department must be made and it should be freed from unnecessary government interference so that it can foster a real people's movement. A model legislation needs to be enacted to achieve this goal.

Factory Sector

Rajasthan has traditionally been an agrarian economy. However, over the past few decades, there has been emphasis on developing industry. The DES has been conducting an annual survey of industries, which covers manufacturing units registered under Sections 2m(i) and 2m(ii) of the Factories Act, 1948 as well as *bidi* and cigar manufacturing establishments. The survey covers activities related to manufacturing processes, repair services, generation and transmission etc. of electricity, gas and water supply and cold storage. A total of 4909 factories were surveyed in 1998-99 and the total employment in these units was 2,51,520.

Mineral Production in Districts

Rajasthan enjoys virtual monopoly in the production of minerals like copper ore, limestone, iron ore, gypsum, wallastonite, silica sand etc., contributing over 70 per cent of the total production in the country.

---

12. Statistical Abstract Rajasthan, 2000, pp. 156-161.

13. *ibid*, p.173.

Infrastructure

Electricity and Power

Of the total installed capacity of state-owned generators of 1554.35 MW (revised), Kota Thermal Power Station contributed 850 MW, Suratgarh Thermal Power Station 500 MW and the Mahi Hydel Project 140 MW. The remainder came from other small capacity hydel, gas and wind projects.

The total consumption of electricity in the state touched 1625 crore Kwh in 1999-2000. Table 1.14 gives the share of electricity consumption of eight major districts, which account for 55 per cent of the total consumption in the state.

TABLE 1.14

Consumption of Electricity by Major Districts, 1999-2000

Districts	*(Crore Kwh)*
Jaipur	238.8
Alwar	113.9
Jodhpur	102.3
Jhunjhunu	94.1
Nagaur	89.7
Chittorgarh	88.7
Udaipur	81.9
Sikar	80.9
Total of eight districts	890.3

Source: Statistical Abstract, Rajasthan, 2000, p. 225.

In 1999-2000, only three districts consumed more than 100 crore Kwh of electricity: Jaipur, Alwar and Jodhpur. The fact that eight districts accounted for more than half of the total electricity consumption in the state is an indication of the relative backwardness of other 24 districts. This imbalance can be corrected by rapid socio-economic growth in other districts.

Road Development

The total length of National Highways (NH) in Rajasthan was 4505 km in 2000-2001, out of which nine districts have more than 200 km of NH each. They are Jaipur, Nagaur, Bikaner, Udaipur, Ajmer, Churu, Chittorgarh, Jodhpur and Pali. The total length of PWD roads in Rajasthan was estimated at 87,642 km in 1999-2000, out of which only five districts had road-length above 4000 km each – Jodhpur (highest with 5825 km), Barmer, Nagaur, Pali and Jaipur. Dholpur district had the lowest length of roads (1133 km) in that year. The state needs to give high priority to road development in its growth strategy for the Tenth Plan period. Given the high capital intensity of road construction and the severe resource constraints being faced by the state government, private investment – through Build-Operate-Transfer (BOT) and Build-Operate-Lease-Transfer (BOLT) – alone can help in the development of infrastructure, particularly roads. However, the mindset of the bureaucracy needs to be changed to enable this.

Communications

Communications play a key role in socio-economic development in modern times. Table 1.15 shows the situation with regard to communication facilities in eight districts in 1999-2000.

TABLE 1.15

Communication Facilities in Eight Districts, 1999-2000

District	*Post Offices*	*Telegraph Offices*	*Telephone Exchanges*	*Public Call Offices (Rural)*
Ajmer	430	61	81	989
Alwar	492	82	100	1073
Barmer	479	104	64	896
Jaipur	599	143	150	859
Jhunjhunu	413	106	69	839
Nagaur	542	165	98	1026
Sikar	467	153	85	773
Udaipur	493	85	79	1136
Total of eight districts	3915 (38)	899 (39)	726 (37)	1791 (32)
Rajasthan	**10394**	**2310**	**1958**	**23727**

Note: Figures in parentheses show cumulative percentage of these districts.

Source: Statistical Abstract, Rajasthan, 2000, p.252

Eight of the state's 32 districts had more than one-third of the various communication facilities.

Social Sector Development

Education

There were 69,174 schools/educational institutions (up to senior secondary level) in the state in 1999-2000. Jaipur had the largest number of institutions (4919) and Sirohi the lowest (832). Nearly 1.08 crore students were enrolled in these institutions, of which the highest number of 9.7 lakh students were in Jaipur district alone.

There were 279 colleges in the state in 1999-2000, 45 of them in Jaipur district, 22 in Ajmer and 21 in Jhunjhunu. Bundi, Jaisalmer and Baran had only two colleges each (one for boys and the other for girls). Apart from this, there were 24 polytechnics, 97 Industrial Training Institutes (ITIs), seven engineering colleges and six medical colleges in the state in 1997-98. The state has five ayurvedic colleges. Subsidisation of higher, technical and professional education is no more a priority of the state government. However, primary education must continue to receive top priority in the allocation of government resources.

Health

The number of medical institutions increased from 10924 in 1995-96 to 12247 in 1999-2000. Their number exceeded 500 each in seven districts – Jaipur, Nagaur, Udaipur, Jodhpur, Alwar, Pali and Sikar. Out of 219 hospitals in Rajasthan, Jaipur had the maximum number of 27 while Dholpur had only one. Medical facilities need to be improved quantitatively as well as qualitatively. While provision of primary health services must continue to be a responsibility of the state government – through Medicare Relief Societies already functioning in all government hospitals, dispensaries and centres – part of the cost of providing health care must be recovered from all patients who do not fall in the below poverty line (BPL) category.

Drinking Water Schemes for Villages

Villages in Rajasthan are served by various types of drinking water schemes – piped pump and tank schemes, regional schemes, Traditional Source Scheme/ Janta Jal Yojana (TSS/JIY) schemes, *diggies* etc. As of December 2001, 37,603 villages were covered by these drinking water schemes, out of which more than 2000 villages belonged to the districts of Ganganagar, Chittorgarh and Jaipur. However, these schemes are not sufficient to serve the water needs of the state. Therefore, more durable and more effective steps need to be taken, for a lasting solution to the problem of scarcity of drinking water, with particular emphasis on conservation and management of water resources. In the case of drinking water, the subsidy component is more than 76 per cent of the total recurrent costs. Such subsidies need to be gradually phased out. The experience of funding agency, KFW, in providing drinking water in the villages of Churu district (in which rural households share the full cost of providing safe drinking water) needs to be replicated in other districts as well.

Conclusion

It is clear from the preceding sections that presentation that Rajasthan's economy has both strengths and weaknesses. The state has a low per capita income and GSDP; there is heavy dependence of the labour force on agriculture; the state is industrially backward and has inadequate infrastructure facilities. It has only 1.2 per cent of the country's surface and ground water resources, although its share in population is 5.5 per cent and, following the bifurcation of Madhya Pradesh, it is now India's largest state with 10.47 per cent of the geographical area. Its public finances are also under stress.

However, nature has endowed Rajasthan with huge mineral wealth, it has abundant livestock resources and a tradition of culture and craft. Above all, its people are known for their entrepreneurial talents and abilities. Therefore, there is no reason why Rajasthan should not become a prosperous state in the years to come. What is required is proper utilisation, development and conservation of its resources.

A comprehensive study on the physical resource base, capability of people for optimally utilising these resources, constraints on the development of agriculture and industry (including infrastructure bottlenecks), administrative problems, weak market linkages etc. would help in preparing a holistic strategy for accelerating the pace of economic development. Regional imbalances relating to social and economic parameters also need to be highlighted in this study. Planned development of Rajasthan can be accelerated only when problems confronting the people are properly addressed by the government and the people. Rajasthan has large number of crafts in different districts and export of handicrafts has crossed Rs. 6,000 crore. Yet, due largely to large number of middlemen, the craftsmen receive only a small fraction of the total revenue. Similarly, numerous small scale units turn sick because of financial mismanagement and weak backward and forward linkages.

Chapter 2

Macroeconomic Issues

Population Growth and Economic Development

Population growth has a decisive impact on the economic development of a region. After 1951, Rajasthan registered a very high rate of population growth. Between 1901 and 1951, the population of the state increased by only 5.6 million – from 10.3 million to 15.9 million. However, between 1951 and 2001, it increased by 40.6 million – from 15.9 million to 56.5 million. The decadal growth of population during 1981-91 was 28.44 per cent, which declined marginally to 28.33 per cent in 1991-2001. The growth rates for India as a whole during these decades were 23.86 per cent and 21.34 per cent respectively. Naturally, the impact of population growth on economic development would be more significant in Rajasthan than the country as a whole.

Table 2.1 compares the average annual growth rate of population in Rajasthan and some other states and shows the gravity of the situation in Rajasthan.

TABLE 2.1

Average Annual Growth Rate of Population in Selected States

(Per cent)

State	*1981-91*	*1991-2001*
Rajasthan	**2.50**	**2.49**
Bihar	2.10	2.50
Uttar Pradesh	2.28	2.30
Madhya Pradesh	2.41	2.18
Kerala	1.34	0.90
Tamil Nadu	1.43	1.06
India	**2.14**	**1.93**

Source: Provisional Population Totals Paper 1 of 2001, India, pp. 42-43.

Thus, the annual compound growth rate of population has not only been higher in Rajasthan as compared to other states, but it has also become sticky in character. While the population growth rate in Kerala dropped below 1 per cent in the 1990s, the growth rate in Rajasthan during that period is 2.49 per cent.

The causes of high population growth in Rajasthan are the following:

- **Low age of marriage:** The mean age of marriage for girls in Rajasthan was 15.4 years in 1996-97, going as low as 11.1 years in Bhilwara district and 11.7 years in Jodhpur district.[1] Child marriages are common in the state in spite of the law stipulating a minimum age of 18 years for girls and 21 years for boys. Unfortunately, the law enforcement authorities fail to take action even when complaints are lodged. What is needed is a massive social awareness campaign about the evils of child marriages.
- **Low couple protection rate (CPR).** Only one-third of the married couples are adopting some birth control method.
- **Low female literacy.** The female literacy rate in the rural areas is 37.7 per cent. - 23.8 per cent in Banswara district and 25.1 per cent in Jodhpur district. The female literacy rate in the Shergarh *tehsil* of Jodhpur district was only 19.65 per cent, which means that only one out of every five rural women is literate.
- Resistance among certain social groups towards adoption of birth control devices.
- High infant mortality ratio (IMR) of 80 per cent and very high total fertility rate (TFR) of 4.0 also contribute to a high rate of population growth.

1. Concurrent Evaluation of Spacing Method, and MCH Services 1996-97, Family Welfare Department, Rajasthan.

If these issues are not addressed, unchecked population growth may continue in the state. Efforts made by the state government to motivate married couples to adopt family planning have not yielded the desired results. The strategy to control population obviously requires a collaborative effort on the part of government, non-government organisations (NGOs) and social workers. SPRI recently conducted a survey of 400 women in the child-bearing age and found that both illiterate and literate women are, by and large, not aware about various family planning devices, except vasectomy. It was also reported that desire to have a male child is still strong in the rural areas, in spite of bearing four to five children.

Economic Impact of Population Growth

Per Capita NSDP

Higher population growth rate results in lower per capita NSDP. This can be seen from the fact that the per capita NSDP of Rajasthan increased only 9.1 times from Rs. 1,424 in 1980-81 to Rs. 12,914 in 2000-2001 at current prices, while it increased 11.5 times – from Rs. 1,835 to Rs. 21,046 – during the same period in Kerala.[2]

Unemployment Situation

The Planning Commission had estimated that the unemployment rate would accelerate in Rajasthan in the Tenth Plan period (2002-2007) because it was assumed that employment growth during the Ninth Plan period (1997-2002) would be 2.71 per cent per annum, while the labour force growth would be 2.84 per cent. The problem of underemployment also seems to have worsened due to lack of higher income opportunities, though no reliable data is available.

Human Development Index

The Human Development Index (HDI) is calculated on the basis of three parameters - educational status, health status on the basis of average expectation of life at birth, and per capita income. All the three variables are adversely affected by high growth of population. Rajasthan's high population growth was partly responsible for its HDI rank of 13.

Socio-economic Problems

There has been rapid growth in population in urban agglomerations/cities with a population of 100,000 and above during the 1991-2001 period (Table 2.2). Population growth has outstripped the supply of amenities like drinking water, electricity, educational facilities, health facilities, roads, sanitation, sewerage, drainage etc. The cities are bursting at the seams, and slums are proliferating on the periphery of many towns. In fact, most towns and cities in Rajasthan have developed in a haphazard manner, notwithstanding the existence of Urban Improvement Trusts (UITs) and the Jaipur Development Authority (JDA). What is needed is the preparation of a Master Plan for each city with a population of 100,000 or more.

TABLE 2.2

20 UAs/Cities in 2001 in Rajasthan with Population of More than 1 Lakh

UA/City	*Total Population (in lakh)*	*Growth-rate 1991-2001 (Per cent)*
Jaipur	23.2	59.4
Jodhpur UA	8.6	28.5
Kota UA	7.0	31.1
Bikaner	5.3	27.1
Ajmer UA	4.9	21.7
Udaipur	3.9	26.2
Bhilwara	2.8	52.3
Alwar UA	2.7	26.5
Ganganagar UA	2.2	38.0
Bharatpur UA	2.1	30.7
Pali	1.9	37.1
Sikar UA	1.8	25.1
Tonk	1.4	35.3
Hanumangarh	1.3	56.7
Beawar UA	1.3	18.0
Kishangarh	1.2	41.7
Gangapur City UA	1.1	52.9
Sawai Madhopur UA	1.0	31.3
Churu UA	1.0	22.9
Jhunjhunu	1.0	39.2

Source: Provisional Population Totals, Paper 2 of 2001, Rural-Urban Distribution of Population, Rajasthan.

Sectoral Composition of NSDP

Table 2.3 shows the sectoral composition of NSDP at constant (1980-81) prices for 1980-81, 1985-86, 1990-91, 1995-96 and at 1993-94 prices (new series) for 1999-2000 and 2000-01.

This, however, does affect the study of the trend of the relevant data. If the population figures for 1981, 1991 and 2001 are juxtaposed with GSDP generated in these respective years, the per capita sectoral income data may appear as in Table 2.4.

2. Economic Survey 2001-2002, P. S-12

TABLE 2.3

Sectoral Distribution of NSDP

(Per cent)

Sector	1980-81	1985-86	1990-91	1995-96	1999-2000	2000-2001	2001-2002
Primary Sector	52.3	50.3	48.6	36.8	32.33	29.73	31.9
Secondary Sector	18.0	19.1	18.5	25.2	25.70	26.34	28.0
Tertiary Sector	29.7	30.6	32.9	38.0	42.07	43.93	40.1
Total	**100.0**	**100.0**	**100.0**	**100.0**	**100.0**	**100.0**	**100.0**

Source: Estimates of Net State Domestic Product of Rajasthan (By Industrial Origin At Factor Cost) 1954-55 to 1998-99, DES, Jaipur, October 1999, Various Tables & Economic Review 2002-2003 for 1995-96 to 2000-01, p.11.

The per capita income in the primary sector was much higher than in the other sectors in 1980-81 due to an exceptionally good harvest. However, per capita income in this sector rose only by 30 per cent between 1980 and 2001 period against 184 per cent in the secondary sector and 182 per cent in the tertiary sector. The slower growth in per capita income in the primary sector is largely due to the volatile nature of agriculture and successive droughts since 1999-2000.

TABLE 2.4

Sectoral Contribution to Per Capita Income (At 1993-94 Prices)

(Rs.)

Sector	1980-81	1990-91	2000-01
Primary	1802	2879	2358
Secondary	735	1374	2090
Tertiary	1235	2362	3484

Source: Calculated on the basis of sectoral income and number of workers. Estimates of Net State Domestic Product of Rajasthan (By Industrial Origin At Factor Cost) 1954-55 to 1998-99, DES, Jaipur, October 1999, Various Tables & Economic Review 2002-2003 for 1995-96 to 2000-01, p.11.

Table 2.3 shows that the share of the primary sector has gone down from about 52 per cent in 1980-81 to 37 per cent in 1995-96, and further to 31.9 per cent in 2000-2001. This is a normal trend in any economy's development. Along with this, the share of the secondary sector in the economy has increased from 18 per cent to 26 per cent. However, much of this has to do with the rapid growth of the construction and power sectors while the pace of industrialisation has been relatively slow. The tertiary sector has also shown a significant increase in its share from about 30 per cent to 44 per cent, although Rajasthan continues to lag behind most states in terms of the contribution of the tertiary sector to its NSDP.

The growth of the agricultural sector in Rajasthan is highly erratic due to the uncertain nature of the monsoons. Agricultural production drops drastically in the years of scanty rainfall and surges during the years of good rainfall. The violent fluctuations in agricultural output can be seen from Table 2.5.

TABLE 2.5

Average Annual Growth Rate of Agricultural Sector (Constant 1980-81 prices)

Year	% Change Over Previous Year
1982-1983	-0.7
1983-1984	34.3
1987-1988	-20.1
1988-1989	83.9
1991-1992	-15.4
1994-1995	34.3
1998-1999	-8.0
1999-2000	-11.1
2000-2001	-8.7

Source: Estimates of Net State Domestic Product of Rajasthan (By Industrial Origin At Factor Cost) 1954-55 to 1998-99, DES, Jaipur, October 1999, Various Tables & Economic Review 2002-2003 for 1995-96 to 2000-01, p.55.

Gujarat is the only other state which shows such sharp oscillations in farm output. The 83.9 per cent rise in agricultural output in 1988-89 took place against the backdrop of a decline in production in 1987-88. Widespread drought conditions were responsible for the state recording a negative growth in this sector during 1998-2001.

Table 2.6 shows that the growth rate of the agricultural sector was low in 1985-90 and 1990-92 and turned negative during the first two years of the Ninth Plan. This has adversely affected the growth rate of NSDP. In 1985-90, the 7.1 per cent growth rate of NSDP was largely due to higher growth rates in the construction segment of the secondary sector and the tertiary sector. The high 8.8 per cent growth rate in the agricultural sector during the Eighth Plan period resulted in NSDP growth of 7.6 per cent. All sectors, barring the tertiary sector, performed poorly in the Ninth Plan period and this led to a negative growth rate in the per capita income.

The high share of the tertiary sector in NSDP can be attributed to the rapid growth of some of its sub-sectors such as communications, trade, hotels and restaurants, banking and insurance and public administration. The percentage shares of communications in NSDP increased by 26 per cent in 1995-96, and by 19 per cent per annum between 1996 and 1999 at constant (1980-81) prices. Due to the impact of the Fifth Pay Commission recommendations, the share of public administration in NSDP shot up by 31 per cent in 1998-99.[3] Thus, the incomes, particularly for public employees in the service sector, show a steady increase due to rise in pay scales and dearness allowance etc., while the commodity-producing sectors are not able to record good performance. Moreover, the demand for various services is dependent on the performance of the commodity-producing sectors. Thus, as a normal phenomenon, the share of the service sector is bound to increase due to socio-economic changes in the state. The growing service sector is an indication of structural changes in the economy, and this is an inevitable process of change. But this does not undervalue the need for higher growth rates in the commodity-producing sectors, like agriculture and industry, which are the real engines of growth in an economy.

TABLE 2.6

Sectoral Growth Rates in Different Plan Periods

(Per cent)

Sector	*1980-85 PP*-VI*	*1985-90 PP-VII*	*1990-92 Two Annual Plans*	*1992-97 PP-VIII*	*1997-99 First Two Years of IX Plan*
Agriculture	8.2	3.2	2.0	8.8	-3.4
Manufacturing	5.0	6.7	0.4	8.2	-0.2
Construction	1.4	10.2	20.2	2.7	2.6
Primary sector	7.8	3.7	2.3	8.5	-2.1
Secondary sector	2.7	9.1	6.4	7.3	2.6
Tertiary sector	4.8	11.4	3.1	6.7	5.8
NSDP	5.9	7.1	3.3	7.6	1.5
Per Capita Income	3.0	4.5	1.1	5.5	-0.3

Note: PP = Plan period

Source: Estimates of Net State Domestic Product of Rajasthan (By Industrial Origin At Factor Cost) 1954-55 to 1998-99, DES, Jaipur, October 1999, Various Tables & Economic Review 2002-2003 for 1995-96 to 2000-01 p.63.

The incremental capital output ratio (ICOR) is an important indicator for evaluating an economy. However, the Planning Department has not been able to develop either sectoral ICORs or an overall ICOR for the state economy. Expert groups must be set up to estimate Plan-wise and sector-wise ICORs before any attempt is made to formulate the next five-year plan.

Growth-Potential of the Service Sector

The service sector provides a strong link between the producers and the consumers. With the process of economic development gaining momentum, there will be greater scope for various types of services, ranging from insurance, storage and warehousing to health clubs, fitness centres and beauty parlours. The advances made by information technology (IT) has opened new opportunities and had a direct impact on the economy of various states.

The state government claims tourism has great potential for generating additional income and employment. But unlike Kerala – where the state government has promoted tourism, especially rural tourism, in a big way – the Rajasthan government's tourism policies have not been quite as effective.

Rajasthan is also trying to join the ranks of IT-savvy states, with the government establishing technology parks and setting up a new ministry for IT. A comprehensive IT policy was unveiled in April 2000 and the government has decided to earmark 3 per cent of Plan outlay for the IT sector by 2003. Work is under way to create a state-wide Value-Added Network (VAN) for inter and intra-departmental communication. The Department of Information Technology has developed a Rajasthan website which contains comprehensive information regarding the state. The Rajasthan State Agency for Computer Services (Rajcomp) has undertaken computerisation projects in two major hospitals at Jaipur and Jodhpur.

Several institutes have sprung up to teach computer science and computer applications. Computer-training facility is being extended to all *panchayat samiti* headquarters and to all government secondary schools. An IT course module is being initiated as a compulsory course in all degree courses.

Private Sector Investments

Private sector investments have a crucial role to play under economic liberalisation and they are present in all sectors of the economy. Detailed information about private sector investments in the state is not easily available. Some trends can be observed in data from diversified sources. Private sector investment in Rajasthan has been sluggish due to the following reasons:

3. Impact of Fifth Pay Commission on the NSDP of Rajasthan has also been discussed in Chapter 1.

- Time consuming procedures required by the Directorate of Industries.
- Inordinate delay in granting power and water connections, despite the existence of single window clearance systems.
- Indifferent and apathetic attitude of government officials.
- Lack of infrastructural facilities, especially road connectivity.
- Irregular power supply.

Gross Fixed Capital Formation of Private Sector

The value of gross fixed capital formation (GFCF) in the private sector increased from Rs. 1931.5 crore in 1990-91 to Rs. 3862.6 crore in 1995-96 and further to Rs. 5614.7 crore in 1998-99 at current prices, which works out to an annual growth rate of 23.8 per cent over eight years. The share of construction and machinery and equipment was around 50 per cent each in different years.[4] Thus, GFCF increased three-fold over a period of eight years. Construction activity helps in promoting investment activity to a great extent, since it has wider linkages with various industries.

Productive Capital of Industries

Productive capital includes fixed capital and working capital. Though the annual survey of industries (ASI) is not confined to private sector factories, the trend in productive capital in the ASI sector shows that it increased from Rs. 10,580 crore in 1993-94 to Rs. 19,979 crore in 1997-98, but declined to Rs. 15,457 crore in 1998-99.[5] Thus, the decline in productive capital after 1997-98 is a cause for worry and it may reflect the impact of industrial slowdown.

Investment in Small-Scale Sector

Table 2.7 gives some figures relating to the small-scale sector in the state. It indicates that the investment level increased from Rs. 1,759 crore in 1995-96 to Rs. 3,116 crore in 2000-2001, recording an annual linear growth rate of 12.8 per cent.

As this includes the years when there was a recession, it would be more appropriate to examine the level of investments locked in sick industrial units. Out of 221,369 small scale industry (SSI) units in March, 2001, agro and food processing accounted for 20.6 per cent; non-metallic mineral-based products 14.9 per cent; metal industry 12.4 per cent, textiles 11.23 per cent, forest-based industry 12.12 per cent; chemicals 6.9 per cent; leather 5.1 per cent, services 10.4 per cent and others 6.35 per cent.[6]

TABLE 2.7

Small-Scale Sector in Rajasthan

Year	*Number (in lakh)*	*Investment (in Rs. crore)*	*Employment (in lakh)*
1995-1996	1.78	1758.8	6.9
1996-1997	1.86	2034.0	7.2
1997-1998	1.97	2332.9	7.5
1998-1999	2.02	2672.0	7.9
1999-2000	2.12	2930.1	8.2
2000-2001	2.21	3116.1	8.6

Source: Rajasthan Chamber of Commerce & Industry, quoted from *Hindustan Times*, Jaipur Live, March 8, 2002, p.5.

With a total fixed capital of Rs. 996 crore, non-metallic mineral based units accounted for 32 per cent of investment, and the metal industry units for 15 per cent. Despite having the highest number of units, the share of the agro and food units in the total investment was only 15.5 per cent. The share of textile units was 11 per cent.

Role of RFC and RIICO

The total investment supported by these financial institutions every year exceeds the actual disbursements made by them in the corresponding year. Therefore, the actual disbursements of financial assistance made by them give only a broad idea of industrial investments promoted by them. For example, in 2000-2001, the total investment supported by RFC was around Rs 400 crore, while the financial assistance actually disbursed was only Rs. 146 crore. Similarly, RIICO disbursed financial assistance of only Rs. 102 crore in 2000-2001, against an expected investment worth Rs. 171 crore during that year. Nevertheless, these two institutions are playing a crucial role in promoting private investments in Rajasthan.

Investment Through Overseas Investors

Between 1990-91 and 2000-2001, multinational corporations (MNCs), overseas corporate bodies (OCBs)

4. Estimates of Gross Fixed Capital Formation in Rajasthan, 1998-99, DES, Jaipur, June 2000.
5. Report on Annual Survey of Industries Rajasthan 1998-99, released in February 2002, p.12. (DES, Jaipur).
6. Rajasthan Chamber of Commerce & Industry, *Hindustan Times*, March 8, 2002.

and non-resident Indians (NRIs) invested about Rs. 2,000 crore in about 30 companies in Rajasthan. Some of the major companies with investments exceeding Rs. 50 crore each were: Kota-based Samcor Glass Ltd (a United States and South Korea collaboration) (Rs. 210 crore); Bhiwadi-based Indian Shaving Products Ltd (Rs. 119 crore from the United States); Bhiwadi-based Bausch & Lomb (India) (Rs. 70 crore from the United States); and Shahjahanpur-based Maharaja International Ltd. (Rs. 50 crore). Some high-value investment projects were abandoned at a later stage for technical reasons.

Investment Promotion Policy for the State

The state government is preparing a detailed Investment Promotion Policy to accelerate private investment in Rajasthan. It will cover industry, trade and service sectors. Infrastructure development – conversion of land use for industrial purposes, development of industrial parks in the private sector, development of roads and specialised industrial areas and transport – is an essential element of this strategy. In order to promote industry, the obstacles to converting agricultural land into private industrial sites must be removed. In addition, the present level of stamp duty (about 10 per cent) must be reduced. This would reduce under-valuation of property to evade duty. Special areas of strength would be minerals, textiles, agro-based products and bio-technology. A cluster approach needs to be promoted by increasing public-private partnership in setting up the support systems for small-scale enterprises.

Private Investment Under Trade Liberalisation

In the wake of increased competition from cheaper imports and rising production costs at home, the government is devising methods to assist industry and industry, on its part, is also trying to become competitive. As many as 20,000 small industrial units are reported to have sprung up in the state in 1999 and 2000 despite the closure of several other units. These small units have been set up with a total investment of Rs. 511.3 crore, and they have created 75,000 new jobs. Industrial promotion activity is the primary responsibility of RIICO, which has attracted industrial units that have been ordered to shift out Delhi for environmental reasons by offering incentives and preferential treatment. The RFC has also been engaged in industrial promotion activity. However, it is equally important that artisans also be provided with adequate support to enable them to face global competition.

Impact of Drought

Drought is a centuries-old problem in Rajasthan and yet, serious efforts at drought-proofing have not been made. The gravity of the problem can be realised from the fact that in the 45-year period between 1956-57 and 2000-2001, only seven years were free from droughts – 1959-60, 1973-74, 1975-76, 1983-84, 1990-91 and 1994-95. Two years — 1986-87 and 1987-88 – were the worst years, affecting 31,936 and 36,252 villages respectively. Even in 2000-01, 30,583 villages were affected but the sufferings of the people in the mid-1980s was far more severe.

The impact of chronic drought is deep and long lasting. It impoverishes the biotic endowment, accelerates extraction and subsequent depletion of natural resources, erodes agricultural capital, destroys livestock and displaces human population.[7] Since the problem of drought is a chronic issue for the economy of Rajasthan, there is a view that it should not be categorised as a disaster but the drought mitigation strategy should be linked to agricultural and rural development as well as water management and sufficient funds should be earmarked in the Plan for this purpose. This also needs to be linked with a strategy of water management.

As Rajasthan has suffered from the adverse impact of droughts for three successive years between 1999 and 2001, it would help to study the impact on the economy of Rajasthan with special reference to this recent experience.

The Jodhpur-based Central Arid Zone Research Institute (CAZRI) conducted a study on the impact of the 1999-2000 drought in the four worst-affected districts of Jaisalmer, Barmer, Jodhpur and Jalore. A sample survey of some villages was undertaken for documenting the impact of drought on water resources, vegetation, crop production, livestock and socio-economic development.[8]

Water Resources

All the shallow wells in the affected areas dried up in March-April 2000 and the watertable dropped significantly in deep wells. The groundwater also became more saline. In some areas, industrial effluents contaminated water and seriously affected the health of the people as well as livestock.

---

7. Milind Bokil, (CAZRI), "Drought in Rajasthan - In Search of a Perspective", *EPW*, November 25, 2000, p. 4171.
8. L.C. Gupta & Vinod K. Sharma, *Drought In Rajasthan, 1999-2000 & 2000-2001*, pp. 54-58.

Vegetation

Overgrazing by animals, especially sheep and goats adversely affected desert vegetation and the drought had adverse impact on the flowering and fruiting of some varieties of trees.

Crop Production

In several parts of these four districts, the crop production was even less than 10 per cent of the previous year's yield. Fodder scarcity led to a steep rise in its price and the area under irrigated wheat increased in Barmer and Jodhpur districts, because wheat straw is preferred as fodder. This led to an increased depletion of ground water in the wheat-growing districts. In Barmer and Jalore districts, the farmers had to feed mustard and isabgol straw to their cattle.

Livestock

Due to scarcity of water, fodder and feed for the livestock, the selling price of sheep and goats declined drastically. Most of the cattle were also released to face starvation and death. In the arid and semi-arid regions of Rajasthan, fodder shortage increases rapidly during drought periods and this leads to the migration of livestock. It was found that 78 per cent of the livestock migrated from Barmer district during the drought of 1999-2000, 70 per cent from Jaisalmer and 20 per cent from Jodhpur district.

Socio-economic Impact

Due to drought, people had to shift from working in the agricultural sector to temporary and *ad hoc* employment in relief works. Men would migrate in search of better employment avenues, leaving women to toil as labourers in relief works in nearby areas, though this increased the contribution of women to family income. Rural women had to spend more time and energy in fetching water and collecting fuel wood.

Strain on State Finances

Drought also puts tremendous strain on state finances. Land revenue has to be suspended and there is enormous expenditure on relief works to provide employment, arranging food and drinking water.

Table 2.8 shows that the state government has to bear a huge financial burden in drought years. The income from land revenue goes down, and relief expenditure has to be incurred, which sometimes becomes quite cumbersome. The Rs. 1,166 crore spent on relief works in 2000-01 includes the value of food grains made available free of charge under the Food for Work scheme. Drought relief is arranged from the Calamity Relief Fund, National Contingency Calamity Fund, the Prime Minister's Relief Fund, foodgrains from the Centre, diversion of funds from centrally sponsored schemes (CSS) and the money spent by the state government from its own kitty. This also affects the Plan investments adversely.

TABLE 2.8

Impact of Droughts on State Budget: Selected Years

Year	*Affected Districts*	*Population Affected (Crore)*	*Land Revenue Suspended (Rs. Crore)*	*Relief Expenditure (Rs. Crore)*
1986-87	27	2.53	7.03	162.6
1987-88	27	3.17	7.54	622.3
1998-99	20	2.15	1.68	435.8
1999-00	26	2.62	2.28	566.0
2000-01	31	3.30	3.10	1166.2

Source: L.C. Gupta & Vinod K. Sharma, *Drought in Rajasthan, 1999-2000 & 2000-2001*, pp. 54-58.

What is strange is the inability of the state government to formulate a long-term policy to mitigate this problem, initiating relief measures only when drought occurs, but neglecting the problem casually during the years of normal rainfall. It is necessary to develop a long-term perspective on drought and initiate water conservation measures during the years of normal rains. For this, there must be a link between drought-mitigation and rural development. The empowerment of rural masses has to be enhanced, so that they are equal partners in programmes relating to employment and welfare.

While existing programmes like the Desert Development Programme (DDP) and Drought-prone Area Programme (DPAP) need to be implemented properly, sustainable long-term measures are also essential in order to reduce the frequency and intensity of droughts. Proper water management is the lynchpin of a permanent solution to the problem of drought. Measures would include ensuring judicious availability of water for drinking and irrigation purposes, roof top rainwater harvesting and other methods of rainwater conservation, checking on water wastage, changing the cropping pattern in favour of less water-intensive crops, regulating the use of ground water in dark and other critical zones of water shortage, etc. Traditional water storage methods such as tanks, ponds, *nadis*, *tankas*, *khadins*/anicuts, *bawdies* etc. should also be revived. In the long run, however, linking of rivers in some areas may be the best solution. This will involve huge investments and long term planning would be essential.

Non-farm development in rural areas would also help in drought relief as it would provide income to people during the drought years. Stabilisation of sand dunes by planting fodder trees like *khejra* may be useful and, wherever possible, other trees like *ber* shrubs and *rohida* trees etc. may be planted in desert areas. The development plan for the Luni Basin should be taken up with financial and technical assistance from international agencies.

Popular Opinion on Development Issues

After half-a-century of planned development, the common man has started articulating his views on development issues with confidence. People are vocal about bureaucratic delays, lack of funds and corruption in all walks of life. At the same time they are also resigned to the fact that it is difficult to change the prevailing situation, while some more dynamic sections go to the extent of saying that complete transformation and not mere tinkering is the need of the hour. However, they are not able to articulate the contours and content of this transformation. Academicians, therefore, need to take a lead in this area, and give a blueprint of a new future. In fact, while formulating development policies, the state government must take into account the feelings and aspirations of the people.

A survey conducted by the Jaipur-based Indian Institute of Rural Development under the District Poverty Initiative Project in the villages of Jhalawar and Kota districts in 1997-98 gives some indication of what people feel about developmental issues.

Awareness About Developmental Activities

Various activities have been initiated for providing employment opportunities for the rural unemployed youth, and only nine of 143 respondents, showed their ignorance about such initiatives. The respondents did not know the difference between the Integrated Rural Development Programme (IRDP) and the DPIP[9], particularly in Jhalawar, Dag and Manohar Thana blocks. Out of the 120 farmers who were respondents, only half were aware of the activities of the Krishi Vigyan Kendras (KVKs) set up for dissemination of agricultural research. In order to make KVKs and other extension agencies more proactive, it would be desirable to involve panchayati raj institutions (PRIs) and progressive farmers in their working. Cultivators of Jhalawar were familiar with the initiatives taken by the District Horticulture Department for increasing the area under citrus crops and guava. People were also aware of activities related with watershed development.

Awareness About Locally Available Resources

Despite a number of rivers and rivulets in Jhalawar district, the people feel the area faces water scarcity during summers because of lack of serious water conservation efforts. A techno-economic feasibility study needs to be undertaken, preferably by an NGO supported by the state government, to identify a cost-effective rainwater conservation technology.

The people also feel that their area is fast losing its forest cover. Villagers in Kota district also complained about the lack of pastures affecting their cattle wealth. Farmers felt that the growing popularity of mustard and soyabean cultivation is depriving them of adequate fodder for their cattle. The evolution of an ideal integrated farming system in which all the available resources such as land, water and livestock yield maximum returns to the people, is the need of the hour.

Cultivators in the command area of the Chambal irrigation project were worried about the problems of waterlogging and soil salinity due to lack of proper management of the irrigation system. This has already happened in Kota and Bundi districts. Though losses caused by waterlogging have been estimated, long-term and cost-effective solutions to the problem have not been worked out. The villagers very strongly feel the need for the optimum use of their resources and a well-conceived strategy would alter their fate dramatically in the near future.

Perceptions About Primary Education

Only 21 out of 143 respondents were women. While all were in favour of sending their sons to schools, only three women supported the idea of their daughters going to primary schools and none was in favour of enrolling their daughters in upper primary class. Men also had reservations about sending their daughters to schools, especially after they cross the age of 10.

Priorities for Poverty Alleviation

The priorities listed by the villagers should be taken into account while formulating plans for poverty alleviation and rural development.

9. Chapter 1 lists the components of DPIP and its targets. Under this Project, four types of activities are expected to be initiated to help the poor directly or indirectly: (a) income generating sub-projects, (b) land based sub-projects, (wells, tubewells, anicuts,etc.) (c) infrastructure sub-projects like roads and (d) social services. A sub-project has a maximum investment of Rs. 10 lakh.

Participatory Role of Villagers in Development Process

Eighty per cent of the respondents were willing to contribute to the development of their villages, if they are assured of full cooperation of the official machinery. Villagers showed their willingness to contribute their share in the form of labour and materials for the speedy construction of link roads and anicuts. In Kota district, many villagers agreed to share up to 30-35 per cent of the cost of draining out excess water from their fields. They feel that this contribution will help in enhancing their income levels in the long run.

All this indicates that villagers have definite views regarding the potential development of their areas and are willing to contribute towards it. The face of the rural areas can be completely transformed if there is proper coordination in the efforts of the state government, people and activists. This would give meaning to the process of decentralised development, which is the need of the hour.

At the same time, the views expressed by the people must be assessed for feasibility and this study must be funded by the state government. The district authorities will then be expected to incorporate these perceptions in formulating a comprehensive plan for development of various sectors in the area with available physical resources. Programmes so prepared have to be implemented in cooperation with the people or their representatives.

Major Constraints in Development

As noted earlier, a combination of geographical, economic and human factors have combined to keep Rajasthan underdeveloped. 60 per cent of its area is desert and is drought-prone. Moreover, the population of the state is thinly spread over large areas, especially in the western districts, and this makes it difficult to provide basic services in a cost-effective manner.

The state government has not formulated any integrated programme for primary, secondary, higher, technical and professional education. This has caused a mismatch in the need and availability of educational facilities and infrastructure. There is a permanent shortage of water in the state. Not only has there been rapid depletion of groundwater in several places, but the quality of water has also deteriorated. This problem is particularly serious in Nagaur, Pali, Jaipur, Tonk and Bharatpur districts. The state government must work out the cost of defluoridation and identify the water bodies where such task is to be undertaken over the next, say, five years.

Erratic rainfall plays havoc with agriculture, which also falls victim to locust storms. As there is a close relationship between the agricultural sector and the forestry and animal husbandry sectors, all of them are affected. The vagaries of nature also affect sectors like floriculture and horticulture.

The state is liberally endowed with mineral resources but lack of infrastructural facilities has hampered the exploitation of this wealth. Rajasthan is also home to various handicrafts that are world famous but these also suffer from poor infrastructure and lack of backward and forward linkages. Lack of long-term industrial planning in the state has impeded industrial growth. Good quality facilities should be made available in the state to attract private investments. Rajasthan should take a leaf out of the book of states like Maharashtra, Andhra Pradesh, and Gujarat, which have a well thought out industrialisation policy.

Above all, the state will have to remove the greatest obstacle to economic development – the lack of financial resources.

Certain macro-level policy measures are needed for rapid, equitable and sustainable development in Rajasthan.

Policy Measures for Development

Policy for Rapid Development

As has been pointed out earlier, there are wide fluctuations in the growth rate of the state's economy. Steps should, therefore, be taken to achieve a trend growth rate of about 15 per cent at current prices, so that after making adjustment for inflation at 5-6 per cent, there may be real growth rate of 7-8 per cent. Therefore, it is absolutely essential to achieve higher growth rates even in drought years. This will depend on proper planning by which growth in certain sectors of the economy, which are not dependent on the monsoons, can be maintained by raising investment levels. These sectors could be mining, tourism, transport, power, construction, handicrafts and handlooms. Suitable measures can be taken to increase export earnings. This would require formulation of appropriate strategies for all these sectors and incorporating them in the state's five year plans.

Private sector investments should be promoted by providing a package of incentives to prospective entrepreneurs, domestic and foreign. Foreign direct investment should be promoted to the extent possible. Liberal concessions and facilities should be extended to NRIs (especially *Rajasthanis*) in order to persuade them to invest liberally in the state. Two round table conferences of NRIs and state government officials had been organised since 2000 but the NRIs did not show much enthusiasm largely due to apathy of the government departments and uncertainty about the returns on their investment. New investment is the lynchpin of the entire development process, and it should be promoted by all means.

It has also been suggested that, initially, priority may be given to public investment in infrastructure. In fact, such public investment will pull in private investment. This view has been supported by the Reserve Bank of India (RBI) in its *Report on Currency and Finance, 2000-2001*. As the state government's outstanding debt is increasing at a rapid rate, higher growth rate in GSDP in essential to keep indicators like debt-GSDP, revenue deficit-GSDP, GFD-GSDP under strict control. The mounting debt burden can be partly managed by the following measures:

- Debt swapping, with some assistance from the Central government.
- A strategy to compress the revenue expenditure, which will help in reducing the revenue deficit and GFD.
- Increasing the level of capital expenditure.
- Downsizing government.
- Enactment of a Fiscal Responsibility and Budget Management legislation.
- Constitution of a consolidated sinking fund to meet the debt redemption liability, as suggested by the RBI in its *Report on State Finances*.
- Disinvesting in selected PSUs.

Thus, planning needs to be restructured in such a manner that infrastructure gets strengthened first and this will result in the commodity-producing sectors increasing production and productivity at a rapid rate, which would finally trigger the growth of the service sector. Therefore, the state will have to adopt measures to achieve high growth rate by boosting investment in various sectors of the economy and external sources will have to be tapped to achieve this goal. Kerala has recently sought financial assistance from the Asian Development Bank (ADB). The ADB has expressed its intention of doubling the quantum of assistance from $600 million to $1200 million in the near future. This package bears a concessional rate of interest of only 7 per cent. Rajasthan should also prepare a viable plan for rapid economic development with the assistance of international financial institutions, foreign companies and large Indian business houses.

The single most important source of augmenting the state's resources is through externally assisted projects (EAPs), because 70-90 per cent of expenditures on EAPs are reimbursed to the state in the form of additional central assistance (ACA). There is no ceiling on the amount a state can receive as ACA and the amount it can receive by way of external assistance depends on efficiency of project implementation, preparation of project proposals keeping in view donor agency requirements, aggressive follow up of proposals and projection of a positive perception for the state, specially relating to governance and reforms.[10] The external aid should be utilised in an efficient manner by implementing the project for which ACA has been received.

There is no list of comparative advantage for investment in different sectors but some of the areas having comparative advantage are:

- Textiles, particularly handlooms and garments.
- Leather products.
- Handicrafts, gems, gold and silver jewellery, including gem cutting.
- Marble and granite products.
- Crops like oilseeds, spices, fruits (pomegranate, *ber*, citrus fruits), floriculture and medicinal plants.

Equitable Development

Apart from rapid development, the government must also ensure that growth is job-augmenting, rural-oriented and participatory in nature. Skill-formation should be promoted and people must learn new techniques of increasing production and productivity as has been done in China, where they try to reap economies of scale. Rajasthan has advantages in the following trades:

- Computer software.
- Handicrafts,
- Marble statues

10. Draft Tenth Five-Year Plan, Volume III, Planning Commission.

- Leather products
- Toys
- Garments
- Dyeing and printing of textiles
- Stone carving
- Pottery
- Gold and silver ornaments
- Carpet weaving

Further, the possibility of productively using stone dust may be explored. Finally, the craftsmen and sculptors of Rajasthan need to be given training for improving their product designs to cater to domestic and international markets. Bankable projects should be designed to assist them. China does not have small scale sector reservations in areas like textiles, leather goods and toys. India is also proceeding in that direction but more vigorous efforts are needed. For equitable development, Rajasthan must promote the small-scale sector by removing hurdles in its development. It must leverage its traditional base of household industries. There is ample scope for developing mineral-based, cattle-based, forest-based and agro-processing industries in Rajasthan, which would increase the earnings of the people in rural as well as urban areas, and reduce income disparities.

Sustainable Development

A new thrust would be needed for the preservation and protection of natural resources, combining their optimum utilisation and speedy development. The policy and programmes towards sustainable development will encompass areas like land, water, mining, forestry and industry. In this connection the problem of *sem* (waterlogging in the Indira Gandhi Canal area) will have to be solved on a war footing to save large tracts of agricultural land from degradation. This may be done via proper drainage of excessive water. Horizontal drainage in about 16,000 ha of saline and waterlogged areas with financial assistance from Canadian International Development Agency (CIDA), has already been installed in the Chambal Command Area. The feasibility of alternative methods of drainage (bio-drainage, vertical drainage, sub-surface drainage) may be studied and the most cost effective method should be used to solve this problem. The excessive use of ground water is leading to the rapid depletion of the water table in several areas of the state, which are being declared as dark or grey zones. A long-term solution will have to be found and implemented for increasing the supply of water in the state, including reviving traditional methods of rain water harvesting. Introduction of less water-intensive crops has also been suggested earlier. As far as possible, subsidy on drip and sprinkler irrigation must be done away with, and market forces be allowed to determine their prices.

Exploitation of mineral wealth will have to be undertaken in an eco-friendly manner. Cattle management will have to be improved so that it does not lead to unsustainable and unmanageable biotic pressures and imbalances.

Thus, innovative and comprehensive policies will have to be adopted for transforming the economy of Rajasthan.

A Development Model for the Future

Any development model for Rajasthan will have to take into account the development model for India, although it will have to take into account local resources, needs, skills and other issues. Therefore, the development model for Rajasthan should be a resource-based and decentralised model that would lead the state down the path of fast track output and employment growth in the next decade.

The essentials of this model are:

- Preparation of the inventory of physical resources such as land, water, livestock, pastures etc. by an independent agency. This exercise has been already done with the help of NGOs in almost 700 villages of seven DPIP districts within a short span of six months during 1996-97.
- It would focus on the exploitation of local resources as far as possible, so that the growth is stable and continuous. However, activities to be initiated must be demand-driven.
- The pattern of decentralised and participatory development would be more suitable, given the democratic and cooperative traditions in the state. In order to be realistic, plans must be prepared by the existing staff of the PRIs and they should then be integrated into a district plan, and forwarded to the state government. Such plans would incorporate the needs of people and would undertake optimum utilisation of locally available resources. At present district plans are not prepared on these lines. Rather, "the District Planning Committees (DPCs) have only

undertaken post-facto compilation of district-wise disaggregated State Annual Plan Programmes and schemes."[11] Planning at the *gram panchayat* level takes into consideration the development of basic socio-economic infrastructure, i.e., local water resources improvement, link roads, health care and sanitation, pasture and wasteland development, literacy and primary education and specific poverty alleviation and employment interventions. The plan at the *panchayat samiti* level will be in the nature of an overall area development plan based on an integrated view of all programmes relevant to the concerned *panchayat samiti* area. The role of the DPC will be of a guiding and facilitating nature, and it will help in plan formulation at the *panchayat samiti* level with the help of the data, models and project designs etc. suggested by the DPC.

However, acceptance and incorporation of these ingredients of the development model in development plans may not be an easy task, especially due to the rigid attitudes of government officials. Yet in the interest of participatory development it must be given a trial, at least on pilot basis.

Once the question of plan formulation agency gets through, the next task is to take decisions regarding the issues and strategy to be included in the plan frame. Resource-utilisation must be dovetailed with the needs of the people, as also the long-term requirements of the economy.

On the basis of a close study of the development needs of Rajasthan, the following priorities will have to be fixed in the developmental design for Rajasthan:

The following demographic goals have been proposed in the Population Policy of Rajasthan: reduction in TFR from 3.74 in 2001 to 2.10 in 2016; reduction in Crude Birth Rate (CBR) from 29.2 per thousand in 2001 to 18.4 per thousand in 2016; increase in CPR from 42.2 per cent to 68 per cent during this period, and reduction in IMR from 77.4 in 2001 to 56.8 in 2016. It is only by achieving these demographic goals that the state will be able to stabilise its population before 2020. This is necessary for increasing the socio-economic welfare of the people of the state.

- The state will have to give more attention to the development of social and physical infrastructure.
- There must be focus on creating a forward-looking, equitable and non-exploitative society. Therefore, the requirements of the economy, society, and polity will have to be synchronised in the development model for Rajasthan. The state has experienced the negative effects of the feudal past, and there is greater need to build an egalitarian society.
- The investment climate will have to be improved. A comprehensive, long-term plan for wasteland development, post-harvest handling and agro-processing facilities and increased value-addition is necessary. Private sector involvement and market-oriented pricing system would be crucial for this purpose. A renewed thrust to information technology and biotechnology would help in accelerating the process of development.

Some model centres of excellence will have to be created and nurtured, not necessarily under the auspices of the state government. The process of second generation reforms will have to be accelerated. Eco-tourism and heritage tourism will have to be developed. The state will have to be presented as a developmental destination.

Conclusion

This chapter has shown that Rajasthan possesses some inherent strengths and weaknesses. The state, the market and civil society must all share the responsibility for taking the state on the path of prosperity and development. People of the state are accustomed to living under crisis. Not only are they hard working, they also possess necessary skills and strengths to undertake tasks of rapid development in all walks of life. Therefore, with the support of the government, it should be possible to give a facelift to the economy of Rajasthan. What is required is a holistic approach to development by which there is an assured progress in the economy, society and polity. Bureaucrats must be compassionate and receptive to new ideas. The state is on the threshold of major socio-economic changes and all concerned agencies must seize this opportunity to help the state get rid of the BIMARU label that has been stuck on to it. This, however, requires a long-term vision on the part of those stakeholders who make plans and implement them.

---

11. Decentralised Planning - Proposed Plan of Action, by M.M.K. Wali, Member, Rajasthan State Planning Board, 2001, paper presented to SPB of Rajasthan.

Chapter 3

Agriculture

Introduction

Agriculture in Rajasthan is largely dependent on the vagaries of the monsoon. The coefficient of variation in rainfall is very high, from less than 100 mm in Jaisalmer to 1000 mm in some areas of Chittorgarh, Jhalawar, Baran and Kota districts. Cereals, millets, oilseeds, pulses, cotton, seed spices, soyabean, vegetables and arid fruits are the main crops grown in the state. The productivity of most of the agricultural commodities is low as compared to national average. The state, however, ranks number one in the production of *bajra*, *moth*, rapeseed and mustard, coriander, *guar* and cumin. Animal husbandry is also an important source of income for farmers.

Agro-climatic Zones

Rajasthan is spread over four of the 15 agro-climatic zones delineated by the Planning Commission:

- Upper Gangetic Plains: Ganganagar and Hanumangarh districts.
- Central Plateau and Hill Region: Ajmer, Alwar, Banswara, Baran, Bharatpur, Bhilwara, Bundi, Chittorgarh, Dungarpur, Dausa, Jaipur, Kota, Pali, Rajsamand, Sawai Madhopur, Karauli, Tonk, Sirohi and Udaipur.
- Western Plateau and Hill Region: Jhalawar.
- Western Dry Region: Barmer, Bikaner, Churu, Jaisalmer, Jalore, Jhunjhunu, Jodhpur, Nagaur and Sikar.

During the National Agriculture Research Project (NARP), 1981-1993, the Rajasthan government, for the purpose of micro-level planning, categorised the state into 10 agro-climatic zones on the basis of soil type, rainfall pattern and crop features:

I Arid Western Plain

II Irrigated North Western Plain

III Hyper Arid Partially Irrigated Western Plain

IV Transitional Plain of Inland Drainage

V Transitional Plain of Luni Basin

VI Semi Arid Eastern Plain

VII Flood Prone Eastern Plain

VIII Sub-Humid Southern Plain and Aravalli Hills

IX Humid Southern Plain

X Humid South Eastern Plain

The number of *tehsils* included in each zone is given at Appendix A–3.1.

Agro-economic Zones of Rajasthan

Since socio-economic factors directly influence agricultural production, the Planning Commission in its Report of the Committee on *25 Years Perspective Plan For the Development of Rainfed Areas* (1997) divided the country into four agro-economic zones on the basis of certain agro-economic characteristics like level of land productivity, incidence of rural poverty etc. These agro-economic zones have the following features:

- **Zone I:** areas with relatively high productivity, with either high levels of irrigation or high assured rainfall and low incidence of poverty.
- **Zone II:** areas with relatively low productivity, high rainfall, low level of irrigation and high incidence of poverty.
- **Zone III:** areas with low productivity, low rainfall and high incidence of poverty.

- **Zone IV:** ecologically fragile areas of the northern Himalayan belt, north-eastern region and desert areas of Rajasthan and Gujarat. This zone has lot of intra-zonal variations in the levels of productivity, poverty, irrigation, etc.

Rajasthan falls largely in the last three zones.

- **Zone II:** Chittorgarh and Jhalawar.
- **Zone III:** Ajmer, Alwar, Banswara, Bharatpur, Bhilwara, Bundi, Dholpur, Dungarpur, Sri Ganganagar, Jaipur, Jhalawar, Kota, Pali, Sawai Madhopur, Sirohi, Tonk and Udaipur.
- **Zone IV:** the desert districts.

Potential of the Agro-Economic Zones

Zone II

In Chittorgarh, the rocky strata makes the installation of tube wells for irrigation difficult. Therefore, tank and well irrigation will have to be resorted to, although even these are often inadequate. In Jhalawar, irrigation and rainwater management are crucial for crop production.

The region has good potential for horticulture development but adoption of drip irrigation and development of proper marketing and transportation facilities for horticultural products are important. Promotion of drip irrigation is part of the horticulture development programme and is becoming popular. The need for subsidies could be obviated by lifting all levies on raw material required for manufacturing these items and this would bring down their market prices. Cultivation of durum (hard) wheat, which has a good market both within India and abroad, needs to be extended in this zone with appropriate varieties and extension efforts. The agricultural research system should develop high yielding low input varieties of durum which are more remunerative than the *aestivum* wheat. Efforts should be made for durum farming on a contract basis with a buy-back guarantee. Indigenous varieties like *kharchiya*, *malvi* and *ikdania* must be protected and improved.

Zone III

- The irrigated belt comprising Sri Ganganagar (including Hanumangarh) and the northwestern part of Bikaner, face problems of soil salinity and alkalinity. The state government should make concerted efforts on the lines of Uttar Pradesh's Sodic Land Development project funded by the World Bank. The technology for addressing the problem has been developed by Central Soil Salinity Research Institute at Karnal. Sand dunes of varying height need stabilisation and the CAZRI has developed appropriate technologies for adoption.
- In Ajmer, Jaipur and Tonk districts, high velocity summer winds cause soil erosion. Appropriate windbreaks could save cultivated fields to a considerable degree. Mechanical, layer and biological methods have been developed for sand dune fixation. Hedge or micro-wind-break has been found to be an effective mechanical method. A number of grasses, shrubs and trees species have been identified for the biological method of fixation. Suitable species have also been suggested for the Indira Gandhi Nahar Project (IGNP) areas. Technologies for seeding, planting techniques, agro-forestry, cost-effective afforestation and people's participation as a complete package have been emphasised. In the Pushkar area of Ajmer district, there is tremendous potential for the development of floriculture. Windbreaks with varying heights are recommended for plantation.
- In parts of Udaipur, Bhilwara, Chittorgarh and Sirohi districts, barren and cultivable wastelands constitute over 30 per cent of the total area, which need to be reclaimed particularly for permanent pastures and grazing land to support livestock rearing.
- Rose cultivation has good potential in the Udaipur, Pushkar and Haldighati (Rajsamand district) areas. Breeding of high yield and fragrance varieties with proper processing, packing, marketing and transportation is necessary. The State Horticulture Department must undertake a study to work out research and other requirements for distillation and re-distillation processes. The field distillation process developed by the National Botanical Research Institute, Lucknow could be tried and growers provided technologies for packaging. Marketing arrangements may be developed to ensure good returns to the producers.

Zone IV

In the desert areas of Barmer, Bikaner, Churu, Sikar, Jaisalmer, Jalore, Jodhpur, Nagaur and Jhunjhunu, shifting sand dunes and inadequate water availability are major constraints to development, especially in

TABLE 3.1

Land Utilisation Pattern in Rajasthan State

(Area in '000 ha.)

Items	*1960-61*		*1970-71*		*1980-81*		*1990-91*		*1999-2000*		*2000-01*	
	AREA	*% share*	*AREA*	*% share*	*AREA*	*% share*	*AREA*	*% share*	*AREA*	*% share*	*AREA*	*% share*
Geographical Area	33841	100.00	34109	100.00	34227	100.00	34252	100.00	34258	100.00	34265	100.00
Forest	814	2.40	1355	3.97	2088	6.10	2353	6.86	2580	7.53	2606	7.61
Land under non-agricultural use	1095	3.23	1162	3.40	1507	4.40	1490	4.35	1725	5.04	1740	5.08
Barren and uncultivable land	5153	15.22	4716	13.82	2917	8.52	2790.0	8.14	2580	7.53	2566	7.49
Area not available for cultivation	6248	18.46	5878	17.23	4424	12.92	4280	12.49	4305	12.57	4306	12.57
Permanent pasture and other grazing lands	1684	4.97	1807	5.29	1834	5.35	1912	5.59	1714	5.00	1707	4.98
Land under miscellaneous tree crops and groves	16	0.04	9	0.02	24	0.07	22	0.06	14	0.04	14	0.04
Cultivable wasteland	6841	20.21	6112	17.91	6415	18.74	5567	16.25	4988	14.56	4908	14.32
Other uncultivable land excluding fallow land	8541	25.23	7928	23.24	8273	24.17	7501	21.89	6716	19.6	6629	19.34
Other than fallow land	3104	9.17	9326	27.34	2089	6.10	1927	5.62	2511	7.33	2444	7.13
Current fallow land	2022	5.97	1443	4.23	2085	6.09	1814	5.29	2637	7.70	2415	7.05
Total fallow land	5126	15.14	3769	11.04	4174	12.19	3741	10.92	5148	15.03	4859	14.18
Net Area Sown	13112	38.74	15179	44.50	15268	44.60	16377	47.81	15509	45.27	15865	46.30
Total Cropped Area	14013	41.40	16720	49.01	17350	50.69	19380	56.58	19286	56.30	19230	56.12
Area Sown More Than Once	**901**	**2.66 (6.42)**	**1550**	**4.54 (9.27)**	**2082**	**6.08 (12.00)**	**3003**	**8.76 (15.49)**	**3777**	**11.02 (19.58)**	**3365**	**9.82 (17.49)**

Note: Figures in parentheses are percentages to total cropped area or GCA.

Source: Trends in Land Use Statistics, Department of Agriculture.

agro-forestry and animal husbandry which have good potential. CAZRI has developed technologies for arid horticulture, especially of *ber*, pomegranate and *khejri*. This region lacks infrastructure like roads, markets, power, cold storage, banks etc, which impede development.

Ultimately, farm productivity can be raised only by developing water resources. Further, the State Agriculture and Forest Departments must prepare district-wise crop/tree species under a master plan for sustainable natural resource exploitation.

Natural Resources of the State

Land Use Pattern

Table 3.1 shows the decadal changes in the land utilisation pattern from 1960-61 to 2000-01. In 1960-61, 38.74 per cent of the state's reporting area was utilised for crop production. This increased to 46.30 per cent in 2000-01. Thus, within four decades the net cropped area increased by 21 per cent, whereas the gross cropped area showed an increase of 37.3 per cent, largely due to increase in irrigated area. The cultivable wasteland decreased from 20.21 per cent to 14.32 per cent in the same period. This change has been more pronounced in districts covered under the western dry region during the Seventh to Eighth Plan periods. Such decline in cultivable waste and fallow area has been reflected in an increase in the net sown area. The area under forest increased from 2.4 per cent to 7.61 per cent during the same period. However, these data do not provide a realistic picture of the forest cover in Rajasthan as only 11.22 per cent of the forest area is dense forest while 59 per cent area is under scrubs.

One disturbing feature is the significant increase in the area under non-agricultural use. Therefore, appropriate policies are needed to prevent fertile agriculture land being put to non-agricultural use and to properly utilise current fallows. An effective balance between agricultural development and urbanisation needs to be maintained, which will also benefit the environment.

Irrigation

Irrigation is the most important input for sustainable agricultural production. Being an arid to semi-arid state, development of water resources for irrigation has the highest priority in Rajasthan. There are presently 100 major and medium irrigation projects and 4410 minor irrigation schemes/projects in Rajasthan, with a total command area of nearly 25 lakh ha. Over the past two decades, irrigation has also been supported under various schemes such as the National Watershed Development Programme (NWDP), Drought Prone Area Programme (DPAP), Desert Development Programme (DDP), etc. The percentage of irrigated area to net sown area was only 13.36 per cent in 1960-61, which increased to 31 per cent in 2000-01 (Table 3.2). Although the state has made good progress on the irrigation front, more planned and sustained efforts are required for ensuring optimum use of scarce water resources.

TABLE 3.2

Irrigated Area and Irrigation Intensity

Year	*Irrigated area to net sown area (%)*	*Irrigation intensity (%)*
1960-61	13.36	119.01
1970-71	14.07	114.84
1980-81	19.54	125.68
1991-92	28.04	121.21
1997-98	31.75	123.15
1998-99	33.33	122.45
2000-01	31.00	109.31

Source: Agriculture Statistics, State Department of Agriculture, 2001-02.

Table 3.3 shows a high correlation between gross irrigated area and production of foodgrains.

TABLE 3.3

Plan-wise Gross Irrigated Area and Foodgrain Production

Plan	*Gross Irrigated Area (Lakh ha)*	*Foodgrains Production (Lakh tonnes)*
I	14.39	39.98
II	18.29	46.40
III	19.39	47.57
Annual Plan	22.69	48.36
IV	25.35	63.49
V	31.34	70.36
Annual Plan	40.84	52.46
VI	38.80	79.93
VII	42.07	77.77
Annual Plan	49.58	94.57
VIII	58.14	105.65
IX	—	121.94

Source: Agriculture Statistics, State Department of Agriculture, 2001-02.

Canals are the main source of irrigation in the North Western Plain Zone and provide more or less assured irrigation, while the maximum irrigated area in other zones is under wells, canals and tubewells. These areas account for 99 per cent of total tanks in the state. The main sources of irrigation in the Western Dry Region are wells and tube-wells.

As of 1997-98, wells provided irrigation in 29.54 million ha or 55 per cent of the state's total irrigated area. Canals supply irrigation water to 28.11 per cent of the total net irrigated area (1997-98). Tanks and other minor sources are important locally. The state has 2945 reservoirs out of which 202 are major, and are used for irrigation purposes. Barring canals, all other sources of irrigation depend on rains for their recharge. Even the canal systems of a majority of irrigation projects (except Bhakra Nangal Gang) in Rajasthan are also dependent on rain-fed rivers.

Groundwater Resources

Due to the scarcity of surface water, Rajasthan has to depend extensively on ground water resources. The availability of ground water depends upon the nature of rocks and their water bearing characters. Approximately 40 per cent of Rajasthan's area is covered by hard rocks consisting of Archaean crystallines, Aravalli super-group and Delhi super-group, the Erinpura granites, Malami suite of igneous rocks and their equivalent – the Vindhyas and the Deccan Traps.

Ground water development is significantly higher in the eastern region as compared to the western part, where annual ground water recharge is affected by low and erratic rainfall, absence of surface water sources and high evapo-transpiration. The depth of water varies widely across the State. The depth of water is comparatively shallow in areas to the east of the Aravalli than in the west. The depth varies between less than 10 to 25 meters in the eastern part, and between 20 and 80 meters in the western regions. Comparatively shallow water levels have been noticed in the canal command areas of Sri Ganganagar, Banswara, Kota and Bundi districts, whereas the depth is higher in the western districts of Jaisalmer, Bikaner and Jodhpur. The chemical quality of ground water is generally good in the eastern region, while it is brackish or saline in most western districts. This is a major constraint to productivity increase in the western districts.

Rajasthan's districts can be categorised under different heads on the basis of groundwater availability.

- **Safe** - Ajmer, Banswara, Baran, Bharatpur, Bhilwara, Bikaner, Bundi, Chittorgarh, Dausa, Dungarpur, Ganganagar, Hanumangarh, Jaisalmer, Jhalawar, Karauli, Kota, Rajsamand, Sawai-Madhopur, Tonk, Udaipur.

- **Semi-critical** - Barmer, Churu, Dholpur, Pali, Sirohi.
- **Critical** - Alwar, Jodhpur, Nagaur, Sikar.
- **Over-exploited** - Jaipur, Jalore, Jhunjhunu

A recent survey by the Ground Water Department for the 1984 to 2001 period shows the ground water level in Jaipur district fell by 6.68 metres, about 40 cm a year. While there were 11 dark zones in 1984, this increased to 26 in 1998 and further to 80 in 2001 with excessive water mixing. Interestingly, the arid districts of Bikaner (1.74 m), Churu (0.09 m), Sri Ganganagar (5.87 m), Hanumangarh (4.99m) and Jaisalmer (0.27 m) recorded an increase in groundwater levels.

While planning for agriculture development in these districts, it is necessary to ensure that appropriate structures are created for recharge of groundwater in the critical, semi-critical and over-exploited blocks. Every drop of rain water must be conserved.

Wastelands Including Ravines

A total of 27.5 per cent of the state's land area is wasteland of different categories (Table 3.4). District-wise wasteland is given in Appendix A–3.2.

TABLE 3.4

Different Categories of Wasteland in Rajasthan

Category	*Area (lakh ha)*	*% of Total Wasteland*	*% of Total State Area*
Gullies/Ravines	4.0	4.4	1.7
Undulating upland with or without scrub	26.0	28.1	7.6
Waterlogged	0.8	0.8	0.2
Salt affected	1.8	1.9	0.5
Degraded forest	9.5	10.3	2.8
Sandy area	46.0	49.7	13.4
Barren rocky/stony waste/sheet rock area	4.5	4.8	1.3
Total	**92.6**	**100.00**	**27.5**

Source: Resource Atlas of Rajasthan.

Desertic sand covers 49.7 per cent of total wastelands in the state. While all the 11 western districts have desertic sands as a dominating wasteland category, districts falling along the Aravalli hill ranges and the Vindhyas have degraded forests or scrub land with or without scrubs and barren rocky areas.

Programmes for development of cultivable land have helped in reducing the area under cultivable wastelands and increasing the production of various crops. The reduction in area under cultivable wastelands during various Plan periods is given in Table 3.5.

TABLE 3.5

Area Under Cultivable Wastelands

Five Year Plan	*Average Area Under Cultivable Wastelands (000 ha)*
First	Not Available
Second	70.78
Third	65.61
Fourth	60.24
Fifth	64.89
Sixth	61.22
Seventh	58.15
Eighth	51.89
Ninth (up to 1997-98)	50.17

Source: Fifty Years of Agriculture Development in Rajasthan, Directorate of Agriculture, Jaipur.

A coordinated watershed approach is needed to prepare a perspective plan for the development of cultivable and other wasteland, involving the departments of Watershed and Soil Conservation, Agriculture, Horticulture and Forestry.

Five eastern districts – Kota, Bundi, Sawai Madhopur, Dholpur and Bharatpur – have the bulk of ravenous areas. The area along the banks of Chambal and its tributaries namely Kali Sindh, Parvati, Parvan, Mej, Banas, Morel, Gambhiri, Banganga etc. suffer from the problem of land degradation leading to ravenous conditions. Ravines have an adverse effect on agro-economical activities. Due to lack of effective measures of management and reclamation of ravines, they have spread to adjoining arable lands as well. It has been estimated that the rate of encroachment of ravines on arable lands has ranged from 0.5 to 1.07 per cent per year in different situations. About 49 per cent of the ravenous area is under the government. 40 per cent is privately owned and remaining 9 per cent is the property of *gram panchayats.*

Management of Ravenous Areas

District-wise area under ravines in Rajasthan is presented in Table 3.6.

A two-fold strategy is needed for improving and managing ravines, one for government-owned land and *gram panchayat* land, and another for privately-owned land. The government-owned land should be put under permanent vegetation and the government should manage the area for at least five years. The areas can then be handed over to adjoining *gram panchayats*/village

TABLE 3.6

District-wise Area under Ravines

District	*Area in ha*	*Per cent*
Kota	1,32,600	29.3
Bundi	86,000	19.0
Sawai Madhopur	1,30,000	28.8
Bharatpur	53,000	11.7
Jaipur	20,000	4.4
Jhalawar	6,900	1.5
Alwar	10,000	2.2
Tonk	4,400	0.9
Bhilwara	3,300	0.7
Sirohi	1,200	0.2
Ajmer	3,000	0.7
Dungarpur	800	0.2
Banswara	500	0.1
Total	**4,51,700**	**100.0**

Source: Resource Atlas of Rajasthan.

communities to look after and retain earnings for their own community works. A similar approach would be needed for *gram panchayat* land. Bankable watershed development projects could be formulated for privately-owned land whose owners mobilise their own finance. The benefits would go entirely to the owner. Land, if it is of viable size, could be given to individuals on payment and a loan-cum-subsidy scheme could be developed with assistance from the Centre. All restrictions on agro-forestry, marketing, processing, etc. should be removed.

Farm Forestry

Farm forestry is an important activity in watershed development and management. During the Eighth Five-Year Plan, seedlings were raised in departmental nurseries for distribution to farmers, schools, *panchayats*, etc. for plantation. During the Ninth Five-Year Plan, Rs. 5.27 crore was kept for 185 lakh seedlings. While the programme needs to be continued, the nurseries should be promoted as commercial ventures, with subsidy-cum loans to entrepreneurs.

Cropping Pattern in Rajasthan

The major crops in Rajasthan are *bajra, jowar,* maize, *moth, kharif* pulses, guar groundnut, cotton, soyabean, and *kharif* paddy and wheat, gram and *rabi* mustard. The cropping pattern has changed over the last four decades as a result of development of irrigation potential, production technology, market prices, industrial demand etc. Tables 3.7 and 3.8 show the major changes in cropping pattern.

There was a negative growth rate in the area under coarse cereals and *kharif* pulses, whereas there was a moderate growth in area under groundnut. However, there was an increase in growth rate in area under cotton and a very high growth rate in soyabean among *kharif* crops. For *rabi* crops, the compound growth rate was positive for all crops except barley. Surprisingly, the growth rate of area under wheat fell drastically between 1980-81 and 1989-90, perhaps because of nine

TABLE 3.7

Cropping Pattern

(% area)

Cereals	*Crops*	*I Plan*	*II*	*III*	*IV*	*V*	*VI*	*VII*	*VIII*	*IX*	*1997-98*	*1998-99*	*1999-2000*	*2000-01*
Kharif	Jowar	9.48	7.77	7.7	6.53	4.65	5.24	5.64	3.32	3.45	2.51	2.52	3.58	3.50
	Bajra	28.24	29.29	30.08	31.23	23.91	26.69	28.26	23.29	21.92	21.07	19.66	25.43	24.10
	Maize	4.42	4.25	4.68	4.82	4.47	4.98	5.34	4.63	4.43	4.34	4.44	6.02	5.04
	Small millets	0.85	0.56	0.52	0.42	0.37	0.24	0.20	0.11	0.12	0.08	0.08	0.09	0.08
	Total kharif	43.58	42.17	43.56	43.78	34.39	38.00	40.17	32.09	30.62	28.73	27.49	45.73	33.60
Rabi	Wheat	7.87	8.57	7.77	8.94	10.59	10.33	9.99	11.24	12.07	12.00	13.04	17.08	12.01
	Barley	4.58	3.86	3.05	3.02	3.44	1.97	1.51	1.04	0.99	1.18	1.02	1.16	1.17
Rabi Pulses	Gram	8.63	10.83	9.58	8.71	10.41	9.11	7.53	7.00	7.39	9.92	13.28	6.28	3.34
Foodgrains	Total	77.03	78.55	75.98	76.89	72.09	69.67	68.89	62.04	61.21	61.54	63.38	70.66	59.14
Oilseeds Kharif	Sesame	3.72	3.47	3.79	3.04	2.29	2.32	2.14	2.13	1.97	1.20	1.14	1.36	1.20
	Groundnut	0.32	0.57	1.21	1.41	1.72	1.10	1.38	1.24	1.23	1.47	1.56	1.77	1.02
	Soyabean	NA	NA	NA	0.02	0.02	0.05	0.05	0.13	0.20	0.17	0.19	NA	3.42
Rabi	Rapeseed & Mustard	1.39	1.82	1.77	1.83	1.86	3.89	6.40	12.02	11.63	12.60	10.94	16.08	7.29
Others Kharif	Cotton	1.65	1.67	1.61	1.76	1.95	2.08	2.07	2.74	2.96	2.89	3.04	3.75	2.65
	Guar	0.00	0.00	0.00	6.39	11.53	10.91	10.00	9.25	9.36	8.89	7.60	NA	15.89

Source: State Department of Agriculture, Jaipur.

TABLE 3.8

Compound Growth Rate of Area

(Per cent)

Crop	*1952-53 to 1965-66*	*1966-67 to 1979-80*	*1980-81 to 1989-90*	*1990-91 to 1998-99*
Jowar	0.30	-3.21	-0.49	-15.82
Bajra	3.30	3.00	-0.26	-1.12
Maize	3.40	0.40	0.20	-0.32
Kharif Cereals	2.60	-1.44	-0.28	-1.44
Kharif Pulses	2.10	-0.12	-2.28	-0.20
Kharif Foodgrain	2.50	-1.07	-0.67	-1.03
Sesame	2.80	-4.90	-3.32	-10.98
Groundnut	17.70	2.20	3.90	3.30
Soyabean	—	—	41.20	19.60
Kharif Oilseed	5.00	-2.39	1.60	2.20
Guar	—	—	-1.74	-0.64
Cotton	2.70	1.90	-0.62	5.30
Red Chillies	—	1.60	-0.35	-1.23
Wheat	2.00	5.10	-1.12	5.40
Barely	-2.14	-0.18	-6.97	-1.05
Gram	3.60	3.20	-5.14	8.20

Source: Fifty Years of Agriculture Development in Rajasthan, Directorate of Agriculture, Jaipur.

drought years. This has affected the growth rate of other crops too, where the growth rate was negative except that of rapeseed and mustard, (3.40 per cent in 1990-91 to 1998-99). This also indicates that rainfall continues to play a major role in determining the pattern of land allocation.

The cropping pattern is likely to be determined largely by the profitability of each crop, since farmers are now adopting high yielding crops for better income. The crops on which value addition is relatively high will claim a larger share provided the requisite inputs, especially irrigation water and remunerative market prices are available.

Progress of Agricultural Production

The state has made phenomenal progress in crop production, especially after the Green Revolution. The area and production of crops like wheat, rapeseed and mustard, *rabi* pulses, groundnut, soyabean and cotton have shown a secular increase from the First to the Ninth Plan. Crops like *bajra, jowar,* sesame, barley and linseed showed an increase till the end of the Seventh Plan but later exhibited a decelerating trend. The area and production of crops like gram also showed a generally rising trend, though there were fluctuations. Details of the area, production and productivity of major crops is given in Appendices 3.3, 3.4 and 3.5 respectively.

Input Services

The level and growth rates of crop production depend largely on the availability and quality of inputs like seeds, manure/fertilisers, irrigation or level of precipitation, plant protection material etc. Availability of credit is also an important input. The progress in the use of inputs is summarised in Table 3.9.

Seeds: In Rajasthan, the main responsibility of providing certified seeds to farmers rests with the

TABLE 3.9

Plan-wise Progress in the Use of Inputs (Average)

Plan Period	*Area Under HYV Food Crops (lakh ha)*	*Use of Fertilisers (kg/ha)*	*Use of Pesticides (kg/ha) TGM*	*Production of Organic Manure*		
				Rural Compost (lakh tonnes)	*Urban Compost (lakh tonnes)*	*Green Manuring (lakh ha)*
First	NA	0.08	NA			
Second	NA	0.10	0.329			
Third	NA	0.48	0.164			
Annual Plans (1966-67 to 1968-69)	1.57	1.53	NA	12.15	0.47	0.25
Fourth	7.54	3.48	0.321	10.31	0.68	0.27
Fifth	12.76	5.72	0.370	16.45	1.21	83.00*
Sixth	24.65	9.44	0.366	27.88	2.49	0.36
Seventh	25.52	15.29	0.492	41.36	4.28	0.38
Annual Plan (1991-92)	30.05	24.37	0.382	54.26	6.31	0.52
Eighth	33.41	29.29	0.377	60.55	8.28	0.66
Ninth (Average of three years)	37.30 (Average of five years)	39.77	0.372	51.35	6.70	0.61

* There seems to be some error.

Source: Fifty Years of Agricultural Development in Rajasthan, Deptt. of Agriculture, Jaipur.

public sector Rajasthan State Seed Corporation (RSSC). Private seed producers also cater to the farmers as do the National Seeds Corporation (NSC) and State Farm Corporation of India (SFCI), which operate either directly or through the RSSC. Table 3.10 gives the details of different varieties of seeds distributed during the past three Plan periods.

TABLE 3.10

Average Seed Distribution of Major Crops

(in '000 quintals)

Crop	*Sixth Plan*	*Seventh Plan*	*Eighth Plan*	*1998-99*
Paddy	2.08	0.99	0.42	0.30
Jowar	0.81	2.65	0.05	0.05
Bajra	0.42	8.89	0.53	1.12
Maize	2.75	1.72	0.67	2.32
Sesamum	0.13	0.13	0.15	0.05
Groundnut	0.39	1.14	13.34	14.27
Soyabean	0.65	1.77	56.36	10.81
Kharif Pulses	0.60	3.28	1.34	0.53
Cotton	3.33	8.63	11.37	16.52
Total Kharif	11.28	23.59	21.88	34.04
Wheat	79.55	64.39	96.06	140.41
Barley	1.62	3.22	1.50	2.48
Gram	2.86	3.66	4.56	4.35
Mustard	2.93	10.28	11.77	14.92
Total Rabi	87.01	80.13	114.46	162.27
Grand Total	**98.30**	**102.55**	**137.55**	**196.32**

Source: Fifty Years of Agriculture Development in Rajasthan, Directorate of Agriculture, Jaipur.

There appears to be a mismatch in the production of self-pollinated crop variety seed and hybrid seed for different crops other than wheat (Table 3.11). Thus, more importance is being given to wheat seeds in comparison to other crop varieties.

TABLE 3.11

Total Seed Distribution

Crop	*Percentage of Total Seed Distribution*		
	1997-1998	*1998-1999*	*1999-2000*
Paddy	0.38	0.32	0.22
Wheat	50.36	51.71	51.00
Gram	2.62	2.25	2.80
Rapeseed & Mustard	11.03	10.66	9.90
Cotton	13.12	9.68	10.45
Groundnut	0.71	0.77	0.48
Soyabean	3.29	5.13	2.95
Arhar	0.99	0.19	0.20

Source: Fifty Years of Agriculture Development in Rajasthan, Directorate of Agriculture, Jaipur.

Data on high yielding varieties (HYV) seed is available only for the seed distributed by RSSC. Table 3.12 shows Plan-wise area coverage of HYV seed both for *kharif* and *rabi* crops. Though the area under HYV has steadily increased up to the Ninth Plan, the pace seems to have slowed down after the Sixth Plan. Although the area under HYV increased from 0.14 lakh ha in 1966-67, the initial year, to 34.72 lakh ha during the Eighth Plan, this could be attributed to the development of the private sector seed industry. The low coverage under HYV is one of the causes of low production in the state. Besides this, the RSSC is mostly concentrating on self-pollinated crop variety of seed, thus, limiting the scope of vertical improvement in productivity.

TABLE 3.12

Average Area Under High Yielding Varieties

(lakh ha)

Period	*Kharif*	*Rabi*	*Total*
1966-67 to 1968-69 (Annual Plan)	0.49	1.08	1.57
Fourth Plan	2.90	4.64	7.54
Fifth Plan	4.12	8.63	12.76
Sixth Plan	12.97	11.69	24.65
Seventh Plan	13.26	12.26	25.52
Eighth Plan	16.48	16.93	33.41
Ninth Plan (1997-98 to 1999-2000)	16.71	18.02	34.72

Source: Fifty Years of Agriculture Development in Rajasthan, Directorate of Agriculture, Jaipur.

Fertilisers. The soils of Rajasthan are rich in calcium and magnesium carbonate etc., while the presence of nutrients like nitrogen, phosphorous, potash and sulphur vary widely from area to area and, at times, from field to field. Traditionally, Rajasthan's farmers have been using organic manure to increase/ maintain soil fertility. However, the use of fertilisers is now increasing in all major crops and especially cash crops and in those areas where there is adequate availability of water.

Per hectare use of nitrogenous fertilisers varies widely. The total consumption of nitrogenous fertilisers is 5.91 lakh metric tonnes (1997-98) with the highest per hectare consumption of 74.71 kg in Sri Ganganagar district. Most of the soils in the state have medium to high phosphate content but due to the mineral's property to remain in various fixed forms in the soils, it is not readily available to plant roots. Therefore, phosphatic fertilisers are required to be applied, especially in good rainfall areas, or in fields with assured irrigation. The total consumption of phosphatic fertilisers is around 1.9 lakh metric tonnes, with the highest per hectare consumption of 38.98 kg in Kota district.

The soils of Rajasthan have medium to high potassium content. Therefore, the state consumes very low quantities of potassic fertilisers, with total consumption at 55 thousand metric tonnes. The use of potash per hectare is less than 1 kg in most districts.

Per hectare NPK fertiliser consumption was 3.73 kg/ha in 1972-73 against the national average of 17.06 kg/ha. Consumption increased to 46.04 kg/ha in 1999-2000 against the national average of 80 kg/ha. The consumption of fertilisers during the *rabi* season (67.75 kg/ha.) was higher than in the *kharif* season (33.65 kg/ha) in 1999-2000.

Plant Protection. Protection against insects and pests, plant diseases and weeds is an important element of agricultural production. On a conservative estimate, at least 21 per cent of crop losses in India are due to insects and pests, diseases and weeds in *the fields alone*, apart from losses during storage caused by grain pests and rats. This loss has been estimated to be around Rs. 8,000 crore a year.

The pesticide consumption pattern in Rajasthan is similar to that in other parts of India. Pesticide consumption is increasing steadily and is creating a medium for pest breeding and its spread. Because of this, pesticide consumption in cotton crop has been maximum, followed by groundnut, maize, *jowar*, mustard and gram. Vegetables and fruit are grown in small pockets near the townships, but the rate of consumption of pesticides in their production is very high, and in many cases surpass the safer limits of pesticide tolerance.

The consumption of pesticide in crops like cotton, sugarcane, paddy, groundnut, sesamum, etc. is high, but it is very casual in crops like wheat and barley, which are less prone to pests and diseases. Pesticides are applied only when crops like gram and mustard are affected by pests.

Two factors contribute to the increasing use of pesticides – high irrigation intensity coupled with application of high dosage of fertiliser besides climate of the area. The consumption of pesticides in Kota and Baran districts is the highest on this account, followed by Sri Ganganagar, Jaipur, etc.

Consumption of pesticides is negligible in the desert districts because of recurring drought conditions and the yields are not commensurate with the expenditure incurred. Precipitation is good in some years but considerable runoff of rainwater keeps soil moisture to the minimum and there is little scope for pests to multiply.

In the world markets, there is increasing demand for foods which are free of chemical residues. Therefore, it has become imperative for the Indian farmers to minimise – if not totally – avoid the use of chemicals. However, not much headway has been made in Rajasthan for popularising the use of bio-pesticides.

Agriculture Credit and Cooperation. The requirement of credit in the agriculture sector falls under three categories.

- Infrastructure support on community basis, including rural roads, warehouses, cold storage, container services and agro processing units.
- Infrastructure support at the field, laying of irrigation systems, sprinkler, drip, pipeline, land improvement, farm machinery and implements.
- Crop loans for procurement of inputs for the duration of a crop.

Almost all financial institutions are providing advances to farmers for the development of irrigation systems, land improvement and purchase of farm machinery. The loan share goes to the Primary Land Development Bank (PLDB). The contribution of commercial banks to this sector is relatively low. However there is a need to enhance credit flow for infrastructure development at this level.

About 83 per cent share of crop loans is primarily contributed by the Central Cooperative Bank through primary credit services, while the share of commercial banks is around 12 per cent. The share of Regional Rural Banks (RRBs) is extremely low at 5 per cent. However, there is a high rate of default on institutional loans to farmers because frequent drought lead to crop failures. Once a farmer is declared defaulter, he loses his entitlement to borrow from any other cooperative society or a bank.

Disbursement of short-term agriculture credit (crop loan) is done by the State Cooperative Bank through 26 Central Cooperative Banks at the district level with a network of 383 branches and 5,240 PACs at the grass root level. In 2001-2002 (up to 31 January 2002), loan disbursement by the Rajasthan Rajya Sahkari Bhoomi Vikas Bank for minor irrigation schemes and agricultural mechanisation was Rs. 5595.71 lakh and

Rs. 8233.42 lakh respectively against the target of Rs. 8500 lakh and Rs. 11000 lakh. The funding planned for 2002-03 is to the tune of Rs. 27000 lakh, of which Rs. 8500 lakh is meant for minor irrigation.

Commercial banks are reluctant to extend crop loans, while the financial health of cooperative banks is not sound. This results in inadequate provision of credit to the farming community. The credit system can be strengthened thus:

- A state crop credit refinance facility can be established with equity participation by the state government, Rajasthan State Cooperative Federation (RAJFED), Tilam Sangh, Rajasthan State Women's Cooperatives (RSWC), etc.
- The state government can categorise Central Cooperative Banks on the basis of percentage share of farmers in the capital of the bank.

Kisan Credit Card Fourteen banks, 14 RRBs and district-level Central Cooperative Banks have implemented the Kisan Credit Card scheme in Rajasthan. Table 3.13 charts the progress of the scheme.

TABLE 3.13

Distribution of Kisan Credit Cards in Rajasthan

Institutions	*Credit Cards issued (up to December 2001)*	*Sanctioned/Disbursed Amount (Rs. crore)*
Commercial Banks	34,979	150.71
RRBs	19,224	116.56
DCCBs	1,21,796	733.80
Total	1,75,999	1001.07

According to the State Co-operative Department, about 10 lakh members of Gram Seva Samitis were issued credit cards till the end of March 2000 and agricultural loans worth Rs. 831 crore were distributed through these cards till end of February 2000. A target of Rs. 1100 crore of disbursements to the holders of Kisan Credit Cards was set for 2000-01. Distribution of Kisan Credit Cards needs to be completed as soon as possible to cover all farmers.

Cooperatives. The cooperative movement in Rajasthan is nearly a century old. Presently, cooperatives cover activities like short-term credit to agriculturists, long-term credit for improvement of land and providing agricultural equipments to farmers and consumer credit in the urban areas. The state government is committed to the promotion and strengthening of the cooperative movement and the financial support provided by the government through Plan funds has been increasing, though the share of the Plan outlay in the cooperative sector has not risen. While in the First Plan, 5.27 per cent share was kept for the cooperative sector, in the Ninth Five Year Plan this dropped to 0.60 per cent. Table 3.14 shows the progress of the cooperative movement in the state.

TABLE 3.14

Progress of Cooperative Institutions in Rajasthan

(Terminal year of the plans)

Item	*First Plan*	*Third Plan*	*Fifth Plan*	*Eighth Plan*	*Ninth Plan (Target)*
Cooperative societies (all types)	8077	22580	18530	20200	20500
Membership (lakh)	2.74	14.92	39.42	78.82	85
Share capital (Rs crore)	0.98	11.40	83.74	416.90	600
Working capital (Rs crore)	6.38	57.00	609.78	4228.54	5500

Source: Ninth Five Year Plan 1997-2002, Government of Rajasthan, Planning Department.

Despite the encouraging progress, the cooperative sector suffers from numerous weaknesses. The flow of short-term credit has stagnated due to overdue loans, reduced eligibility of Central Cooperative Banks for getting refinance from NABARD, rising cost of credit and servicing of loans, and difficulty being faced by Central Cooperative Banks/PLDBs/credit institutions in meeting their establishment costs. The state government must take steps to strengthen this sector.

Rainfed Agriculture

As pointed out earlier, the net irrigated area in Rajasthan is only 49.07 lakh ha or 31 per cent of net sown area as of 2000-01.

Efforts for the development of rainfed agriculture in Rajasthan were initiated in 1952 but was given a major thrust only in 1970-71 at the Centre's initiative in the form of pilot projects on dryland farming and the Rural Works Programme. The DPAP was started in 1974-75 and in 1977-78, the DDP was also initiated by the Union Ministry of Rural Development. During the Seventh Plan, a Centrally-sponsored scheme of National Watershed Development Programme for Rainfed Agriculture (NWDPRA) was launched in 1986, taking 'watershed' as a basis for development of rainfed agriculture on an integrated basis.

Uncertainty of rainfall as well as its unequal distribution result in poor productivity of unirrigated land and traditional methods of cultivation cannot optimally utilise the rainwater. Table 3.15 shows the difference in yield levels of irrigated and unirrigated areas.

TABLE 3.15

Productivity of Irrigated and Unirrigated Crops in Rajasthan

(Kg/ha)

No.	Crop	1980-81		1990-91		1997-98	
		I	UI	I	UI	I	UI
1.	Paddy	1469	545	3156	1320	2146	1466
2.	Maize	962	871	1142	1338	1420	1254
3.	Wheat	1544	879	2491	1257	2574	1208
4.	Barley	1416	700	1917	1012	1982	1331
5.	Gram	854	567	908	552	944	826
6.	Rapeseed & Mustard	669	766	906	760	796	595
7.	Groundnut	569	368	1390	824	1280	1057
8.	Sugarcane*	4052	2201	530	391	4900	4002
9.	Cotton**	201	59	—	—	236	297

Note: I - Irrigated UI - Unirrigated

* in terms of Gur ** in terms of Lint

Source: Fifty Years of Agriculture Development in Rajasthan, Directorate of Agriculture, Jaipur.

Coarse *kharif* cereals like *bajra, jowar,* small millets and pulses are almost entirely rain-fed crops (Table 3.15(a)).

TABLE 3.15(a)

Productivity of Kharif Crops in Rajasthan (kg/ha)

(Area in lakh ha)

Year	Bajra			Jowar			Kharif Pulses		
	Total Area	Rainfed	Yield	Total Area	Rainfed	Yield	Total Area	Rainfed	Yield
1980	50.32	48.82	226	10.02	9.92	337	18.93	18.85	155
1990	48.55	47.74	513	9.31	9.28	597	19.91	19.86	329
2001	46.36	45.12	744	6.73	6.50	414	16.04	15.74	275

A scientific approach to the development of rainfed areas on 'watershed' basis was adopted at the national level in the 1970s with the following objectives:

- To promote the economic development of the village community through optimum utilisation of natural resources in the watershed, employment generation and development of human and economic resources.
- To encourage restoration of the ecological balance in the watershed. Special emphasis to improve the economic and social condition of the resource poor and disadvantaged sections of the community.
- To increase the production and yield per hectare in rainfed areas.

The state government set up a separate Department of Watershed Development and Soil Conservation (DWDSC) in 1991 to look after all watershed development activities. This has made the watershed development activities more focussed. The Department is currently implementing the following programmes: NWDPRA (being implemented in all the districts barring Sri Ganganagar) covering 193 *panchayat samitis* where irrigation facility is less than 30 per cent of the cropped area; Wasteland Development Programme and other schemes; the DDP (being implemented in 16 desert districts); DPAP (being implemented in 10 districts); Employment Assurance Scheme or EAS (being executed in 28 districts).

It was envisaged that the watershed development programme would lead to an increase in crop productivity in the treated areas. Though substantial sums have been spent on various watershed development schemes, the commensurate achievements have been quite slow (Table 3.16).

TABLE 3.16

Achievements under Watershed Development from 1974-75 to 2000-01

Name of Scheme	Total Area Treated (Lakh ha)	Total Expenditure (Rs. Crore)
NWDPRA (1986-87 to 2000-01)	9.29	291.68
Special Schemes (DPAP and DDP) (1974-75 to 2000-01)	10.21	346.64
Externally Aided Projects (1990-91 to 2000-01)	1.53	135.49
Total	**21.03**	**773.81**

Source: Department of Watershed Development and Soil Conservation.

Though individual watersheds have won National Awards and have been declared best watersheds in the country, this is not a major achievement, considering the problem of rainfed areas. The slow pace of watershed development is attributed to various reasons:

- The concept of 'watershed' was not properly understood by workers at the grass-root levels.
- Shortage of trained personnel to undertake an integrated approach.

- Different agencies implementing watershed programmes following varied guidelines.
- Poor community participation.
- Lack of a mission mode approach.
- Evaluation of the watershed development programme by various non-governmental agencies like Marudhar Academy, Jaipur, Indian Institute of Rural Management (IIRM), Centre for Community Economics and Development Consultant Society (CECOEDECON), have thrown up some findings:
  - Expenditure on construction/engineering works were incurred promptly but not on activities like vegetative nurseries, agro-forestry, crop demonstrations, etc.
  - Vegetative cover has been rather poor and contour bands were not properly laid.
  - The agriculture extension services were not satisfactory.
  - Many activities like organic comfort pit were carried on half-heartedly and animal husbandry development was undertaken without linkages for pasture development.
  - Watershed management work is being carried out by different agencies with different approaches and content.
  - There have been some positive and encouraging results including good pasture development, partial success in vegetative barrier (vetiver), some changes in cropping pattern, improvement of water table in wells, some changes in social and economic awareness, etc.

TABLE 3.17

Loss Due to Famine/Scarcity Condition

Year	*Affected Districts*	*Production of Total Foodgrain (in lakh tonnes)*
1991-1992	30	79.81
1992-1993	12	114.80
1993-1994	25	70.54
1994-1995	—	117.10
1995-1996	29	95.67
1996-1997	21	128.22
1997-1998	24	140.36
1998-1999	20	129.11
1999-2000	26	106.36

Source: Fifty Years of Agriculture Development in Rajasthan, Directorate of Agriculture, Jaipur.

Table 3.17 shows that the highest foodgrain production of 140.36 lakh tonnes was recorded in 1997-98 when 24 of the state's 32 districts were declared drought-affected. There was high production in other drought years as well. It appears that advances in production technologies and drought management have helped maintain grain production at a reasonable level.

State governments are now free to identify and implement programme with location-specific activities. This has made them more responsive and responsible in the implementation of various programmes by integrating schemes of various departments. Some suggestions for the future are:

1. Watershed development programmes must be taken up on an integrated basis, with the involvement of the people right from demarcation of watershed to implementation, monitoring and maintenance of work done in the watershed area.
2. There should be emphasis on programmes like aerial seeding of grasses/bushes/legumes. Livestock-based activities like providing hides and skin for tanneries, leather items and footwear industries, modern slaughter houses, and utilisation of by products for ancillary products should be undertaken. Other thrust areas could be milk-based industries, feed and fodder units, promotion and modernisation of wool carpet industry. These will go a long way in generating employment and enhancing the incomes of people.
3. Fodder banks can provide insurance to feed animals during the drought periods, with the Centre, state and beneficiaries at the *panchayat* level sharing the costs of setting them up.
4. Operational research projects like stabilising and increasing the yield of arid crops and updating technology for the conservation of rainwater in arid areas need to be taken up.
5. Research also needs to be undertaken to develop the farming system and management of limited water for irrigation purposes. There should be proper coordination between State Agriculture Universities, CAZRI and international bodies like ICRISAT. The State Department of Agriculture should coordinate with these organisations and other development departments for effective transfer of technologies.

Horticulture Development

Horticulture activities are labour-intensive and provide immense scope for employment generation and can also be instrumental in diversifying the rural economy. The state Department of Horticulture was carved out from the Agriculture Department in 1989. The state government has given emphasis on popularising horticulture among the farmers during the Ninth Plan. The area and production of fruits and vegetables are given in Table 3.18 while the area and production of various fruits, from 1993-94 to 1997-98 are given in Appendix A–3.6.

TABLE 3.18

Total Area and Production of Fruit and Vegetable Crops

Year	*Fruit Crops (Ha)*	*Vegetable Crop (Ha)*	*Fruits Production (in Tonnes)*	*Vegetable Production (in Tonnes)*
1980-81	NA	37979	NA	105205
1983-84	5130	44728	34888	129368
1990-91	21109	59039	104581	300028
1993-94	20849	67332	250550	363154
1994-95	19825	67670	229603	283357
1995-96	19795	75948	238475	356908
1996-97	20922	82602	267199	398200
1997-98	20318	82141	298069	323945
1998-99	20599	99242	238329	396132
1999-00	20347	94374	240864	343420
2000-01	20661	90392	238035	365172

NA- Not available

Source: Directorate of Horticulture, Government of Rajasthan, Reports of various years.

The Working Group for the Formulation of the Tenth Five Year Plan, 2002-2007, has projected targets for area, production and productivity of fruits, vegetables and spices in Rajasthan during the Plan period (Table 3.19) and suggested the following strategies:

1. Expanding area under fruits, vegetables, spices, medicinal and aromatic plants etc. through watershed development and wasteland area development.
2. Demonstration of improved production techniques and emphasis on organic farming.
3. Providing production inputs like planting material, seed, fertiliser and plant protection measures.
4. Distribution of mini-kits of high yielding new varieties/hybrids of vegetables and spices.
5. Upgradation of technical skills of hali/malies and farms in management technology.
6. Increasing the availability of high yielding planting material of fruits, improved/hybrid seeds of vegetables and spices.
7. Expansion of water saving devices networks.
8. Promotion of inter-cropping in newly established orchards.
9. Regeneration of old or improved orchards.
10. Creation of better opportunities for self-employment.
11. Thrust on minimising post-harvest losses and improvement in quality of produce.
12. Efforts to improve exports of horticulture produce.
13. Major thrust on development of new areas like medicinal and aromatic plants and floriculture.

TABLE 3.19

Projection of Area, Production and Productivity of Fruits, Vegetables and Spices

Crop	*Existing (1995-99)*	*2002 -03*	*2003 -04*	*2004 -05*	*2005 -06*	*2006 -07*
Fruits Area (lakh ha)	0.21	0.50	0.57	0.64	0.72	0.80
Production (lakh tonnes)	2.38	3.65	4.19	4.80	5.47	6.18
Vegetable Area (lakh ha)	1.04	1.30	1.38	1.46	1.54	1.62
Production (lakh tonnes)	4.20	10.40	11.73	13.14	14.63	16.20
Productivity (q/ha)	40	80.00	85.00	90.00	95.00	100.00
Spices Area (lakh ha)	4.42	6.00	6.00	6.25	6.50	6.75
Production (lakh tonnes)	3.59	5.40	6.00	6.87	7.15	8.10
Productivity (q/ha)	8.12	9.00	10.00	11.00	11.00	12.00

Source: Vital Horticulture Statistics 1998-99, Directorate of Horticulture, Government of Rajasthan.

Enhanced targets for production and productivity of vegetables have been suggested in order to improve farmers' incomes and raise nutritional level in food intake. Medicinal and aromatic plants have good potential in the state. *Isabgol* is being grown in around one lakh hectares area in Jodhpur division while production of other crops like *sonamukhi* and *aswagandha* is also increasing. There is need to provide backward and forward linkages to farmers so that their incomes increase on a sustained basis.

In a water-scarce state like Rajasthan, farmers must be motivated to use water-saving devices. Horticulture development should be integrated with watershed development in rainfed areas. In fact, there should be emphasis on growing fruits and vegetables in the rainfed areas. This will encourage farmers to go for new fruit crops with assured money.

The state government has made recommendations on growing suitable fruits on the basis of agro-climatic zones. This plan needs to be dovetailed with other programmes.

Date palm cultivation: Rajasthan's agro-climatic profile makes the cultivation of date palm an attractive proposition and it is under review. Research on date palm was initiated by the CAZRI at Jodhpur. A National Research Centre for Arid horticulture was started at the Rajasthan Agriculture University at Bikaner and research was initiated on collection and maintenance of date palm planting material. Experts are of the view that introduction of date palm has not been successful at the farmers' level. A thorough feasibility study is required on the issue and a strategy must then be prepared to motivate farmers of western districts to take to date palm cultivation.

Floriculture. At present there is no organised production of flowers in the state though roses, marigold, etc. are being grown in certain areas. There is great potential for increasing the area and production of roses in Rajsamand district, especially the Chaitri gulab variety, whose oil and perfume are very popular. A feasibility study needs to be undertaken. There is vast possibility of growing flowers in various parts of the state and the state government needs to encourage this sector in a big way. The export potential can also be tapped once Jaipur airport is upgraded to an International Airport. Till then the present facility linking Jaipur to Dubai can be utilised to export cut-flowers.

Animal Husbandry

The animal husbandry sector comprises animal husbandry (livestock); sheep and wool manufacture; and dairy development. It also includes veterinary education and research, which is the responsibility of the state's agriculture universities.

Animal Husbandry

The total animal population of the state as per 1997 Livestock Census was 5.44 crore which gives a ratio of 1:1 with the human population. Rajasthan has 7 per cent of the country's cattle population. The animal husbandry contributes 19 per cent of the state GDP. The cattle population has been increasing regularly except in 1988 due to the previous year's drought (Table 3.20).

In Rajasthan, animal husbandry is not merely a supplement to agriculture but is a major economic activity, especially in the arid and semi-arid areas. Income from livestock accounts for 33-50 per cent of the income of rural households. A 1990 study by the National Council of Applied Economic Research (NCAER), found that revenue from milk sales alone

TABLE 3.20

Livestock and Poultry Population in Rajasthan (1961 to 1997)

(Lakh)

Livestock Species	*Population*							
	1961	*1966*	*1972*	*1977*	*1983*	*1988*	*1992*	*1997*
A. Livestock								
Cattle	131	131	125	129	135	109	115.95	121.58
Buffaloes	40	42	46	51	60	63	77.46	97.56
Sheep	74	88	86	99	134	99	121.68	143.12
Goat	81	103	122	123	155	126	150.62	169.36
Camels	5.7	6.5	7.5	7.5	7.6	7.2	7.3	6.68
Horses	0.9	0.6	0.5	0.5	0.3	0.3	0.25	0.23
Pig	0.7	0.8	1.2	1.3	1.8	2.03	2.48	3.03
Total Livestock	335	374	389	413	496	409	477.73	543.48
B. Poultry	7.2	8.7	12.3	15.9	22.1	25.8	30.00	43.80

Source: Ninth Five Year Plan 1997-2002, Government of Rajasthan, Planning Department.

accounted for 22 per cent of the family income. Rajasthan produces about 10 per cent of the total milk produced in the country.

The livestock sector is more labour intensive than crop cultivation and accounts for a major share in rural employment with 4.5 per cent annual growth as compared to 1.75 per cent for all sectors and 1.1 per cent for agriculture. This sector has highest potential for employment generation and for income enhancement with low investment. It also provides 35 per cent of the draught power of the nation, as small landholders are not able to use tractors and mechanised equipment. Livestock are also the source of organic manure, the use of which is still substantial.

However, this sector faces problems of low productivity. Almost 60 per cent of all cattle and about 80 per cent of buffaloes are non descript and have very low milk yield. Growth in milk production is, therefore, very slow. The other constraints facing the sector are:

- Small size of land holding and shrinkage in grazing and pasture lands
- Widening demand-supply gap in fodder
- Increasing population of unproductive cattle.
- Lack of scientific and organised breeding programme for cattle.
- Lack of extension and education support.
- All services in livestock sector are funded by the government, resulting in shortage of funds.

Organised efforts on scientific lines for improving livestock will only make this sector economically viable and strong. In the Tenth Plan, the state has proposed a shift from veterinary healthcare to breed improvement. In fact, health care for animals should be a priority item as only a healthy animal can respond to breeding and feeding to increase productivity.

Cattle

The Gir, Rathi and Tharparker breeds are good milch animals; the Nagori and Malvi for draught while Haryana and Kankrej serve both purposes. They are to be found all over the state. Among buffaloes, Murrah is the major breed for milk production and it is mainly found in Jaipur, Alwar and Ganganagar districts. Though some of India's best breeds are found in Rajasthan, yet their milk yield is poor.

One step that is needed is breed improvement on scientific lines to improve livestock productivity. The breeding policy should aim at preservation, promotion and improvement of the local breed through cross breeding with exotic breeds on a selective basis. A master plan may be prepared for this purpose. According to the 1997 Livestock Census, there were 2.12 lakh crossbred cattle in the state and 1.9 crore were of indigenous breeds. Crossbreed cattle increased by 82.4 per cent between 1992 and 1997 while indigenous breeds increased only 4.1 per cent. Out of 89 lakh cows and buffaloes that had breed potential, about 70 lakh are non-descript and give low yields and not only strain the limited biomass resources but are also highly uneconomical to the farmers. The state should take effective steps to preserve and improve the local breeds.

Camel

The camel is an essential asset of the desert economy and is an important source of draught power as well as transport of people and goods. The Bikaneri breed is mainly found in the state. Greater attention needs to be paid to breed improvement. The tendency of local people to breed camels without much attention to genetic improvement should be discouraged.

Goats

The main goat breeds are *Jamanapari, Barbari, Sirohi* and *Marwari*. Goats are a source of milk, meat and hair. A cross-breeding programme has been undertaken with assistance from Switzerland and the bucks of the Alpine and Toganberg breeds have been imported for the purpose. The state government has one goat farm at Ramsar in Ajmer district for the development of the *Sirohi* breed only. The government must frame a plan for other breeds as well and the policy must take into account the vast climatic differences in the state and problems of adaptation, nutrition and health.

Sheep and Wool

According to the Livestock Census of 1997, Rajasthan's sheep population was 143.12 lakh, accounting for 26.33 per cent of the livestock population of the state and about 25 per cent of the sheep population of the country. The estimated wool production in Rajasthan is 160-188 lakh kg, which constitutes about 40 per cent of wool production in the country. The state has eight major breeds – *Chokla, Magra, Nali, Pugal, Jaisalmeri, Marwari, Malpura* and *Sonadi*. There are two lakh sheep breeders in the state and over 20 lakh people are engaged in the wool and woollen sector. About 30 lakh surplus sheep are slaughtered for meat for domestic consumption and export, providing 330 lakh kg. mutton and 40 lakh kg hides per year. The contribution of sheep to the state's economy is significant as annual business in wool production is of the order of Rs 350 crore. Though Rajasthan tops in wool production in India, the quality and yield of wool are both low, with the average production of wool of indigenous sheep only about 1.4 kg a year compared to 5-6 kg in Australia and New Zealand. The inferior genetic quality in sheep and low level of feeding are the reasons for low productivity.

Greater efforts should be made to provide better health services for sheep and feed management should be streamlined. Wastelands could be developed to provide pastures for sheep. Sheep breeders should be given training in breeding, shearing etc. Programmes like breed improvement and development of cross breeds, castration, vaccination and health management should form core activities for wool production. Price support and proper marketing of wool, carpets and mutton would provide good incentive to sheep farmers. The state also needs to give priority to the modernisation of the wool and mutton industries.

Dairy Development

Organised dairy development in the state began in 1971 under Operation Flood. The Rajasthan Cooperative Dairy Federation (RCDF), an apex body of 16 milk unions, was set up in 1978. Dairy development activities in the state have been taken up under the cooperative sector on the lines of AMUL in Gujarat.

The primary activities of the RCDF and the milk unions include strengthening and augmentation of the processing facilities, organisation of the dairy cooperative societies in the milkshed of the milk unions. In addition, breed improvement programmes like cross breeding and upgradation of buffaloes and indigenous cows through artificial insemination and natural methods is being undertaken. It would be desirable to coordinate milkshed and watershed development activities. Assistance from the departments of Animal Husbandry, Agriculture, Watershed and Rural Development should be dovetailed. Milk yield per cattle needs to be monitored so that corrective measures may be taken to increase the unit yield.

Table 3.21 shows that between 1986 and 2001, production of milk and eggs rose by 82 per cent and 195 per cent respectively. In 2000-2001, the per capita milk production was 151 litres. However, the consumption availability of milk does not match the production in different districts. In the western districts, huge quantity of milk is transported to Delhi. Clearly, there is a lot of scope for processing of surplus milk in the western districts.

TABLE 3.21

Animal Products in Rajasthan

Year	*Milk ('000 t)*	*Egg (Million Nos.)*	*Meat ('000 t)*	*Wool (Lakh Kgs.)*
1985-1986	4146	196.58	17.29	160.36
1986-1987	4168	208.83	17.57	181.00
1987-1988	3911	213.12	18.95	165.00
1988-1989	4035	225.00	19.30	170.00
1989-1990	4217	230.00	21.50	162.00
1990-1991	4338	280.00	23.50	160.00
1991-1992	4474	317.00	24.00	164.64
1992-1993	4586	348.20	25.50	167.38
1993-1994	4958	395.70	27.34	170.78
1994-1995	5050	400.00	28.00	173.00
1995-1996	5130	412.00	31.00	176.00
1996-1997	5200	428.00	33.00	178.00
1997-1998	6487	503.66	38.38	188.09
1998-1999	6923	534.36	42.33	188.80
1999-2000	7260	558.22	47.46	192.02
2000-2001	7550	580.00	50.00	196.00

Source: Ninth Five Year Plan 1997-2002, Government of Rajasthan, Planning Department.

It has been estimated that the total livestock population in the state will be 868 lakh by 2020 (Table 3.22).

TABLE 3.22

Projections of Livestock Population up to 2020

(lakh no.)

Livestock	*1997*	*2000*	*2005*	*2010*	*2015*	*2020*
Cattle	121.58	135.96	150.13	165.78	183.05	202.13
Buffalo	97.56	92.46	104.17	116.74	130.82	146.59
Sheep	143.12	144.01	159.80	177.32	196.77	218.33
Goats	169.36	183.54	207.69	235.02	265.93	300.89
Total (Including others)	**543.48**	**556.47**	**621.79**	**694.86**	**776.57**	**867.94**

The state government must undertake massive efforts to meet the feed and fodder requirement for such large livestock population. The State must also improve the productivity of 18 lakh ha of pasture lands and plan for green/dry fodder production involving farmers, *gram panchayats*, NGOs, etc. Fodder production in forest areas can also be taken up on commercial lines, without any damage to forest areas. The idea of fodder bank/depots should be given serious consideration.

Fisheries Development

Rajasthan has several inland water bodies, which offer good potential for development of both semi-intensive and extensive system of culture-based fisheries. During the years of good rainfall fresh water resources to the tune of around 3.30 lakh ha collect in tanks, ponds, and rivers. Besides, there are 0.04 lakh ha brackish water bodies and perennial flowing systems, the 214-km long Indira Gandhi Feeder Canal and about 500 km. under the IGNP in the northwest area. The fish production varies between 12,000 to 14,500 tonnes, depending on the availability of fresh water.

Fisheries development, which were being done under the Fish Farmers Development Agencies (FFDAs) in 15 districts were ended in 1998-99 and the task is now being done by the Department of Fisheries.

The department may consider a programme for excavation-cum-field raising technique for fishery-cum farming in shallow waterlogged areas, wherever feasible. The government should attempt to utilise water bodies for the production of sweet water fish, which fetches a very high price in urban markets and hotels could be tapped as potential customers. The local consumption of fish can also be increased by making fresh fish available at a reasonable price. The government should support fish farmers by providing them input assistance, cold storage facilities, transport and market support. This could be a bankable project to be financed by financial institutions, including NABARD. The state may undertake a study for development of saline and brackish water fisheries in suitable areas, with the Fisheries Department monitoring the per ha yield.

Agricultural Research in Rajasthan

The State Agricultural University is responsible for providing technological solutions to the problems faced by farmers. It does this through its multi-disciplinary experts working in different National Agriculture Research Project (NARP) centres and sub-centres. Rajasthan now has two agricultural universities, one at Bikaner and the other at Udaipur. They have a large number of research stations across the state. However, two agricultural universities have not helped the cause of the state. For more purposeful utilisation of available financial resources, there needs to be better planning and fund provision.

The Rajasthan Agriculture University at Bikaner is supposed to conduct research relating to the arid zones, something which the CAZRI also has the mandate for. Clearly, there is some duplication of effort. Besides, there does not seem to be any effective co-ordination between these organisations. The state government and the Indian Council of Agricultural Research (ICAR), under whose jurisdiction CAZRI falls, should review the functioning of their respective organisations so that their functioning is effective, result-oriented, avoids duplication and saves public money. Some states with more than one agriculture university have established a council to co-ordinate their activities. If it can afford to do so, Rajasthan should also establish such a council after carefully studying its effectiveness.

Though Rajasthan has the highest cattle population, there is no veterinary university in the state. This needs to be given priority and the university at Bikaner may be primarily a veterinary and animal husbandry oriented institution.

Rajasthan has developed an excellent research network to develop location-specific technologies covering all the agro-climatic regions of the state. However, more emphasis has been given on crop sciences and not much on animal husbandry, horticulture, fisheries, processing technologies, residue management, pesticides residue, alternate cropping etc. All research has to be demonstrated to farmers for adoption. This is a weak link in whole system. Now that the universities have identified research mandate agriculture zones, they should reformulate agriculture research programmes accordingly. The research on farming system approach should have direct bearing on increasing production in all agricultural sectors.

The agriculture universities should be encouraged to undertake contractual research for industries as a means of revenue raising. The government could consider giving a grant matching the earnings to augment financial position of the universities. The Plant Varieties Protection Act, 2002 has become a reality and research will be very expensive under the provisions of the World Trade Organisation (WTO) provisions. However, it can also be a source of revenue.

Issues in Agriculture Development

Rajasthan has unique characteristics, which need specific strategies based on agro-climatic features. Some of the issues and strategies are:

Demographic limitations The issues facing the state are:

- Small size of villages (population less than 500 per village)
- Large distances between villages
- High growth rate of population and low literacy levels
- Very limited opportunities for shifting surplus labour force from agriculture to non-agriculture areas.
- High growth rate in population of agricultural labourers including of female agricultural workers
- Problems of employment and under employment. According to the 1991 census, there were 3.2 million marginal workers with sub-optimal work days in a year.
- High concentration of scheduled tribe (ST), scheduled caste (SC) and other weaker sections in the southern part of the state with marginal land holdings.

Food Security: Food security does not imply merely providing food for all. Nutritional security is equally important. The major elements of food security should be:

- accelerated growth in production of foodgrains to meet increasing demand. The increase should be more in the case of coarse grains to meet the energy requirements of the below poverty line (BPL) families at affordable rates.
- increasing production of other components of food, in line with regional needs and demand.
- enhancing productivity of all food commodities to keep the cost of production at reasonable level. This would warrant upgrading technologies and increasing investment in agriculture. Research should emphasise more on *in-situ* nutritional security by producing highly nutritional varieties of food commodities.
- increasing the purchasing power of the masses, particularly of the poor and weaker sections of the society.
- improving post-harvest management and marketing of food items.

Food and nutritional security will have to be continued for some more time on social justice and equity considerations. At 481 grams, the per capita and per day availability of food in Rajasthan is lower than the national average. The per capita availability of cereals has fluctuated while the availability of pulses has been declining over the years. The 2.6 per cent annual average growth rate in the production of cereals and 0.01 per cent in the case of pulses since the early 1980s indicates the need to deal with the food production issue urgently, especially when the population growth rate is higher than food production. The per capita availability of oilseeds (94 grams) and milk (272 grams), however, are higher than the national average. The per capita availability of fruits is less than 10 grams per day against the need of 90 grams and 300 grams for vegetables. In order to make the rural food basket more nutritious and ensure a balanced diet for all, particularly the rural masses, there is need to promote fruit and vegetable production as well as consumption in rural areas.

There is wide inter-district variation in the pattern of food availability. During 1995-96, the per capita availability of cereals varied from 130 gms per day in Barmer to 1099 gms per day in Bundi. The availability of pulses varied from 6 gms per day in Jaisalmer to 240 gms per day in Ganganagar while that for oilseeds varied between one gm per day in Dungarpur to 536 gms per day in Baran. All districts of the state have been found deficient in the availability of vegetables. Barring five districts, all others have been found deficient in the availability of fruits. Except three southern and two western districts, all districts are either surplus or self-sufficient in milk production.

Fodder Security: The livestock population has been increasing by around 4 per cent annually and is expected to touch 622 lakh in 2005 and 868 lakh in 2020. Therefore, the requirement for feed and fodder is increasing on par with the need for food security for the human population. Even in the best rainfall year, the feed and fodder produced in the state falls short of what is required. With a decline in the productivity of grazing land in most parts of the state, the burden of feed and fodder for animals falls on the cultivated land. Besides, the fodder storage system continues on traditional lines. Systematic efforts to minimise the storage loss is important, particularly in the drought years.

Sustainable Production System: There have been wide fluctuations in the production of foodgrains as well as commercial crops. The frequent fall in production leads to low rate of return on investment and results in price instability. This discourages private investment in agriculture. Immediate attention needs to be given to the identification of crop/crop-mix, which minimises the risk, and evaluation of alternative strategies to boost the morale of farmers in the event of high risk.

Livestock Development: Decline in the use of draught animal power, whose utilisation is already low in relation to its supply, is a matter of concern because the use of mechanised equipment on small landholdings is not economical. Tractors dominate in the desert region as, apart from their use in agriculture, they also serve as a means of transportation. Draught animal power has almost entirely been replaced by mechanical power in the northeastern regions of the state. With limited scope for earning by hiring of animal power, there is need to properly plan for the herd composition and size in different agro climate zones of the State. The merger of the Sheep and Wool Department with the Animal Husbandry Department has resulted in all sheep and wool development programmes being drastically curtailed or stopped. Given the large sheep population in the state, this decision needs to be reconsidered.

Irrigation Sector: The present availability of water from the existing and on-going irrigation projects and as per existing inter-state agreement is around 42105 million cubic metres (MCM). The demand for water for non-irrigation purposes domestic use, livestock, industry and power plants) is anticipated to increase to 4773 MCM in 2015 from the present level of 3267 MCM. The availability of water for irrigation purposes would decline to 37332 MCM in 2015 due to decline in the availability of water in some rivers.[1] The state government had prepared a State Water Resource Plan in 2002 based on data available up to 1993 (Table 3.23).

TABLE 3.23

Projections on Water Utilisation

Particulars	*1995*	*2015*	*2045*
Surface water availability (BCM)	21.17	22.17	23.38
Surface water utilisation (BCM)	8.20	12.97	16.87
Ground water utilisation (BCM)	9.45	10.37	10.84
Non-agricultural demand (BCM)	3.29	5.05	8.07
Agriculture area irrigated (Lakh ha)	27.07	50.59	57.00
On-farm irrigation efficiency (%)	27.00	44.20	70.00
Off-farm irrigation efficiency (%)	54.00	61.20	72.00

Note: BCM = billion cubic metres

Source: Vision 2045, Department of Irrigation, Government of Rajasthan.

1. Acharya S.S. (1998) Irrigation In Rajasthan : Prospects and Issues. ARPU, Technical Paper No. 38, ACRP Unit, Planning Commission, Ahmedabad.

In 2001, the state formulated a water policy, which aims to help in ensuring optimum use of surface and ground water resources and check further deterioration. The policy addresses the need to plan water resources according to region-specific requirements and provides for the enactment of rules and regulations that give the state government full control on water. However, there is no indication of any punitive measures to enforce its control. It is unlikely that proposed measures would succeed in regulating groundwater utilisation because the existing enactments on irrigation do not define the ownership of groundwater on the basis of ownership of land. This results in over-exploitation of ground water. However, the state government has not taken any measure to protect the interests of people of all sections of society and, in fact, could not pass a groundwater regulation Bill because of strong opposition from the influential big farmers' lobby.

Ground Water: As already mentioned, ground water exploitation has crossed sustainable limits. Immediate steps to work out an appropriate strategy need to be taken.

Agro-processing: The network for agro-based industries is deplorably weak in the state. In the Ninth Plan the state government provided only Rs. 171.47 lakh for agro-food processing industries and small engineering workshops in rural areas. In order to give this sector a boost, district-wise studies may be undertaken on value addition for agricultural commodities, especially, spices, coarse cereals, milk and other animal products. The KVKs and the state agricultural universities should formulate an action plan to train farmers for undertaking various activities.

Agro-processing has tremendous potential for generating employment at low capital cost. Traditional items like *kachri*, *chutneys*, *papad*, *bari*, pickles, spices, etc. as well as milk-based *mawa* sweets have good demand in the domestic and export markets and need to be produced under improved sanitary conditions. Organic food also has tremendous export potential. Farmers and manufactures must be made aware about technologies and export potential of processed food products. The factors that work in favour of agro-processing in Rajasthan are:

- Availability of local work force and large number of marginal workers
- Availability of raw material like cereals, millets, pulses, fruits, milk, etc.

- Proximity to big cities
- Abundant sunshine for sun-drying etc.

There is a need to identify location specific agro-based industries and to explore the possibilities of modernising the existing capacities to suit international market standards. Some agro-based industries that can be taken up are coir making, *gur* making, colour extraction from the bark of the *babul* in the Bassi-Jaipur area, extraction of sodium carbonate from saline soils in the Kota area, dried *methi,* leaves and powder in the Nagaur area, *papad* making etc.

Seed Supply: It has been estimated that seed requirement is met to the extent of only 3.4 per cent for sorghum, 20.2 per cent for *bajra,* 2.6 per cent for maize, 5.8 per cent for wheat, 0.8 per cent for gram, 8.7 per cent for sesamum, 1.1 per cent for ground nut and 33.1 per cent for mustard. Increasing productivity of crops and organising seed processing facilities would greatly help in making good quality seed and planting material available to farmers at affordable price.

Fertiliser and Manures: The crop residues and farmyard manure are not being returned to the soil in the desired quantities to maintain soil health. There is no proper and systematic storage system for fertiliser and farmyard manure in many areas. Systematic efforts are needed in this direction with the active involvement of farmers and NGOs. The use of *rhizobium* culture, vermi-compost and other forms of organic manure and bio-fertilisers will go a long way in improving and sustaining soil health. The state must provide special incentives to the production and use of super compost and vermiculture, especially in cultivation of pulses. However, plans to increase the use of chemical fertilisers must be done with caution in view of the scarcity of water and the declining response to fertilisers in various crops.

Organic Farming: Though the per hectare fertiliser consumption in Rajasthan is only half of the national average, there has been a significant increase in the consumption of nitrogen and phosphorous, at levels higher than at the national level. This has resulted in a decrease in nutrient use efficiency and increased cost of cultivation. This needs to be corrected with increased emphasis on the use of organic manure, green manuring and bio-fertilisers. The state government should discourage the practice of chemical farming.

There are large parts of the state, particularly the western region, where consumption of fertilisers and pesticides is very low because of scanty rainfall. Farmers largely depend on the use of farmyard manure since there is large animal population in this area. But with the advent of high yielding varieties of plants and emphasis on chemicals, the traditional nutrient supply system has been gradually dying out. Given the insistence in many export markets for pesticide-free products, there is an urgent need to revert to the traditional methods of using organic manure as the main plant nutrient. These traditional practices should be integrated with advances made in the recent past to make them more practical. For example, planting of the *Prosopis Cineraria* (khejri) tree in the fields helps in nitrogen fixation, provides leguminous fodder to animals and also enriches soils by their leaf fall. Inter-cropping with such plants and other suitable crops can be used for increasing, or at least stabilising, agricultural production and may also help to control pests and improve soil fertility.

There are some constraints in popularising organic farming in the state: shortage of resources like farmyard manure, compost, oilcakes, etc.; sandy soils with deficient organic matter restricting microbial activity; high velocity winds causing soil erosion; extremely high summer temperatures; erratic rainfall; low atmospheric humidity and low organic matter in the soil resulting in poor soil moisture retention; low winter temperatures slowing down microbial activities; and shortage of labour in certain areas.

These constraints may be overcome by properly re-orienting the organic farming system and incorporating other alternative systems like bio-dynamic system. Some of the basic principles for successful organic farming at the farm levels are crop rotation, inter cropping, multiple cropping, monitoring of soil fertility, proper selection of trees and fodder, allocation of fodder plot, boundary plantation, alley plantation and horticulture, animal association with farming, proper adoption of traditional practices of irrigation, pest and disease control and storage.

Organic farming may also be combined with integrated nutrient and integrated pest management. Thus, instead of switching entirely to organic farming, farmers may be educated about the need to adopt these methods involving judicious combination of organic matter, bio-fertilisers and other bio-agents, while minimising the use of chemicals.

The state government has taken some initiatives to popularise organic farming through the production and promotion of eco-friendly inputs like bio-fertilisers, bio-agents, bio-pesticides etc. but the efforts need to be accelerated. The Department of Agriculture has selected

67 villages for popularising organic farming practices. It has also organised demonstrations on various crops involving bio-fertilisers like phosphate solubilising bacteria, *Azotobacter* and *Azospirillium*. The initial results of these demonstrations are very encouraging. The Department is also providing incentives to popularise improved organic methods of composting, like vermi-composting, NADEP, super-composting. More laboratories need to be established for this. The government should also prepare a perspective plan for adopting organic farming system and minimising dependence on agro-chemicals.

Plant Protection: Efforts to minimise the infestation of weeds and incidence of diseases and pests is necessary. It is essential that all commercial seeds sold be properly treated. Non-chemical methods like soil solemnisation, crop rotation etc. greatly help in checking soil-borne diseases. Integrated pest management should be given priority. The state has eight integrated pest management laboratories, which prepare bio-agents. The government should give greater attention to the development of technologies and their commercialisation with strict quality control. There is a need for cost effective production of bio-pesticides and bio agents. *Neem*-based local methods should form the standard extension method for mass popularisation of such practices.

Infrastructure Facilities: Inter-regional disparities in basic amenities like electricity supply, roads, communication, banking facilities, organised agricultural markets, etc. need to be minimised. Warehousing facilities need to be expanded in different agro-climatic zones to improve post-harvest management. Private sector involvement in warehouses needs encouragement.

Price Policy: The minimum support price (MSP) is an effective instrument in increasing productivity and production of crops. There are several important crops which are not covered under the MSP policy of the Central government. These include *guar*, *moth*, isabgol, seed spices like cumin, coriander, fenugreek, etc. It is important to either include these crops in the MSP policy of the Central government or have a separate price policy at the state level. The RAJFED could be the procurement agency for these products.

Implementation of Land Ceiling Laws: Out of 87,235 cases identified under land ceiling laws in Rajasthan, 6.03 lakh acre of land was declared surplus, which had to be distributed among the landless. Until September 2001, the state government had taken over 4.9 lakh acre of surplus land which was found suitable for cultivation, whereas 60,270 acre was declared unsuitable for agricultural use. Around 80 per cent of the surplus land found suitable for growing crops (3.98 lakh acre) was distributed among 76,073 landless individuals. Assessment of the economic viability of land for distribution to allotees needs a sample survey, which could also cover the size of the holding and extent of satisfaction for allotees. Land was distributed during 2002 under the Special Land Allotment Campaign and beneficiaries belonged to SC, ST and other BPL categories. 36 per cent of the beneficiaries belonged to the SC/ST groups, who received more than 41 per cent of the total disbursed land.

Getting land declared surplus alone has not in any way helped in raising productivity. Most of the land was low lying wasteland with very little potential of raising crops. Secondly, beneficiaries were so poor that they could neither improve the land, nor mobilise inputs which would improve the productivity of crops.

Distribution of Pass Books to Farmers: There are about 91.83 lakh farm households in the state. On the basis of revenue records available with the *patwaris/tehsildars*, land records have been entered in the passbooks handed over to 80.74 lakh farmers. Thus, about 88 per cent of farmers in Rajasthan have an authentic record of their status as tenants. The task of issuing of passbooks to the remaining farmers may be completed by the Revenue Department shortly.

Computerisation of Land Records : The state government had decided that land records of all the 241 *tehsils* be computerised by March 2002. Data entry was completed in 208 tehsils and computerised record for 194 tehsils has been verified. Work is on in the remaining tehsils and data entry for 94.98 per cent of the land records had been completed by June 2002. Verification of data has been done in 18 out of 32 districts.

Pasture and Gochar Lands: According to the Rajasthan Panchayat (General) Rules, the revenue authorities are supposed to reserve adequate areas for grazing of village cattle, and to ensure that strict action is taken against encroachers. However, the former landlords did not surrender such land to the *panchayats*. Demarcation of grazing land has thus been an extremely difficult task.

There is a positive relationship between the size of holdings and size of cattle holding in the state. According to Revenue Board records, though Rajasthan has nearly 15 per cent of the country's cattle population, the share of permanent pastures and other gochar land is less than 5 per cent. In Ganganagar,

Hanumangarh, Baran, Bharatpur and Alwar, the corresponding ratio was less than 3 per cent till 2001. Besides, the state has more than 2.6 lakh ha of barren and uncultivable land. It, therefore, seems proper to motivate marginal and small farmers to form groups and grow grass on the wasteland with the support of the revenue and forest departments. This would partly solve their problem of not having any demarcated pasture land in their villages.

Policy Issues and Recommendations

Rajasthan has immense potential to leverage agriculture for overall economic growth. The state government, however, needs to take certain policy measures to enhance the pace of development. These are stated as under:

Land Use

The following issues must be considered while framing a State Land Use Policy.

- Land use should be delineated on the basis of arid, semi-arid and assured irrigated areas. Land must be allocated for different uses based upon land capability, land productivity and production goals.
- Land use in urban areas should be carefully planned without adversely affecting the agricultural land.
- Development of infrastructure like irrigation, electricity supply, transportation and communication should be given importance in planning, with optimum utilisation of land resources.
- Due consideration must be given to changes in economic growth, and on limits for the conversion of agricultural land for non-agricultural purposes.
- Wastelands should be developed into productive land, which can provide bio-mass. Such lands could be allotted to landless labour, small and marginal farmers, ex-servicemen, unemployed agriculture graduates, small entrepreneurs, etc.
- Problem/sick soils should be reclaimed with people's participation providing them resource support.
- Proper drainage systems should be developed for flood-prone and low lands.
- Consolidation of land holdings should be undertaken to facilitate mechanisation and social forestry, including allocation of land for grazing. Issues related to land records and tenure-tenancy ownership sales etc. should be addressed simultaneously.
- Cropping patterns and mixed farming should be planned on the basis of suitability of land for growing food crops, cereals, high value crops, fruits, aromatic and medicinal plants, etc. Rotational grazing by animal/livestock and stock feeding should be promoted to prevent degradation of grasslands.
- Priority should be given to the development and protection of forest cover and measures for environmental protection.
- Due consideration should be given to the maintenance of soil health.
- Adequate land should be earmarked for agro-industries, with required facilities being provided.
- The Land Use Board should help the state government in the development of a database on land resources on the basis of revenue records, topo-sheets, aerial photos, satellite imageries, soil survey reports, etc. The state land use planners may take advantage of information available from the State Remote Sensing systems and national organisations like the National Land Use and Conservation Board (NLCB), National Wasteland Development Board (NWDB) and National Afforestation and Eco-Development Board. The state Land Use Board can take up coordination work.
- The National Land Use Policy outline should be taken into consideration while framing the State Land Use Policy.
- Campaigns should be organised to raise awareness about effective conservation management and development of land resources.
- The Land Use Board should periodically monitor the implementation of policy measures and develop programmes in line with new needs and areas in order to prevent any further deterioration of land resources.
- The proposed Land Use Policy should examine the legal support available for enforcement in the form of existing state and Central laws, and to consider the need for a comprehensive legislation to provide some teeth to agencies entrusted with the task of implementation of the policy.

Water Use and Irrigation

The State Water Policy adopted in 1999 addresses a number of issues for maximum development and optimum utilisation of the scarce water resources in the state and has set certain goals and targets for 2045. The policy emphasises the need for a time-bound Action Plan for successful implementation. The policy is based on some assumptions/projections regarding the development of water resources and maximisation of water use efficiencies. A policy on pricing of irrigation water is the need of the hour and will be to the mutual benefit of the users and the state.

Water saving devices like drip and sprinkler systems should be promoted in a big way, *without* resorting to subsidies. However, other measures should be taken to reasonably reduce the cost of production. Alternatively, market forces may be allowed to determine their prices.

Minor irrigation should be under the jurisdiction of the Agriculture Department, for proper on-farm water management. The state government should consider the formation of a Department of Water by merging the departments of Irrigation (dealing with surface and ground water), Public Health and Engineering Department (PHED) (dealing with drinking water) and DWDSC.

Rainfed Agriculture

All agriculture development in rainfed areas should be planned and implemented on a watershed basis only. All plans should be prepared on individual agro-climatic zones basis. Drought management, including contingency cropping, should be given due emphasis for rainfed agriculture

Seeds

The state and Central governments should reorganise the production and distribution of quality seed of various crop varieties by giving more emphasis to the production of seeds for pulses and oilseeds. Similarly, there should be emphasis on the production of hybrid seeds.

Private seed companies do not get the benefit of seed subsidy and this discourages private participation in the sector. Therefore, it would be appropriate to abolish the seed subsidy, especially for crops whose multiplication rate is high or seed rate is very low. Subsidies should be confined only to seeds whose production/multiplication is expensive. A mechanism needs to be developed for testing seeds produced by private agencies before they are sold. A study needs to be undertaken to ascertain the reasons for farmers rejecting some seed varieties. This would provide a feedback to scientists engaged in research. Seed viability is affected by storing and handling conditions. Both the private and public sector should be encouraged to develop modern seed storage facilities.

Efforts for the production and distribution of quality horticulture seeds are grossly inadequate. Attention is also not being paid to the production and distribution of certified/quality seeds of seed spices. Both these issues need to be addressed. Improvement in the variety and availability of *durum* wheat seed needs to be encouraged.

A Seed Grid for specific zones should be established and the ICAR and the state agricultural universities should produce nucleus and breeder seed. Private seed producers may, however be allowed to operate only subject to their own risk and credibility.

Cultivars of varieties are likely to become extinct in near future if proper action is not taken to protect them at different levels. These cultivars constitute a major portion of the national food and nutritional security system. It is, therefore, necessary that appropriate action is taken immediately to document them, and popularise them under organic conditions.

Fertiliser

In order to check the over use of nitrogenous fertilisers, subsidy on it should be phased out and farmers motivated to adopt an integrated nutrient management system with more emphasis on the use of organic manure. Since the cost of fertilisers is taken into consideration while deciding the MSP of agricultural produce, there does not seem to be any justification for continuing fertiliser subsidy.

Since the indiscriminate use of fertilisers has adversely affected the growth of productivity due to degradation of soils, the state government must review its strategy for the use of fertilisers for increasing production and give proper incentive to propagate the integrated use of organic manure with fertilisers. Incentives may also be given for the production of different forms of organic manure

Pesticides

The government may consider the following suggestions to minimise the use of pesticides:

- Provide proper incentive for organising seasonal field schools on pest management for different crops.
- Provide proper incentive for encouraging production and distribution of bio-agents pesticides/plant-based pesticides in the private as well as public sector.
- Organise training camps for farmers at the *panchayat* level to train them in the use of bio-agents/pesticides.
- Encourage proprietors of plant clinics to propagate the use of these bio-pesticides.
- For dissemination of information, regular training programmes have to be organised with KVKs, SAUs, other governmental agencies and NGOs being given the responsibility of being agents of training.

All this will be successful only when a large number of hazardous plant protection chemicals are banned. Only the chemicals which have short duration effect on environment, and which do not have any residual effect on agricultural crop, should be allowed.

Agricultural Marketing

The Fourteenth National Conference on Agricultural Marketing held in February, 2001, made the following recommendations for a regulatory framework for agricultural marketing:

- A regulatory role for the government was considered essential in the context of globalisation and economic liberalisation. It was also suggested that State Marketing Acts, which enable the government to regulate the activities of traders and other functionaries, should continue.
- Producers and sellers should be free to take their produce anywhere in the country.
- To facilitate physical movement of the produce for marketing, sale through a representative sample should be adopted, and the purchaser should make his own arrangements to lift the stock.
- Management of the Agricultural Produce Market Committee (APMC) should be in the hands of the representatives of the cultivators and traders with cultivators forming the majority.
- If the various stakeholders agree, sale on credit basis in the regulated market should be allowed with the responsibility of final payment being placed on the APMC.

Farmers in Rajasthan are not able to cope with the new challenges in domestic and external markets because they are not organised and there is no effective cooperative movement in the field of agricultural marketing as in Maharashtra, Gujarat and Karnataka. In order to help farmers and create a conducive environment for higher private investment in agriculture, the state government has recently taken some important decisions:

- Abolition of sales tax, transport and octroi check posts throughout the state.
- Ending controls on the movement of any agriculture commodity within the state.
- Multi-point market fees have been revoked, and these fees are now levied at the first point only.
- A system of permanent license has been started for traders operating in APMCs, instead of their being required to renew licenses annually.
- Fertiliser retail trade up to 10 tonnes and seed retail trade up to 10 quintals have been delicensed.
- There is no monopoly procurement scheme, no state levies, nor any price controls operating within the state.

The National Conference on Agricultural Marketing made the following suggestions for broad-basing and modernising agricultural marketing:

- Agri-Business Consortiums should be organised to compete with multinational companies to upgrade grading, packaging, branding, etc. The State Marketing Board should help farmers in providing management expertise on a paid basis.
- The State Marketing Board should take up marketing of aromatic and medicinal plants and organise patenting of plant wealth and protecting farmers' rights.
- Provisions of the Multi-State Cooperative Act may be enforced to strengthen the cooperative movement, which will also help in improving the marketing systems.
- Marketing of livestock should also be organised on the lines of marketing crops. This should not be left entirely to the private sector.
- Farmers should be covered with insurance.

Horticulture

Commercial floriculture needs organised cultivation, processing, packaging and marketing. It has tremendous potential for export. Problems in commercial cultivation and expansion of area need immediate attention.

Animal Husbandry

The state must adopt a breeding policy to take advantage of native breeds and avoid the use of imported semen for breed improvement. To support the animal husbandry sector, fodder crops should be encouraged on lands which do not give profitable yields.

Agro-Industries

Fruit and Vegetable Processing: There is tremendous potential to enlarge the processing base in Rajasthan with increased production of quality fruits and vegetables in the near future.

Dairy Processing: Although the state government is giving full support to the modernisation of dairy plants, a lot more needs to be done like production and processing of organic milk and exploring its export potential.

Cotton Ginning: The state needs to upgrade and modernise ginning and pressing units to meet international standards. This will greatly help textile industry of Rajasthan in producing better quality fibre and cloth. The same is true for wool processing.

Slaughter Houses: This sector also needs modernisation of slaughter houses and processing plants, to produce better disease-free meat and by products.

Tanneries: Improvement of the 150 registered small scale tanning units and 200 unorganised tanning centres will help in controlling pollution and improving the quality of products.

Edible Oil: The state government must encourage the establishment of improved *ghani* edible oil manufacturing facilities.

Brewing: The state has great potential for the development of this industry as the raw material is readily available. The movement of cereal-based alcohol should be freely allowed.

Coarse Cereals: National food security can be strengthened by promoting production of coarse cereals. The promotion of cultivation of coarse cereals in Rajasthan must be considered with reference to the efficient management of natural resources, nutrition and agro-biodiversity.

In view of the easy availability of wheat and rice, the use of coarse cereals, especially *bajra, jowar* and barley has declined, leading to abundant marketable surplus of these commodities and this has resulted in reduced profitability for farmers. Therefore, the surplus production of *bajra* should be used for the manufacture of ethanol fuel (which is under the consideration of the Central government as well). Since this will face stiff competition with the ethanol produced from sugarcane in Haryana, Punjab, Uttar Pradesh, Madhya Pradesh and Maharashtra, a cost-effective method of producing ethanol must be found and administrative measures like ban on ethanol from other states and incentives to units producing ethanol from *bajra* need to be taken. Similarly, barley can be used by the malt industry and the government can extend incentives such as exemption from market fees and relaxation in sales tax for a limited period.

The Department of Industry should regularly monitor the usage of coarse cereals by factories in order to assess the requirement of these commodities for industrial use. Research needs to be undertaken into the industrial usage of coarse cereals in order to evolve high yielding and nutritious varieties. The task can be assigned to the state-level research institutes.

Food Processing

Food processing and grading facilities should be set up at producing centres in rural areas and the government should give attractive incentives for at least five years to entrepreneurs. Food processing should be monitored by the Department of Agriculture. The department of Agriculture, Horticulture, Watershed, Food Processing and Animal Husbandry and Dairying may be integrated under a Principal Secretary to the government.

Agriculture Extension

Agriculture extension should also give adequate emphasis to on-farm water management in irrigated areas and soil and moisture conservation practices in the rainfed areas. Contingency cropping and drought management should be a part of the education for extension workers and farmers, so that they can take prompt decisions when faced with any contingencies.

Agriculture extension itself needs reorientation. However, there is a lot of overlapping of extension efforts due to a multiplicity of extension agencies.

Various agencies involved in the transfer of technology should be assigned specific districts, blocks and villages for dissemination of production technologies. Training for farmers should include education about production requirements in line with the demands of the domestic and export market.

Management of Agriculture

The concept of agri-business should be implemented at the district level for management in agriculture with farmers' participation. The agri-business plan prepared for Bikaner should be examined and replicated for other districts. The assistance of the Dr. M.S. Swaminathan Research Foundation, Chennai, may be obtained for this. The state government could also consider the concept of agri-clinics to provide efficient and timely support to farmers. The government should extend all support to the clinics and even give them the responsibility of implementing some component of schemes to propagate IPM and INMS, which would not only reduce cost of cultivation but would also be eco-friendly. Further, the state government should encourage students graduating in agriculture and animal husbandry to prepare bankable projects for which commercial banks and cooperative banks can provide finances at low interest rate. Tax exemptions could be given to the agri-clinics.

Funds of the Department of Rural Development should be used for activities related with agricultural development, particularly the creation of infrastructure facilities and rural services.

The state government will have to take some tough long-term measures for sustainable development. These relate to agriculture and food management, surplus food stocks and rural employment. Bold initiatives to reduce the cost of production and improve quality will go a long way in improving the competitive strength of farmers under the WTO regime.

Export

There should be emphasis on spices, medicinal plants, mushroom, asparagus, agro-forestry, sericulture, apiculture, etc. in line with local needs and the demand of domestic and export markets. The state government must constitute an expert group to suggest an appropriate export strategy based on a direct relationship between exporters and farmers, thus avoiding middlemen. This could be attempted under RAJFED. Such strategy may include making farmers aware about the market value of their produce, both in the domestic and international market. The government may also establish market surveillance centres for the collection and transfer of market price information to help farmers. The export strategy may also include creation of infrastructural facilities at production and export centres for storage, cold storage, packaging, transport, etc.

Organic Farming

Production of organically grown pulses, cotton, soyabean, and spices should be encouraged on a priority basis. For this, large-scale production and utilisation of organic manure, bio-fertilisers and bio-pesticides should be undertaken with appropriate quality control. State Agriculture Universities should be entrusted with the responsibility of monitoring the quality of all agricultural produce, particularly for pesticide residues. Quality certificates may also be given for organically produced food.

Conclusion

Clearly a lot needs to be achieved in the next 45 years: the surface water utilisation has to be increased by 60 per cent; distribution system efficiency has to be improved to 74 per cent; and average on-farm irrigation efficiency has to be significantly increased to about 70 per cent. There is also need for sustainability of water resources and ensuring water quality to meet the future drinking water and irrigation requirements. The State Water Policy and Plan list the actions initiated to integrate and solve problems relating to water resource development and management.

Major thrust needs to be given to the State Water Policy and proposed State Land Use Policy in order to achieve the long-term goals of sustainable agricultural development.

To achieve the objectives of the Tenth Plan, more emphasis should be given on agro climatic zonal planning. In the last two Plans, the Planning Commission has categorically suggested the urgent need for agro climatic zonal planning for agriculture development. This warrants the preparation of a suitable Action Plan for the next decade.

APPENDIX A–3.1

Agro Climatic Zones of Rajasthan

Name of Zone	*Districts and Number of Tehsils in each Zone*	*Total Tehsils*
Arid Western Plain	Barmer (8), Parts of Jodhpur (3)	11
Irrigated North Western Plain	Ganganagar (9), Hanumangarh (7)	16
Hyper Arid Partially Irrigated Western Plain	Bikaner (6), Jaisalmer (3), parts of Churu (4)	13
Transitional Plain of Inland Drainage	Nagaur (10), Sikar (6), Jhunjhunu (5), parts of Churu (3)	24
Transitional Plain of Luni Basin	Jalore (5), Pali (7), parts of Sirohi (3), Jodhpur (3)	18
Semi Arid Eastern Plain	Jaipur (13), Ajmer (9), Dausa (5), Tonk (7)	34
Flood-Prone Eastern Plain	Alwar (12), Bharatpur (10), Dholpur (5), Karuli (5), parts of Sawai Madhopur (3)	35
Sub-Humid Southern Plain & Aravali Hills	Bhilwara (11), Rajsamand (7), parts of Udaipur (6), parts of Chittorgarh (9), parts of Sirohi (2)	35
Humid Southern Plain	Dungarpur (4), Banswara (5), parts of Udaipur (4), parts of Chittorgarh (3)	16
Humid Southern Eastern Plain	Kota (5), Baran (8), Bundi (5), Jhalawar (6), parts of Sawai Madhopur (2)	26

* Figure in parenthesis are number of tehsils in a district.

Source: Report of the Rajasthan Agricultural University-Highlight of Research, 1997.

APPENDIX A–3.2

District-wise Available Wasteland

(Area in Sq.Km)

District	*Geographical Area*	*Available Wasteland*
Ajmer	8481	1488.70
Alwar	8380	1158.48
Banswara	5037	1174.98
Barmer	28387	8922.99
Bharatpur	5066	360.95
Bhilwara	10456	1041.47
Bikaner	27244	13247.27
Bundi	5550	620.85
Chittorgarh	10856	588.93
Churu	16830	1152.04
Dholpur	3034	909.99
Dungarpur	3770	746.81
Ganganagar	20634	2562.62
Jaipur and Dausa	14538	1499.11
Jaisalmer	38401	32245.19
Jalore	10640	1217.63
Jhalawar	6219	1319.50
Jhunjhunu	5928	412.74
Jodhpur	22850	5135.40
Kota & Baran	12436	612.64
Nagaur	17718	1398.39
Pali	12387	1131.85
Sawai Madhopur	10057	1483.52
Sikar	7732	307.33
Sirohi	5136	444.74
Tonk	7194	1107.94
Udaipur & Rajsamand	17279	4172.21
Total	**342239**	**86464.27**

Source: Resource Atlas of Rajasthan.

APPENDIX A–3.3

Plan-wise Area under Crops in Rajasthan

(Area in lakh ha)

Plan Period	*Cereals*	*Pulses*	*Oilseeds*	*Cotton*	*Guar*	*Spices*	*Others*	*Total*
First	65.64	24.60	7.24	1.93	—	13.81	—	113.22
Second	75.20	32.8	9.23	2.30	—	18.01	—	137.72
Third	81.39	32.31	11.10	2.41	16.67	22.42	—	149.63
Annual Plan	84.95	31.93	11.44	2.56	7.60	1.50	14.55	154.53
Fourth	91.12	34.60	11.04	2.88	10.44	1.72	11.70	163.50
Fifth	81.54	39.86	10.89	3.28	19.42	2.60	10.80	168.39
Sixth	90.97	35.09	14.85	3.77	19.75	2.47	14.05	180.95
Seventh	88.71	29.55	20.29	3.55	17.16	3.06	9.33	171.65
Annual Plan	87.14	32.57	33.15	4.65	18.24	2.86	8.75	187.36
Eighth	88.87	35.41	36.31	5.48	18.54	4.36	11.37	200.34
1997-98	93.57	43.81	44.19	6.45	19.85	5.13	10.25	223.25
1998-99	88.31	46.14	43.04	6.45	16.12	4.43	9.52	214.01
1999-00	84.80	24.79	36.35	5.83	26.48	3.69	10.92	192.86
2000-01	89.84	23.73	26.46	5.10	30.56	4.41	7.22	187.22

Source: Department of Agriculture, Govt. of Rajasthan, 2002.

APPENDIX A–3.4

Plan-wise Production of Crops in Rajasthan

(Average Production in lakh tonnes)

Plan Period	*Cereals*	*Pulses*	*Oilseeds*	*Guar*	*Cotton*	*Spices*
First	32.37	7.61	2.09	—	1.31	—
Second	33.67	12.73	2.27	—	1.63	—
Third	37.06	10.51	2.56	—	1.72	—
Annual Plan	38.45	9.91	2.27	—	1.94	—

Contd...

APPENDIX A–3.4 (Contd. ...)

Plan-wise Production of Crops in Rajasthan

(Average Production in lakh tonnes)

Plan Period	Cereals	Pulses	Oilseeds	Guar	Cotton	Spices
Fourth	50.36	12.94	3.72	2.75	2.62	—
Fifth	52.42	17.94	4.43	5.79	4.31	1.74
Sixth	65.27	14.66	7.97	3.87	4.77	1.49
Seventh	65.86	11.93	13.60	2.64	5.96	2.11
Annual Plan	81.40	13.18	25.31	2.04	8.45	2.30
Eighth	89.67	15.59	28.75	5.18	10.86	3.11
1997-98	114.03	26.33	33.00	7.34	8.68	4.17
1998-99	107.89	24.44	38.16	3.12	8.72	3.54
1999-2000	97.93	8.92	34.05	5.00	15.00	3.09
2000-01	93.08	7.26	20.32	4.81	8.05	3.57
Four year average of Ninth Plan	102.48	16.71	31.38	4.42	8.82	3.60

Source: Department of Agriculture, Govt. of Rajasthan, 2002.

APPENDIX A–3.5

Plan-wise Productivity of Crops in Rajasthan

(Productivity in Kg/ha)

Plan Period	Cereals	Pulses	Oilseeds	Guar	Cotton	Spices
First	493	309	289	—	116	—
Second	448	386	246	—	121	—
Third	455	325	231	—	122	—
Annual Plan	453	310	198	—	129	—
Fourth	555	374	337	264	155	—
Fifth	643	450	407	298	224	669
Sixth	717	418	537	196	215	603
Seventh	743	404	670	154	285	690
Eighth	1009	440	792	154	285	713
1997-98	1219	601	747	370	229	802
1998-99	1188	530	887	194	230	796
1999-2000	1155	360	937	88	287	671
2000-01	1036	306	768	157	268	—
Four year average of Ninth Plan	1150	483	837	190	252	—

Source: Department of Agriculture, Govt. of Rajasthan, 2002.

APPENDIX A–3.6

Area (ha) and Production (tonnes) of Fruits in Rajasthan (1993-94 to 1997-98)

Area in ha.
Production in tonnes

Fruits	1993-94		1994-95		1996-97		1996-97		1997-98	
	Area	Prod.	Area	Prod.	Area	Prod.	Area	Prod.	Area	Prod.
Mango	7180	58347	6977	50470	7058	51615	7010	45856	6924	58296
Lemon	3401	19283	3167	30600	3222	31237	3169	29168	3095	32891
Guava	1731	23218	1646	28241	1587	27255	1593	22071	1651	23835
Pomegranate	271	3763	380	2674	389	2800	427	3939	458	4601
Jamun	NA	2774	NA	1870	NA	3075	NA	NA	NA	NA
Ber	811	8322	784	10866	749	9958	883	8291	881	16705
Oranges	2123	41292	2299	32273	2247	38397	3473	71480	3163	75046
Musambi	560	14183	561	5361	619	6001	566	10718	492	10328
Kinnu	2856	51367	2150	39644	2078	39448	1948	44516	1963	40708
Malta	384	6737	372	5161	249	3533	313	5226	214	4101
Grapes	32	268	29	250	25	278	23	173	29	267
Alu Bukhara	2	30	0	0	0	0	0	0	0	0
Sapota/Cheeku	9	75	9	60	15	102	15	91	14	235
Banana	71	988	77	1219	65	1405	57	848	65	867
Datepalm	54	343	0	0	12	0	0	0	0	0
Phalsa	54	89	55	96	54	135	53	450	22	350
Aonla	0	0	0	0	50	417	27	292	22	170
Mulbery	44	176	43	211	37	84	45	134	42	153
Custard Apple	556	10641	580	10101	586	10500	582	10215	573	10534
Nashpati	NA	151	NA	10100	NA	10500	NA	NA	NA	NA
Adu	NA	14	NA	100	NA	83	NA	NA	NA	NA
Khirani	26	157	21	45	23	42	23	127	11	40
Papaya	324	7912	359	9729	390	11460	380	11258	396	15488

Source: Department of Agriculture, Government of Rajasthan.

Chapter 4

Industrial and Mineral Sector Development

Introduction

Until 1960, Rajasthan virtually had no place on the industrial map of India. Some strategies were worked out to increase investment in public sector industries and to promote private sector investment in different districts, which gradually led to the development of industries in the state. However, Rajasthan still ranks quite low among Indian states in terms of industrial development.

Growth of Industries

Contribution to NSDP

Table 4.1 shows the contribution of industries to the NSDP from 1960-61 to 2000-2001.

TABLE 4.1

Contribution of Industries to NSDP of Rajasthan

(Measured at 1993-94 prices)

Year	*Value (Rs. Crore)*			
	Registered Units	*Unregistered Units*	*Total*	*Share in NSDP (Per cent)*
1960-1961	167.7	788.1	955.80	12.5
1965-1966	257.8	802.1	1059.9	12.8
1970-1971	303.1	786.9	1090.0	9.4
1975-1976	362.8	921.5	1284.3	10.6
1980-1981	465.2	940.9	1306.1	10.2
1985-1986	650.8	1288.7	1939.5	12.2
1990-1991	1665.4	1520.5	3185.9	11.0
1995-1996	2998.4	1880.0	4878.4	14.2
1996-1997	2725.2	1840.1	4565.3	11.6
1997-1998	3428.8	2491.4	5920.2	13.4
1998-1999	2953.7	2526.8	5480.5	12.0
1999-2000	2865.7	2470.7	5336.4	12.1
2000-2001	3987.3	2475.6	6462.9	14.8

Source: Economic Review (various issues), Directorate of Economics and Statistics, Government of Rajasthan.

During this period, the contribution of industry to NSDP has hovered in the 10.6 per cent to 15 per cent range. The percentage share of unregistered units in SDP has declined, despite an increase in the volume and value of output.

Industrial Growth Rate

In the 1961-71 decade, the linear growth rate in industrial production in Rajasthan was only 2.2 per cent. This increased to 3.9 per cent in 1971-81 and 6.5 per cent in 1981-91, though the growth rate of output in the unregistered sub-sector was rather slow. During 1991-2001, industrial production recorded a linear growth rate of 10.3 per cent. Thus industrial production has recorded a steady growth. However, the contribution of the manufacturing sector to the NSDP is still less than 15 per cent.

The total contribution of the secondary sector to NSDP rose from 20 per cent in 1960-61 to 28 per cent in 2000-01. However, this is not an indication of movement towards a modern economy in Rajasthan as the primary sector still continues to be higher than the share of the secondary sector.

Industrial Growth Rate During the Ninth Five Year Plan

Given the fluctuations in agricultural production in the state, the industrial and service sectors have to grow rapidly if the growth of NSDP has to touch 6-7 per cent. An industrially backward state like Rajasthan requires an annual growth rate of at least 15 per cent in industrial production.

In order to reduce the gap between Rajasthan and more developed states like Maharashtra, Gujarat, Andhra Pradesh and Karnataka, agricultural production must increase at 4 per cent per year (trend rate) over the next 10 years and industrial production at 15 per cent, which would alone contribute about 40 per cent of the NSDP growth rate.

Employment

In 1960-61, total employment in industries and mines was estimated at 6.2 lakh (i.e., 8 per cent of the total number of workers) and this increased to 10.26 lakh by 1998-99, a rise of 64 per cent. Though this growth may appear impressive, industry's percentage share in total employment is not significant. In short, industries have not emerged as an important sector either in terms of output or employment.

Policies and Strategies of Industrial Development

Development of new industrial investment in any region requires an investor-friendly environment. Despite the limited potential of industrial development in the state, the government has taken initiatives to woo investors like concessions in sales tax, land and building tax, octroi, subsidy on new investment and simpler procedures. However, all these efforts have not evoked much response.

Policies

In the various policies enunciated over the past four decades, the following objectives have been a common thread:

- Minimising regional imbalances in the distribution of industries.
- Promotion of medium and large-scale industrial units.
- Increase in employment through development of small industries, *khadi*, handloom and handicrafts.
- Development of infrastructure.
- Emphasis on agro-based and mineral based industries, wherever possible.

In addition, the industrial policies of 1994 and 1998 have mentioned the commitment of the state government to adopt investor-friendly measures with a vision to achieve the following goals:

- Simplification of rules and procedures relating to granting permission to new entrepreneurs, and timely delivery of services.
- Achieving global competitiveness through increasing productivity of capital and labour.
- Enhancing the contribution of industries to NSDP, employment and exports.

The 1998 Industrial Policy clearly states that top priority will be given to infrastructure development, development of thrust sectors such as gems and jewellery, hosiery, ceramics, auto-ancillary, software technology and textiles. The state government has also included electronics, leather goods, agro-based industries, woollen cloth, handicrafts and dimensional stone (marble etc.) in the list of thrust sectors.

The main features of the 1998 Industrial Policy are:

- Greater stress on new agro-industries, which would receive reimbursement of 50 per cent of the *mandi* fees. The ceiling on capital investment subsidy was also raised to Rs. 3 crore.
- Generous financial aid, training and facilities for women entrepreneurs.
- Giving thrust sector status to 11 industries and giving them higher sales tax exemption.
- Full sales tax and octroi exemption for industrial units which propose to use fly ash and stone slurry as raw material.
- Increase in the limit for sanction of loans by the RFC at the field level from Rs. 2 lakh to Rs. 20 lakh. Where all formalities are in order, loan will be sanctioned within 30 days. Appraisal of application for financial assistance will be done within seven days.
- No need for permission from any power corporation for installing captive power plant.
- The Rajasthan Pollution Board will have a regulatory as well as a promotional role.
- New units will enjoy land and building tax exemption for four years.
- Under a Single Window Clearance Scheme, empowered committees have been set up at the district and state levels and a Board of Infrastructure and Investment Promotion has been set up for facilitating statutory approvals/ clearances of applications submitted by prospective investors.

It was assumed that the Tenth Five Year Plan would initiate industrial development across the state along the lines of the guidelines provided in the 1998 policy statement. In order to do this, land allotment rules for industrial units are being simplified and made more transparent. Under the 1998 Industrial Policy, monitoring of progress of applications by potential entrepreneurs is done at the district and state levels. Depending on the cost of a project, the General Manager, District Industries Centre, Directorate of Industries and the Bureau of Industrial Promotion and Investment (BIPI), through their escort officers, now ensure that all procedures to facilitate production in the new units are completed within the given time frame.

Single Window Clearance Scheme

In order to minimise the hassles faced by new entrepreneurs, the Department of Industries introduced a Single Window Clearance Scheme in 1998. An entrepreneur now has to submit a composite application form containing requests for clearances relating to allotment of industrial plot (inclusive of land conversion), permission from the Director of Factories and Boilers, Pollution Control Board, power connection, water connection etc. either to the General Manager, District Industries Centre or to BIPI. Empowered Committees have been constituted at the district or state level (depending on the cost of the project) which forward such requests to the concerned agency, which is obliged to accept or reject the application within a given time frame, failing which the Empowered Committee is authorised to issue the letter of sanction.

Strategies

To be meaningful, a strategy must incorporate both macro-level and micro-level measures for promoting industrial development. Macro-level measures taken by the state government have focussed largely on fiscal incentives, institutional framework, infrastructure inputs, subsidies, a resolve to provide land, water and power for new industrial units etc. To this end, the state government has attempted to develop industrial areas/estates across the state, and thus 'create' a climate for ensuring balanced regional dispersal of industrial units.

For the first time, micro level strategies were initiated in 1999-2000, with a focus on the following:

- Extending subsidy for new industrial units in the 'no industry' districts of Sirohi, Barmer and Jaisalmer.
- Focus on forward linkages such as proximity of markets like Jaipur and Delhi.
- Development of agro-based industries in the command area of the Indira Gandhi Canal Project after techno-economic appraisal of each project.
- Formation of the Indian Institute of Crafts and Design through a memorandum of understanding (MoU) signed with the National Institute of Design, Ahmedabad, and the National Institute of Fashion Technology, Delhi, for the training of design managers to take over the task of developing modern design and growth centres for crafts.

All these macro-level measures were adopted on the assumption that entrepreneurs will be encouraged to invest in different parts of the state. It was also assumed that fiscal incentives and provision of infrastructure will help all locations and all types of industries uniformly. The location-specific issues were overlooked in such macro-level strategies. This lack of attention to micro-level resulted in the sickness of large number of industrial units in the state.

Industrial and Mineral Sector

The Plan expenditure on industries in Rajasthan increased from a modest Rs. 5.4 crore in the First Plan to Rs. 1200 crore in the Eighth Plan. The total outlay for the Tenth Plan is 1113.56 crore for industries & minerals, 300.09 crore for industries 813.47 crore for minerals.

Growth Centres

Growth centres are set up under a centrally sponsored scheme. Guidelines and norms for setting up growth centres are provided to all states by the Central government. Of the eight proposals for growth centres at Bharatpur, Sawai Madhopur, Bhilwara, Jhalawar, Bikaner, Sirohi, Ajmer and Alwar, the Centre approved only four at Bikaner, Jhalawar, Bhilwara and Abu Road in October 1989. In February 1992, a growth centre at Dholpur was also approved.

A sum of Rs. 30 crore was to be spent on each growth centre during a three-year period. The state government was required to allot land and the necessary facilities. While the state government's initial response to the scheme was encouraging, the centres went into decline due to the following reasons:

- Lack of land for the development of industrial units;
- lack of coordination among different government agencies and departments;
- too many decision-making levels; and

- lack of interest on the part of the bureaucracy in implementing the scheme and ensuring various linkages.

Institutional Set-up for Industrial Development

The following institutions have been set up to facilitate the development of industries in the public and private sector in Rajasthan:

- Directorate of Industries (the nodal agency).
- Bureau of Industrial Promotion.
- Department of State Enterprises.
- Rajasthan Khadi and Village Industries Board (KVIB).
- Rajasthan Small Industrial Corporation (RSIC).
- Rajasthan Industrial Investment Development Corporation. (RIICO)
- Rajasthan Financial Corporation. (RFC)
- Rajasthan Handloom Development Corporation. (RHDC)

Their main role is to catalyse industrial development in different parts of Rajasthan. However, while other agencies/institutions are directly dependent on financial support from the state government, RFC and RHDC are operating under heavy losses and have to seek support from banks and other financial institutions.

A. Small Scale Industrial Units

The small-scale industry (SSI) sector has witnessed massive growth between 1980-81 and 2000-01. The number of registered small-scale units increased from 70,100 to 2.21 lakh while cumulative employment rose from 2.7 lakh to 8.6 lakh during this period. The total investment in 1980-81 stood at Rs. 208.6 crore, which increased 15-fold to Rs. 3,116 crore by 2000-01.

Plan allocations for the SSI sector increased from Rs. 49 lakh during the Fourth Plan to Rs. 5.4 crore in the Eighth Flan and Rs. 171 crore in the Ninth Plan. Of the Rs. 171 crore in the Ninth Plan, Rs. 13.1 crore was earmarked for subsidies on testing equipment and diesel generator sets.

Despite the robust growth in the sector, the average investment per small-scale unit was less than Rs. 1.5 lakh even in 2000-01, whereas the average level of employment was less than four persons. No small-scale unit can expect to be viable with such a small level of investment.

Over 60 per cent of the investment in small-scale units was concentrated in six districts — Jaipur, Alwar, Udaipur, Jodhpur, Ajmer and Bhilwara. On the other hand, Jaisalmer, Barmer, Jalore, Sirohi, Bikaner, Banswara, Dungarpur, Dholpur, Sawai Madhopur, Dausa etc. have meagre industrial investment. Thus small industries are concentrated in only six districts.

B. Medium and Large Industrial Units

As of 31 March 2001, Rajasthan had 394 medium and large-scale industrial units, with total investment to the tune of Rs. 14,343 crore, which was 29 per cent higher than the investment level of Rs. 11,118 crore in March 1995. Jaipur and Alwar accounted for 35 per cent of such investment, whereas the combined share of the 11 districts of Jhunjhunu, Sawai Madhopur, Bundi, Dausa, Dungarpur, Dholpur, Jaisalmer, Jhalawar, Karauli, Hanumangarh and Baran was less than 5.6 per cent. Further, Banswara, Sikar, Tonk, Barmer, Churu and Jalore accounted for even less.

Sectoral Distribution of Industrial Units

Since the Rajasthan economy is dominated by agricultural and mineral production, industrial production in the state is also based on these two sectors.

SSI Units

Out of 2.21 lakh SSI units, 21 per cent were engaged in agro-processing (oil mills, *dal* mills, flour mills etc.) while 15 per cent were based on non-metallic mineral products. These two categories of SSI units accounted for a total investment of Rs. 1480 crore, which was 47.5 per cent of the total investment in SSI units. However, the average capital invested in these units was very meagre to enable them to operate on an efficient scale.

Forest-based SSI units constituted nearly 12 per cent of all the units, but their capital base was only Rs. 113.51 crore. The relative size of average investment in chemical industries was high (Rs. 2.52 lakh per unit) while that in leather units were very small (Table 4.2).

Medium and Large Scale Industrial Units

Table 4.3 shows distribution of medium and large-scale units according to their product lines. Agro-processing units dominate, but on account of concentration of textile mills in Kishangarh, Beawer, Bhilwara, Gulabpura, Banswara, such units outnumber all other types of medium and large units.

Rajasthan also has some important cement factories located in Bundi, Ajmer, Kota, Chittorgarh, Pali and Udaipur districts, whose average investment was estimated at Rs. 1.18 crore. Their combined investment constitutes 21.5 per cent of the total investment till March 2001.

TABLE 4.2

Sectoral Distribution of Registered SSI Units

(up to March 2001)

Name of Sector	*No. of Units*	*Fixed Capital (Rs. crore)*
Agro-food processing	45705	483.71
Non-metallic/mineral product	32880	996.44
Metal industry	27397	470.27
Textile	24861	348.02
Forest-based industry	26842	113.51
Leather	11303	16.21
Chemical	15215	384.04
Machine Electrical industry	9007	194.6
Miscellaneous	5148	30.79
Service	23011	78.77
Total	**221369**	**3116.36**

TABLE 4.3

Sectoral Distribution of Large and Medium Units

(as on 31 March 2001)

Classification	*No. of Units*	*Fixed Capital (Rs. lakh)*
Machine tools and parts	17	44353.99
Agro-food and allied products	61	321649.80
Electronics and related products	13	27579.22
Electrical and allied products	14	63346.74
Textile	95	32922.96
Cement and cement products	26	309192.34
Chemical gases, lubricants and plastics	53	54267.35
Metal and allied products	26	93134.85
Automobiles and parts	8	50820.91
Ceramics and glass wares	3	6327.00
Drugs and pharmaceuticals	11	11396.28
Minerals, stones, lime and products	51	31635.81
Leather/footwear	2	1287.27
Miscellaneous Industries	7	10096.87
Heavy machinery/structural industries	3	8994.00
Unclassified	4	368340.47
Total	**394**	**1434355.86**

Source: Economic Review 2001, Department of Economics and Statistics, Government of Rajasthan

Industrial Growth in Districts

When Rajasthan was formed in 1950, there were quite a few textile units in Ajmer (at Beawer) and Kota, some silica/soap stone processing units at Dausa, Bundi etc. and a few marble processing units in Makrana in Nagaur district. The total contribution of the manufacturing sub-sector to the NSDP was less than 3 per cent in 1961.

After 1961, Kota emerged as an industrial city with the establishment of numerous large-scale industrial units. Several SSI units were set up in Bhilwara, Jodhpur, Jaipur, Alwar and Pali, while Ganganagar and Chittorgarh grew as agro-processing and cement producing centres respectively.

However, industrial growth in Rajasthan is concentrated only in a few pockets. In 1970, 48.7 per cent of 1022 factories were located only in three districts – Jaipur, Ajmer and Ganganagar. According to the Annual Survey of Industries (ASI), by 1998-99, Jodhpur, Pali, Alwar, Bhilwara and Udaipur districts also saw the establishment of large number of industrial units, although Jaipur still had the largest share. The average size of industrial units measured in terms of fixed capital continued to be significantly higher in Kota than in other districts.

Four districts – Jaipur, Bhilwara, Alwar and Jodhpur—had 46 per cent of industrial units, whereas their share in industrial employment in 1998-99 was 41.5 per cent. The combined share of industrial units in Baran, Dholpur, Jaisalmer, Jhalawar and Jhunjhunu was only 0.07 per cent, and their combined share in the value of output was just 2.1 in 1998-99 (Table 4.4). Total employment rose from 1.11 lakh in 1970 to 1.75 lakh in 1998-99, with the top four industrialised districts accounting for over 71 per cent. Jodhpur, Bhilwara and Alwar recorded a huge spurt in industrial employment, while in Jaipur employment showed a decline of 17.5 per cent.

As late as 1992-93, the value of goods produced in the factories of Rajasthan was only Rs.12.6 crore, with Alwar, Jaipur and Kota districts accounting for 13.4, 23.9 and 10.4 per cent of the total value. In 1998-99, Alwar, Jaipur, Jodhpur and Bhilwara districts contributed nearly 51.37 per cent of the total value of industrial output (which was Rs. 21.6 crore), with Alwar and Jaipur accounting for 17.8 per cent and 15.8 per cent respectively of the total value.

Table 4.4 shows the industrial scenario in the eight most backward districts.

TABLE 4.4

Industrial Units and Value of Output in Eight Least Industrialised Districts

(1998-99)

District	*Number of Factories*	*Percentage of Total*	*Value of Output (Rs. lakh)*	*Percentage of Total*
Sawai Madhopur	14	0.03	6.8	0.3
Jalore	10	0.02	2.4	0.1
Jhunjhunu	10	0.02	22.4	1.0
Jhalawar	9	0.02	12.7	0.5
Dungarpur	6	0.01	11.0	0.5
Baran	5	0.01	12.2	0.5
Dholpur	4	0.01	2.4	0.1
Jaisalmer	3	0.01	0.2	Neg
Total	**61**	**0.13**	**67.7**	**3.0**

Source: Economic Review 2000, Department of Economics and Statistics, Government of Rajasthan.

Minerals of Rajasthan

Mining contributed less than 0.5 per cent of the NSDP of Rajasthan until 1970-71. Later, its contribution steadily increased and reached 2.2 per cent in 2000-01. In value terms (measured at 1993-94 prices), NSDP from the mining sector increased from Rs. 39.38 crore in 1970-71 to Rs.1003 crore in 2000-01. Rajasthan has a dominant share in the production of quite a few minerals (Table 4.5). The reserves of minerals in the state is given in Appendix A–4.1.

TABLE 4.5

Production of Minerals in Rajasthan

(1999-2000)

Mineral	*India ('000 Tonnes)*	*Rajasthan ('000 Tonnes)*	*Rajasthan's Share in National Production*
Wollastonite	116.95	116.95	100
Zinc	359.51	359.51	100
Asbestos	21.14	21.14	100
Soapstone	550.63	550.63	100
Rock phosphate	1461.48	1461.48	100
Ball clay	594.02	594.02	100
Gypsum	3287.78	3242.06	99
Calcite	59.37	57.79	97
Felspar	161.80	123.98	96
Jasper	5.44	5.01	92
Marble	4754.03	4278.63	90
Lead	62.86	50.73	89
Sandstone	19953.87	16196.1	81
Flagi limestone	2313.72	1619.6	70

Source: Raj Darpan (http/www.rajgovt.org/itwork/mineral policy.htm).

Besides these, Rajasthan is an important producer of copper ore, granite, phosphorite and some other minerals, though the contribution of these minerals in the total value added is negligible. Petroleum and gas reserves have been found in the western districts of Barmer, Jaisalmer, parts of Bikaner and Nagaur districts, and these can be profitably used for generating power. This would also provide employment to people of these districts. During 1950, only 15 types of major minerals and six minor minerals were produced across the state. By 1993, their number rose to 42 and 23 respectively. During this period the number of mineral and royalty leases rose from 1250 to 12,175, exclusive of 19,251 quarry licenses issued to firms engaged in mining.

There are no primary deposits of precious metals like gold and silver in Rajasthan, although Hindustan Zinc Ltd. (Udaipur) and Hindustan Copper Ltd. (Khetri) extract a small quantity of silver.

Table 4.6 shows growth trends in mineral production and employment between 1950-51 and 2000-01.

TABLE 4.6

Growth Trends in Mineral Production, Revenue and Employment

Year	*Mineral Production (lakh tonnes)*			*Employment (persons)*	*Revenue (Rs. lakh)*
	Major	*Minor*	*Total*	*Total*	*Total*
1950-51	6.67	8.87	15.54	32,250	48.02
1980-81	59.28	196.43	255.71	133,658	2,760.69
1990-91	147.76	283.72	431.48	337,551	7,858.98
1994-95	184.59	322.56	507.15	356,137	18,275.06
1998-99	285.85	557.81	843.66	365,455	30,614.65
2000-01	303.92	441.67	745.59	316,220	37,000.94

Source: Economic Review (various years), Department of Economics and Statistics, Government of Rajasthan.

It is clear that between 1950-51 and 2000-2001 employment in the mineral sector has increased rather moderately as compared to production, implying that productivity per worker has risen significantly. Revenue from the mineral sector has increased 80 times during this period. Such revenue can be raised further with the help of a carefully conceived mineral policy.

Until 1992-93, Rajasthan contributed 55.5 per cent of India's total silver metal production of 4.6 tonnes in India, but this ratio declined to 8 per cent by 1998-99 in spite of the fact that the state is supposed to rank second in the country in the production of silver ore. Rajasthan also does not have substantial deposits or production of other ferrous minerals like iron ore, tungsten, gold hematile, magnetite etc. Yet, the state has numerous minerals that may support industrialisation in a major way.

Mineral Based Industries

Copper, Lead and Zinc

Rajasthan has good deposits of copper, lead and zinc. Lead and zinc are extracted in the Javar Rajpura-Dariba and Agucha mines near Udaipur. These are used in producing zinc at the Debari Zinc Smelter near Udaipur and Chanderia Super Smelter near Chittorgarh. These two smelters produce 35,000 tonnes of lead and 119,000 tonnes of zinc every year. In 1998-99, large deposits of zinc and lead were discovered in the Rampura Agucha area of Bhilwara district, which would promote the zinc and lead based industry in that region in a major way. A decision has already been taken to install a private sector zinc smelter at Chanderia.

Around 31,000 copper rods and an equal number of cathodes are produced annually at Hindustan Copper Ltd., a Central government unit located at Khetri in Jhunjhunu district.

Limestone and Cement

Rajasthan has huge deposits of steel grade and cement grade limestone. Jaisalmer district has plenty of steel grade limestone, whose proven quantity has been estimated at around 550 million tonnes. Rajasthan State Minerals and Metals (RSMM) has been appointed as the sole government agent to ensure steel melting shop grade limestone mining in collaboration with Steel Authority of India Ltd. (SAIL).

Cement grade limestone deposits are available in Chittorgarh, Bundi, Bhilwara, Kota, Nagaur, Pali, Jodhpur, Jhunjhunu, Jaisalmer, Jaipur and Banswara districts. The state has a policy to lease out cement grade limestone mines only for captive use in cement plants.

Apart from limestone, Rajasthan also has reserves of calcium oxide, silica magnesia etc. which are also required for cement production.

Rajasthan has 17 large and medium cement units, with a combined production capacity of 12.3 million tonnes a year, 14 of them producing only Portland cement. In addition, there were numerous mini cement plants but they have closed down because they could not compete with large plants and became sick. However, the production of cement in the state accounts for nearly 11 per cent of the country's production.

Ceramic Industry

Rajasthan has abundant slip clay, pottery clay, retort clay, terracotta clay, pipe clay, bleaching clay, bonding clay etc., which are used for manufacturing bricks, tiles, statues, insulators, porcelain (via a mixture of clay with felspar and quartz) etc. Glass and ceramic units are among the thrust sectors identified in the 1998 Industrial Policy.

Units which manufacture plain bricks, tiles, blue pottery, sanitary pipes, insulated bricks, ceramic wall tiles, bone china pottery, stone wares, insulators, stonewares etc. are located across the state but are concentrated in Jaipur, Bikaner, Bhilwara, Abu Road and Bhiwandi. Rajasthan is a major producer of felspar, quartz and bentonite, which are the raw materials for ceramic industry. However, about 60 per cent of these minerals are sent out of Rajasthan for processing. Large Indian players must be encouraged to set up their plants in Rajasthan so as to facilitate production of high quality pottery, insulators, ceramic wall tiles etc., to thwart competition from multinational corporations.

The installed capacity of Modern Insulators Ltd. at Abu Road is 5,000 million pieces, but the unit seems to have become defunct. Classical Tiles for manufacturing ceramic glaze tiles (at Abu Road), Regal Potteries (Jaipur), Feather Touch Ceramics (Alwar), all produce bone china potteries on a fairly large scale. However, most of these units have to face stiff competition from bigger players in the national market. Though the ceramic units of Rajasthan have lower cost advantage than their larger competitors, they have failed to woo new consumers due to their inability to develop new designs or improve packaging.

Rock Phosphate

Rajasthan has nearly 80 million tonnes of rock phosphate reserves. The rock phosphate available in the state has 20 to 35 per cent quantum of P_2O_5 and it can be profitably used to produce fertilisers, especially super phosphates. Presently there are 13 fertiliser producing units in the state, with eight located in Udaipur division and two in Kota division. The two units at Kota – Sriram Fertilisers and Chemicals and Chambal Fetilisers and Chemicals – produce urea on a large scale while the rest produce super phosphate.

Other mineral-based units include those engaged in stone crushing, marble tiles and floorings, granite tiles, processing of soapstone and semi-precious stones like garnets processing) etc. Sandstone carving and marble statue making units also employ a large number of workers. However, marble and granite units at Abu Road, Udaipur, Chittorgarh, Jalore, Kishangarh, Makrana, Rajsamand, Rajnagar, Char Bhuja, Jaipur and other places are facing a serious problem of demand recession, which has thrown several thousand workers out of jobs.

Multinational Corporations

Notwithstanding a relatively slow pace of industrial investment in Rajasthan, MNCs set up 41 industrial units in the state between 1990-91 and 1998-99, involving a total investment of Rs.3,480 crore. Prominent projects were CEMCORE Glass Ltd. (two units of Rs.1010 crore), MICO Ltd. (Rs. 250 crore), Copper Automobile Products (Rs. 120 crore) and Asian Consolidated Ltd. (Rs. 125 crore).

However, in view of the vast potential of agro-based and mineral-based industries, this investment is grossly inadequate, and the government must analyse the reasons for low levels of foreign investment in the state.

Prospects of Industrial and Mineral Sector Development

Despite numerous concessions and incentives offered by the government to prospective entrepreneurs and a conference of Non-Resident Rajasthanis (NRRs) to reiterate its commitment to boosting industrial development, Rajasthan has not been able to emerge as an industrially developed state. Many NRRs have set up large industrial units in other states and invested in the United Kingdom United States, Kenya and Thailand but the government has not been able to interest them in investing in their home state.

In 1975-76, the gross capital formation in the manufacturing sector was Rs. 39.22 crore and in mineral units Rs. 31.82 crore. In 1999-2000, this had increased to Rs. 2551.8 crore in the manufacturing sector and Rs. 37.85 crore in the mineral sector. Thus, while investment in the manufacturing units recorded a substantial increase during the 25-year period, it was dismally low in the minerals sector. Besides, only 28.3 per cent of gross investment was from the private sector, with the public sector accounting for the majority of investment. However, steps like the formation of Export Promotion Industrial Parks (EPIPs) at Jaipur and Jodhpur and Special Economic Zones (SEZs) for gems and jewellery, the constitution of empowered committees and provision of escort services could pull in more private investment.

Mineral development can get a big boost in Rajasthan, given its virtual monopoly in respect of several minerals, provided the technology used in mineral production is modernised, and wastage of minerals is minimised. Shortage of power and other inputs has resulted in the capacity of a large number of industrial units located in Rajasthan not being optimally utilised.

The following steps are needed to develop agro-based and mineral-based industries in the state.

- Identification of all the resources available in the state which are used as 'base raw materials' for industries in different regions and evolution of a region-specific programme for their exploitation in the short and long term.
- Estimation of fixed and working capital needs for industries in each category and for each region.
- Carefully evolve an input-output design for industries to be started over a period. This would include their needs for raw materials, labour, machinery and equipment, training and, above all, power.
- A careful analysis of the impact of external factors on the state's industrial economy with focus on the following industries is also needed: readymade garments; gems and jewellery; marble and granite processing; limestone; dairy products and edible oil mills.

The Freight Disadvantage

The quality of the limestone found in the western districts of Rajasthan is comparable to that imported by steel mills from Jordan. Yet, due to very high freight costs and cheaper prices of imported limestone, steel mills located in eastern India prefer the latter to limestone sourced from Rajasthan. Limestone procured from Jaisalmer for the Vishakhapatnam Steel Plant will cost around Rs. 1,650 per tonne against Rs. 1,350 per tonne for imported limestone, which is inclusive of shipping cost.

- The state government must, in collaboration with the representatives of all categories of industry, identify the problems facing them, work out solutions and evolve a priority-based policy. Implementation of such an industrial policy must be done in cooperation with industry. Such collaboration will, hopefully, free the industrialisation strategy from bottlenecks created by bureaucracy.

- For the future development of industries, a professional approach is required to ascertain the value addition that industrial development policies would provide. For each new unit, careful computation of financial parameters such as cost-benefit ratio, internal rate of return etc., have to be calculated which will help in working out the increase in income which both public and private sector investment would generate for the NSDP.

Rajasthan's Strengths

Though industrial development in Rajasthan has been erratic, the state has certain factors working to its advantage.

Political stability: Unlike some other states, Rajasthan has had stable governments and this is an important factor in attracting investment.

Peaceful industrial relations: Labour unrest is quite negligible in Rajasthan. The number of industrial disputes in the state dropped from 51 in 1995-96 to 31 in 1998-99, out of which 10 pertained to textile units involving only 6,672 workers.

Plentiful land: The state has ample land which can be put to use. A substantial part of Rajasthan falls in the National Capital Region (NCR).

Rich heritage: The state has rich tradition of handicrafts, gems and jewellery, and other artefacts. These can be significant foreign exchange earners with a little investment in the development of new designs and training.

Problems Concerning Industrial and Mining Sector

The failure or success of industries is determined by the following factors:

- Proper selection of site for the plant.
- Availability of adequate capital and labour.
- Availability of power at reasonable tariff.
- Overall cost of production, which determines the competitive strength of the unit concerned.
- Proximity to the market.
- Labour laws.
- Quality of management.
- Attitude and policy of the government.

As long as these factors remain favourable, industrial units will flourish. Since industrial sickness has been increasing in Rajasthan and investment in new industrial units has virtually ceased, a careful analysis of their problems needs to be undertaken without delay.

According to the chairman of the Twelfth Finance Commission, C. Rangarajan,[1] 41,159 IEMs were received in all the states between August 1991 and December 2000, of which only 2,113 (5 per cent) were received in Rajasthan. The proposed investment in these units was Rs. 35,713 crore, which was less than 4 per cent of the total proposed investment for the whole country. Further, out of 3,567 LoIs issued for all states, only 2.66 per cent were issued in Rajasthan during this period, and the proposed investment in these units was only 1.5 per cent of the aggregated investment proposed for India as a whole.

Industrial Sickness

As of 31 March 2000, there were 7560 sick SSI units and 88 non-SSI units. (See Appendix A–4.2) Among the notable large units which have turned sick are cement manufacturer Jaipur Udyog Ltd. at Sawai Madhopur, synthetic fibre unit, J.K. Synthetics Ltd. and Instrumentation Ltd. at Kota and Modern Insulators at Abu Road.

A Problem of Definition

There is a problem of definition in relation to industrial sickness, which could be responsible for under-reporting of sick units. The state government's Industries Department considers only those units as sick which have failed to meet their financial obligations to a bank or the RFC. A visit to various industrial estates set up by RIICO shows that 60 to 70 per cent of SSI units are non-functional or closed. Yet, these units are listed as operative in the records of the Industries Department.

Most of the sick industrial units are mini-cement plants, granite cutting and polishing units, oil mills, mini steel plants, yarn spinning mills and readymade garment units. Their sickness can be attributed to the non-availability or shortage of raw materials and power, though overstaffing and related high establishment costs as well as bad financial management and labour problems are also factors in some cases.

There are some sector-specific reasons as well. Mini cement plants have become sick primarily due to failure of vertical shaft kiln technology which was advocated for them without its viability being assessed. Granite units suffered a setback due to marketing constraints, while the edible oil sector has become a victim of a

1. *The Hindu*: Survey of Indian Industry, 2001.

liberalised import policy. Marble units have become sick because of the variation in the commercial tax rates (including royalty) between Rajasthan and neighbouring Gujarat, which has a lower tax rate.

Unfortunately, the state government has made no attempt to diagnose the problem of industrial sickness or work out solutions to improve the competitiveness of industrial units in the state. Financial institutions, for their part, are largely concerned only with the recovery of their loans, and do not seem to bother about the financial viability of a project while sanctioning a loan. If the government is not proactive in taking measures to help industry, the problem of industrial sickness in the state is likely to increase. However, according to a special formula recently adopted by the state government for facilitating the revival of sick units, clarity and transparency have been introduced for the new management which buys any sick unit, especially in matters relating to outstanding dues.

Low Productivity

Table 4.7 shows the per capita value added in industries in Rajasthan is much lower than that in other states. This is because a majority of the industrial units in the state use obsolete technology.

TABLE 4.7

State-wise Per Worker Value Added in Industries

(1997-98)

State	*Value Added (Rs.)*	*Rank*
Andhra Pradesh	1578	8
Assam	500	16
Bihar	972	14
Gujarat	3092	2
Haryana	2476	3
Himachal Pradesh	1842	6
Jammu & Kashmir	222	17
Karnataka	1715	7
Kerala	1032	13
Madhya Pradesh	1124	10
Maharashtra	3862	1
Orissa	1072	12
Punjab	2051	5
Rajasthan	**1077**	11
Tamil Nadu	2235	4
Uttar Pradesh	891	15
West Bengal	1274	9

Source: Report on Currency & Finance, Reserve Bank of India, 2000-01.

Regional Imbalances

Though all regions of Rajasthan have resources that enable them to develop evenly, industrial development is concentrated in a few eastern districts only and there has been little effort to exploit the mineral resources found in the western and southern districts.[2] The main reason for this is their distance from the markets and ports, which pushes up transportation costs.

Official Apathy

Unlike Gujarat, Haryana, Punjab and Maharashtra, the Rajasthan bureaucracy has not been very supportive to the potential investors. What is required is an integrated and holistic approach – making available backward and forward linkages – for each new unit. Even where RIICO has created infrastructure (including link roads), no effective monitoring is done to ensure that the required inputs are available on time.

Shortage of Power and Water

The total availability of power in Rajasthan is a little over 3,000 MW in 2002. While the demand for power has been rising at an annual rate of 7 per cent, the availability of power has failed to keep pace with this growth and has stagnated at this level over the past few years. Hopefully, the power supply position will improve in the next few years in view of the additional power generation capacity of 1200 MW which is being installed. The power situation will further improve if the lignite and gas reserves in the western districts are used for power generation.

Given the perennial water scarcity in Rajasthan, water-intensive industries face a serious problem. Water shortage will also hamper the use of lignite deposits in Barmer and Jaisalmer districts for power generation.

Obsolete Technology and High Cost

Outdated technology has resulted in a sizeable proportion of minerals extracted across the state going waste. The use of obsolete technology and small scale of production in the mineral-based and agro-based industries have pushed up the cost of production.

Connectivity of Mines and Quarries

The connectivity of mines and quarries with industrial or processing plants is highly unsatisfactory. Though approach roads are being built under the Jawahar Rozgar Yojana (JRY), Apna Gaon Apna Kaam

2. For instance, in 2000-01, almost 50 per cent of the 5325 medium and large industrial units were located in Jaipur, Jodhpur, Alwar and Ajmer districts whereas in Churu, Baran, Dausa, Dungarpur, Jaisalmer, Jhalawar, Karauli, Jhunjhunu and Tonk the total number of such units was only 112 (2 per cent). This was also the case with small industries (Annual Survey of Industries, 2002-03, GoR).

Schemes etc., a lot more needs to be done. A comprehensive survey needs to be done and a Master Plan prepared to provide motorable roads for mines and quarries located even in remote areas.

Lack of Market Linkages

Linking villages with industrial sites is important for fostering industrial development. For this there must be a good road network and all metre gauge rail lines should be converted into broad gauge. This would facilitate marketing of industrial products not only within the state but in other parts of the country as well.

In fact, those responsible for industrial development could take some lessons from what is being done in other states and in China.

A Leaf from the Chinese Book

The Chinese policy towards industrial development has the following features:

- Rewarding units which start production before schedule and penalties for those who delay it.
- Simplified tax system.
- Prompt response of law enforcing officials.
- Cooperative bureaucracy.
- Creation of quality infrastructure before allotment of industrial sites.
- Single window approach for approvals as well as access to all facilities and inputs for an industrial unit.
- Good industrial relations. In case of any disagreement, the local labour bureau looks into the problem and offers a prompt solution.
- No trouble for law-abiding industries.
- Low interest rate
- Quick disposal of pending problems.

Prospects of Agro-based and Mineral Based Industries

There is a lot of scope for the development of agro-based and mineral-based industries in Rajasthan.

(1) **Leather**: Though Rajasthan has 12 per cent of the nation's livestock, more than 60 per cent of the hides and skins are sent out of the state for processing. If leather goods industries could be developed in the state, it will give sufficient income and employment.

(2) **Ceramic and Glass**: Rajasthan has vast deposits of felspar, quartz and bentonite but over 60 per cent of these minerals are sent out of the state for processing. There is ample scope for developing ceramic and glass industries based on modern technology. Rajasthan non-Farm Development Agency (RUDA) has already started the process of facilitating the development of leather, ceramic and glass industries in the state.

(3) **Agro Processing**: Medicinal plants, spices horticultural crops, pulses etc. have vast potential in different parts of Rajasthan. Their processing will generate employment and enhance incomes in areas rich in these crops. The state government has already set up agro parks at Kota, Sriganganagar and Jodhpur to give a boost to agro-food activities in Rajasthan.

Though there are small scale units to process pulses and oilseeds in Kota, Bharatpur, Alwar and Jaipur, agro-based processing units could be set up in the rural areas of such districts, where adequate agricultural products are produced. Table 4.8 shows the prospects of setting up such units as a cottage industry.

TABLE 4.8

Districts with Adequate Production	*Products to be Processed*
Churu, Sikar, Hanumangarh, Jhunjhunu	Gram
Chittorgarh, Jaipur, Sawai Madhopur, Bikaner, Tonk	Ground Nut
Jodhpur, Tonk, Dholpur, Bharatpur, Sawai Madhopur	Red Chillies
Pali	Heena (Mehandi)

Industrially backward districts like Dholpur, Tonk, Sawai Madhopur, Hanumangarh, Sikar, Churu, Jhunjhunu, Bikaner and even villages in other districts can benefit if semi-processed agricultural products are directly sold by farmers in the neighbouring markets. This would also help in developing non-farm activities in the industrially backward regions of Rajasthan.

(4) **Milk-processing:** Production of milk in Rajasthan has risen over the past one decade at an annual rate of 6 per cent. The price fetched by processed milk is much higher than that of fluid milk. If the milk cooperatives scattered over Ajmer, Sriganganagar, Bikaner and Hanumangarh can motivate dairy operators to spare a part of total milk production for producing milk products, they can expect to enhance their income. Dairy operators in the Bassi and Chomu areas of Jaipur who sell both fluid milk and *mawa* to the sweet makers of Jaipur earn 20 per cent more than those who sell only fluid milk.

Marble and Granite Industry

Rajasthan is the country's largest producer of marble and granite. Between 1991-92 and 1996-97, exports of these products rose from Rs. 3.6 crore to Rs. 87 crore. There are good prospects of increasing the production as well as exports of these as new marble and high quality granite deposits have been found in Udaipur, Bhilwara, Jaipur, Banswara, Jalore, Sirohi, and Ajmer districts. Sand stone available in Dholpur and Jodhpur districts and flooring stone available in Sawai Madhopur, Karauli and Kota district are being polished and marketed on a large scale in Rajasthan and other states.

Public Sector Enterprises

Rajasthan has 24 state-level public sector enterprises (SLPEs). These include seven statutory corporations/ boards set up under Special Act(s) of Legislature, 15 companies registered under the Companies Act, 1956 and two departmental undertakings. The list of these enterprises is given in Appendix A–4.3. Total investment in these SLPEs in the form of paid-up equity and term loans as on March 31, 1998 was about Rs. 9,000 crore. Capital investment, which is represented by paid-up capital reserves/surplus, and term loan minus accumulated losses in these enterprises as on March 31, 1998 stood at around Rs. 9,500 crore. The contribution of these enterprises to the exchequer in the form of royalty, excise duty, cess, income tax and dividend, etc. was approximately Rs. 500 crore in 1997-98. About one lakh people are employed in these state enterprises. Return on capital investment during the 1997-98 was only 6.1 per cent. The statement showing capital investment in 23 public sector enterprises as on March 31,1998 is available in Appendix A–4.4. Fourteen of these state enterprises have net worth in excess of 100 per cent. Appendix A–4.5 gives the net worth of these enterprises for 1994-95 to 1997-98. Of the 24 SLPEs, four units (Rajasthan Electronics, Rajasthan State Tungsten Development Corporation, Rajasthan State Chemical Works and Rajasthan Government Salt Works) have turned sick and been merged with other companies or closed. The Rajasthan State Electricity Board (RSEB) has been reorganised, and it is premature to evaluate the performance of the five power corporations set up in the past two years.

One disturbing fact is the growing losses of some units, which have resulted in their mounting liabilities. Profit after tax as a ratio of paid up capital is negative in respect of Rajasthan State Roadways Transport Corporation (RSTC), RFC, Ganganagar Sugar Mills, Rajasthan Agro Industries Corporation, Rajasthan Tourism Development Corporation (RTDC) and RHDC, while the Rajasthan Land Development Corporation has recently emerged as a profit-making unit. This has put a strain on the state exchequer. The PSUs in Rajasthan have to bear a heavy burden of salaries and interest payment. No serious attempts have been made to increase the turnover of these SLPEs and to cut costs. The aggregate debts on all the state PSUs is about Rs. 1,238 crore. While the Rajasthan Agro Industries Corporation and Rajasthan Land Development Corporation have been closed down, no attempt has been made to do the same for the persistently loss-bearing PSUs. Unlike the Central government, the state government has not prepared any disinvestment policy.

Yet, there are examples of good performance. These include Rajasthan State Warehouse Corporation, Rajasthan Small Industries Corporation Ltd. (RAJSICO), RIICO, Rajasthan State Agriculture Marketing Board (RSAMB), Rajasthan State Mines & Minerals Ltd (RSMM), Rajasthan State Bridge and Construction Corporation (RSBCC), Seeds Corporation, Jal Vikas Nigam etc. The SLPEs have played an important role in the state's industrial and infrastructure development, especially the RSEB, RIICO, RFC, RSMM and the Rajasthan State Mineral Development Corporation Ltd (RSMDC). The role of Rajasthan Rajya Paryatan Nigam Limited in promoting tourism and RAJSICO in promoting the handicraft sector and export infrastructure has also been noteworthy.

The state government has recently embarked upon the task of restructuring the SLPEs. The RSEB has been unbundled into five new companies. The RSMM and RSMDC have been merged. The Nirwan Committee, set up in 2001 to enquire into the performance of all SLPEs, recommended that Ganganagar Sugar Mills, Rajasthan State Hotel Corporation and the RTDC be fully disinvested.

There is a lot of state government intervention in the functioning of state enterprises through the Boards of these enterprises as well as through funding. Most of the administrative decisions meant for government departments are imposed on them, thereby restricting their operational freedom.

It would be desirable to immediately undertake an exercise to restructure SLPEs, both at the state level as well as individual enterprise level. At the state level, strategic options of merging, amalgamating and unbundling various state enterprises need to be explored to foster synergy. At the enterprise level options of divestment, privatisation and objective review deserve serious and immediate consideration. The state government may hire the services of renowned consultants for suggesting strategic options.

Secondly, the heads of the state enterprises are generally government officials appointed by the state government. The tenure is usually quite short and this creates various problems. The SLPEs must be managed on professional lines and must increase their level of efficiency.

In 1994, the NCAER had suggested that each SLPE should be subjected to a SWOT (strengths, weaknesses, opportunities, threats) analysis and that the state government decide on closure or continuance on a case-to-case basis. Some SLPEs – the Dholpur Glass Factory, State Cooperative Consumer Federation, Forest Development Corporation etc. – were closed down. Such an exercise needs to be done for the rest of the SLPEs as well.

New Directions for Industrial and Mineral Development

Any strategy of industrial development must be based on the raw materials available within the state. For this, the state government must smoothen the way for private sector investment and address the problem of industrial sickness. The following suggestions are worth considering:

- Availability of power must be ensured.
- An in-depth and sector specific study of the factors responsible for industrial sickness must be carried out. Steps must then be taken to
  - (a) prevent the problem of incipient sickness,
  - (b) redress the problems of non-functional and sick units
  - (c) create a corpus fund exclusively for the revival of sick units, which will be used to offer relief and concessions to sick units which can be revived[3]
  - (d) offer reward to industrial units which register an improvement in their performance continuously for at least five years,
  - (e) penalise industrial units which do not start production within two years after their registration and reward those which start production before the stipulated time
  - (f) develop an investor-friendly approach for small and medium industrial units, and provide immediate redressal of their problems
  - (g) motivate the industrialists to strengthen their competitive advantage
  - (h) ensure that the tax policy enables industries in Rajasthan to enjoy parity with the neighbouring states
  - (i) ensure that SLPEs reduce their establishment costs so as to increase profits.

3. However, such corpus fund would not be available for units which have turned sick due to technological obsolescence, financial mismanagement low productivity etc.

The Forest Department and the mineral sector are constantly at loggerheads, and this has jeopardised the development of minerals in Rajasthan, especially in the forest areas. While protection of the environment is important, a solution to the present impasse needs to be worked out. One solution could be the delineation of mineral-rich areas which are located in forests but which have no trees at all. The two sectors are not mutually exclusive and development of both is necessary for Rajasthan's economic development.

Action Plan for Industries and Minerals Sector

The state government needs to bring about a change in its approach to the development of the industries and mining sector. A medium-term strategy for this sector needs to be evolved on the basis of potential and prospects, constraints and priorities. The idea is to bring about minor modifications, which would increase investment, income and employment in industries and mining.

Action Plan for Industries

Despite a very attractive Industrial Policy of 1998, the response of new investors has so far not been encouraging. What is now needed is the implementation of such policy statements. The following actions need to be taken immediately:

- Greater emphasis on the promotion of agro-processing units (oil mills etc.) processing of milk, fruits, etc., and ensuring that the larger share of value addition goes to farmers, industrialists as well as consumers.
- Promotion of region-specific industries with a thrust on making optimum use of raw material available in that region. This would reduce regional concentration of industries.

- A detailed study of the factors which inhibit investment of private capital and immediate corrective measures.
- Ensure availability of power and adequate access to backward and forward linkages for new industrial units.
- A more investor-friendly and transparent approach and operationalising the single window clearance scheme.
- A thorough analysis of the factors responsible for industrial sickness. If policies or the attitude of bureaucracy are responsible, corrective action must be initiated immediately. On the other hand, if sickness is an outcome of financial or other mismanagement, then strict legal action must be taken.
- A time-bound strategy to turn SLPEs into commercial units must be developed immediately Managers of loss-making PSEs must be made more accountable and non-performance needs to be dealt with severely. All PSEs which do not perform well by the end of Tenth Plan must be closed down.
- The state government's involvement in industrial development process needs to be restricted to infrastructure development and facilitation.

Action Plan for Mining Sector

Mining Sector

Lignite, gas, petroleum, marble, granite, limestone, soapstone and other minerals in which the state enjoys comparative advantage must be extracted in the most economical manner and industrial units must be set up to ensure high value addition. This would require the introduction of new technology in extraction of minerals, so that wastage is minimised.

Paradigm Shifts in Policy for Mining Sector

- Clearly design an eco-friendly leasing policy
- Techno-economic survey of mineral deposits
- Promoting private investment in exploration and extraction of minerals
- Revival of mineral based industrial units like mini-cement plants
- Economic use of slurry and debris
- Improvement in mineral extraction technology to minimise wastage

- The leasing policy must draw a fine balance between mineral exploitation and environmental factors.
- There must be intensive techno-economic survey of minerals in the western districts and private sector investment promoted since the prospects of agricultural development in this region are limited. This would require the development of investor-friendly policies for mining sector.
- Over the next five years, the state government must evolve a rational policy for revival of mini cement units.
- The government must also evolve a policy for promoting economic use of marble slurry and debris accumulated in the mining zones.
- Mining technology needs to be upgraded in order to minimise wastage.
- In order to attract foreign direct investment (FDI) in the mining sector, there should be a clear leasing policy, concessions must to be offered to MNCs on their capital investment, connectivity of mines to markets/processing sites should be improved and an investor-friendly attitude should be inculcated among the bureaucracy.

Such policy would also encourage investment by domestic companies as well.

APPENDIX A–4.1

Reserves of Minerals in Rajasthan

(In '000 Tonnes)

Mineral	*Recoverable Reserves as on 1.4.1995*			
	Proved	*Probable*	*Possible*	*Total*
Asbestos (T)	2649476	2463322	3887412	9000210
Ball Clay	4175	3525	17723	25425
Barytes	141	170	927	1238
Bauxite	—	—	319	319
Bentonite	33806	105118	136116	275040
Calcite (T)	1211906	1163446	995912	3371264
China Clay	15914	12325	176879	205118
Copper Ore	22275	34464	48235	104974
Metal	188	336	485	1009
Corundum (T)	—	—	11925	11925
Diatomite	—	—	1520	1520
Dolomite	42547	114315	37567	194429
Feldspar (T)	3654244	3507696	13454985	20616925
Fireclay	7636	3497	19612	30745
Fluorite	1021	150	294	1465
Fuller's Earth	—	350	189709	190059
Garnet	14	34	5097	5145
Granite ('000 Cum)	—	4	201692	201696
Graphite (T)	128902	567	372307	501776
Gypsum	20167	28347	43646	92160
Kyanite	5	4	12	21
Lead & Zinc Ore	63642	35836	55797	155275
Lead Metal	746	467	714	1927
Zinc Metal	4425	2127	2743	9295
Limestone	1082989	3937578	4723372	9743939
Magnesite	1336	1353	2798	5487
Marble	2184	109475	451467	563126
Mica (T)	—	—	1589	1589
Manganese Ore	—	—	430	430
Ochre	1551	4162	8995	14708
Phosphorite	62956	747	15003	78706
Potash* (M.T.)	—	16935.76	3461.72	20397.48
Pyrite	13677	22917	3620	40204
Pyrophylite	81	171	231	783
Quartz/Silica sand	12900	50014	67590	130504
Silver Ore (T)	743690900	38893900	35951150	147214950
Metal (T)	2010.79	1547.24	1143.35	4701.38
Soapstone	66517	31353	72470	170340
Tungsten	—			
Ore (T)	—	722750	12750471	13473221
W.O.3 (T)	—	924	58304	59528
Vermiculite (T)	—	2600	13030	15630
Wollastonite	1519	2769	511	4799

Note: Figure rounded off, M.T. : Million Tonnes, *Conditional resources

Source: IBM, Indian Minerals Year Book 1998 & 1999.

APPENDIX A–4.2

Sick Industrial Units

(As of March, 2000)

State	*SSI*	*Non-SSI*
West Bengal	143893	241
Bihar	26909	79
Uttar Pradesh	21235	232
Andhra Pradesh	12461	400
Tamil Nadu	11602	285
Assam	11445	48
Maharashtra	9115	580
Kerala	9017	76
Rajasthan	**7560**	**88**
Orissa	7444	60
Tripura	7170	3
Madhya Pradesh	6072	163
Gujarat	5928	281
Manipur	5577	2
Karnataka	5416	218
Delhi	3309	79
Haryana	2952	101
Jammu & Kashmir	2002	9
Punjab	1897	90
Pondichery	1052	15
Others	2179	114

Source: IBM, Indian Minerals Year Book 1998 & 1999.

APPENDIX A–4.3

List of Public Enterprises

(A) Statutory Corporations/Boards
1. Rajasthan State Electricity Board
2. Rajasthan State Road Transport Corporation
3. Rajasthan Financial Corporation
4. Rajasthan Land Development Corporation
5. Rajasthan Housing Board
6. Rajasthan State Warehousing Corporation
7. Rajasthan State Agriculture Marketing Board

(B) Registered Companies
8. Rajasthan State Industrial Development and Investment Corporation Ltd.
9. Rajasthan State Mines and Minerals Ltd.
10. Rajasthan State Mineral Development Corporation Ltd.
11. Rajasthan State Tungsten Development Corporation Ltd.
12. Rajasthan Electronics Ltd.
13. The Rajasthan Small Industries Corporation Ltd.
14. Rajasthan State Handloom Development Corporation Ltd.
15. Rajasthan Rajya Paryatan Vikas Nigam Ltd.
16. Rajasthan State Hotels Corporation Ltd.
17. Rajasthan State Seeds Corporation Ltd.
18. Rajasthan State Agro Industries Corporation Ltd.
19. Rajasthan State Bridge and Construction Corporation Ltd.
20. Rajasthan Jal Vikas Nigam Ltd.
21. Rajasthan State Ganganagar Sugar Mills Ltd.
22. Rajasthan State Power Corporation Limited

(C) Departmental Undertakings
23. Rajasthan State Chemicals Works, Didwana (Sodium Sulphate Works)
24. Rajasthan Government Salts Works, Didwana

APPENDIX A–4.4

Consolidated Position of Capital Structure of State Public Enterprises

(Rs. lakh)

	1994-95	1995-96	1996-97	1997-98
Capital Structure				
(a) Paid-up Capital				
(i) State Government	104394.74	135458.52	147530.17	222460.17
(ii) Others	11384.64	12154.91	13472.06	15171.45
(iii) Total	115779.38	147613.43	161002.23	237631.62
(a) Reserves and Surplus	31994.77	51593.94	65914.82	78150.02
(c) Term Loans				
(i) State Government	186549.63	196769.50	193278.80	139037.22
(ii) Others	314468.00	328803.41	397645.32	522078.94
(iii) Total	501017.63	525572.91	590924.126	61116.16
(d) Total Resources (a+b+c)	648791.78	724880.28	817841.18	976897.80
(e) Fixed Assets (Net)	384477.36	364036.74	384689.61	442402.20
(f) Current Assets				
(i) Cash and Bank Balance	58872.33	48223.50	53543.32	73987.35
(ii) Debtors	72181.54	91923.03	109747.52	123758.58
(iii) Inventories	44318.17	64720.25	82151.82	103447.42
(iv) Loans and Advances	126576.47	139266.14	152267.77	164455.13
(v) Others	118337.86	215007.89	262465.186	327097.14
(vi) Total	420286.37	559140.81	60175.61	796045.62
(g) Current Liabilities	210118.66	245584.18	266861.75	294400.26
(h) Net Current Assets (f-g)	210167.71	313556.63	393313.86	501645.36
(i) Intangible Assets				
(i) Accumulated Losses	52012.41	44201.30	33406.78	28928.14
(ii) Others	2134.30	2985.61	3430.92	3922.10
(iii) Total	54146.71	47186.91	36837.70	32850.24
(i) Total utilisation (e+h+i)	648791.78	724780.28	817841.17	976897.80
(k) Capital Invested (a+b+c-i(i))	596779.37	680578.98	784434.39	947969.66
(l) Capital employed (e+f)	804763.73	923177.55	1047865.22	1238447.82
(m) Capital formation during the year	16839.77	-20452.82	23772.74	54715.55
(n) Net worth (a+b-i(i)))	95761.74	155006.07	193510.27	286853.50
(o) %age of Net Worth to Paid-up Capital	82.71	105.10	120.19	120.71

APPENDIX A–4.5

Net Worth of State Public Enterprises (1994-95 to 1997-98)

(% of net worth to capital > 100%) based on the year 1997-98

Name of Enterprise	*Accounting Year*	*Paid up Capital*	*Net Worth*	*% of Net Worth to Capital*
Rajasthan State Electricity Board	1994-95	62309.00	31317.53	50.26
	1995-96	91309.00	81819.36	89.61
	1996-97	102759.00	107189.06	104.31
	1997-98	177459.00	197527.86	111.31
Rajasthan State Road Transport	1994-95	10795.25	13075.61	121.12
	1995-96	10795.25	13879.32	128.57
	1996-97	10795.25	14283.13	132.31
	1997-98	10795.25	11875.50	110.01
Rajasthan Financial Corporation	1994-95	9107.70	12054.96	132.36
	1995-96	9107.70	13212.82	145.07
	1996-97	9107.70	14200.64	155.92
	1997-98	9107.70	13794.78	151.46
Rajasthan State Warehousing Corporation	1994-95	567.65	1552.94	273.57
	1995-96	640.26	1958.77	305.93
	1996-97	690.26	2221.04	321.77
	1997-98	725.26	2509.29	345.98
Rajasthan Land Development Corporation	1994-95	2051.45	1334.95	65.07
	1995-96	2051.45	-3660.88	-178.45
	1996-97	2051.45	4816.39	234.78
	1997-98	2051.45	5898.65	287.54

Contd...

...*Contd*...

(% of net worth to capital > 100%) based on the year 1997-98

Name of Enterprise	*Accounting Year*	*Paid up Capital*	*Net Worth*	*% of Net Worth to Capital*
Rajasthan State Ganganagar Sugar Mills Ltd.	1994-95	364.73	477.19	130.83
	1995-96	364.73	490.32	134.43
	1996-97	364.73	514.52	141.07
	1997-98	364.73	511.23	140.17
Rajasthan State Mines and Minerals Ltd.	1994-95	6172.60	10265.17	166.30
	1995-96	6172.60	11156.80	180.75
	1996-97	6172.60	12101.33	196.05
	1997-98	6172.60	13095.49	212.16
Rajasthan State Industrial Development and Investment Corporation Limited	1994-95	14040.25	16256.28	115.78
	1995-96	14890.25	18474.27	124.07
	1996-97	15440.25	19986.86	129.45
	1997-98	15560.25	20711.77	133.11
Rajasthan Small Industries Corporation Ltd.	1994-95	546.40	428.26	78.38
	1995-96	546.40	652.71	119.46
	1996-97	546.40	838.99	153.55
	1997-98	546.40	1222.63	223.76
Rajasthan State Hotels Corporation Ltd.	1994-95	106.75	144.20	135.08
	1995-96	106.75	158.59	148.56
	1996-97	106.75	163.71	153.36
	1997-98	106.75	158.55	148.52
Rajasthan Rajya Paryatan Vikas Nigam Ltd.	1994-95	1383.84	1610.71	116.39
	1995-96	1383.84	2268.84	163.95
	1996-97	1383.84	1796.02	129.79
	1997-98	1383.84	1810.79	130.85
Rajasthan State Seeds Corporation Ltd.	1994-95	233.72	-213.40	-91.31
	1995-96	634.73	577.86	91.04
	1996-97	634.74	850.59	134.01
	1997-98	634.28	1007.85	158.90
Rajasthan State Bridge and Construction Corporation Ltd.	1994-95	500.00	933.78	186.76
	1995-96	1000.00	1819.35	181.94
	1996-97	1000.00	2436.76	243.68
	1997-98	1000.00	2783.85	278.39
Rajasthan Jal Vikas Nigam Ltd.	1994-95	127.00	118.70	93.46
	1995-96	127.00	138.06	108.71
	1996-97	127.00	138.47	109.03
	1997-98	127.00	157.28	123.84

APPENDIX A–4.6

Position of Employment in State-level Public Sector Enterprises (Excluding RSEB) as on 31.03.2000

(No.)

S.No	*Name of PSU*	*Managerial*	*Non-Managerial*	*Total*
CATEGORY - A		2068	32277	34345
1.	Rajasthan Warehousing Corporation	19	615	634
2.	Rajasthan State Mines & Minerals Development Corporation Ltd.	218	1413	1631
3.	Rajasthan State Mineral Development Corporation Ltd.	154	633	787
4.	Rajasthan State Industrial Development & Investment Corporation Ltd.	214	1158	1372
5.	Rajasthan Small Industries Corporation Ltd.	92	403	495
6.	Rajasthan Financial Corporation	444	604	1048
7.	Rajasthan State Seeds Corporation Ltd.	34	188	222
8.	Rajasthan State Road Transport Corporation	348	25192	25540
9.	Rajasthan State Agriculture Marketing Board	147	789	936
10.	Rajasthan Housing Board*	266	971	1237
11.	Rajasthan State Bride and Construction Corporation Ltd.	132	301	433
CATEGORY - B		279	3659	3938
1.	Rajasthan State Ganganagar Sugar Mills Ltd.	74	2397	2471
2.	Rajasthan State Hotels Corporation Ltd.	23	127	150
3.	Rajasthan Tourism Development Corporation Ltd.	182	1135	1317

Contd...

...Contd...

(No.)

S.No	Name of PSU	Managerial	Non-Managerial	Total
CATEGORY - C		14	348	362
1.	Rajasthan Handloom Development Corporation Ltd.	5	274	279
2.	Rajasthan Land Development Corporation	5	16	21
3.	Rajasthan Jal Vikas Nigam Ltd.	3	53	56
4.	Rajasthan State Agro Industries Corporation Ltd.	—	—	—
5.	Rajasthan Electronics Ltd.	1	5	6
6.	Rajasthan State Tungsten Development Corporation Ltd.	—	—	—
7.	Rajasthan Tanneries Limited	Closed		

* Relates to 1998-99.

APPENDIX A–4.7

Net Profit/Loss of Public Sector Undertakings during the Year 1996-97 to 1999-2000

(Rs. in lakh)

S.No.	Name of PSU	1996-97	1997-98	1998-99	1999-2000
CATEGORY – A					
1.	Rajasthan State Warehousing Corporation	222.05	192.68	507.47	642.35
2.	Rajasthan State Mines & Minerals Ltd.	1273.14	1292.06	1635.50	1710.43
3.	Rajasthan State Mineral Corporation Ltd.	26.91	22.32	520.43	672.86
4.	Rajasthan State Industrial Development and Investment Corporation Ltd.	1181.74	968.91	61.24	51.37
5.	Rajasthan Small Industries Corporation Ltd.*	205.44	385.98	464.80	512.61
6.	Rajasthan Financial Corporation	-1714.25	-1537.75	-545.88	339.95
7.	Rajasthan State Seeds Corporation Ltd.	273.35	148.75	181.43	160.56
8.	Rajasthan State Road Transport Corporation	677.65	-1823.70	-3747.51	-7064.97
9.	Rajasthan State Agriculture Marketing Board	760.07	716.18	507.47	831.79
10.	Rajasthan Housing Board	84.09	91.03	30.89	10.27
11.	Rajasthan Bridge and Construction Corporation Ltd.	778.91	417.73	198.01	241.01
CATEGORY - B					
1.	Rajasthan State Ganganagar Sugar Mills Ltd.*	1.72	3.40	17.63	13.78
2.	Rajasthan State Hotels Corporation Ltd.	10.99	-2.99	-37.97	-10.17
3.	Rajasthan Tourism Dev. Corporation Ltd.*	23.98	23.40	-98.10	Under Finalisation
CATEGORY – C					
1.	Rajasthan State Handloom Dev. Corporation Ltd.	-304.90	-271.16	-435.32	-533.01
2.	Rajasthan Land Development Corporation	17.30	60.10	130.54	138.79
3.	Rajasthan Jal Vikas Nigam Ltd.	0.96	18.53	21.29	12.98
4.	Rajasthan State Agro Industries Corporation Ltd.	-74.70	-78.59	-139.98	Closed
5.	Rajasthan Electronics Ltd.	-11.15	-11.32	-14.49	-15.13
6.	Rajasthan State Tungsten Corporation Ltd.	-0.41	-15.82	-3.0	-5.33
7.	Rajasthan Tanneries Ltd.	Closed			

* Division/Activity wise profit/loss appended.

Chapter 5

Handloom and Handicrafts

Handloom and handicrafts constitute the largest part of Indian cottage industries. Handicrafts help preserve traditional art and culture, while the handloom sub-sector is an important source of employment generation. It is estimated that there are 4 million handloom units all over the country, which contribute 20 per cent of the total textiles made in India and approximately Rs. 1,500 crore worth of export earnings, although these figures do not suggest that the contribution of this decentralised sector to the state NSDP and employment has been significant.

Handlooms, handicrafts, khadi and village industries constitute an important part of the non-formal sector of Rajasthan's economy. However, they have not been given an important place in Plan allocations. Because they are not organised, they are unable to influence government policies to a significant extent. Their regional distribution is also uneven.

However, there is sufficient scope for the development of this sector in Rajasthan, since there is a lot of demand for their products in the rural areas. What is required is a new approach to the sector, with a long-term perspective, involving reorientation in product designs, aggressive marketing and a customer-friendly approach. These segments of the non-formal sector must get what is due to them in Plan allocations and should be protected from the onslaught of the organised sector.

Plan Allocation for the Decentralised Industrial Sector

Though the three sub-sectors are labour-intensive, employing more than 6.5 lakh persons in Rajasthan, not enough resources have been provided for raising the income of artisans. During the initial five Plans, khadi units, village industries and handloom were allocated around Rs. 60 lakh and the focus of policymakers was only on providing subsidy for procurement of yarn, modernisation of looms and purchase of *khadi*.

These allocations were substantially raised in the subsequent Plans. In the Sixth Plan, apart from the RHDC, Rs. 2 crore was allocated for the cooperative sector in handloom while Rs. 3 crore was allotted for khadi and village industries. The outlays were substantially enhanced in the Ninth Plan, with Rs. 8.5 crore for the cooperative sector in handlooms, Rs. 19 crore for the RHDC, Rs. 10.09 for khadi and village industries and Rs. 10 lakh for handicrafts.

In the Tenth Plan, an outlay of Rs. 18.85 crore is proposed for khadi and village industries, while a decision has been taken to provide only managerial subsidy for cooperatives in handlooms. An outlay of Rs. 2.64 crore has been provided for various programmes to be initiated by the RHDC.

However, government assistance has not helped in strengthening the sector and the income of workers is barely enough for their subsistence.

Handloom

According to a survey conducted by the Directorate of Industries in 1997-98, about 66,000 weavers operate nearly 33,000 handlooms in Rajasthan and produce 62.8 million sq. meters of cloth from cotton, woollen, silk and synthetic fibre. A total of 98.5 per cent of the handloom units are operated by families, which work on more than 27,600 handlooms and produce 45.8 million sq. mts. of cloth every year. The handloom cloth produced in 1997-98 was more than the production of mill-made cloth in the state in 1997-98 — 47.2 million sq. meters.

Characteristics of Handloom Sector

A handloom unit is generally operated by two members of a household. The regional distribution of handloom units in the state is highly skewed, with 34 per cent of the units concentrated in three districts of Barmer (4856), Jodhpur (2569) and Bikaner (2008) and very few in the predominantly tribal districts of Banswara, Dungarpur and Udaipur. The other districts where the handloom sub-sector is contributing modestly to employment are Churu, Nagaur, Jaipur and Kota.

A wide variety of handloom cloth is produced in the state. While the handloom workers in Kota produce *doria* and *moonga saris* with a considerably high value addition, a majority of handloom units manufacture medium quality *dhotis*, towels, *lungis*, carpets, bed covers, barrack blankets etc. In Barmer, Jaisalmer and Bikaner, however, handloom weavers also prepare *khes* (a woollen sheet) and dress material which are in high demand both within the country and outside. However, there has been very little attempt to increase exports.

The RHDC set up in 1984, caters to the requirements of individual weavers. In addition, cooperative societies of weavers have been organised to help procure yarn and provide assistance in marketing. As of March 2000, 815 such cooperative societies had been registered, of which 23 per cent were in Jaipur district alone. However, only 25.6 per cent of such societies are functional, while 39 per cent have turned defunct. Sixteen per cent of the cooperatives were liquidated within six to eight years of their inception. With some assistance from the government, 159 weavers' cooperative societies can be made functional. Table 5.1 lists the districts where more than 65 per cent of societies were non-functional.

TABLE 5.1

Functional and Non Functional Weavers' Societies (March, 1998)

District	*No. of Registered Primary Societies*	*% of Non Functional Societies*
Jaipur	190	80.5
Pali	37	92
Nagaur	21	100
Sirohi	7	71.5
Barmer	30	70
Bikaner	20	65
Jhunjhunu	30	93.3
Dungarpur	14	92.9
Ajmer	45	87
Alwar	26	88.5
Banswara	6	93.7

Source: Statistical Abstract, 1999, Department of Economics and Statistics, Government of Rajasthan.

Even where the weavers' cooperative societies are functional, there are several dummy members, gross financial and administrative lapses, and manipulation of purchases and sales. According to the Audit Report prepared by the Cooperative Department for 1999-2000 and 2000-2001 for 27 weavers' societies in Jaipur, products worth Rs. 11.24 lakh and Rs. 5.95 lakh were 'purchased' from three non-existent societies.

Policies for Development of the Handloom Sector

The state government has taken various steps to help the handloom sub-sector.

- Fairs and exhibitions are regularly held at the national, regional and district levels to exhibit products of handloom and create demand.
- State government offices and corporations have been directed to purchase specified cotton, silk and woollen cloth only from the handloom sector.
- The RHDC and the Rajasthan State Bunkar Cooperative Sangh (RSBCS) have production centres covering all the districts. While the RHDC has 51 centres, the RSBCS has 17 centres which produce cotton, silk and woollen handloom cloth and exhibit them at their show rooms. Most of these production centres have been set up in areas having high concentration of weavers.
- Apart from government purchases, the state government has also taken steps to market handloom products. The RHDC has set up 19 marketing centres or show rooms, including five at Delhi, Ahmedabad, Kolkata, Hyderabad and Kanpur, while the RSBCS has set up 21 show rooms, including one at Mumbai.
- A project package scheme has been initiated for BPL weavers, especially those from the SC/ST population and women. A cluster approach has been adopted to improve both quality and productivity. Financial assistance in the form of subsidy and loan is given to weavers for modernisation of looms, training, development of new designs, construction of work-sheds etc. Twenty-eight such schemes are being implemented in different districts with financial support from the RHDC as well as the National Handloom Development Corporation (NHDC). The schemes encompass a variety of handloom products ranging from jacquard, turkish towels, embroidered cloth to tie-and-dye products and silk cloth, *tussar* and woollen tweed. The total number of beneficiaries

from these schemes is estimated at 4,650 and the total cost at Rs. 9.79 crore.

- Under the Mill Gate Rate Scheme, the NHDC offers 100 per cent subsidy on handling charges paid by handloom weavers in procuring raw material, especially yarn. Reimbursement of these charges is made by any one of the following agencies: RHDC, RSBCS, primary Bunkar Cooperative Societies, the Handloom Development Centre and recognised export houses.

The Development Commissioner, Handlooms, Government of India, has introduced numerous schemes for the welfare of handloom weavers, which include part reimbursement of the medical bills paid by a weaver. Since 1997-98, the Central government also shares the premium paid by a handloom weaver on life insurance policy.

Deen Dayal Handloom Promotion Scheme

The Deen Dayal Hathkargha Protsahan Yojana initiated by the Central government incorporates the following elements for promoting the handloom sector:

(a) Inputs: Financial assistance in the form of margin money to avail credit. The Central government will provide Rs. 2000, the state government Rs.1000 and the concerned weaver Rs. 1000. Financial assistance is also provided for training to enable weavers to switch over from low to high value added items. The weavers have to organise themselves into self-help groups, membership of which can range from 25 to 100.

(b) Infrastructure support for eligible district or state level primary cooperatives or apex agencies.

(c) Design Development in collaboration with the National Institute of Design and National Institute of Fashion Technology.

(d) Publicity and marketing incentives for handloom products.

(e) Transport subsidy for partly meeting the cost of transportation of finished goods, which is limited to the weavers in the northeast, Sikkim and Jammu and Kashmir.

(f) Strengthening of handloom organisations.

In addition, the state government has taken the following steps to help weavers:

- RFC-sponsored financial assistance to SC weavers. The RHDC will act as a nodal agency, which will assist weavers in procuring yarn and act as an assured buyer of their products. It will recover the cost from the sale proceeds.
- Under the 1998 Industrial Policy, a decision has been taken to gradually phase out the non-competitive products (such as *dhoti*, towels etc.) and promote only those handloom products which are commercially viable.
- The Policy also outlines measures to ensure easy access of weavers to adequate credit.
- The state government has also decided to evolve a mechanism for disseminating information on designs and technical developments.

Problems Facing the Handloom Sub-sector

There has been no long-term programme to develop the handloom sub-sector. Weavers, acting individually, are not able to procure yarn on time and properly market their products and cooperatives have performed dismally. Weavers remain unaware of consumer preferences and there is no agency which collects such information. Products like *janta dhoti*, towels, dusters, towelling cloth etc. are produced in huge quantities without assessing demand. A close study of the sector would reveal that it faces the following problems:

- Inadequate capital, which leads to delays in procurement of yarn.
- Piling of unsold stock with the RSBCS and its agencies and the sale depots of RHDC. According to annual reports of the RHDC, the closing stock in its sale depots was worth Rs. 1.1 crore in 1987-88 and rose to Rs. 2.56 crore in 1997-98.The unsold stock with the RSBCS rose from Rs. 3.98 crore in 1994-95 to Rs. 4.17 crore in 1999-2000.
- High cost of handloom cloth and lack of level playing field with mill cloth.
- The weavers' cooperatives do not have a market-friendly approach. Though exhibitions and fairs do push up sales occasionally, a lasting demand for such products has not been created.
- The RHDC is not managed as a professional organisation. It is running under heavy losses, which has jeopardised its plans to take a lead role in developing this sector. The RSBCS, the apex cooperative of weavers, spent about 60 per cent of its budget on salaries and allowances in 1994-95 and this has risen to 74 per cent by 1999-2000.

Vision for the Future

The handloom sub-sector faces stiff competition from mill cloth, because the mill sector has economies of scale. Efforts should be made to create demand for handloom cloth, introduce new designs and help the sector adopt a customer-oriented approach. Such a demand-driven approach will solve the problem of unsold stock. Attempts also need to be made to raise the productivity of labour. Both the RHDC and the RSBCS must cut their establishment costs or else face liquidation. In the face of globalisation, the handloom sector can survive only if it raises the efficiency of weavers and reorganises the apex bodies.

Khadi and Village Industries

Khadi and village industries have a long history in Rajasthan. Village industries such as blacksmithy, carpentry, leather works thrived, as their products had a local market. Woollen khadi is common in the western districts, such as Jaisalmer, Bikaner, Barmer, Jodhpur and Nagaur, and it is gaining popularity in Jaipur district as well.

Khadi

The pace of development of *khadi* in Rajasthan has been rather slow. The total value of *khadi* produced in the entire state rose from Rs. 21.75 crore in 1988-89 to Rs. 39.42 crore in 1995-96, a linear growth rate of 11.6 per cent. However, it has slipped since and the total value was estimated at Rs. 23.51 crore during 2003-04.

The total employment in *khadi* units, which was about 165,000 in 1988-89, started declining after 1993-94 and stood at 98,500 in 1999-2000, a decline of 40 per cent since 1988-89. Table 5.2 shows production and employment scenario.

Interestingly, in spite of a decline in production and employment, the per worker output in value terms has steadily increased between 1988-89 and 1999-2000. The output-labour ratio has increased in respect of both woollen and cotton *khadi*, but the growth in cotton *khadi* has been relatively higher, perhaps due to increasing demand in urban areas. The decline in the production of cotton *khadi* is also lesser than that of woollen *khadi* in 1999-2000.

There are various problems facing the *khadi* units in Rajasthan. Nearly 75 per cent of production of woollen *khadi* is concentrated in the four districts of Bikaner, Jaipur, Jaisalmer and Nagaur. Bikaner and Jaipur presently account for 57.4 per cent of production and 48 per cent of employment, with Bikaner accounting for 40 per cent of employment. However, cotton *khadi* units are more evenly dispersed. Jaipur and Dausa districts account for 43.2 per cent of production and 25.3 per cent of employment.

TABLE 5.2

Production and Employment in Khadi

S.No.		1988-89	1995-96	1999-2000
A	Production (Rs. lakh)			
	Woollen Khadi	1,458	2,134	1,702
	Cotton Khadi	717	1,808	1,758
	Total	**2,175**	**3,942**	**3,460**
B	Employment (persons per year)			
	Woollen Khadi	120,47	85,349	66,229
	Cotton Khadi	444,719	35,551	32,242
	Total	**165,193**	**120,900**	**98,471**
C	Productivity per worker (Rs.)			
	Woollen Khadi	1,210	2,500	2,570
	Cotton Khadi	1,603	5,086	5,453
	Average	**1,316**	**3,260**	**3,514**

Source: Statistical Abstract (various issues) Department of Economics and Statistics, Government of Rajasthan.

There was wide inter-district variation in labour productivity of woollen *khadi* units in 1999-2000 — ranging from Rs. 8132 in Jaipur to Rs 1475 in Nagaur. The productivity per worker was Rs. 2030 in Bikaner and Rs. 1550 in Jaisalmer. Cotton *khadi* units also saw wide variations in productivity, ranging from Rs. 10,047 in Dausa to Rs. 5739 in Bikaner, with Jaipur at Rs. 7652.

The Rajasthan Khadi and Village Industries Board (KVIB) used to collect and publish district-wise data about the income of khadi unit workers, but it is no longer being done. In 1988-89 the average net annual income per worker was Rs. 404 in the case of woollen *khadi*, and Rs. 888 for cotton *khadi*, which increased to Rs. 677 for woollen *khadi* and Rs. 1457 for cotton *khadi* for 1994-95. Clearly, the average earning per worker is extremely low and their profession cannot help them move above the poverty line.

The state government has not played a pro-active role in designing policies for improving the lot of *khadi* workers. The total subsidy for promoting *khadi* has fallen from Rs. 66 lakh in 1990-91 to less than Rs. 3 lakh now. Though the KVIB provides loans to khadi units, subsidies and loans have registered a declining trend on account of mounting overdues. Outstanding loans of *khadi* units increased from Rs. 2.62 crore in 1988-89 to Rs. 6.54 crore in 1994-95 and is estimated to have touched Rs. 10 crore in March 2000. In such a situation, the government may find it difficult to revive the sector and artisans will not have adequate funds even to maintain the level of production. The lack of funds forces *khadi* producers to rely on the yarn supplied by various private outlets and, as a result, the scale of their operations remains very small.

Vision for the Future

In the face of fierce competition from the mill and handloom sectors, the prospects of the *khadi* units in Rajasthan will remain bleak unless there is a total reorientation in approach and product innovation carried out. In a free market environment, *khadi* units can withstand competition only if productivity per worker is substantially raised. The KVIB has to shift its role from facilitation to innovation, while retaining the traditional philosophy underlying the *khadi* movement. The following suggestions merit serious consideration:

- Studying the prospects of developing *khadi* units in districts where its production is low, and providing necessary help for increasing production. Equitable spatial distribution of *khadi* units will broaden the base of the state economy.
- Improving the quality of woollen yarn.
- Improving the design of cotton *khadi*, and ensuring a linking of the cotton and silk *khadi* units with the garment industry, to tap the urban markets.
- Developing a customer friendly approach.
- Ensuring a better deal for *khadi* workers through grassroot organisations, which will strengthen their bargaining power.
- Raising the Plan allocation for *khadi* industries so as to increase their production and employment levels.

Village Industries

The village industries, spread across Rajasthan, employ 3.22 lakh workers but the value of products prepared by these units was estimated at a mere Rs. 450 crore in 1999-2000, which was only 1.03 per cent of the NSDP. Table 5.3 gives the production and employment in village industries.

The production of village industries has generally grown at a significantly higher rate than the increase in employment. However, such values have been measured at current prices, which partly reflect increase in prices. Overall, per artisan value of output contributed by village industries has shown an upward trend. During the 12 years under review, the percentage of part-time workers to total workers has ranged from 45 per cent in 1993-94 to 40 per cent in other years.

TABLE 5.3

Production and Employment in Village Industries

Year	*Production Value (Rs. Crore)*	*Increase Per cent*	*Employment (Persons)*	*Increase Per cent*
1988-89	136.76	—	267,676	—
1989-90	161.58	18.1	284,645	6.3
1990-91	183.38	13.5	297,654	4.6
1991-92	202.64	10.5	304,386	2.3
1992-93	233.45	15.2	305,670	0.4
1993-94	197.61	(-)15.3	254,936	(-)17.6
1994-95	229.86	16.3	265,164	4.0
1995-96	260.48	13.3	274,652	3.6
1996-97	324.61	24.6	283,294	3.1
1997-98	340.35	4.8	287,494	1.5
1998-99	407.96	19.8	302,575	5.2
1999-00	450.00	10.3	327,000	8.1

Source: Statistical Abstract (various issues) Department of Economics and Statistics, Government of Rajasthan.

The value of village industries has been estimated on the basis of data collected under the auspices of the KVIB. It, however, does not represent the profitability of units. It would be possible to estimate the net income accruing to workers engaged in village industries only if the KVIB improves its database on actual output, and the value of various products contributed by village industries, cost of producing each product and the profitability of each unit.

Inter-Regional Variations in Labour Productivity

Table 5.4 shows the predominant position of village industries in districts like Jaipur, Jodhpur, Udaipur, Chittorgarh and Alwar, which together share 31.5 per cent in the total value of village industry products and provide employment to nearly 30 per cent of village industry workers.

Village industries do not seem to be important either in terms of production or employment, in Hanumangarh, Bikaner, Baran, Jalore and Kota, partly because agriculture or mining provide alternative sources of employment in these districts. In Jaisalmer, sparse population means the village industries do not have much to add to the economy.

Village industries in Rajasthan do not seem to have enough scope for development because they suffer from the following weaknesses:

TABLE 5.4

District-wise Distribution of Production and Employment in Village Industries (1999-2000)

Productivity (value per worker) in Rs.	*District*	*Production Value (Rs. crore)*	*%*	*Employment (persons)*	*%*
15306	Jaipur	36.8	8.2	24043	7.4
19054	Jodhpur	31.2	6.9	16385	5.1
13991	Chittorgarh	25.66	5.7	18341	5.7
13592	Udaipur	24.82	5.5	18258	5.7
12204	Alwar	23.28	5.2	19076	5.9
12872	Nagaur	22.77	5.1	17690	5.5
16204	Ajmer	20.66	4.6	12752	4.0
11508	Banswara	18.46	4.1	16038	5.0
12310	Bharatpur	15.51	3.4	12604	3.9
12565	Sawai Madhopur	13.13	2.9	10451	3.2
11734	Barmer	12.25	2.7	10439	3.2
12816	Dungarpur	11.04	2.5	8614	2.7

Source: Statistical Abstract, 2001, Department of Economics and Statistics, Government of Rajasthan.

- Lack of dynamism among artisans, as a result of which they do not develop new product designs.
- Low productivity, which prevents artisans from competing with bigger players in the market.
- Though these industries are labour intensive, the low prices their products fetch means that workers do not receive adequate returns commensurate with their labour.

KVIB does not seem to have been able to evolve a market-friendly approach to develop village industries in Rajasthan and nor does it seem to have plans to do so. A perspective plan is needed to train the artisans so as to enable them to improve their efficiency.

So far, the KVIB has only acted as a facilitator for disbursing loans and subsidies and organising exhibitions. It needs to develop a long-term plan for developing new techniques and designs and aggressively capturing the rural as well as urban markets. An attempt also needs to be made to encourage the children of these artisans to continue in their traditional occupations, adopting new techniques and designs.

Handicrafts

While village industries meet day-to-day needs of consumers in the rural and urban areas, handicrafts are more artistic and represent a region's heritage. Rajasthan has a range of handicrafts: silver ornaments made by tribal women (Banswara, Dungarpur, Sirohi etc.) traditional costumes, embroidery work, tie-and-dye saris and scarves (Jodhpur and Jaipur), blue and black pottery (Jaipur), kundan work (Bikaner and Jaipur), stone carving and marble statues (Ajmer, Jaipur, Dausa and Rajsamand) gold jewellery (Jaipur, Bikaner), miniature paintings, engraved brassware, etc. They have a great income-generating potential.

Proper planning for development of handicrafts would not only increase the income of craftsmen, but could also help reduce regional imbalances.

Development of Handicrafts in Rajasthan

The history of handicrafts in the erstwhile princely states of Rajasthan can be traced to the Stone Age. Excavations of the Indus Valley civilisation in Kalibanga (now in Hanumangarh district) reveal that the area had been an important centre of ceramic industry. In later ages, gold and silver ornaments, block printing, stone carving, wood crafts, etc. were made. The rulers of the princely states patronised these crafts, a role that was taken over by the state government after integration of these principalities with the Indian Union. The Directorate of Industries serves as the focal point for formulating and implementing policies for the development of the sector.

Handicrafts of Rajasthan

The handicrafts made in Rajasthan fall into 18 broad categories.[1] Leather shoes, wood craft, pottery, fibre craft and metal craft have maximum number of units. Table 5.5. give the district-wise distribution of handicrafts.

Leather craft is the most prevalent handicraft in Rajasthan, although it is concentrated in a few districts (Sikar, Barmer, Bundi, Jaisalmer and Udaipur). Barmer is widely known for its artistic needle and crochet work and 70 per cent of needle craft units are located here. Sikar, Tonk, Bhilwara, Bharatpur, Udaipur and Barmer are also popular centres for artistic woodwork. Jaipur, Dausa and Alwar are famous for jewellery, stone work and blue pottery. Though over 51 per cent of handicraft units are located in Barmer, Bhilwara, Tonk, Sikar, Jodhpur and Udaipur, Jaipur tops in terms of value addition and exports.

All these data relate to 1991-92 when the Census Survey of Artisans and Handicraft Units in Rajasthan was conducted. No attempt has been made by the Directorate of Industries to update the data since then.

---

1. Leather craft; Wood craft; Pottery; Weaving; Needle and crochet work; Fibre craft; Metal craft; Stone craft; Jewellery; Textile dyeing and printing; Readymade garments and made ups; Edible oil (Kolhu); Painting; Hand made paper; Glass ware; Horn products; Cotton carding; and others.

TABLE 5.5

District-wise Distribution of Important Handicrafts 1991-92

District	*No. of Units*				
	Leather Craft	*Wood Craft*	*Needle & Crochet Work*	*Pottery*	*Fibre Craft*
Ajmer	1530	736	64	793	347
Barmer	2272	1092	7127	940	118
Bhilwara	1901	1765	14	1638	647
Bundi	1501	592	—	724	452
Ganganagar	1029	685	144	295	64
Jaisalmer	1667	80	35	210	141
Jodhpur	1000	521	—	126	156
Pali	1497	599	—	794	79
Sikar	2603	1123	—	695	709
Tonk	1401	1579	10	1684	843
Udaipur	1770	1122	—	1271	692
Bharatpur	548	1054	—	1313	1009
Banswara	633	37	—	647	745

Source: Census Survey of Artisans and Handicraft Units in Rajasthan, 1991-92, Directorate of Industries, Government of Rajasthan.

Employment: The Census Survey revealed that 1.49 lakh persons were engaged in handicrafts all over the state in 1991-92. Barmer accounted for 15 per cent of such employment, Jodhpur (8.4 per cent), Tonk (7 per cent) and Sikar (9 per cent). Table 5.6 shows the crafts-wise share in employment.

TABLE 5.6

Employment in Crafts Sectors

Handicraft	*Employment (% of total)*
Leather	25.45
Pottery	15.13
Wood craft	14.38
Weaving	14.36
Needle work	9.75
Fibre craft	7.44
Metal craft	5.25
Stone craft	2.31
Jewellery	1.98
Textile dyeing and printing	1.94
Others	2.01

Source: Census Survey of Artisans and Handicraft Units in Rajasthan, 1991-92, Directorate of Industries, Government of Rajasthan.

Analysis of Income

According to the Census Survey, the total income of all the 86,000 units was estimated at Rs. 84.15 crore. This yielded an average income of Rs. 9785 per unit to artisans. With an average employment of 1.73 persons per unit, per person income was estimated at a mere Rs. 5657, which meant that a person employed in a handicraft unit was, on an average, living below the poverty line.

Seventeen per cent of these units had an annual income of Rs. 3357 only while 37.7 per cent units received an average income of Rs. 4950. A small fraction of 2.92 per cent of handicraft units earned Rs. 60,000 per year. Textile dyeing and jewellery units generally earned much higher income than leather craft, needle and crochet units. Painters also earned more than other types of crafts.

There are many reasons for such low earnings, the main one being the existence of many middlemen between the artisan and the consumer. Even where handicrafts are marketed by government emporia, high establishment costs take up most of the sale proceeds and the craftsmen continue to get low prices. There is lack of a market-friendly approach, especially in the case of leather shoes, wood-craft products, horn products, carpet weaving, fibre crafts, needle and crochet work etc. Artisans have not prepared themselves to woo new customers. New designs are often provided by middlemen, who appropriate a major part of the earnings. Even in the case of gold jewellery, big showrooms located at Jaipur, Jodhpur and Bikaner result in the goldsmiths not getting a reasonable share in profits. In some cases, there is stiff competition from the big players.

CHANGING TASTES

Kota doria saris was in high demand in Kolkata, Mumbai, Chennai, etc and fetched high prices. However, it is now facing stiff challenge from moonga doria made of synthetic fibre, which is cheaper. This is working to the detriment of local craftsmen.

Export of Handicrafts

Export of handicrafts from Rajasthan has been steadily rising and the state has an important contribution to handicraft exports from India (Table 5.7).

TABLE 5.7

Exports of Handicrafts* from India and Rajasthan

(Value in Rs. crore)

Year	*India*	*Rajasthan*	*Rajasthan's Share %*
1990-91	713	63	8.8
1991-92	1065	86	8.1
1992-93	1412	148	10.5
1993-94	1970	143	7.3
1994-95	3020	304	10.0
1996-97	3569	458	12.0
1997-98	4306	517	12.0

* Including handloom cloth.

Source: Economic Review, Department of Economics and Statistics, Government of Rajasthan.

Problems of Handicrafts Sub-sector

- The processing of hides/skins and seasoning of timber are still done on traditional lines, resulting in considerable waste of raw material and increasing the cost of production.
- A lack of backward and forward linkages.

Back-ward Linkages
• Credit, of which 80 per cent is needed for working capital
• Timely availability of raw material
• Upgradation of skills via training
• Development of new designs
Forward Linkages
• Pricing of handicraft products
• Market-friendly approach

- Multiplicity of middlemen, especially in high-value and export-oriented products.
- Threat from the organised sector in case of textile dyeing and printing, jewellery, blue pottery, readymade garments, carpet making, doria etc. Several artisans are forced to sell their products to such organised units since they had earlier taken loans from them.

In 1995, the state government set up an Institute of Crafts and Designs at Jaipur to help handicraft units in evolving new designs as well as marketing their products. The government has also initiated a policy of assisting craftsmen in selling their products in *haats*.

Vision for the Future

The contribution of handicrafts to state income and employment is negligible. However, its share in the country's export trade is steadily rising. There is ample scope to increase these exports and thus enhance the income of artisans. This would require a carefully designed policy for the handicrafts sub-sector and a road map will have to be prepared for a decade with the following features:

- Organising craftsmen to meet the challenges of bigger players.
- Developing market outlets for handicraft products owned and operated by craftsmen, thus minimising the role of middlemen.
- Development of new product designs with the active involvement of the Institute of Crafts and Design and other agencies and facilitating training of craftsmen.
- Development of an export-oriented approach with a target of Rs.1000 crore of exports by 2004-2005. This would require the use of cost-effective technology in these units.
- Develop a database on the cost structure of each handicraft product, its profitability and the actual share of earnings going to craftsmen as well as on direct and indirect employment in this sub-sector. Such data must be updated regularly.
- Making profitable use of marble slurry, sand stone wastes and stone rubbish in the making of statues and expanding the market for shellac products, clay-based sanitary works, kundan work etc. (See Appendix A–5.1).
- Raising the share of handicrafts in Plan allocations. Such allocations should be geared to strengthening the infrastructure available for the sector.

New Approach for the Decentralised Industrial Sector

The decentralised industrial sector has so far thrived largely on subsidy received from the state government. Given the inadequate capital base, low productivity, and weak marketing linkages, products of these units have not become popular even in the domestic markets. What is needed is a strategy with the following features:

- Downsizing the RHDC, Khadi Gramodyog Board and RSBCS so as to reduce their expenditure on salaries, allowances and perks to a maximum limit of 30 per cent in the next 10 years.
- Gradual phasing out of subsidies by the end of Eleventh Five Year Plan. But this strategy has to be supported by a market-friendly and consumer-oriented approach. There should be innovations in design and packaging. To achieve this end, *khadi* and handloom units could organise fashion shows to woo the urban clientele.
- Attempts need to be made to adopt new technology in order to increase productivity per worker.

- Vertical integration of different activities – procurement of raw materials, production of finished products and marketing – has to be ensured. This would help workers in getting a larger share in profits. Two major steps have been initiated to popularise handicrafts. Handicraft counters have been opened at all hotels and the midway points on the highways. *Shilp melas* have been organised at Jaipur, Jodhpur and Udaipur to demonstrate handicraft items. These need to be made effective.
- Master craftsmen must be involved in training youth in traditional art and culture.
- A comprehensive database for all units comprising the decentralised industrial sector must be prepared before a strategy for its development is evolved and put to action.

APPENDIX A–5.1

Important Handicrafts of Rajasthan

Name of the Craft	*District Identified*
Marble statues, kitchen-ware and decoration pieces	Jaipur, Ajmer, Rajsamand
Tribal ornaments and silver ware	Banswara, Udaipur, Sirohi, Baran
Traditional costumes	Jaipur, Jodhpur, Barmer
Embroidery works	Jaipur, Jaisalmer, Barmer
Light-weight shoes (*jutian*)	Tonk, Jaipur
Tie & Dye scarves and saris	Jaipur, Jodhpur
Sandalwood crafts	Jaipur
Shellac and lac ware bangles, toys etc.	Sawai Madhopur, Karauli, Jaipur
Stone carving and *jalees*	Dausa, Rajsamand
Blue and black pottery	Jaipur
Hand made paper	Jaipur
Woollen carpets and *durries*	Bikaner, Dausa, Tonk and Jaipur
Camel leather goods	Barmer, Jaisalmer
Wooden crafts : toys and furniture	Jaisalmer, Barmer & Sawai Madhopur
Leather toys	Jhalawar
Artistic water containers	Jodhpur
Iron ware	Nagaur
Handmade paintings and proto-types	Ajmer (Kishangarh), Bundi, Kota, Chittorgarh, Jaipur
Kundan and *meenakari* work (gold and silver)	Jaipur
Decorators made of precious and semi-precious stones	Jaipur
Doria saris and dress material	Kota
Gem-stone cutting and polishing	Jaipur
Sanitary wares made from clay	Barmer
Odhanas	Jhunjhunu, Jodhpur
Rose perfume	Rajsamand
Quilts made of cotton and silk	Jaipur
Brass wares	Jaipur

Chapter 6

Roads and Transport

Status of Roads in Rajasthan

The economy of a region and its transport infrastructure are closely inter-related. In Rajasthan, a number of important industrial centres have come into existence and this has led to an increase in road length across the state.

As of 2000-01, the total length of roads in Rajasthan is 151,865 km, of which 87,462 km is maintained by the public works department or PWD (including 4637 km of National Highways) and 64,403 km has been constructed and is maintained by other departments (Appendix A–6.1). The length of PWD roads in 1949 was a mere 13,553 km. Of the total road length, 89.6 per cent is surfaced, while only 10.4 per cent is unsurfaced. The roads constructed by departments like the Rajasthan Housing Board, RIICO, JDA, Urban Improvement Trusts (UITs), municipalities, railways, Forest Department, Irrigation Department, RSEB, Manufacturing Engineering Section (MES) etc. do not cater to general traffic. Nor do most of the roads constructed by village panchayat samitis and the Rajasthan State Agriculture and Marketing Board (RSAMB).

In spite of the increase in road length over the years, Rajasthan's road density compares poorly to the national average. Against the national average of 66.8 km of roads for every 100 sq km of area, Rajasthan has only an average of 38 km of roads. The road length per lakh of population is 254.3 km, which is lesser than smaller states like Orissa, Punjab, Himachal Pradesh and Goa and puts it at the eighteenth rank. Fifty-two per cent of the villages are still not linked by all weather roads and only 47 per cent villages are linked by bituminous treated (BT) and metal roads (Appendix A–6.2).

Seventy-seven per cent of Rajasthan's population live in rural areas, where roads were primarily built to serve the needs of slow-moving/animal-drawn traffic. But the state has now a number of large cities like Jaipur, Jodhpur, Kota, Bikaner, Ajmer and Udaipur, which are located on the high traffic density National Highways or State Highways. Because of growing traffic congestion, bypasses have to be provided to these cities for smooth and accident-free corridors. Bypasses must also be provided for industrial towns like Bhilwara, Alwar, Pali, Beawar and Bharatpur. Funds for these projects will mostly come from the budgetary support of the state government or external assistance.

District-wise Road Length

The district-wise distribution of roads in Rajasthan is rather uneven (Appendix A–6.3). Kota, Jaipur, Bhilwara, Bundi, Jodhpur, Jhunjhunu, Pali, Dausa, Alwar and Udaipur had a significantly high density of roads, whereas Jaisalmer, Jhalawar, Bikaner, Sawai Madhopur, Ganganagar and Barmer had extremely low road connectivity. Economically backward districts suffer the most in allocation of resources for roads. Of the road length of 87,462 km, the shares of National Highways and State Highways is a mere 5.2 per cent and 10 per cent respectively, whereas major district roads (MDRs) constituted only 6.56 per cent. Thus, more than 63.5 per cent roads are village roads.

The state needs special treatment in allocation of funds for upgrading and maintenance of the existing road network, because habitations are widely dispersed and it has a long international border. A number of programmes are being launched in the state by the government and funding agencies, and it is now possible to specially earmark dedicated funds for the road sector in Rajasthan.

Road Development Plans

Three long-term Road Development Plans have been implemented over the last 60 years, which set out the agenda for development of roads and road transport across the country – Nagpur Plan (1943-61), Bombay Plan (1961-81), and Lucknow Plan (1981-2001). Preparations for the next 20-year plan for road development are under way. It is, therefore, necessary to assess past achievements and plan for future requirements (Appendix A–6.4)

National Highways and State Highways carry 80 per cent of the total traffic even though they constitute just 8 per cent of the total network. Hardly 5 per cent of the National Highways network is four-laned and 15 per cent is still single laned.

For balanced development and the economic integration of Rajasthan, it is essential that the vast hinterland be provided connectivity. The development of an extensive high quality road network is, therefore, the need of the hour.

The main thrust in Rajasthan should be to augment the capacity of high-density corridors by providing four lane roads and having two lane roads on all National/ State Highways. The condition of National Highways in Rajasthan is not in line with prescribed specifications and this needs to be addressed.

During the Ninth Five-Year Plan, villages having population above 1,000 (1991 census) were to be connected with all-weather roads and 75 per cent of all villages with population between 500-1,000 were to be connected with all-weather roads. Unfortunately, these targets could not be achieved, mainly because of inadequate funding. But with adequate financial provisions in the new Central Road Fund (CRF) Act, this lacuna could be addressed.

Funds for the Road Sector

The share of the road sector in total Plan allocation for India as a whole has steadily declined from 6.7 per cent in the First Plan to 3 per cent in the Eighth Plan. This has to be viewed in the context of the growth of freight traffic from 6 billion tonne km in 1951 to 350 billion tonne km in 1994 and passenger traffic from 23 billion passenger km to 1,500 billion passenger km.

Like other state governments, the Rajasthan government has also gone in for institutional financing and involvement of the private sector through the build-operate-transfer (BOT) model to develop the roads sector. It plans to mobilise private investment of Rs. 1,000 crore during the Tenth Plan period. A new BOT policy is on the anvil, which is contemplating providing legal protection to private parties, entitling them to seek justice in courts if there is any violation of the agreement by any party.

Unlike power and telecommunications, where user charges are a substantial source of revenue, the roads sector in India relies almost exclusively on funds provided by the Central and state budgets. Toll roads are only now being implemented. Though the total volume of road user taxation in India (mainly taxes on fuels and vehicles) is 2.1 per cent of GDP and compares favourably with other countries, actual expenditure on roads as a percentage of road user taxes is only 48 per cent. In the absence of earmarking, there has been persistent under funding of the road sector. A major casualty of the financing constraints is expenditure on maintenance, which is only 60 per cent of the desired level.

The Central government is implementing some mega road projects – the Golden Quadrilateral and North South East West Corridors under the National Highway Development Plan (NHDP) and the linking of villages under the Pradhan Mantri Gram Sadak Yojana (PMGSY). Implementing such mega projects requires a change in traditional methods of project execution and management. Management has to be more professional and the adoption of latest technology and materials is of vital importance.

The Golden Quadrilateral and the North South East West Corridors of the NHDP will result in Rajasthan getting 1,200 km length of four-laned highways, involving around Rs. 5,300 crore worth of investment.

National Highways

Eleven National Highways, totalling 4,481 km, pass through Rajasthan. The state thus, ranks third in terms of National Highway network after Uttar Pradesh (4,883 km) and Madhya Pradesh (4,608 km) (Appendix A–6.13). The National Highway network in Rajasthan covers practically every district, excepting Banswara, Hanumangarh, Jhunjhunu and Sawai Madhopur The position of National Highways passing through the state is given in Appendix A–6.14.

For better connectivity with the National Highway system in the state, the state government has proposed additional lengths of new National Highways (Appendix A–6.15), adding another 4,109 km to the network in the state.

Only 240 km of the National Highways in Rajasthan are four-laned (5 per cent). Fifty-five per cent are two-laned and 38 per cent are single-laned (Appendix A–6.16). An exception is the Delhi-Jaipur highway, which has recently been upgraded and is now a properly designed divided highway. According to a Traffic Volume Survey conducted in April 2001, the maximum average daily traffic (ADT) of 46,037 passenger car units (PCUs) or 23,274 vehicles was observed on the Jaipur-Bagru section of this highway. The National Highway from Delhi to Ahmedabad via Jaipur, Ajmer and Udaipur has the highest traffic density in Rajasthan and hence this section was taken up for upgrading on priority basis.

State Highways

The total network of State Highways in Rajasthan is only 8,898 km. But this network is not evenly distributed across the state, either in terms of location, density or per head of the population. Urban areas have been better served than rural areas. As per available records, 43 per cent of all villages and 21 per cent of larger villages (>1,000 population) are yet to be connected to the all-weather road network (Appendix A–6.2).

A large proportion of the State Highways are not suitable to bear heavy flow of traffic and need to be upgraded and renewed as per their prescribed specifications. This is primarily a responsibility of the state government. An action plan has to be prepared for four-laning of high traffic density corridors (more than 15,000 PCUs a day). Besides, capacity relief on some corridors through paved shoulders, 2.5 m wide on either side, of two-lane sections may also be required and will save lot of investments. For medium traffic corridors (5,000-15,000 PCU a day), single lanes should be widened to two lanes and poor quality two-lanes should be upgraded. This would save time on land acquisition, shifting/relocation of utilities etc. which will otherwise be required.

Rural Roads

Rajasthan has 68,392 km of village roads. As of now, 97 per cent of villages with population of more than 1500 and 78 per cent of villages with population between 1000 and 1500 are connected by road. However, there are wide variations in the accessibility of different districts. It is necessary to prepare Master Plans for each district providing an efficient network based on a hierarchy of settlements and growth centres in order to develop rural roads in a planned manner. Use of locally available materials and low cost technologies should be encouraged.

Maintenance of rural roads tends to get neglected due to inadequate funds. The RSAMB constructs and maintains a large number of link roads. Additional funds are being generated through a levy on agriculture produce being brought to the market.

Like other states, Rajasthan too is using the funds available under the PMGSY to provide rural connectivity. Around Rs. 400 crore was pumped in for this task during 2001-02, and nearly Rs. 840 crore is likely to be sent under PMGSY by 2007. A sum of Rs. 99.61 crore has been sanctioned to connect 340 villages with a regular road and works to connect 339 villages have already been taken up. The successful completion of the PMGSY is expected to bring about a complete transformation in the rural economy of the state. To implement these programmes, availability of funds must be ensured at the proper time. It will be better to conduct an institutional development strategy study in view of massive programmes under PMGSY and the Rural Infrastructure Development Fund (RIDF) works.

Maintenance of Roads

To mitigate the problem of ribbon development or development along the roadside, there is an urgent need to regulate the development of land along highways as well as main roads of cities, urban areas and the state road network. Legislation is required to facilitate proper functioning of highways and main roads. The allocation for maintenance of road should be realistic in respect to the direct/indirect revenue earned by road sector.

Roadside Amenities

Roadside amenities are necessary for long distance travel. No such provisions exist on the State Highways network in Rajasthan, though there are some on the National Highways. It has been decided to create such amenities (parking areas, eating places and rest rooms, drinking water, first aid facilities, telephone booths, toilet facilities, petrol pumps, repair/spare parts shops) at about 100 km intervals along the National Highways. Similar facilities could be provided along State Highways. Given the resource constraints and the growing traffic, the government must consider inviting private entrepreneurs to finance and manage such amenities.

For selecting suitable sites for such complexes along the National Highways and State Highways, multi-disciplinary teams were set up for each state with the respective Chief Engineers as conveners and representatives of the Ministry of Road Transport and Highways (MoRTH) and the Indian Oil Corporation as members. The recommendations of these committees were prioritised in the joint inter-ministerial meetings of MoRTH. It was decided to take up development complexes in each state. These facilities are to be jointly financed by MoRTH and the Ministry of Tourism. The cost of land acquisition and infrastructure would be borne by MoRTH and the cost of buildings by the Department of Tourism. The complexes would be run by the state Tourism Departments. Rajasthan has a dominant share of tourist traffic and can hope to get a large share of such funds. Rajasthan needs such complexes along its National Highways and State Highways network because it will cater to the traffic on the Golden Quadrilateral and North South East West corridors.

Central Road Fund

The Central Road Fund was created in 1929 for providing additional resources for the development of roads. In 1977, it was decided that a minimum of 3.5 paise per litre of petrol consumed was to be set apart for this fund, out of the custom and excise duty levied on petrol. The amount so accrued was being distributed in an 80:20 ratio between state and Central schemes, after defraying the cost of administration of the fund. The amount, however, has been insufficient to meet the growing demands of the states for development of state roads, as well as the Centrally sponsored schemes.

In recognition of the need for funds for the road infrastructure sector, the Union Budget of 1998-99 provided for a levy of additional excise duty and additional customs duty of Re. 1 per litre on petrol and diesel while the 1999-2000 Budget levied an additional duty of Re. 1.00 per litre on imported and domestic high speed diesel oil. Revenues from these two levies are to accrue to a dedicated non-lapsable Central Road Fund. The total accruals from the two levies are estimated to be Rs. 6000 crore a year.

Fifty per cent of the cess levied on high speed diesel will be used for rural roads. The remaining 50 per cent of the cess on high speed diesel and the entire cess collected on petrol will be allocated thus:

- 57.5 per cent of the sum for the development and maintenance of National Highways.
- 12.5 per cent for the construction of road underbridges/overbridges and erection of safety works at unmanned railroad crossings.
- The balance 30 per cent for the development of roads other than National Highways. Out of this, 10 per cent of total share of state roads shall be kept as reserve by the Central government for allocation to states for implementation of the scheme of Roads of Economic and Interstate Importance.

The Central government issued instructions for the formulation of state sector schemes for 2000-2001 to be financed from this Fund. The Centre will give administrative approval to the projects, while the state governments will give the technical and financial approvals.

Rajasthan has also benefited from the programme. Administrative sanction has been given for 109 works to the tune of Rs. 147.335 crore for 2001-02. This covered 109 works for a total length of 1,408.85 km and 152 cross drainage works. The PWD had spent Rs. 22.52 crore up to the end of December 2001. Works taken under CRF in Rajasthan given in Appendix A–6.22.

Problems Relating to Roads in Rajasthan

Overloading on Roads and Vehicles

Overloading of vehicles is one of the main reasons for the poor quality of roads in India. A study on a few state highways found that 12 to 40 per cent of commercial vehicles exceeded the prescribed laden weight of 22 tonnes by as much as 6 to 16 tonnes, taking gross weight in the range of 26-38 tonnes. The effect of overloaded vehicles on the road varies on the basis of the fourth power of axle weight. A 10-tonne axle will cause 16 times the damage as would be caused by a single 5-tonne axle. Besides, inadequate road width means higher repetitions of load on the same road.

In Rajasthan, most roads are of 3 metres width and 16 cm crust thickness with two coats of surface dressing. According to the Indian Roads Congress (IRC) Code, these roads are unsuited even for a single commercial vehicle per day.

However, unauthorised overloaded vehicles are a common sight on Rajasthan's roads. Three-wheeler tempos carry passengers almost two or three times more than their capacity. Tractors are being used more a commercial goods carriers, with large trolleys being attached to them. Apart from being a traffic hazard, they also result in revenue loss to the government. Ninety-eight per cent of the truck fleet comprises two-axle rigid chassis vehicles and they carry 90 per cent of freight tonnage on the National and State Highways network. Overloading of these vehicles is common, leading to premature deterioration of roads.

Negligence in Maintenance and Poor Funding

Road maintenance constitutes one of the most important components of the entire road system, yet it is by far the most neglected one. In India, the expenditure on maintenance is 35 per cent of the capital cost, against 96 per cent in the United States, 128 per cent in Japan and 82 per cent in Germany.

The magnitude of work involved in the maintenance of roads is very large but the funds available are not enough to meet the requirements, often being less than one-fourth of what is needed.

If the roads sector is well managed, it need not depend on any other source of funds. All that is needed is proper realisation of fees for driving license, vehicle registration and parking, passenger tax and goods tax, user charges for roads, rent for roadside plantation lease, fee for roadside commercial activity (petrol pump, hotel, motel, *dhaba*, shops, industries, laying optic fibre cable, installation of hoarding, etc).

Primary and secondary roads must get their due share from the collection of levies by the *mandi samiti* etc. Tertiary road construction and maintenance must be funded by locally realised road revenue.

Lack of Appropriate Traffic Rules

Encroachment on National and State Highways is a serious problem, which not only causes traffic hazards but also affects the quality of the roads. Improper drainage results in failure of the pavement. In urban areas, the laying of water pipes, electricity cables, sewer pipes, telephone cables, etc. result in frequent digging, thereby disturbing the homogeneity of the pavement and its efficient drainage.

Tendering System

The PWD has been following a system of tendering laid down in the PWD manual, which is very old. However, there has been a sea change in the medium of publicity, which can bring greater transparency into the process and healthier competition. Therefore, it is necessary to review and refine the present system relating tenders and contracts.

Suggested New Procedure

A. Single Agency

Once the administrative approval for a work is accorded, the work should be assigned as a single job (including the components of electrification, roadside development, approach road landscaping, way side motel, etc.) to an agency through proper competition. The current piecemeal approach results in a bridge or road facility being completed, but the necessary toll station or some other component remains incomplete, which often delays the opening of the facility to traffic.

B. Specifications as part of the Document

The present practice is to describe the items of the work in the Schedule of Quantities and to just attach a specification number. The bidder finds it difficult to understand what exactly is covered under the item and this often leads to speculative bidding. It is advisable to have a separate volume of tender documents so that the bidders can work out rates after understanding the scope of the work.

C. Involvement of the Agencies in the Finalisation of the Bid Document

Sometimes the PWD may not include some items in the bid document by oversight, resulting in extra items at a later stage, which may lead to disputes. It would be a good idea to involve prospective bidders in the formulation of the bid documents right from the beginning. The tender items will thus cover a number of ancillary works which are likely to be lost sight of by an inexperienced junior engineer, who normally prepares such documents.

D. Issue of Material by the Department

The system of issuing material by the PWD suffers from some drawbacks. Agencies generally raise claims against the PWD for non-procurement on time. This wastes a lot of time and effort on the part of both the department and the agency. A lot of working capital of the Department is locked up in the procurement of material and there is a lot of duplication in the process of tendering for procurement. A lot of staff has to be maintained for storing material resulting in extra cost.

E. Publicity

The tender notices are presently published in local and regional papers, and there are complaints about inadequate or restricted publicity. To overcome this problem and bring in transparency, tender notices could be publicised on the PWD website. In addition, a shorter version of the notice with reference to the website could be advertised in the newspapers on an appointed day. The fixed part of terms and conditions of the contract can be made available on the website while only the variable part – the bill of quantities and information relating to work – may be made available on payment of fee.

F. Bid Opening

The bids received should be opened on a fixed day of the week in any PWD division/circle. This would avoid postponement of opening of technical/financial offers. Also, long custody of the sealed envelopes/tender boxes would not be required.

G. Comparative Statement

The comparative statement must be made within 24 hours of the financial bid opening, and if, possible, displayed on the website.

H. Processing Time

Rules for maximum time to be taken at any level for processing the tenders should be laid down and strictly followed. No negotiation should be allowed at any level. The lowest offer may be rejected only if found unworkable.

I. Validity Extension

As far as possible, no extension of the validity period of the tender should be necessary for processing time. The working season should not be lost by undue delay in finalisation of the tender.

J. Quality of Work and Quality Assurance Plan

The agency should be allowed to procure only material of certified quality. Preparation of a quality assurance plan before starting work should be insisted upon and execution of various items of work as per the approved QA plan needs to be ensured by supervisory staff employed by both the PWD and the agency. The defect liability clause in the agreement should be properly implemented.

K. General Reforms

Photographs and video recording of the place of work before commencement and after completion of the project should form an essential part of the documents submitted by the agency with the first/final bill as the case may be. Complaints about the work and its progress from any quarter should be investigated and investigations completed before the work is over. A flying squad for investigating such complaints could be considered. Maintenance of general quality is the responsibility of the agency.

Road construction can be either labour intensive or mechanised or a combination of both, depending on the importance of the road and the availability of finances. With rapid industrialisation and huge investments in the roads sector, construction of roads is increasingly becoming mechanised. The state PWD needs to gear itself to faster decision making and taking initiatives to remove bottlenecks.

Present System of Responsibility for State Roads

The PWD is responsible for planning, surveying, designing, construction and maintenance of all state roads, bridges and buildings. It was also responsible for the National Highways network in the state, till the National Highways Authority of India (NHAI) was set up. Seventy-two per cent of PWD's activities are estimated to be in the roads sector and only 28 per cent in the buildings sector. With the proposed increase in rural connectivity, the activities of the PWD will increase and will require organisational restructuring.

Organisational Structure of PWD

The PWD is under the charge of a Cabinet Minister and is headed by a Secretary. The Head Office has three chief engineers (CE) handling buildings, roads and highways. The CE (Roads) is responsible for rural roads under the PMGSY, all Plan works of state roads, drought relief and RIDF works. The CE (National Highways) is responsible for all National Highways works executed by the PWD on behalf of MoRTH, except those which are under the jurisdiction of the NHAI. The CE (NH) liaisons with the MoRTH and represents the state government on matters related to the National Highways.

Financial Resources

Like most government organisations, the PWD does not have its own sources of revenue, but depends on budget allocations from the state and Central governments and on loans or grants from international funding institutions. Whatever revenue it earns, in the form of agency fees for work executed for other departments and fees for renting equipment to contractors, are passed on to the state exchequer.

The PWD has been involving the private sector in the development of roads sector, as consultants and contractors and developers under BOT schemes. However, the government has not been able to attract enough private investment, because of problems like lack of access controlled roads and recovery of tolls. In Rajasthan 10 schemes to the tune of Rs 91.89 crore have been completed by the private sector and opened to traffic so far. The Rajasthan State Road Development and Construction Corporation (RSRDCC) has also taken up four schemes costing Rs. 19 crore. Besides this, three more schemes of the value of Rs 25.21 crore are in progress. Ten more such schemes costing Rs 450 crore are proposed to be taken up.

The RSRDCC has constructed toll-financed bridges and bypasses through institutional financing from organisations like NABARD, with government pitching in with seed money of 30 per cent of the construction cost in the form of loan or grants.

State Road Policy

The Rajasthan Road Policy of 1994 adopted the national target of connecting all villages with population of more than 1,000 (1991 base), by BT roads, upgrading connections to *panchayat* headquarters to BT stage, widening and upgrading major State Highways and major district roads, construction of major missing links, construction of bypasses and construction of missing bridges and drainage crossings and overpasses. The PWD identified the status of road connections to villages with a 1000-plus population, the total road length required to connect still unconnected villages, construction or upgrading 4,035 bridges and major drainage works and the cost involved.

A planning exercise through a Strategic Options Study (SOS) for development of roads was completed in 1995 with World Bank assistance. This study covered 21,415 km of selected National Highways, State Highways and major district roads. This study prioritised road sections for improvement on the basis of current traffic volume/capacity ratio, percentage of commercial traffic, missing links and roads in poor condition but having high percentage of commercial traffic. The study also conducted origin-destination surveys but did not make any traffic projections or undertake any economic analysis of the proposed priorities. Even after these studies the PWD has not been able to evolve a long-term programme of road development in the state due to lack of clear directions from the state government about upgrading existing roads, construction of new roads and maintenance of existing roads. The entire system is working on an *ad hoc* basis.

Quality Control

The PWD has a Manual of Orders, with specific norms for various officers responsible for the quality and measurements of the works. Unfortunately, these provisions are not being strictly followed and, therefore, it is not possible to pin the responsibility for defective work. The practice of keeping an inspection book at the work site is also ignored. There are clear instructions in the Manual that copies of notes recorded should be submitted to the next higher officer for information, and to the subordinate officer for compliance. The responsibility of checking the quality and measurements of works lies with the Executive Engineer and Assistant Engineer but this does not debar the Superintending Engineer from checking any work as a test check. According to contractual obligations, the contractor is responsible for execution of works in line with specifications. He is supposed to maintain qualified technical staff and set up a laboratory to carry out required tests as suggested in the specifications.

Mere conformity to specifications is also not a guarantee of quality. It is necessary to move to a Quality Assurance (QA) phase, with emphasis on planned and systematic working. Statistical process control techniques must be employed which will ensure that the specified requirements are adhered to rather than lapses being detected after work is completed. The main emphasis should be on prevention of defects rather than their detection through subsequent inspections or tests. Provisions in codes of practice and the contract documents have to be followed. They specify design criteria, practical rules, technical specifications, testing and acceptance criteria and workmanship.

All these strategies depend on human skill or their successful and reliable application, which eventually determines the quality of work. The basic desire to produce quality work must be internalised by everyone connected with PWD projects. In the process of quality systems, training of young engineers, workmen and everyone connected with the execution of works is necessary.

It is necessary that materials be tested before their use in the construction work, and rejected if found unsuitable. For this purpose, quality control wings were created in PWD in 1977. Over the years, it has been found that the system of quality control staff touring sites for checking, taking samples and reporting to higher officers has largely resulted in post-execution probes, which, in turn, diverts the attention of field staff. However, it is necessary to have central control to keep the field staff on their guard. There is need to plan an in-built quality control mechanism in the field staff itself. The role of quality control staff should be complimentary and not that of policing. All procedures should be fully documented to demonstrate conformance to the required quality norms and the effective operation of the quality system.

Suggestions for PWD

The PWD must reorganise itself into a result-oriented organisation, with a very efficient design section where the latest technical inputs are available. There should be regular interaction between the design engineers and the people responsible for construction for a regular feedback. A separate wing in the head office has to be created for this. Some of the field sectors may have to be abolished to accommodate the expenditure on this account.

A pilot plan may be permitted for upgrading of State Highways from single lane and intermediate lane to double lane carriageway as per the priority stretches. Zonal offices headed by additional chief engineers may be abolished. Their presence has diluted the position and utility of the supervising engineers. They do not serve any useful function. In fact, the supervision sector has become too top heavy and is proving to be absolutely unproductive. The additional chief engineers can be accommodated in the head office of the chief engineers and be assigned separate duties like designing, specification drafting etc. The cadre may ultimately get abolished in due course of time. By doing so, many assisting levels like supervising engineers, executive engineers, assistant engineers and junior engineers will also get reduced. Similarly the ministerial staff will also reduce. This will result in reduction of non-productive expenditure.

Rail Network in Rajasthan

Rajasthan has the largest rail network after Uttar Pradesh, but the majority of the length of this railway system belonged to rulers of the former states of Jaipur, Jodhpur, Bikaner and Mewar. Most of areas of present day Rajasthan remain without this facility. The district headquarters of Jhalawar, Banswara, Karauli, Sirohi, Rajsamand and Tonk remain unconnected with any railway line even today. The districts of Kota, Sawai Madhopur, Alwar, Bharatpur, Sikar, Chittorgarh, Bhilwara, Pali, Nagaur, Bundi and others have rail connectivity because they happen to be on the main lines from Delhi to Mumbai and Ahmedabad.

Public Transport System

Being a backward state with low rail and road connectivity, the transport system in Rajasthan has also been underdeveloped. Since ancient times, people used camel carts and bullock carts for transportation of passengers and goods, but over the past few decades, trucks, passenger buses, jongas/jeeps and taxis have become popular means of transportation.

Over the past few decades, the state has witnessed a huge increase in the number of private cars, jeeps, contract and taxi carriages, state carriages, private and public carriers to the extent of 107 per cent (Table 6.1).

TABLE 6.1

Number of Registered Motor Vehicles in Rajasthan

Vehicle Type	*1990-91*	*1998-99*	*Increase (%)*
Private cars/jeeps	91,601	209,633	129
Contract & Taxi carriage	26,432	53,489	102
State carriages	23,288	43,892	88
Private and public carriers	71,280	133,125	87
Total	**212,601**	**440,139**	**107**

Note: These vehicles exclude motorcycles, scooters and three wheelers.

Source: Basic Statistics-Rajasthan.

Rajasthan State Road Transport Corporation

The Rajasthan State Road Transport Corporation (RSRTC) was set up in 1964 with a fleet of 421 buses with the objective of providing efficient, adequate, economical, safe and well-coordinated passenger transport service. The fleet has increased to 4754. The Corporation operates 2624 routes covering 4.47 lakh km and transports 9.70 lakh passengers daily. It not only connects all 32 districts of Rajasthan but also provides links with other states. Of the fleet of 4702 buses, 4489 are RSRTC's own buses and 213 are private buses hired on contract (on km. basis). RSRTC's punctuality is 98.5 per cent, while the break down rate was 0.14 in 2002-03 and accident rate 0.13.

RSRTC provides a mix of ordinary and suburban services to rural and short distance passengers as well as air-conditioned, deluxe and express services for long distance passengers. In Jaipur city, about 200 city buses cater to commuters. The Corporation manages its operations from 48 depots spread across the state. It also provides tour services to places of tourist interest and religious centres, like Jaisalmer, Nathdwara, Sawai Madhopur, Pali, Sirohi etc. RSRTC has decided to set up sub-depots at Jaisalmer and Sawai Madhopur to cater to the tourist rush.

Till 1996-97, RSRTC was in profit but it started running into losses since 1997-98 because of concessional fares for various categories of passengers as well as clandestine operation of unauthorised private vehicles. However, the RSRTC has reduced the loss burden by Rs. 20.02 crore in 2002-03.

Absence of Transport Policy

The provision of low cost, comfortable and speedy transport facilities is important for the social and economic development of a region. However, this warrants a rational approach which must have the following components: minimum hazards; comfortable journey; minimum loss to the operator; low cost; and punctuality.

Rajasthan has no transport policy to ensure good service to the people and regulate private transport operators. In the absence of such policy, it is difficult to develop any vision for this sector.

Neglect of Some Important Routes

A study has to be conducted to ascertain the demand for transport services, commuters' preferences and problems. Some important tourist centres located in Pali, Bundi, Kota, Sirohi, Jalore, Jaisalmer and Jhalawar districts have been so far neglected by bus operators, including the RSRTC. Likewise, frequency of buses between the divisional/district headquarters and important industrial and trade centres also has to be dovetailed with the increasing demand for such services.

Increase in Unauthorised Private Transporters

There are no accurate figures of unauthorised vehicles plying on nationalised routes, but in 2000-01 there were an estimated 3856 video coaches, 818 mini buses, 5370 jeeps and jongas and 130 other vehicles. This totals 10,174 against 4754 vehicles of RSRTC. The financial loss incurred by RSRTC due to the illegal operation of these vehicles on nationalised routes will be almost equal to the total annual turnover. It has thus become imperative to analyse the increasing role of unauthorised transporters and the impact on the state's tax revenue, RSRTC's income and passenger services.

The main reason for the popularity of these private vehicles is the lower fares they charge. They can afford to do this because their expenditure on staff is very low, they do not have to spend on the bus-stand, public facilities or provide concessional fares. However, this advantage is offset by the fact that they are more prone to accidents.

Regular campaigns and vigilance by the Transport Department and the police is required to control the unauthorised private vehicles. People, especially those living in rural areas, must be educated about the hazards involved in travelling by unauthorised vehicles.

Since the RSRTC is a public sector undertaking, it functions with a service orientation and not a profit orientation. Besides it has an extremely high establishment cost, with the total cost incurred on salaries, allowances and provident fund increasing from Rs.15.5 lakh in 1964-65 to Rs. 240 crore in 1999-2000. Besides, recurring costs on fuel, lubricants and auto spare parts have also shown enormous increase.

From time to time, the RSRTC raises its fares, with the permission of the state government. The latest revision was done in December 1997. However, this resulted in a drastic fall in occupancy, with the load factor declining from 74 per cent in 1996-97 to 62.3 per cent in 2000-01. A one per cent fall in load factor reduces the revenue of RSRTC by Rs. 2.50 lakh per day. This indicates that the cumulative losses of the Corporation are likely to be still more alarming if fares are raised further.

Thus, partly due to negligence of the Transport Department and the police, and partly on account of lack of professional approach of the RSRTC itself, the Corporation is now in a dismal financial position and it would not be wrong to state that it has become a sick unit, and may meet the same fate as similar corporations in Delhi, Punjab, Haryana, Uttar Pradesh and Karnataka. Its future depends on the policies of the state government which has to either provide full support to the Corporation and permit it to be run properly, or to let its ailment become more serious.

In the light of all this, the entire road transport sector has to be reviewed. The functioning of the RSRTC should be analysed carefully and its relevance examined. Such review would also cover the role of private sector to supplement/replace the transport services presently provided by the RSRTC.

A committee headed by a member of Rajasthan State Planning Board had reviewed the working of all state-owned corporations in 2001. The committee observed that a lot needs to be done to make the RSRTC more accountable while fulfilling its social responsibilities. The committee suggested that a suitable agency be identified to study the entire transport sector. It also suggested dividing the nationalised routes in Rajasthan into three or four zones and ensure that high density routes cross-subsidise the low density routes. Unbundling the RSRTC was another suggestion given.

The government should consider privatisation of the transport sector through organised corporate and cooperative bodies, which will help to curb unauthorised and hazardous modes of transport and improve the availability as well as quality of transport facilities in the State.

APPENDIX A–6.1

Rajasthan at a Glance

S.No.	Item	Year	Unit	Particulars
1	Area	2001	Sq Km	342239
2	Population	2001	Number	56473122
	(a) Urban	2001	Number	13205444
	(b) Rural	2001	Number	43267678
	Sex Ratio (Female to male)	2001	No. per '000 male	922
	Density	2001	Per Sq Km	165
3	Cities and Town	2001	Number	222
4	Villages	2001	Number	41353
5	**Roads (PWD)**	**2000-01**	**Km**	**89701**
	Other Dept. Roads	2000-01	Km	64403
	Length of Roads per 100 sq km (PWD)	**2000-01**	**Km**	**26.21**
	Length of Roads (Total)	2000-01	Km	151865
	Length of Roads per 100 sq km (Total)	2000-01	km	**45.02**
	National average (Roads per 100 sq km)		km	**66.8**
6	Village Panchayats	2001	Number	9184
7	Index Numbers			
	(i) Ajmer (Base 1982)	2000	Index	433
	(ii) Jaipur (Base 1982)	2000	Index	403
	(iii) Bhilwara (Base 1982)	2000	Index	439
8	Districts	2001	Number	32
9	Sub-Divisions	2001	Number	104
10	Tehsils	2001	Number	241
11	Panchayat Samitis	2001	Number	237
12	Number of Villages	2001	Number	41353

APPENDIX A–6.2

Village Connectivity in Rajasthan as on 31 March 2001

District	Total Village	Connected by				Unconnected	Unconnected BT	Sanctioned BT	Not Sanctioned BT
		BT	MR	GR	Total				
Ajmer	985	568	104	154	826	159	417	23	394
Alwar	1946	1020	43	155	1218	728	926	9	917
Banswara	1431	596	52	146	794	637	835	30	805
Baran	1070	329	23	97	449	621	741	26	715
Barmer	1625	570	29	385	984	641	1055	18	1037
Bharatpur	1345	640	27	75	742	603	705	33	672
Bhilwara	1565	527	66	325	918	647	1038	26	1012
Bikaner	580	364	7	54	425	155	216	7	209
Bundi	826	299	19	55	373	453	527	14	513
Chittorgarh	2172	669	83	234	986	1186	1503	25	1478
Churu	926	518	33	19	570	356	408	14	394
Dausa	1009	348	20	72	440	569	661	12	649
Dholpur	551	254	20	51	325	226	297	15	282
Dungarpur	846	419	63	69	551	295	427	24	403
Ganganagar	2908	1364	4	17	1385	1523	1544	10	1534
Hanumangarh	1530	785	4	1	790	740	745	8	737
Jaipur	2131	1105	64	117	1286	845	1026	19	1007
Jaisalmer	518	208	3	80	291	227	310	13	297
Jalore	665	405	50	141	596	69	260	20	240

Contd...

...Contd...

District	Total Village	Connected by				Unconnected	Unconnected BT	Sanctioned BT	Not Sanctioned BT
		BT	MR	GR	Total				
Jhalawar	1448	298	32	70	400	1048	1150	17	1133
Jhunjhunu	824	479	37	91	607	217	345	16	329
Jodhpur	860	648	29	129	806	54	212	28	184
Karauli	741	335	56	19	410	331	406	34	372
Kota	811	331	22	40	393	418	480	13	467
Nagaur	1374	730	92	186	1008	366	644	47	597
Pali	904	571	60	155	786	118	333	18	315
Rajsamand	873	383	55	129	567	306	490	15	475
Sawai Madhopur	723	245	22	32	299	424	478	35	443
Sikar	931	467	100	90	657	274	464	31	433
Sirohi	446	237	19	71	327	119	209	7	202
Tonk	1019	304	21	66	391	628	715	11	704
Udaipur	2306	750	87	256	1093	1213	1556	48	1508
Total	**37889**	**16766**	**1346**	**3581**	**21693**	**16196**	**21123**	**666**	**20457**

APPENDIX A-6.3

Districtwise Road Length (as on 31 March 2001)

(Length in km)

District	Area sq km	BT	MR	GR	FW	Total	NH	SH	MDR	ODR	Village Roads	VR/100 Sq km
Ajmer	8481	2732	81	31		2844	242	362	256	592	1392	16.41
Alwar	8380	3379	105	156		3640	35	483	261	404	2487	29.68
Banswara	5037	1476	110	121		1707		258	80	25	1344	26.68
Baran	6955	1118	52	315	11	1496	232	74	153	153	884	12.71
Barmer	28387	4187	238	793		5218	189	546	233	619	3631	12.79
Bharatpur	5066	1940	53	6		1999	71	237	227	330	1134	22.38
Bhilwara	10455	2680	357	838	13	3888	129	249	459	149	2902	27.76
Bikaner	27244	3233	87	316	10	3646	325	228	184	302	2607	9.57
Bundi	5550	1228	95	187		1510	107	321		131	851	15.33
Chittorgarh	10856	2501	178	162		2841	202	331	135	266	1907	17.57
Churu	16830	2752	203	145		3100	239	528	269	234	1830	10.87
Dausa	2950	1236	83	273		1592	88	143	82	341	938	31.80
Dholpur	3034	1006	83	49		1138	28	152	60	72	826	27.22
Dungarpur	3770	1299	156	63		1518	34	106	159	157	1062	28.17
Ganganagar	20634	3225	11	92		3328	124	288		430	2486	12.05
Hanumangarh		2460	23	44		2527		202	106	462	1757	
Jaipur	11580	3856	164	44	42	4106	401	427	151	169	2958	25.54
Jaisalmer	38401	3083	42	731		3856	196	23	129	684	2824	7.35
Jalore	10640	2194	180	268	18	2660	41	314	175	382	1748	16.43
Jhalawar	6219	1128	116	144		1388	126	197	157	286	622	10.00
Jhunjhunu	5928	2069	267	140		2476		278	142	514	1542	26.01
Jodhpur	22850	4708	226	1004		5938	218	525	333	1967	2895	12.67
Karauli		1231	164	105	2	1502	4	172	198	234	894	
Kota	5481	1419	78	139	2	1638	120	149	197	302	870	15.87
Nagaur	17718	3774	533	731		5038	330	723	177	442	3366	19.00
Pali	12387	3177	440	1028		4645	218	171	360	1330	2566	20.72
Rajsamand	4768	1438	214	231		1883	155	55	148	360	1165	24.43
Sawai Madhopur	10065	976	86	149		1211		228	91	159	733	7.28
Sikar	7732	2033	168	308		2509	191	273	187	87	1771	22.90
Sirohi	5136	1274	78	97		1449	143	176	25	265	840	16.36
Tonk	7194	1452	37	185	8	1682	109	203	202	144	1024	14.23
Udaipur	12511	3179	197	106	7	3489	250	292	403	808	1736	13.88
Rajasthan	**342239**	**73443**	**4905**	**9001**	**113**	**87462**	**4547**	**8714**	**5739**	**12800**	**55592**	

Note: BT = Bitumen treated; MR = Metallic roads; GR = Gravel roads; FW = Fair weather roads

Source: Basic Statistics, Rajasthan, 2001.

APPENDIX A–6.4

ROAD DEVELOPMENT PLANS

Targets and Achievements of Nagpur Plan were almost Achieved by 1961

Nagpur Plan Targets (km)	*Achievements By 1961 (km)*
26715	22636
6680	
86825	62052
90145	113483
133580	111961
198755	388841
10149	
532700	709122

Targets and Achievements of 1961-81 Plan

Category	*Bombay Plan Targets (km)*	*Achievements By 1981 (km)*
National Highways	51500	31737
State Highways	112650	95491
Major District Roads	241400	153000
Rural Roads		912684
(a) Other District roads	289680	
(b) Village Roads	362100	
Total	**1057330**	**1192912**

Targets and Achievements of 1981-2001 Plan

Category	*1981-2001 Plan Targets (km)*	*Achievements By 1981 (km) Up to 3/97*	*Shortfall (km)*
National Highways	66000	34058	31942
Expressways	2000		2000
State Highways	144400	128000	16000
Others	2510000	1728000	8E+06
Total	**2722000**	**1890058**	**831942**

APPENDIX A–6.5

Expenditure on Roads in Various Plans

(Rs. in crore)

No.	*Year*	*State Plan Expenditure*	*Road Expenditure*	*% of Plan Expenditure*	*Plan*
1.	1951-56	54.14	4.98	9.20	First
2.	1956-61	102.74	10.07	9.80	Second
3.	1961-66	202.70	9.62	4.75	Third
4.	1966-69	136.75	4.29	3.14	Three One year Planns
5.	1969-74	303.49	9.97	3.29	Fourth
6.	1974-79	867.94	38.20	4.40	Fifth
7.	1979-80	295.38	12.99	4.40	Annual plan
8.	1980-85	1747.53	65.85	3.77	Sixth
9.	1985-90	3106.18	89.93	2.90	Seventh
10.	1990-91	956.00	35.32	3.69	Annual plan
11.	1991-92	1166.00	51.01	4.37	Annual plan
12.	1992-97	11500.00	701.69	6.10	Eighth
Ninth Five Year Plan 1997-2002					
13.	1997-98	3987.35	206.97	5.19	Annual plan
14.	1998-99	3832.83	194.39	5.07	Annual plan
15.	1999-00	3600.95	104.46	2.90	Annual plan
16.	2000-01	4412.00	268.60	6.09	Annual plan
17.	2001-02 (B.E)	4441.09	166.86	3.76	Annual plan

Contd...

...Contd...

APPENDIX A–6.6

Progress of Roads in Rajasthan from 1949 to 2001

Year	*BT*	*WBM*	*Gravel*	*FWR*	*Total*
1949	766	4378	2037	6372	13553
1951	868	4560	3286	8625	17339
1956	3152	5636	4508	9222	22518
1961	7474	5681	4830	8716	26701
1966	11558	5743	6486	6841	30628
1971	14308	5647	6462	5335	31752
1976	20938	4933	8244	3693	37808
1981	27700	3657	7539	2298	41194
1985	33479	4138	10269	925	48811
1986	34777	4210	10560	889	50436
1987	36369	4159	10326	836	51690
1988	38459	4584	9948	532	53523
1989	40541	4759	10075	426	55801
1990	42059	4415	10078	404	56956
1991	43932	4034	10026	358	58350
1992	45797	3834	9958	324	59913
1993	47451	3587	10219	263	61520
1994	49138	3395	10256	289	63078
1995	51507	3398	10513	269	65687
1996	53652	4744	11620	213	70229
1997	58265	5388	11139	155	74947
1998	65398	5766	10288	106	81558
1999	69911	5165	9859	73	85008
2000	72281	4886	9193	113	86473
2001	73443	4905	9001	113	87462

APPENDIX A–6.7

Length of Roads in Rajasthan as per Nagpur Classification from 1956 to 2001

(Length in Km)

Year	NH	SH	MDR	ODR	VR	Total
1956	648	3824	3936	8224	5886	22518
1961	998	3846	4697	10100	7060	26701
1966	1256	4409	4851	11157	8955	30628
1969	1256	8430	4355	8277	9058	31376
1971	1256	8643	4373	8398	9082	31752
1974	2089	8739	4697	8775	9532	33832
1976	2089	7265	4258	15023	9173	37808
1979	2110	7499	3716	14969	11453	39747
1980	2110	7666	3746	14980	11897	40399
1981	2533	7274	3754	14840	12793	41194
1985	2521	7457	3616	14819	20398	48811
1989	2840	7235	3596	14992	27138	55801
1990	2840	7235	3596	14996	28289	56956
1991	2840	7247	3604	14987	29672	58350
1992	2840	7136	3936	15054	31241	60207
1993	2846	7151	3638	15068	32818	61521
1994	2846	8720	3212	14394	33906	63078
1995	2846	9810	5549	12143	35339	65687
1996	2846	10006	5707	12615	39044	70218
1997	2846	10047	5820	12684	43550	74947
1998	2964	9990	5789	12766	50049	81558
1999	2964	9966	5947	12766	53365	85008
2000	4453	8898	5741	12971	54410	86473
2001	4547	8714	5739	12800	55662	87462

APPENDIX A–6.8

Registration of Motor Vehicles in Rajasthan

(in No's)

Type of Vehicle	1996-97	1997-98	1998-99	2000-01
Motorised Rickshaws		90	90	
Auto/Motorised Cycle & Scooters	1325605	1472889	1643867	2010821
Tempo				
(i) Goods Vehicles	2422	2882	4136	6930
(ii) Passenger Vehicles	5231	5527	6184	7480
Auto Rickshaws	29207	31971	36151	43136
Car/Station Wagons	91965	101768	112882	143308
Jeep	74698	85410	96751	112012
Tractors	248375	276100	306608	355822
Trailers	46233	48155	50292	53584
Taxis	14476	15593	17248	20527
Buses/Mini Buses	36443	40239	43892	49244
Trucks	107899	116213	122805	137118
Others	2978	2962	2999	3388
Total	**1985532**	**2199799**	**2443905**	**2943370**

Note: Growth of Registered vehicles in the year 2000-01 over 1996-97 is 48.24 per cent.

Indicator: The availability of vehicles per thousand person increased from 45 in 1996-97 to 67 in 2000-01 (48.24 per cent increase) while availability of road increased 1.70 km to 1.96 km per thousand person (15.29 per cent).

APPENDIX A–6.9

Growth of Revenue and Expenditure on Roads in India

Year	Road Revenue Million Rupees	Expenditure %age of Road Revenue	Expenditure on Roads In Million Rupees
1950-51	610		—
1960-61	1669	66	1098
1970-71	16832	37	2567
1980-81	23876	51	12093
1983-84	40420	42	17000
1984-85	44730	43	19100
1985-86	52790	40	21230
1986-87	63150	40	25100
1987-88	82100	32	26380
1990-91	121844	35	38990

Allocation as Percentage of Total Plan Outlay

Year	Five Year Plan	Transport Sector	Road Sector
1951-56	1st Plan	24.5	6.5
1956-61	2nd Plan	27.1	5.5
1961-66	3rd Plan	18.6	4.0
1969-74	4th Plan	10.2	5.5
1974-78	5th Plan	13.8	3.5
1980-85	6th Plan	12.4	3.5
1985-90	7th Plan	12.6	2.9
1992-97	8th Plan	13.1	3.0

APPENDIX A–6.10

National Highways Development Project

Golden Quadrilateral
North-South Corridor
East-West Corridor
National Highway No.

Corridor	Passing Through National Highways (Nos.)	Length (in km)
Golden Quadrilateral (GQ)		
Delhi - Calcutta	2	1,469
Calcutta - Chennai	5,6,60	1,751
Chennai - Mumbai	4,7,46	1,278
Mumbai - Delhi	8,79,76	1,454
GQ Total		5,952
North South Corridor (NS)		
Srinagar - Kanyakumari and Salem - Cochin spur	1A,1,2,3,75,26,7,47	4,000
East West Corridor (EW)		
Silchar - Porbandar	54,36,37,31,57,28,25, 76,14,15,8A,8B	3,300
NS & EW Corridors Total		**7,300**
	NHDP TOTAL	**13,252**

NHDP - Implementation Status as on February, 2001
(All lengths in km)

	GQ	NS & EW	Total
Already Four Laned	629	648	1277
Under Implementation	1408	272	1680
For award of Civil works contracts (by 6/2001)	3797	403	4200

Note : Total Legth of GQ on realignment is 5,834 km but taken as 5,952 km. NS&EW Corridors have, however, been kept as 7,300 km, as before, because the alignment finalisation is in progress.

Source: National Highways Development Project (NHDP).

APPENDIX A–6.11

North-South and East-West Corridors

- Out of the total 7300 km, work on 648 km of the Corridors has already been completed and work on another stretch of 272 km is underway.
- 'No work has been taken up under the East-West corridor in Rajasthan. Highways development under Golden Quadrilateral i.e. Jaipur-Chittorgarh-Bhilwara-Udaipur has been completed'.

Corridor	From	To	Passing Through
North-South 4000 Km (with a spur to Cochin)	Kashmir	Kanyakumari	Jammu-Jalandhar-Delhi-Mathura-Agra-Gwalior-Jhansi-Nagpur-Hyderabad-Bangalore-Hosur-Salem-Kanyakumari
East-West 3465 Km	Silchar	Porbandar	Silchar-Guwahati-Siliguri-Purnea-Muzaffarpur-Lucknow-Kanpur-Jhansi-Udaipur-Palanpur-Rajkot-Porbandar

Note: Total length of NS&EW Corridors has been taken as 7,300 km, as before, because the alignment finalisation is in progress.

APPENDIX A–6.12

National Highways Proposed for Four/Six Lanes on NHDP

(All lengths in km)

State	*Golden Quadrilateral*	*Corridors*		*Corridor Total*	*NHDP Total*
		North-South	*East-West*		
Andhra Pradesh	1000	753		753	1753
Assam			758	758	758
Bihar	200		517	517	717
Delhi	25	34		34	59
Gujarat	498		654	654	1152
Haryana	175	254		254	429
Himachal Pradesh		14		14	14
Jammu & Kashmir		405		405	405
Jharkhand	192				192
Karnataka	686	125		125	811
Kerala		160		160	160
Madhya Pradesh		524	142	666	666
Maharashtra	487	232		232	719
Orissa	437				437
Punjab		296		296	296
Rajasthan	688	32	480	512	1200
Tamil Nadu	275	851		851	1126
Uttar Pradesh	752	268	548	816	1568
West Bengal	471		366	366	837
Lengths of Inter-state/ Bypasses/State Roads/ Roads/MDRs	66				66
Total	**5952**	**3948**	**3465**	**7413**	**13365**

APPENDIX A–6.13

List of National Highways Passing Through States As on 31 March 2001

Name of State	*National Highway No.*	*Total Length (Km)*	*Area*	*Length per 100 sq km*	*Length before bifurcation*
Andhra Pradesh	4,5,7,9,16,18,43,63,202,205,214 and 219	4038	275068	1.47	
Arunachal Pradesh	52,52A and 153	392	83743	0.47	
Assam	31,31B,31C,36,37,37A,38,39,44, 51,52,52A, 52B,53,54,61,62,151, 152,153 and 154	2836	78438	3.62	
Bihar	2,19,28,28A,30,30A,31,57,77,78,80,81,83, 84,85, 98,99,100,101,102,103,104,105,106 and 107	3301	173877	1.90	5131
Chandigarh	21	24	114	21.05	
Chhattisgarh	6,12A,16,43,78,200,202,216 and 217	1830			
Delhi	1,2,8,10 and 24	72	1483	4.86	
Goa	4A,17,17A and 17B	269	3814	7.05	
Gujarat	NE-1,6,8,8A,8B,8C,8D,8E,14,15 and 59	2461	196024	1.26	
Haryana	1,2,8,10,21A,22,65,71,71A,72 and 73	1361	44212	3.08	
Himachal Pradesh	1A,20,21,21A,22,70,72 and 88	1188	55673	2.13	
Jammu & Kashmir	1A,1B,1C, and 13 Ext	823	222236	0.37	
Jharkhand	2,6,23,31,32,33,75,78,80,98,99 and 100	1614			
Karnataka	4,4A,7,9,13,48,63,206,207,209,212 and 218	3570	191791	1.86	
Kerala	17,47,47A,49,208,212,213 and 220	1440	38863	3.71	
Madhya Pradesh	3,7,12,12A,25,26,27,59,69,75,76, 78,79,86,92 and 200	4608	443446	1.40	6223
Maharashtra	3,4,4B,6,7,8,9,13,16,17,50,59,204 and 211	3626	307690	1.18	
Manipur	39,53 and 150	954	22327	4.27	

Contd...

...Contd...

Name of State	*National Highway No.*	*Total Length (Km)*	*Area*	*Length per 100 sq km*	*Length before bifurcation*
Meghalaya	40,44,51 and 62	717	22429	3.20	
Mizoram	44A,54,54A,54B,150 and 154	927	21081	4.40	
Nagaland	36,39,61 and 150	369	16579	2.23	
Orissa	5,5A,6,23,42,43,60,200,201,203,215 and 217	3301	155707	2.12	
Pondicherry	45A and 66	53	495	10.71	
Punjab	1,1A,10,15,20,21,22,64,70,71 and 95	1553	50362	3.08	
Rajasthan	**3,8,11,11A,12,14,15,65,76,79,89 and 90**	**4481**	**342239**	1.31	
Sikkim	31A	62	7096	0.87	
Tamil Nadu	4,5,7,7A,45,45A,45B,46,47,49,66,67,68,205, 207,208, 209,210,219 and 220	3758	130058	2.89	
Tripura	44 and 44A	400	10486	3.81	
Uttaranchal	58,72,73,74,87 and 94	875			
Uttar Pradesh	2,2A,3,7,11,19,24,24A,25,25A,26,27,28,29, 56,56A,56B		294411	1.60	4883
	58,72,73,74,75,76,86,87,91,92,93,96 and 97	4883			
West Bengal	2,,6,31,31A,31C,32,34,35,41,55,60,80 and 81	1951	88752	2.20	
	Total	57737			

APPENDIX A–6.14

National Highways in Rajasthan As on 31 March 2001

NH No.	*Route*	*Length (km)*
8	Delhi-Jaipur-Ajmer-Udaipur-Ahmedabad (Golden Quadrilateral)	676.92
3	Agra-Dholpur-Bombay (North-South Corridor)	28.29
11	Agra - Bharatpur - Jaipur - Sikar -Bikaner	520.50
11A	Dausa - Manoharpur	62.00
11AA	Dausa - Lalsot - Kothoon	81.00
12	Jaipur - Tonk - Kota - Jhalawar - - Bhopal - Jabalpur	411.50
14	Beawar-Bar-Pali-Sirohi-Pindwara – up to Gujarat Border (East-West Corridor)	306.38
15	Pathankot-Sri Ganganagar-Bikaner-Jaisalmer-Barmer-Sanchore	874.31
65	Ambala-Hisar-Churu-Fatehpur-Nagaur-Jodhpur-Pali	496.40
76	Pindwara-Udaipur-Mangalwar-Chittorgarh-Kota-Shivpuri (East-West Corridor)	580.00
79	Ajmer-Bhilwara-Chittorgarh-Neemuch-Indore (Golden Quadrilateral)	228.00
89	Bikaner-Nokha - Nagaur-Merta - Pushkar - Ajmer	278.00
90	Baran-Aklera	94.00
	TOTAL	**4637.30**

APPENDIX A–6.15

New National Highways Proposed by State Government to MoRTH

NH No.	*Route*	*Length (km)*
1	Ratangarh-Sardarshahar-Pallu-Hanumangarh-Sadulshahar (SH7) (Linking NH11 and NH10 Punjab link)	238
2	Bhiwadi-Alwar-Rajgarh-Hindaun-Karauli-Gangapur-Sawai Madhopur-Indergarh-Kota- (Linking NH8, NH11and NH12)	457
3	Kosi-Kama-Deeg-Bharatpur-Roopwas-Sepau-Dholpur (Linking NH2 and NH3)	139
4	Tonk-Sawai Madhopur-Shivpuri (SH 30) (Linking NH@ and NH12)	112
5	Deoli-Nasirabad (SH26) (Linking NH12 and NH79)	98
6	Nimbahera-Pratapgarh-Banswara-Jhalod (SH4) (Linking NH79 with NH in Gujarat-Tribal area)	217
7	Sanchore-Abu Road-Sarupganj-Kotra-Kherwara-Dungarpur-Sagwara-Banswara-Ratlam (Tribal area)	423
8	Gaumti Chauraha-Desuri-Sadri-Sanderao-Ahore-Jalore-Barmer (SH16) (Linking NH8 with NH15)	306
9	Bar-Jodhpur (SH5) (Linking NH14 with NH65)	125
10	Phalodi-Balotra-Jalore-Sirohi (SH39) (Linking NH14 and NH15)	343
11	Phalodi-Nagaur-Kuchaman-Jaipur (SH2) (Linking NH15-NH65-Nh89-NH8-NH11-NH12)	395
12	Nawa-Dudu-Phagi-Lalsot-Gangapur-Karauli-Sarmathura-Dholpur (SH2) (Linking NH12 and NH3)	360
13	Nagaur-Deedwana-Sikar-Jhunjhunu-Pilani-Luharu (Linking NH89-NH15-Nh11)	280
14	Jhunjhunu-Singhana-Narnol-Rewari	77
15	Jodhpur-Pokran	150
16	Jodhpur - Balotra - Barmer	204
17	Kirki Chowki-Bhinder-Salumber-Aspur-Dungarpur	146
18	Kishangarh-Nasirabad	39
	TOTAL	**4109**

APPENDIX A–6.16

Status of National Highways As Regards the Carriageway Width in Rajasthan

(Km.)

NH No.	*6-Lane*	*4-Lane*	*2-Lane withpaved shoulders*	*2-Lane*	*Intermediate Lane*	*Single Lane*	*Missing Links*	*Total*
3		2.00		26.29				28.29
8		155.00		521.92				676.92
11		10.20	16.00	494.30				520.50
11A				18.60			43.40	62.00
12		25.03	7.70	313.45	28.145	37.18		411.50
14				292.38	14.000			306.38
15		8.20		297.28	567.600	1.57		874.65
65		1.70	2.00		71.900	42.40		118.00
65 Ext		10.00	1.00	109.00	138.900	97.00	19.00	374.90
76		24.00		108.00	230.200	216.40		578.60
79		4.00	6.00	211.60				221.60
89				27.50	155.000	93.50		276.00
90								
Total		**240.13**	**32.70**	**2420.32**	**1205.745**	**488.05**	**62.40**	**4449.34**

APPENDIX A-6.17

Daywise Traffic by Survey Location

Section	*Survey Location*	*Daily Traffic Volume in PCUs/Day* *Day-1 Mon*	*Day-2 Tue*	*Day-3 Wed*	*Day-4 Thu*	*Day-5 Fri*	*Day-6 Sat*	*Day-7 Sun*	*ADT Vehicle*	*April, 2001 PCUs*	*Nov., 2000 PCUs*
Kotputli-Chandwaji	Km 206	29238	31528	31319	32363	30796	30446	31205	13576	30985	33310
Chandwaji-Amer	Km 246	17593	17240	18696	17938	18803	17965	18171	9493	18059	30461
Jaipur-Bagru	Km 276	42466	42250	47506	47058	46545	47611	47244	23274	46037	52025
Bagru-Dudu	Km 325	26203	30407	31561	32136	30994	32014	33458	11420	31258	35983
Dudu-Kishangarh	Km 357	30468	22046	32020	32776	34167	33017	37368	12108	32694	43849

APPENDIX A-6.18

Traffic Composition in Percentage by Mode by Survey Point

Mode	*Km 206*	*Km 246*	*Km 276*	*Km 325*	*Km 357*
SC/MC/Moped	7.31	16.17	22.40	2.27	3.81
Auto Rickshaw	0.02	0.20	0.60	0.01	0.07
Tempo/Vikram	0.05	0.37	0.55	0.04	0.05
Car/Jeep/(OT)	10.96	11.77	8.65	5.25	5.82
Car/Jeep/(NT)	15.02	22.84	11.86	12.36	11.86
Stad. Roadways	3.86	7.62	4.09	5.38	6.24
Mini Bus	0.38	0.99	3.82	0.41	0.53
Other Bus	0.88	1.24	0.44	0.10	0.03
Other Passenger	0.20	0.10	0.15	0.08	0.09
LCA/Tempo	7.13	4.46	3.70	4.48	4.61
2-Axle Trucks	35.28	25.78	24.82	44.56	41.34
3-Axle Trucks	5.91	2.64	4.64	9.56	9.40
Multi Axle Trucks	4.92	0.85	3.92	7.85	7.89
Oil/Gas Tankers	3.04	1.67	3.50	6.51	6.82
Tractors	1.97	0.94	1.79	0.51	0.56
Other Goods	0.65	0.19	0.10	0.03	0.69
Cycle	2.06	0.97	4.31	0.13	0.16
Cycle Rickshaw	0.14	0.11	0.40	0.01	0.01
Animal Drawn	0.22	0.06	0.22	0.01	
Other Slow	0.03	1.02	0.03		

APPENDIX A–6.19

Traffic Census and Carriage Widths of State Highways

Lengths in km

Name of SH	*SH No*	*Section*	*Traffic in PCU*	*Single Lane*	*Intermediate Lane*	*Double Lane*	*Four Lane*
Jhalawar-Indore	1	Jhalawar-Indore		30			
Rajakhera-Sarmathura-Karauli-	2	Rajakhera-Dholpur					
Gangapur-Lalsot-Phagi-Dudu-		Dholpur-Gangapur	10565				
Nagaur-Phalodi		Gangapur-Dudu	3966				
		Dudu-Nagaur	3447				
		Nagaur-Phalodi	9680	326	366.2	14	
Jaipur-Jobner-Nawan-	2A	Jaipur-Jobner	5446				
Kuchaman-Khatu		Jobner-Nawan	6236				
		Nawan-Kuchaman	2269	65	70		11.13
Ganganagar-Padampur-Raisingnagar	3	Ganganagar-Padampur	3408				
Anupgarh-Chhatargarh-Bikaner		Padampur-Bikaner	6060	54	383.2	120.5	6
Ajmer-Nasirabad-Bhilwara-	4	Ajmer-Nasirabad	12899				
Chittorgarh-Pratapgarh-Banswara		Nasirabad-Bhilwara	22717				
		Bhilwara-Chittorgarh	30641				
		Chittorgarh-Banswara	2989		198.8	237.2	3.3
Bar-Bilara-Jodhpur-Dechu-Pokaran	5	Bar-Bilara	7000				
		Bilara-Jodhpur	6515				
		Jodhpur-Pokaran	9649		2.5	293.7	
Dungargarh-Sardarshahar-	6	Dungargarh-Sardarshahar-	3785				
Taranagar-Rajgarh-Hisar		Sardarshahar-Rajgarh	5425	114	67		
Sardarshahar-Sattasar via Lunkaransar	6A	Sardarshahar-Sattasar	1580				
Sarwar-Kishangarh-Deedwana-Sujangarh-	7	Sarwar-Deedwana	3215				
Talchhapar-Ratangarh-Sardarshahar-		Deedwana-Talchhapar	7064				
Hanumangarh-Sadulshahar-Abohar		Talchhapar-Ratangarh	9043				
		Ratangarh-Hanumangarh	6770	47	379	80.7	
Kishangarh-Nasirabad	7A	Kishangarh-Nasirabad	32770			37.4	
Sadulshahar-Ganganagar-Karanpur	7B	Sadulshahar-Ganganagar	7332				
		Ganganagar-Karanpur	6388	29	34	4	
Sikar-Nawalgarh-Jhunjhnu-Chirawa-	8	Sikar-Nawalgarh	11549				
Sujangarh-Luharu		Nawalgarh-Jhunjhunu	8776				
		Jhunjhunu-Luharu	5807	12	80	30	
Sikar-Panchkodi via Danta Ramgarh Renwal	8A	Sikar- Danta Ramgarh	6307	47	38		
Renwal-Chomu-Chandwaji	8B	Renwal-Chomu	3899				
		Chomu-Chandwaji	7388	11	24	2	
Udaipur-Dabok-Kapasan-Chittorgarh	9	Udaipur-Chittorgarh	20092	73	78	150.4	18
Ladpura-Bundi		Chittorgarh-Bundi					
Katunda-Bhainsrodgarh-Chechat-Ramganjmandi	9A	Katunda-Ramganjmandi	3230	138.4	10		
Kotda-Kherwara-Dungarpur-Sagwara-Banswara-	10	Kotda-Kherwara	4527				

Contd...

...*Contd*...

Lengths in km

Name of SH	*SH No*	*Section*	*Traffic in PCU*	*Single Lane*	*Intermediate Lane*	*Double Lane*	*Four Lane*
Ratlam		Dungarpur-Sagwara	7330				
		Banswara-Ratlam	2625	149	157.23	8	
Sanchore-Raniwara-Mandar-Abu Road	11	Sanchore-Raniwara	5596				
		Mandar-Abu Road	3302	75.2	25	7	
Jaipur-Sanganer-Diggi-Malpura-Kekri-Shahpura-	12	Sanganer-Malpura	14681				
Bhilwara-Kankroli		Malpura-Kekri	2697				
		Kekri-Bhilwara	3800				
		Bhilwara-Kankroli	5329	26	115	96	
Alwar-Shahpura-Kanwat-Neem Ka Thana-	13	Alwar-Shahpura	13487				
Khetri-Singhana-Chirawa-Pilani-Rajgarh		Shahpura—Neem Ka Thana	3820				
		Neem Ka Thana-Khetri	5076				
		Khetri-Pilani	3407	62	211.92	7	
Bharatpur-Deeg-Nagar-Alwar-Behror-Narnaul	14	Bharatpur-Deeg-Nagar	4337				
		Nagar-Alwar	14800				
		Alwar-Behror	4300	9	157.35	16	
Dewari-Dabok-Mangalwar-Badi Sadri-Neemuch	15	Dewari-Dabok-Mangalwar	1873				
		Mangalwar—Neemuch	6507	78	11	75	
Barmer-Sindri-Jalore-Sanderao-Sadri-	16	Barmer-Sindri-Jalore	2761				
Desuri-Amartiya		Sanderao-Sadri	4625				
		Desuri-Amartiya	9760	185	105	9	
Kota-Baran-Shivpuri (MP Border)	17			130	46	6	
Ajmer-Badi Ghati-Bherunda-Degana-Tarneu-	18	Ajmer-Degana	6398				
Deedwana		Degana-Degana	2542	115	23	24	
Indergarh-Itawa-Mangrol-Baran-Khanpur-	19	Indergarh—Baran	2669				
Jhalawar-Bhawani Mandi-Dug-Agar		Baran-Jhalawar	4200				
		Jhalawar-Bhawani Mandi	6800	298.6	20	8	
Baran-Aklera via Atru Chhipa Barod	19A	Baran-Aklera	3307	86	7		
Mangrol-Rajpura	19B	Mangrol-Rajpura		15.5			
Sikar-Sujangarh-Tal Chhapar-Nokha	20	Sikar-Tal Chhapar	2036	87	102	2	
Dantiwara-Pipar City-Merta City-Parwatsar	21	Dantiwara-Pipar City	4535				
		Pipar City- Merta City					
		Merta City-Parwatsar		117	61	3	
Mandrail-Karauli-Hindaun-Mahua-Kherli-Nagar-	22	Mandrail-Karauli	2890				
Pahari		Karauli-Hindaun	10617				
		Hindaun-Mahua		22	30.3	38.56	
Bharatpur-Roopwas-Sepau-Dholpur	23	Bharatpur-Roopwas	4692				
		Sepau-Dholpur			63.15	2	

Contd...

...Contd...

Lengths in km

Name of SH	*SH No*	*Section*	*Traffic in PCU*	*Single Lane*	*Intermediate Lane*	*Double Lane*	*Four Lane*
Bharoti-Gangapur-Hindon-Bharatpur-Mathura	24	Bharoti-Gangapur	2607				
		Hindon-Bharatpur	11840				
		Bharatpur-Mathura	5522	86	76.4	6	1
Dharuhera-Tijara-Alwar-Rajgarh-Mandawar-	25	Dharuhera-Tijara-Alwar					
Mahua		Alwar-Mandawar-Mahua		88	35	28	
Nasirabad-Kekri-Devali	26	Nasirabad-Kekri-Devali	4277	6	18	74	
Sirohi-Mandar-Deesa	27	Sirohi-Mandar	8629		47.4	24	
Jodhpur-Balotra-Sindri-Chitalwana	28	Jodhpur-Balotra	13604				
		Balotra-Sindri-Chitalwana	5120	68	138	14.5	5.5
Balotra-Gadra Road via Bayatu	28A	Balotra-Gadra Road	3532	13	82	2	
Bundi-Lakheri-SWM-Dausa-Siriska	29	Bundi-Lakheri	7030				
		SWM-Dausa-Siriska	5925	20.2	71.8	18	2
Tonk-SWM-Palighat-Shivpuri	30	Tonk-SWM	711				
		SWMt-Shivpuri	1130	21	65	25.77	
Jalore-Bhinmal-Raniwara	31			12	92	3	
Sadri-Lasadiya-Aspur-Salumber-Udaipur-	32	Sadri-Aspur-Salumber	2281				
Gogunda-Ranakpur		Salumber-Udaipur-	19986				
		Udaipur-Ranakpur	2933	35	208	3	
Jaswant Garh - Pindwara	32A			53	9		
Bhensrodgarh-Lakheri	33	Bhensrodgarh-Lakheri	3309	79	32	6	5
Tonk-Kota via Nainwa, Khatgar, K Patan	34	Khatgar, K Patan	3010	100	10		
Mahua-Laxman Garh-Ram Garh-Delhi	35	Mahua-Laxman Garh	9649				
		Ram Garh-Delhi	4652	61	16.1	10	
Fatehpur-Churu-Taranagar-Sahawa-Nauhar-	36	Fatehpur-Churu	8750				
Hanuman Garh		Churu-Taranagar	2445				
		Taranagar-Nauhar-	6762				
		Nauhar-Hanuman Garh	6277	147.6	38.7	25.3	5
Chomu-Divrata-Khandela-Udaipur Wati	37	Chomu-Udaipur Wati	5354	176.2	28	8	
Chomu-Khejrodi Mod	37A	Chomu-Khejrodi Mod	10507	14	5		
Sirohi-Kalandri-Ramseen-Jalore-Siwana-Balotra-	38	Sirohi-Jalore	3515				
Pachpadra-Shergarh-Dechu-Phalodi		alore-Siwana-Balotra-	6304				
		Balotra-Phalodi	2328	203	44	5	
Satur-Jahajpur-Shahpura-Vijaynagar-Beawar-	39	Satur-Jahajpur-Shahpura	3835				
Merta City-Nagaur		Shahpura-Vijaynagar	3132				
		Vijaynagar-Beawar	4427				
		Merta City-Nagaur	5486	154	50	5	
				3738.7	**3932.05**	**1529.03**	**56.93**

APPENDIX A–6.20

State Highways in Rajasthan as on 31.03.2001

S.No.	*SH No.*	*Route*	*Length (km)*
1	1	Jhalawar - Indore	30
2	2	Rajakhera-Sarmathura-Karauli-Gangapur-Lalsot -Chaksu-Phagi-Dudu-Khatu-Nagaur-Phalodi	692
3	2A	Jaipur-Khatu-Panchkodi-Lunwa-Nawa-Kuchaman -Budsu-Toshina	135
4	3	Ganganagar-padampur-Raisinghnagar-Anupgarh -Chhatargarh-Sattasar-Bikaner	255
5	4	Nimbahera-Chhoti Sadri-Pratapgarh-Banswara **(Ajmer-Bhilwara-Chittorgarh-Nimbahera is part of NH79)**	230
6	5	Bar-Dechhu-Pokran	307
7	6	Dungargarh-Sardarshahar-Taranagar-Rajgarh-Hisar	159
8	6A	Sardarshahar-Sattasar via Lunkaransar	138
9	7	Sarwad-Kishangarh-Deedwana-Sujangarh-Talchhaper -Ratangarh-Sardarshahar-Hanumangarh -Sadulshahar-Abohar (Punjab)	558
10	7A	Kishangarh-Nasirabad (**This section is part of NH79)**	38
11	7B	Sadulshahar-Karanpur via ShriGanganagar-Mirjanwala	87
12	8	Sikar-Nawalgarh-Jhunjhunu-Chidawa-Surajgarh-Luharu	124
13	8A	Sikar-Panchkodi via Dataramgarh-Renwal	85
14	8B	Renwal-Chandwaji via Chomu	63
15	9	Udaipur-Dabok-Mavli-Bhopalsagar-Kapasan -Chittorgarh-Ladpura-Bundi	151
16	9A	Katunda-Chhatarpur via Bhensrodgarh-Barodia -Chechat-Ramganjmandi	130
17	10	Kotda-Kherwara-Dungarpur-Sagwara-Banswara-Ratlam	315
18	11	Sanchore-Raniwara-Mandar-Abu Road	108
19	12	Jaipur-Diggi-Malpura-Kekri-Shahpura -Mandal-Bhilwara-Kankroli	307
20	13	Alwar-Shahpura-Kanwat-Neem ka Thana-Khetri-Singhana -Chidawa-Pilani-Rajgarh	281
21	14	Bharatpur-Deeg-Nagar-Alwar-Behror-Narnol	185
22	15	Dewari-Dabok-Mangalwar-Bari Sadri **(Dabok-Mangalwar is NH76)**-Chhoti Sadri-Neemuch	77
23	16	Barmer-Sindri-Jalore-Sanderao-Sadri-Desuri-Amritia	305
24	18	Ajmer-Bari Ghati-Bherunda-Degana-Tarneu-Deedwana	148
25	19	Indergarh-Itawa-Mangral-Baran-Khanpur-Jhalawar -Bhanimandi-Dug-Agar	324
26	19A	Baran-Aklera via Atru-Chhipa Barod **(Declared as NH90)**	94
27	19B	Mangrol-Rajpura	16

Contd...

...*Contd*...

S.No.	*SH No.*	*Route*	*Length (km)*
28	20	Sikar-Sujangarh-Talchhper-Nokha	171
29	21	Dantiwara-pipad City-Merta City-Parbatsar	155
30	22	Mandrail-Karauli-Hindaun-Mahua-Khedli-Nagar-Pahadi	83
31	23	Bharatpur-Rupwas-Sepau-Dholpur	63
32	24	Bharonti-Mathura via Gangapur-Hindon-Bharatpur	165
33	25	Dharuhera-Tijara-Alwar-Rajgarh-Mandawar-mahua	279
34	26	Nasirabad—Kekdi-Devli	132
35	27	Sirohi-Mandar-Deesa up to Border	72
36	28	Jodhpur-Balotara-Sindri-Chittalwara	226
37	28A	Balotara-Gadra Road via Bayatu	183
38	29	Bundi-Lakheri-Sawai Madhopur-Dausa-Sariska	274
39	30	Tonk-Sawai Madhopur-Pali Ghat-Shivpuri	112
40	31	Jalore-Bhinmal-Raniwara up to Border	107
41	32	Sadri-Banswara via Ranakpur-Gogunda -Udaipur-Salumber-Aspur	216
42	33	Bhensrodgarh-Lakheri via Kota-Keshoraipatan -Kapren-Laban	127
43	34	Tonk-Kota via Nagar-Nainwa-Khatgarh-K'Patan	110
44	35	Mahua-Delhi via Laxman Garh-Ramgarh	86
45	36	Fatepur-Ganganagar via Churu-Taranagar -Sahawa-Nohar-Hanumangarh	199
46	37	Chomu-Churu via Divrala-Khandela-Udaipurwati	206
47	37A	Chomu-Khejrodi-Mand Road	19
48	38	Sirohi-Phalodi via Kalindri-Ramsin-Jalore-Siwana -Balotra-Pachpadre-Shergarh-Dhechu	254
49	39	Satur-Nagaur via Jahajpur-Shahpura-Vijaynagar -Biawer-Merta City	317
		TOTAL	**8898**
		Breakup is as under	
		B.T. Road Length = 8861	
		W.B.M Road Length = 10	
		Gravelled Length = 10	
		Fair Weather Road Length = 17	

APPENDIX A–6.21

Road Length in Relation to Area and Population in India as on 31.03.1997

States/UTs	*Total Road Length (km)*	*Area (sq.km)*	*Population (Lakh)*	*Road Length (km)*	
				Per 100sq km	*Per 1 Lakh Population*
All India	**2465877**	**3291080**	**9552**	**74.9**	**258.2**
Andhra Pradesh	178012	275068	734	64.7	242.5
Arunachal Pradesh	14092	83743	11	16.8	1281.1
Assam	68418	78438	253	87.2	270.4
Bihar	88352	173877	952	50.8	92.8
Goa	8563	3814	15	224.5	570.9
Gujarat	90896	196024	464	46.4	195.9
Haryana	28164	44212	180	63.7	156.5
Himachal Pradesh	30193	55673	62	54.2	487.0
Jammu & Kashmir	21446	222236	93	9.7	230.6
Karnataka	144012	191791	503	75.1	286.3
Kerala	145704	38863	315	374.9	462.6
Madhya Pradesh	200137	443446	760	45.1	263.3
Maharashtra	361893	307690	883	117.6	409.8
Manipur	10941	22327	23	49.0	475.7
Meghalaya	8480	22429	22	37.8	385.5
Mizoram	4829	21081	9	22.9	536.6
Nagaland	18356	16579	15	110.7	1223.7
Orissa	262703	155707	349	168.7	752.7
Punjab	64352	50362	238	127.8	270.4
Rajasthan	**129674**	**342239**	**510**	**37.9**	**254.3**
Sikkim	1834	7096	5	25.8	366.8
Tamil Nadu	206503	130058	603	158.8	342.5
Tripura	14729	10486	34	140.5	433.2
Uttar Pradesh	255467	294411	1607	86.8	159.0
West Bengal	75435	88752	761	85.0	99.1
Total (States)	**2433185**	**3276402**	**9401**	**74.3**	**258.8**
Union Territories					
Andaman & Nicobar	1317	8249	4	16.0	329.3
Chandigarh	1753	114	8	1537.7	219.1
D&N Haveli	533	491	2	108.6	266.5
Daman & Diu	101	3814	1	2.6	101.0
Delhi	26582	1483	125	1792.4	212.7
Lakshadweep	1	32	1	3.1	1.0
Pondicherry	2405	495	10	485.9	240.5
Total (UTs)	**32692**	**14678**	**151**	**222.7**	**216.5**

APPENDIX A–6.22

Works under CRF in Rajasthan

District	*Adm. Sanction in Lakh*	*No. of Jobs*	*Road Length*	*CD Works Number*	*Expenditure 31.12.2001*
Ajmer	330.00	4	30.00	22	63.12
Alwar	447.00	4	39.30	10	56.77
Banswara	310.00	4	52.00		156.50
Baran	445.00	2	2.00	1	
Barmer	360.00	2	38.00	5	35.87
Bharatpur	450.00	4	43.00	1	145.80
Bhilwara	274.00	3	31.55	17	51.20
Bikaner	170.00	2	17.00		56.48
Bundi	270.00	3	29.00		38.86
Chittorgarh	280.00	2	19.50		72.17
Churu	475.00	4	52.00		93.92
Dausa	300.00	3	25.00		82.02
Dholpur	539.00	4	66.00		23.05
Dungarpur	255.00	3	46.00		161.33
Hanumangarh	300.00	2	30.00		129.86
Jaipur	405.00	3	42.00	3	62.53
Jaisalmer	360.00	3	36.50	5	97.31
Jalore	320.00	3	33.00	1	67.40
Jhalawar	560.00	3	66.00	1	71.74
Jhunjhunu	350.00	2	35.00		44.03
Jodhpur	1570.00	5	120.00	18	190.08
Karauli	350.00	3	33.00	14	58.86
Kota	386.00	4	36.00		64.57
Nagaur	1635.00	6	147.00	10	53.23
Pali	990.00	4	60.00		87.57
Rajsamand	350.00	3	35.00	1	107.65
Sikar	408.50	4	48.50	1	56.01
Sirohi	510.00	4	47.00		127.57
Sawai Madhopur	260.00	4	26.00	11	45.03
Sri Ganganagar	288.00	2	34.00	12	141.20
Tonk	335.00	5	45.50		61.04
Udaipur	451.00	3	44.00	19	26.24
Total	**14733.50**	**107**	**1408.85**	**152**	**2252.62**

APPENDIX A–6.23

Powers Delegated to PWD Officers

Ref No	*Nature of Power*	*To whom Delegated*	*Limits of Financial Power (in Rs)*
1	To accord technical sanction to detailed, revised or supplementary estimates for original, deposit and contribution work, subject to the condition that fresh administrative sanction is sought if the detailed, revised or supplementary estimates exceed the original by 20 per cent or more.	CE ACE SE EE AE	Full Powers Full Powers Up to 25 lakh Up to 7 lakh Up to 0.25 lakh
1A	For conducting detailed investigation and preparation of designs and drawings, use of consultancy services may be availed, for works costing more than 50 lakh wherever necessary and to pay the consultancy fees.	CE	Full Powers
2	To accord administrative approval to projects of original works.	Admin Dept CE SE	Up to 5 lakh Up to 2 lakh Up to 0.5 lakh
27	To sanction execution of works departmentally	Admin Dept CE ACE SE EE AE	Up to 200 lakh Up to 100 lakh Up to 50 lakh Up to 7 lakh Up to 2 lakh Up to 0.1 lakh
28	To accept tenders for the execution of sanctioned work and for rate contracts (Area-wise, for repairs, maintenance and petty works, including supply of materials for these works).	Admin Dept CE ACE SE EE AE	Up to 500 lakh Up to 200 lakh Up to 100 lakh Up to 25 lakh Up to 7 lakh Up to 0.25 lakh
40/41	To execute the instruments (contracts) relating to acceptance of tenders on behalf of the Governor	EE AE	Full Powers Up to 0.5 lakh
51	To sanction subject to budget provision the purchase of stores including tools and plants and spare parts of machinery from firms after calling for competitive tenders including the sanction of necessary estimates.	CE ACE SE EE AE	Full Powers Up to 25 lakh Up to 5 lakh Up to 1 lakh Up to 0.25 lakh

APPENDIX A–6.24

Number of PWD Officers and Technical Staff

	Position	*Head Office*	*Zones*	*Total*
Civil Engineers	Chief Engineer	3		3
	Additional Chief Engineer		6	6
	Superintending Engineer	6	24	30
	Executive Engineer	13	128	141
	Assistant Engineer	82	732	814
	Junior Engineer			1016
Mechanical Engineers	Superintending Engineer		2	2
	Executive Engineer	1	9	10
	Assistant Engineer			72
	Junior Engineer			97
Electrical Engineers	Superintending Engineer		2	2
	Executive Engineer		6	6
	Assistant Engineer			50
	Junior Engineer			52
Architects	Architects			8
	Assistant Architects			8
	Horticulturists/Garden Supdt			8
	Technical Officers/Assistants			16
				2341

Chapter 7

Power Development in Rajasthan

Power is an extremely important infrastructure for economic development. Good quality and affordable power is a crucial determinant of competitiveness of industries and the attractiveness of nations as investment destinations. Rajasthan has a decisive advantage over other states in terms of power potential. It is ironical that the state's lignite and hydrocarbon resources have not been properly exploited for power generation, and a detailed economic and technical feasibility study of the lignite and gas reserves is yet to be made for ascertaining the potential of power generation.

Demand and Availability of Power

Rajasthan has made substantial progress in the availability of power, which increased from 36.7 million units (MU) in 1956 to 23,809 MU in 2000-2001. Over the past few years, the state government has attempted to further increase availability. However, bridging the energy gap of 13 per cent (55 per cent peak demand) is a Herculean task. Table 7.1 charts the progress in power development over the years.

According to the Sixteenth Power Survey, Rajasthan had a projected energy requirement of 26,890 MU and peak demand of 4,514 MW in 2000-2001, against which actual availability was 23,809 MU and 2,916 MW. Thus, there was an energy shortage of 12.94 per cent and peak demand shortage of 54.80 per cent. The state has been meeting the peak demand shortage through load management in the form of shifting of agricultural load to off-peak hours and imposing power cut on industrial consumers during the peak load hours. Power is being provided to farmers in three blocks of six to seven hours per day, especially in the *rabi* season.

The state had been purchasing power at the rate of Rs. 74.82 crore per month between April 1990 and November 1998. This average purchase has increased to Rs. 195.45 crore per month from December 1998 to March 2002. A budget of Rs. 2400 crore has been sanctioned for the purchase of electricity during 2002-03. Hopefully, the demand-supply mismatch will be substantially reduced with the likely commissioning of various power projects during the Tenth Plan period, which should increase the availability of power.

TABLE 7.1

Progress in Power Development in Rajasthan

Particulars	*1950*	*1999-2000*
Per capita energy consumption (in units)	1.50	302.49
Rural electrification (No./%)	16/0.05	37285/93.66 (2001-02)
Well electrification (No.)	47 (1955-56)	599020
Harijan basti electrification (No.)	1120 (1973-74)	18919
Installed capacity (MW)	13.27	3998 (2000-01)
Energy availability (MU)	36.707	24250
Peak load (MW)	7.48	3583
Electricity sales (MU)	50.96 (1955-56)	16100
No. of consumers	34518	5322172
Connected load (MW)	49 (1955-56)	11409
Sub-transmission and distribution lines (km)	1783	382697
Extra high voltage sub-station (No./capacity (MVW))	—	217/15794.5
Extra high voltage line (km)	—	16884

Source: Power Scenario in Rajasthan in Retrospect and Prospects during 1999-2000, RSEB, Jaipur.

Future Scenario

The Sixteenth Power Survey has projected a peak demand of 6,772 MW for 2006-07 as against the projected availability of 4,634 MW. This requires the state to make substantial investments in order to bridge this peak shortage of 46 per cent. The survey also projects a normal demand of 40,341 MU as against the availability of 32,993 MU, a shortage of 22 per cent.

Energy demand from the industrial sector seems to have marginally declined in the past four years. This may be partly on account of slowdown in industrial activity, and partly due to setting up of captive power generation plants by industry to get over the problem of high tariff and unreliable supply.

Power Distribution Losses

Table 7.2 shows the losses incurred by the Rajasthan Vidyut Vitaran companies (distribution companies or DISCOMs).

TABLE 7.2

Per Unit Revenue and Expenditure

Vitaran Company	*Cost Per Unit (Paise)*	*Revenue Per Unit (Paise)*	*Deficit/Unit (Paise)*
Jaipur	390	332	58
Ajmer	363	318	45
Jodhpur	380	296	84

Note: Average loss/unit : 60 Paise
Source: Rajasthan Vidyut Vitaran Companies.

On the eve of power sector reforms in 1998, transmission and distribution (T&D) losses were estimated at 37 per cent. In 2000-01, the T&D losses of all the three DISCOMs were estimated at 42 per cent. These losses are projected to be reduced to 28 per cent by 2006-07. Various initiatives such as strengthening of the transmission and sub-transmission network, providing meters on all 11 KV feeders, conducting energy audit, installation of capacitor banks, providing aerial bunched conductors in theft-prone areas, improvement of metering system by providing meter boxes and replacement of defective meters, controlling theft and increasing vigilance checking, renovation and modernisation (R&M) of lines and equipment etc. have been taken to reduce T&D losses. Table 7.3 indicates the loss reduction programme envisaged in the Tenth Plan.

The rise in 2002-03 was due to the drought, which resulted in substantial increase in agricultural consumption of power. However, various initiatives taken in selected urban and industrial areas have helped reduce T&D losses in 2002-03 over 2000-01 (Table 7.4).

One important exercise that needs to be initiated immediately is to generate data on T&D losses incurred by each retail unit or a sub division which is responsible for billing and revenue realisation. Without this, corrective measures for T&D losses cannot be planned in a technically correct manner. Though media reports estimate losses in some districts as ranging between 55 per cent and 60 per cent, the state government does not seem to have district-wise data.

TABLE 7.3

Actual and Targeted Loss Reduction (2000-01 to 2006-07)

FY	*Actual*			*Target*			
	2000-01	*2001-02*	*2002-03*	*2003-04*	*2004-05*	*2005-06*	*2006-07*
T&D losses in %	42	39.52	40.89	37.89	34.81	31.60	27.88

Source: Sixteenth Power Survey of India, 2000.

TABLE 7.4

Achievements in Reducing T&D Losses

Area	*% Losses*		*Reduction over Two Years*
	2000-01	*2002-03*	
Urban			
Jaipur city	24.6	19.5	5.1
Alwar	32.9	26.6	6.4
Kota city	31.5	25.4	6.1
Jodhpur city	27.8	22.8	5.0
Industrial			
VKIA, Jaipur	4.4	1.6	2.8
Bhiwadi, Alwar	3.3	1.2	2.1
Sitapura, Jaipur	3.2	1.0	2.1
Kota	4.2	1.9	2.3

Source: Rajasthan Vidyut Vitaran Companies.

Presently, there is no system to evaluate whether the expenditure incurred on reduction in T&D losses is appropriate nor has its rate of return been estimated.[1] There is also urgent need for establishing a monitoring system to see whether the desired results are being obtained.

The T&D losses comprise both technical losses and losses due to pilferage of electricity. The technical losses could be further categorised into construction/ augmentation of T&D systems involving large investments and those not involving large investments such as balancing of loads on the three phases,

1. The Jaipur DISCOM has decided to install 2,500 capacitors in all the low tension lines at a total cost of Rs. 3 crore under the Union government's Accelerated Power Development Project. This is expected to raise the DISCOM's revenue by about Rs. 7 crore. Such work will be undertaken in other cities after evaluating its success in Jaipur.

minimising transformation losses, reducing contact losses and preventing leakages as also reducing losses due to poor power factor. The areas not involving major investments should be taken up immediately and this will yield significant reductions in T&D losses.

In view of the financial constraints, units accounting for higher commercial losses should be tackled first. A rate of return has to be determined for each T&D project. Besides, the deadlines for the completion of power projects should be tight in order to contain escalation in costs.

Power Factor and T&D Losses

Improving the power factor of T&D systems is also an important factor in reducing T&D losses. For this, data on the existing power factors of all subdivisions has to be collected.

The induction motors used in agricultural pump sets and industries have a low power factor. Though industries are required to maintain good power factors, yet no effort seems to have been seriously made in respect of agricultural pump sets. It is high time that serious efforts are made to improve the power factor of agricultural pump sets. Alternatively, the Bureau of Indian Standards specifications may be modified in order to help in improving the low power factor in the electrical systems.

Power theft and pilferage is done by either hooking on to the overhead power lines or tampering with the meters. Both are criminal offences and can be checked only by strict and foolproof monitoring. Use of bunch conductors may prevent theft from overhead lines. A large number of energy meters remain out of order at any given point of time. The time taken for their repair/replacement needs to be reduced. T&D losses must be scaled down within five to seven years, since they are not only a burden on the state exchequer, but they also penalise the honest consumers.

Power generation takes up a large share of investment in the power sector. A proper balance between generation, transmission as also distribution is required and such rationalisation would also help in scaling down T & D losses.

Plant Load Factor

The various power generating units have improved their plant load factor (PLF) over the years (Table 7.5), with the Kota Thermal Plant being awarded for achieving a steady improvement in PLF.

TABLE 7.5

Improvement in Plant Load Factor

(Per cent)

Year	*Kota Thermal Power Station*	*Suratgarh Super Thermal Unit*
1991	59.79	—
1998-1999	78.82	71.24
1999-2000	84.57	74.43
2000-2001	86.45	80.24
2001-2002	85.30	85.04
2002-2003	88.02	88.94

Source: Power Scenario in Rajasthan, RSEB, Jaipur.

State's Resources for Power Generation

Rajasthan does not have the raw material required for generation of thermal and atomic power. The state has to spend huge amounts on the transportation of coal for its thermal plants, while its degree of freedom to increase the capacity of atomic power generation is severely limited.

However, recent surveys conducted by Gas Authority of India Ltd (GAIL), Oil and Natural Gas Corporation (ONGC), Shell and other agencies have shown that there are huge deposits of lignite and gas (coal bed methane gas and natural gas) which can help the state overcome its present shortage of power and would also meet prospective demand.

Lignite: Rajasthan has an estimated 2000 million tonnes (mt) of surface lignite deposits. These deposits are sufficient to generate 3000 MW of power in the next five to seven years, if generation is undertaken at the pitheads. There are also large deep-seated deposits of lignite, but the potential of power generation from these and the cost of such generation have to be determined.

Methane Gas: According to an assessment done by the Prime Minister's Office, south Barmer area alone has potential to generate 3500 MW of power using methane gas as fuel. However, technical and financial feasibility of such generation needs to be determined.

Heavy Oil: It is estimated that Rajasthan has deposits of around 15 billion tonnes of heavy oil and bitumen. These can sustain 8000-10,000 MW of power generation. However, these reserves can be developed only if the public sector Oil India Ltd. (OIL), which holds the petroleum exploration licence, sheds its preference for companies from Venezuela, Colombia, Europe or the United States and gives a chance to Indian companies for exploration. The policies of the multinational companies in exploring and extracting heavy oil in the western districts of Rajasthan does not seem to be transparent. However, in view of the uncertainty on this front, no decisive policy to extract heavy oil can be made, nor can the state be sure about the quantum of power that can be generated from such resources.

During the past four decades, 118 wells have been dug for exploration of oil in western Rajasthan at a cost of Rs. 900 crore. However, not much oil has been found, although ONGC itself has spent around Rs. 340 crore in the 1958-2002 period, while OIL has spent over Rs. 368 crore in the 1984-2002 period and struck oil only in three wells in the Baghewala area of Jaisalmer district. OIL has also found natural gas and has collaborated with a Venezuelan company for extracting oil and natural gas in the area.

Multinational oil companies, Cairn Energy and Shell, have, however, made significant discoveries of oil in the South Barmer area. Reserves in a part of the area are assessed at 155 million barrels of good quality oil.

Gas: The area with most potential in Jaisalmer is held by ONGC, which has sub-let exploration to Phoenix Overseas, a multinational. However, this company has not commenced its survey even after five years. OIL, on the other hand, is capping its new wells and is negotiating for higher rates with the Rajasthan government. Meanwhile, the state was forced to use diesel in its Ramgarh Power Plant, which is gas-based. Thus, various steps need to be taken to leverage the huge deposits of lignite, gas and oil for power generation in the state. This would require adequate supply of water. Apart from feasibility studies, it is necessary to persuade the Central government to adopt a clear policy on permitting MNCs, Central PSUs or private Indian companies to explore and extract these reserves for generating power in a manner that the state also gets its due share from these ventures. Sites for power generation must be selected in such a manner that power is available in the most cost effective way.

These attempts need to be taken with the long-term perspective of not only bridging the present demand-supply gap, but also ultimately creating surplus power over the next 10 or 15 years, providing a source of revenue for the state.

The state government, on its part, can formulate a policy which encourages major Indian players to invest in power generation, transmission and distribution. During the first three years of power sector reforms, the state government invested about Rs. 4,000 crore in the power sector, but much more investment is required to meet the growing demand for power. The power sector is the most capital-intensive sector, with an incremental capital-output ratio (ICOR) of 42.

Hydel Generation

In the sixties, the bulk of power generation in the country was through hydro-electricity (hydel). With the gradual shift to thermal-based power, the bulk of power generation comes from coal-based power stations and partly from gas-based power stations. The advantage of having a higher share of hydel power is that it would be possible to regulate the generation in line with variations in demand. Thermal/nuclear power stations generally operate as base load stations. A higher hydro mix helps in meeting the morning and evening peaks hours. Besides, it is eco-friendly. However, Rajasthan cannot expect to meet its rising demand for power from hydel sources, since it is a water-scarce state. The present capacity of hydel power generation in Rajasthan is 987 MW. However, this does not mean that there is no scope for expanding the state's capacity to generate hydel power. All that the state has to do is take recourse to sources of hydel power which are certain. Currently, the state is forced to depend largely on the cheap power generated in neighbouring states like Gujarat, Madhya Pradesh, Punjab and Himachal Pradesh. A cost-benefit analysis of such power availability would be required.

Nuclear Power

It is believed, worldwide, that nuclear power will decline drastically in the decades to come. Nuclear power generation is constrained by high capital costs and increasingly stifling regulations. France is the only country in Europe where 75 per cent of the electricity generated is through nuclear power. However, India and China are committed to expand nuclear power in order to reduce their dependence on hydrocarbons. Rajasthan gets 342 MW from the Rajasthan Atomic Power Project (RAPP) and Narora Atomic Power Station (NAPS). The Nuclear Power Corporation is now planning to install an additional 2 × 220 MW units at RAPP.

Wind Energy

Wind energy is a perennial and environmentally friendly source of power. However, the scope for wind energy in Rajasthan is rather limited compared to the coastal states. Jaisalmer district is technically most suited for setting up such plants because of high wind velocity. The Indian Institute of Tropical Meteorology has assessed the gross potential wind energy in the state at 1200 MW, although 400 MW can be harnessed with existing technology. The Rajasthan Energy

Development Agency (REDA) has received proposals for generation of more than 225 MW of wind energy in the state. Five plants have been set up with a total capacity of 14 MW. Procedures for clearance need to be streamlined and standardised so that the proposals can be implemented soon. Apart from standardising tariff for non-conventional energy, the power purchase agreement should also be standardised.

Solar Energy

Rajasthan has the highest solar insolence in the country and this makes it a suitable location for solar power projects. A 140 MW integrated solar and combined cycle project based on parabolic trough technology is being set up at Mathania in Jodhpur district at a cost of Rs. 600 crore, with financial assistance from Global Environment Facility (GEF) and German funding agency, KFW. The initial higher cost of solar power projects has so far hampered solar energy development, but since it is eco-friendly and involves only a one-time expenditure, it could be promoted more aggressively, if grants and loans from abroad could be liberally available.

Power Consumption Patterns

The per capita consumption of power in Rajasthan has grown from 124 kWh in 1985-86 to 329 kWh in 1998-99. This is much lower than consumption in many other states like the Punjab (861 kWh), Haryana (503 kWh), Madhya Pradesh (398 kWh) and Gujarat (724 kWh). The industrial sector accounts for 35 per cent of the total consumption, agriculture sector 30 per cent, and the domestic sector 20 per cent. Between 1994 and 1999, the domestic sector has shown the highest annual growth rate of electricity consumption of 11 per cent and the share of the agriculture sector has risen from 6 per cent to 11 per cent in 2000-01. However, the share of industry has declined considerably – from 43 per cent in 1990-91 to 35 per cent in 2000-01. This is not a happy augury either for the industry or for the power sector, because the bulk of the revenues come from industry. The compound annual growth rate (CAGR) of energy demand in the industrial sector between 1994 and 1999 was around 2 per cent. In fact, there has been negative growth in energy demand of the industrial sector in 1998-1999, 1999-2000 and 2000-01. Table 7.6 gives the sector-wise shares in consumption of energy.

Captive Power Generation

There is an estimated 500 MW of captive power capacity in Rajasthan. Captive generation has both advantages and disadvantages. While generation for captive use should not be restricted, often such captive supply becomes a cover for commercial sale of power and this can have serious implications. The entire edifice of power supply in India is based on the principle of cross subsidy and till such subsidy is reduced or eliminated through tariff rationalisation, free access for sale to only select consumers would be inviting disaster as it would jeopardise the operations of the DISCOMs. The DISCOMs in Rajasthan cater to more than 56 lakh consumers in different segments. Allowing cherry picking of just bulk industrial commercial consumers having demand of more than 3 MVA would lead to virtual collapse of the distribution system as they contribute more than 22 per cent to revenues of the DISCOMs. Besides, even operations would suffer. Not only would domestic and agriculture consumers suffer, even the remaining industrial consumers would face problems.

TABLE 7.6

Sector-Wise Power Consumption in Rajasthan (%)

Year	*Agriculture*	*Industrial*	*Domestic*	*Commercial*	*Others*	*Total*
1990-91	28.36	42.82	10.69	5.09	13.04	100.00
1994-95	30.43	40.26	13.50	4.87	10.94	100.00
2000-01	30.62	35.16	20.56	6.16	7.5	100.00

Source: RSEB Annual Report, various years.

However, if captive plants are generously allowed, industries would face fewer power cuts and hence the power companies would stand to gain financially. Besides, setting up of additional generating capacity is becoming very difficult as financial institutions are unwilling to lend for power projects, without foolproof escrow mechanism from the power corporations. But captive power plants do not suffer from this handicap. If the quality of power improves as a result of additions through captive generation, many industrial units that have installed captive plants may like to use them as standby arrangements only. Hence, effectively, the overall industrial load may not decrease with captive generation. Rather, with adequate and reliable power, lot of suppressed demand of industry may be unlocked and new industries may be attracted to the state. Thus, the fear of loss of revenue by liberally allowing captive plants may turn out to be unfounded. Instead of adopting an obstructive policy towards captive generation, the DISCOMs should create congenial conditions and appropriate power tariff structure so that industrial consumers are not tempted to switch over to captive generation.

The 1998 Industrial Policy freely permits captive power plants to be set up and permission from the state's power corporation is no longer required.

Natural Gas

Rajasthan has commenced work on the fifth unit of 250 MW at the gas-based Suratgarh Power Plant, sixth unit of 195 MW at the Kota Power Plant and 2 × 37.5 MW units at the Ramgarh gas-based Power Plant. For Ramgarh, the additional availability of only 2 lakh million standard cubic meters per day (MSCMD) of natural gas has been confirmed by OIL against a requirement of 5 lakh MSCMD. The gap is to be met by high speed diesel. The lacklustre progress in exploring petroleum and gas reserves has proved to be a major bottleneck. While Pakistan has been exploiting its gas deposits for years, very little has been achieved in Rajasthan because of extraneous considerations. Due to harsh weather conditions, senior officials do not wish to be posted in the desert areas. The private sector could perhaps be involved in this effort. Rajasthan has also signed a MoU for buying power from two mega projects — 1200 MW from the 6 × 660 MW Hirma project in Orissa and 500 MW from the 4 × 500 MW Pipavav project located in Gujarat. The fate of the Hirma project is uncertain, as the foreign partner, Mirant Corporation, has exited from the project due to slow progress.

Measures to Improve Power Scenario

Besides liberalising the establishment of captive power plants, the Rajasthan government has taken the following steps to improve the availability of power in the state:

- Uninterrupted supply of power will be ensured for export-oriented units set up in the EPIPs.
- All industrial areas on rural feeders will be connected to urban/industrial feeders in a phased manner for better quality of power and the cost will be borne by RIICO.
- Land for private power plants will be allotted by RIICO close to the grid station, at rates applicable for industrial land on priority basis.
- Provisional fuel surcharge will be revised on a quarterly basis to avoid an undue burden on industrial units at a later stage.
- Reduction in contract demand to units supplying surplus power to power corporations will be freely permitted. Where the contract demand is reduced to zero, no minimum charge will be levied.
- New large industrial consumers will be required to pay for the first six months on the basis of actual consumption, and for the next six months on the basis of actual consumption or 50 per cent of the minimum charges, whichever is higher.
- To deal with the problem of fly-ash from thermal power stations, efforts have been made to promote the use of fly ash for building material. The results of these initiatives will be visible only over the next five or six years.
- Rebate in tariff to industrial consumers.

Rationalisation of Power Tariff

After power sector reforms were initiated in Rajasthan, attempts have been made by the state-owned power companies to rationalise power tariffs. However, even a hike in domestic and commercial tariffs and reduction in subsidy for the agricultural sector has not helped in reducing the losses of power companies, largely due to huge T&D losses.

There is a direct and positive correlation between tariffs and power theft, but the state government has made no attempt to analyse this. If T & D losses can be significantly reduced, power tariffs in Rajasthan may be rationalised, and honest consumers may not have any ground for criticising power companies for increased tariffs.

Power Sector Reforms in Rajasthan

Power sector reforms were necessitated by the mounting burden of losses of the RSEB, which was attributed to overstaffing, heavy T&D losses and non-payment of bills by many public, semi-government and private units. Loss of credibility had also hampered the RSEB's attempts to mobilise adequate funds for improving power availability in the state.

Power sector reforms were initiated in 1998, when the World Bank agreed to provide adequate funds for power development in the state. The reforms were expected to lead to a reduction in establishment costs, rationalisation of power tariff; mobilisation of private capital for power generation and transmission; and lower capital–power generation ratio.

In order to achieve these goals, the state government decided to unbundle the RSEB and form five corporations - two for generation and transmission and three for distribution. The goal of reducing the establishment costs has not been achieved and it is hoped that the corporations take appropriate action to reduce losses.

The state government has done well in sparing about Rs. 4,000 crore for the development of power sector, and has also allocated Rs. 7,777 crore for this sector during the Tenth Plan. However, the expected mobilisation of private sector funds for generation/transmission has not happened. The per unit revenue deficit has been successfully been brought down from 100 paise in 1999-2000 to 60 paise in 2001-2002. Revenue collection of the DISCOMs has also marginally improved and has helped reduce their deficit from Rs.1,678 crore in 1999-2000 to Rs.1,250 crore in 2001-02.

The state government must analyse the factors responsible for hampering the flow of private capital into power sector, and take appropriate steps to overcome these problems. Urgent efforts are necessary to reduce the administrative costs associated with generation and distribution of power. Power companies must be managed on commercial lines with the objective of eliminating their dependence on the government for covering up their losses.

Reforms are now a reality. A thorough review of the performance of power companies is needed, focusing on capital and labour productivity vis-à-vis the climate for increasing private sector investment in the power sector. The World Bank had not intended that power sector reforms be confined to the restructuring of the RSEB. A major challenge facing the five public sector power companies is that of reducing pilferage which continues to remain high.

A high-level power committee must be constituted to regularly report on all matters relating to generation, transmission, distribution, pricing, investment etc.

The Rajasthan State Electricity Regulatory Commission (RSERC) was set up in April 2000. The Commission will issue licences for transmission and supply of power. It also reserves the rights for ascertaining the methodology, procedures for collecting expected revenue and for determining tariff.

Nursery Scheme

The RSEB had become financially unviable because of high subsidies and pilferage. The RSERC should be allowed to operate independently, and given full backing so that the task might be achieved in a phased manner. The political leadership should avoid making announcements about tariff etc.

Agricultural subsidy is the most politically sensitive issue. Rajasthan had taken the lead in introducing a nursery scheme under which electricity connections are given out of turn to farmers who pay a higher fee. The initial capital cost is around 10 times higher than the cost of an ordinary agricultural connection and the tariff was also 100 per cent higher. The scheme had become quite popular with the farmers and more than 80,000 connections had already been given under this category. Unfortunately, the scheme was abolished in 1999-2000. It raises serious doubts about the determination to reduce subsidies. This scheme needs to be revived as it would not only create a proper climate for reduction of subsidies in ordinary agricultural connections but would also help curbing theft. With the waiting time for agricultural connections averaging 12 to 13 years, theft is bound to increase in the absence of any out of turn scheme.

The major problem with the nursery scheme was that the basic premise that those ready to pay more could jump the queue was given up and those opting for the nursery scheme later returned to the general category for tariff. Therefore, there was no reduction in subsidy. Such a scheme would be appropriate only if higher tariff could be continued, at least for the time equivalent to the normal waiting time for an agriculture connection.

Boom Scheme

Unchecked privatisation can be problematic. The advantages/disadvantages of privatisation varies from activity to activity. The greatest advantage that privatisation brings into distribution is efficiency, which, in turn, would lead to improved finances.

In 2000, tenders were invited for the construction of 132 KV and 220 KV grid stations in the private sector on a Build-Own-Operate-Maintain (BOOM) basis, involving an investment of Rs. 1,200 crore. Leading national companies participated in the scheme as the rates were quite competitive and even the RFC had agreed to finance the project. The requirement of grid stations for the next ten years was to be completed in 18 months. It would mean a saving of about 19 crore units a year which means an additional availability of about 142 MW every year. Unfortunately, the scheme was not properly structured. It needs to be thoroughly reviewed, as it would not only reduce technical losses, but would bring in private sector participation in a big way. Besides, 33 KV grid substations could also be brought under the BOOM scheme.

ANNEXURE 1

Oil, Gas and Lignite Fields of Rajasthan

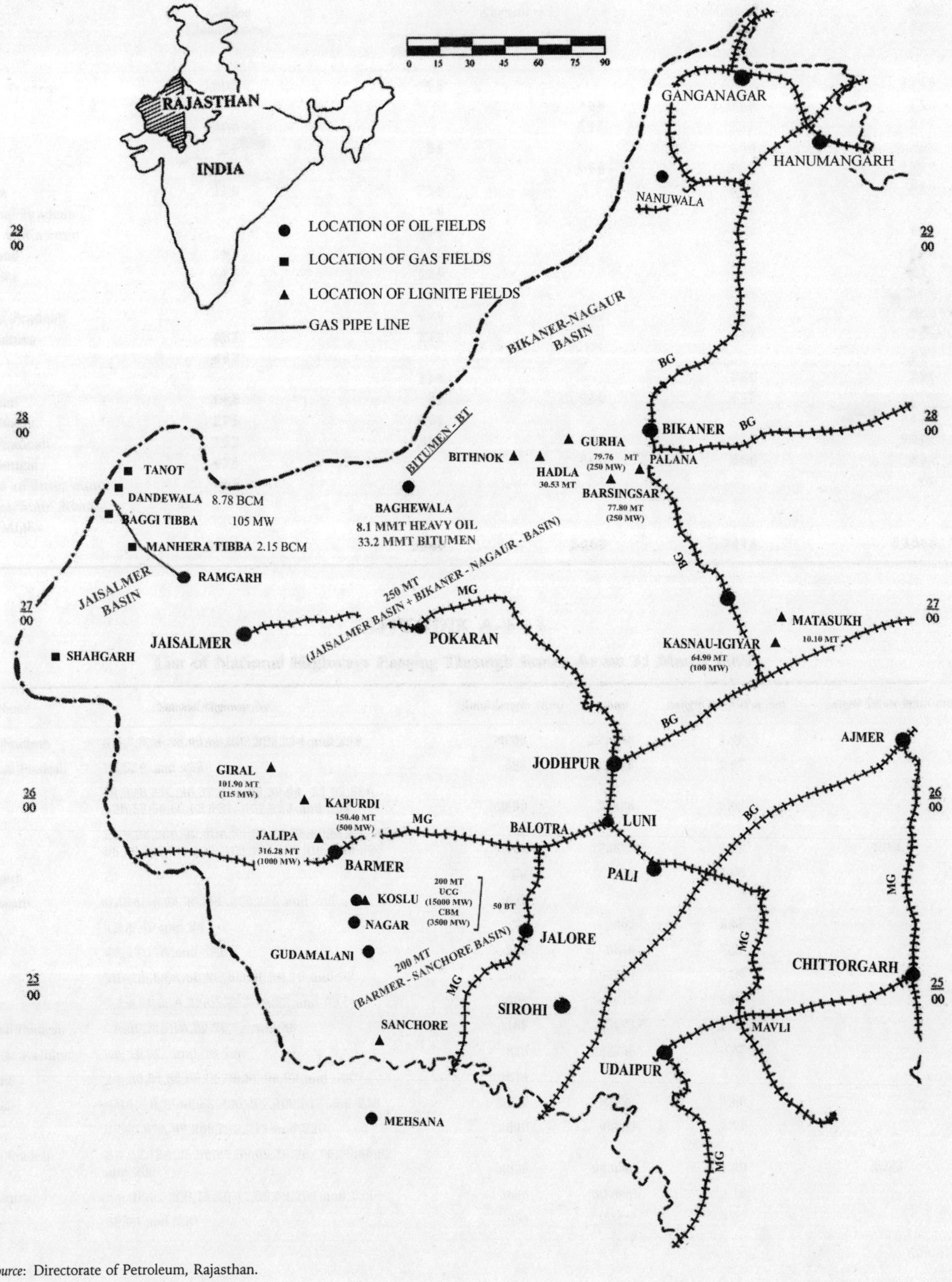

Source: Directorate of Petroleum, Rajasthan.

Chapter 8

Urban Infrastructure and Basic Services

Introduction

Rajasthan ranks twenty-first in India in terms of urbanisation, with over 23 per cent of its population living in urban areas. Urbanisation is largely the result of the migration of people from villages to towns and cities in search of better employment prospects, education, market, tourism, transport and other facilities, although this process has partly been supported by natural growth of urban population as well. The process of urbanisation is expected to increase, due to the current pace of migration and will be facilitated with the development of urban infrastructure being undertaken by the Rajasthan government. Data from the 1961, 1971 and 1981 Census indicate that about 30 per cent of the state's enumerated population was migrant population. Most of the migration is from neighbouring states of Uttar Pradesh, Madhya Pradesh, Punjab, Haryana and Gujarat.

Urbanisation puts urban resources, services and infrastructure under tremendous strain and requires the extension of various services and amenities. Rapid urbanisation has led to an alarming deterioration in the quality of life of urban dwellers, who have to cope with poor sanitation and disposal of solid waste, water shortage, pollution, poor transport system, frequent epidemics, inadequate health facilities etc. The deficiency of proper housing facilities results in the proliferation of *kuchchee bastis* (shanty towns)/slums and lack of support for the social and economic development of disadvantaged population.

Growth of Urban Population

Rajasthan has been recording a very high rate of population growth, especially in the urban areas. The urban population increased from 7.2 million in 1981 to over 10 million in 1991 and further to 15.1 million in 2001. Most population projections indicate the urban population would increase to 22 million in 2011 and over 29 million in 2021. The annual average increase in urban population is estimated at 500,000 in the 1991-2001 decade and is expected to be over 600,000 in 2001-2011 and 800,000 in 2011-2021. The exponential growth in urban population is due to both natural growth as well as inmigration (Table 8.1).

TABLE 8.1

Urban Population Growth in Rajasthan

Year	*Total Population (million)*	*Urban Population (million)*	*% of Urban Population*	*Total Decadal Increase (%)*	*Urban Population Increase (%)*
1951	16.0	2.96	18.50	—	—
1961	20	3.25	16.28	25.0	9.8
1971	25	4.55	17.63	29.0	40.0
1981	34	7.22	21.05	32.9	58.7
1991	44	10.06	22.88	28.3	39.3
2001	56	15.1	23.38	28.3	31.2

Source: Report of The Second State Finance Commission, Rajasthan.

In 2001, 75,57,650 people were living in 20 cities and towns with 100,000 and above population [Appendix A–8.1]. As much as 70.04 per cent of the total urban population lived in six large cities covered under the Rajasthan Urban Infrastructure Development Programme (RUIDP).[1] The remaining 30 per cent is spread unevenly over 14 towns, with the maximum of 280,000 in Bhilwara followed by Alwar (266,000) and the minimum in Churu (102,000) and Jhunjhunu (100,000). Towns with relatively high population should receive the attention of planners on priority

1. The Rajasthan Urban Infrastructure Development Project (RUIDP) is being implemented in Jaipur, Jodhpur, Kota, Bikaner, Ajmer and Jodhpur with assistance from the Asian Development Bank.

basis to avoid the crisis relating housing, water supply, sewerage and basic amenities etc. in the future.

Slum/*Kuchchee Basti* Population

According to provisional figures of Census 2001, the slum population in Rajasthan's towns and urban agglomerations (UAs) is estimated at 1.2 million. There has been a growth of *kuchchee bastees* (shanty towns with minimum drinking water and electricity facilities) in the urban areas especially in large cities like Jaipur, Jodhpur, Kota, Ajmer, etc. and this has led to a deterioration in the environment and put a strain on urban infrastructure. These *bastees* develop through encroachments, largely by the in-migrant population. In due course of time, the number of such people increases and they build *pucca* or semi-*pucca* houses. Eventually, it becomes difficult to relocate such huge numbers of people and these areas are 'regularised' and basic infrastructure is provided. The regularisation and non-regularisation of these areas depends on the policy of the state government as well as political pressure.

Urban Poor

According to the Planning Commission, the below poverty line (BPL) population in the urban areas of Rajasthan is higher than in the rural areas. Urban poverty was estimated at 19.85 per cent in 1999-2000 against 13.74 per cent in rural poverty, a difference of seven percentage points. This is an alarming situation, considering the income-enhancing potential of self-employment and small and tiny enterprise is very low and this may generate feelings of insecurity and frustration. Hence, there is an urgent need for proper implementation of urban poverty and slum development/improvement programmes, along with related socio-welfare programmes.

Drinking Water

Nearly 94 per cent of the urban water supply schemes are based on ground water sources. However, this is under tremendous strain because of overexploitation of ground water and low rate of replenishment due to frequent failure of rains. A survey carried out by the Ground Water Department showed that the water level declined in 26 districts, ranging from (-) 1.66 to (-) 8.66 meters between 1998 and 2001.

Further, the water is brackish and has excessive fluoride. A little over 70 per cent towns (157 UAs), have no access to surface water for drinking purposes. In most towns, deep wells and hand pumps are used to exploit underground water. As high as 69 per cent UAs are dependent on deep wells, in which water levels are falling every year. In 30.62 per cent UAs, hand pumps are also used along with deep wells. Such conditions pose a serious challenge of supplying safe drinking water.

TABLE 8.2

Status of Ground Water Situation in Blocks

	1998	*2001*
Total number of blocks	237	237
Overexploited blocks	41	86
Critical (dark) blocks	26	80
Semi-critical (gray) blocks	34	21
Safe blocks	135	49
Fully saline water (Taranagar Block)	1	1

Source: Report of The Group on The Estimation of Ground Water Resources of Rajasthan, Ground Water Department, 2001.

Demand For Water

Table 8.3. shows the trend of demand for water for domestic, industrial, livestock and other purposes.

TABLE 8.3

Water Demand for Different Sectors

(cubic mm/year)

Year	*Domestic*	*Industrial*	*Livestock*	*Others*	*Total*
1995	2002.0	47.2	1069.0	167.0	3285.2
2005	2584.0	57.2	910.0	645.0	4196.2
2015	3176.0	71.4	1089.0	715.0	5051.4

Source: Water Resources Planning for the State of Rajasthan, Tahal & WAPCOS, 1998.

Domestic water demand, both existing as well as projected, shows a sharp increasing trend from 1991 to 2015 (Table 8.4).

Status of Water Supply and Sanitation

Going by the findings of the NSS 54th Round, the drinking water, sanitation and hygiene situation in the urban areas of Rajasthan needs urgent attention. Though 88.2 per cent of urban households have access to principal drinking water, there is insufficient supply from the principal source of water (taps) for up to five months in a year. Besides, the quality of drinking water from the principal source was reported to be satisfactory in 94.1 per cent of urban households against 97.9 per cent of rural households.

TABLE 8.4

Demand for Domestic Water in Rajasthan

Year	*Population (thousands)*	*Net Demand*		*Gross Demand Cubic mm/year*
		Cubic mm/year	*Lcpd*	
	Cities			
1991	5053.99	372.8	199.0	621.4
1995	5629.24	418.4	200.0	697.3
2005	7023.36	529.4	203.0	853.8
2015	8296.94	632.8	2052.2	988.6
	Towns			
1991	5032.56	251.4	125.7	419
1995	5981.84	303.4	127.5	505.4
2005	8886.24	458.8	130.2	739.5
2015	12418.59	651.2	132.5	1017.5

Source: Water Resources Planning for the State of Rajasthan, Tahal-WAPCOS, 1998.

Up to 16.1 per cent of urban households have no bathrooms and 87.3 per cent had sole access to latrines, while 12.7 per cent of urban households shared latrines. Only 4.8 per cent urban households took their waste to community dumping spots, while 44 per cent took it to individual dumping spots.

- There is no identified place for solid waste disposal and this leads to environmental pollution and health hazards. Places for dumping solid waste should be identified and managed properly. Local bodies should take up recycling of waste material with the use of advanced technology.
- Recent constructions have individual septic tanks and soak pits. However, this may be difficult in the future with the size of plots shrinking.
- The PHED and the Ground Water Board should plan for alternative sources of drinking water supply.
- The PHED needs to plan for comprehensive schemes for water distribution in consonance with the land use plan, 2001.
- An integrated drainage and sewerage plan for cities and towns should be prepared and implemented.
- Installation of sewage treatment plants (STP) is necessary.

According to information available from the Database Management Information, Public Health Engineering Department (PHED), 59.47 per cent of the total towns/cities have been partially covered by drinking water supply which require extension network and capacity augmentation for drinking water supply. More than 14 per cent partially covered towns require extension of the distribution network. Besides, 13.96 per cent fully covered towns need service level augmentation. The service even in 12.16 per cent towns identified as fully covered and not requiring any augmentation, may need to be reviewed due to natural growth and in-migration of population. It calls for better operation and maintenance and better quality of services.

Data for 2001 available from the Master Plans of towns/cities from the Town Planning Department indicate increasing demand for drinking water and decreasing level of water supply. The demand-supply gap will widen with the increasing urban population and will be further aggravated by the frequent occurrence of droughts.

All the 222 towns are reported to have access to safe drinking water supplied by the PHED and other schemes of water supply (Appendix A–8.3). However, in view of the increasing demand, extension of the prevalent network, capacity and service augmentation in water supply are needed in almost all urban areas.

The existing water supply situation calls for the revival of traditional water conservation methods to reduce the pressure on underground water, raise the water level and also rejuvenate the ecological equilibrium.

Water Supply Schemes

The state government is implementing various water supply schemes and reforms are under way to optimally utilise scarce water resources. To meet the increasing demand for water, urban development, tourism, recreation, etc. different schemes like the Rs. 1100 crore Beesalpur scheme for Jaipur city and the Rs. 166.50 crore Chambal scheme for cities like Jaipur and Ajmer, towns and villages of Bharatpur and Dholpur districts. The Rs. 135.05 crore Rajiv Gandhi Jalothan Canal Project (Phase III) will also cover provision for water supply to 729 problematic villages and towns of Jodhpur, Barmer and Jaisalmer districts. Schemes worth Rs. 61.03 crore for 61 fluoride-affected villages of the Nasirabad area of Ajmer district, Rs. 43.99 crore to cover 232 villages of the Bhinay-Masuda area, Vijay Nagar, Gulabpura towns; and Rs. 44.35 crore to cover 94 villages of Kekadi and Sarwad areas in Ajmer district have also been sanctioned. The Churu-Bisau project worth Rs. 119.05 crore will cater to the needs of 168 villages and three towns/cities of Churu and Jhunjhunu districts. The Rs. 153 crore Jawai-Jodhpur project and Rs. 45.70 crore worth of water consolidation schemes for Jodhpur city are in progress. The Rs. 77 crore Mansi-Wakal (Phase I) project for Udaipur city has also been approved.

Besides villages, nine towns/cities were provided with drinking water through railways and road during the drought years. A contingency plan of Rs. 210.90 crore was sanctioned to make drinking water available during summer months, which includes installation of hand pumps, tube wells, private wells, etc. A total Rs. 1868.67 crore was spent on various drinking water schemes by the PHED in 2001 (Appendix A–8.7).

A total expenditure of Rs. 4311.25 crore has so far been incurred on drinking water schemes under various five-year Plans. It includes Rs. 1432.15 crore for urban drinking water schemes and Rs. 2879.10 crore for rural drinking water schemes. The Rs. 173.89 crore spent on urban drinking water is 39.34 per cent of the total state government budget of Rs. 442.03 crore (Appendix A–8.8).

Commissioning of Hand Pumps and Tube-Wells

According to the PHED Database Information, as of April 2000, 81.31 per cent households had service connections for water supply in urban areas. There were 16,611 stand posts, 1,681 other spot sources and 21,683 hand pumps available for drinking water supply. Hand pumps and tube wells commissioned by PHED and other agencies are listed in Table 8.5.

TABLE 8.5

Commissioning of Hand Pumps and Tube-wells

Particulars	*1998-99*	*1999-2000*	*2000-01*	*2001-02*	*2002-03*	*2003-(up to July 2003)*
Tube wells	757	911	1371	1307	1776	721
Hand pumps	11990	13279	15229	12636	17574	5782

Source: PHED, GoR, Jaipur, 2001.

The maintenance of hand pumps in 22 districts is the responsibility of panchayat samitis, while the PHED is entrusted with the task in the remaining 10 desert districts. Every year a special maintenance drive is launched to ensure the smooth operation of hand pumps, especially during the summer months.

Water Tariff

During the 1991-2000 period, the PHED spent three times its revenue for meeting the rising demand for drinking water. The revenue-expenditure gap has progressively risen over the years (Appendix A–8.9). Drinking water tariffs, especially in urban areas, need to be rationalised in order to reduce this gap. The state government is paying more than 74 per cent subsidy for the maintenance of drinking water supply schemes.

Water tariffs in most cities are much lower than the cost of supply. Some organisations like the Bangalore Water Supply and Sewerage Board (BWSSB) have taken the initiative to revise water rates by almost 20 per cent every year since 1991, so as to recover costs, on a no loss no profit basis. Service agencies which have taken loans from financial institutions like the Housing and Urban Development Corporations (HUDCO) have also revised their water rates.[2] The municipalities of Vishakhapatnam, Chennai, Tirupur, Alandur, and Pune have either revised their water tariffs or are in the process of doing so. In 1999, the Confederation of Indian Industries (CII) called for raising water charges to meet the operation and maintenance (O&M) costs. All the projects commissioned under the Financial Institution Reform and Expansion (FIRE) programme have an in-built conditionality regarding commercialisation of urban infrastructure projects.[3] Public-private partnerships (PPPs) have led to cost savings for many public agencies. Thus, there is case for revision of water tariffs in Rajasthan.

Rajasthan has a long history of philanthropic organisations contributing to the supply of drinking water, by constructing tanks, *bawaries*, wells and *tankas* from where anyone could fetch drinking water. During the past few decades, with the State assuming this role of supplying water, the *tankas* and *bawaries* have been totally abandoned. Obviously the consumers have to pay for ensuring adequate supply of drinking water.

Thus, with growing urbanisation, the demand for water for both domestic and commercial use has also been increasing. However, organised water supply is not sufficient to meet these needs. The ground water table in cities is depleting rapidly and there is no dependable surface water source in the vicinity of any city.

Water Treatment

Though all 222 towns have been fully or partially covered with water supply facilities, there is a problem of excessive content of chloride, fluoride and nitrate. Chlorination treatment of water supply is expected to be adopted in 163 towns. Multiple forms of water treatment have been attempted in 59 towns. Supply of good quality of drinking water must receive special attention in the state.

The strategy for ensuring the supply of state drinking water could involve the following:

2. M. Mehta M 'Pricing Of Water Supply', *All India Housing Development Association Journal*, February 1993
3. *Standing Committee on Finance*, Ministry of Finance, Government of India, 1999.

TABLE 8.6

Type of Municipal Bodies

Criteria	*Category*	*Number*
Population of more then 500,000	Municipal Corporation	03
Population above 100,000 and below 500,000	Municipal Council	11
Population above 50,000 and less then 100,000 and district headquarter ULB or having per capita income of more than Rs. 200 per annum	Municipal Board 2nd class	39
Population above 25,000 and less then 50,000 and having per capita income of Rs. 150 per annum or more	Municipal Board 3rd class	58
Population less than 25,000	Municipal Board 4th class	72

Source: Annual Progress Report-1997, Directorate of Local Bodies, Jaipur.

- A detailed inventory and plotting of all habitations.
- Plotting of existing ground water sources and examination of their capacities.
- Detailed field hydro-geological surveys for the location and design of additional ground water structures.
- In cases where the quality of water is not in line with national drinking water standards, water of lower specifications may be allowed to be supplied, provided it does not have the potential of causing a health hazard.
- Construction of roof-top rain water harvesting structures in new houses should be made mandatory in urban areas and should be encouraged in existing buildings, if possible.
- Storm water drainage recharge and liquid waste recycling through the aquifer systems should be the responsibility of the municipal bodies.
- Ground water protection zones should be identified and notified. Setting up of any industry or other likely sources of pollution in such areas should be prohibited.
- All drinking water schemes may initially be funded by the government but the users should share part of the expenditure. This will give a sense of ownership.
- Excessive fluoride content and salinity are the main problems relating to quality of water. Since community treatment plants have not been successful because of constraints like power availability, emphasis should be on implementation of household-based treatment methods or regional water supply systems.

Municipal Bodies of Rajasthan

There are 183 urban local bodies (ULBs) in Rajasthan (Table 8.6).

Urban Schemes

All the ULBs operate according to the guidelines provided by the Directorate of Local Bodies (DLB) which has several cells to facilitate their working. The major function of the Project Cell is to collect funds from the Central and state governments and disburse them to the municipal bodies/District Collector. It is utilised for various schemes like the Swarna Jayanti Shahri Rozgar Yojana (SJSRY), National Slum Development Programme, Slum Environment Improvement, conversion of dry into flush latrines, Balika Samridhdhi Yojana (BSY), Apna Ghar Yojana, Sahbhagi Nagar Vikas Yojana, Core Services, fire fighting service, the slum improvement components of the Eleventh Finance Commission award, reimbursement of octroi and state Finance Commission Grants etc. (Appendix A–8.11) The directorate organises training programmes for officers of ULBs, Centre for Development Studies (CDS), community organisations etc. at the state, district and project levels.

Functions of ULBs

Under the Rajasthan Municipality Rule, 1974, municipalities/councils/corporations give sanction for the allotment of land for schools, public institutions, Central/state government offices and house construction. Approval for the purchase of land even by government departments is sought from ULBs.

Municipal bodies are vested with various functions delegated to them by the state government. These broadly relate to public health including water supply, sewerage and sanitation, eradication of communicable diseases; welfare activities including public facilities such as primary education and recreation; regulatory functions related to prescribing and enforcing building bye-laws, removal of encroachments on public land, registration of births and deaths; public safety including fire protection, street lighting, etc.; public works include measures such as construction and maintenance of inner city roads; and development functions related to town planning and development of commercial markets etc. Public works are carried out by the JDA, UITs and Housing Boards. Drinking water supply is the responsibility of the PHED. Various departments of the state government often assign various functions to municipalities on their own, or on agency basis, such as family planning, nutrition, slum improvement, disease and epidemic control etc. Details about the functions of ULBs are given in Appendix A–8.10.

The Eleventh Finance Commission has also looked into the existing power of municipalities to raise financial resources, including levying of additional taxes by municipalities and the powers, authority and responsibilities of municipalities under the Constitution. This was done in order to recommend grants to states for financing local governments.

However, it appears that the ULBs in Rajasthan have neither been empowered to raise their tax rates nor have they taken any initiative in this direction. The withdrawal of octroi has placed the ULBs in a precarious financial position.

The 74th Constitution Amendment, 1992 for the first time conferred constitutional status on municipalities. Accordingly, the Rajasthan Municipality Act, 1959 was amended to extend reservation in municipal bodies to scheduled caste/scheduled tribe population, women and other backward classes. Elections are held regularly and on schedule.

Following the 74th Amendment, a detailed exercise has been undertaken for the transfer of functions listed under the Twelfth Schedule of the Constitution. A cabinet sub-committee was formed to deliberate on the issue, and to propose modalities for transfer of functions to the municipalities. After discussion of its recommendations, the government has decided to transfer the identified functions, along with necessary funds and functionaries and detailed modalities are being worked out.

State Finance Commission

The first State Finance Commission (SFC) was constituted in 1994 to formulate and suggest the grant-in-aid to be provided to panchayati raj institutions (PRIs) and ULBs. The norms and other modalities to meet the fund requirements for activities related to urban development have been fixed. The Commission recommended that 2.18 per cent of the net tax proceeds of the state should be devolved to PRIs and ULBs, according to the ratio of population (77.27 per cent for PRIs and 22.73 per cent for ULBs). The SFC recommended the following grants for the ULBs.

General Purpose Grant: Sixty per cent of the funds for ULBs should be allocated to different categories of ULBs in proportion to their population, as a grant given for general purpose.

Development Loans: The state government should set up a Municipal Financial Corporation (MFC) and provide a corpus fund of Rs. 150 lakh each year from the 20 per cent funds earmarked for development assistance to be given to ULBs. The MFC will provide loans to eligible ULBs on the basis of their financial status and repayment capacity. The SFC has also suggested that 75 per cent of the lending resources should be earmarked for municipal corporations and councils and 25 per cent for the municipal boards.

Development Grant: Twenty per cent of the ULBs' share of funds should be kept for the development activities of which Rs. 150 lakh will be given to the MFC every year. The remaining amount should be given as a development grant to ULBs with poor financial and resource base.

Incentive Grant and Matching Grant: Twenty per cent of the ULBs' share is earmarked for the Incentive Grant and Matching Grant for eligible ULBs. A sum of Rs. 146 lakh is to be kept as incentive grant for eligible ULBs on the basis of performance in activities under the award schemes to be formulated for this purpose. The state government will determine the necessary indicators for the award scheme. The remaining amount is being given to weaker ULBs as Matching Grant assistance as per the suggestions made by the Tenth Finance Commission. Table 8.7 gives details of the grants given under SFC during the last five years.

Second State Finance Commission: The Second SFC, constituted in 1999, recommended that 2.25 per cent of the net tax proceeds should be distributed between PRIs and ULBs, according to their population. It recommended that Rs. 199.82 crore be devolved to ULBs between 2000-01 and 2004-05. Table 8.8 details the funds transferred to ULBs during last three years.

A sum of Rs. 27.6 crore has been kept in the Annual Plan 2003-04.

TABLE 8.7

State Finance Commission Grant to ULBs

(Rs. lakh)

Year	*General Purpose Grant*	*Development Grant*	*Development Loan*	*Matching Grant*	*Incentive Grant*
1995-96	755.40	101.80	150.00	—	146.00
1996-97	891.00	147.00	—	151.00	146.00
1997-98	1050.60	200.20	—	204.20	146.00
1998-99	1237.80	262.20	—	250.00	—
1999-00	1378.90	168.10	—	—	—
Total	5113.70	879.30	150.00	605.20	438.00

Source: Annual Plan, 2000-2001, Directorate of Local Bodies, Rajasthan, Jaipur.

TABLE 8.8

Funds Released to ULBs

Year	*(Rs. in crore)*
2000-01	23.90
2001-02	27.61
2002-03	27.61

Tenth Finance Commission Grant: This grant is given to ULBs for core services in line with the recommendations of the Tenth Finance Commission. Table 8.9 gives the amount given under the Tenth Finance Commission recommendations to ULBs during 1996-97 to 1999-2000.

TABLE 8.9

Tenth Finance Commission Grant to ULBs

(Rs. lakh)

Year	*Amount Proposed by TFC*	*Amount Given*
1996-97	1080.00	1080.00
1997-98	1080.00	810.00
1998-99	1079.00	1079.00
1999-00	1079.00	1349.00
Total	**4318.00**	**4318.00**

Source: Annual Plan, 2000-2001, Directorate of Local Bodies, Rajasthan, Jaipur.

Eleventh Finance Commission Grants: The Eleventh Finance Commission recommended grant of Rs. 22 crore for fire fighting services, Rs. 40 crore for Slum Improvement Programme and Rs. 19.8 crore a year (approximately Rs. 99.421 crore for the period 2000-04) for core services. The action plan of each programme was prepared by the concerned department and approved by the State-Level Empowered Committee. The implementation of the approved activities is being carried out in agreed phases and on the basis of the availability of funds. Table 8.10 gives details of the funds provided to ULBs.

TABLE 8.10

Eleventh Finance Commission Grants to ULBs

(2001-03) (Rs. lakh)

	2000-01	*2001-02*	*2002-03*
Grant for core services	994.16	2982.48	994.16
Grant for fire services	—	780.00	440.00
Grant for slum improvement	—	1600.00	400.00

Other grants (Private sector participation) An amount of Rs. 225 lakh was transferred to the PHED in 1998-99 against the water charges of the public taps. Presently, a token provision is being kept for this purpose.

Special grant-in-aid for urban renewal: Special financial assistance is provided to ULBs for meeting the cost involved in removal of encroachments on municipal land. Land acquired for the implementation of development programme can be very expensive. A sum of Rs. 1000 lakh was allocated in the Annual Plan 2000-01 for acquiring land, of which Rs. 400 lakh was transferred to the municipal council of Udaipur, while Rs. 100 lakh was earmarked in the Annual Plan 2001-02 and transferred to the municipal corporations of Baran, Rajakheda, Shree Madhopur, Reengas and the municipality of Jodhpur. Presently, a token provision is being kept for this purpose.

Reimbursement of Octroi: The Rajasthan government abolished octroi on 1 August 1998, and this is being reimbursed to all ULBs through the state grant. It was given to the ULBs by making an increment of 10 per cent per year over collection of octroi in 1997-98. In 1999-2000, Rs. 320.65 crore was allocated to the ULBs and a provision of Rs. 352.73

crore was made for 2000-2001. The state government has taken effective steps to make the octroi grant available to all ULBs. The sanction of whole amount (as per the approved Plan ceiling) with a break up of monthly instalments is issued in the beginning of every year. The sanction order mentions the fact that the concerned treasury shall credit the monthly instalment in the public deposit account of the respective ULBs.

General Grant: The general grant is distributed to all the municipal committees/corporation/ municipalities in two instalments. A sum of Rs. 2106.13 lakh was distributed as general grant to all municipal corporations/councils at the rate of Rs. 12.50 per head, and to second class municipalities at the rate of Rs.25 per head, while the third and fourth class municipalities received funds at the rate of Rs. 37.50 per head in 2000-2001.

Own Resource Mobilisation: The state government has given high priority to improve and enhance the ULBs' "own income revenue". The views of selected ULBs representatives and officers were sought on this matter at various fora. A sub-working group on this subject was also constituted during the preparation of the Tenth Five Year Plan. Currently, a task force constituted for state finances is also considering this issue.

Land Use Conversion: Section 173 (A) of the Rajasthan Municipalities Act, 1959 has been modified to make state government permission mandatory for the conversion of any type of land. The Land Utilisation Conversion Act, 2000, has also been enacted.

Regularisation of *Kuchchee Bastis*: In 1999, the state government decided to regularise *kuchchee bastis* which had come up on or before 15 August 1998. This provided security of land tenure to the existing residents of these areas.

According to a survey conducted to assess the number of existing slums and gather information on the family status characteristics, there were 2,113 *kuchchee bastis* in the state, with 2,37,474 families. Out of these, possessions of 63,817 families were found eligible for regularisation. Up to March 2003, 51,473 *pattas* (legal titles) have been allotted against very nominal charges. To protect the rights of women, it was decided to issue *pattas* in the joint name of husband and wife. The maximum limit of regularisation was raised from 50 sq. yards to 300 sq. yards so that a maximum number of people might benefit. After regularisation, the work of providing basic civic amenities like roads, drains, electricity etc. has been started.

Conversion of Agricultural Land: In the urban areas, cooperative societies and individuals have sold out plots on agricultural land without any approval by any competent authority. To regularise construction on such agricultural land, the state government promulgated an ordinance on 17 June 1999 to amend the Land Revenue Act 1956, Rajasthan Agriculture Act, 1955, Rajasthan Urban Improvement Trust Act, 1959, Rajasthan Municipality Act 1959 and Jaipur Development Authority Act of 1982. Of 41,395 cases, 1,093 have been resolved. Regularisation of such agricultural land yielded Rs.1.15 crore in 2000 and Rs. 8.75 crore in 2001.

- Settlement committees have been constituted to resolve the disputes and complicated cases. The state government has provided powers under Section 170 and 203 of the Rajasthan Municipalities Act to competent authorities to check encroachments on government land.
- Under the revised order for regularisation of *kuchchee bastis* issued on 24 July 2000, *pattas* are to be issued free of cost to Harijans and tribals residing in these areas for the last 20 years or more.
- The state government has asked all presiding officers of ULBs to convene meetings every month to resolve the disputes and complicated cases.
- Under Section 297 of the Rajasthan Municipalities Act, a leaseholder of a municipal corporation/council/municipality who deposits past dues by 31 December 2000 would be given a rebate of 50 per cent on the interest on principal money.
- It has been decided that the income of a ULBs could be raised through hoardings installed on annual contract basis.
- The Rajasthan Municipalities Act has been amended to ban the use of polythene of up to 20 microns.
- Sections 7 and 18 of the Rajasthan Municipalities (Land Abolition) Rule, 1974 have been amended to allow the state government to provide rebate in charges for regularisation of *kuchchee bastis.*

However, all these legal provisions vest enormous powers in the hands of officials. The resultant procedural hurdles do not serve much purpose, and given the growing demand for houses, conversion of agricultural land into residential land continues to remain a major problem in cities.

It, therefore, seems desirable to simplify the process of land conversion. The UITs and JDA should adopt the Haryana model of land conversion, according to which any individual or group of individuals can be granted a right for developing a colony provided that they have adequate land and capital, abide by the relevant rules, such as payment of periphery and conversion charges to the concerned body. The JDA has attempted this approach and land has been given to the private sector for construction of residential houses for NRIs, including the development works. The work on this project is in progress. The local authority can stipulate that a certain percentage of the plots so converted will be allotted to the weaker sections at a concessional rate.

The procedure for collecting taxes must be taxpayer friendly. The existing house tax system needs a thorough review and the possibility of adopting the Patna model should be explored.

Stamp Duty: Stamp duty is generally levied on the value of a property sale transaction. Table 8.11 shows the rates of stamp duty in some major states.

TABLE 8.11

Stamp Duty on Transfer of Properties

State	*Area*	*Stamp Duty (%)*
Andhra Pradesh	Urban Areas & Municipal Areas	8
	Other Areas	6
Delhi		8
Gujarat	Rural Areas	12.5
	Urban Areas	8
Rajasthan		11.5
Haryana	Rural Areas	12.5
	Urban Areas	15.5
Karnataka	Bangalore	10
	Other Cities	9
Kerala	Municipal Areas	8.5
	Rural Areas	6
Maharashtra	Less than Rs.5.0 lakh	1.7
	Rs.5-10 lakh	3.8
	Rs.10-20 lakh	5.94
Orissa	Urban Areas	12.7
	Rural Areas	10.7
Punjab		7.0
Tamil Nadu	Urban Areas	8.0
	Rural Areas	7.0
West Bengal	Calcutta	8.0
	Other Areas	6.0
Uttar Pradesh	General	8.0
	Developed Areas	10.0

Source: Department of Urban Local Bodies, Government of Rajasthan.

Stamp duty rates are very high in Haryana, Rajasthan, Orissa and Gujarat. In Gujarat, the stamp duty in rural areas is higher than in urban areas, while in some states including Rajasthan, Andhra Pradesh and Maharashtra, there is no stamp duty on the registration of rural properties.

The Rajasthan government is attempting to simplify and rationalise stamp duty. District-level committee rates have been rationalised and the process of computerisation of registration of the documents have also been taken up in selected cities and towns. Review of stamp duty payable on items such as housing loans, mortgages security and amalgamation of companies etc. is under consideration. High rates of stamp duty only encourage under-valuation of property transactions. As a result, the actual revenue accruing to the state exchequer is very low.

Financial Transfers to ULBS

Inter-governmental financial transfers are a significant source of revenue. The Tenth Finance Commission and the SFCs have made recommendations in this regard. The purposes for which the per capita grant is given under the recommendations of the Tenth Finance Commission are purchase of sanitary equipment; street lighting; improvement of *kuchchee bastis*; construction of roads, drains, and improvement of fire fighting services

The recommendations of the SFC as per the 74th Amendment are:

- A total of 2.18 per cent of the net state tax proceeds should be given to the ULBs. Of this, 1.68 per cent is meant for PRIs and 0.50 per cent for ULBs.
- Share in sales tax, registration and stamp duty on the sale of immovable property in urban areas, motor vehicles tax, entertainment tax and abolition of octroi exemptions on the goods consumed by the RSEB and PHED should be provided to ULBs.
- ULBs should be compensated by the state government for revenue loss due to abolition of exemption of octroi on the goods consumed by industries in the first five years of their operation.
- Formation of a Local Finance Corporation with a seed capital of Rs. 150 crore a year for five years to finance the development works of the ULBs and to raise funds from financial institutions.

A high-powered committee should be set up immediately to go into the whole gamut of legal issues, fund devolution, taxation powers and responsibility to generate own resources by ULBs and its recommendation should be implemented at the earliest.

RUIDP Report on Resource Mobilisation

The RUIDP Report, 1998, has given the following suggestions for enhancing the financial resources of ULBs.

Land/Building or House Tax: Land and building tax was levied in 11 cities with population of over 150,000 (1991 Census). The total revenue generated in 1996-97 was Rs. 32 crore, with Jaipur contributing more than half the share. At least 10 per cent of this revenue may be transferred to the ULBs of the city/ town. Many towns and cities (Kota, Udaipur, to name just two) are not levying this tax. The tax is grossly under-utilised because the annual rental value (ARV), the base of the tax, does not reflect the market rent. The tax was, therefore, abolished in 2003.

There is need for discussions on issues relating to taxes on land, building, house, street, profession and other issues relating to revenue realisation. There is need to make these sources more vibrant and also to ensure that processes are simple, transparent and tax payer friendly.

In 2002, in line with the recommendations of the Administrative Reforms Commission, simplified house tax assessment proposals were prepared by the Local Self Government Department. An area-based simplified assessment procedure of house tax was proposed and the government has taken a decision to implement the revised house tax plan from 1 April 2003. The proposed scheme is objective and extremely simple.

Database for property tax, profession/vocation tax and fees/charges: A comprehensive and reliable database must be prepared through compulsory self-assessment by landlords/occupants. The details submitted may be counterchecked and reconciled by municipal officials.

Profession Tax: Since the state government has already levied profession tax, it should consider a formula for sharing the proceeds with ULBs.

Non-tax sources: The revenue from non-tax sources, including proceeds accruing from sale of land and UIT contribution of 15 per cent of its sale of land, are of great importance to the urban areas. Certain aspects of the license fees and rental property are also important.

License Fees: Revenue from license fees for trade or commercial activity has immense potential but this source has remained under-utilised. It is necessary to take advantage of this potential.

Trade License Rates: The rates of trade licenses in Rajasthan are low and are not revised periodically. In Udaipur, rates fixed 20 years ago are still in operation. Periodic rate enhancement of at least 10 per cent would be more reasonable than sharp increases at long intervals. Despite the huge increase in trading activities, the number of licenses issued has been stagnant in many cities. This shows that the coverage of the tax has been limited, leading to loss of revenue.

Municipal Rental Property: An area-based rental system consistent with the market rents may be considered over the present method of long leases. The total inventory of the rental property may be prepared on the basis of age of construction, area, year of leasing, rents obtained, etc. to help future planning. Municipal properties, which have proved to be unproductive and do not generate adequate income, may be sold at the market rate and the sum may be put in the fixed deposit. The state government has decided to give shops/plots which were provided on rent, fees, and license basis, 99-year leases on a one-time payment of rent/lease money. This will enhance the income of the concerned ULB and provide the right of ownership to the tenant.

Revenue Loss: Heavy loss of revenue is incurred due to under-assessment of house/property for tax purposes and also delay in collecting taxes/fees.

New Sources of Revenue: Additional resource mobilisation efforts should be taken, which could take the form of new taxes/levies at the municipal and state levels by suitably amending the Municipal Act. It is necessary to introduce other levies as composite levies as has been done in many states. In Vadodara and Ahmedabad in Gujarat, a portion of the property tax rate is earmarked for general city purposes. The rate also includes designated percentages covering other purposes, including a water tax, education tax, health cess, etc. Cess is an earmarked additional levy for a specific purpose.

Street Tax: Investment in a city's infrastructure enhances the value of land and buildings and this leads to higher rental and capital values. Cities/towns are justified in taking advantage of the rising property values (in terms of rental and capital). In Mumbai, the corporation introduced the street tax on the basis of the annual rental value of the property. It has also constituted a road development fund and earmarked the revenue yield for the development of local roads. The collection mechanism of the tax has to be effective so that arrears do not accumulate.

Municipal Bonds: ULBs could use municipal bonds for selected services, for which costs can be recovered. The steps taken in Ahmedabad to use municipal bonds to finance the city's infrastructure could be studied. Municipal bonds require a return at least equal to the market rate of interest. This situation assumes a reliable delivery of the service and a high degree of credibility with the local body as well as an effective mechanism of cost recovery. However, Jaipur is the only city in Rajasthan in a position to issue such bonds.

Other sources: Other sources include betterment levy, vacant land tax, vehicle registration fees, levy on cultural shows (for priced admissions only), conversion charges from single to multi-storey buildings, etc.

Shared taxes: There is a strong case for additional transfers from the state government to the municipalities. Fifty per cent of the country's GDP is generated from the urban areas by nearly one-third of the population.

Share in sales tax: ULBs can be given a share in the sales tax in the form of an urban development surcharge on certain selected commodities like petrol and petroleum products; automobiles and auto components; refrigerators and related equipment; and building material.

Non-conventional methods of raising resources: Some cities in Andhra Pradesh, Karnataka and Kerala levy a nominal monthly fee of Rs. 10 per household for garbage disposal. This may be replicated in Rajasthan's cities as well. With building activity on the rise, huge quantities of building debris and waste material will accumulate in the city. Since removal involves tremendous costs, municipal authorities can recover the cost from the house builder or developer.

Entertainment tax: This is a shared tax constituting part of the general revenues and has remained stagnant over several years. An increase in this share can be built into the system.

Grants-in-aid: A block grant at the rate of Rs. 12.50 per capita for general purposes is given to tide over a budgetary crisis of local bodies. These grants are given in addition to those recommended by the SFC

These recommendations need to be considered in their totality by a high-powered committee and their legal aspects examined along with the responsibilities of these bodies. ULBs need to receive mandatory legal powers for levying different taxes, and grants to these bodies should be given only when ULBs have collected these taxes.

Operations and Maintenance

Municipal expenditure can be categorised into three main components: wages and salaries; operations and maintenance (O&M); and interest payments. Though expenditure on O&M accounts for only one-fifth of the total expenditure of municipal services, most local bodies fail to recover the costs.[4] According to a National Institute of Public Finance and Policy (NIPFP) report, *Trends and Structure of Urban Local Bodies in the Context of Urbanisation in India*, per capita revenue expenditure in ULBs was Rs. 165.07 for sewerage and drainage and Rs. 5.40 for street lighting. Total per capita expenditure on core services has been Rs. 497.24 in the case of Rajasthan against Rs. 747.02 at the country level. The O&M of basic infrastructure and services in urban areas are under serious fiscal stress, making it difficult to even manage existing services, while the question of augmenting them does not arise at all. With extremely low or practically non-existent user charges, there is little or no increase in the revenue base of ULBs which, barring a few exceptions, are becoming increasingly dependent on government support for their O&M requirements.

Besides resource constraints, municipal administrations are also beset with the problems of ineffective local governance, inefficient management practices, poor planning process, lack of periodical revision of municipal tax rates/user charges, and poor information system. They are burdened with excess manpower, staff responsibilities are unclear and often fragmented and their capabilities and motivation to deal with the increasingly complex urban needs are severely limited.

Lack of Sanitation Facilities

There has been gross neglect of sanitation services, not just over the last few years, but over decades. Many cities do not have sewerage systems, and even where they do exist, their capacities are not adequate to cope with the increasing requirements. During the International Drinking Water Supply and Sanitation Decade (1981-90), it was recommended that almost 100

4. India Infrastructure Report, 2001; **3i Network, Oxford University Press.

per cent population in Class I urban centres of the country be covered by proper sewerage and sewerage treatment facilities. However, a number of cities in the state, including the developed ones, are only partially covered by sewerage services.

In Rajasthan, 4 million urban population did not have access to sanitation facilities in 1991. The number rose to 4.8 million in 1996 and to 5.8 million in 2001, and is expected to increase to 7.1 million in 2006 and 8.8 million by 2011. One of the reasons for insufficient sanitation facilities is poverty and the higher priority that poor people give to other necessities of life. In order to reduce the health hazards posed by improper disposal of human waste, septic tanks and private toilets are urgently needed.

A similar situation exists with regard to the disposal of waste water in housing units. Only 50 per cent of houses have a system of pipes carrying waste water to the roadside drains. The rest dispose their waste water either on open land or streets with no drains. This creates an unhygienic environment around the house, which is not only a health hazard but also leads to disputes among neighbours.

Solid Waste Management

Solid waste generation in India's urban areas varies between 294 grams and 484 grams per capita per day. On an average, around 40-60 per cent of total waste generated remains uncollected, which becomes one of the biggest sources of pollution. Rajasthan's cities are no exception.

Rajasthan's cities and towns lack a proper solid waste management system. There is no network of door-to-door collection of solid waste. Most of the garbage is dumped on unofficial municipal collecting points, which are of inadequate capacity, or adjacent to the road. Often people dump garbage in open grounds, ponds and nearby drains which causes blockage.

Collection of such garbage is also poor. Jaipur generates about 400 tonnes of solid waste every day, but only 40 per cent is collected. The garbage that is collected is transported to dumping sites at the periphery of the city. The indiscriminate dumping of waste in the nearest available low-lying area often causes damage to the soil. No city in Rajasthan practises scientific methods of sanitary landfill or conversion of waste into compost or energy. None of the cities have arrangements to separate garbage before collection. In large cities, therefore, the landfill sites and garbage bins attract a large number of poor people who scavenge for bits of metal, paper and plastic to supply to the recycling trade.

Solid waste management and sewerage/sanitation need to be undertaken according to the best practices available elsewhere. Making compost out of solid waste and making this available to farmers is one solution and Central loan and subsidy or even external funding should be sought for this purpose.

Overstaffing, low output and public dissatisfaction characterise the urban solid waste management sector. It is, therefore, necessary to improve the quality of service and reduce the operating costs. The sector will be able to deliver satisfactory services to urban dwellers only with appropriate institutional reforms like privatisation and rationalisation of the existing staff. This sector has the potential to recover costs by providing service for a fee at the household level and from the sale of compost. Hence, both financial and economic internal rates of return are viable, although with proper appraisal.

In 2001, a policy on solid waste management was formulated. Work is under way on installing waste management plant and machinery with private sector cooperation for 20 Class-1 cities with population of 100,000 and above. A biomedical waste disposal and treatment plant has started functioning in Jaipur. This project is being implemented as a public-private partnership on a Build-Own-Operate (BOO) basis. Efforts are being made to establish such plants in other cities with population of 100,000 and above.

Drainage Control

Drainage is a serious problem in many cities because of the inadequacy of drainage facilities, poor maintenance by the line agencies and encroachment on the drainage channels for construction and dumping of waste in drains. During monsoons, some areas get waterlogged for days together, which increases the mosquito menace and also causes damage to life and property. The cities facing serious drainage problems are Ajmer, Kota, Bikaner, Jodhpur and Jaipur.

Relation with Parastatal Agencies

The state government has not paid sufficient attention to the requisite change in the institutional arrangements for urban infrastructure and the role of municipal governments *vis-à-vis* those of parastatal agencies. Municipal bodies are assisted by parastatal agencies, operating either at the state or city level to carry out various functions including water supply and sanitation. Such agencies like the PHED, JDA, UITs etc., usually undertake land acquisition and development works, and take up income yielding projects such as marketplaces and commercial complexes. Municipal bodies have largely been left only with the functions of garbage collection/disposal, street lighting, maintenance of inner city roads, and registration of births and deaths, which yield no revenue. That is the reason for their poor financial health.

Municipal Finances

The state of municipal finances in India suggests that the present revenues of ULBs are insufficient to meet the growing expenditure. Municipal expenditures are thus constrained by the level of resources available. In Rajasthan, municipal revenues are extremely low and do not permit ULBs to take up the required programmes such as sanitation, cleanliness, streetlights, drainage, etc. Often repairs and maintenance of services are poor and expenditure on capital works is postponed (Appendix A–8.12). Even though ULBs are now authorised to impose additional taxes to mobilise revenue, yet they have not taken any initiative so far in this direction.

Resource Mobilisation

Urban areas are governed by the Rajasthan Municipalities Act, 1959, which lays down the sources of revenue to be utilised and the functions to be performed. However, there are wide variations among the municipal bodies in utilising their designated sources of revenue. ULBs have so far failed to tap the tax potential under their jurisdiction. Although the SFCs have touched upon a variety of aspects on resource mobilisation, yet not much headway has been made. A reliable database needs to be created and updated periodically. This should be followed by a comprehensive study on the restructuring of the municipal finances that includes a management information system (MIS) and training programmes to make the ULBs more service oriented.

The revenue from conventional sources like the property tax (house tax), professional/vocation tax and trade/commerce license fees as well as sewerage and household garbage charges etc. may be collected along with immediate action for improving the quality of their services.

A uniform Municipal Corporation Act, if promulgated, may help overcome many of the structural deficiencies. Revenue from the new sources like the street tax, municipal bonds and an appropriate share from state taxes like entertainment tax, surcharge on stamp duty and levy of surcharge on selective commodities subject to sales tax, betterment charge, charge on conversion of agriculture land to non-agriculture use, charge on the conversion of the buildings from single to multi-storey, taxing priced entertainment, etc. should be considered, for enhancing the revenue of ULBs (Details in Appendix A–8.13).

BOX 8.1

Guidelines to Reform Property Tax

The Union Ministry of Urban Development has issued guidelines to reform property tax. These are: substitution of the existing ARV system by a mix of capital value (CV) and area detail system by decomposing property tax into land tax and building tax; and introduction of user charges for directly chargeable services such as water supply, waste management etc. with direct relation to cost recovery for other services through a building tax on the basis of area details of buildings.

Other suggestions concern the modality for relating building tax to cost of services, determination of tax liability, tax exemptions, property tax record management, assessment cycle of property tax, system of appeals, etc. Building tax is proposed to be levied by adopting an area-based property tax system on the Patna and Andhra Pradesh patterns. While the Andhra Pradesh model uses the values obtained through sample survey of prevailing market rents for different categories of properties in terms of location, quality of construction, land use, age and physical area, the Patna model uses values arrived at suo moto. The guidelines hence suggest a mix of these two models.

Role and Responsibilities of ULBs in Public-Private Partnerships

Public-private partnerships in the provision of municipal services have become common and there have been several experiments across the country (See Box 8.1). These experiments could be replicated in Rajasthan after a careful study.

The PPP model has also been initiated in the Jaipur Municipal Corporation (JMC). The work of garbage transportation, maintenance of streetlights, sewer lines and parks has been given on contract basis and the results were found to be better than before. The Centre for Development Studies is working in the field of solid waste management. Initially, the JMC was providing a mutually agreed grant per household to CDS. Later, CDS started collecting Rs. 20 per month per household for door-to-door collection and segregation of solid

BOX 8.2

Successful Public-Private Partnersips

Rajkot: The Rajkot Municipal Corporation (RMC) has given the maintenance of streetlights, cleaning of public toilets, maintenance of gardens, afforestation, etc. to private contractors and has also undertaken various entertainment projects. The RMC has been able to save a significant amount of money and has also been able to narrow the demand-supply gaps in the provision of services.

CIDCO, Mumbai: The public sector City and Industrial Development Corporation (CIDCO), Mumbai has given the collection of its various service charges to Senior Citizens Clubs whom it pays 1 per cent as commission. Collecting the service charges on its own would cost CIDCO three times more. Sweeping of roads, garbage collection and disposal, maintenance of drains, spraying of insecticides, etc. have been assigned to 15 contractors on a yearly basis. The work is supervised by CIDCO's sanitary inspectors. The cost to CIDCO for seven townships is only Rs. 42.6 lakh against the Rs. 1 crore that it would have had to incur if it had done the work departmentally.

Alandur, Tamil Nadu: The Alandur Sewerage Project is proposed to be implemented on the PPP pattern. There will be a construction contract for the sewage collection system, whereas the treatment plants will be managed on a build-operate-transfer (BOT) basis. O&M for the collection system as well as treatment plant will also be on a contract basis. Cost recovery will be made through sewerage tax, sewerage charge, connection charge, general revenues and state government support. The expected gains from more efficient and cost-effective working are likely to be large.

BOX 8.3

Suggested Provisions for Involving the Private Sector

Local bodies should primarily concentrate on essential urban services such as water supply, sewerage, drainage, and solid waste disposal. The Municipal Acts do permit 'any person' to deliver specific services, including construction and maintenance of water works, purchasing or taking on lease any water works, and storing and conveyance of water. With the passing of the 74th Constitution Amendment Act, a majority of states have amended their respective Municipal Acts. According to the amended municipal legislations in Maharashtra, the municipality may either discharge such duty or perform it through any agency. Thus, inserting specific clauses enabling the involvement of the private sector will go a long way in improving the quality of services in the urban areas of the country.

waste. The work of privatisation of these activities in other ULBs is also being initiated. PPPs have also been initiated in the JDA and other UITs.

Municipal Accounting Systems

The existing system of single cash accounting in ULBs in Rajasthan does not address the financial position of municipal bodies. Suitable changes in the accounting system have been an important issue in municipal financial management. The state government has introduced double entry accounting system in the JMC on a pilot basis. It has been working successfully for the last two years. A similar system is being introduced in five other ULBs.

Devolution of additional taxes, rationalised user charges and fiscal autonomy to ULBs to set their own rates are urgently required. Proper standards and transparent accounting systems have to be put in place before municipalities can go public for collecting funds without state support. In short, ULBs have to develop their financial credibility and embark upon a way to a self-reliant system without government guarantees.

A committee of experts needs to be set up to introduce a computerised accounting system for all municipalities. This could be done by the Central government and the Central and state governments should make the adoption of a computerised accounting system mandatory for claiming financial assistance.

APPENDIX A–8.1

Towns of Rajasthan (Population of One Lakh and Above, 1991 and 2001)

City	*Population of Cities*			*Growth Rate*		*Sex Ratio 2001*
	Person	*Male*	*Female*	*1981-91*	*1991-2001*	
2	3	4	5	6	7	8
Jaipur	2324319	123711	1084608	49.56	59.37	875
Jodhpur	856034	455860	400174	31.59	28.48	878
Kota	704731	374570	330161	50.00	31.14	881
Bikaner	529007	282450	246557	44.69	27.08	873
Ajmer	490138	256379	233759	7.22	21.71	912
Udaipur	389317	205319	183998	32.67	26.17	896
Sub Total	**5293549**					
Bhilwara	280185	148642	131543	50.02	52.30	885
Alwar	265850	143238	122612	44.14	26.51	856
Ganganagar	222833	121877	100956	30.55	37.99	828
Bharatpur	205104	110148	94956	49.02	30.74	862
Pali	187571	99258	88313	49.44	37.07	890
Sikar	195506	96646	88860	44.00	25.11	919
Tonk	135663	70135	65528	29.08	35.34	934
Hanumangarh	129654	69583	60071	37.73	56.71	863
Beawar	125923	65569	60354	18.58	17.99	920
Kishangarh	116156	61025	55131	32.11	41.74	903
Gangapur city	105336	56088	49248	49.67	52.91	878
Sawai Madhopur	101994	53942	48052	31.49	31.28	891
Churu	101853	53099	48754	33.48	22.93	918
Jhunjhunu	100476	52814	47662	53.01	39.19	902

APPENDIX A–8.2

Water Demand and Supply in Selected Towns

Name of town	*Population*		*Water Demand*	*Water Supply PHED*
	2001	*2011 (Projected)*		
Ajmer Zone				
Beawar	167500	—	—	19 lakh gallons/day
Bikaner Zone				
Bikaner	—	—	—	5 million gallons/day
Nokha	70000	—	—	2.5 lakh gallons/day
Sardarshahar	107930	—	30 gallons/individual/day	18 gallons/individual/day
Churu	91215	—	—	12 lakh gallons/day
Sujangarh	99500	—	29.69 gallons/individual/day	13.19 gallons/individual/day
Deedwana	43000	55000	15 lakh gallons/day	.70 lakh gallons/day
Jaipur Zone				
Fatehpur	95000		NA	11.75 gallons/individual/day
Sikar	203000	NA	NA	16 lakh gallons/day
Jhunjhunu	105175	150000	—	6.01 lakh gallons/day
Shahpura	30000	50000	NA	241.9 lakh gallons/day
Deeg	43116	54545	29.69 gallons/individual/day	14.29 gallons/individual/day
Pali	180000	225000	54 lakh gallons/day	25 lakh gallons/day
Jodhpur Zone				
Balotra	70000	100000	Not available	5.5 lakh gallons/day
Sumerpur-Sheoganj	70000	NA	20 gallons/individual/day	10 gallons/individual/day
Kota Zone				
Ramganjmandi	55000	—	—	2.12 lakh gallons/day
Bundi	105000	—	24 lakh gallons/day	12 lakh gallons/day
Anta	27000	37800	NA	2.19 lakh gallons/day
Pratapgarh	37500	47000	21.997 gallons/individual/day	8.79 gallons/individual/day
Deoli	26000	38000	NA	3.6 lakh gallons/day
Alwar Zone				
Alwar	NA	NA	49.49 gallons/individual/day	19.79 gallons/individual/day
Nimbahera	64642	—	30 gallons/individual/day	22 gallons/individual/day

Source: Draft Master Plan, Town Planning Department, GoR, 1985 & 2000.

APPENDIX A–8.3

Water Supply Status in Towns

Particulars	*Number*	*Percentage*
Town fully covered requires no augmentation	27	12.16
Town fully covered requires service level augmentation	31	13.96
Town partially covered requires extension of distribution network	32	14.41
Town partially covered requires extension network and capacity augmentation	132	59.47
Total	222	100

Source: Database Management Information, PHED, GoR 2000.

APPENDIX A–8.4

Water Supply Interval

7 Towns having interval of water supply	96 hours
10 Towns having interval of water supply	72 hours
29 Towns having interval of water supply	48 hours
176 Towns having interval of water supply	24 hours

Source: PHED, GoR 2002.

APPENDIX A–8.5

Water Supply Connections

Water supply	*Jaipur*	*Ajmer*	*Udaipur*	*Kota*	*Bikaner*	*Jodhpur*
Own PHED connection	53.6	73.0	71.1	63.1	79.9	90.1
PHED supply from neighbours	2.8	3.9	1.2	2.4	1.4	1.3
Stand post, public hand pump, water tanker, supplier	20.6	14.3	22.1	14.8	18.0	7.6
Traditional sources (well, pond, tanks)	7.5	1.6	0.9	3.8	0.7	0.4
Private tube-wells and private hand pumps	15.5	7.2	4.7	16.0	0.0	0.7
Total	100	100	100	100	100	100

Source: RUIDP Consultants' Survey.

APPENDIX A–8.6

Schemes Being Implemented by PHED

The details of ongoing major projects are given below:

Rajiv Gandhi Lift Canal Project (Second Phase) for Jodhpur city and rural areas. This project has been sanctioned with a revised cost of Rs. 94.47 crore. This scheme will cater the demand of projected population of 14.40 lakh in the year 2011.The project is being executed on single responsibility basis. Work orders have been issued to M/s SPML and survey work is completed. Raising of canal by CR stone dowel masonry is completed in a length of 14.4 Km. Approval for drawings & designs is under process. Supply of 4069m steel pipes of 1626mm dia. has been completed. Rs. 28.01 Crore spent till July 2003. The project is proposed to be completed by December 2004.Bisalpur-Jaipur project had been originally sanctioned costing Rs. 1100 crore. A meeting was held under the chairmanship of Hon'ble Chief Minister on 16-11-02 wherein first phase of the project costing Rs. 690 crore and its funding pattern has been approved. It was decided that the project shall be implemented under RUIDP. Till date appropriate necessary action regarding settlement of involuntary effected persons is in full swing. An amount of Rs. 10.00 crore has been spent which includes payment to Railways and JDA. Action is being taken up by RUIDP for tendering for major components of the project. Mansi-Wakal project for Udaipur city has been sanctioned costing Rs. 60.00 crore to provide 36 mld water to Udaipur city and Hindustan Zinc Ltd. in the ratio of 70:30. The project is being executed by M/s HZL and the work is under progress. Allotment of diversion of 2.5 hectares forestland for mining of masonry stone for constriction of dam has been approved in principle with certain conditions by Forest Department, Lucknow vide letter dated 21-07-03. Total expenditure incurred up to June 2003 is Rs. 23. 16 Crore. The construction of dam is targeted to be completed by February 2004. Payment of Rs. 3.32 crore has been made to RVPNL against their demand note. RVPNL has started the work.First phase of Gandheli Sahwa project (German aided) with a revised cost of Rs. 399.27 crore is under execution. This was further revised for a cost of Rs. 402.57 crore taking provision of benefiting additional 12 villages of Tara Nagar tehsil. It was renamed as APANI YOJNA. By this scheme 65 habs of Nohar tehsil, 52 of Rawatsar, 105 of Sardarshahar 37 of Rajgarh tehsil, 98 of Taranagar and 13 of Churu tehsil (i.e. total 370 habitations) will be benefited. Up to June 2003, 286 villages have been commissioned incurring an expenditure of Rs. 356 crore. The proposed date of completion is March 2004. Chambal Bharatpur Dholpur project of Rs. 166.50 for districts of Bharatpur & Dholpur with Chambal river has been sanctioned. This will benefit 212 villages of Bharatpur & Dholpur & City of Bharatpur (phase-I). Detailed work order for the execution has been issued on 05.12.02 to M/s Essar Projects Ltd. Mumbai. The firm has started topographical survey, design, soil investigation and detailed engineering work. Land acquisition work is under progress. Up to July-2003 an expenditure of Rs 3.19 Crore has been incurred. The project is proposed to be completed by May-2005. Barmer Lift Project costing Rs. 424.91 crore has been framed to cover the demand of 573 villages, 1684 Dhanis and Barmer City. Survey work under progress. The proposal has been sent to GoI for funding under ARWSP (DDP).Bhageri Ka Naka Project amounting to Rs. 128.40 crore is sanctioned to benefit 206 villages of tehsil Nathdwara, Girwa, Rajsamand & Railmagara. Under the project a dam of 311.68 MCFT on Banas river on upstream of Nansamand Dam near village Manchind will be constructed by Irrigation Deptt., for which an amount of Rs. 5.10 crore has been deposited. The work - orders for transmission main and other works from intake to Nathdwara headworks has been issued to the firm. Work is under progress. Survey work for preparation of Technical packages of various regional schemes from different headworks is under process. Till date an expenditure of Rs. 8.01 crore has been incurred.

Chambal Sawai Madhopur-Nadauti Project is under execution to cover the water demand of 1067 villages and 3 towns (50% water demand) of District Sawai Madhopur & Karauli covering the areas of tehsils Khandaer, Chauth Ka Barwaada , Bonli, Malarana Dungar, Sawai Madhopur, Sapotara, Gangapur, Bamanwas, Hindon, Nadauti, Karauli and TodaBhim. Phase–I of Rs. 240.88 crore has been sanctioned. The project proposes to cover 215 villages of District Sawai Madhopur and 385 villages of District Karauli. Tender for work under single point responsibility basis has been invited and are under process. The single responsibility work mainly includes works from in take well at Chambal river to Toda Bhim. The technical bids have been opened and are under consideration. The project is proposed to be completed by March 2006. Till date an expenditure incurred on the project is Rs. 0.12 crore. Churu–Bisau Project amounting to Rs.119.04 crore is under execution which targets to cover 3 towns i.e. Churu, Ratannagar and Bisau and 169 villages (i.e. 84 villages of district Churu & 85 villages of district Jhunjhunu). The project is targeted to be completed by March 2004. Total expenditure incurred on the project is up to June-2003 is Rs. 69.40 crore. Dudu–Bisalpur Project has been prepared to cover the demand for the Year 2016 of 1488 villages of tehsils Phagi, Chaksu, Dudu, Fulera, Bassi, Malpura, Todaraisingh, Pipaloo (Tonk), Niwai and Nawa and seven urban towns viz. Chaksu, Sambhar-Lake, Fulera, Naraina, Malpura, Niwai and Todaraisingh. The project is proposed to be completed in two phases. In phase – I,693 villages will be benefited and in phase-II, 795 villages & 7 towns will be benefited. Tenders for transmissions mains have been invited and have been being processed. The project is proposed to be completed by June 2005.

APPENDIX A–8.7

Major Drinking Water Schemes of Surface Water

Drinking Water Schemes	*Sanctioned Cost in Crore*
Bharatpur from Chambal	166.50
Mansi Wakal by HZL (Ph.l)	60.00
F.C.P. Kekri Sarawar 94 villages (Revised)	44.35
F.C.P. Nasirabad 61 villages	61.03
F.C.P. Bhinay Masoda	43.99
R.G.L.C. Phase II Jodhpur (Revised)	94.47
Churu Bissau Project	119.04
Bageri Ka Naka (Rajsamand) 206 villages	128.40
Bisalpur-Dudu WS Project(1352 villages)	216.55
Chambal-Baler-S. Madhopur WS Project	240.88
Bhilwara-Kankrolia Ghati	29.13
Barmer Lift Canal WS Project	424.91
Churu Jhunjhunu (Phase II) WS Project	405.08
Apani Yojana	402.57
Jaipur (Bisalpur)	1100.00
Jawai Jodhpur P/L Project	153.00
TOTAL	**3689.90**

Source: PHED, GoR, Jaipur, Rajasthan, 2001.

APPENDIX A–8.8

Budget of Drinking Water Under Five Year Plans

(Rs. in Crore)

Five Year Plans	*Urban Area*	*Rural Area*	*Total*
First Five Year Plan (1951-56)	0.88	0.005	0.885
Second Five Year Plan (1956-61)	4.79	0.15	4.94
Third Five Year Plan (1961-66)	4.64	2.89	7.53
1966-69	2.58	2.30	4.88
Fourth Five Year Plan (1969-74)	11.50	20.92	32.42
1974-75	2.37	5.905	8.275
Fifth Five Year Plan (1975-80)	22.89	54.86	77.75
Sixth Five Year Plan (1980-85)	63.74	248.34	312.08
Seventh Five Year Plan (1985-90)	178.67	398.84	577.51
1990-92	99.84	196.61	296.45
Eighth Five Year Plan (1992-97)	632.14	919.54	1551.68
Ninth Five Year Plan (97-upto Dec. 2000)	408.11	1028.74	1436.85
Total	**1432.15**	**2879.10**	**4311.25**

Source: Annual Progress Report, PHED, Jaipur, Rajasthan, 2000-2001.

APPENDIX A–8.9

Income and Expenditure of PHED in Rajasthan

(Rs. lakh)

Year	*Sewerage Schemes (Revenue)*	*Sewerage & Service Fees (Revenue)*	*Urban Water Supply Scheme Income and Expenditure*			*Total Urban & Rural Revenue*	*Expenditure on UWSS (Urban Water Supply Schemes)*				*Total Expenditure on Urban & Rural*
			Water Connection	*Public Tap*	*Total*		*Direct Expend.*	*Indirect Expend.*	*Interest on Insurance Loan*	*Total Expend.*	
1991-92	39.66	11.27	3707.47	150.00	3857.47	4925.57	8453.99	297.85	384.18	9436.02	15644.86
1992-93	54.00	34.06	3770.14	150.00	3920.14	5266.43	9764.43	733.07	491.84	10989.34	18012.21
1993-94	56.91	29.40	3902.58	150.00	4052.50	5568.28	12295.80	732.74	985.75	14014.26	24542.70
1994-95	56.10	33.10	4417.43	150.00	4567.43	6542.41	14149.38	719.45	1079.89	15948.72	26699.51
1995-96	80.22	30.90	5172.57	150.00	5322.57	7576.22	17689.68	720.11	1111.75	19521.54	31563.28
1996-97	70.90	122.03	5361.53	150.00	5511.53	7845.11	20684.88	723.66	1448.72	22857.26	37200.25
1997-98	80.43	93.07	6769.25	150.00	6919.25	9679.20	24717.16	716.71	1600.38	27034.25	43802.41
1998-99	92.36	86.00	8514.28	225.00	8739.28	12160.58	29508.67	719.56	1725.79	31954.02	52924.46
1999-00	119.31	43.04	8851.35	225.00	9076.35	12572.32	31752.87	708.06	1998.59	34459.52	56544.19
2000-01	70.07	6.00	6544.58	—	6544.58	8517.16	26061.93	—	1289.51	27351.44	46252.85

Source: Pragati Vivaranika, PHED; Jaipur, 2000-2001.

APPENDIX A–8.10

Functions of Directorate Local Bodies

Under the Directorate Local Bodies, Jaipur, its Engineering Cell gives consent to the technical proposals of more than Rs. 15 lakh, supervision of the work of committee constituted for the house construction in Mount Abu, take measures related to the damage caused by excessive rain, examine the proposals for taking loan by Municipalities from financing institutions, provide advice related to development work of Municipalities, and adhere to the technical standard of State/Central Government.

Accounts cell give its consent to general grant, special grant, other assistance (for the consumer of Public taps), and grant for State Finance Commission award, improvement of fire fighting services, core services and for the reimbursement of Octroi against abolition. It has the responsibility of accounting and auditing for the Auditor General report.

Other functions of DLB are:

- To prepare and submit the Annual Plan and Five Year Plan proposals and send it to the planning department.
- To compile the financial-physical data of Municipal bodies.
- Compilation of income-expenditure statement of Municipal bodies and to prepare the yearly progress report.
- To prepare the proposal for special scheme and tribal sub-plan and transmission of the information to the concerning departments.
- To prepare the budget speech of governor and the consolidated report and works related to the State level coordination committee meeting.
- To extend and shorten the area limit of Municipalities and examine the proposals for the formation of new ULBs.
- To issue the consent to Divisional commissioner committee for establishing the statue on public places.
- Solve the public litigations and complaints received from the office of Chief Minister etc.

Vigilance Cell is aimed at effective governance by controlling fraudulent practices in all the Municipal Corporations/Council/Municipalities of the state. Various types of grants and other assistance provided to the Municipal Corporations/Council/Municipalities are monitored and inspected for proper utilisation of it. Against the misuse of power and financial irregularities or corruption, under the Municipality Act 1959, Section 63, action is initiated against the defaulters.

APPENDIX A–8.11

Details about the Various Programmes/Schemes Being Implemented by the Local Self-Government Department in the Urban Areas

1. National Slum Development Programme

This programme was launched in the year 1996-97 by providing an additional central assistance with 70% loan and 30 per cent grant. The basic objective of this programme is to create and develop the basic physical amenities viz. water taps, wells, hand pumps, street lights, community bathrooms/latrines, garbage collection, disposable bins, physical infrastructure (viz. Road, Sewerage, Storm Water Drainage, Electricity) and social infrastructure (like Housing/Shelter facilities, education centres, healthcare centres, community hall etc). A sum of Rs. 5245.00 lakh was kept for IX Plan period. Against this Rs. 6178.00 lakh were transferred Urban Local Bodies during IX plan period. A sum of Rs. 1627.00 lakh was kept for 2002-03. Against this, a sum of Rs.1402.00 lakh was transferred to ULBs.

Apna Ghar Yojna

As per guidelines of NSDP, at least 10 per cent amount of total allocation should be spent on Shelter/Shelter Upgradation activities.

A provision of formulating a suitable scheme for shelter/shelter up-gradation by state has been mentioned in the guidelines of NSDP. A scheme named "Apana Ghar" was framed by the department in the year 2000-01 comprising of loan, subsidy and individual beneficiaries' share for constructing a dwelling housing unit. The Housing Unit will have 1 Room, Kitchen, Latrine and Bathroom along with provision of open space for constructing additional room in future. The total unit cost of a dwelling unit Rs. 40,000 has a component of Rs. 25,000 loan, Rs. 10000 subsidy from NSDP and Rs. 5000 as individual beneficiaries share. This yojana has a provision of providing loan only on the guarantee of the land *pattas*. The shifted/to be shifted slums and *basties* will be given priority in implementation. A priority order in the line of (1) BPL families (2) SC/ST families, (3) Widow/Divorced women, (4) OBC, (5) other urban poor and general families has been prescribed in the instructions and guidelines of this scheme. This yojana will be implemented in all Urban Towns but in the first phase, priority will be accorded to Divisional and District Headquarters. ULBs, Housing Boards, JDA and UITs are implementing the scheme.

An administrative sanction of construction of 47 houses in the Azad Nagar *Kuchchee Bastee* of Jaipur city has been issued. Till now, subsidy for construction of 61 houses has been sanctioned. About 2600 application were got prepared by JDA. Out of this loan sanctioned and disbursement in 993 cases. An amount of Rs. 6.60 lakh has been made available for construction of 66 houses in Jodhpur city. 1780 houses were constructed by UIT, Kota for allotting them to slum dwellers under Apna Ghar Yojana.

2. Valmiki Ambedkar Awas Yojana

The Government of India has launched a new scheme named as "Valmiki Ambedkar Awas Yojana" in Dec. 2001. In this yojana, loan and subsidy is provided to the BPL/SCs/STs/Economically weaker section for constructing one room dwelling housing unit. The loan and subsidy part will be 1:1. A unit cost of Rs. 50,000 has been fixed for the cities having population in the range of 10-50 lakh and Rs. 40,000 for the other cities. Accordingly Jaipur city will come in the range of unit cost of Rs. 50000 with Rs. 25000 subsidy (50%) and other cities coming in the range of unit cost of Rs. 40000 will have a subsidy element of Rs. 20000. The implementing guidelines of this scheme have been issued to all concerned ULBs. This yojana is being implemented with the association of HUDCO. Presently, the field operation of this yojana has been started in the Jaipur, Jodhpur and Kota city of the State.

3. Environment Improvement of Slums

This programme, included in the 20-point programme, is aimed for the improvement of environment of urban slums. Under this programme, basic facilities like roads, drains, electricity and drinking water are provided to slum dwellers. Up to 1995-1996 basic facilities were provided to about 90-95 per cent of the urban slums identified in 1981. The scheme was dropped in 1996-97 when NSDP programme was launched by Government of India. The scheme was re-started at in 1999-2000 and a provision of Rs. 100.00 lakh was kept in 1999-2000 and Rs. 50.00 lakh in 2000-01 but no funds were received during these two years. At present no provision is being kept under this programme but ULBs are benefiting the slum population with their own resources.

4. Sahabhagi Nagar Vikas Yojana

This programme was launched in 1994 and the execution started in 1995-96. The scheme offers 50 per cent state share and 50 per cent public contribution or 30 per cent public contribution, 20 per cent ULBs/UITs/JDA share and 50 per cent Govt. share. The scheme creates not only a great sense of people's participation in development works, but also doubles the amount of investment in infrastructural work in the urban areas.

A sum of Rs. 10000.00 lakh was kept for IX Plan period. Against this, a sum of Rs. 2325.00 lakh was transferred to District Collectors up to 1999-2000. From the year 2000-01 onwards, no provision is being kept in Annual Plans.

During 1995-96 to 2001-02, 4374 works were sanctioned and 3747 works were completed.

5. Low Cost Sanitation Programme (LCSP)

This scheme is aimed at achieving minimum basic sanitation requirement and liberation of scavengers. In this scheme dry latrine is converted into flush one. This programme is being implemented in the state from 1981-82 under PCR Act. Besides conversion of dry latrine into flush ones, construction of new flush latrine was also included in this programme as per guidelines issued by GoI in 1989-90. The GoI share/HUDCO loan is directly provided to municipalities. A target of conversion/construction of 242424 latrines during IX Plan period was kept. Against this, 171175 latrines were converted/constructed. In Annual Plan 2002-03, 10965 latrines were converted/constructed.

6. Swarna Jayanti Shahari Rozgar Yojana

This programme was started from 1.12.97 in place of earlier Urban Poverty Alleviation Schemes namely NRY, UBSP and PMI - UPEP with a 75 per cent: 25 per cent centre/state share. The basic objective of this programme is to provide self employment opportunities and to develop the various basic and physical amenities and social services for the socio/economic upliftment of BPL families with association (NHC) of the community structure like Neighborhood group (NHGs), Neighborhood Committees and Community Development Society (CDS). The CDS is the focal point for the purpose of identification of beneficiaries, preparation of applications, monitoring recovery and generally providing whatever other support necessary to the programme. The CDS also identify projects suitable for that particular area. This programme has two components namely Urban Self Employment Programme and Urban Wage Employment Programme. The description of the different components of USEP and UWEP are mentioned below: -

A. Urban Self Employment Programme (USEP): This component provides the loan and subsidy for self employment and development of women and children in urban areas and grants for skill upgradation, thrift and credit societies, community structure and infrastructure.

(i) *Self Employment Programme* - The objective of this programme is to generate additional employment for unemployed and under employed BPL persons. The maximum cost of the project is Rs. 50,000 with maximum allowable subsidy of Rs. 7500 or 15 per cent cost of the project, whichever is less. The beneficiary is required to contribute 5 per cent margin money of the project cost and rest amount is disbursed as a bank loan. A target of benefiting 29317 persons was kept for IX Plan period, against this, 29341 persons were benefited. A target of benefiting 5000 persons was kept in 2002-2003. Against this target 5149 persons were benefited.

(ii) *Training and Skill Development* - This component is confined to BPL beneficiaries who have got education up to ninth standard. The unit cost allowed for training is Rs. 2000 per trainee including material cost, trainers fee, other miscellaneous expenses to be incurred by the training institution and monthly stipend to trainee. The training is provided in variety of services and manufacturing trades as well as in local skills and craft. The total training period for skill upgradation may very from two to six months, subject to minimum of 300 hours.

There is a provision to provide a tool kit to the trainee (if needed) after completion of training satisfactory. The cost of the tool kit should not exceed Rs. 600/-. A target of imparting training to 13010 persons was kept for IX Plan period. Against this target 13425 persons were benefited. In 2002-03 a target of benefiting 2000 persons was kept and 1304 persons were benefited.

(iii) *Development of women and children in Urban Areas (DWCUA):* Under this component, a group of Urban poor women (BPL) can take up an economic activity suited to their skill, training aptitude and local condition. The DWCUA group should consist of at least 10 urban poor women to be eligible for subsidy under this scheme. The group can select its own organiser from amongst the members. The DWCUA group is entitled to a subsidy of Rs. 1,25,000 (or 50 per cent of the cost of the project whichever is less) and the bank loan of the same amount.

If DWCUA group decides to set itself as thrift and credit society (T&C), besides its entrepreneurial activity, the group shall also be entitled to a lump-sum grant of Rs. 25,000 as revolving fund at the rate of 1000 per member. The revolving fund shall also be available to a simple T&C society even if the society is not engaged in DWCUA. This revolving fund is meant for the use of purchase of raw material, marketing, infrastructure support of income generation and other group activity. A thrift and credit society is entitled for payment of revolving fund after one year of its constitution.

The implementation of these components is being geared up. The department is organising capacity building and awareness activities for these components under the UNICEF assistance plan for poor activities with a stress on NGOs associations and strong community participation.

During 1999-2000 to 2001-02 (IX Plan period) 1200 Self-help groups (SHGs) were constituted out of which 134 were converted in to Thrift and credit societies (T&Cs). In 2002-03, 412 SHGs were constituted out of which 132 converted into T&Cs. 48 DWCUA groups were constituted during 2000-01 to 2002-03.

Community structure: Under this scheme, medical camps, formal education centers and awareness camps are organised in urban areas. Progress achieved under this component is as follows:

Camps Organised	*1999-2000*	*2000-01*	*2001-02*	*2002-03*
Medical Camps	432	810	1088	1201
Awareness Camps	167	540	880	996

Basic structure: Under this component to raise the income of urban BPL, structure like hawkers market, packing, designing and advertisement for the sale of product etc. are taken up by local bodies.

B. Urban Wage Employment Programme (UWEP): This programme is aimed to create and develop useful assets pertaining to the basic physical and social amenities by providing employment to the persons living below poverty line in urban areas. This programme is applicable to those urban local bodies having a population of less than 5 lakh, as per 1991 census. Material Labour ratio required to be maintained 60:40. A target of generating 16.12 lakh employment mandays was fixed for the IX Plan period. Against this target, 14.46 lakh mandays were generated.

7. Fire Fighting Grant (FFC)

Eleventh Finance Commission recommended providing 2200.00 lakh to ULBs in coming 3-4 years for strengthening the existing fire services and establishing the new fire stations/centres for providing fire fighting services. In this context, an action plan was prepared by the Department and approved by State Level Empower Committee (SLEC). A sum of Rs. 780.00 lakh in Annual Plan 2001-02 and Rs. 440.00 lakh in 2002-03 was received by the department and the activities are being taken as per approved action plan.

8. Eleventh Finance Commission Grant- For Slum Improvement

Slums are the integral part of cities and towns. Of late, necessity to accelerate the process of development was being felt to provide basic amenities and core services in urban slums. The EFC acceded to the demand of Rajasthan State for providing funds under Slum Improvement and allocated a sum of Rs. 4000 lakh for the period 2000-2004 with a provision of providing 800 lakh per year. No funds were provided in Annual Plan 2000-01 under this programme. A sum of Rs. 2400.00 lakh was kept in 2001-02. Out of which 1600.00 lakh was provided during this year. A sum of Rs. 800.00 lakh was kept for 2002-03. Out which Rs. 400.00 lakh was provided to Urban Local Bodies.

9. Eleventh Finance Commission Grant- For Core Services

Maintenance of core services is the obligatory function of ULBs. The XI Finance Commission recommended Rs. 9940.00 lakh for providing core services in urban areas for 2000- 2004. A sum of Rs. 4970.80 lakh was received by the department from 2000-01 to 2002-03 and same was transferred to ULBs.

10. State Finance Commission Grant (SFC)

As per recommendation of Second State Finance Commission, a sum of Rs. 2389.52. lakh in 2000-01, Rs. 2760.79 lakh in 2001-02, Rs. 2760.79 lakh in 2002-03 was transferred to Urban Local Bodies.

11. Octroi Grant

The Govt. of Rajasthan has abolished octroi from 1 Aug. 1998. This grant is being reimbursed to all ULBs through the state grant. This grant is given to ULBs after making an increment of 10 percent per annum of the income earned by ULBs in 1997-98. A sum of Rs. 12380.83 lakh was transferred to ULBs during 1998-99 to 2000-01 (IX Plan Period). A sum of Rs. 38888.04 lakh was provided to ULBs in 2002-2003.

12. Special Grant-in-Aid for Urban Renewal

A sum or Rs. 1000.00 lakh was kept in Annual Plan 2000-01 out of which Rs. 400.00 lakh were transferred to municipal council, Udaipur. A sum or Rs. 100.00 lakh was kept in Annual Plan 2001-02 and the same was transferred to Nagarpalika Baran, Rajakheda, Shree Madhopur, Reengas and Nagar Nigam, Jodhpur. Presently, a token provision is being kept for this purpose.

13. Chief Minister's Employment Scheme (CMES)

This scheme was announced by the Hon'ble Chief Minister of the state on 12.10.99 to provide the Kiosks to unemployed youth to take/carry out the self employment activities. Initially a target of constructing 1 lakh kiosks in coming four years was kept. Later it was decided that besides constructing kiosks, land/place can also be provided to allottee and kiosks of certain type design will be constructed by allottee himself. 37444 kiosk/land were allotted during the period 2000-01 to 2003-04 (up to July 2003).

14. Urs Fair

A sum of Rs. 445 lakh was made available to municipal council Ajmer and municipal board Sarwad during the year 1998-99, to provided basic facilities to pilgrims visiting 786 Urs fair at Ajmer.

15. Balika Samridhdhi Yojana (BSY)

BSY is a 100 percent CSS scheme. It is a part of long term strategy to change social attitude and behavioural practice toward the girl child while raising her status. A grant amount of Rs. 500 is deposited in the name of the girl child born on or after 15.8.97 in BPL families up to 2 girl child as per revised guidelines. Besides this, the BSY has a provision of providing scholarship up to class 1-10 at the different rates prescribed for each class under the revised guidelines. But this department is not dealing this segment. The benefit of BSY will be restricted to only 2 girl children in each household irrespective of the total number of children in the house. No amount was received during last three years. Keeping in view the adequate unspent balance a token sum of Rs. 0.01 lakh is being proposed as central share in Annual Plans. 12838 girl child have been benefited up to 2002-03.

16. Antyoday Anna Yojana

Government of India launched Antyoday Anna Yojana. Under this scheme 25 kg. wheat at the rate of Rs. 2 per kg or rice at the rate of Rs. 3 per kg is provided to each identified BPL family. This scheme has been revised recently and the total weight has been increased to about 35 kg.

Food and Civil Supplies Department of Government of Rajasthan is implementing the Antyoday Anna Yojana. Rural Development Department for rural areas and Local Self Government Department for the urban areas have done the selection of the families for this yojana. 30269 poor families have been identified in the 183 ULBs. A yellow ration card or specific seal marked on ration card have been provided to each of these families for the purpose.

An additional target of 1,86,500 families have been given by Government of India recently. Out of this, a target of 15094 additional families has been fixed for urban areas i.e. for 183 ULBs. Accordingly, the department of LSG has issued a circular to all ULBs and other concerned to select the additional families of given number mentioned in the circular (in proportion to BPL families) under this yojana. The process of selection of additional families has been almost completed.

APPENDIX A–8.12

Income and Expenditure of ULBs

	Income Rs. (in lakh)				*Expenditure Rs. (in lakh)*		
Items	*1996-97*	*1998-99*	*1999-2000*	*Items*	*1996-97*	*1998-99*	*1999-2000*
Land and House tax	943.75	1054.16	1243.86	General administration	3463.99	3737.90	4773.13
Octroi and Road tax	24452.72	26490.81	20.53	Octroi	3461.59	3602.89	4375.51
Vehicle tax	9.77	5.30	10.13	Land and House tax	131.04	353.78	385.73
Passenger tax	96.47	100.87	110.85	Other taxes	61.69	215.88	233.02
Terminal tax	12.78	12.35	10.09	Public welfare and Public Health	12917.39	14308.95	18435.45
Other tax	17.05	36.80	80.72	Public Protection	339.85	353.85	463.37
Upvidhion	1987.41	1193.47	1040.45	Medical	58.34	56.98	80.54
Asset	659.75	599.42	688.33	Electricity	2106.35	2378.52	2357.76
Ordinances	68.53	64.67	64.15	Water	189.62	260.70	281.55
Sanitation	141.70	142.89	138.38	Cattle house	105.98	134.90	141.65
Water works	44.47	46.27	138.88	Education	65.05	128.37	155.93
Interest on investment	423.24	434.52	523.05	Garden	639.32	659.38	832.46
Yearly general grant	1209.74	2087.92	2105.65	Public repair	865.04	993.79	1082.02
Special Aid (for drains and roads)	359.36	539.24	—	Development work	13130.07	15089.09	10932.89
Reimbursement of Octroi	—	1167.07	32065.72	Purchase of new property	546.31	489.78	476.48
Miscellaneous (aavartak)	1265.15	1187.23	1004.66	Return of Loans	433.37	383.11	533.91
Land sale	2989.51	2749.15	3199.77	Miscellaneous expenditure	5139.37	6060.70	5684.14
Special assistance and loan	5392.19	7247.04	5396.13				
Miscellaneous (anavartak)	4448.99	5679.90	4834.11				
Total	**44522.58**	**50839.08**	**52675.46**		**43654.27**	**49208.57**	**51225.54**

Source: Annual Progress Reports (1997—2001).

APPENDIX A–8.13

Plan Outlay and Expenditure During the Ninth Plan (1997-98 up to 2000)

Name of Scheme	*Ninth Plan (1997-2000 Approved Outlay)*	*Annual Plan 1997-98*			*Annual Plan 1998-99*			*Annual Plan 1999-2000*		
		Original Outlay	*Revised Outlay*	*Expenditure*	*Original Outlay*	*Revised Outlay*	*Expenditure*	*Original Outlay*	*Revised Outlay*	*Expenditure*
2	3	4	5	6	7	8	9	10	11	12
Swarna Jayanti Shahari Rozgar Yojana (SJSRY)	5000.00	1100.00	481.22	460.22	1000.00	200.00	200.00	400.00	200.00	80.71
i) UBSP	500.00									
ii) N.R.Y.	2000.00									
iii) PMI-UPEP	2500.00									
National Slum Development Programme (NSDP)	5245.00	1049.00	1345.0	1270.25	1048.00	1345.00	1345.0	1345.00	1479.0	1479.0
Sahbhagi Nagar Vikas Yojana	—	—	—	—	—	—	—	—	—	—
Low Cost Sanitation	10000.00	1500.00	1500.00	1500.00	1500.00	425.00	425.00	800.00	400.00	400.00
State Finance Commission	11107.00	1751.00	1751.0	1600.0	1750.00	1750.00	1750.0	2431.00	2431.0	1547.0
Tenth Finance Commission (TFC)	6475.00	1080.00	1080.0	810.00	1079.00	1079.00	1079.0	1079.00	1079.0	1349.0
Fire Fighting Equipment grant	444.00	125.00	125.00	56.25	150.00	150.00	150.00	125.00	293.75	293.75
Environment Improvement of Urban Slums (EIUS)	—	—	—	—	—	—	—	100.00	1.00	0.00
Urs Fair, Ajmer	—	—	—	—	—	445.00	445.00	—	—	—
Reimbursement of Octroi Grant	—	—	—	—	—	19433.6	19433.60	32066.0	32066.	32065.92
Special Grant-in-aid for Urban Renewal	—	—	—	—	—	—	—	—	—	—
Total: (1-11)	**45271.00**	**6905.00**	**6582.22**	**5997.62**	**6827.00**	**25027.60**	**25027.60**	**38446.00**	**37949.75**	**37215.38**

APPENDIX A–8.14

Central Assistance

Sub-Heading	*Actual Expenditure*		
	1996-97	*1997-98*	*1999-2000*
Low Cost Latrines (Harijan Kast Mukt Yojana)			
Nehru Rozgar Yojana	335.39	202.28	
Prime Minister Coordination Urban Poverty Upshaman Programme	485.92	1678.74	
Swarna Jayanti Shahari Rozgar Yojana	—	100.03	572.73
Basic services for urban poor		—	
Balika Samridhdhi Yojana		—	63.31
Total	**899.85**	**471.05**	**626.04**

Source: Annual Progress Reports (1997-98, 1998-99 and 2000-2001).

Chapter 9

Telecommunications

Till 1984, the telecommunications sector in Rajasthan remained undeveloped – largely due to the low level of investment in this area and outdated equipment. However, the fast-changing economy of the state as well as increasing globalisation brought forth the realisation that this sector needed to be developed fast. A modest beginning was made in 1984 when the private sector was permitted to enter the sector. Cellular and paging services were initiated under the private sector.

Like other states, Rajasthan's telecom growth too was influenced by the Central government, which formulates and implements the telecom policy for the entire country. Obviously, expansion as well as qualitative improvement of telecom services in the state has largely depended on the overall policy changes by the Central government. A major policy breakthrough was made in 1994 when the Central government announced its National Telecom Policy (NTP-94).

Present Scenario

The Rajasthan telecom circle is divided into 24 secondary switching stations, each covering one or two revenue districts of the state (see Appendix A–9.1).

Demographic Details

Telecom penetration can be analysed in terms of the number of telephones (either fixed or mobile) per 1,000 population. This is also known as teledensity.

- Area in Sq.km. - 3,42,239
- Population (2001 census) - 56,473,122
- No. of revenue districts - 32
- Telephone density - 23.5 (Per 1,000 persons)
- Area-wise telephone density - 3.88 (per sq.km.)
- Staff per 1,000 telephones - 11.32

Situation Analysis

TABLE 9.1

Status of Telecommunication in Rajasthan as on 31 March 2001

Equipped exchange capacity	17,18,426
Telephone connections	13,26,286
Waiting list	1,22,315
No. of telecommunication exchanges	2061
FAX capacity	1,16,000
STD stations	1,626
Stn. on reliable media	993
Village Public Telephones (VPTs)	23,825
VPTs with STD	707
STD PCOs	27,199
Local PCOs	5,695
Telecom centres	80
Departmental telegraph offices	42
Central telegraph offices	5
Customer service centres	90

Source: BSNL (For details see Appendix A–9.3).

As mentioned earlier, until 1984, the telecom sector in India was wholly under government control and growth was very slow. However, at this point, policy-makers realised that the state monopoly was a major constraining factor in spurring internal growth and developing global competitiveness. Add to this lack of resources, technology and trained personnel as well as political expediency and the task appeared even more difficult.

Telecom service liberalisation began in 1984 when the private sector was allowed to manufacture customer premise equipment. In 1992, services were also opened to the private sector. At that stage, the government also unbundled basic and value added services, especially cellular and paging services. The key growth driver in this sector was the NTP-94.

Present Status of Rural Telecom Services

Although the number of villages with a phone link has increased over the years, rural connectivity continues to remain a matter of great concern. Even in villages where phone connections are provided, there are many flaws:

- Often, the connections do not work
- They are not accessible to the public
- A majority of these phones are devoid of long distance facility
- A large number of villages do not have any PCOs

During the Eighth Five Year Plan, the government decided that its main objective in the development of the telecom sector would be accessibility, and not the provision of an individual phone. Therefore, the attempt was to provide one pay phone per village. The quality of service, however, remained poor. This was largely due to non-reliable media in rural areas.[1]

Some commonly faced problems were:-

- Delay in connections even when payments had been made long ago.
- To use a phone during an emergency, villagers had to go to another village or even a town as phones in their own village were not functional.
- Absence of STD and PCOs.
- Old and faulty apparatus, and broken cables are a common sight in rural areas.

Current System of Fixed Service Provision

If district-wise planned net capacity and direct exchange line (DEL) are juxtaposed with actual achievement, a large gap is observed. In fact, it is quite disconcerting to note that only 13.3 per cent out of the planned net capacity and 15.8 per cent of the planned DELs have been achieved till now.

Apart from the state-controlled Bharat Sanchar Nigam Limited's (BSNL) efforts, the private sector too has taken up the job of providing fixed line services, which are supposed to be more reliable. At present, the only private company that provides fixed line connections in the state is Shyam Telelink Ltd., but so far it has covered only three districts – Jaipur, Jodhpur and Ajmer. In Jaipur, it is providing Level 4 services, in Jodhpur it is ready with Level 3 and in Ajmer it has recently started Level 2 services. It is expected to cover more districts of the state soon. Thus, fixed service provision through a reliable medium, i.e. optical fibre cabling, is currently available in only three districts of Rajasthan.

Status of Mobile Services

Cellular services were introduced in India in May 1991 when the Central government announced its intention of awarding licences to the private sector for providing cellular phones in four major cities – Delhi, Mumbai, Kolkata and Chennai. BSNL launched its cellular services in Rajasthan in November 2002. Presently, mobile services are available in 47 stations across 24 districts of the state

The private operators currently providing cellular connections in Rajasthan are: OASIS/Hexacom India Ltd.; Essar Telecommunications; Shyam Telelink Ltd. OASIS and Essar provide mobile connections based on GSM (Global System for Mobile Communication) technology through which the subscriber can operate from anywhere within the country or outside. Shyam Telelink offers citymobile connections with its 'Rainbow' services, which is based on CDMA (Code Division Multiple Access) technology. With this type of connection, subscribers get mobility only within the range of the city and not beyond. Shyam Telelink provides mainly two types of connections: wireless and wireline.

Pattern of Growth of Telephony and Internet

Pattern of Growth of Telephony: Over the past five years, an increase in the number of telegraph offices, telephone exchanges and PCOs (both rural and urban) is an indicator of satisfactory growth in the telecom circle of Rajasthan.

Pattern of Growth of Internet: At present, the Rajasthan Telecom Circle has one Internet node at Jaipur, access to which is available on local charge basis from all over the state. The Jaipur node can be accessed by dialling 172222 (for TCP/IP access and 172223 for terminal dial up-access) from the entire Rajasthan circle. Currently, the following services are available: TCP/IP access (PSTN dial up); ISDN dial up; leased

1. The connection cables are laid through overhead installation mode rather than through the underground cabling system, which is quite prone to frequent damages caused by lightening, thunderstorm, heavy rainfall or even with high wind velocity.

line access. At present, Internet nodes of BSNL are available in all district headquarters.

The growth pattern of Internet in the state cannot be judged properly over the last five years, because BSNL has been providing Internet services for just one year. Still the targetted plan was achieved in a very short span of time, which is a good sign of progress in Internet connectivity and services in the state. Apart from the government's efforts to popularise Internet usage among its subscribers, private operators are also being encouraged to provide better Internet services. More and more companies are emerging as Internet Service Providers (ISP) these days. The mushrooming of cyber cafes is a result of this growth momentum.

Quality of Services in Rural and Urban Areas

The quality of services in both rural as well as urban areas can be assessed on the basis of the following indicators:

- Number of faults per 100 stations per month
- Percentage of faults cleared on the same day
- Percentage of faults cleared in one week
- Percentage of effective trunk calls
- Number of faults per 100 telex lines per month
- Number of telegrams sent by post per 1,000 telegrams
- Number of telegrams delivered within 12 daylight hours
- Average revenue per DEL per month.

Performance Trends

The quality of services in Rajasthan's rural and urban areas can be compared with five neighbouring states – Haryana, Madhya Pradesh, Punjab, Uttar Pradesh and Gujarat – on the basis of the above factors. These are summarised in Appendix A–9.4

Plan for Villages

The state government has made efforts to cover all villages in the state (Table 9.2).

Out of 39,000 targetted connections, BSNL has covered approximately 23,000 villages where it has provided VPTs. At present, BSNL has no more VPT targets and the rest of the villages have been left for the private sector to cover.

TABLE 9.2

Plan of DoT and DTS for VPTs in Last Five Years and Their Level of Acheivement

SSAs	*No. of VPTs*	*No. of Villages*	*Percentage Covered*	*No. of Telephones Per 1000 Population*
Ajmer	989	1018	97.15	36.8
Alwar	1103	1949	56.6	21.9
Banswara	1350	2334	57.8	12.3
Barmer	898	1918	46.8	12.75
Bharatpur	1229	2153	56.9	13.54
Bhilwara	1180	1680	70.2	22.1
Bikaner	539	700	77.0	28.7
Bundi	518	834	62.1	13.8
Chittorgarh	786	2183	36.0	16.1
Churu	684	931	73.5	18.2
Jaisalmer	374	571	65.5	17.4
Jaipur	1499	3172	47.2	41.7
Jhalawar	705	1454	48.5	11.7
Jhunjhunu	842	856	98.4	23.4
Jodhpur	826	1064	77.6	31.4
Kota	1423	1883	75.6	29.5
Nagaur	1044	1476	70.7	16.7
Pali	779	930	83.8	32.6
Sawai Madhopur	924	1469	62.9	12.8
Sikar	781	976	80.0	19.8
Sirohi	891	1144	77.9	19.3
Sri Ganganagar	1879	4440	42.32	30.7
Tonk	664	1036	64.10	13.5
Udaipur	1926	3312	58.1	24.4
Total	**23833**	**39483**	**60.36**	**23.96**

* VPTs = Village Public Telephones.

New Telecom Policy, 1999

In its NTP-99, the Central government came out with a new policy framework for cellular mobile service providers (CMSPs), which brought certain changes in their licence conditions. The most striking feature of NTP-99 was that it replaced the payment of licence fees to the government by a revenue-sharing scheme. The other important features were:

- Direct connectivity between licensed CMSPs and any other type of service provider (including other CMSP) in their area of operation, including permitting sharing of infrastructure with any other type of service provider.
- Interconnectivity between different service providers in different service areas to be reviewed in consultation with the Telecom Regulatory Authority of India (TRAI).

- The CMSPs to be allowed to directly interconnect with Videsh Sanchar Nigam Limited (VSNL) after opening of national long distance from January 1, 2000.
- The CMSPs to be permitted to provide mobile telephony services including permission to carry their own long distance tariff within their service area without seeking an additional licence.

The key objectives of the NTP-99 were:

- Availability of telephone on demand.
- Teledensity of 7 per cent by 2005 and 15 per cent by 2010.
- To provide Internet access to all district headquarters by 2000.
- To provide high-speed data and multimedia capabilities using technologies including ISDN (Integrated Service Digital Network) to all towns with a population greater than 2 lakh by the year 2002.
- Provision of world-class services at reasonable rates.
- Emergence of India as a major manufacturing/exporting base of equipment.

Highlights of NTP-99

- It allowed operators to carry their own intra circle traffic without seeking an additional licence.
- Operators could interconnect with any other service provider, including another cable service provider which was not allowed earlier.
- Direct interconnectivity between licensed service provider in their area of operation and sharing of infrastructure with any other type of service provider was possible under NTP-99.
- Direct interconnectivity to VSNL was also possible, after domestic long distance was opened up.
- Operators could apply for licences for any number of areas.
- Licence fee was restructured as a one-time entry fee and recurring revenue share.
- Entry of more operators would be based on the recommendation of the TRAI and the situation would be reviewed every two years.
- Licences were to be available for 20 years and further extendable for another 10 years.
- Both voice and data traffic could be carried by the service provider.
- Providing services would require a payment of a one-time entry fee (as a percentage of the original licence bid) and licence fee, based on revenue share. The number of players, their mode of selection, appropriate level of entry fee and percentage of revenue share were to be recommended by the TRAI.

Likely Benefits to the State Under NTP-99's Universal Service Obligations (USOs)

NTP-99's USOs has undoubtedly opened the state telecom circle's doors to private operators who can now provide fixed-line or mobile services. The obligation to pay a huge amount of money to the government to get their licences to operate in the circle has been relaxed to a greater extent. The increased teledensity in the last two years is an outcome of NTP-99.

Competitive Scenario

With the telecom sector in Rajasthan flooded with several service providing companies, the state-owned BSNL has been facing stiff competition and BSNL was forced to slash long distance STD call rates by 62 per cent from 14 January 2002. Due to this drastic rate cut, BSNL will initially have to suffer a 13 per cent loss in its annual revenue, i.e. a loss of Rs. 3,000 crore out of Rs. 23,000 crore.

BSNL was forced to take such a decision because India's first long distance service providing private company, Bharti Tele-Ventures announced a 50 per cent cut in STD rates from 26 January 2002. In such a situation, BSNL, whose 54 per cent of the total revenue, i.e. Rs. 12,441 crore, is from long distance calls, had no other option but to cut rates drastically by 50-62 per cent. Moreover, in order to clear the traffic, BSNL has also planned to invest Rs.500 crore, which will take the total expenditure to Rs.3,500 crore. Apart from this, it will be investing another Rs.12,000 crore to modernise and expand its network.

Information Technology (IT) in the Government

In the first phase of computerisation in Rajasthan, which began as early as in 1985-86, the objective was confined to automating basic clerical operations. This phase was fairly successful. One of the outcomes of this step was that IT awareness spread at all levels of the state machinery. However, the computerisation effort resulted in islands of computing resource getting formed in specific locations, especially at the departmental headquarters. There were little or no linkages among the computing resource islands. Further, the computerisation plans did not explicitly include customer orientation.

Nevertheless, the success achieved in the initial phase of computerisation has made the government departments and agencies more ambitious. They are beginning to take a hard look at their roles in the years to come, and are willing to talk about re-engineering their processes through enterprise-wide information systems. The government departments want their IT plans to be part of the overall planning process so as to improve the efficiency and effectiveness of their service delivery systems.

The second phase of the IT plan for the state should now focus on the use of IT in enhancing the quality of government services, creating a responsive and transparent administration, thus facilitating empowerment of people and satisfying their right to information.

The following policy initiatives were planned in order to achieve the overall objectives:

- Each department would prepare a Five-Year IT Plan. This plan would address the extent of computerisation of its core activities, need for hardware and software resources, manpower requirement and training of employees.
- From 1999-2000, 1 per cent of the total Plan outlay is being earmarked for deploying in the IT sector. It is envisaged that by 2003, 3 per cent of the total Plan outlay would be earmarked for the IT sector. Appropriate minor heads for accounting investments in the IT sector would be created for each department. The expenditure control under this head will be with the Administrative Secretary.
- In the near future, speed and accuracy of communication will be a strategic factor in determining the success and effectiveness of any organisation. Therefore, the government will make it necessary for all departments and PSUs to use the state-wide Value Added Network (VAN) for inter and intra departmental data, voice and video communication.
- An integrated IT centre will be created in each of the 32 districts in the state by 2005. This centre will provide multifarious facilities to the district administration and to the general public. Wherever possible, the establishment and running of the district-based IT centres would be outsourced to the private sector. The Department of Information Technology (DoIT) would carry out the selection procedures and post selection benchmarking. A logical extension of this hub would be downward linkages to the *tehsil* and panchayat samiti levels.
- In each district, data warehouses having local content would be created. These centres will provide information on the government's activities to citizens through information kiosks. In order to have a large spread of the information kiosks in the state, private sector participation would be actively pursued. Access to the data warehouses through the private sector information kiosks would be on cost plus basis, so that it is financially viable for the private entrepreneur. DoIT would determine the end user costs and also carry out regular benchmarking of the facilities.
- The government would introduce IT at all points of contact between it and the citizens by 2003. All forms requiring submission of information, while applying for any service or clearance from the government, would also be made available electronically. Each public dealing department would list out the contact points and the level of information interchange between it and the people. The information kiosks would enable the people to carry out this kind of information interchange with the government.
- To attain the overall objectives of electronic governance, high-end computing facilities comprising state-of-the-art computer network and other related communication peripherals would be installed at the state secretariat. Linkages between the secretariat network and the state-wide VAN would provide e-mail, voice, data and video communication facility to the Chief Minister, Cabinet members, chief secretary and high-level dignitaries.
- Computerisation projects of revenue-earning departments and agencies having high level of public contact would be fully operational by 2002. The government would examine and adopt the National Policy on Data Security, Privacy and Data Protection Act and other legal frameworks including cyber laws as and when the same come in force.

- In the Annual Confidential Reports of government employees, a column on contribution to IT utilisation in the department/organisation would be introduced.
- Computer proficiency of a specified level would be stipulated as an essential qualification for all appointments in the government. In case of new entrants to government service, computer training of at least 'O' level certification would be made a mandatory component of the induction level training. In case of serving employees, confirmation of services would be done only after they passed the basic computer test. This would be applicable to all service rules barring class IV employees.
- The government would establish IT training centres, aimed at the existing government employees, in each district headquarter by 2002. These training centres would be an integral part of the district-based IT centres.
- As recommended in the 'National IT Action Plan', the government would establish framework contracts with leading IT service vendors so as to avail a wide range of IT consultancy, specialist services and IT products at lower cost and with a shortened procurement cycle. To minimise the technological obsolescence factor and to avoid a large upfront expenditure, computer hardware would be largely procured through leasing
- The DoIT, the nodal agency for computerisation in the state, will be further strengthened so that it becomes the strategic vehicle to implement these IT policy initiatives. RAJCOMP would be converted into a corporation to act as high-end technology consultant and training facilitator.
- Government personnel would be sent on regular high-end computer training courses so that they would remain in touch with the emerging and cutting edge technology.
- With the Internet emerging as a powerful communication medium, public dealing government departments would create their websites under the umbrella of the Government of Rajasthan's website. All government circulars, notifications, tenders, etc. would be published on the website on regular basis. All examinations and recruitment notifications, selection results would also be published on the website.
- In order to monitor that IT resources are being used at the optimal levels, regular and structured IT audit shall be carried out by team comprising officers of DoIT and the concerned department.
- The role of the Committee of Information Technology Projects Approval (CITPA) would be strengthened. All departments shall be required to submit comprehensive report on the execution of IT projects to CITPA on regular basis.
- The private sector would be encouraged to donate computers and related items to public utilities, especially hospitals. Discarded computer items lying in various departments would also be made available to such utilities.
- The government would take initiatives to establish an inter-state IT exchange panel. Regular seminars and conferences would be organised where interaction with the officers of other states as well as the private sector will take place.
- State-level awards will be given to government departments/PSUs for outstanding usage of IT. The selection of the departments/PSUs for the award will be done by CITPA.

Rajasthan's IT Policy

IT has become the driving force behind human development and growth in the new millennium. Rajasthan is one of the pioneering states in the country to have designated IT as a priority thrust area. The state government envisages IT as a force multiplier to enhance the welfare of its people and accelerate economic growth. As part of this commitment, it unveiled a comprehensive 'IT Policy' in April 2000.

To provide greater focus and impetus to implement the IT Policy and to make Rajasthan a major IT hub in the country, the state government has recently constituted a high-level IT Task Force.

The broad objectives of the state's IT Policy are as follows:

- Positioning the state as an attractive location for development and growth of the IT industry and related services for rapid economic growth and improvement in the overall economy of the state.
- Creation and continuous upgradation of IT infrastructure in the state through government-private sector joint efforts.

- Continuous effort toward the development of human resource for IT by increasing its reach both in terms of quality and spatial coverage, and to improve the employability of educated youth of the state.
- Encouraging IT-driven electronic commerce.
- Encouraging electronic governance

The following strategies are recommended to achieve these objectives:

- Positioning the state as an attractive location for the development and growth of the IT industry
  - It would be the explicit objective of the government to provide an enabling environment as a facilitator/catalyst and to let the entrepreneurial skills of the private sector flourish.
  - IT industry will be a priority sector for investments.
  - Suitable tax concessions and financial incentives will continuously be given to industries in the IT sector.
  - Land at concessional rates would be given to IT companies and there would be no restrictions on land use for IT industries.
  - Complete one-stop service will be provided to all IT units within a time-bound schedule.
  - The state government will endeavour to ensure availability of finances for IT projects.
  - There would be minimal regulatory inspections for IT industries.
  - State-level awards will be given to IT companies with outstanding performance in exports and in domestic segments.
  - All software industries including services and training institutions in IT, will be given industry status.
- Creation and continuous upgrading of IT infrastructure in the state through government-private sector joint efforts. The state government is aware of the fact that to position the state as an attractive location for the IT industry, there is a need to create and continuously upgrade IT infrastructure. The state government is also aware that this task cannot be done by it alone and, in fact, should be attempted jointly with the private sector. It is the intention of the state government to act primarily as a facilitator to let the private sector establish quality infrastructure within a time bound framework and to ensure redressal of any constraints/problems in this regard.
  - The government will persuade BSNL, VSNL and other service providers to extend their network infrastructure up to the level of gram *panchayats* by the end of the Tenth Five-Year Plan.
  - The state government will ensure creation of pertinent government data warehouses and try to provide relevant information to citizens at all levels.
  - Free 'Right of way' will continue to be provided to all service providers on priority basis.
  - The state government is of the opinion that rather than creating closed user group and intranets, the Internet should be encouraged. Citizens, even at the *gram panchayat* level, should be able to log on to the Internet by the end of the Tenth Five-Year Plan.
  - High quality basic amenities/facilities and state-of-the-art infrastructure would be made available to promote the establishment of offices of major national and international IT companies in the state,
  - The state government will encourage the private sector to set up IT training centres and Internet access centres at all places including government schools, colleges and government offices.
- Continuous efforts in developing human resource for IT. The state government is aware that the goal of creating an IT-driven and knowledge-based society in the state cannot be achieved without building core competencies in human resource development with substantial inputs of information technology knowledge. The following strategies are recommended for this:

Training for IT within Government

- Training needs for higher management, middle management and field level functionaries and operational staff are different and the training content and delivery media have to be accordingly planned for each category. All these categories are proposed to be provided appropriate training by the end of the Tenth Five Year Plan.

- To cover all the employees, the government would establish IT training centres at each district headquarters
- Suitable incentive programmes shall be devised for the state government employees to get trained in IT.
- Chief Information Officers (CIOs) will be nominated in all the departments and appropriate training will be provided to the CIOs. Their role as IT facilitators will be clearly defined. They would be in charge of the IT Cells in their respective departments, primarily responsible for training different levels of government employees and identifying the IT needs of their respective departments.
- In the Annual Confidential Reports of government employees, a column would be introduced for evaluation regarding contribution to utilisation of IT in the department/organisation.
- IT would be one of the components of foundation courses for state/subordinate services.

Training and Orientation of Citizens

- It is the explicit intention of the state government that the rural population and other weaker sections of the society should not get excluded from the IT revolution. They should be provided with facilities and opportunities, which are within their reach and are affordable, to gain IT literacy. IT awareness programmes will be launched with the help of panchayati raj institutions and district administration so that they cover all sections of the society, especially in rural areas. The private sector would be proactively involved to maximise the coverage area.
- Standard syllabi and use of local language will be made mandatory for all such courses.
- Local public representatives will be extensively trained and will be involved in imparting training programmes to the rural masses.
- Innovative tools like touch screens, Interactive Voice Response Systems (IVRS), etc., would be used for training programmes and government-citizen interfaces.

IT Education for Professionals

- IT education modules would be made an integral and compulsory part of school and college syllabi.
- Special high-end IT courses would be run at ITIs and polytechnic colleges. Infrastructure and other facilities shall be made available with the active association of the private sector.
- The state government would endeavour to enforce widely accepted quality standards as adopted by the Ministry of Information Technology at the Centre. Appropriate rating mechanisms will be put in place to ascertain the quality standards of private IT institutions.
- The state government would encourage the expansion of new private engineering colleges, MCA and BCA courses.
- Syllabi of all high-end IT courses would be standardised across the state and shall be continuously upgraded to suit the prevailing IT trends.
- An Indian Institute of Information Technology (IIIT) will be set up in the state with the assistance of the private sector.
- Major IT companies would be encouraged to set up technological institutions in association with universities in colleges.
- The state government will support private sector initiatives in setting up virtual institutes on the Internet aimed at providing distance learning and vocational and trade specific education/training.
- The state government will launch online testing and evaluation programmes to assess the quality of students passing out of private institutions.
- Floor space in government schools/ colleges will be made available to private IT training institutes after office hours for providing IT training.

Electronic Commerce

It is the government's objective to provide proper institutional mechanisms for e-commerce. By the end of the Tenth Five-Year Plan, government procurement of goods and services will be done electronically.

Electronic Governance

The main objectives of the e-governance initiatives are:

- Bringing transparency in government operations and government-public interface.
- Improving the efficiency and effectiveness of the government's service delivery systems.
- Increasing control over malpractices and leakages through the use of IT and thus helping in providing a clean administration.
- Improving efficiency and economy of administration.
- Better dissemination of information to public.
- Improving financial management.

Computerisation of Individual Departments and Inter-departmental Communication (G2G)

- The complete computerisation of revenue-earning and public dealing departments would be taken up on a priority basis. While preparing the IT plan, each revenue-earning department shall project the increase in revenue due to better monitoring made possible through automated systems. A portion of such projected increase in revenue shall be earmarked to creating IT infrastructure in each department. By the end of the Tenth Five-Year Plan, all such revenue earning and public dealing departments are proposed to be fully automated and networked.
- A comprehensive and structured project methodology will be adopted for all IT projects in the state. The various steps would be: System Study and Design, Software Development, User Training, Database Creation and Hardware Procurement, and User Interface. Hardware shall only be procured when all other components have been successfully carried out. Emphasis would be given on database creation, back-end system computerisation and process automation for all major government departments.
- In order to ensure efficient utilisation of hardware and software resources, IT audit shall be made compulsory.
- Input-output formats and business processes, including manual process of all major departments, would be redesigned to suit the effective application of IT. A business process re-engineering strategy will be used in all administrative departments during the Tenth Five-Year Plan.
- Appropriate upgrading protocols will be devised for timely and continuous upgrading of different databases.
- A state-wide communication network would be set up for inter/intra-departmental information interchange and the government would promote the use of e-mails, electronic delivery of databases.
- The state government will develop common data protocols, infrastructure and system standards which will enable information and data to be shared and integrated horizontally and vertically across agencies, reducing the multiple collection and processing of the same data

Government-Citizen Interactions (G2C)

- During the Tenth Five-Year Plan, the government would introduce IT at all points of contact between it and the citizen. Use of local language and user-friendly formats and procedures will be encouraged while designing such systems. The interface should be responsive and should convey an appropriate image of the government.
- All forms requiring submission of information, while applying for any

service or clearance from the government, may be made available for electronic access and submission. Appropriate cyber laws will be framed to facilitate online transactions between citizens and the government.

- All government circulars, notifications, tenders, etc. would be published on the website on a regular basis. All examinations and recruitment notifications, and selection results would be published on the website by the concerned departments.
- Appropriate systems would be devised for IT-enabled citizen-department interface. The CIOs and head of departments of respective departments would be responsible for responding to citizen's grievances/inquiries. All departments would have to execute effective online Public Grievance Redressal Systems by the end of the Tenth Five-Year Plan.
- State-level awards would be given to government departments/PSUs every year for outstanding usage of IT.

Action Plan for the State

A. Positioning Rajasthan as an Attractive Location for IT Investment

The state government has already taken several steps aimed at making Rajasthan an attractive location for the development of the IT industry.

The Ministry of Information Technology has set up a Software Technology Park of India (STPI) at Jaipur. STPI is an autonomous society and has the mandate to promote software exports from the country. STPI has also set up a satellite earth station under the state-led initiatives in association with RIICO. This earth station functions as an international gateway and provides worldwide reliable high-speed data communication (HSDC) services at internationally competitive rates. The software units to be located in this Park will be governed by the STPI scheme of the Ministry of Information Technology.

For minimising the gestation period for new IT projects 'plug and play' built up modules are being offered at the IT PARK. Also "one point government clearance" is being offered to set up a unit under 'STP' Scheme.

To set up an Advanced Software Training Institute, land up to 5 acres is being offered at a concessional rate of Rs. 200 per sq. metre (50 per cent of the prevailing land rate) at the IT Park, Jaipur. As an affirmation of the state government's commitment, it is planning to take following policy initiatives:

- Sales tax on software will be fixed at a rate not above the uniform floor rate announced by the state government.
- The sales tax on leasing of computers and its accessories will be fixed at a rate not above the uniform floor rate announced by the state government.
- The rate of tax on inter-state sales of computers, parts, accessories and computer consumables would be fixed not above the uniform floor rate announced by the state government.
- Commercial buildings which are fully dedicated to the software/IT industry will be exempted from land and building tax on a case-to-case basis by the Empowered Committee on investment chaired by the Chief Secretary. If the use of the building changes, this exemption would automatically get revoked.
- Software units have already been permitted to be set up in urban areas. As a further liberalisation step, software units will be permitted to be set up in residential plots without change in land use.
- Property transactions in designated IT parks will be exempted from stamp duty.
- A percentage of the sales tax receipts from the IT industry would be earmarked for strengthening IT infrastructure in the state.
- Power supply companies would endeavour to ensure uninterrupted supply of power. There will be no requirement to take permission from such a company regarding installation of DG sets of any capacity for captive use up to 50 per cent of the industry's demand.
- Promotional campaigns and visits targeting investments into IT industry from countries like Singapore, the United States, Japan, the United Kingdom and Sweden would be undertaken with support from embassies, Central government and industry/trade development organisations of these countries.
- Complete one-stop service will be provided by BIP to all IT units *within a time-bound schedule.*

- The definition of IT software and IT hardware will be modified in all state Acts in line with the approved policy of the Central government.
- The sales tax on CD-ROMs, Optical Disc Media or Magnetic Media containing text, data or multimedia will be fixed at a rate not above the uniform floor rate announced by the state government.
- IT software and IT services companies, being the constituents of the knowledge industry, will be exempted from routine inspection by inspectors like those for Factory & Boiler, Excise, Labour, Pollution, Environment, Industry, Electricity etc. in line with the approved policy of the Government of India.
- IT software and IT services shall be deemed as manufacturing activity for the purpose of incentives for the industry in line with the approved policy of the Central government. Depreciation norms and loan for capital investments and working capital requirements will be in line with the approved policy of the Central government.
- The state financial institutions (FIs) and banks, in line with the approved policy of the Central government, shall treat IT software and IT services as priority sectors.
- State FIs and banks will be allowed to invest in the form of equity in line with the approved policy of the Central government.
- All promotional and liberalised policy instruments available to the IT software and IT services sector will be made available to the IT-enabled services, including the information content industry by classifying IT-enabled services as tantamount to IT software and IT services in line with the approved policy of the Central government.
- State-level awards will be given to IT companies with outstanding performance in exports and in domestic segments. Permission to use agricultural land for non-agricultural purpose will not be required in case the entire piece of land and building constructed thereon is to be used exclusively for setting up an IT industry, subject to the approval by the Empowered Committee on investment chaired by the Chief Secretary.
- The Board of Infrastructure Development & Investment Promotion (BIDI), headed by the Chief Minister, will review IT sector-related projects regularly. Decisions on all investment proposals will be taken within 30 days by all concerned departments.
- There will be one common application form for setting up IT units in the state. The single window system set up for private investment proposals would be applicable to IT proposals as well.
- All software industries including services and training institutions in IT will be entitled to industry status. Such units shall be eligible for all concessions and incentives applicable to industries. For the purpose of this clause, accredited training institutions will also be eligible to claim industry status, subject to certain norms which will enable them to obtain term loans and bank finance at industry rates.
- RIICO shall create a separate area for setting up a corporate and registered headquarters for major IT national and multinational companies in Rajasthan. Land shall be allotted at industrial rates. Up to 20 per cent of the utility area can be used for creating residential accommodation. Such buildings shall be exempted from payment of land and building tax for five years from date of completion. Out of these, the first five companies (pioneering units) would be given land at 50 per cent of the selling price.
- The state government would encourage the flow of investments including FDI and provide full support wherever required. The state government will offer a customised package of incentives for prestigious investment proposals, for example, projects where total investments are more than Rs. 10 crore or a Fortune 500 company is implementing the project. All such proposals shall be received by BIP and put up to the BIDI for approval on a case-to-case merit basis. Before putting up the case to BIDI, recommendations of DoIT will be obtained.
- The state FIs (RIICO and RFC) will provide term loans and equity on priority to units at a reduced rate of promoter's contribution that will not exceed 30 per cent of the total project cost considering the merit of each.
- The state FIs will consider a security margin of 30 per cent of the total assets on case-to-case basis.
- Interest subsidy scheme available to other industries would be made applicable for both computer hardware and software sectors.

- A venture capital fund (VCF) will be created to encourage innovative IT projects/software projects. RIICO is actively considering setting up a VCF with a corpus of Rs. 16 crore. The state government and SIDBI are financing this fund jointly.
- Software industries will be treated as industrial (and not commercial) consumers and electricity tariff applicable to the industrial consumers will be levied on such industries.
- Bar coding machines keep track of prices on the same items by different vendors. Therefore, to encourage the use of bar coding machines in the trade and industry, the sales tax shall be fixed not above the uniform floor rate announced by the state government.

B. Developing Core Competencies in Human Resource Development

The state government is quite aware that the goal of creating an IT-driven and knowledge-based society in the state cannot be achieved without building core competencies in human resource development with substantial inputs of information technology knowledge.

The IT Action Plan submitted by the IT Task Force set up by the Central government has, in its report, specially highlighted the need to take up a proactive drive for 'IT for all by 2008'. It has recommended that the government should launch 'OPERATION KNOWLEDGE' with an aim to universalise computer literacy and also to spread the use computers and IT in education. The key initiatives proposed by the Task Force are:

- Launching of three schemes - Vidyarthi Computer Scheme, Shikshak Computer Scheme and School Computer Scheme.
- Computers and Internet access in every school, polytechnic, college, university and public hospital in the country.
- Networking of all universities, engineering colleges, medical colleges and other institutions of higher learning in the country.
- Initiating a 'Teach the Teachers' programme for upgrading the IT knowledge and skills of teachers on a regular basis.
- Pilot projects in some lead districts, which have attained universal literacy, with an aim of achieving universal computer literacy in all the secondary schools in these districts. These pilot projects would be joint initiatives of local educational institutions, the state government and the Centre.

In view of the lower than national average levels of technical and IT education facilities in Rajasthan, several education centres will be identified with the purpose of making them models of IT-based education. The state government will take preparatory steps so that the time lag between the planning and implementation of national policy is reduced.

The state government's goal is to provide the rural population and other weaker sections facilities and opportunities which are within their reach, in order to make them IT literate. By 2001-2002, the state government plans to run IT centres in all ITIs/ polytechnics located at panchayat samiti headquarters. These IT centres will run short-term six-month long courses. On completion of the course, the Board of Technical Education would provide certificates to successful candidates, which will be given weightage in all government and public sector jobs. The government intends to provide scholarships on sliding scales for needy students.

The state government is alive to the potential of computers as a teaching tool, especially in schools. At present it runs a Central government-funded scheme, 'Computer Literacy and Studies in School (CLASS)', in 135 government senior secondary schools. It also runs another scheme, 'DIET', at 27 locations, where computer training is provided to teachers. The state government plans to take steps to strengthen these schemes so that by 2004-2005, computer training is started in all government senior secondary schools. The state government plans to approach the Central government for financial assistance to implement the plan. The state government will also try to prepare standardised computer syllabi. It will take necessary steps to use computers and multimedia technology to enrich the existing curriculum in senior secondary level schools.

No amount of hardware and software resource can be a substitute for teachers. The state government will take up computer training of at least 10 per cent of teachers in Higher Secondary schools. Progressively, one or two teachers in all other schools will be provided with computer training. To provide incentives to such teachers, the state government intends to provide two advance increments to all the teachers who qualify the proficiency tests. IT centres to be created at district and *tehsil* levels will be used as resource centres for providing computer training to the teachers under this scheme.

An IT course module will be made a compulsory component of all degree courses. At present, computer application course as part of the vocational module is being run in 16 out of 53 government colleges under a University Grants Commission (UGC) programme. This programme will be implemented in the remaining 41 government colleges in phases with the financial assistance of UGC. The state government will provide financial assistance to aided colleges to help them create necessary computing resources and launch this course. A uniform IT module syllabus shall be prepared by the DoIT in consultation with the Department of College Education, universities and other agencies.

The private sector will be encouraged to donate old and used PCs and other items to schools. All government colleges, universities and research institutes will be encouraged to connect to the Internet. They will also be encouraged to have their own websites for information dissemination. DoIT/RAJCOMP would give requisite training for development of such websites. Necessary budget provision shall be made for this purpose.

Private parties will be welcome to set up Internet cafes in colleges and universities. Space shall be provided free by the institution but computer hardware and software would have to be installed by the company, which will be allowed to determine the rates of access to individuals. For the initial three years, this facility would be made available on a rent-free basis.

Internet is making distance learning very cost effective. With Internet connectivity being made available in the districts, distance learning through virtual institutes/universities would be possible for a wide range of subjects. The state government will support the private sector in setting up virtual institutes on the Internet aimed at providing vocational and trade specific education/training.

The 'National IT Action Plan' envisages that Internet connectivity would be provided to every district of the country by 26 January 2000. The state government will take initiatives to pressurise DoT and VSNL to expedite connectivity at the district level in the first phase itself. Subsequently, at least one Internet kiosk would be installed in every panchayat samiti through the state's VAN.

Floor space in government schools and colleges will be made available to private IT training institutes after office hours for providing IT training. No rent will be charged for the first three years. Thereafter, rent will be payable at the rate of 50 per cent of the rent as assessed by the PWD. An Indian Institute of Information Technology (IIIT) will be set up in the state with the assistance of private sector. The state government will provide land for this institute free of cost. It will also allocate Rs. 10 crore towards construction of the building. No rent will be charged for the first five years. Thereafter, the charged rent will be spent on the maintenance of the campus.

C. Creation and Upgradation of IT Infrastructure in the State

The state government is aware of the fact that to position the state as an attractive location for the IT industry, there is a need to create and continuously upgrade IT infrastructure. It is also aware that it cannot do this task alone and needs the participation of the private sector. Therefore, it plans to act primarily as a facilitator to let the entrepreneurial skills of the private sector flourish. As part of this exercise the state government would take initiatives to invite private sector participation in setting up a state-wide value added network. This network will provide data, voice and video communication to the government bodies, PSUs and the private sector. This network will be built on a Build, Own, Operate (BOO) basis. The VAN project would be conceived, designed and executed in a phased manner and will act as the backbone of the IT policy implementation. Subsequently, the reach of the network would be extended to panchayat samiti headquarters.

As envisaged in the National IT Action Plan, the government would encourage the private sector to become ISPs in the districts. If need be, it shall persuade DoT and VSNL to extend optical fibre links to the districts on priority basis.

The state government would encourage internet access through cable TV network in line with the approved policy of the Central government. The RSEB would even consider granting permission to ISPs for putting their cables over its transmission line structures on mutually agreed and negotiated terms and conditions.

As and when private ISPs are permitted by the Central government, right of way will be made available by government departments and institutions such as the PWD, Irrigation Department, power supply companies, municipal corporations, zilla parishads, and so on. Repair of roads would, however, be the responsibility of the service provider. The rates for use would be determined on the basis of open tenders.

RSEB would lease the spare capacity for data transmission to ISPs, the state government or DOT in line with the approved policy of the Central government.

An Electronics Complex encompassing Electronics Hardware Technology Park (EHTP) is being developed by RIICO at Kukas, Jaipur with facilities like quality power, reliable facilities for data, voice and video communication, customs clearance for export and import as well as social infrastructure including housing, school, recreational facilities, shopping complex, banks, post-offices and hospitals.

APPENDIX A–9.1

Rajasthan Telecom Circle

Plan of Net Capacity, DELs and New Exchanges 2001-02
(As on 31-08-2001)

Fixed Service Provision

SSA	Net Capacity		DELs		New Exch.
	Plan	Achievement	Plan	Achievement	Plan
AJ	14,200	2352	15,000	2,277	1
ALW	9,000	844	12,000	2,080	4
BSW	9,000	1364	7,500	1,586	1
BMR	5,100	-328	6,000	757	7
BTP	11,000	1828	12,000	3,269	7
BLW	9,500	16	12,000	1,145	4
BIK	7,400	4952	10,500	1,480	4
BND	2,800	0	3,000	363	2
CTT	9,800	608	9,000	1,769	1
CRU	7,000	400	12,000	1,355	10
JSL	1,500	0	1,900	588	4
JP	33,000	6928	31,000	4,907	—
JLW	3,300	56	3,000	140	4
JJN	11,700	-712	13,000	1,094	3
JDP	17,000	5190	17,500	3,037	11
KTH	12,100	1148	12,000	1,945	8
NGR	13,100	168	13,000	3,118	7
PLI	10,000	-348	15,000	3,264	1
SWM	2,800	1408	4,200	1,142	2
SIK	17,000	1136	15,000	660	5
SRO	11,500	2868	11,000	1,715	3
SGR	15,000	2344	22,000	2,081	8
TNK	2,000	-1040	3,500	199	1
UPR	14,500	2096	15,000	3,719	2
Total	**249,300**	**33,278**	**276,100**	**43,690**	**100**
Status		**1,751,704**		**1,369,978**	

APPENDIX A–9.2

Plan of Mobile Services

Rajasthan Telecom Circle IMPCS-main Project

S.No.	Name of District	No. of IMPCS Lines		Total Lines
		Phase-I	Phase-II	
1.	Ajmer	2000	3000	5000
2.	Alwar	2000	3000	5000
3.	Banswara	1000	1600	2600
4.	Baran	0	1000	1000
5.	Barmer	500	800	1300
6.	Beawar	500	800	1300
7.	Bharatpur	1000	1600	2600
8.	Bhilwara	1500	2500	4000
9.	Bhiwadi	1000	1600	2600
10.	Bikaner	3500	5600	9100
11.	Bundi	0	1000	1000
12.	Chittorgarh	500	800	1300
13.	Churu	1000	1600	2600
14.	Dausa	0	1000	1000
15.	Dholpur	500	800	1300

Contd...

...Contd...

S.No.	Name of District	No. of IMPCS Lines		Total Lines
		Phase-I	Phase-II	
16.	Dungerpur	0	1000	1000
17.	Hanumangarh	500	800	1300
18.	Jaipur	11000	18000	29000
19.	Jaisalmer	500	800	1300
20.	Jalore	0	1000	1000
21.	Jhalawar	0	1000	1000
22.	Jhunjhunu	1000	1600	2600
23.	Jodhpur	3000	4750	7750
24.	Kankroli	1000	1600	2600
25.	Rajsamand	0	1000	1000
26.	Karauli	0	1000	1000
27.	Kota	4000	6400	10400
28.	Madanganj	500	800	1300
29.	Makrana	500	800	1300
30.	Mt. Abu	500	800	1300
31.	Nagaur	500	800	1300
32.	Nathdwara	500	800	1300
33.	Pali	2000	3000	5000
34.	Ramganj Mandi	500	800	1300
35.	Sikar	1000	1600	2600
36.	Sirohi	500	800	1300
37.	Sriganganagar	2000	3000	5000
38.	SWM	1000	1600	2600
39.	Tonk	500	800	1300
40.	Udaipur	4000	6400	10400
	Total	**50000**	**87650**	**134650**

APPENDIX A–9.3

Bharat Sanchar Nigam Limited

Rajasthan Telecom Circle

SSA Name	SSA Head	Area Head	Revenue District Covered
Alwar	GMTD, ALWAR	GMTD, ALWAR	ALWAR
Ajmer	GMTD, AJMER	GMTD, AJMER	AJMER
Banswara	TDM, BANSWARA	GM(SOUTH), UDAIPUR	BANSWARA, DUNGARPUR
Bharatpur	TDM, BHARATPUR	GM(WEST), JODHPUR	BHARATPUR, DHOLPUR
Bhilwara	GMTD, BHILWARA	GMTD, BHILWARA	BHILWARA
Bikaner	GMTD, BIKANER	GMTD, BIKANER	BIKANER
Barmer	TDM, BARMER	GM(WEST), JODHPUR	BARMER
Bundi	TDE, BUNDI	GMTD, KOTA	BUNDI
Chittorgarh	TDM, CHITTORGARH	GM(SOUTH), UDAIPUR	CHITTORGARGH
Churu	TDM, CHURU	GM(WEST), JODHPUR	CHURU
Jaipur	PGMTD, JAIPUR	PGMTD, JAIPUR	JAIPUR, DAUSA
Jaisalmer	TDE, JAISALMER	GM(WEST), JODHPUR	JAISALMER
Jhalawar	TDE, JHALAWAR	GMTD, KOTA	JHALAWAR
Jhunjhunu	GMTD, JHUNJHUNU	GMTD, JHUNJHUNU	JHUNJHUNU

Contd...

...*Contd*...

SSA Name	*SSA Head*	*Area Head*	*Revenue District Covered*
Jodhpur	GMTD, JODHPUR	GMTD, JODHPUR	JODHPUR
Kota	GMTD, KOTA	GMTD, KOTA	KOTA, BARA
Nagaur	TDM, NAGAUR	GM(WEST), JODHPUR	NAGAUR
Pali Marwar	GMTD ,PALI	GMTD ,PALI	PALI
Sawai Madhopur	TDM, SAWAIMADHOPUR	GM(SOUTH), UDAIPUR	SAWAI MADHOPUR
Sri Ganganagar	GMTD, SRIGANGANAGAR	GMTD, SRIGANGANAGAR	SRIGANGANAGAR, HANUMANGARH
Sikar	GMTD, SIKAR	GMTD, SIKAR	SIKAR
Sirohi	GMTD, SIROHI	GMTD, SIROHI	SIROHI, JALORE
Tonk	TDE, TONK	GM(SOUTH), UDAIPUR	TONK
Udaipur	GMTD, UDAIPUR	GMTD, UDAIPUR	UDAIPUR, RAJSAMAND

APPENDIX A-9.4

(i) No. of Complaints Per 100 Stations Per Month

(System of less than 1,000 lines)

State	*1997-98*	*1998-99*
Rajasthan	**12.3**	**13.6**
Haryana	10.4	11.1
Madhya Pradesh	10.3	10.0
Punjab	13.0	11.9
Uttar Pradesh	16.0	15.5
Gujarat	18.2	17.5
All India	12.1	12.1

Inference: Number of complaints received in Rajasthan is not alarmingly high.

(ii) No. of Complaints Per 100 Stations Per Month

(for system of more than 1,000 lines)

State	*1997-98*	*1998-99*
Rajasthan	**26.0**	**27.8**
Haryana	19.4	19.6
Madhya Pradesh	20.1	18.8
Punjab	27.7	21.2
Uttar Pradesh	22.2	18.8
Gujarat	31.3	28.2
All India	22.0	10.8

Inference: For stations having more than 1,000 lines. Rajasthan receives more complaints than the neighbouring states.

(iii) No. of Faults Per 100 Stations Per Month

(for system of less than 1,000 lines)

State	*1997-98*	*1998-99*
Rajasthan	**11.8**	**10.9**
Haryana	9.0	9.7
Madhya Pradesh	9.4	9.2
Punjab	10.9	9.3
Uttar Pradesh	12.1	13.5
Gujarat	16.1	15.5
All India	10.8	10.8

Inference: Faults in Rajasthan are less than developed states like Gujarat, but are equal to All-India level.

(iv) No. of Faults Per 100 Station/Month

(for system more than 1,000 lines)

State	*1997-98*	*1998-99*
Rajasthan	**22.0**	**22.8**
Haryana	16.8	16.6
Madhya Pradesh	17.1	15.2
Punjab	19.8	18.4
Uttar Pradesh	20.0	16.5
Gujarat	26.1	24.5
All India	18.6	18.0

(v) Percentage of Faults Cleared on Same Day

State	*1997-98*	*1998-99*
Rajasthan	**63.8**	**49.5**
Haryana	68.1	65.9
Madhya Pradesh	55.7	56.0
Punjab	54.6	58.0
Uttar Pradesh	67.5	75.0
Gujarat	53.7	53.5
All India	55.3	53.2

Inference: As compared to the neighbouring states, promptness in redressal of faults in Rajasthan is less.

(vi) Percentage of Faults Cleared by the Next Day

State	*1997-98*	*1998-99*
Rajasthan	**81.2**	**76.5**
Haryana	88.1	82.9
Madhya Pradesh	76.4	72.6
Punjab	74.8	75.8
Uttar Pradesh	88.6	89.1
Gujarat	81.8	83.2
All India	71.1	76.2

(vii) Percentage of Faults Cleared within Seven Days

State	*1997-98*	*1998-99*
Rajasthan	**93.0**	**93.5**
Haryana	96.6	92.7
Madhya Pradesh	94.6	86.7
Punjab	96.4	97.6
Uttar Pradesh	98.7	98.8
Gujarat	96.8	97.6
All India	94.0	93.4

Inference: In Punjab, U.P. and Gujarat, faults are generally cleared with more delay than in Rajasthan.

(viii) No. of Repeat Faults Per 100 Stations Per Month

State	*1997-98*	*1998-99*
Rajasthan	**0.3**	**0.2**
Haryana	0.7	0.6
Madhya Pradesh	0.5	0.6
Punjab	0.5	0.5
Uttar Pradesh	0.4	0.4
Gujarat	2.0	1.9
All India	1.3	1.2

(ix) Percentage of Trunk Efficiency (Excluding demand/No delay calls)

State	*1997-98*	*1998-99*
Rajasthan	**77.8**	**79.2**
Haryana	92.1	83.0
Madhya Pradesh	79.1	80.2
Punjab	87.7	90.6
Uttar Pradesh	83.2	81.4
Gujarat	82.4	85.6
All India	81.5	82.7

(x) Percentage of Success Calls to Operator Services

State	*1997-98*	*1998-99*
Rajasthan	**88.1**	**81.7**
Haryana	92.1	83.0
Madhya Pradesh	79.1	80.2
Punjab	87.7	90.6
Uttar Pradesh	83.2	81.4
Gujarat	94.6	93.3
All India	67.9	62.1

Chapter 10

Tourism Industry

Tourism has come to be recognised as an 'industry' given its cascading effect on the economy. This fact has been acknowledged in India, particularly in Rajasthan, resulting in a major focus on the promotion and development of tourism. To this end, Rajasthan has taken the lead in introducing several new concepts, including that of heritage hotels. The Department of Tourism has been marketing local fairs and festivals as tourist attractions, and tapping the high-end segment of tourists through the Palace on Wheels train.

Rajasthan's rich cultural heritage and diverse tourism products attract both foreign and domestic tourists to the state. The Jaipur and Udaipur districts figure among India's top ten popular destinations for foreign tourists. Other states like Gujarat, Uttar Pradesh, Meghalaya etc., are following Rajasthan's example in developing their tourism industry, while Rajasthan is searching for new ways of attracting tourists.

Despite immense potential and various efforts, Rajasthan's share of foreign tourist arrivals in India has been declining over the last decade, though overall number of tourists has been increasing. However, there has been a rise in domestic tourist arrivals, though the country has been hit by various calamities. Following the 9/11 terrorist attacks in New York, the tourism industry has been on the look out for new potential markets in South East Asia, other neighbouring countries, as also domestic markets, devising new marketing techniques and attractive tourists packages.

Nature of Tourist Arrivals in Rajasthan

Owing to its unique topography, history and culture, customs and relatively peaceful environment, Rajasthan has been able to attract a large number of tourists. It has showcased a unique mix of products, ranging from the Golden Triangle (the Delhi-Jaipur-Agra circuit), Palace on Wheels, Desert Triangle (the Jodhpur, Jaisalmer and Bikaner circuit), heritage hotels, pastoral fairs and festivals.

In the initial years of the development of the tourism industry in the country, Rajasthan reaped the advantage of proximity to Delhi, which is one of the major ports of entry for foreign tourists. The recent years have witnessed an increase in the flow of both domestic as well as foreign tourists. Foreign tourists comprise 7.79 per cent of total tourists arrivals in Rajasthan.

Jaipur, Udaipur, Jodhpur, Pushkar, Ajmer, Jaisalmer and Mount Abu are the popular tourist destinations in Rajasthan. Besides Jaipur and Udaipur, foreign tourists also go to Jodhpur, Pushkar, Ajmer, and Jaisalmer in large numbers. Domestic tourists prefer Mount Abu, Ajmer, Pushkar, Jaipur and Udaipur. Rajasthan has important pilgrimage centres for Jainism, Islam and Hinduism and tourism and religion combine to draw crowds to places like Mount Abu, Delwara, Ranakpur, Ramdeora, Deshnok, Pushkar, Ajmer and Nathdwara. Indian nationals also come to Rajasthan for business, education and leisure.

French and British tourists form the majority of foreign tourists in Rajasthan, followed by Germans, Americans and Italians.[1] Foreign tourists mainly come for leisure and exploring the culture and customs of the people and many take time to learn the language, folk dances, music, local musical instruments etc.

---

1. Around 31 per cent of these tourists visited Rajasthan in 2000. 92 per cent of the French visiting India come to Rajasthan. This share in total arrivals is also high in the case of Italians (68.5 per cent), Germans (58.3 per cent), Swiss (44.6 per cent), Australians (31.8 per cent), Japanese (22.51 per cent) and Americans (15 per cent). In 1999, more than 43 per cent tourists coming to India came from the United Kingdom, United States, France, Italy, Canada, Germany, Australia, Switzerland and Japan.

Rajasthan ranks fifth in foreign tourist arrivals after Delhi, Maharashtra, Uttar Pradesh and Tamil Nadu. However, the state lags far behind these states in infrastructure development. Also, the airports at Delhi and Mumbai (Maharashtra) are the main ports of entry for the foreign tourists; whereas Uttar Pradesh and Tamil Nadu have their own international airports. Still, due to proximity to Delhi and good connecting links (air, road, and rail) between Jaipur-Delhi, Rajasthan has impressive number of foreign visitors.

Undivided Uttar Pradesh, Andhra Pradesh and Karnataka reported more than 10 million tourist arrivals in 1999. According to provisional figures for the top ten states in domestic tourism in 1999, domestic tourists in Rajasthan were only one-seventh of that in Uttar Pradesh. Uttar Pradesh has an advantage because of the large number of pilgrimage centres on the banks of the Ganga.

There is a disappointment about the future prospects of the tourism industry among people associated with and dependent on it. There has been a decline in the number of high-income group foreign tourists, while the middle-income level travellers are still coming to Rajasthan. Five-star hotels have suffered more than the two-star and one-star hotels and paying guest accommodations. Hotel occupancy used to be in the ratio of 70:30 for foreign and domestic tourists but this situation has reversed now. There has been an estimated overall 30-40 per cent loss of business between 1998 and 2001.

As a consequence, the industry and government have announced various concessions to domestic travellers. There are reports on increased tourist traffic in Jaisalmer with 90 per cent hotel bookings and increased business for camel safari organisers during the Christmas and New Year celebrations in 2002.

Status of Hotel Infrastructure

The state government has contributed to the development of hotel infrastructure through Rajasthan Tourism Development Corporation (RTDC) hotels at all major tourist centres. The private sector has also pitched in to cater to the needs of tourists. The annual tourist volume is estimated at 77 lakh. Foreign tourist arrivals peak in winter for foreign and domestic tourists increase during the summer. A total of 43,952 beds are available (including RTDC hotels) all over the state. The approved hotels constitute only around 9 per cent of the total hotels in Rajasthan. Heritage hotels constitute a large share of approved hotels in the state and account for 51.6 per cent of all heritage hotels in India.

Since Udaipur, Jaipur and Mount Abu are the preferred destinations for all kinds of tourists, they account for a major chunk of hotels and bed capacities, followed by Jaisalmer, Jodhpur, Bikaner, Ajmer, Kota, Alwar, Chittorgarh and Bharatpur.

This clearly shows that private sector investment in developing hotels follow the trail of tourists. RTDC's share in total hotel accommodation in the state is only 4.38 per cent. The state government can easily withdraw from the hotel business, as the private sector has consolidated its position in this area. Further, to ensure private sector investment and services to the tourists, the government needs to design norms for establishing low budget hotels and motels, making some mandatory provisions for minimum facilities to be provided by them.[2]

Employment Scenario

Globally, tourism accounts for 8 per cent of world employment and 11 per cent of global GDP. Tourism generates employment both directly and indirectly, with indirect employment being many times more than the direct employment. The Central government estimated direct employment in tourism at 17.28 million in 2000-2001 as compared to 15.50 million in 1999-2000 and 14.39 million in 1998-99.

It is estimated that while Rs. 10 lakh invested in the energy sector creates 47.5 direct jobs, 44.6 jobs in agriculture and 12.6 jobs in the manufacturing sector, the same amount generates 89 direct and indirect jobs in the tourism sector. Hence, tourism has immense scope for employment generation in urban and rural areas. To this end, the state government needs to conduct an exercise to estimate the employment potential of the tourism industry, and explore the possibilities of additional employment generation in the urban and rural areas.

Transport Networking

Rajasthan, because of its topography, has been facing problems in developing proper road and rail infrastructure. While the south-eastern and northern parts of the state have good communication linkages, the western areas are poorly linked.

2. Toilets for men and women must be constructed in the vicinity of all categories of hotels, which should have access from the approach road to hotel. The maintenance of these toilets will be the responsibility of hotels.

Interestingly, the infrastructure development index of popular tourist districts is lower than the districts with industrial development, such as Bundi, Chittorgarh, Kota and Jaipur.

Road transport is extremely crucial for movement of tourists. Bus services in some lesser-known routes needs a complete overhaul. The bus services between Jaipur-Delhi, Jaipur-Agra, Jaipur-Udaipur, Jaipur-Jodhpur, etc. are the best among various services.

The rail connections within the state are not adequate as a multiple gauge system still prevails. The programme of uni-gauge system was abandoned which has had an adverse impact on the development of tourism.

Role of Government Agencies in Tourism Development

The Central government has supported the development of tourism in the states through many legislative and administrative measures. The tourist centres or sites in Rajasthan are under the control of either the Central or state governments.

Following the establishment of the Indian Tourism Development Corporation (ITDC), the state government also set up the RTDC—the implementing agency of the Department of Tourism. The state government has provided financial support to the developmental activities of the RTDC. The Central Government provides financial assistance for tourism development projects, under various Centrally-sponsored schemes. In 2001, the Central government released Rs. 7 crore for the development of tourism in Rajasthan. The state government uses the marketing infrastructure created by the Central government abroad to market its products. The Central and state governments are preparing publicity material for promotion of tourism independently of each other.

The tourism industry got a boost with the establishment of the RTDC and the state's tourism sector has progressed well with diverse products being launched by the Tourism Department. RTDC has tried to achieve its objectives by establishing a network of tourist accommodation in all important tourist centres and providing midway facilities along important national highways and major link roads.

The state government has made separate allocations of funds in successive five-year Plans since the Fifth Plan to enhance development-related activities in the tourism sector. It started investing in transport facilities in the Fourth Plan, when it spent Rs. 1.63 crore for the purpose. In the Fifth Plan outlay of Rs. 4 crore, the government focussed on creating tourist accommodation, and a chain of RTDC hotels was established in the state. In the Sixth Plan, the government focused on developing the tourist centres. Almost 60 per cent of the budget outlay on tourism was provided to increase the share capital of RTDC so as to strengthen it.

The focus of the Seventh Plan was also on strengthening the RTDC, which shared 50 per cent of the total revised allocations. In the Eighth Plan, the government shifted its focus to developing new products and other activities, which took up almost 50 per cent of total Plan outlay, leaving 30 per cent for the share capital of RTDC. The Ninth Plan planned for many developmental activities, providing an increased outlay of Rs. 30310 lakh. Training of tourism industry personnel has also been on the agenda.

The share of tourism in the Eighth and Ninth Plans was around 0.4 per cent of the total outlay for Rajasthan, which cannot be termed as a significant hike over earlier plans. The share of tourism in the earlier Plans was 0.14 per cent in the Fifth Plan, 0.25 per cent in the Sixth Plan and 0.19 per cent in the Seventh Plan. The progress in the Ninth Plan shows that development of the Desert Triangle, Palace on Wheels, upgrading of Jaipur airport, etc. have not been started. The Tourism Department attributes this lack of progress to the funds constraint facing the state government.

The state government has proposed private sector participation in developing tourist areas and improving accommodation facilities. However, it is uncertain about the volume of such private investment, given the present decline in tourist inflow.

The government must focus on core sector development, such as providing improved accessibility to all tourist sites, good communication network etc. This must be done in a planned and phased manner, clearly defining the private and public components.

The RTDC hotels have not performed up to the mark, and have, therefore, been running into losses. The new policy of the government emphasises the privatisation of these in order to attract private investment in developing more hotels and motels in areas where they are economically feasible. Though private sector investment in the hotel industry is higher than public sector investment, yet the policy seeks interventions only in such areas where the private sector is reluctant to initiate development. The state government set up a Rajiv Gandhi Mission For Tourism Development in 2000.

Product Mix/Product Design

Rajasthan boasts of a variety of architectural marvels like forts, fortresses, temples, palaces, besides natural features like lakes, hills/mountains desert and forests etc. The state also has a rich tradition of folk music and folklore, which have universal appeal. The Department of Tourism has tried to use market fairs and festivals, which are celebrated by the local people, to attract tourists. These fairs and festivals have become popular with tourists and managing these events has become a major thrust area for the Department.

The Department is also trying to woo organisers of various events/shows (like the Mr. Grasim International pageant) and film producers to showcase Rajasthan. The RTDC signed an MoU with the producer of the film *Talaash* to use the Palace on Wheels for shooting. Developing various tourist circuits in popular places and along important highways will boost the economy of the rural areas and small towns and can further consolidate the present product mix further.

Marketing

The state government has established a network of tourist information bureaus (TIBs) in important tourist centres within the state and in other cities as well. Publicity material on various tourist attractions of the state has been printed with relevant material like hotels and their tariff, transport facilities etc. but, though affordable, this material is not popular with the tourists. Most of the tourists coming to Rajasthan already have literature on the state before they come.

The condition of the various TIBs is deplorable, with inadequate staff. The government needs to strengthen these TIBs by deploying the required manpower and providing multiple facilities for tourists, so as to make them as reliable centres for providing information to all categories of tourists.

Overseas marketing[3] is done under the umbrella of the Union government and also by participating in travel marts. The other avenues of marketing are liaisons with travel agencies operating in India and abroad. However, the most effective marketing strategy is to give the tourist value for money. Tourists must be treated with respect by all those they come into contact with - the common man, shopkeepers, taxi drivers, guides, hotel staff, bus/rail staff, etc.

Policy Initiatives

The state government is striving for planned development of tourism. The state policy on tourism was announced in 2001 and the government is taking action to implement it. The policy envisages an increased role for the private sector, and limiting the government to policy-making, regulation and being a catalyst, wherever required. The policy aims at generating employment in the state, particularly in the rural areas and is geared at benefiting the least advantaged group of people, such as women, unemployed, backward castes and classes. The Shekhawati region is being developed for farm tourism. The *havelis* in the rural areas are extremely popular with tourists and this has pulled in private sector investment in the area.

Though the National Tourism Policy talks about rationalisation of taxes for the industry, capping all the taxes together at 20 per cent, the state policy is silent on this. The policy provides incentives to the hotel industry in selected areas, but the initiatives are inadequate at the moment, and need to be formulated with greater vigour.

The state policy advocates private sector involvement in infrastructure development, and joint ventures with RTDC to develop state-owned properties. It also addresses the problems of inadequate transport facilities. The policy envisages attracting financial and technical support from outside the state for improving roads; introducing package tours, and providing air-conditioned luxury coaches and cars to promote tourism. The Department of Tourism has signed an MoU with RSRTC. Also, Rajasthan Roadways has introduced high tech buses on the Jaipur-Delhi route. It is planning to introduce more such buses on other important routes. The good intentions reflected in the policy can be effectively implemented only when the decision-making process is fast, and government has a clear-cut roadmap to implement it.

Infrastructure development is crucial for accelerating progress in the tourism sector. The roads around hotels/temples/tourist sites can be handed over to the agencies managing these for their maintenance and upkeep, something the industry is willing to take up. They may be provided additional tax concessions for this work.

---

3. The central government has increased the marketing budget for tourism for overseas publicity to woo pilgrim tourists.

Incentives

The Central and state governments offer various incentives to the tourism industry in the form of lower stamp duty, land conversion rates, rebates on luxury tax, entertainment tax on films, and providing finances with some interest subsidy. These measures have also been incorporated in the 1998 Industrial Policy of the state government.

All these incentives generally relate to the hotel industry. However, the hotel industry and tour operators say they do not require these concessions. The private sector has the funds and the willingness to invest in improving infrastructure facilities, if the government is willing to cooperate. What it requires for growth is a debureaucratised environment, proper infrastructure, and conservation of historical sites. There is a need to rationalise the tax structure for the industry, as the present rates are leading to evasion and corruption. The tour operators are seeking the rationalisation of tax on transport and easing accessibility to national parks.

Some steps such as the increase in the exemption limit for luxury tax invites mixed reactions, with the lower-end hotels appreciating the move, while the five-star hotels appear unaffected. However, industry wants total withdrawal of this tax. Private sector players complain that though tourism has got industry status, the commensurate benefits are not extended to it. For example, the hotels are paying electricity bills at commercial rates, instead of industrial rates.

Tourism entrepreneurs find it difficult to avail of various subsidies and tax exemptions, as the concerned authorities take time to approve the requests. Besides, it also breeds corruption. They feel it is better not to get such subsidies and exemptions sanctioned where the process involves government bureaucracy.

Tourist Police

Rajasthan has taken the initiative in deploying tourist assistance police at important tourist centres to instil a sense of security among visitors, especially foreign tourists. The Tourist Assistance Force (TAF) is still in the formation stage. The tourism industry feels that deployment of this police force has reduced the activities of *lapkas* (the touts and tourism mafia) and harassment of tourists.

The TAF has been given certain tasks and powers, but the problems facing women tourists, who face sexual harassment, has been ignored. If the state can implement the TAF scheme at all tourist places, it will be able to curb rising crimes against tourists and will discourage criminals coming from outside the state.

Constraints to Tourism Development in Rajasthan

Despite its many tourist attractions, tourism has not been developed to its full potential in Rajasthan because of the following constraints:

- Poor infrastructure.
- Inadequate and lopsided information.
- Marketing lacunae.
- Paucity of funds for tourism development.
- Negligence towards ethnic tourist centres.
- Inadequate and inappropriate distribution of the human resources of the Department of Tourism.
- Apathetic public attitude towards tourists.
- Safety concerns.
- Higher taxation on private sector tourist service providers.
- Ambiguous state policies.

Infrastructure

Tourism development in Rajasthan requires well-maintained access roads, hygiene-conscious eating places, clean staying facilities and reliable communication links.

In Rajasthan, most infrastructure development has been concentrated around industrial districts, while tourist destinations have been neglected in this respect. The maintenance of link roads, other than national and state highways, is extremely poor. The broad framework of road development must take into account the need to link tourist destinations in different parts of the state. Apart from roads, tourists visiting Rajasthan have stressed the need to provide basic amenities like clean toilets, markets, petrol pumps, bus stops and railway stations at all places of tourist interest. The government has successfully played a promoter's role in developing wayside facilities on important roads and this has encouraged the private sector to do so as well.

Other problems faced by tourists are the limited availability of foreign exchange facilities, which appear confined to three-star/five-star hotels and selected banks only. A widespread network of ATMs is also lacking in all cities of tourists interest. Tourists are also unhappy with the state of cities, which they would like to be cleaner, with better traffic management.

Information

The Department of Tourism has a network of 42 TIBs in 21 districts and in Delhi, Mumbai, Kolkata and Chennai. Ten of these centres are not working while the remaining 32 functional centres, some of which are located in Jaipur, Udaipur, Jaisalmer, Jodhpur, Ajmer, Mount Abu, Sirohi, Bikaner and Chittorgarh, do not function properly because of inadequate staff. The 24-hour TIBs at the railway stations are the best managed ones, as they provide facilities to tourists to book hotels to suit their budget and also look into the problems they face during their stay.

Tourists do not rate these centres highly as information available is not updated and complete and they do not counsel tourists on accommodation reservations, tour planning, or provide exhaustive information on various packages and options available to them.

Tourists need dependable and practical information. However, while the government-produced material does contain exhaustive information on the attractions of a particular region, it lacks in information on transport facilities, their frequency and the approximate tariff structure for each mode of transport. The government is now encouraging the private sector to bring out good publicity material on the tourism products in the state.

Marketing

The Central government advertises the tourism products of Rajasthan through the Internet, print and electronic media, travel marts, etc. The Rajasthan government advertises the products in travel marts, magazines and newspapers. It is also using local newspapers for publicity, which seems inappropriate. These funds can be better utilised for national and international publicity. The Planning Commission has increased the publicity budget from Rs. 25 crore to Rs. 51 crore at the request of the Ministry of Tourism. There are many Internet sites on Rajasthan, which provide detailed information on tourist places, hotels, travel facilities, calendar of events, etc. However, widespread target-oriented marketing in a planned manner is hampered due to the lack of funds. So acute is the funds scarcity that the Department could not aggressively market the state in the United States after former president Bill Clinton's visit. The Department needs to adopt a more aggressive and target-oriented marketing strategy and more funds need to be allotted for this.

Paucity of funds for tourism development activities: The 60 per cent of total Ninth Five Year Plan budget allocated for the Department of Tourism is not made available to it, apparently because the government is not in a position to provide for the sanctioned Plan budgets.

Inadequate and inappropriate distribution of human resources: Of the 206 sanctioned posts in the Tourism Department, only 163 are filled. Of the 43 vacant posts, 25 are in the category of tourist officers/ assistant tourist officer and this is what is responsible for the sorry state of the TIBs. Even the functional TIBs lack adequate and qualified manpower and sometimes people who cannot communicate with tourists are deputed to man these centres.

The success of the Department's efforts is reflected through the level of satisfaction of the tourists. The very purpose of the tourist centre is defeated if tourists do not get proper reception. Hence, trained tourist officers provide the crucial link between government initiatives and the tourists.

General public attitude towards tourists: Tourists to Rajasthan are reported to have had unpleasant experiences with the general public, who subject them to stares, assault them and harass female tourists. Foreign tourists are often cheated. However, the situation was believed to be worse in Delhi, Uttar Pradesh and Mumbai.

Safety Concerns: The state government presently has no legal provisions to give protection to the visiting tourists. The TAF has been deployed at important places of tourist interest, and it has the same powers as the local police. A close networking between local and tourist police needs to be established in this initial stage. The expansion of this force to other important tourist centres is being planned but the overburdened Police Department is finding it difficult to spare trained and qualified persons for the job.

Taxation: The hotel industry is subjected to numerous taxes – stamp duty, entertainment tax, luxury tax, etc. The luxury tax is said to be very high and is passed on to the tourists. The hotel owners have raised this issue at various levels and in 2001 the Central government reduced luxury tax while the state government also raised the threshold for exemption from luxury tax.[4]

---

4. In the 2001, the Central government reiterated its determination to lessen the tax burden on the hotel industry by announcing cent per cent exemption from service tax. The government announced continuation of exemption from service tax for the financial year 2002-03. In the budget, expenditure tax is limited to only room charges of Rs. 3,000 or above per day against the (existing limit of Rs. 2,000).

Similarly, exemption of entertainment tax of up to 75 per cent, to films shot in Rajasthan does not mean much as the Department of Tourism delays decisions and is arbitrary in its approach.

Ambiguous government policies: Lack of clarity and frequent changes in government policies can adversely affect the tourism sector. One example of this lack of coordination is the Central government's sudden decision to increase the entrance fees to famous monuments, which was enforced with immediate effect and later reduced. Such decisions affect the business of tour operators and travel agents as the profit margins on tour packages sold in advance get reduced considerably. It also creates negative publicity for the country. Such decisions need proper planning and must be implemented over a reasonable timeframe. The Central government is considering bringing tourism under the Concurrent List of the Constitution to facilitate better coordination and cooperation between the Central and state governments.

Action Plan For Development of Tourism in Rajasthan

- Jaipur must be developed as a nodal point for tourists and the following steps need to be taken for this:
  - Road, rail, air connections must be provided with all major cities like Delhi, Ahmedabad, Mumbai, Agra, Kolkata, Chennai, etc.
  - Jaipur airport should be upgraded to the status of international airport at the earliest. A Delhi-Dubai flight is now routed through Jaipur and a Jaipur-Bangkok flight has been started.
  - Well-equipped 'tourist service centres' should be set up at all railway stations, the airport, bus stands and all National Highways passing through Jaipur. These tourist service centres must provide information on places of tourist interest, foreign exchange counters/ATMs, telephone/Internet facilities, toilets, handicraft shops, booking facility for buses, trains and airlines as well as package tours and hotels, facilities for renting cars and hiring taxis, providing information on extension of visas etc.
  - The project on developing Jaipur as a 'heritage city' on the lines of Lyons in France and Leicester in the United Kingdom must continue. Work on cleaning up the city should be continued and a participatory system of keeping cities clean should be introduced. The Asia Urbs Programme has sanctioned Rs. 2.25 crore for waste management and sanitation and traffic improvement.
  - Increase the strength of the TAF, so that it can be deployed at railway stations, bus stops and important markets frequently visited by tourists.
  - Jaipur should be connected with all the major tourist centres – Jodhpur, Bikaner, Kota, Bundi, Bharatpur, Sirohi etc. – with good roads, where rail and air routes are not yet developed.
  - Various tourist sites within Jaipur should be linked well, for example, through the introduction of double-decker sightseeing buses as has been done in Chandigarh and London. The Tourism Department has put up a proposal to this effect.
  - The government needs to enact a Rajasthan Tourists' Act which will cover all kinds of crimes and forms of harassment (beggars, *lapkas*, shopkeepers, drivers, etc.) that tourists face in the state.
  - The appearance of the entrance of the city either by rail or road must be pleasant. The government has decided to cityscape all the entry points of Jaipur.
- A task force must be constituted to conduct a situational analysis of the tourism industry across the state. The possibilities of setting up autonomous organisations at the local level for improving the tourism infrastructure, especially for pilgrimage, should be explored. The task force should also study the requirements of tourists, availability of facilities for measuring the demand-supply mismatch, get feedback from tourists about the quality and cost of different services/facilities and the behaviour of tourist industry personnel, suggest policy interventions to promote the tourism industry and to identify the areas in which private sector investment can be promoted.
- Sub-circuits should be developed on all major circuits like Delhi, Jaipur, Agra, Jodhpur-Jaisalmer, Bikaner and major tourist cities. For example, Jaipur is a major circuit and places around it — Lohargal, Khatu Shyamji, Salaser, etc.— can be developed as sub-circuits. Six

tourism circuits have been identified in the 2002-03 budget for development to international standards. This will require the documentation of all heritage sites, natural scenic beauty of the area, and special fairs. Development works, which can serve as examples for others to emulate, also need to be highlighted.

- New products need to be developed. Some new products have already been developed: the Rajasthan Canal Safari on the Indira Gandhi Canal; Palace on Waves; water parks; ropeways and Apna Utsavs. The Apna Utsavs have been planned by the Tourism Department in various districts. The Department should amalgamate this concept with the local fairs to ensure people's participation and preservation of local customs and culture. The Alwar *Utsav* held from February 8-10 every year has been extremely successful. Hence the Tourism Department has decided to include it in the annual tourist calendar. Other new potential products could be:
  - Training modules on handicrafts, paintings, Indian cuisine, etc. can be developed for foreigners and Indians. Tourists have expressed their desire for this and this will help in promoting the culture of Rajasthan.
  - Excursion spots can be developed for promoting weekend tourism and picnics. Special emphasis can be placed on developing games parks for children.
  - Since health tourism has a lot of potential, ayurvedic health resorts and Yoga centres can be developed.
  - Tourists can be allowed to plant saplings named after them or their relatives and encouraged to contribute to the cause of education or any other community development activity.
- The private sector and local people must be involved in developing Rajasthan as an attractive tourist destination. To this end, the following steps can be taken:
  - Conservation of historical monuments can be jointly done by the government and the private sector, with the latter taking the responsibility of maintenance. Facilities should be provided to the tourists near the tourist sites for a nominal fee.
  - Privatisation of transport, including tourist transport, through organised corporate and cooperative bodies, can improve the availability and quality of these services.
  - Individuals, NGOs and private sector can be asked to manage the TIBs.[5]
  - Trusts and caretakers can be entrusted with the task of conserving old religious sites and shrines as is being done at Nathdwara.
  - The area around monuments/temples etc. can be developed with the involvement of the governing trust, private sector and local community and a nominal fee may be charged for this purpose.
  - Suitable and eligible persons from the local community can be appointed as vigilante assistants in places where the tourist police cannot be deployed. They will help tourists with queries and guard them against beggars and touts. A token monthly payment can be made from the entrance fee collected for that particular tourist site.
  - The concept of ethnic tourism needs to be taken to the village level. Special short-term courses in hospitality, cooking, serving etc. should be organised for them. Emphasis must be laid on involving women in such activities. Village resorts must be given to the community, especially the educated youth, to develop, with whatever state assistance in terms of finances and planning they require.[6] Readymade bankable projects can also be used for mobilising finance for this purpose.
  - Development of basic amenities likes toilets must be taken up. Pay and use toilets on the lines of Sulabh Shauchalayas can be built along highways and major roads as well as in market areas.
- Various steps need to be taken on the publicity front:

---

5. In Udaipur, a British national, has taken initiative of publishing a monthly magazine, Out and About Udaipur, which provides information required by tourists. Now he has opened a tourist information centre where he provides information without any charges. His income comes from the sale of the magazine and advertisements.

6. The Shekhawati Festival is being organised jointly by the M.R. Morarka Foundation, a NGO, and the Department of Tourism from 13 to 17 February every year. This will focus on popularising rural arts, crafts, culture and games.

- Publicise intensively the wide range of products through travel agencies, tour operators, travel marts, travel magazines and guides.
- Prize/incentive schemes should be announced to promote tourism.
- The government must focus more on religious and historical tourism combined with some elements of leisure tourism to make a complete package and promote family tourism.
- Printed, audio-visual and other technical aids can be used to popularise folklore, fairs and festivals, customs and other cultural practices.

- The existing Hotel Management Institute and other food and craft institutes can be equipped further to train people in the following areas:
  - Hotel management.
  - Tours management.
  - Tourism product marketing.
  - Foreign language courses.
  - History and culture of Rajasthan, government policies on tourism, etc. for guides.
  - Sensitivity and compassion towards tourists for drivers and other assisting staff.
- Awareness should be created among the general public to treat tourists as their honoured guests. The people need to be made aware of the need for conserving the state's heritage and be sensitive to the degradation of symbols of history, maintain law and order and observing community discipline. The media can be involved in educating the public about better behaviour towards tourists.

  The Department of Tourism, in co-operation with Rajasthan Board of Secondary Education, Directorates of Secondary Education and Archaeology and Museum Department, has initiated a joint programme to encourage and educate schoolchildren to conserve the heritage of Rajasthan. This will be done through organising students into groups called 'Cultural Heritage Seva-Vahini'.
- A plan to clean all cities which are the favourite destinations of tourists needs to be put in place. The residents of the cities must participate in keeping cities clean and the government may have to introduce strict rules in this regard. Clean toilet facilities must be provided at all important places and additional funds for this purpose may be made available to ULBs.
- The process of quarterly permits for tourist vehicles must be simplified so that visitors are not harassed.
- The system of entrance fees to all the monuments must be designed in a manner that the tourists are not required to queue up at each monument. Instead, a single card for various monuments can be issued for a fee.
- The video and camera charges for monuments must be abolished and the entrance fees can be hiked slightly to include these charges.
- Clean budget class hotels need to be promoted.
- Wildlife tourism must be prominently advertised along with the image of Rajasthan as a desert state.

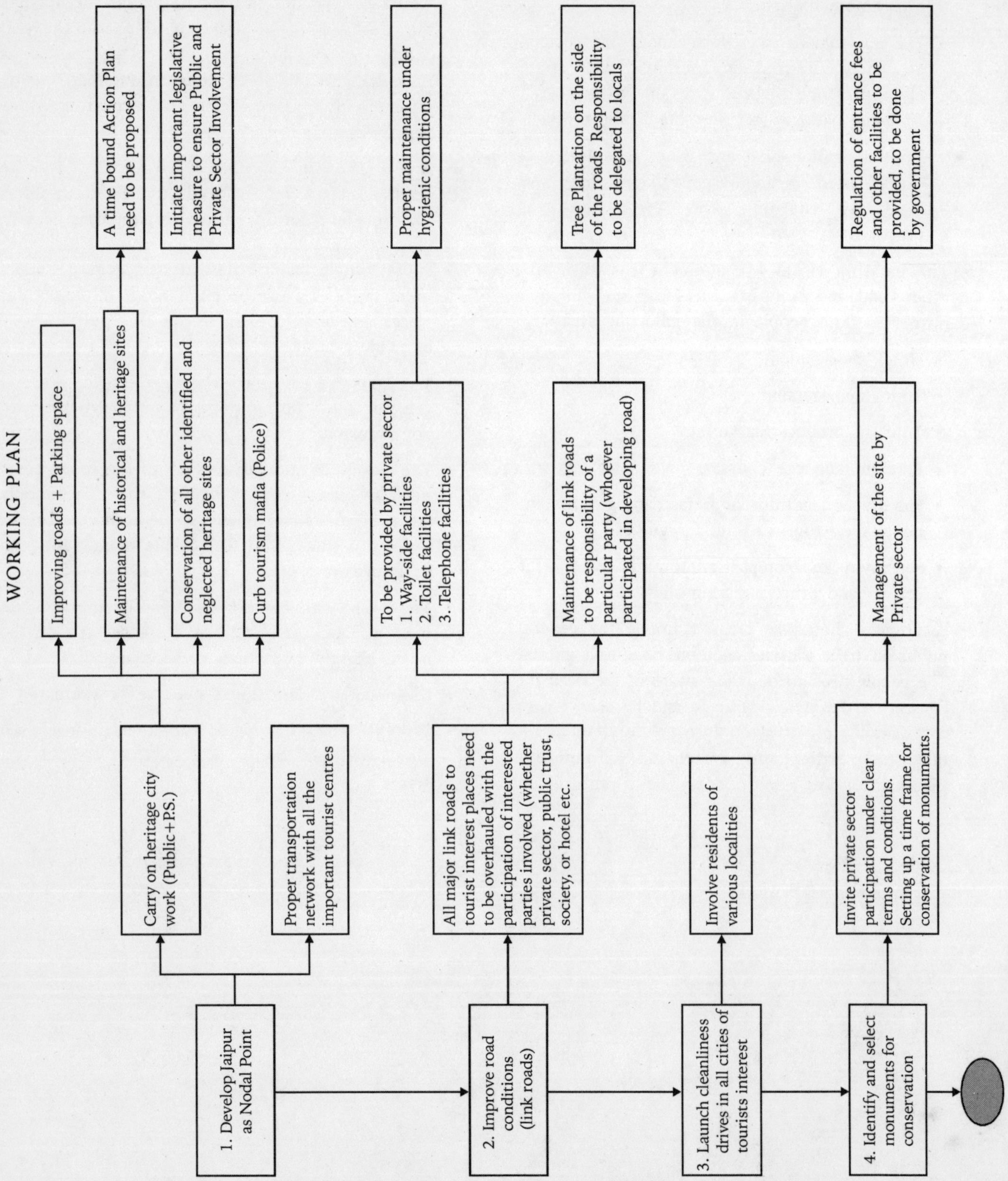
WORKING PLAN
1. Develop Jaipur as Nodal Point
Carry on heritage city work (Public+P.S.)
Proper transportation network with all the important tourist centres
Improving roads + Parking space
Maintenance of historical and heritage sites
Conservation of all other identified and neglected heritage sites
Curb tourism mafia (Police)
A time bound Action Plan need to be proposed
Initiate important legislative measure to ensure Public and Private Sector Involvement
2. Improve road conditions (link roads)
All major link roads to tourist interest places need to be overhauled with the participation of interested parties involved (whether private sector, public trust, society, or hotel etc.
To be provided by private sector 1. Way-side facilities 2. Toilet facilities 3. Telephone facilities
Maintenance of link roads to be responsibility of a particular party (whoever participated in developing road)
Proper maintenance under hygienic conditions
Tree Plantation on the side of the roads. Responsibility to be delegated to locals
3. Launch cleanliness drives in all cities of tourists interest
Involve residents of various localities
4. Identify and select monuments for conservation
Invite private sector participation under clear terms and conditions. Setting up a time frame for conservation of monuments.
Management of the site by Private sector
Regulation of entrance fees and other facilities to be provided, to be done by government

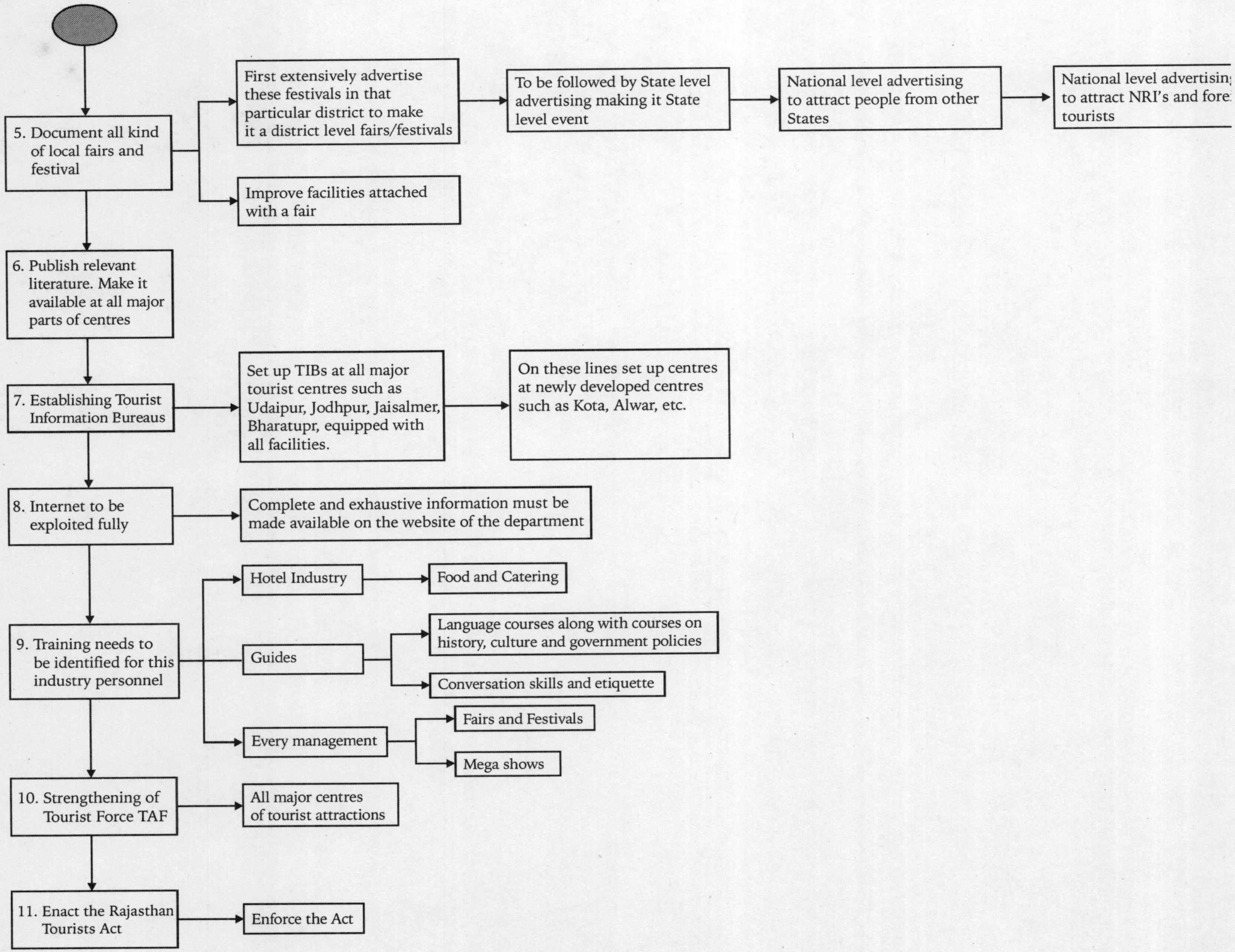

Note: 1. Financial resources required to implement this working plan can e generated by involving private sector, concerned trusts and the public.

2. Personnel will be required for Tourist Information Bureaus.

DESERT CIRCUIT & ITS SUB-CIRCUITS

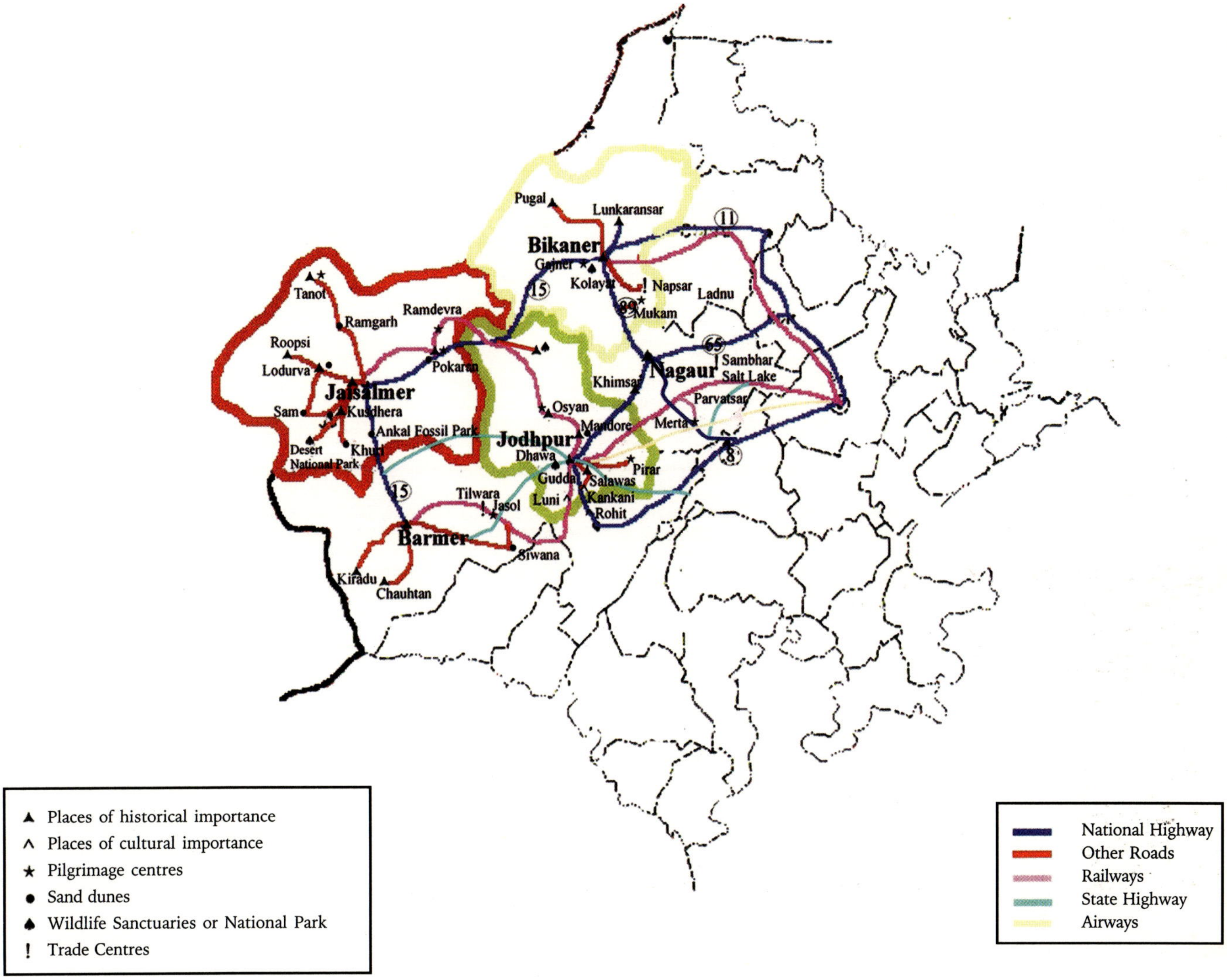

Note: The tourism in the state can be further boosted by developing sub-circuits on the popular major circuits such as golden triangle, desert triangle etc. As an example, desert circuit has been depicted in the map with the potential other destinations around major tourist cities in the circuit. The major tourist destinations and other potential destinations (which can be developed as sub-circuits) around these are as follows:-

(1) Bikaner

(a) Pugal, (b) Lunkaransar, (c) Gajner, (d) Kolayat, (e) Napsar, (f) Mukam

(2) Jaisalmer

(a) Kulahera, (b) Pokharan, (c) Ramdevra, (d) Tanot, (e) Roopsi, (f) sam, (g) Khuri

(3) Jodhpur

(a) Kankani, (b) Salawas, (c) Pipar, (d) Dhawa, (e) Osiyan, (f) Rohit

The tourist attraction in and around these major cities can be linked as a sub-circuit by developing good road links, as presently there is very little connectivity between these destinations. The nearby districts of Nagaur and Barmer can also be developed as sub-circuits to desert circuits to boost the economy of these districts.

APPENDIX A–10.1

Domestic Tourist Arrivals in Rajasthan

Name of the Place	*2000*	*1999*	*1998*	*1997*	*1996*	*1995*	*1994*	*1993*	*1992*	*1991*
Mount Abu	1254770	1338431	1056113	1391832	1124432	1139885	906015	965731	927963	668944
Ajmer	1088000	766497	783782	493596	527008	501476	423912	478977	537325	467512
Pushkar	951000	731124	679303	700515	702604	662699	505357	654827	481102	421299
Jaipur	745476	613511	616315	700358	659694	662879	666417	623578	720953	473247
Udaipur	735333	578622	575088	638987	621516	646547	644995	688188	675403	585672
Nathdwara	462837	464136	326749	281161	231776	236392	200000	249412	246342	215393
Jodhpur	370993	352707	364870	427549	418232	440447	461695	527617	531926	465186
Jhalawar	189694	128703	124615	183812	47680	14289	—	—	—	—
Bikaner	182477	225678	205976	196168	168075	169772	160089	147186	127933	114283
Chittorgarh	120145	150108	327874	240872	182400	152164	153839	200170	173940	155326
Bharatpur	118079	104247	112394	118310	118479	119221	117574	135985	159514	140960
Banswara	109053	111872	96137	76200	76101	74812	50000	59996	65115	58159
S.Madhopur	89391	62080	84961	77238	67693	67384	53242	65721	65039	50088
Alwar	76934	53958	47360	50747	49751	48683	30173	57004	48444	42001
Jhunjhunu	68192	61027	66205	63085	57997	54782	55181	47344	16591	13520
Jaisalmer	58578	35157	52889	69184	79901	85831	76029	254490	225797	201739
Ranakpur	56949	55520	55756	55320	57000	56700	52649	117441	113000	100000
Kota	53874	53017	83212	102162	87583	87066	99488	123465	121641	110716
Rishabhdeo	36893	16021	10629	8754	8057	8000	12747	15527	4941	4409
Bundi	30433	29293	11333	2661	2016	2145	2035	13545	3045	2660
Sariska	15559	11949	10706	5864	4876	4732	13300	17487	6814	6034
Sikar	8136	5952	7952	14912	6140	6668	6904	7205	7168	—
Baharor	5754	6417	8189	10004	7005	4624	4175	—	—	—
Other Spots	543865	717520	690946	379044	418646	—	—	—	—	—
TOTAL	**7374391**	**6675528**	**6403310**	**6290115**	**5726441**	**5248862**	**4699886**	**5454321**	**5263121**	**4299907**

APPENDIX A–10.2

Foreign Tourist Arrivals in Rajasthan

Place	*2000*	*1999*	*1998*	*1997*	*1996*	*1995*	*1994*	*1993*	*1992*	*1991*
Jaipur	154756	129955	150971	184112	148535	150497	111497	146555	170817	155011
Udaipur	77174	78708	78267	84284	82610	86506	73083	85225	79871	72773
Jodhpur	67845	47807	49007	49221	48462	50388	56740	61612	69792	64216
Pushkar	52011	49279	38150	50198	48993	39325	14710	18863	14876	13964
Ajmer	51344	45202	48808	60066	56126	47651	46024	10326	14828	10744
Jaisalmer	50732	50283	52299	57166	49486	48001	42672	44736	49624	42866
Jhunjhunu	28818	25346	30233	26641	24237	22279	15719	17306	16284	15520
Bikaner	28441	22215	26752	25479	19983	18403	15983	15914	15086	14074
Ranakpur	23816	21676	23976	301	350	650	936	45400	41439	38611
Mount Abu	14427	13413	14259	15818	13785	11044	10119	24387	23313	21762
Bharatpur	11262	10626	14638	16265	30323	31351	24794	45360	25379	23000
Sariska	10854	9551	8325	1280	1193	901	487	1293	1225	1178
Bundi	10568	10342	3818	1431	582	538	705	202	247	344
S. Madhopur	8869	6750	8602	4704	6399	6197	9430	10623	14284	10274
Alwar	8235	7934	12465	1837	2427	1805	391	430	607	501
Chittorgarh	8164	5886	10453	13357	18240	17153	12700	9087	6355	6153
Kota	1775	1523	1834	2156	857	833	787	2505	2965	2695
Sikar	527	337	574	803	480	489	291	269	245	—
Banswara	263	338	306	256	260	236	—	125	121	10
Nathdwara	300	166	37	—	—	—	—	—	—	—
Siliserh	206	254	404	394	480	428	240	450	419	371
Jhalawar	82	41	47	95	47	38				
Bahror	66	49	84	80	72	36	26			
Rishabhdeo	22	52	28	25	13	—	7	70	25	20
Other Spots	12543	24952	17032	9091	7006					
TOTAL	**623100**	**562685**	**591369**	**605060**	**560946**	**534749**	**436801**	**540738**	**547802**	**494109**

APPENDIX A-10.3

Tourist Arrival in Rajasthan by Countries of Origin

Figures in Nos

Nationality	Rajasthan		India		Rajasthan			
	Arrivals In 1999#	Arrivals in 2000	Arrivals in 1999*	Arrivals in 2000$	% of Tourist Arrival over India in 1999	% of Tourist Arrival over India in 2000	% Nationality Share 1999	% Nationality Share 2000
France	78982	88223	85891	89565	92	98.5	14.04	14.16
U.K.	70526	68019	345085	354217	20.4	19.2	12.53	10.92
Germany	49589	48719	85033	84989	58.3	57.32	8.81	7.82
U.S.A.	37838	45938	251926	309309	15	14.85	6.72	7.37
Italy	36021	36171	52613	52529	68.5	68.86	6.4	5.81
Australia	23214	25844	73041	90465	31.8	28.57	4.13	4.15
Japan	17897	24555	79373	79167	22.5	31.02	3.18	3.94
Switzerland	15547	18966	34824	31402	44.6	60.4	2.76	3.04
Canada	10351	16776	82892	98259	12.5	17.07	1.84	2.69
Bangladesh	7689	8413	414359	441168	1.9	1.91	1.37	1.35
Others	215031	241476	976889	1010087	22.01	23.91	38.22	38.75
TOTAL	**562685**	**623100**	**2481926**	**2641157**	**22.67**	**23.59**		

Source: * Tourist Statistics: DoT, GoI' 1999; # Tourist Statistics: DoT, GoR' 2000; $ Tourist Arrivals In India: Highlights' 2000.

Tourist Arrival in Rajasthan *vis-à-vis* India

Figures in Nos

Year	Foreign			Domestic			Total	
	Rajasthan	India	State Share	Rajasthan	India	State Share	Rajasthan	India
2000#	623100	2641157	23.59	7434391	N.A.	—	8057491	—
1999*	562685	2481926	22.67	6675528	176082442	3.79	7238213	178564368
1998	591369	2358629	25.07	6403310	168196000	3.81	6994679	170554629
1997	605060	2374094	25.49	6290115	159877008	3.93	6895175	162251102
1996	560946	2287860	24.52	5726441	140119672	4.09	6287387	142407532
1995	534749	2123683	25.18	5248862	136643600	3.84	5783611	138767283

Source: * Tourist Statistics: DoT, GoI' 1999, # Tourist Statistics: DoT, GoR' 2000.

APPENDIX A-10.4

Outlay for the Tourism Sector in Five Year Plans

Rs Lakh

		Fifth Plan 1974-79	Sixth Plan 1980-85	Seventh Plan 1985-90	Eighth Plan 1992-97	Ninth Plan 1997-2002
1	Direction and Administration	40	44.58	100	258	640
2	Share Capital To RTDC		475.27	500	1195	
	Share Capital To RSHC			150		
	Land Bank With RTDC					450
	Total (2)		**475.27**	**650**	**1195**	**450**
3	Tourist Transport Services	33.5	0.01			
	Tourist Accommodation	236.5	0.01			
	Dev. Of Tourist Centres	60	163.63	317	1198	4000
	Share For C.S.S.				150	300
	Incentives For Tourist Trade Activities				455	5
	Fairs & Festivals			50	110	400
	Development of Places Through DC's					200
	Tourist Police/Home Guard					50
	Consultancy Charges				25	150

Contd...

...Contd...

Rs Lakh

	Fifth Plan 1974-79	Sixth Plan 1980-85	Seventh Plan 1985-90	Eighth Plan 1992-97	Ninth Plan 1997-2002
Desert Triangle					19380
Computer Network					100
Land Bank With RTDC					450
Upgradation of Jaipur Airport					920
Development of Palace on Wheels					100
Construction of Paryatan Bhawan					450
Dev. of Tourist Circuits					400
Total (3)	**330**	**163.65**	**367**	**1938**	**26905**
4 RITTMAN Regional Chapter					50
Bldg. of FCI's					250
Sub. for Wage & Salary FCI					300
Sub/GIA for Tourism Units					65
Total (4)					**665**
5 Tourist Information & Publicity	20	102	259.6		1900
Printing of Literature for Intl. Market					200
Total (5)	**20**	**102**	**259.6**		**2100**
6 Others	10	14.5		78	
TOTAL	**400**	**800**	**1292**	**3889**	**30310**
% of Total State Budget Outlay	**0.14%**	**0.25%**	**0.19%**	**0.37**	**0.40%**

Source: Plan Documents: Planning Department, Rajasthan.

APPENDIX A-10.5

No. of Foreign Tourist in India *vis-à-vis* Rajasthan and Kerala

(In Nos)

Year	India^	% Change	Rajasthan*	% Change	Share Over India	%Change in Share	Kerala#	Share Over India	% Change in Share
1991	1677508	—	494150	—	29.46	—	69309	4.13	—
1992	1867651	11.33	547802	10.86	29.33	-0.44	90635	4.85	17.43
1993	1764830	-5.51	540738	-1.29	30.64	4.47	95209	5.39	11.13
1994	1886433	6.89	436801	-19.22	23.15	-24.45	104568	5.54	2.78
1995	2123683	12.58	534749	22.42	25.18	8.77	142972	6.73	21.48
1996	2287860	7.73	560946	4.9	24.52	-2.62	176855	7.73	14.86
1997	2374094	3.77	605060	7.86	25.49	3.96	182427	7.68	-0.65
1998	2358629	-0.65	591369	-2.26	25.07	-1.65	189941	8.05	4.82
1999	2481928	5.23	562685	-4.85	22.67	-9.57	202173	8.15	1.24
2000	2641157	6.42	623100	10.74	23.59	4.06	209893@	7.95	-2.45

Source: * Tourist Statistics: DoT, GoR

\# Tourism Vision 2025: Kerala

@ Provisional figures

^ Tourist Statistics 1999: DoT, GoI.

APPENDIX A–10.6

Profiles of Major Tourists Centres

Place	*Population**	*Domestic Tourist Arrivals**2000*	*Foreign Tourist Arrivals**2000*	*Total Tourist Arrivals 2000*	*Infrastructure Development Index****
Mount Abu	22045	1254770	14427	1269197	105.55
Ajmer	490138	1088000	51344	1139344	90.89
Pushkar	14789	951000	52011	1003011	90.89
Jaipur	2324319	745476	154756	900232	94.45
Udaipur	389317	735333	77174	812507	90.63
Nathdwara	37007	462837	300	463137	90.63
Jodhpur	856034	370993	67845	438838	79.56
Jhalawar	48049	189694	82	189776	87.99
Bikaner	529007	182477	28441	210918	92.11
Chittorgarh	96028	120145	8164	128309	99.93
Bharatpur	205104	118079	11262	129341	91.63
Banswara	87277	109053	263	109316	84.86
S.Madhopur	101994	89391	8869	98260	77.14
Alwar	265850	76934	8235	85169	92.5
Jhunjhunu	100476	68192	28818	97010	82.73
Jaisalmer	85286	58578	50732	109310	73.6
Ranakpur	18194	56949	23816	80765	90.63
Kota	695899	53874	1775	55649	98.23
Rishabhdeo	8023	36893	22	36915	90.63
Bundi	88312	30433	10568	41001	107.96
Sariska	76934	15559	10854	26413	91.63
Sikar	185506	8136	527	8663	84.47
Bahror	22829	5754	66	5820	92.5

Source: * Final figures: Census 2001, Directorate of Census
** Tourist Statistics, DoT, GoR
*** CMIE Report: Profiles of Districts, October 2000.

APPENDIX A–10.7

Infrastructure Profile of States

State/UT	*Infrastructure Development Index*	*Villages Electrified (Per cent)*	*Road Length (Per 100 Sq. km.)*	*Railway Route length (Per 100 Sq. km.)*	*Telephone (Per 100 Persons)*	*Post Office (Per Lakh Population)*	*Bank Branches (Per Lakh Population)*
Delhi	730.62	100	1796.08	11.55	12.5	4.6	10.79
Maharashtra	106.77	100	117.61	1.8	4.1	13.88	6.76
Uttar Pradesh	112.04	77.20	86.77	3.02	1.01	12.6	5.44
Tamil Nadu	142.62	100	158.78	3.07	3.43	19.89	7.79
Rajasthan	**87.27**	**88.56**	**37.89**	**1.72**	**1.72**	**20.15**	**6.25**
Goa	171.57	100	231.43	2.14	—	—	25.63
Karnataka	106.12	98.51	75.09	1.59	2.79	19.43	9.13
Kerala	162.42	100	374.95	2.7	4.18	15.77	10.15
West Bengal	102.09	77.21	19.63	4.25	1.56	11.29	5.53
Madhya Pradesh.	86.66	94.37	45.13	1.33	1.18	14.73	5.68
INDIA	**100**	**85.95**	**75.01**	**1.91**	**2.15**	—	**6.65**

Source: CMIE Report: Profiles of Districts, Oct' 2000.

Chapter 11

State Finances

The financial position of Rajasthan, like that of several other states of India, has deteriorated greatly in the recent past, due to recurring droughts and scarcity conditions in different parts of the state. The fiscal imbalance is reflected in rising revenue and fiscal deficits, interest liabilities, outstanding debt etc., both in absolute terms and as percentage of GSDP. State finances took a turn for the worse from 1998-99, following the implementation of the recommendations of Fifth Pay Commission, which greatly increased the burden of salaries and pensions. As a result, the revenue deficit increased by 415 per cent in a single year (from Rs. 582 crore in 1997-98 to Rs. 2996 crore in 1998-99) and the fiscal deficit by 102 per cent during the same period (from Rs. 2552 crore in 1997-98 to Rs. 5151 crore in 1998-99). This increase in gross fiscal deficit is a cause of serious concern because the revenue deficit was 68 per cent of the gross fiscal deficit in 1999-2000 and nearly two-thirds of the net borrowings of the government in that year were used to finance current expenditure, which is very much on the higher side. The interest payment liability in 2002-2003 (BE) was Rs. 4373 crore, which is 30.5 per cent of revenue receipts, and even exceeds the revenue deficit of Rs. 3902 crore for that period.

FIGURE 11.1

Trends in Revenue Expenditure and Revenue Deficits

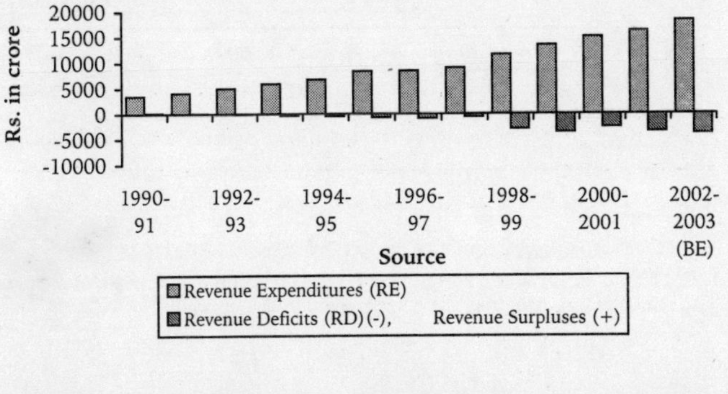

The outstanding debt in 2000-2001 was estimated as Rs. 33,874 crore, which is 44.3 per cent of GSDP and is likely to be 46.1 per cent as per the estimates for 2002-2003. The ratio would rise further if the amount of guarantees or contingent liabilities is added to it.[1]

FISCAL PROBLEMS OF RAJASTHAN

The important issues relating to state finances are:

- Capital outlay in the state has declined to a low level of Rs. 2570 crore in 2002-2003 (BE), which is only one-third of the gross fiscal deficit level for the same period. The fact that revenue deficit was 55.7 per cent of the gross fiscal deficit for 2002-03 (BE) shows that the quality of fiscal deficit is not satisfactory. From 1998-99 onwards, the amount of capital outlay has been less than the amount of revenue deficit, which has a negative effect on the state's development process.
- Balance from Current Revenues (BCR)[2] has been negative in recent years, which means that the government had to depend heavily on borrowings for meeting its entire Plan expenditures as well as some of its non-Plan revenue expenditures.
- The return on investment (ROI)[3] has been very low, moving in the narrow range of 0.21 per cent to 0.46 per cent during 1999-2000 to 2000-01. Such poor returns on investments make the fiscal situation quite fragile and unsustainable as investments are funded from borrowings at high rates of interest.

1. In the two years following 2000-01, the outstanding debt of the Rajasthan government has crossed Rs. 46,000 crore.
2. Revenue receipts minus Non-Plan revenue expenditure and Plan assistance grants.
3. The ratio of earnings to the capital employed.

- The state government's financial assets are less than the level of its financial liabilities. The asset-liability ratio was estimated as 0.63 in 2000-01, which is an indicator of the vulnerability of state finances. While assets comprise mainly capital expenditures, liabilities include financial resources mobilised by the state government such as internal borrowings, loans from the Central government and receipts from the public account (small savings, provident funds, deposits, reserve funds, suspense amount and remittances etc.).
- A huge amount of money is blocked in incomplete government projects, the level of which has gone up from Rs. 1038 crore in 1996-97 to Rs. 2670 crore in 2000-01.
- Plan financing is constrained by extreme paucity of funds. The gaps between proposed Plan outlays, revised outlays and actual outlays have been increasing and the uncertainty has started adversely affecting the planning process.

TABLE 11.1

Approved Outlay and Actual Plan Expenditure

Plan	*Approved Outlay (Rs. Crore)*	*Actual Expenditure (Rs. Crore)*
First Plan	64.5	54.1
Second Plan	105.3	102.7
Third Plan	236.0	212.7
Annual Plans (1966-69)	132.7	136.8
Fourth Plan	306.2	308.8
Fifth Plan	847.2	857.6
Annual Plan (1979-80)	275.0	290.2
Sixth Plan	2,025	2,130.7
Seventh Plan	3,000	3,106.2
Annual Plan (1990-91)	956	975.6
Annual Plan (1991-92)	1,166	1,178.4
Eighth Plan	11,500	11,999
Ninth Plan	27,650	19,836
	(Earlier Plan)	(Possible)
Annual Plan (1997-98)	3,504	3,987.4
Annual Plan (1998-99)	4,300	3,832.8
Annual Plan (1999-2000)	5,022	3,601
Annual Plan (2000-01)	4,146	3,773
Annual Plan (2001-02)	4,516	4,342.3
Annual Plan (2002-03)	5,623	4370.78 (RE)
2003-04	4258	5504.52 (RE)

- In addition, there are problems of the poor financial performance of state-owned enterprises (including cooperative enterprises), heavy financial burden of merit and non-merit subsidies, Centrally-sponsored schemes and Central schemes etc., which are adversely affecting the state's finances. Of the Rs 4373 crore of subsidies in 1993-94, 28 per cent were on account of merit subsidies and 72 per cent on account of non-merit subsidies. An in-depth study of these issues is necessary to find solutions and to put state finances on a sound footing.

Though Rajasthan is only facing 'fiscal stress' and not a situation of 'fiscal alarm' like that of Uttar Pradesh, where the outstanding liabilities in March 2002 had reached Rs. 79439 crore,[4] which was more than twice that of Rajasthan's level of Rs. 35,741 crore, this is causing a lot of anxiety for the state's policy makers.

Trends in Fiscal Indicators

Table 11.2 shows the trends in the revenue account[5] between 1990-91 and 2002-03 (BE).

TABLE 11.2

Trends in Revenue Receipts, Revenue Expenditure and Revenue Deficits

(Rs. crore)

Year	*Revenue Receipts*	*Revenue Expenditure*	*Revenue Deficit (-)/Surplus (+)*
1990-1991	3647.9	3479.9	+168.0
1991-1992	4128.8	4080.2	+48.6
1992-1993	4887.5	4997.0	-109.5
1993-1994	5596.9	5897.6	-300.7
1994-1995	6321.7	6746.5	-424.8
1995-1996	7629.7	8331.6	-701.9
1996-1997	7559.7	8425.7	-866.0
1997-1998	8404.2	8986.1	-581.9
1998-1999	8579.3	11575.6	-2996.3
1999-2000	9789.6	13429.6	-3640.0
2000-2001	12401.8	15035.4	-2633.6
2001-2002 (RE)	12665.0	16175.0	-3510.0
2002-2003 (BE)	14312.5	18214.4	-3901.9

TABLE 11.3

Variations in Estimates of Revenue Account

(Rs. Crore)

Year	*Revenue Receipts*			*Revenue Expenditure*			*Revenue Deficit*		
	BE	*RE*	*Actuals*	*BE*	*RE*	*Actuals*	*BE*	*RE*	*Actuals*
1999-2000	10165	10006	9790	13557	13866	13430	3392	3860	3640

4. State Finances: A Study of Budgets of 2001-02, RBI January 2002.
5. Trends in variable like tax/GSDP ratio, revenue deficit, fiscal deficit and outstanding liabilities have been given in the appendix for selected years.

FIGURE 11.2

Budget Estimates, RE and Actuals for the Year 1999-2000

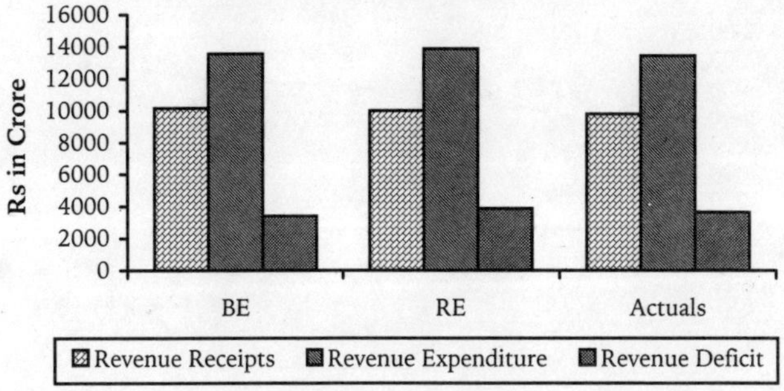

Source: Rajasthan Budget, 1999-2000; 2000-2001; and 2001-2002.

Table 11.3 shows wide variations among budget estimates, revised estimates and actuals for 1999-2000 and exhibits glaring inconsistency in the data used by the state government while depicting the financial scenario. The implementation of the Fifth Pay Commission recommendations led to an exponential increase in the revenue deficit, which stood at Rs. 3902 crore in 2002-2003 (BE) and put the fiscal stability of the state in a precarious position.

FIGURE 11.3

Trends in Revenue Receipts and Revenue Deficits

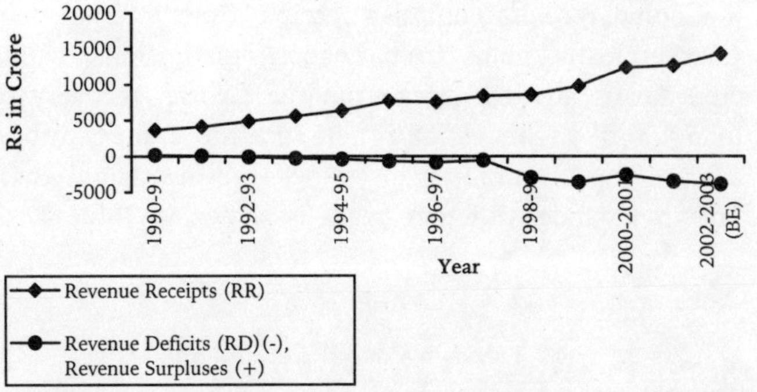

Revenue receipts include tax revenues and non-tax revenues. Tax revenues comprise of own tax revenues such as sales tax, state excise, stamp duty and registration fee, taxes on vehicles etc., and state's share in Central taxes. Table 11.4 compares the tax/GSDP ratio of Rajasthan with that of some other states.

Thus, the tax-GSDP ratio for Rajasthan was lower than that of Tamil Nadu, Gujarat and Maharashtra, but it was higher than that of Bihar, Madhya Pradesh and Uttar Pradesh and was at the same level as that of West Bengal. Improving revenues from own taxes is an imperative for the state exchequer.

TABLE 11.4

Tax-GSDP Ratio of Rajasthan vis-à-vis Other States

Tax/GSDP Ratio (Average 1994-95 to 1996-97)	*Per cent*
Rajasthan	**5.33**
Bihar	3.83
Gujarat	7.29
Madhya Pradesh	4.94
Uttar Pradesh	4.66
Maharashtra	6.55
Tamil Nadu	8.47
West Bengal	5.39

Source: EFC Report, June 2000, p. 219.

FIGURE 11.4

Tax/GSDP Ratio (Average 1994-95 to 1996-97)

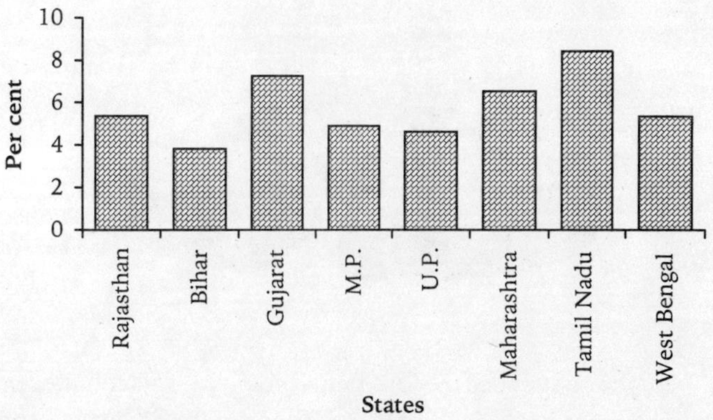

Under non-tax revenues, there have been wide fluctuations in the receipts under own non-tax revenues (interest receipts, dividends and profit, revenues from general services, social services and economic services and grants-in-aid from the Centre under the Eleventh Finance Commission award). The revenues from own non-tax sources increased by 16.3 per cent in 1999-2000 over 1998-99 and by only 7.2 per cent in 2000-2001. The grants-in-aid from the Centre rose by 13.4 per cent in 1999-2000 and by 71.9 per cent in 2000-01. However, they are likely to remain at a lower level in 2001-02 (RE) and 2002-03 (BE).

There has been a significant rise the expenditure on interest payment liabilities and salaries and wages as a ratio to revenue receipts between 1995-96 and 2000-01 (Table 11.5). Clearly, these two heads of expenditure constitute a heavy burden on state finances. This is unsustainable in the long run and the problem needs to be addressed.

TABLE 11.5

Interest Payment Liability and Wages and Salaries in Relation to Revenue Receipts

Year	*Interest Payment (Rs. crore)*	*Wages & Salaries (Rs. crore)*	*Revenue Receipts (Rs. crore)*	*Interest Payment/ Revenue Receipts (%)*	*Wages & Salaries/ Revenue Receipts (%)*
1995-1996	1233.8	2665.8	7629.7	16.2	34.9
1996-1997	1553.1	3088.9	7559.7	20.5	40.9
1997-1998	1896.7	3395.2	8404.2	22.6	40.4
1998-1999	2242.9	4736.8	8579.3	26.1	55.2
1999-2000	2825.2	5043.0	9789.6	28.9	51.5
2000-2001 (RE)	3378.4	5266.0	12507.1	27.0	42.1
2001-2002 (BE)	3980.2	5827.1	13189.1	30.2	44.2

FIGURE 11.5

Interest Payment Liability and Wages and Salaries in Relation to Revenue Receipts for the Year 2001-02 (BE)

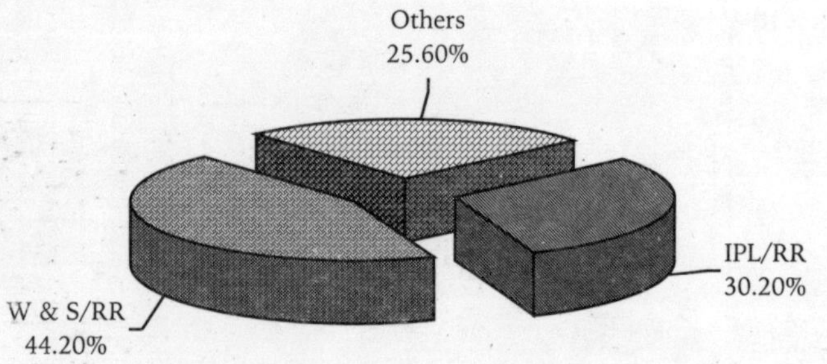

If the expenditure on pensions and miscellaneous general services is added to these expenditures, the strain on state revenues becomes quite formidable. In 2000-2001, the amount under this head was Rs. 1692.8 crore, which was 27 per cent higher than the previous year. It is likely to cross Rs. 2000 crore in 2002-2003 (BE).

FIGURE 11.6

Interest Payment Liability (IPL)

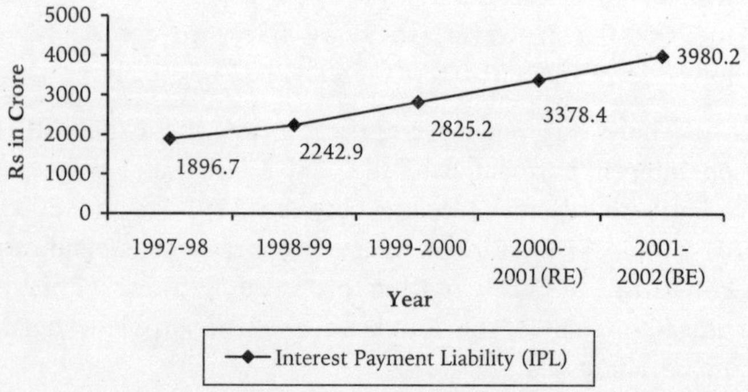

FIGURE 11.7

Wages and Salaries

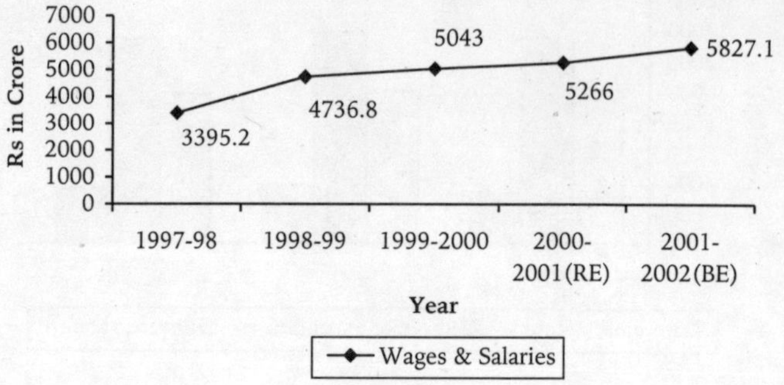

FIGURE 11.8

Pension & Misc. General Services

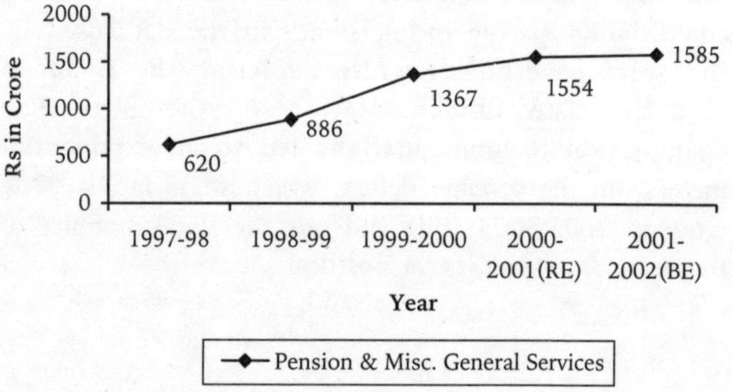

Capital Receipts

Capital receipts comprise receipts from internal debt (market loans, loans from financial institutions, banks etc.), loans and advances from the Centre, recovery of loans and advances and net receipts under public account (mainly from small savings, provident fund etc.). The trend under different heads is shown in Table 11.6.

TABLE 11.6

Trend in Capital Receipts

(Rs. crore)

Year	*Internal Debt of the State Government*	*Recovery of Loans and Advances*	*Loans and Advances from the Centre*	*Net Public Accounts*	*Total Capital Receipts*
1995-96	2961.8	402.1	1140.2	895.0	5399.1
1996-97	5205.2	315.1	1489.9	829.6	7839.8
1997-98	3769.0	887.8	1879.3	1216.4	7752.6
1998-99	5023.0	80.5	1963.5	1418.8	8485.8
1999-00	8060.4	120.0	3354.6	1574.8	13109.8
2000-01	7640.8	123.8	2693.9	1141.1	11599.6
2001-02 (RE)	8430.4	71.0	3531.4	1126.9	13159.7
2002-03 (BE)	5275.6	106.6	4105.1	1286.0	10773.3

Source: Budget at a Glance, Government of Rajasthan, 1997-98 to 2002-2003.

FIGURE 11.9

Trend in Capital Receipts

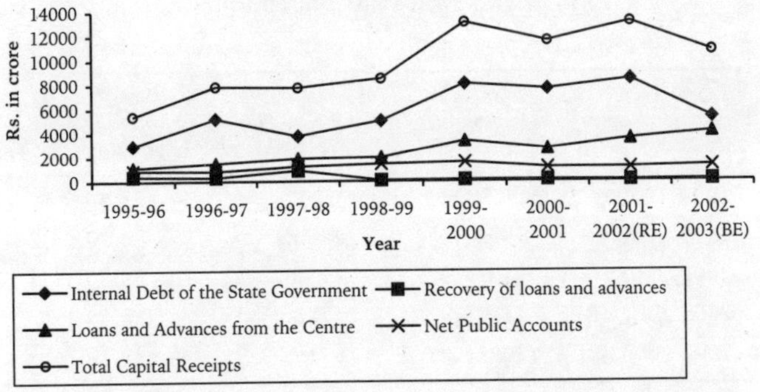

Total capital receipts reached the maximum level of Rs. 13,160 crore in 2001-2002 (RE) of which internal debt was 64 per cent. The state government is now relying more on the Centre for loans and advances due to its rising deficits. Capital receipts in 1999-2000 were 2.4 times the level of 1995-96. Consequently, the burden of internal liability is bound to increase by a large margin particularly because a large part of such receipts now consists of loans. With the shift towards market-determined interest rates, the interest liability has shot up significantly for the state.

Capital Expenditure

Capital expenditure includes capital outlay on general, social and economic services, repayment of loans by the state government and loans and advances by the state government. Thus, there is a difference between capital expenditure and capital outlay. It is the capital outlay that really affects the growth process in an economy and, therefore, needs to be raised at a faster rate. Table 11.7 depicts the recent trend in capital expenditure in the state.

TABLE 11.7

Trend in Capital Expenditure

(Rs. crore)

Year	*Capital Outlay or Investment*	*Public Debt (Non-plan) or Repayment of Loans by the State*	*Loans and Advances Given by the State*	*Total Capital Expenditure (Rounding off up to One Decimal Place)*
1995-96	1757.6	2625.5	517.0	4900.2
1996-97	1657.9	4896.8	297.8	6852.4
1997-98	2507.0	4354.9	351.0	7212.9
1998-99	1792.0	3513.4	443.0	5748.4
1999-00	1517.3	7132.8	324.1	8974.2
2000-01	1384.1	7341.9	419.3	9145.3
2001-02(RE)	2080.0	8236.2	234.3	10550.5
2002-03(BE)	2569.7	4994.3	641.5	8205.5

Source: Budget at a Glance, Government of Rajasthan, various years

FIGURE 11.10

Trend in Capital Expenditure

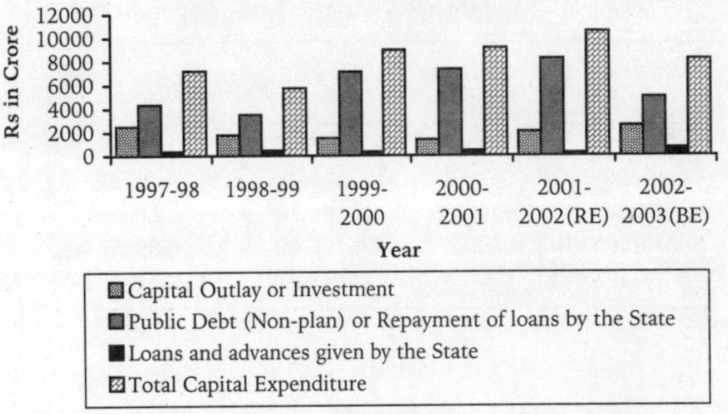

Capital outlay is a very important component of total capital expenditure. It was at its highest level of Rs. 2,507 crore in 1997-98. It went down in subsequent years and is likely to be Rs. 2,570 crore in 2002-03 (BE). Since it is earmarked for investment outlay under general, social and economic services related with Plan, non-Plan and Centrally-sponsored schemes, a decline in capital outlay is a cause of worry, especially at current prices since the decline in real terms would be much more.

The amount of capital outlay has been less than the amount of revenue deficit from 1998-99 onwards, due to burgeoning revenue expenditure.

FIGURE 11.11

Correlation between Capital Outlay with Revenue Deficit

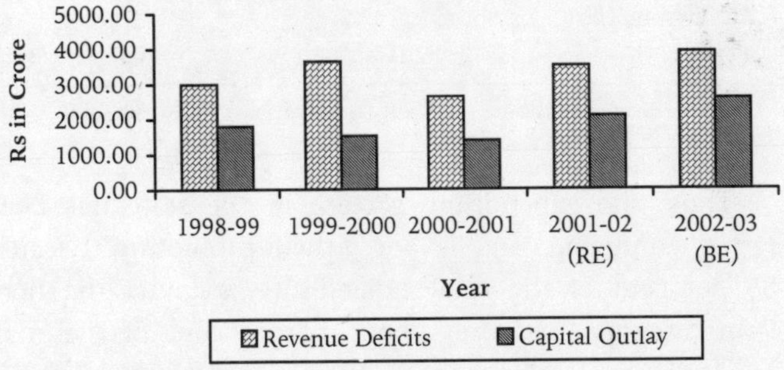

Thus, there is an urgent need for restructuring public expenditure in the state so that more funds can be diverted towards capital outlay for developmental purposes. Capital outlay in 2002-2003 (BE) is estimated to be about 9.7 per cent of the total expenditure (revenue and capital) in the state, while it was only 7.8 per cent in 2001-2002 (RE). It needs to be raised much more in future by devising suitable growth-oriented expenditure under the Plan, non-Plan and Centrally-sponsored schemes categories. Table 11.9 shows the expenditure under these three categories in 2000-01.

TABLE 11.8

Capital Expenditure vis-à-vis Total Expenditure

Year	*Total Capital Expenditure*	*Total Expenditure*	*Capital Expenditure/ Total Expenditure (%)*
1998-1999	5748.4	17324	33.20
1999-2000	8974.2	22403.7	40.10
2000-2001	9145.3	24180.7	37.80
2001-2002 (RE)	10550.5	26725.6	39.50
2002-2003 (BE)	8205.5	26419.9	31.10

FIGURE 11.12

Capital Expenditure/Total Expenditure

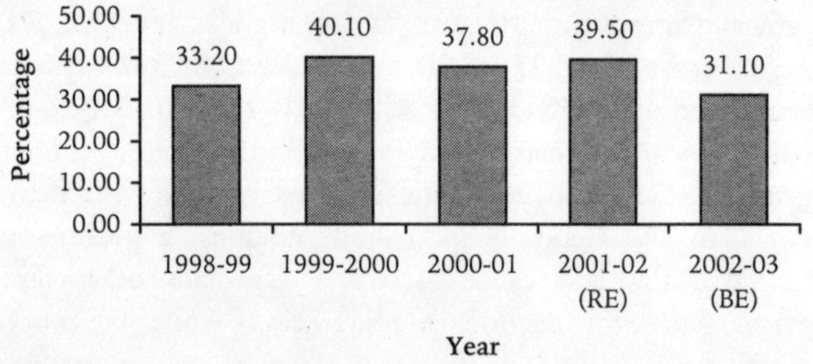

TABLE 11.9

Total Expenditure Under Plan, Non-Plan and CSS in 2000-2001

(Rs. crore)

Category	*Actual*	*% of Total Expenditure*
Plan expenditure	2759.4	11.4
Non-Plan expenditure	20679.0	85.5
CSS expenditure	742.3	3.1
Total	**24180.7**	**100.0**

Source: Economic Review, 2000-01, Government of Rajasthan.

Thus, the expenditure pattern in the state has been rather confusing, and is not growth-promoting, because 85 per cent of the total expenditure is under the non-Plan category, and only about 11 per cent of the total expenditure is devoted to Plan expenditure. This is borne out by Table 11.10 which shows Plan and non-Plan expenditure from 1998-99 to 2002-03.

Plan Financing in Rajasthan

Though it is a crucial part of the planning process, plan financing has been the weakest link in the management of state finances in Rajasthan. Since actual data for resource mobilisation for the Ninth Plan are not available, the data available for the Eighth Five Year Plan has been reviewed (Table 11.11). The various sources of Plan finance are: BCR, contribution from public enterprises, small savings, state provident fund, market borrowings including negotiated loans from financial institutions, miscellaneous capital receipts, Central assistance (normal and from externally aided projects) and additional resource mobilisation etc.

TABLE 11.10

Plan and Non-Plan Expenditures

(Rs. Crore)

Year	*Non Plan Expenditure*	*Total Expenditure (Plan+Non Plan+ CSS Exp.)*	*Non-Plan Expenditure/Total Expenditure (%)*
1998-1999	13772	17324	79.50
1999-2000	19057.5	22403.7	85.10
2000-2001	20679	24180.7	85.50
2001-2002 (RE)	22212.9	26725.6	83.10
2002-2003 (BE)	20916.5	26419.9	79.20

FIGURE 11.13

Non-Plan Expenditure as Percentage of Total Expenditure

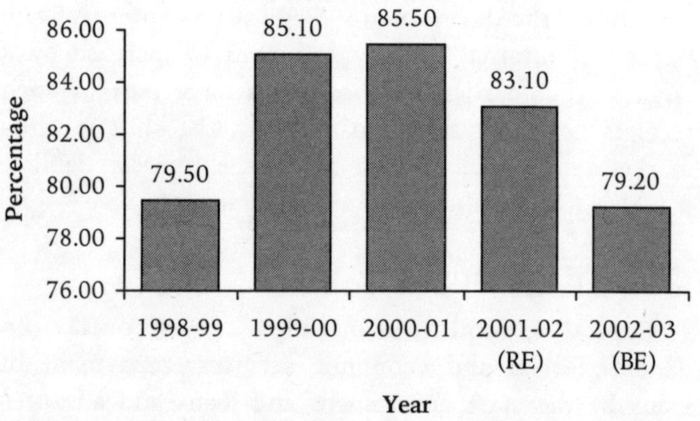

TABLE 11.11

Sources of Plan Financing

Particulars	*Rs. crore (at 1991-92 prices)*
BCR	583.9
Contribution from Public Enterprises	-379.5
Market Borrowings	1269.0
Small Savings	1832.0
State PF	1521.7
Institutional Loan	493.6
Misc. Capital Receipts	-833.6
Plan Revenue Deficits – Aid	752.1
Additional Resource Mobilisation	2827.6
Central Assistance	
General Externally	1770.0
Aided Projects	1663.1
Total	**11500.0**

FIGURE 11.14

Eight Five Year Plan

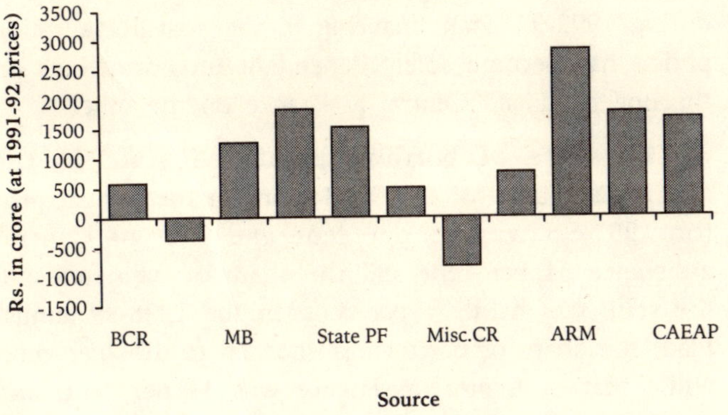

The most notable feature in the sources of financing the Eighth Plan has been the wide gap between Plan projections and the actual realisation under different heads of financing. There have been serious shortfalls in achieving the targets, especially under BCR, contribution from public enterprises and Central assistance under externally aided projects (EAP). Inter-Plan financial patterns in different states are generally not comparable because the published data are not based on uniform price levels.

TABLE 11.12

Projected and Actual Outlay Over Various Plans

Plan	*Projected Outlay (Rs. crore)*	*Actual Expenditure (Rs. crore)*
First	64.5	54.1
Second	105.3	102.7
Third	236	212.7
Annual Plan(1966-69)	132.7	136.8
Fourth	306.2	308.8
Fifth	847.2	857.6
Sixth	2025	2130.7
Seventh	3000	3106.2
1990-91	956	975.6
1992-93	1166	1178.4
Eighth	11500	11999
Ninth (revised proposals)	22525.83 (at 1996-97 prices)	16319.74
Tenth	27318 (at 2001-02 prices)	
2002-2003	5160	4431
2003-04	4258	6044.37

However, on the basis of the information available with the Planning Commission, some important results of Plan financing in Rajasthan can be shown.

TABLE 11.13 (a)

Sixth Plan Financing Pattern (1980-85)

(Rs. crore) (at 1979-80 prices)

	BCR	*Contribution from Public Enterprises*	*Small Savings*	*PF*	*Misc. Capital Receipts*	*Adjustment of Overdrafts etc.*	*Market Borrowings and Negotiated Loans*	*Total State Resources*	*Central Assistance*	*Total Resources*
Plan Estimate	1027.0	-159.3	114.2	99.9	-114.1	-34.0	464.9	1388.7	626.3	2025.0
Latest Estimate	503.5	-238.3	144.0	90.0	-43.6	20.5	401.8	877.8	688.5	1566.2
Shortfall (+) Surplus (-)(%)	51.0	49.7	-26.2	10.0	-61.8	-160.2	13.6	37.2	-9.9	22.7

TABLE 11.13 (b)

Seventh Plan Financing Pattern (1985-90)

(at 1984-85 prices)

	BCR	*Contribution from Public Enterprises*	*Small Savings*	*PF*	*Misc. Capital Receipts*	*Adjustment of Overdrafts etc.*	*Market Borrowings and Negotiated Loans*	*Total State Resources*	*Central Assistance*	*Total Resources*
Plan Estimate	719.6	-402.2	503.6	397.9	-247.2	0.0	888.4	1860.4	1139.8	3000.0
Latest Estimate	-6.0	-9.0	511.2	579.5	-620.1	-22.8	NA	NA	NA	NA
Shortfall (+) Surplus (-)(%)	100.8	-97.8	-1.5	-45.6	150.9	—	NA	NA	NA	NA

Plan-Financing in the Pre-Liberalisation Period

The following tables present the financing patterns of the Sixth and Seventh Plans.[6]

In the Sixth Plan period, there was a shortfall of 51 per cent under BCR, about 50 per cent under contribution from public enterprises and 23 per cent in the total resources, when annual figures for latest estimates are deflated at 1979-80 prices. On the other hand, there were surpluses under small savings and miscellaneous capital receipts. In the Seventh Plan period too, there were heavy shortfalls to the extent of 101 per cent under BCR. BCR was slightly negative by Rs. 6 crore, when it was estimated to be positive to the extent of Rs. 719.6 crore. Similarly, there were heavy shortfalls under miscellaneous capital receipts. These results too have been obtained after deflating the annual figures for latest estimates at 1984-85 prices.

The broad conclusion is that Plan finance deviated drastically in the pre-liberalisation era from the earlier projections. Importantly, the BCR position continued to deteriorate at a fast rate and consequently the dependence on borrowings continued to rise at a very high rate.

Plan Financing in the Post-liberalisation Period

Table 11.13 (c) shows the financing pattern of the Eighth Plan.

TABLE 11.13 (c)

Financing Pattern of the Eighth Plan

	Percentage Share of Central Assistance	*Percentage Share of State's Own Funds*	*Percentage Share of State's Borrowings*	*Total*
Total Outlay (at 1991-92 prices) (Rs.11,500 crore) (Projected)	36.4	19.1	44.5	100.0
Total Outlay (Rs.8,810 crore) (Released) (at 1991-92 prices)	39.2	-15.1	75.9	100.0

There was a shortfall of 23.4 per cent in the realised outlay in the Eighth Plan of Rajasthan over the projected outlay at 1991-92 prices. Moreover, the percentage share of own funds of the state became negative to the extent of 15 per cent as compared to the projected positive level of 19 per cent. As a result, the contribution of borrowings increased to 76 per cent against the projected level of only 44.5 per cent. Thus, three-fourths of the Eighth Plan financing was done through borrowings during 1992-97. Plan financing in the post-liberalisation period has become solely dependent on borrowings on the one hand and Central assistance on the other.

The share of borrowings of the state in the anticipated outlay of Rs. 3748 crore in the annual plan for 1997-98 was 68 per cent and that of Central assistance 31 per cent and the share of own funds of the state was hardly 1 per cent. In the 1998-99 annual Plan, the share of borrowings shot up to 104 per cent, while that of Central assistance was 33 per cent, and own funds contributed negatively to the extent of about 37 per cent (for the approved outlay of Rs. 4,300 crore at current prices for the Plan).[7]

Financing of the Ninth Plan

Table 11.13 (d) shows the pattern of financing of the Ninth Plan.

TABLE 11.13 (d)

Pattern of Financing of Ninth Plan

(calculated at 1996-97 prices) (%)

	Central Assistance	*State's Own Funds*	*Borrowings of the State*	*Total*
Anticipated share	43.34	5.70	50.96	100.0
Actual realisation	32.97	-94.87	161.90	100.0

Source: "State Government Finances – A Survey of Recent Trends" by N. J. Kurian in *Economic and Political Weekly*, 8 May 1999.

Thus, the share of Central assistance in resources actually mobilised for the Ninth Plan, at around 33 per cent, is lower than the anticipated share of 43 per cent. This is primarily due to lower utilisation of Central assistance earmarked for EAPs. However, what is really disturbing is the large negative contribution of the state in resources mobilised for the Ninth Plan.

The size of the Ninth Plan was fixed at Rs. 27,650 crore at current prices, but the actual outlay was Rs. 19,414 crore due to heavy shortfall under EAPs, the impact of Fifth Pay Commission award and reduced Central tax transfers and lower revenue from own taxes, and increased expenditure due to recurring droughts.[8] Thus, there was an overall shortfall of Rs. 8236 crore, of which shortfall in external assistance was about Rs. 3,000 crore. There has been a marked reluctance

6. Amaresh Bagchi and Tapas Sen, "Budgetary Trends and Plan Financing in the States", in *State Finances in India*, Edited by Amaresh Bagchi, J.L. Bajaj and William A. Byrd, 1992, Tables 2.8 & 2.9.

7. N.J. Kurian, "State Government Finances - A Survey of Recent Trends", *Economic and Political Weekly*, 8 May 1999, Pp. 1118-1119.

8. State Planning Department, May, 2002.

among funding agencies to sanction new projects after the nuclear tests in May 1998. Expenditures under the EAPs have been lower than projected in the original proposals. Thus, exogenous factors have affected the financing of Ninth Plan in an adverse manner. Moreover, the state could not mobilise resources for financing the Plan, as it had to cope with recurrent droughts for which substantial amount resources had to be earmarked every year. The budget speeches of the successive Finance Ministers in the 1997-2002 period carried the following estimates of the net yield from additional resource mobilisation (ARM) measures, which refer to resources to be mobilised through fresh tax and non-tax measures only (Table 11.14).

TABLE 11.14

Additional Resource Mobilisation Measures

Year	*Rs. crore*	*Sources*
1997-1998	118	Luxury tax, profession tax, entertainment tax etc.
1998-1999	20	Non-tax revenue
1999-2000	662	Land Revenue, stamps and registration fees, sales tax, taxes on vehicles, electricity duties, entertainment tax, etc and non-tax revenue.
2000-2001	106	Sales tax, tax on vehicles, electricity duties, entertainment tax and other taxes.
2001-2002	72	Various taxes such as irrigation water rates, commercial tax, etc.
Total	**978**	

Source: State Finances, Annual Studies by RBI for these years

Table 11.14 indicates that the state government undertook a major effort towards ARM only in 1999-2000. ARM measures in other years were rather inadequate. Thus, Plan financing poses a serious challenge and dilemma for planners and policy-makers. In order to step up the growth rate of NSDP, successively larger Plans have to be formulated, but due to inadequate capacity for ARM measures, there is greater reliance on borrowing. In future, far more efforts would have to be devoted towards utilisation of external funds for financing developmental projects, particularly in infrastructure sectors like power, roads etc.

Trends in Various Types of Deficits

Table 11.15 shows that the revenue deficit in 2001-02 was more than five times that of 1995-96, while the gross fiscal deficit during the same period was about twice the previous level. The revenue deficit was 27 per cent of gross fiscal deficit in 1995-96, and increased to 61 per cent in 2001-02, which shows a deterioration in the severity of the problem. Revenue deficit as a ratio of GSDP was 0.9 per cent in 1997-98, which rose to 4.1 per cent in 1998-99 and rose to 4.8 per cent in 2000-01, before falling to 4 per cent in 2001-2002. On the other hand, gross fiscal deficit as a ratio of GSDP was 4 per cent in 1997-98, which rose to 7.1 per cent in 1998-99 and remained at that level in 2001-02. In the revised estimates for 2001-2002, it has been estimated at a level of 6.8 per cent.[9] Fiscal experts have emphasised the importance of reducing GFD as a ratio of GSDP in order to improve the financial position of the government. But to achieve this objective, it is essential that the growth rate of GSDP be increased by adopting growth-oriented policies.

TABLE 11.15

Trends in Various Deficits
1995-96 to 2002-2003 (BE)

(Rs. crore)

Year	*Revenue Deficit*	*Budgetary Deficit*	*Gross Fiscal Deficit*	*Interest Payment Liability*	*Primary Deficit*
(1)	(2)	(3)	(4)	(5)	6=(4)-(5)
1995-1996	701.8	202.9	2574.3	1233.8	1340.5
1996-97	865.9	121.4 (surplus)	2506.5	1553.1	953.4
1997-1998	581.8	42.1	2552.0	1896.7	655.3
1998-1999	2996.3	258.9	5150.9	2242.9	2908.0
1999-2000	3639.9	495.7	5361.2	2825.2	2536.0
2000-2001	2633.6	179.3	4313.2	3339.2	973.9
2001-2002(RE)	3510.0	900.8	5753.3	3913.0	1840.4
2002-2003(BE)	3901.9	1334.1	7006.5	4372.9	2633.6

Source: Annual Studies by RBI on State Finances.

Table 11.16 compares the position of revenue deficits and gross fiscal deficits as a ratio of GSDP in Rajasthan and some other states.

TABLE 11.16

Comparative Position of
Deficits in Some States (1999-2000)

(Percentages)

State	*Revenue Deficit (Rs. crore)*	*Gross Fiscal Deficit (Rs. crore)*	*GSDP (1993-94 series at current prices)*	*RD/ GSDP %*	*GFD/ GSDP %*
Rajasthan	**3,640**	**5,361**	**74,452**	**4.9**	**7.2**
Uttar Pradesh	7,253	11,099	187,642	3.9	5.9
Maharashtra	4,269	11,706	240,224	1.8	4.9
Gujarat	3,617	6,792	107,606	3.4	6.3
Punjab	2,727	3,195	62,700	4.3	5.1
West Bengal	9,287	11,666	133,211	7.0	8.8

Source: State Finances, RBI, 2001-02, January 2002; Economic Review 2001-02, Rajasthan.

9. In this context GSDP has been measured at 1993-94 prices.

The position of states like Uttar Pradesh, Maharashtra, Gujarat and Punjab was better than Rajasthan in terms of revenue deficit and fiscal deficits as a ratio of GSDP in 1999-2000. But the situation of West Bengal was much worse than Rajasthan. The gross fiscal deficit has crossed Rs. 11,000 crore in the case of Uttar Pradesh, Maharashtra and West Bengal for 1999-2000, which is more than twice the level of Rajasthan. Thus, seen in absolute terms, the gross fiscal deficit in Rajasthan has been considerably lower than in some of the economically advanced states. However, the ratios of revenue and fiscal deficits to GSDP have been significantly higher than in other states.

Projections of Deficits for Tenth Plan Period

Table 11.17 presents the proportions of revenue deficit and gross fiscal deficit to GSDP for the period 1995-96 to 2001-02. There does not seem to be any marked improvement in the situation. There is a growing support amongst fiscal experts for the view that between 2002 and 2007, the revenue deficit should be reduced to zero level, and fiscal deficit should also be brought down to around 2-3 per cent of GSDP, at both the Centre and the states. Thus, desired targets for reducing revenue deficit and gross fiscal deficit have to be indicated by the government during the Tenth Plan period. Another option is to achieve a very high growth rate of GSDP, though this may prove a daunting task.

The Eleventh Finance Commission has suggested a simple formula to stabilise the debt-GSDP ratio at the state level which would lead to control over the level of gross fiscal deficit as well. The formula is:

$f_t = a_t \ (g/1+g)$

Where f_t = gross fiscal deficit as a ratio of GSDP

a_t= Debt as a ratio of GSDP

and g = Growth rate of GSDP at current prices

suppose a_t = 42%, and g = 20%

then f_t should be

= 0.42(0.20/1.20) = 0.42/6 = 0.07 = 7%

This relationship is very crucial to control the level of gross fiscal deficit. It shows that the ratio between gross fiscal deficit and GSDP can be 7 per cent, in case debt/GSDP ratio is to be stabilised at 42 per cent, and the annual growth rate of the economy needs to be 20 per cent. In case the growth rate is only 5 per cent at current prices, the permissible level of gross fiscal deficit as a ratio of GSDP would be only 2 per cent. Thus, Rajasthan will have to achieve a higher growth rate to sustain a higher level of gross fiscal deficit. The state must face the challenge of achieving a sustained higher growth rate in the Tenth Plan period to improve its fiscal sustainability.

TABLE 11.17

Ratio of Revenue and Fiscal Deficits to GSDP

Year	*Fiscal Deficit as % of GSDP*	*Revenue Deficit as % of GSDP*
1995-96	5.4	1.5
1996-97	4.3	1.5
1997-98	4	0.9
1998-99	7.1	4.1
1999-2000	7.2	4.9
2000-01	5.6	3.4
2001-02 (RE)	6.7	4.1

Source: Economic Review, Various Years, Government of Rajasthan.

FIGURE 11.15

Trends in RD, BD, GFD & PD from 1995-96 to 2002-2003 (BE)

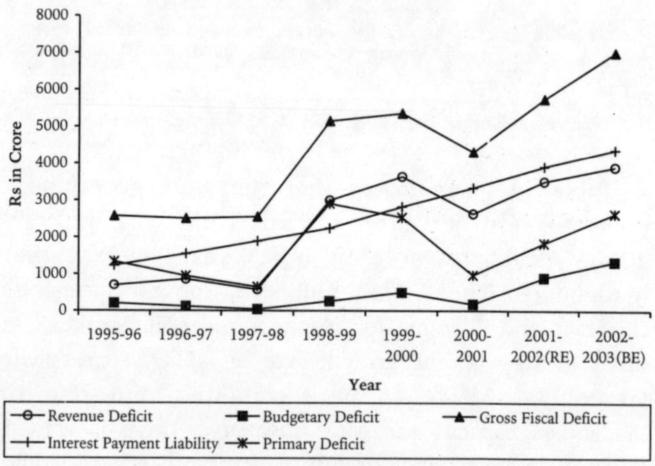

Resource Mobilisation Options

The state government can consider various options for the mobilisation of additional resources.

Tax Revenue

The Eleventh Finance Commission has suggested a method of estimating the taxable capacity of the state by taking the aggregate revenue from all taxes that it can raise under its constitutional powers, and setting up a relationship between tax revenue and variables that influence the tax base as also exogenous factors that determine the tax yield. Therefore, for estimating the tax revenues of Rajasthan for the Tenth Plan period, the Commission suggested that the state's total own tax revenue should be estimated normatively for the base year 1999-2000. For this, the trend growth rate of the total own tax revenue was calculated for 1987-99, which was applied to the actual revenue for 1998-99 to derive the base year tax revenue figures for 1999-2000. The Commission suggested some adjustments in the base year figure (actual figure+Rs.169 crore), because the average tax-GSDP figure for that year was below the relevant group average. The Commission then applied the prescriptive per annum growth rate of tax-revenue of 18.20 per cent to indicate the level of tax-revenue of Rajasthan for subsequent years (GSDP growth rate per annum was estimated at 14 per cent and 'tax-revenue prescriptive buoyancy' was estimated at 1.30 for Rajasthan; hence the annual growth rate of own tax revenue of 14 X 1.30 = 18.20 per cent). Detailed projections of tax-revenue for individual years for the Tenth Plan period are not given here, because much would depend on the actual economic growth in various sectors of the economy in different years of the Plan. In case the GSDP increases at the rate of 14 per cent at current prices every year, there is a possibility of having a higher growth rate in the tax revenues of the state due to tax buoyancy of 1.3.

The Eleventh Finance Commission has, however, indicated that the state's share in Central tax revenues would increase by 16.6 per cent every year and may go up from Rs. 2,959 crore in 2000-2001 to Rs. 5,474 crore in 2004-05. But there are several constraints that need consideration. In 2001-02 (BE), the state's share in Central taxes was estimated at Rs. 3,380 crore, but due to lower realisations of Central tax revenues at the national level that year, there is likely to be a shortfall of more than Rs. 600 crore in the revised estimates for that year. Therefore, it would be quite risky to make precise predictions regarding tax-revenues (own as well as share in Central taxes during the period 2002-2007).

Non-tax Revenue

The position of non-tax revenues in Rajasthan is, by and large, unsatisfactory. Non-tax revenue includes return on capital invested (in the form of dividends, interests and profits), user charges, royalty from minerals, receipts from forestry and receipts from irrigation etc. The return on investment came down from 0.46 per cent in 1996-97 to 0.21 per cent in 1999-2000 and 2000-2001. Such returns are not sustainable, especially when the investments are funded from borrowings. Total subsidies in Rajasthan have been estimated at Rs. 4,373 crore for 1993-94, out of which Rs. 1,230 crore (28 per cent) was merit subsidies and Rs. 3,143 crore was non-merit subsidies. User charges for social services like education, medical and public health and water supply and sanitation and economic services like agriculture, cooperation, irrigation, power etc. need to be raised in a gradual and selective manner. Per capita non-merit subsidies in 1993-94 were to the tune of Rs. 319 on social services and Rs. 356 on economic services.[10] The Finance Department has highlighted a serious revenue-expenditure gap in services like irrigation and drinking water. The revenue from major and medium irrigation projects was 6.5 per cent of their O&M expenditure in 2000-01, while it was 19.3 per cent in the case of drinking water. This situation is a cause of concern and needs immediate remedial action. Thus, non-tax revenue from user charges have very little potential of helping the state exchequer in reducing deficits.

Restructuring of State PSUs

It is also necessary to ensure reasonable returns on investments in irrigation projects, power projects, transport undertakings, departmental undertakings and public sector enterprises. Radical restructuring of the state PSUs to improve their financial performance is necessary on the lines of Central PSUs. Table 11.18 shows the position of accumulated losses of some state-level PSEs in Rajasthan as on 31 March 1998.

TABLE 11.18

Losses of State-Level PSEs in Rajasthan

(Rs. crore)

PSE	*Losses*
Rajasthan State Electricity Board	172.9
Rajasthan Financial Corporation	74.9
Rajasthan State Agro Industries Corporation Ltd.	21.5
Rajasthan Handloom Development Corporation Ltd.	12.8
Rajasthan Mineral Development Corporation Ltd.	3.4
Rajasthan Electronics Ltd.	2.3
Rajasthan Tungsten Development Corporation Ltd.	1.5
Total	**289.3**

Source: Public Enterprises Profile 1997-98, BPE, State Enterprises Deptt., Jaipur, P-20.

Note: Complete list of PSEs and their performance are presented in Chapter 4, Appendix A-4.7.

10. D.K. Srivastava & Tapas K. Sen, *Government Subsidies in India*, 1997, NIPFP, New Delhi.

The RSEB alone had shown about 60 per cent of the accumulated losses of the SLPEs as on 31 March 1998. If the power subsidy given by the state government is also factored in, the amount of losses would increase further. The report of the Comptroller and Auditor General (CAG) (commercial) for the year ended 31 March 2001 indicates that the accumulated losses of the RHDC, RSRTC and RFC exceeded their paid-up capital for the period ending 31 March, 2001 (30 September 2001 in the case of RSRTC). The Raj Singh Nirwan Committee, in its report of December 2001, has suggested closure of seven perpetually loss-making units and suggested the privatisation of two other.[11] Mergers, redistribution of work and partial privatisation have been recommended for 11 others. The committee has recommended the adoption of a voluntary retirement scheme for RAJSICO and recommended the division of the RSRTC into separate companies on a regional or area-basis, conversion of the Housing Board into a corporation and its partial privatisation.[12]

As state finances are closely linked to the financial performance of the SLPEs, a policy of selective disinvestment may be tried out. However, all out efforts should be made to improve their financial performance.

Notwithstanding the heavy losses of many PSUs, the state government has not prepared any policy for disinvestment of such units. During the Tenth Five Year Plan, the state government will have to show strong political will to reduce non-merit subsidies and improve the commercial and financial performance of the SLPEs. The recommendations of the Raj Singh Nirwan Committee should be implemented without delay. Privatisation and corporatisation are the essential ingredients of the economic reform process, which should now percolate to the state level as well.

Financial Implications of 73rd and 74th Amendments

The 73rd and 74th Constitutional Amendment Acts, 1992, give a larger role to *panchayats* and ULBs in the development process, and mandates the transfer of functions, funds and functionaries to them. Naturally, the local bodies would need more financial resources to carry out their increasing responsibilities. Funds for financing the activities of rural and urban local bodies are quite inadequate for the tasks assigned to them, because their own sources of revenue (such as taxes, duties, tolls, fees, fines etc.) as ratio of their total needs/expenditure are very meagre. They, therefore, have to depend largely on transfers from state tax revenues and grants-in-aid.

The Second State Finance Commission Report made the following suggestions to improve the finances of ULBs.[13]:

- House tax, which is collected at present from only 66 of 183 municipalities, should be collected regularly from all the municipalities on the new area-basis.
- The state government should compensate ULBs for loss caused by abolition of octroi.
- The ULBs should explore the possibilities of levying various discretionary taxes they are empowered to and recover user charges for various services.
- ULBs should try to reduce staff costs by contracting out various functions.

Rural local bodies also have scope to raise revenue through various sources.

- Zilla parishads can impose surcharge up to 5 per cent on stamp duty on sale of property in rural areas. The Finance Department needs to lay down the required procedure for this.
- The mandi committees should recover surcharge on market fees on agricultural produce and the Agriculture Department must issue necessary instructions. Part of this revenue must be transferred to the local body.
- The condition that *panchayats* must contribute an amount equivalent to 25 per cent of the share of grants awarded by the Eleventh Finance Commission should be relaxed so that these rural local bodies can utilise the grants awarded to them.

Table 11.19 shows the position regarding own revenues as a ratio of total revenues for all PRIs and ULBs for 1990-91 and 1997-98.

Table 11.20 shows the amount of own resources as a percentage of total revenue of the ULBs from 1995-96 to 1999-2000.

11. Details of the PSUs are in chapter on industrial and mineral development.
12. Press Report in *Dainik Bhaskar*, 3 December 2001.
13. A more detailed discussion of this issue can be found in the chapter on urban infrastructure.

TABLE 11.19

Revenues of Local Bodies in Rajasthan

(Rs. crore)

Year	*Panchayati Raj Institutions*	*Urban Local Bodies*
1990-91		
Own Revenues	24.3	124.8
Total Revenues	754.5	168.0
Own Revenue/ Total Revenue (%)	3.2	74.35
1997-98		
Own Revenues	30.7	380.2
Total Revenues	1520.2	510.0
Own Revenue/ Total Revenue (%)	2.0	74.5

Source: Eleventh Finance Commission Report, June 2000, p. 230 & p. 248.

TABLE 11.20

Own Resources and Total Resources of ULBs

(Rs. Crore)

Year	*Own Resources (Tax Revenue + Non-tax Revenue, Internal)*	*Total Resource (Own + External Income)*	*Own Resources as % of Total Resources*
1995-96	284.6	382.3	74.4
1996-97	334.8	441.1	75.9
1997-98	341.9	485.6	70.4
1998-99	184.4	551.5	33.4
1999-00	119.4	518.3	23.0

Source: Report of the Second Finance Commission of the State, August 2001, p. 142.

Thus, the share of own resources as a proportion of total resources has declined from 76 per cent in 1996-97 to 23 per cent in 1999-2000. Own resources include obligatory taxes like octroi and house tax and discretionary taxes like tax on vehicles, tolls, passenger tax and other taxes and the internal income from properties, fines and penalties, water works, sale of land etc.

TABLE 11.21

Own Resources and Total Resources for PRIs

(Rs. Crore)

Year	*Own Resources*	*Total Resources*	*Own Resources as a Proportion of Total Resources (%)*
1995-96	23.8	992.4	2.40
1996-97	32.5	1286.3	2.52
1997-98	31.8	1199.4	2.65
1998-99	31.8	1521.1	2.09
1999-00	36.6	1679.0	2.18

Source: ibid, p. 133.

FIGURE 11.16

Amount of Own Resources in Proportion to Total Resources for Panchayati Raj Institutions (PRI's)

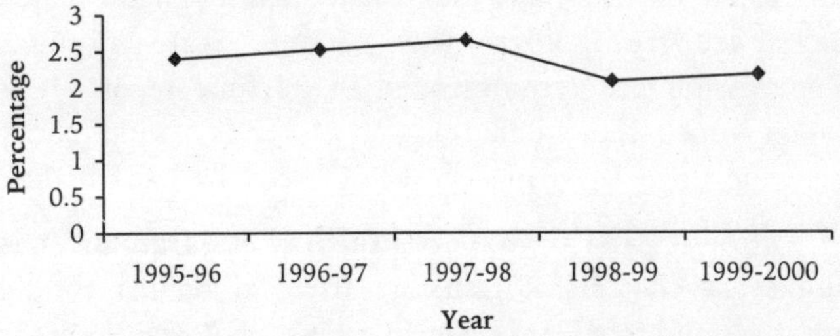

The own revenues of PRIs stagnated around the Rs. 32 crore mark from 1996-97 to 1998-99. The proportion of own resources to total resources has been around only 2.5 per cent for all PRIs taken together. Table 11.21 shows that the share of own revenues as a ratio of total revenues of PRIs in 1990-91 was 3.2 per cent, which declined to 2.2 per cent in 1999-2000. Rural local bodies are more financially stressed than ULBs in Rajasthan. The ratio of own revenues to total revenues for PRIs in Kerala for 1997-98 was 10.1 per cent, which was five times that of Rajasthan. Kerala could do so by giving large grants under the revenue account to local bodies, for which it was later compensated by higher Central grants-in-aid. State Finance Commissions now examine the revenue-sharing arrangement between the state governments and local bodies and also review the entire gamut of issues relating to taxation powers, transfers and their mechanism, borrowing powers of local bodies etc. The second SFC of Rajasthan recommended a total devolution of Rs.794.43 crore to PRIs and ULBs for the 2000-2005 period with the share of PRIs fixed at Rs. 594.61 crore and that of ULBs at Rs. 199.82 crore. Since 1998-99, there has been an increase in the revenue deficit mainly due to the cascading effects of removal of octroi, abolition of state lotteries and implementation of the recommendations of Fifth Pay Commission as well as abnormal expenditure on relief works in famine affected areas.

The Eleventh Finance Commission has recommended an annual transfer of Rs. 1,600 crore to *panchayats* and Rs. 400 crore to municipalities for each of the five years from 2000 to 2005, which would be distributed among the states on the following criteria and weights: population (40 per cent); index of decentralisation on the basis of 10 parameters related with the functioning of the local bodies, etc (20 per cent); distance from highest per capita income (20 per cent); revenue effort by local bodies (10 per cent); geographical area (10 per cent).

On the basis of these criteria, Rajasthan's total share in the allocation for *panchayats* would be 4.92 per cent (or Rs. 98.19 crore a year) and 4.97 per cent (or Rs. 19.88 crore a year) for municipalities. This would be apart from what the Second State Finance Commission has recommended in its final report. It is to be hoped that such transfer of funds would partly ease the financial stringency being faced by local bodies.

Eminent fiscal expert Indira Rajaraman has suggested that fiscal transfers to local bodies should not be interpreted narrowly in terms of flows from the Tenth and Eleventh Finance Commissions only, but the massive annual developmental flows from the Central government for rural areas must also be taken into account. This amount was Rs. 16,000 crore for 2001-02 (BE), which was 10 times the Eleventh Finance Commission's annual provision of Rs. 1,600 crore for *panchayats*. Therefore, there is a need for more cautious interpretation regarding the flow of funds to rural and urban local bodies and developmental efforts for these areas. But there is no doubt about the fact that the own revenues of the PRIs, especially the *gram panchayats* are extremely meagre and need to be enhanced substantially.

Trends in Finance Commission Transfers

The proportion of Rajasthan in successive Finance Commission transfers increased from 5.03 per cent in 1995-2000 to 5.42 per cent in 2000-2005. Thus, the Eleventh Finance Commission was more liberal towards Rajasthan as compared to the Tenth Finance Commission.

TABLE 11.22

Finance Commission Transfers to Rajasthan as Percentage of Total Transfers to All States

Finance Commission	*%*
1950-51 to 1955-56	2.60
1957-58 to 1960-61	4.57
1961-62 to 1965-66	NA
Fourth Finance Commission	4.52
Fifth Finance Commission	4.99
Sixth Finance Commission	5.87
Seventh Finance Commission	4.33
Eighth Finance Commission	4.25
Ninth I Report	4.77
Ninth II Report	6.15
Tenth Finance Commission	5.03
Eleventh Finance Commission	5.42

FIGURE 11.17

Trends in Finance Commision (FC) Transfers to Rajasthan as Percentage of Total Transfers to all States

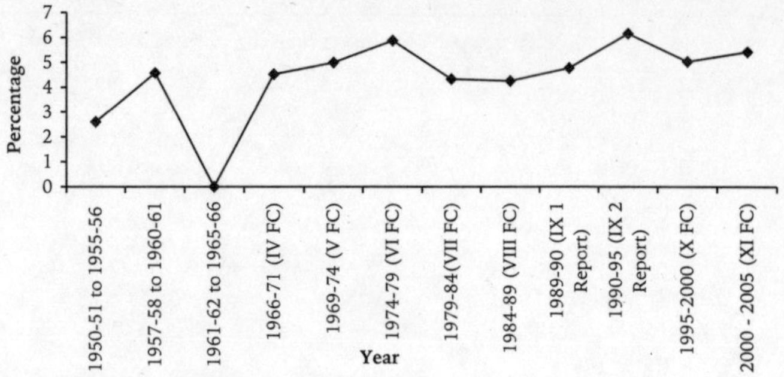

Expenditure Compression

Revenue Expenditure

Controlling unproductive or wasteful expenditure is an effective way of addressing the problem of fiscal stress being faced by Central and state governments alike. But there are difficulties in identifying pockets of wasteful expenditure and in implementing the harsh measures needed to cut them drastically.

For 2000-2001, the total revenue expenditure was Rs. 15,035 crore, of which 9.7 per cent was under the Plan category, 87.5 per cent was under non-Plan category and 2.8 per cent was under the Centrally-sponsored schemes category. The major scope for expenditure compression, therefore, lies in the non-Plan category. Non-Plan expenditure has two components – developmental (under social and economic services) and non-developmental (under various general services such as organs of the State, fiscal services, interest payments, administrative services, pensions, etc. and payments to local bodies).

Interest payments account for half of the non-Plan non-developmental revenue expenditure of Rs. 6,578 crore, pensions about one-fourth and administrative services one-sixth. Thus, 90 per cent of non-Plan non-developmental expenditure is absorbed under these three items. As these expenditures are, by and large, committed in nature, it is not easy to reduce them. Efforts are already being made to reduce interest liability. The establishment of Debt Amortisation and Guarantee Redemption Funds has been suggested, but resource constraints do not permit this right now. The state government is curbing recruitment for services like police, education, health and medicine, so that social sector expenditure is not drastically affected. These sectors constitute 64 per cent of the total staff of the government. Compression of expenditure on salaries and pension warrants downsizing of government, which can be done only in the long run. The recent decision of the state government to introduce a participatory pension scheme for new employees may limit the pension liability

NCAER has suggested that Rajasthan should try to limit the growth rate of the non-interest component of revenue expenditure of 10 per cent a year over the next few years so as to reduce the revenue deficit-GSDP ratio as well as gross fiscal deficit-GSDP ratio in future.[14] The non-interest expenditure under general services (excluding grants-in-aid by the state government) increased from Rs. 640.7 crore in 1990-91 to Rs. 3,228 crore in 2000-2001 resulting in a compound annual growth rate of 17.5 per cent, which was on the higher side. It should be reduced to a level of 10 per cent as far as possible. The state government has already started implementing these recommendations.

Capital Expenditure

Table 11.23 presents data on capital expenditure for the past five years.

TABLE 11.23

Trends in Capital Expenditure

(Rs. Crore)

Year	*Plan*	*Non-Plan*	*Centrally-Sponsored Schemes*	*Total Capital Expenditure*
1998-99	1845.3	3640.0	263.1	5748.4
1999-00	1488.0	7270.6	215.5	8947.1
2000-01	1301.8	7528.9	314.6	9145.3
2001-02 (RE)	1655.1	8404.4	491.0	10550.5
2002-03 (BE)	2411.5	5275.2	518.8	8205.5

FIGURE 11.18

Capital Expenditure - Plan - Non-Plan

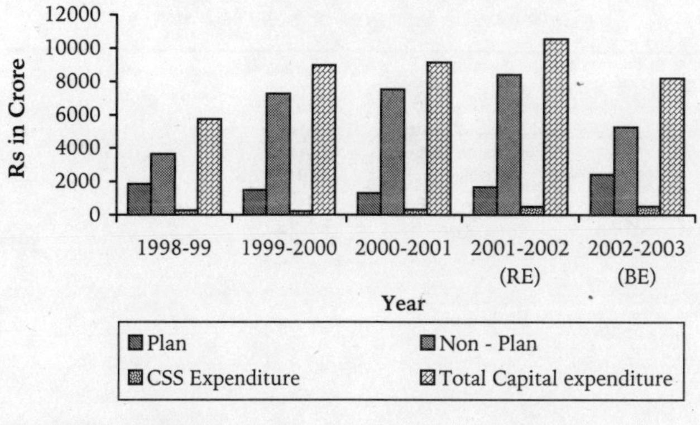

14. Finances of the Northern States in the New Millennium - Status and Prospects, July 2001

Thus, non-Plan capital expenditure was around 80 per cent of the total expenditure in 2001-02 (RE). There has been consistent increase in it since 1998-99.

Capital outlay on investment includes liquidation of public debt (non-Plan) and advances given to various bodies. In 2002-2003 (BE), capital outlay or investment was 31.3 per cent of total capital expenditure. About 60.9 per cent of total capital expenditure was used for repayment of public debt (internal debt and Central loans) and the rest 7.8 per cent was given as loans and advances by the state government to various bodies. Thus, annual capital outlay has been a very small part of the total annual capital expenditure in Rajasthan.

Table 11.24 shows the ratio of capital outlay to total capital expenditure from 1998-99.

TABLE 11.24

Ratio of Capital Outlay to Capital Expenditure

Year	*(%)*
1998-99	31.2
1999-00	16.9
2000-01	15.1
2001-02 (RE)	19.7
2002-03 (BE)	31.3

Thus, capital outlay as a ratio of total capital expenditure came down from 31 per cent in 1998-99 to 15 per cent in 2000-2001, which was a substantial decline. Clearly, there is no scope for compression of capital expenditure. On the contrary, capital outlay, which is an important component of capital expenditure, has to be enhanced for economic development. Repayment of existing loans and advances by the government are committed payments, and cannot be reduced by the government at will. There is a need for proper planning and proper execution of capital projects in various sectors, which will expedite their completion and minimise time and cost over-runs.

Public Borrowings in Rajasthan

The various categories of public loans are: internal debt (market borrowings, loans from financial institutions, ways and means advances from the RBI); Central loans comprising non-Plan loans (of which small savings form a major part), Plan loans, sponsored schemes loans, Centrally-sponsored scheme loans, ways and means advances and other loans; and other liabilities (provident fund, reserve funds and deposits. Table 11.25 shows the state's outstanding liabilities.

TABLE 11.25

Balance of Outstanding Debt and Other Liabilities as on 31 March

(Rs. crore)

Item	*1999-2000*	*2000-2001*	*2001-2002(RE)*	*2002-2003(BE)*
Internal debt	7515.0	8283.2	9204.8	10198.1
Central loans	12480.7	14705.3	17509.3	20902.5
Other Liabilities	10015.1	10885.4	12003.3	13279.2
Total	**30010.8**	**33873.9**	**38717.4**	**44379.8**

Source: Finance Department, GoR, June 2002.

FIGURE 11.19

Balance of Outstanding Debt and Other Liabilities as on 31 March Every Year

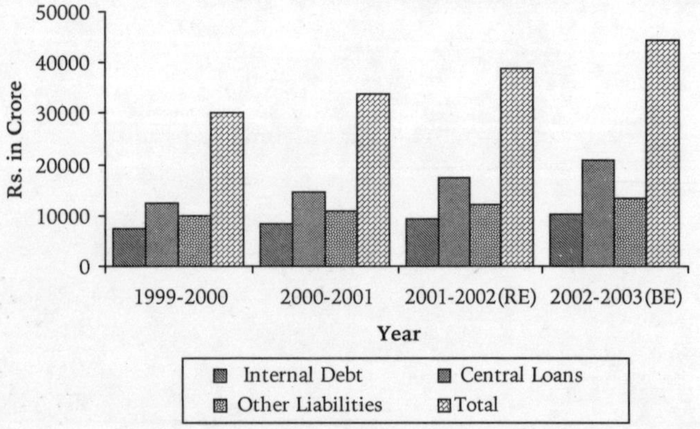

The outstanding debt and other liabilities were Rs. 6,546 crore on 31 March 1991, which increased to Rs. 14,104 crore on 31 March 1996 and are likely to reach a level of Rs. 46,000 crore on 31 March 2003 (BE). Thus, the outstanding debt and liabilities have increased seven-fold over a period of 12 years. The debt-GSDP ratio has gone up from 31.6 per cent in 1990-91 to 40.3 per cent in 1999-2000 and is likely to touch 48 per cent in 2002-2003 (BE).

At the end of March 2002, all the major states had a heavy burden of outstanding debt (Table 11.26).

TABLE 11.26

Outstanding Debt Liabilities of States (March 2002)

States	*Outstanding Liabilities as on March 2002 (BE)*	
	Amount in Rs. Crore	*Percentage share in total of all States*
Uttar Pradesh	79,439	13.4
West Bengal	57,358	9.7
Maharashtra	51,554	8.7
Andhra Pradesh	44,994	7.6
Bihar	38,983	6.6
Gujarat	38,815	6.5
Rajasthan	**35,741**	**6.0**

FIGURE 11.20

Outstanding Liabilities as on March 2002 (BE)

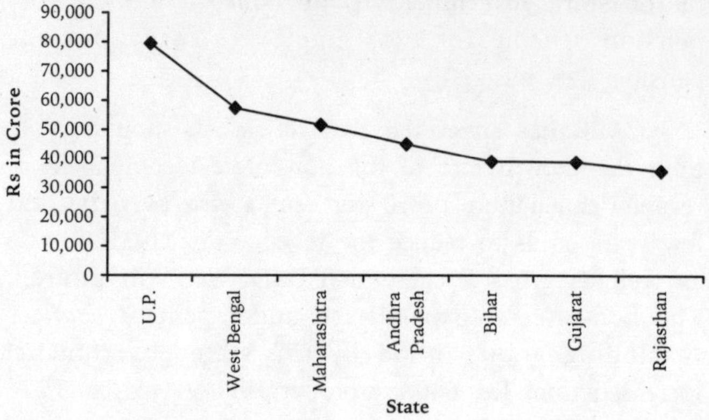

FIGURE 11.21

Ratio of Outstanding Liabilities as a Ratio of GSDP

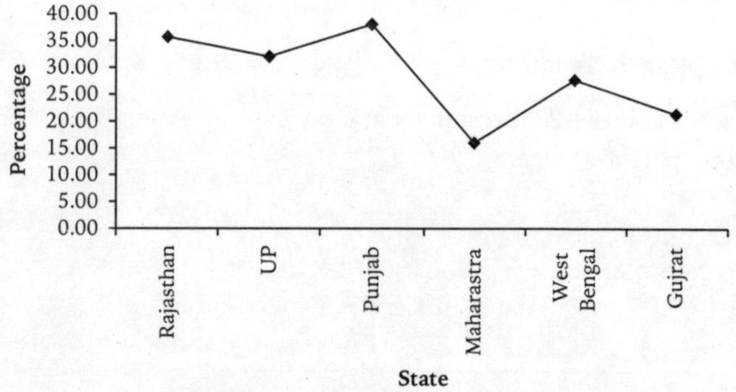

These seven states accounted for a little more than half of the outstanding debt of all the states in the country. The debt burden of Uttar Pradesh, West Bengal, Andhra Pradesh and Maharashtra has been more alarming than that of Rajasthan. However, Rajasthan's debt position was gloomier when seen as percentage of GSDP (Table 11.27).

TABLE 11.27

Debt-GSDP Position of Selected States

State	*Outstanding Liabilities as at End March 2000 (Rs. crore)*	*GSDP on (1993-94 New Series at Current Prices (1999-2000)*	*Ratio of Outstanding Liabilities as a Ratio of GSDP(%)*
Rajasthan	**26,683**	**74,452**	**35.8**
UP	59,969	187,642	31.9
Punjab	23,661	62,700	37.7
Maharashtra	38,300	241,224	15.9
West Bengal	37,007	133,211	27.8
Gujarat	22,984	107,606	21.3

Source: Same as under table 11.7.

Further, the gravity of this problem has been rising rapidly in Rajasthan, with the total outstanding debt, guarantees and interest liability touching a record level of 60 per cent of GSDP in 2000-01 (Table 11.28).

TABLE 11.28

Outstanding Debt and Interest Liabilities in Rajasthan

(Rs. Crore)

Year	*Outstanding Debt (year-end)*	*Outstanding guarantees (including interest) (year-end)*	*Debt + guarantees + interest (2+3)*	*GSDP at current prices*	*% (4)/(5)*
1	*2*	*3*	*4*	*5*	*6*
1996-97	16776	5754	22530	57516	39.2
1997-98	19261	7240	26501	64061	41.4
1998-99	24170	9203	33373	72974	45.7
1999-00	30011	11270	41281	74452	55.4
2000-01(Q)	33874	11954	45828	76440	60.0

Source: Report of the Comptroller and Auditor General of India, for the year ended 31-March, 2001 (Civil), GoR, p. 7, and GSDP Data from DES, Jaipur, May 2002 document.

FIGURE 11.22

Total Outstanding/Liability including Guarantees and Interest Payments

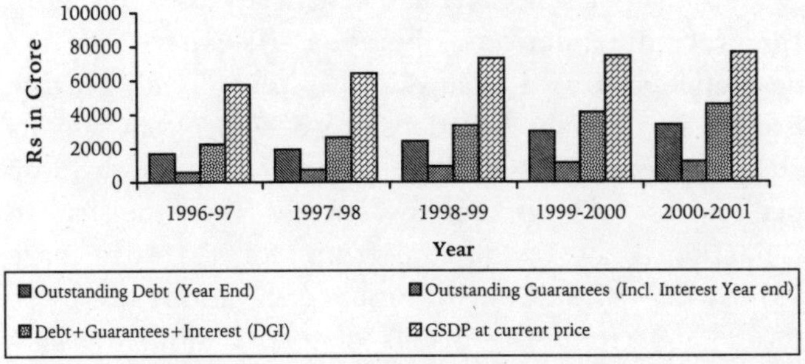

Another cause of worry in Rajasthan is the fact that the interest payment liability in 2002-2003 (BE) was estimated at 31 per cent of revenue receipts, though established norms say this should normally not exceed 18 per cent of revenue receipts, while the outstanding debt should not normally exceed 27 per cent of GSDP. Outstanding guarantees (including interest) must also be estimated to ascertain the impact of contingent liabilities. The amount of outstanding guarantees (including interest) increased from Rs. 5,754 crore in 1996-97 to Rs. 11,954 crore in 2000-2001, according to the CAG Report for 2001. In 2000-01, the outstanding guarantees were 96 per cent of the revenue receipts, compelling the government to announce an administrative ceiling on guarantees.

Under this arrangement, the total of loans and guarantees on the last day of any financial year will not exceed double the amount of estimated receipts in the Consolidated Fund of Rajasthan for the financial year, and the outstanding guarantees issued by the state government will not exceed the amount of receipts in the state's Consolidated Fund. Thus, the outstanding debt, outstanding guarantees and interest liability indicate the need for a high degree of fiscal responsibility on the part of the state government so that the state does not fall into a debt trap.

The Eleventh Finance Commission has indicated that the repayments of Central loans by Rajasthan during 2000-2005 would be to the tune of Rs. 2,488.1 crore, of which repayment of Plan loans would be Rs. 1,551.1 crore and of non-Plan loans would be Rs. 937 crore. These payments relate to loans received from the Centre and other loans outstanding as on 31 March 1999.

The issue of outstanding debt and other liabilities of a state is a very complex issue and has no easy solutions. Some states are close to financial bankruptcy and they are not even in a position to make regular salary payments to their employees. Former Union home secretary Madhav Godbole has even suggested that fiscal emergency may be imposed in Maharashtra under Article 360 of the Constitution because the total outstanding debt and liabilities of the state (including budgetary debt and borrowings through special purpose vehicles and contingent liabilities) has reached an alarming level. If timely steps are not taken, Rajasthan may face a similar situation in the course of the Tenth Plan period.

Going by past experience, (under which the annual increase in debt liability had been Rs. 5,000 crore) the total outstanding debt of Rajasthan at the end of March 2007 may cross the level of Rs. 65,000 crore. Even if the GSDP increases at a moderate rate of 8 to 9 per cent per annum at current prices during 2000-2007, the state may face much worse fiscal situation at the end of the Tenth Plan period, because various fiscal parameters like the revenue deficit-GSDP ratio, gross fiscal deficit-GSDP ratio and debt-GSDP ratio would also deteriorate.

Only large ULBs such as municipal corporations can raise development loans from financial bodies and corporations with the permission of the state government. The first State Finance Commission had recommended development loans of Rs. 1.50 crore each year between 1995-96 and 1999-2000 for various ULBs provided they had good resource base and income. However, this has not made a major difference to their financial viability, because their need for funds far exceeds their resources, and the abolition of octroi in 1998 had an adverse impact on their revenues. Moreover, revenue realisation from house tax is low and a lot of rationalisation is needed with regard to house tax, lease money, registration and stamp fees, land conversion charges, land development charges, etc., so that both state and local bodies finances can benefit. A more co-ordinated and rational approach is needed for this purpose.

Impact of the Fifth Pay Commission

The implementation of the Fifth Pay Commission's recommendations has adversely affected the fiscal position of the Centre and the states. While governments were quick to implement recommendations relating to increase in pay and retirement age etc. they did not implement recommendations regarding downsizing of government and abolition of vacant posts.

Rajasthan has seen a huge increase in salaries and wages, which was around 40 per cent in 1998-99 over the previous year, following the implementation of the Pay Commission recommendations. Since then, the expenditure on this account has been *rising* at an annual growth rate of around 7 per cent. The payments under pensions and miscellaneous general services also increased by 43 per cent in 1998-99 (Table 11.29)

If the state government does not step up its resource mobilisation significantly in the next few years, it may find it increasingly difficult to make regular salary and pension payments.

TABLE 11.29

Growth in Payments of Salaries and Wages, Pensions and Misc. General Services

(Rs. crore)

Item	*1997-98*	*1998-99*	*1999-00*	*2000-01(RE)*	*2001-02 (BE)*
Salaries and wages	3395 (9.9)	4737 (39.5)	5043 (6.5)	5266 (4.4)	5827 (10.7)
Pensions and misc. general services (such as state lotteries)	620 (23.89)	886 (42.9)	1367 (54.3)	1554 (13.7)	1585 (2)

Note: Figures in parenthesis are percentage rise over the previous year.

Source: Finance Department, Government of Rajasthan.

Impact of Eleventh Finance Commission Recommendations

The Eleventh Finance Commission recommended that 29.5 per cent of the net proceeds of the Central taxes should devolve to the states. Of this, 1.5 per cent will go to states that do not collect sales taxes on sugar, textiles and tobacco while states which collect these taxes would get their share only from the 28 per cent component. The Commission imposed a cap of 37.5 per cent on the ratio of total Central revenue receipts (tax and non-tax) to be transferred to the states.

Rajasthan has been a net beneficiary as a result of the recommendations, because its share in tax devolution increased from 4.97 per cent (Tenth Finance Commission recommendations) to 5.47 per cent and its share in total Central devolution increased from 5.03 per cent to 5.42 per cent respectively. Total transfers to Rajasthan have gone up from Rs. 11,401 crore (following the Tenth Finance Commission) to Rs. 23,589 crore. The details of total Central transfers to Rajasthan for 2000-2005 are indicated in Table 11.30.

TABLE 11.30

Various Components of Total Transfers to Rajasthan during 2000-2005

(Rs. crore)

State	*Share in Central Taxes*	*Grants-in-aid*					*Total Central Transfers*
		Non-Plan Revenue Deficit	*Upgradation and Special Problems*	*For Local Bodies: Panchayats*	*For Local Bodies: Municipalities*	*Relief Expenditure*	
(1)	(2)	(3)	(4)	(5)	(6)	(7)	(8)=total of (2) to (7)
Rajasthan	**20595.9 (5.47)**	**1244.7 (3.52)**	**299.8 (6.03)**	**490.9 (6.14)**	**99.4 (4.97)**	**857.9 (10.39)**	**23588.6 (5.42)**
All States	376318.0	35359.1	4972.6	8000.0	2000.0	8255.7	434905.4

Note: Figures in parentheses are percentage rise over the previous year.

Source: Finance Department, Government of Rajasthan.

Thus, Rajasthan got a much higher share under the head of relief expenditure, which was about 10.4 per cent of the total amount provided for all the 25 major states. However, the Finance Commission also suggested that Rajasthan improve its own tax-GSDP ratio from the existing level of 5.33 per cent (average for 1994-95 to 1996-97) and try to attain fiscal self-reliance by raising its own revenues (tax and non-tax) as a ratio of its revenue expenditure. In the Commission's Supplementary Report, an Incentive Fund was created for Central transfers to states on the basis of the medium-term monitorable state fiscal reforms programme. Under this, states were required to reduce their revenue deficits as a proportion of their revenue receipts by at least 5 per cent annually between 2000 and 2005 to be eligible for its share from the Incentive Fund. The shares, fixed on the basis of the population in 1971, were in ascending order, the total amount being Rs. 251.63 crore for 2000-2005 for Rajasthan. As Rajasthan's revenue deficit-revenue receipts ratio came down from 37.2 per cent in 1999-2000 to about 21.2 per cent in 2000-2001, the state got a sum of Rs. 171.68 crore in 2000-2001 from the Incentive Fund. It is likely to get Rs. 92.80 crore for 2001-2002 also. However, going by present indications, the revenue deficit-revenue receipts ratio is likely to remain in the range of 27-28 per cent during 2001-2002 and 2002-2003, Therefore, the state will have to improve its fiscal performance in the near future to keep the momentum of reducing the revenue deficit-revenue receipts ratio as was done in 2000-2001.

Causes of Fiscal Malaise

Although the fiscal health of all states have deteriorated more or less due to identical reasons (growth in revenue expenditures outpacing revenue receipts, high revenue and fiscal deficits, increasing interest payment liabilities, lack of adequate resource mobilisation, and dwindling Central transfers), in the case of Rajasthan there are some factors unique to it. Several decisions taken during the past three decades have placed a heavy burden on the state exchequer.

- Employees got earned leave for 30 days in a year. In 1976, the then government decided to give cash payment for one month's salary in two years. This was later changed to four years by another government. Despite this, the step has brought an annual burden of about Rs. 100 crore.
- The decision, in 1998, to give salary equivalent to Central employees placed a burden of about Rs. 1,300 crore in 1998-99.
- In 1992, the government initiated the scheme of giving three promotions to all employees (including non-gazetted employees) after nine, 18 and 27 years of service. This has increased the pension burden from Rs. 236 crore in 1990-91 to Rs. 1,693 crore in 2000-2001 and it is likely to shoot up to Rs. 2,028 crore in 2002-2003 (BE).
- In 1997, the Central government revised the pay-scale of employees and fitment allowance was raised from 20 per cent to 40 per cent. This placed an additional burden of Rs. 600 crore a year on the state government.
- In 1998, the state government revised pay scales, raised allowances and reduced taxes just before the Assembly elections.
- The state government reduced the retirement age in 1998 from 60 to 58 years (with the intention of providing more job opportunities for the youth), but it also placed an additional burden of Rs. 750 crore on the state on account of payment of pension, provident fund, gratuity etc. which could have been delayed by two years.

Later, due to the worsening financial position of the exchequer due to rising expenditures for drought relief and lower growth rates, the government did take measures to cut establishment expenditure by reducing the number of staff cars, telephone facilities and travel facilities etc., but this has not helped much. It thus seems appropriate to search for options which may improve the fiscal situation.

Fiscal Policy For The Future

Two observations need to be made before suggesting a fiscal policy for Rajasthan. First, the problem is structural and chronic in nature. Second, the growth rate of the economy has not picked up during the last few years, even at current prices, and that has led to a worsening of various fiscal parameters in the state. Therefore, any scheme of fiscal reforms will have to address these constraints, especially ensuring a higher growth rate of around 14-15 per cent at current prices in order to make a positive dent on fiscal variables like revenue deficit, gross fiscal deficit, debt-GSDP ratio etc. The following fiscal measures should be taken to improve the finances of the state in the short run as well as the long term.

Short-term Measures

Short-term measures are necessary to stabilise the state's fiscal position. Such measures should focus on additional resource mobilisation and control over non-productive and wasteful expenditure. The state government has requested the Centre to convert the overdrafts from RBI into medium-term loans to give some respite. The state should be permitted to resort to more market borrowings, given the difficult financial situation.

Additional Resource Mobilisation: Tax administration should be strengthened and streamlined for better tax collections. An additional sum of about Rs. 150 crore (5 per cent more than the present level) can be collected from sales tax alone, provided necessary steps are taken for this purpose. High rates of stamps and registration fee, land conversion charges etc. lead to tax evasion and hence lower collections. Stamp and registration fee of 11 per cent may be reduced to 7 per cent so as to ensure higher tax compliance. More revenue can also be generated by reducing T&D losses in electricity and improving the distribution system. Experts have suggested that the implementation of value-added tax (VAT) at the state level will lead to a rise in revenues from electricity duty, entertainment tax, taxes on vehicles and on goods and passengers, hotel receipts tax etc. Many more services may be brought under the tax net at that time. Therefore, the exercise for switch-over from indirect taxes on goods and services towards VAT should be initiated immediately. Some fiscal analysts feel that rich and well-to-do farmers should also be brought under the tax net, but strong political will is needed to implement that.

Expenditure Restructuring and Reduction: Downsizing or rightsizing of government is essential to compress non-Plan non-development expenditure on salaries and wages. Vacancies created by natural attrition should be filled up only partially for the next few years. In 2001, the state government did the right thing by deciding to increase the number of employees only in the police, education and health departments for the time being. The government should try to control further rises in salary, dearness allowance, bonus etc., till there is a substantial improvement in state finances.

Since expenditure on drought relief is a major cause of the financial strain, Rajasthan should be included in the category of special category states so that the Central Plan assistance is available to it in the ratio of 90 per cent grant and 10 per cent loan against the current 30 per cent grant and 70 per cent as loan. However, this matter needs to be studied carefully before a final decision is taken.

In 2001, the Centre decided that additional 20 per cent of small savings would be transferred to the states on the condition that they would prepay part of debt to the Centre. The interest rate on such borrowings would be 8.5 per cent per annum and it can be used to retire older debt that bears an interest rate of 10 per cent and more. This debt swap facility will ease financial burden on the States to some extent.

Medium-Term/Long-Term Measures

As the present financial position of the state is the result of policies pursued over several years in the past, more sustained measures would be needed to put finances back on track.

- The state must take harsh measures to improve its financial position. It must fix targets for reducing revenue deficit to zero level, and gross fiscal deficit to around 2-3 per cent of GSDP by 2006-2007. For this, a Fiscal Responsibility and Budget Management legislation, on the pattern of the Central legislation, should be considered. It would be appropriate if the revenue deficit-GSDP and gross fiscal deficit-GSDP ratio reduced by at least half per cent of GSDP every year. Moreover, the debt-GSDP ratio should be controlled at a level of 50 per cent by 2011 (including the state government guarantees). This will help in reducing the level of contingent liabilities. The state has taken administrative measures to put a ceiling on guarantees in 1999. However, this would warrant the adoption of some tough measures.
- The government should try to raise capital outlay by attracting foreign direct investment and NRI investment. To do this, it should formulate attractive incentive packages and create a hassle-free environment for entrepreneurs. Though some steps have been taken, progress has been slow.
- In order to attain a high growth rate of GSDP, investment level has to be raised by attracting domestic and foreign private investment. Aid from foreign lending institutions like the World Bank would also be helpful in this regard. The state should speed up the pace of second generation reforms in sectors like infrastructure and the social sector. There is tremendous growth potential in sectors like mining, cattle, tourism, exports, handicrafts, gems and jewellery, textiles, herbal medicines, etc., which should be exploited to the maximum extent. Higher income in these

sectors would add to buoyancy of revenues. One such option is the exploitation of lignite, gas and minerals in the western districts.

- State-level PSUs must be restructured so that their financial performance improves and their dependence on the state exchequer reduces. The process of disinvestment and other reforms must be initiated so as to raise finances and utilise them for investment in other channels.
- Non-merit subsidies should be cut in order to reduce the revenue deficit. There is scope for raising user charges especially for those sections that can afford to pay for services. At the same time, efforts should be made to keep costs in various departments and government services under control.

Role of Oil, Gas and Lignite in Resource Mobilisation

The Eleventh Report of the Administrative Reforms Commission (December 2001) has pointed out that if Rajasthan exploits its vast resources of petroleum, gas lignite in right earnest, it would facilitate rapid growth of the economy in several ways.

- It would help in generating an additional 20,000 MW of power, which will benefit diverse sectors like agriculture, industry, mining etc., and give a fillip to economic growth. This, in turn, will create more employment opportunities, raise income levels and, consequently, the standard of living of the people. Preliminary surveys have shown that if power is generated in the lignite-rich districts of western Rajasthan at the pit-head, 3000 MW of electricity can be generated within four to five years.
- Rajasthan would become a power surplus state and be in a position to earn revenue of Rs. 650 crore per year from the sale of about 1000 MW of surplus electricity, besides saving Rs. 1100 crore a year, which is now spent on purchasing power. Moreover, the state would be able to generate additional revenue of Rs. 110 crore a year by way of royalty and sales tax from lignite. Similarly, more revenue could be obtained every year from recoverable light oil and underground coal gasification in Barmer district and power generation from methane gas.

Thus, this vast reservoir of hidden wealth needs to be exploited without further loss of time.

Since the problem of distressed state finances is common to all states, this issue needs to be discussed in depth at the national level by the representatives of the Centre, states, Planning Commission, National Development Council, Ministry of Finance, RBI, and suitable policy decisions should be taken to solve the problem on a larger scale and a lasting basis. This requires preparation of a roadmap with suitable milestones, which all states, including Rajasthan, must adopt with the help of the Central government.

APPENDIX A–11.1

Trends in Tax/GSDP Ratio, Revenue Deficit, Fiscal Deficit and Outstanding Liabilities from 1990-91 to 2002-2003 (BE) for Selected Years

Year	*Tax-GSDP Ratio (%)*	*Revenue Deficit (-) Revenue Surplus (+) (Rs. crore)*	*Fiscal Deficit (-) (Rs. crore)*	*Outstanding Liabilities (Rs. crore)*
1990-91	5.87	+168	-544.8	6,546
1995-96	5.77	-701.9	-2574.3	14,104
1999-2000	6.09	-3640.0	-5361.2	30,011
2000-2001	6.93	-2633.6	-4313.2	33,874
2001-2002 (RE)	6.72	-3510.0	-5753.3	38,717
2002-2003 (BE)	7.30	-3901.9	-7006.5	44,380

Source: Finance Department of Rajasthan, June 2002.

Chapter 12

Governance in Rajasthan

The historical background and geographical conditions of a state have a direct bearing on the way it is governed. In addition, the socio-economic conditions of a state determine and, in turn, are affected by, the nature and quality of governance.

Rajasthan came into being as a result of the process of integration of about two dozen princely states and chieftainships between 1948 and 1956. All these princely states varied greatly in size, population, administrative system, and social and economic development.

BOX 12.1

Stages in the Formation of Present-day Rajasthan

18 March 1948: Merger of the formerly princely states of Alwar, Bharatpur, Dholpur and Karauli into Matsya Union.

25 March 1948: Kota, Bundi, Jhalawar, Banswara, Dungarpur, Pratapgarh, Kishangarh, Tonk and Shahpura states merged to form the Rajasthan Union.

18 April 1948: Merger of Udaipur in the Rajasthan Union resulting in the United State of Rajasthan.

30 March 1949: The princely states of Jaipur, Jodhpur, Bikaner and Jaisalmer merged into Rajasthan.

15 May 1949: Merger of Matsya Union into Rajasthan.

7 February 1950: Princely State of Sirohi integrated into Rajasthan. Abu and Dilwara *tehsils* of Sirohi were transferred to Bombay.

1 November 1956: Final stage in the formation of Rajasthan when the Centrally–administered area of Ajmer, Abu and Dilwara *tehsils* of Bombay and Sunel Tappa of Madhya Pradesh were merged in Rajasthan and Sironj *tehsil* of Rajasthan (an enclave in the state of Madhya Pradesh) was transferred to Madhya Pradesh in line with the recommendations of the States' Reorganisation Commission.

Though the ruling dynasties of Rajasthan took pride in their glorious traditions of bravery and heroism, all this had dissipated over the years. The rulers had been leading a sort of sheltered existence under Mughal rule. Later, when Rajputana was being ravaged by Maratha chieftains, the native rulers readily accepted British supremacy for protection. The British never tried to interfere with the feudal order, which manifested itself in luxurious lifestyles, absence of definite rules and procedures in land administration, existence of intermediaries known as *jagirdars*, imposition of several heads of cess and taxes known as *lag-bag* and prevalence of forced labour (*begar*) etc. Moving from this feudalistic order toward a new democratic social order was a formidable task before the new state.

Geographical Conditions

Rajasthan is roughly rhombic in shape and extends between $23^{0}3'$ and $30^{0}12'$ North latitudes and $69^{0}30'$ and $78^{0}17'$ East longitudes over an area of 342,239 sq. km. The Aravali range, the oldest mountain system in the world stretching diagonally from the south-west of the state to the north-east, divides the state in two parts. To the west of the Aravali range lies the desert and semi-desert areas of Jodhpur and Bikaner divisions. The desert is not flat and the area is dotted with sand dunes and small hillocks. To the east of the Aravalis lies the fertile plain area and in the south-east is the elevated plain. The Aravalis form the watershed and the Luni and Sukhri rivers draining the western region fall into the Gulf of Cambay and Kutch and the Arabian Sea, while the rivers in the south and eastern side (Banas, Kothari, Khari, Chambal, Kalisindh, Parvati etc.) join the Yamuna-Gangetic system. The Mahi and Sabarmati rivers are the important rivers of the southern region.

INITIAL PROBLEMS AND DIFFICULTIES

The physical features and geographical conditions have combined with the age-old feudal system to influence the course of development of the state. Large parts of the state are desert and semi-desert areas. Rainfall is scanty and the state has meagre water resources. This resulted in frequent drought and famines, leading to the problem of chronic food shortage.

Given the diverse conditions in the various constituents of Rajasthan, the first task before the state government was to set up a uniform administrative system and integration of the services. The system of *jagirdars*, *zamindars* and *biswedars* and the absence of a well-established revenue and land tenure system was an issue demanding the new state's attention. The other serious problems were the worsening law and order situation, the menace of dacoits and the *jagirdari* system.

Land Reforms and Abolition of Intermediaries

Rajasthan has made far-reaching achievements in the sphere of abolition of intermediaries and land reforms, completely transforming the system from an outdated and exploitative feudalistic order to a democratic modern system conferring due rights and protection to the tiller of land.

Earlier, there was no uniformity in laws, procedures and administrative processes in the integrating units. These variations were still higher in case of land relations, land laws and land administration. The land tenures and land revenue system was characterised by the preponderance of intermediaries, absence of well-defined rights of tenants, prevalence of kind rents and rack-renting, existence of several fees and exactions (*lag-bag*), besides rent and prevalence of the system of forced unpaid labour (*begar*) from the people.

Huge areas of land had been assigned to grantees of various categories known as *jagirdar*, *mafidar*, *inamdar* etc. The *jagirdari* system prevailed in 60 per cent of the total area of the state, increasing to as much as 80 per cent in some of the erstwhile princely states. The *jagirdari* system gave rise to two categories of land in terms of revenue administration – areas which were directly under the state (known as *khalsa*) and those which were assigned to *jagirdars* (non-*khalsa*). Revenue administration and land tenures varied greatly in these two areas. The condition of the tenants in non-*khalsa* areas was much worse, and majority of the cultivators were tenants-at-will, with no fixed tenure, while rents were also unfair.

While the *jagirdars* paid a fixed amount as tribute to the state for the *jagir* area, the *zamindars* and *biswedars* paid fixed land revenue to the state. They were free to realise rents from the tenants at whatever rates they pleased and the system of recovery of rent or revenue in kind (*latai, batai, kunta, khara* etc.) was prevailing in many areas.

The unfair conditions that tenants, especially those in the non-*khalsa* areas, had to face immediately engaged the attention of the government in the newly-formed state. Keeping in mind the land policy enunciated at the national level, the state government also laid down priorities and proceeded to take effective measures in the direction of:

- abolition of intermediaries and bringing the tenant into a direct relationship with the state;
- introducing a uniform system of tenancy, land revenue and land settlement all over the state;
- undertaking immediate steps during the intervening period for protection of tenants and sub-tenants from ejection and unlawful exactions;
- taking up survey and settlement operations;
- making land records systematic and ensuring their regular maintenance; and
- introducing a uniform revenue administration and revenue courts in the state.

Abolition of Intermediaries

The first major step in the direction of land reforms was the enactment of the Rajasthan Land Reforms and Resumption of Jagirs Act, 1952, which provided for resumption of *jagirs*, vesting of all rights, title and interest of *jagirdars* in the state government free from all encumbrances, along with assessment and payment of compensation and rehabilitation grant to *jagirdars*, allotment of *khudkasht* (land for self-cultivation) to *jagirdars* and the rights of the tenants of *jagir* lands. After the resumption of *jagirs*, the tenants of *jagir* lands became *khatedar* tenants of the state, with transferable and inheritable rights. The *zamindari and biswedari* estates were abolished under the Rajasthan Zamindari and Biswedari Abolition Act 1959, bringing similar relief to the tenants in these areas.

Tenancy and Revenue Legislation

The most important enactments concerning land revenue administration and land tenures are the Rajasthan Tenancy Act, 1955 and the Rajasthan Land

Revenue Act, 1956. The Rajasthan Tenancy Act conferred more rights to tenants over their land. The law provided for only two classes of tenants – *khatedar* and *gair-khatedar*. A large majority of the cultivators, who were holding land as tenants, or as sub-tenant or tenant of *khudkasht*, became *khatedar* tenants overnight on 15 October 1955, when the new law became applicable. The law provided for the acquisition of *khatedari* rights by the sub-tenants and tenants of *khudkasht* recorded as such in the annual registers. Initially, this was done only on an application for acquiring *khatedari* rights by the sub-tenant or tenant of *khudkasht*, but the process was later made automatic so as to afford the benefit of the provision to these tillers of land. The law also provides for the acquisition of *khatedari* rights by the *ghair-khatedar* tenants also after a certain period and on fulfilling of certain conditions. These progressive measures helped the cultivators become real owners of their land enjoying rights of inheritance, transfer, gift and mortgage etc. This comes close to the much–acclaimed Operation Berga of West Bengal. Other salutary provisions of the Act concerned restriction on transfer of lands of tenants belonging to scheduled caste and scheduled tribes and automatic extinction of usufructuary mortgage after the prescribed period and restoration of the land to the tenant without any encumbrance.

The Rajasthan Land Revenue Act, 1956 provides for the appointment of revenue courts and officers, specifies their powers and duties, preparation and maintenance of land records and survey and settlement operations etc. Other important enactments enforced by the state government related to consolidation of holdings, land utilisation, agricultural loans, relief of agricultural indebtedness and imposition of ceiling on land holdings. All these measures went a long way in amelioration of the conditions of cultivators in the state.

The programme of consolidation of land holdings was started in the state in the late 1950s under the Rajasthan Holdings (Consolidation and Prevention of Fragmentation) Act, 1954. The programme was taken up in selected *tehsils* in some districts (Sriganganagar, Kota, Jaipur, Sawai Madhopur etc.). There were practical difficulties and a lot of complaints of inequitable adjustment of rights, corruption and nepotism, difficulties in transfer of possession. The biggest hurdle was the emotional attachment of tenants to their lands and widespread dissatisfaction, resulting in litigation. The programme was, therefore, abandoned. There are no proposals for re-starting this programme.

ERA OF POLITICAL STABILITY

The period 1949-54 was marked by political instability in the state with frequent change in governments.

BOX 12.2

Change in Governments in Rajasthan

7 April 1949 to 4 January 1951: Government headed by Hira Lal Shastri, the first Premier of Rajasthan.

5 January 1951 to 25 April 1951: A caretaker government under C.S. Venkatachar, ICS

26 April 1951 to 3 March 1952: Jai Narain Vyas functioned as Premier.

3 March 1952 to 1 October 1952: Tika Ram Paliwal was the Chief Minister of the first democratically elected government following the first general elections.

1 October 1952 to 13 November 1954: Jai Narain Vyas replaced Tika Ram Paliwal as Chief Minister but lost in a confidence motion in the state assembly.

13 November 1954: Mohan Lal Sukhadia took over as Chief Minister.

The accession of Mohan Lal Sukhadia to the Chief Minister's office in 1954 ushered in an era of political stability in the state, and he continued as Chief Minister till 8 July 1971 with a brief intervening period of President's Rule from 14 March 1967 to 26 April 1967. This period saw a coming together of political will and bureaucratic innovation, which contributed to the state's development. The credit for several measures of administrative reforms and innovations, planned development, administrative vigilance and launching of *panchayati raj* can be traced to this period.

PLANNED DEVELOPMENT

Rajasthan entered the era of planned development through five-year plans with the initial handicaps mentioned earlier. However, the state government, working with the support of the Central Government and the Planning Commission, was able to overcome these handicaps and the state proceeded on the road to planned development with a measure of confidence and concern for the common man. The political stability in the state proved to be a boon in this regard. Table 12.1 presents the progress in successive plans.

The Tenth Plan has proposed an outlay of Rs. 31831.75 crore.

The state has made significant strides in various spheres of the economy. As a result of the Green

Revolution, Rajasthan has changed from being a food-deficit state to a food-surplus one. Food production increased from 33.86 lakh tonnes in 1952 to 140.48 lakh tonnes in 1997-98. The index of agricultural production (base year 1979-80 to 1981-82 average) has increased to 257 in 1998-99 from 100 in 1979-80. The White Revolution has made significant contribution to the state income and per capita income. The percentage of irrigated area and availability of power have significantly increased. Some socio-economic indicators presented in Table 12.2 exhibit the progress and development in these spheres.

TABLE 12.1

Progress in Successive Five-Year Plans

(Rs. in crore)

Item	*Outlay*	*Total Expenditure*
First Five Year Plan	64.50	54.15
Second Five Year Plan	105.27	102.74
Third Five Year Plan	236.00	212.70
Three Annual Plans	132.72	136.76
Fourth Five Year Plan	306.21	308.79
Fifth Five Year Plan	847.16	857.62
Annual Plan	275.00	290.19
Sixth Five Year Plan	2025.00	2120.45
Seventh Five Year Plan	3000.00	3106.18
Annual Plan	961.53	973.22
Annual Plan	1170.00	1184.41
Eighth Five Year Plan	11500.00	11998.97
Ninth Five Year Plan	27650.00	19532.32

Source: Some facts about Rajasthan (2000): Directorate of Economics and Statistics, Rajasthan, Jaipur.

MEANING AND SCOPE OF GOOD GOVERNANCE

Governance is an all-inclusive term covering various aspects of the organisation and structure of government which have an impact on the efficiency of government and the delivery of public services and incorporates accountability, transparency, financial devolution, political/administrative decentralisation and corruption and administrative vigilance.

According to Adrian Leftwich, good governance has three levels of meaning: systemic, political and administrative.[1]

"First, from a broad point of view, the concept of governance is wider than that of government which conventionally refers to the formal institutional structure and location of authoritative decision-making in the modern state. Governance, on the other hand, refers to a looser and wider distribution of both internal and external political and economic power.

"The second, more limited and obviously political sense of good governance clearly presupposes such a regime. But it also explicitly means a state enjoying legitimacy and authority, derived from a democratic mandate and based on the traditional liberal notion of a clear separation of legislative executive and judicial powers.

"Thirdly, from a narrow administrative point of view, good governance means an efficient, independent, accountable and open public service. This is the World Bank's position which is outlined in its latest definition statement on Governance and Development which treats good governance as synonymous with sound development management ... The World Bank document focuses on four main areas of

TABLE 12.2

Some Socio-economic Indicators

Indicators	*1998-99*	*As Compared to*
Index of Food Production	208.30	100 } Base year 1979-80 to 1981-82 av.
Index of Oilseeds Production	619.34	100
Index of Agricultural Production	257.71	100
Percentage of irrigated area	34.22 %	11% (1956-57)
Per capita power availability (units)	480.98	
Percentage of electrified villages	95.63	
Villages covered under safe drinking water supply schemes	37,556	37889 (total)
Road length per 100 sq km.	24.84	
Road length per lakh of population	157.58	
Infant Mortality Rate (1997) per 1000	85	71 (All India)
Birth Rate (Oct. 1998) per 1000	32.1	27.2 (All India)
Death Rate (Oct. 1998) per 1000	8.9	8.9 (All India)
Per Capita Income at constant prices (Base year 1993-94)	7,694	9739 (All India)

Source: Some facts about Rajasthan (2000), Basic Statistics Rajasthan 2001: Directorate of Economics & Statistics Jaipur.

1. Development and Social Change Vol. 25 No.2 July 1994.

public administration in general and public sector management in particular viz. (i) accountability (ii) legal framework for development (iii) information and (iv) transparency".

The new economic policy and the economic liberalisation process introduced in 1991 and the decentralisation of powers and functions to rural and urban local bodies through the 73rd and 74th Constitution Amendment Acts in 1992 have necessitated the re-examination of various issues related to governance, including redefinition of the role and responsibilities of the government.

"Government must become more caring, more compassionate and more responsive to the concerns of these sections who have hitherto remained far removed from government. Renewing governance will, therefore, no longer be a matter of economic indicators, but a matter of human beings, their lives and their aspirations."[2]

Tackling Corruption

Good governance is based on the premise that effective steps are taken by the government to check corruption and ensure, transparency, in administration. The Rajasthan government has taken several steps in this direction.

- Right to Information Act has been implemented at all levels.
- Citizens' charters have been issued in 28 departments.
- Effective steps have been taken to abolish inspector raj, especially in areas where there were complaints of harassment.
- Chief vigilance officers have been appointed in 28 departments with a Chief Vigilance Commissioner.

ADMINISTRATIVE INNOVATIONS AND REFORMS

Having successfully tided over the various initial problems, the state government devoted its attention to the important task of setting up a uniform administrative system and continuous improvements for better governance. A number of committees were appointed from time to time to recommend administrative reforms measures, the important ones being the Departmental Procedures Committee, 1954, Administrative Enquiry Committee, 1956, State Economy Committee, 1956, Committee on Training, and the Committee on Technical Department, the last two set up to suggest measures to relieve senior technical officers of their routine administrative duties.

Among the significant administrative and innovative measures taken in the initial years were:

- Establishment of Organisation and Methods (O&M) section in the Secretariat in May 1955 to create consciousness about the need for administrative improvement, examination of rules and procedures, codification/compilation of government orders and rules, laying guidelines and monitoring tours and inspections. Initially, the activities of the O&M section were confined to the Secretariat but its scope was extended to the Departmental and District Offices in 1961. The O&M Section, in fact, was the precursor of the present Department of Administrative Reforms in the Secretariat.
- A separate department of anti-corruption was set up in 1957 under the Additional Inspector General of Police to inquire into and proceed against complaints of corruption, misappropriation and embezzlements etc. by public servants. The Department has been strengthened from time to time and is presently headed by an Indian Police Service officer of the rank of Director-General of Police.
- Considerable emphasis has been laid on periodical inspections and tours by officers and submission of quarterly/half yearly/yearly reports.
- An officer-oriented system of working or cell system was introduced in the Secretariat to expedite disposal of work. Emphasis has been laid on speedy disposal of files, reducing of number of levels and increasing accountability.
- Detailed instructions were issued defining the role of District Collectors in relation to district-level officers of other departments particularly with a view to coordination. These instructions were revised after the introduction of panchayati raj in 1959.

Administrative Reforms Committee/Commission

The Union government has been paying considerable attention to administrative innovation and reforms,

2. P. Chidambaram, Foreword in Banerjie, Ajit M. and Chadrasekara, K.A. (ed) *Renewing Governance: Issues and Options*, Tata McGraw Hill, 1996.

setting up special bodies to examine the administrative framework and suggesting improvements. An important step in this direction was the setting up of an Administrative Reforms Commission (ARC) in the late 1960s under the chairmanship of Morarji Desai. The Commission published 19 reports, which contained about 600 recommendations. The process of reforms continued and the landmark steps were the setting up of the Sarkaria Commission on Centre-State relations, 1983, the Economic Reforms Administration Commission 1984 and the 73rd and 74th Constitutional Amendments 1993. The government of Rajasthan has also been taking steps for administrative reforms.

H.C. Mathur Committee: In Rajasthan, the first major step in this direction was the setting up of the Administrative Reforms Committee in July 1963 under the chairmanship of H.C. Mathur. The Committee submitted its report in September 1963. The report contained 233 recommendations covering government at the state level, field administration, personnel administration, financial matters, administrative procedures, technical efficiency and internal evaluation, *panchayati raj* and municipalities and public relations.

G.K. Bhanot Committee: In 1994, another Administrative Reforms Committee was appointed under the chairmanship of G.K. Bhanot. All the members of the Committee were senior officers of the level of Secretary to the government. The Committee submitted nine reports on financial administration, public health engineering department, energy, medical and health, primary and secondary education, printing and stationery, inspectors in various departments, licences and permits, and revenue administration.

However, the implementation of the recommendations is not very encouraging. There was initial enthusiasm but that petered out with the passage of time and ultimately the exercise was abandoned.

Shiv Charan Mathur Commission: In May 1999, yet another Administrative Reforms Commission was appointed under the chairmanship of Shiv Charan Mathur. The Commission submitted 11 reports on revenue administration, registration and stamps, tax on urban property, transfer policy of state civil services, redressal of public grievances, power sector reforms, *panchayati raj*, police, economy in the use of government vehicles, utilisation of lignite, coal bed methane gas and petroleum for power generation and mobilisation of additional resources in the state, etc. The Commission examined other aspects and spheres of administration and submitted 13 reports. The state government, however, could not take steps for their implementation. A committee of three senior ministers was appointed to examine the recommendations and suggest action but progress has not been very encouraging.

The S.C. Mathur Commission has emphasised the following aspects in its approach:

- Reduction/elimination of individual discretion in administrative decisions and procedures with a view to minimising the charges of misuse of authority and corruption.
- Accountability of government functionaries at all levels, not only to the higher authorities, audit and the legislature, but also to the public.
- Transparency and right to information.
- Responsiveness of public services to the common man with a sense of responsibility.
- Simplification of rules and procedures.
- A people-friendly approach of the administration to fulfil its real objective of good governance; and
- The adoption of 'Destination – Common Man" as the ideal of good administration.

Having enunciated these general attributes of good governance, the Commission observed that instead of making generalisations on theories and principles of the administration, it would also make specific practical and recommendations that can be implemented.

The tardy implementation notwithstanding, the process served to focus attention on the need for improvement in administration, which got reflected in the various measures adopted by the state government.

A basic weakness of the process of administrative reforms at the national as well as the state level has been the absence of follow–up machinery, as a result of which action on the recommendations of various reports continue for only some time. The present Department of Administrative Reforms in the state has proved unequal to the task.

The state government appointed a cabinet sub-committee to examine the recommendations of the Mathur Commission and suggest steps for implementing these. The sub-committee, as was apprehended, could not function continuously and did not make significant progress.

Community Development Programme and National Extension Service

Rural development has been accepted as the sheet anchor of economic development in India. The first major step towards integrated development of rural areas was the launching of Community Development Programme on 2 October 1952 in selected blocks in different states. Over the years, it was extended to more and more blocks. In Rajasthan, the programme was initiated in seven blocks to begin with and later extended to other blocks.

The programme envisaged overall development of the rural areas through the development of agriculture, animal husbandry, cooperatives, rural industries and social services, particularly education and health. The programme was implemented with the involvement of the village *panchayats* as the *panchayat*, village school and village cooperative society were considered to be the basic institutions for change and development. People's participation was an important ingredient of the programme. Thus, Rajasthan has been a pioneering state in evolving decentralised governance. In 2002, the *panchayat* laws were made more flexible to ensure that weaker sections of the community get a fair representation in the PRIs.

The National Extension Service (NES) programme, which was a wider application of the Community Development concept to cover the entire rural area, was initiated in 1952. The entire state of Rajasthan was covered by the Community Development and NES programme, with all the development blocks categorised into three stages – pre-extension intensive, development, and post-intensive development. The programme generated considerable interest and enthusiasm among the rural people and served to create an urge for social and economic development. These two programmes dominated the rural development scenario during the first two Five-Year Plan periods.

Employment Generation Poverty Alleviation and Special Area Programmes

Schemes for providing wage employment to the poor and the landless were taken up in the Third Five-Year Plan. In the Fourth and Fifth Plans, special programmes like Agriculture Area Development Programme and the Minimum Needs Programme were launched. From the Sixth Plan onwards, special emphasis was placed on poverty alleviation and employment generation programmes. Various schemes have been implemented in Rajasthan in pursuance of these policies and programmes at the national level. Important among them are: special programmes for small and marginal farmers, Intensive Agriculture District Programme (IADP), Local Development Works Programme (LDWP), Drought Prone Areas Programme (DPAP), Desert Development Programme (DDP), Tribal Development Programme (TDP), Food for Work Programme, Integrated Rural Development Programme (IRDP), National Rural Employment Programme (NREP), Rural Landless Employment Guarantee Programme (RLEGP), Million Well Scheme (MWS), Jawahar Rozgar Yojana (JRY) later converted into the Jawahar Gram Samridhdhi Yojana (JGSY), Indira Awas Yojana (IAY) and Employment Assurance Scheme (EAS). The IRDP has been merged with some sub-schemes viz. Training of Rural Youth for Self-Employment (TRYSEM), Development of Women and Children in Rural Areas (DWACRA), MWS etc. and has now been re-named as the Swarnajayanti Gram Swarozgar Yojana (SGSY). The thrust of the poverty alleviation and employment generation schemes has been on helping the below-poverty line (BPL) families to cross the poverty line, and creation of permanent community assets in rural areas.

Before the IRDP was launched in 1980, the state government had introduced a novel scheme for the welfare of the poor, known as Antyodaya and was targeted at five poorest families in each village.

DEMOCRATIC DECENTRALISATION AND PANCHAYATI RAJ

Given the overwhelming response to the Community Development and NES programme, the Central government wanted to evaluate it and put it on a sound future course. The Committee on Plan Projects (COPP) of the National Development Council (NDC) constituted a study team under the chairmanship of Balwant Rai Mehta to study the Programme and make recommendations for ensuring economy and efficiency. The study team was also entrusted with the task of looking at the reorganisation of the district administration, so that democratic bodies, by pre-determined stages, should take over the entire general administration and development work at the district, sub-division and *panchayat* level.

The Mehta Report, submitted in November 1957, recommended a revolutionary programme of democratic decentralisation (now known as panchayati raj) through democratically elected bodies, and envisaged a fundamental change in the administrative set-up from district to the village level. The study team recommended a three-tier set-up of organically linked democratic institutions at the village, block and district level and devolution of powers and functions to them. The report was considered by the NDC which decided that state governments should accelerate the process for establishment of democratic institutions in the light of their own situations, and the process of democratisation should be completed as speedily as possible.

Panchayati Raj in Rajasthan

Rajasthan introduced panchayati raj on 2 October 1959 and has the distinction of being one of the pioneers in this, along with Andhra Pradesh. The state government took speedy decisions and expeditious action in respect of the necessary legislative measures, formation of rules and regulations, elections and constitution of panchayati raj bodies, transfer of powers and functions, training of officials and non-officials, devolution of resources and issue of timely orders and instructions.

The panchayati raj system prior to the 73rd Amendment Act was governed by the Rajasthan Panchayat Act, 1953. The Rajasthan Panchayat Samitis and Zilla Parishads Act, 1959 was passed to provide for the establishment of panchayat samitis at the block level and zilla parishads at the district level and necessary amendments were made to the Rajasthan Panchayat Act, 1953. Thus, a three-tier system comprising gram panchayats, panchayat samitis and zilla parishads was established in the state. The *sarpanch* and members (ward *panchas*) of the gram panchayat were directly elected. The *sarpanchs* of the gram panchayat were ex-officio members of the panchayat samiti and the *pradhans* (chairpersons) of the panchayat samitis became the ex-officio members of the zilla parishads. There were no direct elections for the members of the panchayat samiti/zilla parishad. The *pradhan* of the panchayat samiti was elected by an electoral college comprising members of the panchayat samiti and panchayat while the *pramukh* (chairperson) of the zilla parishad was elected by an electoral college comprising the members of the panchayat samitis and zilla parishads. There were provisions for co-opting women and members belonging to scheduled caste/tribe at each level in case members of these categories were not already represented in the institution through election or ex-officio membership.

The panchayat samiti at the block level was the most important institution with executive powers and functions. The zilla parishads had only a supervisory and coordinating role. The village-level *panchayats* functioned as agencies for the implementation of various programmes with certain original powers and functions. Over the past few years, PRIs in Rajasthan have got more powers and, for the first time, pasture management committees have been constituted under each gram panchayat. During 2000-01 and 2001-02, Rs. 81.24 crore and Rs. 94 crore respectively have been transferred for strengthening the PRIs.

Unfortunately, the country's experience with panchayati raj was not entirely satisfactory. The Ashok Mehta Committee has acknowledged that the period of ascendancy of panchayati raj lasted for only five years, from 1959 to 1964. It was followed by a period of stagnation till 1969 and from 1970 onwards the system declined.

Rajasthan was not an exception to this unhappy situation. The ascendancy of panchayati raj in the state continued till the first half of sixties when two *panchayat* general elections were held in 1962 and 1965, after which the momentum petered out. This was reflected in the dwindling allocation of financial resources, withdrawal of powers and functions and postponement of *panchayat* elections, on one pretext or the other. Complete elections to all tiers of PRIs were not held for 16 years up to 1981. This naturally compromised the position of PRIs and resulted in loss of credibility of these institutions in the public.

In 1981, the state government declared a 20-Resolution Programme for the state, of which the first resolution included elections to PRIs at all levels. Complete elections were held from 10 December 1981 to 10 January 1982 and new PRIs constituted. A Panchayati Raj Sammelan (conference) was held on 30 January 1982 in which several announcements were made for strengthening panchayati raj in the state. This was followed by a conference of the panchayat samiti *pradhans* and *pramukhs* of zilla parishads on 19-20 July 1983.

The measures adopted for revitalisation of PRIs included transfer of more functions and powers to them, sanction of additional staff and officers, emphasis on training of officials and non-officials and issue of instructions for periodical review of functioning and removal of difficulties. On the occasion of the celebrations of the silver jubilee of panchayati raj on 7 October 1984, several decisions for strengthening the system were taken, an important one of which was the establishment of a panchayati raj institute, named the

Indira Gandhi Panchayati Raj and Gramin Vikas Sansthan, for continuous study and research on the subject and for training of officials and non-officials. After initial enthusiasm, there was a period when the Institute was neglected but it has again started receiving proper attention.

However, the efforts to revitalise panchayati raj could not be sustained for long and it declined again.

In spite of the fluctuating fortunes of panchayati raj in the country, there was the realisation that it has great potential of strengthening grassroots democracy. Several committees were appointed by the Central Government to examine the system and make recommendations on various aspects. Important among these are the Ashok Mehta Committee (1978), G.V.K. Rao Committee (1985) and L.M. Singhvi Committee (1986). In Rajasthan, a comprehensive study on panchayati raj was undertaken by the Sadik Ali Study Team (1964) which made several recommendations on elections, functioning powers, resources, transferred schemes, coordination, supervision and control etc. Other Committees which reported on one or more aspects of panchayati raj were the Girdhari Lal Vyas Committee (1973), S.P. Singh Bhandari Committee and Harlal Singh Kharra Committee (1990).

Causes of Stagnation and Decline of PRIs

The causes for stagnation and decline of PRIs have been identified as absence of regular elections, prolonged suppressions and supercessions, inadequate devolution of powers and functions, inadequate devolution of financial resources to match the assigned duties and responsibilities and insufficient representation of weaker sections. An important factor impeding the progress of PRIs has been an absence of political will because, as the L.M. Singhvi Committee Report pointed out, the potential of PRIs as centres of people's power made elected representatives to the state legislature and Parliaments jealous and they saw themselves being dependent on panchayati raj functionaries. The Committee also felt that PRIs declined "because of lack of conceptual clarity, absence of political will and denial of national priority, lack of continuous process of research, evaluation, feedback and correction." It recommended "that local self-government should be constitutionally recognised, protected and preserved by the inclusion of a new chapter in the Constitution and that local self-government should be constitutionally proclaimed as the third tier of government."

In the mid-1980s, the Union government held regional conferences of PRI representatives to discuss the existing status and future of these institutions. Regional workshops/seminars of District Collectors were organised to discuss decentralised planning, district administration and implementation of development programmes. The most important outcome of these deliberations was the decision to further strengthen panchayati raj and initiate action in that direction including an amendment to the Constitution to provide constitutional status to PRIs. The Constitution (64th Amendment) Bill was introduced in the monsoon session of Parliament in 1989 but its passage by both houses of Parliament was delayed for various reasons. Finally, in December 1992, the Constitution (73rd Amendment) Act was passed and came into effect on 20 April 1993.

The 73rd Constitutional Amendment made specific provisions about the Constitution, term, elections, functions and resources etc. of PRIs. It ensured the following:

- basic uniformity of the three-tier panchayati raj system in the country, except in the states having population of less than two million, which were allowed to adopt a two tier system.
- uniform fixed term of five years for PRIs;
- direct election of all members of PRIs;
- reservation of seats for members of scheduled caste/tribe in the membership as well as the post of chairpersons in proportion to their population. Reservation of seats for other backward classes (OBC) was left to the state legislatures;
- reservation of one-third seats in the membership and chairperson post for women;
- devolution of powers and functions to PRIs in respect of preparation and implementation of plans for economic development and social justice;
- addition of the Eleventh Schedule to the Constitution specifying the 29 functions and schemes to be entrusted to PRIs;
- independent and timely elections to PRIs through the State Election Commission;
- setting up of State Finance Commissions (SFC) every five years to make recommendations in respect of financial devolution and resources etc for PRIs; and

- widening of the scope of the National Finance Commission to include recommendations in respect of PRIs on the basis of recommendations of the SFC.

In pursuance of the 73rd Constitutional Amendment, the Rajasthan government enacted the Rajasthan Panchayati Raj Act, 1994, which came into force on 23 April 1994. Apart from making provisions for the mandatory implementation of the Constitutional amendment, the Act makes provisions on matters left to the state legislature. The notable features of the Rajasthan Panchayati Raj Act, 1994 are:

- Detailed provisions in respect of *gram sabha* and ward *sabha* (assembly of all adult members) about their meetings at regular intervals, quorum procedure, subjects to be discussed and follow-up.
- Constitution of vigilance committees by *panchayats*. (The provision has now been amended to allow the constitution of such committees at panchayat samiti/zilla parishad level).
- Reservation of seats for OBCs in the membership as well as post of chairpersons of PRIs (which has been increased to 21 per cent from 15 per cent).
- Ex-officio membership of the chairpersons of the lower body in the next higher body (introduced by a subsequent amendment). The *sarpanch* of the gram panchayat is now the ex-officio member of the panchayat samiti and the *pradhan* of panchayat samitis the ex-officio member of the zilla parishad.
- Detailed list of the functions of panchayat, panchayat samiti and zilla parishad in Schedules I, II and III under Sections 50, 51 and 52 of the Act.
- Disqualification of persons with more than two children from contesting elections to PRIs.
- Disqualifying persons with criminal background from contesting elections to PRIs (added by subsequent amendment).

Elections to PRIs, under the new Act, were held in January 1995. In these elections, 1,19,419 representatives were elected for 31 zilla parishads, 237 panchayat samitis and 9,185 gram panchayats. Of these, 38,791 were women, 20,712 from scheduled castes, 18,092 scheduled tribes and 14,981 OBCs. The second round of elections was held in January 2000.

The gram sabha and ward sabha have been viewed as the basic institutions of panchayati raj and steps have been taken to ensure that meetings are held on fixed days viz. 26 January, 1 May, 15 August and 2 October. Detailed instructions have been issued for the conduct of meetings, subjects to be discussed and follow-up of the decisions.

So far 16 programmes/activities have been transferred to the PRIs. These include elementary education together with programmes of literacy and universalisation of elementary education (UEE). Other decisions include the constitution of District Planning Committees under the chairmanship of the *zilla parishad pramukh*, making the *pramukh* the chairman of the District Rural Development Agency (DRDA), devolution of funds to PRIs as per the interim recommendations of the Second State Finance Commission and constitution of a task force under the Development Commissioner and Additional Chief Secretary for strengthening local bodies.

These decisions, however, are mostly in the nature of peripheral actions and cannot be considered as going sufficiently far in the direction of empowering PRIs. Even after seven years of the coming into force of the new panchayati raj system, all the activities and programmes enlisted in the Eleventh Schedule of the Constitution and Schedules I, II and III of the Rajasthan Panchayati Raj Act, 1994 have not been transferred to PRIs. The DRDA is still continuing as a separate agency, undermining the position of the zilla parishad. There is a general feeling among the elected representatives of PRIs that the government is hesitant in the matter of devolution of powers and functions and matching resources to PRIs. Looking to the present position of devolution of functions and resources, this feeling does not seem to be unfounded.

The S.C. Mathur Administrative Reforms Commission, in its Seventh Report on Panchayati Raj, submitted on 15 July 2001 made several recommendations, some of which are:

- Revamp the entire functioning of PRIs so that they can function as institutions of self-governance in its true sense.
- Revive the old system of direct elections only at the gram panchayat level and representation of chairpersons of the lower tier in the next higher tier and persuading the Central government to bring in an amendment to this effect in the Constitution.

- Merge DRDAs with zilla parishads; upgrade the post of project director to that of district development commissioner who should be higher in status and scale than the district collector; de-link development administration from revenue administration.
- Revive *nyaya panchayats* to ensure faster and cheaper settlement of small disputes at the village level.
- Allow PRIs and ULBs to assume the role of district government which should function as the third tier of government at the district level.
- Allow PRIs to have statutory entitlement to a share in the total revenue of the state and give them powers to generate their own resources to fulfil the constitutional mandate of planning and implementation of schemes. At least 30 per cent of the state revenue should be allocated to PRIs. There should be 'untied' grants also to PRIs.
- Make compulsory the levying of certain taxes by the appropriate level of local bodies, like house tax, entertainment tax, vehicle tax profession tax, tax on industries business and fairs, cess on land revenue and education cess etc. so that they get over their reluctance and hesitation in levying taxes due to their proximity to the people.
- Take up a massive programme of construction of residential houses for employees at the village and block level with loan assistance from HUDCO for creating village/block civil lines. The scheme could be made self-financing from the rents recoverable from the employees/functionaries.
- Create income-generating assets for PRIs with loans from the Panchayat Finance Corporation. A massive programme of construction of office buildings for PRIs should also be taken up with institutional finance.

A task force should be constituted to look into these recommendations and prescribe action for their implementation.

74TH CONSTITUTIONAL AMENDMENT AND ULBs

The Constitution (74th Amendment) Act, 1992, which came into effect on 20 April 1993, makes provisions for ULBs identical to those made by the 73rd Constitutional Amendment for PRIs. The Twelfth Schedule has been added which enlists the functions and schemes which may be entrusted to ULBs. Apart from the various municipal functions, the Twelfth Schedule includes planning for economic and social development, urban forestry, environmental and ecological aspects, safeguarding the interests of weaker sections and urban poverty alleviation.

The law relating to ULBs is contained in the Rajasthan Municipalities Act, 1959. Necessary amendments were made in 1994 in pursuance of the 74th Constitutional Amendment and to provide for matters left to the state legislature. Reservation for OBCs has been provided in membership and the post of chairpersons initially at 15 per cent, which was subsequently enhanced to 21 per cent.

Article 43 ZD of the 74th Amendment Act provides for the constitution of District Planning Committees for each district to consolidate the plans prepared by the PRIs and ULBs and to prepare a draft development plan for the district as a whole.

At present, there are 183 ULBs in the state. Two elections to the ULBs have been held under the amended law. The ULBs are carrying out various municipal functions and implementing related schemes which include strengthening of fire services, low cost sanitation, participatory urban development, national slum development and environment development. The programmes for welfare of weaker sections and urban poverty alleviation being implemented by ULBs include the Swarna Jayanti Shahri Rozgar Yojana, Urban Self Employment Programme, Training for Skill Upgradation, Self-help Groups, Basic Infrastructure and Mukhya Mantri Rozgar Yojana. An extensive programme for regularisation of *kuchchee bastees* (shanty towns) and for regularisation of conversion of agricultural land into residential/commercial use has been taken up after simplification of the rules and procedures. A month-long campaign, *'Prashasan Shaharon Ke Sang'* (Administration In Cooperation With Cities), was held from 26 January 2002 for sorting out various problems of the people in urban areas on the spot.

STATE FINANCE COMMISSION

In pursuance of Article 243 I and 243 Y of the Constitution and provisions of the Rajasthan Panchayati Raj Act 1959 and the Rajasthan Municipalities Act 1959 (as amended in 1994), the first State Finance Commission (SFC) was set up on 23 April 1994 for making recommendations on financial devolution and grants-in-aid and for improving the financial position of rural and urban local bodies.

In its report, submitted on 30 December 1995, the Commission observed that the time was not yet ripe for assigning some of the state-level taxes to the PRIs or ULBs. Instead, it recommended a share of 2.18 per cent of the net state tax proceeds to be devolved to these bodies and distribution of this share amongst the PRIs and ULBs in the ratio of 3.4:1 in proportion to the rural/urban population according to the 1991 census. This grant was to be an additionality and all allocations under Plan and non-Plan were to continue to flow to the PRIs and ULBs, with the same norms for increase, independent of this additional transfer.

In case of PRIs, the grants recommended by the SFC are establishment grant, maintenance grant, start up grant, matching grant, general purposes grant and incentive grant. In the case of ULBs, the devolution recommended includes general purposes grant, development grant, development loan, incentive grant and matching grant.

During the 1995-2000 period, the PRIs got a total of Rs. 517.82 crore, of which Rs. 212.22 crore was from the award of the Tenth Finance Commission and Rs. 305.60 was from the SFC award. The ULBs got a total of Rs. 133.07 crore (Rs. 43.18 crore from the Tenth Finance Commission grant and Rs. 89.89 crore from the SFC grant).

Apart from the recommendations about financial devolution to PRIs and ULBs, the SFC has made a number of recommendations relating to financial resources, financial management, administration, training, physical infrastructure and environmental improvement etc. An important recommendation relates to the establishment of a financial corporation to look after the credit and technical needs of PRIs. While the state government has accepted all the recommendations of the SFC and devolution of funds started accordingly, the recommendation about a Panchayati Raj Financial Corporation, though accepted, has not yet been implemented.

The second SFC was established on 7 May 1999 and it submitted its Interim Report on 23 February 2001. In line with its recommendation, the state government has made financial devolutions for 2000-2001 and provided for devolutions for 2001-2002. The Commission's final report has not yet been made public.

DECENTRALISED PLANNING: DISTRICT PLANNING

Decentralised planning, planning from below and district planning have been receiving the attention of the Central government and the state government since the 1950s, starting with the Community Development Programme and National Extension Service. It continued through the pilot project in growth centres, guidelines issued by the Planning Commission in 1969, the Dantwala Committee Report of 1978 and, finally, the Hanumantha Rao Report on district planning in 1984. There has been continuous deliberation at the national and state levels for decentralisation of the planning process based on local assessment of resources and needs. The efforts included block level planning, district planning and regional planning.

In Rajasthan, a beginning in decentralised planning was made at the time of the formulation of the Third Five Year Plan by attempting to involve local bodies in the exercise. The process of planning at the district level and at the block level and integration of the block plans and district plans into the state Plan was carried out more systematically in the Fourth Plan. The Planning Department issued circulars on 23 April 1965 and 4 June 1965 with detailed instructions and guidelines to the *vikas adhikaris* of panchayat samitis, secretaries of the *zilla parishads* and the district collectors for preparation of block-level plans and their integration at the district level. A committee called the District Planning Committee was constituted under the chairmanship of the Collector for coordinating the planning process at the district level in respect of PRIs as well as other departments.

Despite all sincerity and earnestness of the state government, the experience of 'planning from below' in Rajasthan was not successful in having any marked impact on the process of economic planning. It was at the best an attempt for aggregation of block Plans into the district Plan without adherence to the principles of planning. The exercise was nearly abandoned in the subsequent five-year Plans till the focus on decentralised planning was revived in the late 1980s.

After the 73rd and 74th Constitutional Amendments, district planning through the PRIs and ULBs has been constitutionally recognised. Section 121 of the Rajasthan Panchayati Raj Act, 1994 provides for the constitution of a District Planning Committee in each district to consolidate the Plans prepared by the PRIs and ULBs in the district, and to prepare a draft development Plan for the district as a whole. The law further provides that in preparing this draft development Plan, the District Planning Committee must give consideration to matters of common interest between PRIs and ULBs, including spatial planning, sharing of water and other physical and natural resources, integrated development of infrastructure and environmental conservation and the extent and type of available resources whether financial or otherwise.

Orders for the constitution of District Planning Committees under the chairmanship of the *zilla parishad pramukhs* were issued in July 1996, with 25 members, of whom 20 members are elected from among the members of zilla parishads and municipalities in proportion to the rural and urban population of the district, while five members are nominated by the government. These are the District Collector, additional Collector (development), Chief Executive Officer and additional chief executive officer of the zilla parishad, and the District Planning Officer, who is the member-secretary.

In spite of the detailed specific provisions in the Constitution and the Rajasthan Panchayati Raj Act, 1994, the District Planning Committees are still not functional and the provisions for district planning still remain on paper and are yet to be translated into action. Orders were issued on 15 November 1999 for the constitution of District Planning and Coordination Committees under the chairmanship of the Collector to assist the District Planning Committees in their work. This goes against the spirit of the Constitution and dilutes the position of the District Planning Committees under the chairmanship of the *pramukh* of the zilla parishads. The Development Commissioner issued instructions, on 17 September 2001, for the review by the District Planning Committees of the progress of the Ninth Plan and for discussions on the approach to the Tenth Five-Year Plan of various departments. The process of decentralised planning or district planning, thus, still remains a distant dream and has not even reached the stage at which it was at the time of the formulation of the Fourth Five Year Plan. A definite and systematic approach is urgently needed in respect of district planning, covering indication of financial resources, delegation of decision-making powers at the district level, encouraging local participation and initiative, making official functionaries accountable to the district planning body, incentives for augmenting local resources and preparation of perspective Plans and annual Plans.

It has been suggested that apart from the District Planning Committee, some other committees should be formed at the block and *gram panchayat* levels so as to formulate local plans keeping in view the local resources and requirements. Suitable formats should be devised for each level with detailed instructions and guidelines.

Costs and Benefits of Decentralisation

Democratic decentralisation has now been accepted in principle and practice and has been granted Constitutional recognition. The concept represents decentralisation of power and functions to local levels. Closely related to decentralisation of administration and development is the subject of decentralised planning or district planning.

The benefits or merits of decentralisation have been widely discussed from time to time. The obvious advantages are mobilisation of local resources, realistic assessment of needs and resources, greater possibilities of people's participation, adaptation to local conditions, sychronising various programmes under simultaneous implementation and removal of regional disparities. The importance of local enthusiasm, which decentralisation is capable of generating, cannot be over-emphasised. The local governing institutions (PRIs and ULBs) will certainly gain in strength and effectiveness through these advantages.

However, decentralisation also has its costs. The most important aspect of costs relates to the provision of adequate infrastructure and technical competence at the relevant local levels. In most of the cases, infrastructure could be provided by decentralisation of the existing set-up. There may be a marginal increase in the costs which will be more than compensated by the advantages flowing from decentralisation. The greatest drawback appears to be the reluctance of the higher levels (of the political and bureaucratic establishments) in parting with their powers and functions. Once this hurdle is overcome, the decks for genuine and effective decentralisation will automatically get cleared.

RECENT MEASURES FOR GOOD GOVERNANCE

The Ashok Gehlot government took several measures towards good governance, especially ensuring transparency, accountability and responsiveness in the administration, empowering women and welfare of the weaker sections.

Transparency in Government

Two important steps in the direction of transparency in administration are the Citizen's Charters and enactment of the Rajasthan Right to Information Act, 2000.

Citizens' Charters have been finalised and issued in 28 departments with public dealing functions with a view to familiarising people about their rights, entitlements and procedures. Demystification of administrative procedures is the objective of such charters. Some of the important departments which have issued Citizens' Charters are Revenue, Home, Medical and Health, Food and Civil Supplies, Labour, Transport, Panchayati Raj and Rural Development. Commercial Taxes, Registration and Stamps, Animal Husbandry, Irrigation, Command Area Development and Anti Corruption Bureau etc. Instructions have been issued for publicising the Citizens' Charters and displaying them at conspicuous places.

The salient features of the various Citizens' Charters are:

- rights of the citizens in relation to the department;
- identification of various activities of the department in relation to the citizen;
- accessibility of the various rules and procedures; making them easily available to the public;
- simplification of rules and procedures;
- identifying various services and facilities to be extended to the people;
- specifying the authorities whom the citizen should approach for specific work/services;
- stipulating time limits for the disposal of various application;
- specifying the authorities whom people can approach for redressal of complaints about delay or inaction.
- propagation of the rules laws and procedures for the benefit of the people; and
- exhibiting important provisions of the charter at conspicuous places in the various offices as also in public places.

The provisions of the citizens' charter should be made legally enforceable and justifiable. All government forms should be simplified and contain instructions for filling them and documents to be attached. Forms should be allowed to be copied/printed freely to ensure their easy availability.

In reality, the Citizens' Charters are not being faithfully and consciously implemented and they have not had any significant effect on the ground. This creates a feeling that the government is not serious about implementing them. It is essential that the charters are translated into action. There has to be a political will and administrative vigilance to ensure this.

Right to Information

The Rajasthan Right to Information Act, 2000, which came into force from 26 January 2001, provides for the right of access to information relating to the affairs of the state and public bodies by means of obtaining certified copies of documents, or inspection of accessible records, or inspection of public works, or taking of samples of material from public works. Every citizen has the right to obtain information from the in-charge of the office, who is liable to provide information. Failure to do so will attract disciplinary action by the disciplinary authority. Rules have been framed in pursuance of the Act and the Chief Secretary has written to all Secretaries and heads of departments to ensure that the objectives of the Act are fully implemented. The Act provides for first and second appeal against an order of any authority refusing information. It also provides for penalty for the defaulting officer in administrative proceedings. These are salutary provisions, but in order to make this right really effective, it is suggested that be made legally enforceable and justifiable.

Computerisation of land records is being done progressively in order to make copies of revenue records available promptly. Other departments have also taken up computerisation of records. Simplification of rules and procedures has been taken up simultaneously in various departments. Powers of inspectors of various departments have been drastically curtailed with a view to reducing individual discretion and arbitrariness.

As in the case of the Citizens' Charters, there is a general feeling that the provisions of the Act and Rules are not being sincerely implemented. It is very necessary to create a sense of urgency about this important legislative measure to ensure that it is faithfully implemented.

Accountability in Government

Conscientious steps have been taken to ensure accountability and eliminate corruption in public life. The Anti-Corruption Bureau has been strengthened. Vigilance Officers have been appointed in 22 major departments, particularly in the revenue-earning departments. The Home Commissioner has been designated as the Chief Vigilance Officer of the state and he supervises the functioning of the Vigilance Officers in various departments. Provisions of the service rules are being invoked for compulsory retirement of employees/officers with doubtful integrity and proven incompetence.

Responsive Administration

Redressal of public grievances: The system of redressal of public grievances includes a Department of Removal of Public Grievances at the state level under the charge of Secretary, Administrative Reforms, who functions as Commissioner for Removal of Public Grievances; Public Grievances cum Vigilance Committees at the district and sub-division level; and Public Grievances Removal Cell in the Chief Minister's Secretariat. Cases of serious complaints are pursued by the Chief Minister's Office till they are finally disposed. Apart from the usual monitoring system for removal of public grievances, monitoring and follow-up from Chief Minister's Office imparts a sense of seriousness and urgency to the entire exercise.

The S.C. Mathur Commission examined the existing system of grievance redressal in detail and, finding it inadequate, recommended restructuring of the entire system under the Chief Ministers' Secretariat.

BOX 12.3

Disposal Campaigns

With a view to disposing of pending matters and grievances on the spot, special campaigns were organised in 2001 for three months in the rural areas and for one month in the urban areas. These special campaigns known as *'Prashasan Gaon Ke Sang'* and *'Prashasan Shaharon Ke Sang'* (i.e. Administration in Cooperation with the Villages/ Towns) were preceded by detailed preparation and instructions, wide publicity and foolproof arrangements for sorting out matters on the spot by the concerned officials. These campaigns have certainly helped in the disposal of pending matters and providing much needed relief to the people.

Under the *Prashasan Gaon Ke Sang* campaign, concerted efforts were made to include participation of rural people in governance A novel approach was taken by the district administration to hear grievances of people and redress them swiftly. At these camps, the district administration tried to resolve matters related to land, old age pension, and drought. *Khatedari* rights were instantly conferred on deserving farmers during these campaigns.

Between October 2001 and January 2002, 66 lakh rural families were given various types of relief and 44 lakh pending revenue cases were solved.

In June 2002, under a special land allotment campaign, 5,126 scheduled tribe families were allotted 5,682 acres of land, 14,169 scheduled caste families got 15,316 acres of agricultural land and 17,139 other poor families were allotted 20,374 acres of agricultural land.

Panchayat laws have been made more flexible to facilitate participation of rural people in the democratic processes.

As a part of rural development strategy, 16 lakh Kisan Credit Cards have been distributed to farmers through the network of cooperative banks between January 1999 and December 2001.

Pending matters of municipalities relating to sanitation, cleanliness, house tax, regularisation of colonies, drainage etc. were taken up by the concerned officials. Under the *Prashasan Shaharon Ke Sang* from January 2002 to February 2002, 14,898 city dwellers were given titles for residential houses in different cities. Likewise, many *kuchchee bastees* were regularised, providing relief to 41,000 households living in these colonies. It is estimated that under the campaign, more than 1.1 million city dwellers were given the opportunity to present their grievances before the administration and their problems were resolved.

Welfare and Empowerment of Women

Several steps have been taken for the welfare and empowerment of women. The Rajasthan State Women's Commission was constituted on 15 May 1999 and the State Women's Policy was announced on 8 May 2000. Reservation for women in government services has been increased from 20 per cent to 30 per cent. There is also reservation of 25 per cent seats for women in technical courses. Special emphasis has been laid on education of the girl child and appropriate incentives are being provided to the girl students. Self-help Groups (SHGs) are being formed to promote thrift and micro credit amongst women and a total of 9654 SHGs had been formed till March 2001.

Appreciating the problems of working women, the Rajasthan Civil Service (conduct) Rules have been amended to deal strictly with male employees who harass or misbehave with women employees. Zilla Mahila Sahayata Samitis have been constituted at each district headquarters to prevent atrocities against women.

Welfare of Weaker Sections

Apart from the various on-going schemes and programmes for the welfare of scheduled castes, scheduled tribes, OBCs and minorities and BPL families, the state government has taken certain special measures for the welfare of all weaker sections. These include expansion of the coverage of social security schemes of pensions to the old, disabled, widows and destitutes; setting up of a State Minorities Finance and Development Corporation; increase in economic assistance to scheduled castes/scheduled tribes/OBCs, minorities and *safai karmacharis*; implementation of the scheme for liberation of municipal workers from scavenging and their rehabilitation and expansion of educational facilities to scheduled castes/scheduled tribes/OBCs.

A social worker has been appointed as Commissioner for the Disabled to look after the task of promoting the welfare of disabled persons and has also been entrusted with the task of looking after other social security schemes.

All BPL families are provided free medical treatment at government medical institutions through Medicare Relief Cards.

The Mukhya Mantri Jeevan Raksha Kosh has been set up for providing secondary and tertiary level treatment completely free of cost to BPL patients, irrespective of the cost. Persons who do not belong to BPL category but whose income is below Rs. 24,000 a year, are provided assistance from the Chief Minister's Relief Fund.

Other measures for ensuring good governance include the constitution of the Rajasthan State Human Rights Commission; adoption of a mission approach for water management, population control, tourism development, social security schemes including women and child development and elementary education and literacy; appointment of task forces for financial management, panchayati raj and rural development, agriculture development, information technology, telecom and e-governance, and sustainable development. These measures have created a good impact. In fact, while the expected good governance has not become a reality at the macro level, there have been some extremely useful initiatives at the micro levels. These initiatives, whether in the areas of infrastructure development or revenue administration or primary education, are expected to go a long way in providing responsible and transparent governance to the people of Rajasthan.

SUGGESTIONS FOR ACTION/MEASURES FOR GOOD GOVERNANCE

- In order to achieve the objective of good governance, government must become more caring, compassionate and responsive: Conscious efforts have to be made in this direction.
- Steps must be taken for the all round socio-economic development of the area and the people, through a holistic approach.
- The development activities and ameliorative measures must pay special attention to the poor, deprived sections of the society and welfare of the weaker sections.
- Steps must be taken to review and revitalise poverty alleviation and employment generation programmes with a view to achieving the goal of alleviation of poverty.
- The 73rd and 74th Constitutional Amendments have paved the way for devolution of real power to the people though PRIs and ULBs.
- Effective steps must be taken for the devolution of powers and functions to PRIs along with corresponding devolution of physical and financial resources.
- Education and health must constitute the prime areas of concern for ensuring better quality of life for the people.
- Intensive efforts are necessary for the universalisation of elementary education and achieving 100 per cent literacy both for boys and girls.
- In spite of the multiplication of medical institutions, medical and health care facilities are yet to reach the common man, particularly in the far-flung and interior areas. Effective measures must be taken to extend medical and health care facilities to the remote areas of the state, with particular emphasis on benefiting the BPL families, weaker sections, senior citizens and rural areas.
- Steps for the empowerment of women and welfare of weaker sections should be accorded high priority.
- NGO and private initiatives and participation of people can make a significant contribution in the delivery of services, particularly in the sphere of education and health care. Such initiatives should be encouraged as part of the government policy for awareness creation, monitoring of development activities and appraisal of benefits.
- Recommended administrative reforms measures should be examined closely and implemented. It is necessary to have a permanent machinery at the state level to monitor and pursue the process of administrative reforms.

- Since there is no visible impact of the enactment of the Right to Information Act, steps should be taken to propagate its provisions and translate into action the idea of transparency in administration at all levels.
- Every government department must publish an annual report containing detailed information on its organisation, functions, programmes financial allocations, their utilisation and other important information relevant to the public.
- Measures should be adopted to generate awareness about Citizens' Charters and to see that they are implemented in letter and spirit.
- The goals of accountability and responsiveness of administration have to be always kept in mind, and concerted measures should be taken to ensure these attributes at all levels of administration.
- Rooting out of corruption from all levels and in all spheres has to be pursued in a determined manner. There should be no tolerance of corruption and a war against corruption has to be waged on all fronts.
- The number of cases in courts is constantly increasing. leading to delayed disposal and harassment of the public. Steps should be taken for expeditious disposal of cases and reduction in the number of pending cases in the civil, revenue and criminal courts. Nyaya Panchayats and Lok Adalats can play a significant role in this regard.
- A people-friendly government and administration should be the avowed objective for every office and every government functionary. Publication of all relevant information and making this available, opening of reception counters fully equipped with necessary information and facilities, maintenance of office discipline, timely disposal of matters, simplification of rules and procedures, reduction of discretionary powers to the minimum and an efficient mechanism for redressal of public grievances will go a long way in this direction.
- The following measures need to be taken to reduce the hassles in submission of forms to government offices:
  - All forms should be simple and comprehensible to a lay person and the cost of the form should be included in the fees charged for the service.
  - The concerned department must print the list of all documents which the applicant is required to enclose with the form. The official receiving the form along with its enclosures must point out lapses, if any, while accepting the documents.
  - The requirement of depositing postal orders and stamp papers should be replaced by a pay order or account payee cheque.
  - Transparency needs to be maintained while receiving forms and scrutinising them.
  - Decision on the application filed by any individual must be notified within a specified period. An applicant must have a right to know the reasons for rejection of the application.
- The following additional steps are necessary in order to minimise corruption and make the entire system people friendly:
  - All industrial licensing should be ended.
  - All restrictions on trading, movement, marketing, processing and stocking of agricultural commodities must be removed.
  - Restrictions on land sales/transfers should be ended.
  - Physical exchange and voluntary consolidation of lands should be allowed and recorded without payment of stamp duty, or at a nominal rate.

Chapter 13

Women

The status of women in a society is an indicator of the level of development of any civilization. In this respect, Indian society is caught between tradition and modernity, between respect for women and exploitation, and between restrictive patriarchal values and progressive ideals. Rajasthan society is, by and large, patrilineal and follows the system of patrilocality i.e., transfer of a woman to the residence of her husband after marriage. Hence, daughters generally do not inherit immovable assets, and instead, are given a portion of the movable property as dowry. This results in the preference for the male child and discrimination against the girl child, whether it is in matters of food and nutrition, healthcare, education, freedom, rights and justice.

Though the Constitution stipulates equality for all citizens, irrespective of gender, caste, religion, race, and place of birth, women still do not enjoy equality in many spheres.

Despite India having one of the largest health care systems in the world and the existence of the Integrated Child Development Scheme (ICDS), infant and child mortality rates among girls is still very high. The situation is worse in Rajasthan. More than 68 per cent of women are married before 18 years of age. Although enrolment of girls in schools has increased, the rising dropout rate is worrying. Women are mostly found in marginal and casual employment, and that too mostly in agriculture and the informal sectors, constituting almost 90 per cent of the total marginal workers. They are still subjected to violence and exploitation.

Gender Related Demographic Indicators

Life expectancy at birth has improved for both men and women. The trend from 1971 to 1991 shows a higher percentage gain for women. This is due to better survival chances at older ages. The age-specific death rates, which show a greater risk of death for females during infancy, early childhood and during the prime life until the age of 30, support this finding.

TABLE 13.1

Life Expectancy at Birth

Year	*Male*	*Female*
1971	50.5	49.0
1981	55.4	55.7
1991	58.1	58.6

Source: Registrar General of India. Data for 2001 are not presently available.

TABLE 13.2

Age-specific Death Rates in Rajasthan, 1991

Age Group	*Male*	*Female*
0-4 yrs.	25.9	26.5
5-9 yrs.	1.8	2.3
10-14 yrs.	1.3	1.4
15-19 yrs.	1.1	2.6
20-24 yrs.	2.4	2.8
25-29 yrs.	1.9	2.7
30-34 yrs.	2.2	2.3
35-39 yrs.	4.3	3.2
40-44 yrs.	5.8	2.5
45-49 yrs.	11.6	2.6

Source: Census of India, 1991, Series-21, Rajasthan.

Economic deprivation and gender discrimination lead to higher mortality for females, besides reducing women's access to resources that ensure their survival and health. Girls face the maximum discrimination in the allocation of food and medical care in the first two years of their life. Twice as much is spent on medical care of male infants than on females. During the reproductive years, women go through a vicious cycle of malnutrition, anaemia and unregulated fertility, which takes a heavy toll of their lives. Malnutrition during pregnancy and lactation results in the birth of underweight babies and, consequently, high infant mortality rates and increasing chances of maternal mortality.

Sex Ratio

Sex ratio is considered to be an important and sensitive indicator of the status of women. This indicator becomes more important in Rajasthan, where several factors work to result in the marginalisation of women.

TABLE 13.3

Sex Ratio

Sex Ratio	*1991*	*2001*
India	**927**	**933**
Rajasthan	**910**	**922**
Urban	879	890
Rural	919	932
0-6 yrs.	917	909

Source: Census of India 2001.

According to the 2001 Census estimates, Rajasthan has registered an improvement in the sex ratio over 1991 (Table 13.3), though it is still behind the national average of 933. What is worrying is the fact that the sex ratio in the 0-6 years age group has actually registered a decline since 1991. The sex ratio among children enrolled in anganwadi centres is 877, which is proof of discrimination against the girl child.

Sex ratio and poverty have an inverse relation. This challenges the conventional notion that the poor neglect their girl children. Statistics show that the sex ratio among BPL households is better than in APL households and the adverse sex ratio in the age group 0-6 is higher in relatively more prosperous regions and among the better-off households. Though rural society is considered to be orthodox, this is belied by the fact that the adverse sex ratio is more marked in urban areas as compared to rural areas. The skewed sex ratio in urban areas is mainly due to sex determination of the foetus and female foeticide, facilities for which are more readily available in the urban areas.

Age at Marriage

The mean age at marriage for girls in Rajasthan is 15.1 years and mean age at cohabitation is 16.2 years. Though the legal age of marriage is 18, 68.3 per cent of women in the age group of 20-24 years were found to have been married before 18 years. This is due to strong and deep-rooted social pressures. Early marriage results in early child bearing, with all its attendant risks. The risk of maternal mortality in teenage pregnancy is almost ten times more. Early marriage also results in girls not continuing with education, which limits their employment opportunities. The majority are, therefore, confined to domestic drudgery, with no decision-making powers even within the household.

Total Fertility Rate

The Total Fertility Rate (TFR) for Rajasthan is higher than the national average. With a high Infant Mortality Rate (IMR) of 80 and an under-five mortality rate of 114.9, there is a tendency for women to bear more children. Most mothers in Rajasthan, especially in the rural areas, lose one or more children. The mortality in children belonging to scheduled castes, scheduled tribes and OBCs is higher than in other social groups, as a result of which the TFR in these groups is also higher. The total wanted fertility rate is 2.57 as against the TFR of almost 3.78.

Child Mortality

Infant and child mortality are much higher in rural than in urban areas. The female neonatal mortality is the only indicator in which the urban areas fare better. This is due to increased risk for male infants and better

TABLE 13.4

Reproductive and Child Health Indicators of Select States

Indicators	*Rajasthan*	*Punjab*	*Uttar Pradesh*	*Bihar*	*Andhra Pradesh*	*Kerala*	*India*
% of women aged 20-24 years married at the age of 18	68.3	11.6	62.4	71.0	64.3	17.0	50
TFR	3.78	2.21	3.99	3.49	2.25	1.96	2.85
IMR	80.4	57.1	86.7	72.9	65.8	16.3	67.6
Under-5 mortality rate	114.9	72.1	122.5	105.1	85.5	18.8	94.9

Source: NFHS-2.

survival chances for female infants. The under-five mortality rate is higher for the girls than boys, reflecting the neglect of the girl child.

TABLE 13.5

Childhood Mortality

Background Characteristics	*Neonatal Mortality*	*Infant Mortality*	*Under 5 Mortality*
Urban	45.6	68.9	93.9
Rural	56.3	93.1	133.2
Male	51.5	88.9	115.7
Female	50.4	87.2	134.9
Mother			
Illiterate	57.7	94.6	136.5
Literate	34.5	52.8	65.43
Region			
Western	57.9	94.9	122.3
North-Eastern	50.8	82.4	123.1
Southern	55.2	86.3	122.0
South-Eastern	56.2	94.9	141.7

Source: NFHS-2

Physical Quality of Life Index

The physical quality of life index uses three measures – IMR, life expectancy at age one and literacy for population aged 15 and above. This index has improved considerably for women in Rajasthan but it is still below the national average and the index for most other states.

Women and Employment

While income levels are generally low, women's access to income and control over economic resources is even worse. Although most women are engaged in work, their work tends to be invisible and unrecorded. The total employment of women in the organised sector is less than 4 per cent. In spite of their valuable contribution to household income, both in the agriculture and non-farm sectors, women have little or no control over decisions relating to their income. Less than one out of every seven persons employed in the formal economy are women and women are generally paid less than men for the same job. Though the government is aware of this discrimination, it has done little to correct this.

Women also have to bear the double burden of domestic chores in addition to their work. Therefore, any strategy to improve women's access to paid work must also consider how to reduce their domestic burden. The usual fallout of this double burden is that children, especially the girl child, is often made to take up these chores, like fetching water, collecting fuel wood and fodder, tending to livestock etc. In the process, children's education suffers and this becomes the cause of continued poverty and large families.

Table 13.7 shows work participation rates in Rajasthan vis-à-vis some other states. In Rajasthan, the working life of a rural female worker is 24.6 years and that of the urban female worker is 11.6 years. Work participation rates (WPR) peak in the 25-29 years age group. This is closely related to years spent in formal education that determines age at entry into the labour market. High levels of WPR are recorded among currently married females, illiterate females, scheduled caste and scheduled tribe women. Female WPR varies inversely with the income of a household.

TABLE 13.6

Physical Quality of Life Indicators

Year	*Rajasthan*		*India*		*Punjab*		*Uttar Pradesh*		*Bihar*		*Andhra Pradesh*		*Kerala*	
	Rural	*Urban*	*Rural*	*Urban*	*Rural*	*Urban*	*Rural*	*Urban*	*Rural*	*Urban*	*Rural*	*Urban*	*Rural*	*Urban*
1971														
Male	34	65	41	66	54	69	28	55	—	—	43	65	72	75
Female	22	50	28	56	40	61	13	42	—	—	35	59	66	73
1981														
Male	40	76	49	66	59	78	37	63	52	75	50	78	84	95
Female	31	70	38	59	55	78	25	55	36	64	45	72	85	90
1991														
Male	50	73	57	75	66	77	49	66	55	73	56	73	87	87
Female	39	63	47	71	60	74	35	60	40	62	57	69	89	88

TABLE 13.7

Work Participation Rates in Select States (1991) (%)

	Rural		*Urban*	
	Male	*Female*	*Male*	*Female*
Rajasthan	**54.0**	**45.7**	**49.0**	**16.3**
Haryana	46.3	27.1	51.9	15.2
Uttar Pradesh	52.2	21.9	48.2	10.2
Bihar	51.1	17.2	43.9	6.9
Andhra Pradesh	63.1	52.1	54.4	19.9
Kerala	53.7	23.8	55.9	20.3
INDIA	55.3	32.8	52.1	15.5

Source: Census of India, 1991, Series-21, Rajasthan.

TABLE 13.8

Work Participation Rates, 1991

(000's)

	Total Main Workers	*Marginal Workers*	*Non Workers*
Male	11,182	178	11,683
Female	2,733	3,011	15,219

Source: Census of India, 1991, Series-21, Rajasthan.

Female WPR is highest in agricultural labour households in the rural areas and casual labour households in the urban areas. It is also higher in female-headed households and among migrants. Women earn two-thirds to three-fourths of male wages in farm and non-farm occupations for similar tasks and similar hours of work. There is a strong labour market segmentation, with women at the bottom of the hierarchy, less access to training and skill development and less opportunities to attain upward mobility. Women occupy the lower ranks of piece-rate or home-based workers, with low returns and without legal protection. Their job is also generally hazardous.

Women as workers and home-makers bear the major brunt of urban poverty. The poor working and living conditions lead to an overall deterioration in their health. Unemployment figures do not throw much light on disguised unemployment among women. Working women contribute a much larger share of their household income to household expenditure as compared to men. Rural poverty and male migration to the cities increase female headship in the family, and leads to an increase in the ranks of 'cultivators' and 'agricultural labourers'.

Due to the additional burden of domestic work and pressure to retain employment, women usually keep away from trade union activities. Many trade unions also do not pay adequate attention to gender issues in the workplace.

TABLE 13.9

Sectoral and Gender Distribution of Main Workers (%)

	Cultivation	*Agri. Labour*	*Livestock Forestry etc.*
Male	56.2	8.0	1.9
Female	69.3	18.2	1.3

Source: Census of India, 1991, Series-21, Rajasthan.

Some Special Employment Programmes Benefiting Women

Integrated Rural Development Programme

Development of Women & Children in Rural Areas

Employment Generation through SHGs.

Jawahar Rozgar Yojana

Employment Assurance Scheme

Urbanisation and Industrialisation

Rajasthan's frequent droughts and consequent lack of economic activity in the rural areas lead to men migrating to cities for employment. This increases women's vulnerability to reproductive morbidity because of reproductive tract infections and sexually transmitted diseases, since the men are involved in sexual relations with sex workers and contract sexually transmitted diseases which they pass on to their wives. Their work burden also increases in the absence of the male. Rapid and unchecked industrialisation has adversely affected the living and environmental conditions, with harmful consequences for health, especially women's health.

Similarly, depletion of forest cover and scanty rainfall has increased the workload of women who have to travel longer distances to fetch water, fodder and fuel.

CONSTITUTIONAL PROVISIONS

The Constitution grants equality to women and also enjoins the State to take steps to address the social, economic, educational and political disadvantages they face. In addition, there have been various legislations which are aimed at helping women. The Hindu Marriage Act, 1955, allows Hindu women to seek divorce on various grounds. The Hindu Succession Act, 1956, has given Hindu women the same rights as men in the matter of succession, The Hindu Minority and Guardianship Act, 1956, provided the mother with the natural custody of a child below five years of age. The Hindu Adoption and Maintenance Act, 1956, allows women to adopt children without the consent of the husband and for single women to adopt children. It also allows the adoption of girls. The Dowry Prohibition Act, 1961, makes the act of giving, abetting or taking dowry is a cognisable, non-bailable offence. In addition to these women-specific legislations, there are various provisions in the Indian Penal Code and the Criminal Procedure Code, which are guaranteed to protect women's interests.

Government Policies Related to Women's Development

The Central Social Welfare Board (CSWB) was set up in 1953 to act as an apex body on social welfare. It pointed to the absence of any government machinery at most levels for welfare activities, and proposed involving voluntary organisations in the task. Mahila Mandals (women's groups) were proposed as delivery mechanisms for essential services. This was expected to motivate women to participate in the political and development process. The Second to the Fifth Five-Year Plans continued to reflect the same welfare approach, though they also accorded priority to education, besides taking measures to improve maternal and child health and nutrition services, etc. The growing emphasis on population control highlighted women's reproductive rather than productive roles.

The Sixth Five-Year Plan is regarded as a landmark for women's development. It adopted a multi-disciplinary approach with a three-pronged thrust on health, education and employment of women. A Women's Welfare and Development Bureau was set up as a nodal point. Special cells for women were set up in the Ministries of Labour and Employment and Rural Development in order to promote and strengthen women's participation in the economy.

The Seventh Plan continued development programmes for women, with the objective of raising their economic and social status and bringing them into the mainstream of national development. The basic thrust was on the identification and promotion of beneficiary-oriented programmes, which extended direct benefits to women.

Some of the policy initiatives undertaken during the Eighth Plan period were: setting up of the National Commission for Women in 1992 to safeguard the interests of women; the establishment of the Rashtriya Mahila Kosh (RMK) in 1993; and the adoption of the National Nutrition Policy. The Ninth Plan made a major commitment of empowering women as agents of socio-economic change and development.

Policies for Women in Rajasthan

The five-year Plans for Rajasthan were formulated on lines of the national Plans. The Fifth Five-Year Plan of the state emphasised nutrition for children and women. The Sixth Plan had a separate chapter on women and children. In the Eighth Plan, development of women laid emphasis on education of women and the girl child. It also had beneficiary-oriented schemes like IRDP, JRY, Indira Awas Yojana.

The state's Ninth Plan had a specific focus on empowerment of women and other socially disadvantaged groups, through convergence of services, with focus on education, health and employment. As the organised sector offers limited employment potential for women, special training courses for women were planned. There was specific allocation of resources for women's development which was 0.16 per cent of the total Plan outlay. This was an additional amount over the allocation for various schemes aimed at benefiting women.

Protective Legal Provisions for Women in the Workplace

Factories Act, 1948: No woman or child to be employed in any part of a factory for pressing action.

Employee's State Insurance Act, 1948: Claim for maternity benefits.

Plantation Labour Act, 1951: Separate toilet facilities for women and fully equipped crèche facilities wherever 50 or more women are employed.

Mines Act, 1952: Separate urinals for women; crèche facilities; women and children not to work below the ground; women not be put on night duty.

Maternity Benefits Act, 1961: Twelve weeks maternity leave for women who put in 160 days of work within 12 months of the expected date of delivery.

Mines Crèche Rules, 1948: Crèche facilities; medical examination of children once a month and of nursing mothers once in two months.

Contract Labour Act, 1952: Minimum wages; service conditions at par with regular workers; women not to be required to work beyond nine hours.

Equal Remuneration Act, 1976: Equal pay for men and women for similar or same work; no discrimination in recruitment and service conditions, promotions, training, transfers, etc.

Building and Other Construction Workers Act, 1966: Representation of a women member on the Building and other Construction Workers Welfare Board.

Policy and Machinery for Women's Advancement in Rajasthan

The state government formulated a Women's Policy in 2002 and set up various institutions for women's welfare and development: the Department of Women and Child Development (DWCD); State Women's Commission; and Department of Social Welfare.

The DWCD is responsible for mainstreaming of women into development by raising their overall status. It formulates various policies and programmes, recommends the enactment/amendment of legislations affecting women and coordinates the efforts of both government and non-government organisations to improve the position of women.

The four-member Women's Commission was established on 15 May 1998. Its main functions are:

- To investigate any kind of misbehaviour/ill-treatment against women and make recommendations to the government about the proceedings of the case.
- To make the existing enactments/amendments/legislations in favour of women more effective.
- To stop any discrimination against women in various public services and public undertakings.
- To take necessary steps for the development and empowerment of women, and to make recommendations to the government in this regard.
- To study the relative social, economic and political status of women and provide impetus to the issue of women's rights with the help of statistics.

The Commission is running a gender cell with assistance from UNICEF.

The Commission has been given powers of a civil court to settle cases and it can direct the state government to initiate legal proceedings in any case where it feels injustice has been done to women. The state government is bound to act on the recommendations and suggestions of the Commission, and to report to the Commission within three months. The Commission is empowered to investigate any case of atrocity against women and to execute various actions to curb any kind of violence, crime and exploitation against women. The Women's Commission in Rajasthan is one of the most powerful women's commissions in the country after that of Kerala.

Women's Policy

The objectives of the Women's Policy is:

- To implement programmes and policies that are gender-just and enable women to exercise their Constitutional rights.
- To appreciate the productive role of women in the economic, social and political spheres.
- To understand and work towards the special needs of women and adolescent girls, especially those in adverse situations and belonging to socially disadvantaged groups.
- To adopt a life cycle and holistic approach to address the health and nutrition needs of women.
- To promote literacy among women and adolescent girls. To focus on illiterate and neo-literate girls and women so as to provide them with opportunities for fundamental and continuing education.
- To propagate gender sensitivity in all government departments at all levels and to create a congenial and enabling environment to make political leaders, policymakers and media gender-sensitive.
- To promote and support women in the political process and to facilitate the reach of women to various governmental and non-governmental agencies, which promote the active role of women in development.

Government Schemes for Women's Development

The DWCD implements various schemes to provide basic facilities for improving the lives of children and women, and, in the process, ensure their physical, mental and psychological development. Many of these are schemes which have been initiated by the Central government as Centrally-sponsored or Central schemes.

The **Integrated Child Development Scheme (ICDS)** was started in 1975 and is presently in its third phase, which is being supported by the World Bank. It is operational in all districts of Rajasthan. Its target population is children in the 0-6 years age group, pregnant and lactating women and adolescent girls in the 11-18 years age group in seven districts. The programme focuses on supplementary nutrition, immunisation, health checkups, distribution of iron folic acid tablets, vitamin-A doses, Oral Rehydration Solution (ORS) packets and safe delivery kits, health education, pre-school non-formal education and referral services.

Barring the supplementary nutrition component, ICDS has not been very successful in the areas of health check ups, health education and referral services. The design of the programme is faulty. According to the guidelines, a severely undernourished child should get double the amount of supplementary nutrition. However, severely undernourished children are unable to consume even the regular stipulated amount of food.

There are centres where more children are enrolled than are required. Children in the 3-6 years age group outnumber those in the 0-3 years age group, as mothers do not leave toddlers in the centres. Besides, the food incentive is better utilised by the older children. There is also a gender bias in the enrolment of children, with more boys being enrolled.

Health education is limited only to pregnant and lactating women. It should be given to all women of the community every fortnight and should also focus on adolescent girls all over the state and not only in select districts.

The **Self-Help Group (SHG) scheme** aims at inculcating the habit of savings and cooperation among the poor rural women and to help them in taking credit from banks, NABARD etc. Women are provided training to this effect. Till February 2001 there were 18,827 SHGs with a membership of 2.82 lakh women.

The DWCD provides funds at the rate of Rs.1,000 per couple for group marriages among the socially disadvantaged groups. As of 2001, 4,148 couples have benefited through this scheme started in 1996-97.

Started in 1984, the **Women's Development Programme** is operational in all districts. Its objective is the economic and social empowerment of women through information, education and training. The programme ensures participation of women in various women-oriented schemes run by various departments. The focus areas of the scheme are education, training, health, nutrition, family welfare, employment and economic development. It attempts to generate a sense of confidence among rural women and bring about a change in their thinking and beliefs through awareness generation programmes on various issues like dowry, child marriages, family planning, savings, social forestry, literacy, AIDS, violence against women and exploitation of women through focus group discussions, film shows, street plays, camps etc. The programme initially showed signs of promise. However, the momentum was lost because of loose organisational structure and lack of proper coordination between the partner governmental and non-governmental organisations.

The LADLI scheme for adolescent girls operates on the premise that the social development of adolescent girls should be in accordance with their needs and abilities and they are capable of determining their own interests and benefits. It operates through the formation of adolescent girl groups, camps and fairs, training of adolescent girls in traditional skills like weaving, knitting etc. as well as non-traditional male-dominated occupations like gardening, repairing of hand pumps, first aid etc. Till February 2001, 18,600 girls had been covered under the scheme which has been completed in 19 districts. Such training is important for the advancement of women, and adolescent girls are the right targets. However, it is important to sustain such schemes and provide training on an on-going basis. The trainees could be enabled to become trainers with or without the project.

The **Mahila Rajgir Yojana (Women Masons Scheme)** was started in 10 districts in 1996-97 with the joint effort of the DWCD, Panchayati Raj Department, the Union Ministry of Rural Development and UNICEF. The project was later extended to 13 districts and has been completed in all of them.

The **District Women Assistance Committee** scheme was started in 1997-98 to provide help to the women in distress and to ensure prosecution of perpetrators of these crimes. The committees are set up under the District Collector. Till February 2001, 2,740 cases were received and 1,961 disposed of. This is a rather small number for four years of operation. This shows that a large number of cases of violence and atrocities against women are not reported. It is also possible people do not know of the existence of such a committee or that it is not yet seen as being effective.

The **Integrated Population Development Programme** is operational in seven districts with assistance from the UNFPA. It focuses on reproductive and child health services, adolescent girls' needs, development of SHGs and joint training programmes of DWCD, Health Department and Education Department. A Women's Resource Centre has been set up under this project, which works in the areas of gender training, documentation and dissemination of information, research and analysis and advocacy. This is done through studies on various subjects relating to women as well as training on these issues and aims to bring about attitudinal change among policymakers and create a gender sensitive environment.

The **Integrated Women's Employment Programme (Indira Mahila Yojana)** is a Centrally-sponsored scheme which aims to create awareness among women about various governmental and non-governmental schemes, educate them to make use of these and encourage them to take up various income generating activities.

Various Women Awareness Centres have been set up at the level of anganwadis. Women SHGs have been formed and bank loans on easy terms provided to them. NGOs have also been involved to facilitate the process of formation of SHGs and provision of loans from banks. Till February 2001, 1572 groups had been organised.

SHGs are functioning very well in some of the rural areas. Women who earlier had no access to money find it extremely helpful to have a source from where they can get easy loans and also save money. This is a form of economic empowerment, which also incorporates social change.

Under the **NORAD-assisted Programme**, which is an income generation programme, funding agency Norwegian Agency for Development Cooperation (NORAD) assisted in the setting up of training-cum-production centres, which provide training to poor and needy women in the 18-45 years age in emerging non-traditional areas. This is implemented by the Central government, and state government sends proposals for it.

STEP (Science and Technology Entrepreneur Park provides a comprehensive package for upgrading of skills of women from low-income groups through training, extension inputs, market linkages etc. in the traditional sectors of agriculture, dairying, handicrafts, handlooms etc. The Rajasthan Cooperative Dairy Federation received Rs. 7.26 crore as grant till 2001, under which Women Dairy Cooperatives are running in ten districts.

The **National Women's Fund** was set up for meeting the need for loans among women in the unorganised sector and develop a simple repayment system. Loans are mainly given for productive and economic activities.

These are various income generation schemes aimed at economic empowerment of women. However, these schemes are not availed of, given the poor literacy levels among women and their lack of decision-making power. Often women are made proxy beneficiaries while the husband or a male relative uses the loan. There is, therefore, no material difference to the status of woman or her position within the household. Some mechanism has to be evolved to check these malpractices, so that benefits reach the groups at whom they are targeted.

The **Balika Samridhdhi Yojana** is meant to change the attitude of society towards the girl child, prevent female foeticide and infanticide and increase the enrolment of girls in school. Under the scheme, girl children born to BPL families (a maximum of two children) after 15 August 1997 get Rs.550 which is deposited in a bank. When the girl is enrolled in school, she is given an annual scholarship of Rs. 300-1000/- for classes I to X. A total of 31,169 girl children in Rajasthan had benefited under the scheme till February 2001.

Under the **Rashtriya Matruteva Sahayata Yojana or National Motherhood Benefit Scheme**, initiated on 31 October 2000, women from BPL families are given Rs. 500 for the initial two live births.

The **Mahila Shakti Award** is given on International Women's Day (8 March) to a bonafide resident of Rajasthan working in the field of women's development for at least 10 years. The award carries a gift cheque of Rs.11,000 and a citation.

In 1996, the chief minister announced reservation for women in government services - 20 per cent in ordinary services and 10 per cent in the police services.

Thus, there is no dearth of schemes for women. What is needed is effective implementation of these. The DWCD needs to publish statistics relating to the implementation. This will help in promoting effective schemes and doing away with redundant ones.

Schemes of The Social Welfare Department

Hostel facilities for working women: As of 2001, 33 hostels have been built. However, the living conditions are not uniformly good. These hostels should be seen by working women as welcome interventions of the government on their behalf and not as facilities used by them when they have no choice. Suitable recreational facilities should be made available for women residents in these hostels. In fact, these can act as a platform for addressing the needs of majority of women who have parallel to, or lower economic status.

Women's Home: Shelter homes are provided for exploited women and undertrials. Girl children who stay in Kishori Grah, the shelter home for exploited women and undertrials, are transferred here when they turn 18 and stay here till they get married or can support themselves. The women in these homes are provided security and rehabilitation along with free housing, food, clothing, medical facilities, vocational training etc. A sum of Rs. 5,000 is provided to each woman for marriage. As of 2001, 342 residents have been married and 5,404 have been handed over to their guardians. The young women in these homes need psychological counselling. The home should be looked upon as an enabling institution to help women cope and get on with their lives when they leave the home.

The Department of Social Welfare runs nine short stay homes which provide refuge to women affected by adverse family circumstances, victims of violence and marital discord. Such women and their children are provided shelter for short periods of time till they are able to be on their own.

The government provides Rs. 5,000 for the marriage of daughters of widows or destitute women from the socio-economically weaker sections of society.

The Department provides grant-in-aid to various organisations for promoting women's welfare. Aid is also provided for day care centres to widows/unwed mothers/abandoned and helpless women. The Department also provides a widow pension of Rs. 200 per month.

The Department of Social Welfare provides grants-in-aid to various organisations handling different aspects of welfare of women and children. The Social Welfare Board is expected to play the role of an apex body to assist voluntary agencies and to improve and develop welfare programmes. These activities cover women as well as they are seen to be hampered by social customs and values. However, there is a lot of overlap between the work of the Department of Social Welfare and those of Community Development, Health, Labour, Rural Development, etc. The role of the Social Welfare Department is thus restricted to providing only grants-in-aid.

The **Women Resource Centre (WRC)** has been set up to sponsor studies on women and submit its findings and recommendations to the state government. It also organises training programmes.

Literacy and Education

India has the largest number of illiterate women in the world. Only 54.16 per cent of women are literate. Out of 100 girls who enrol in class I, nearly 60 per cent drop out before Class V. There are various factors behind this lack of girls' education. On the supply side, the lack of schools close to the home often acts as a barrier. Absence of separate toilet facilities, lack of schools for girls only in the higher classes and dearth of lady teachers are other barriers. On the demand side, cost is a major inhibiting factor, especially in a culture where boy's education is valued more. Even in cases where education is free, direct costs related to books, uniforms etc. and the opportunity costs incurred because the girl child is not available for domestic chores discourage parents from sending girls to school. Cultural norms also stand in the way of girls' education.

TABLE 13.10

Female Literacy - Rajasthan vis-à-vis Few Other States

	Female Literacy	*Male Literacy*
Rajasthan	**44.34**	**76.46**
Haryana	56.31	79.25
Bihar	33.57	60.32
Uttar Pradesh	42.98	70.23
Madhya Pradesh	50.28	76.80
Gujarat	58.6	80.50
Andhra Pradesh	51.17	70.85
Kerala	87.86	94.20
Tamil Nadu	64.55	82.33
INDIA	**54.16**	**75.85**

Source: Census 2001

There are marked gender disparities in literacy and education. Rajasthan has seen an impressive rise in female literacy between 1991 and 2001, registering an increase of 23.9 percentage points which is higher than that of male literacy (21.39 per cent). However, female literacy in the state is below 50 per cent. The gender gap in literacy within the country is highest for Rajasthan.

Though primary school enrolment in Rajasthan is higher than the national average, girls' enrolment was below the all-India figure (Table 13.11). The retention rate of girls in the upper primary stage is quite low, because of the high drop out rate, which ranges from 34.58 in Nagaur district to 74.17 in Karauli district. The enrolment for girls is worse in the western desert region and in the south-eastern tribal belt. There are nine districts in the state where more than 40 per cent girls are not availing of primary education.

Enrolment of girls in upper primary and secondary levels drops sharply. The enrolment of girls in the secondary stage was only 2.74 per cent in 1996-97, increasing to 3.20 per cent in 1998-99. This is because girls are pulled out to work at home and are married off early. The percentage of girls from socially disadvantaged groups is negligible.

TABLE 13.11

Gender-wise Gross Enrolment Ratio in Selected States

	Primary		*Upper Primary*	
	Girls	*Boys*	*Girls*	*Boys*
Rajasthan	**75.3**	**129.3**	**32.0**	**79.7**
India	**93.3**	**114.5**	**54.5**	**79.5**
Bihar	55.4	93.0	21.9	47.5
Uttar Pradesh	72.2	104.3	34.9	72.3
Madhya Pradesh	88.9	112.9	43.3	91.6
Gujarat	106.8	158.3	61.5	81.1
Maharashtra	120.2	125.5	77.2	92.4
Andhra Pradesh	89.9	99.6	41.8	57.3
Kerala	95.4	98.4	101.5	105.1

Source: DPEP.

TABLE 13.12

Drop-out Rate for Girls in Select Districts (1998-99)

District	*Drop Out Rate*
Alwar	70.75
Bhilwara	65.06
Jhalawar	70.75
Jhunjhunu	44.07
Kota	56.32
Nagaur	34.58
Sikar	53.75
Sirohi	73.78
Sri Ganganagar	53.73
Tonk	64.7
Dholpur	70.32
Karauli	74.17
Churu	64.4

Source: DPEP, Jaipur.

TABLE 13.13

Causes for Low Enrolment of Girls

Reasons	*% of Deprived Children*
Domestic chores	65.50
Seasonal migration	3.54
Poverty	8.89
Lack of facilities	5.91
Prolonged illness	0.39
Handicaps (physical/mental)	0.96
Social handicaps	7.74

Source: DPEP, Jaipur.

The state's two main education projects – Lok Jumbish and Shiksha Karmi – both of which have special provisions for women have had a positive impact on education levels. However, all posts reserved for women within the project are not filled up for want of educated women workers.

Literacy and Sex Ratio

Though literacy levels and sex ratio normally have a positive correlation, the 2001 Census shows that in Rajasthan the sex ratio was worse in districts with high literacy rate.

TABLE 13.14

Literacy and Sex Ratio

District	*Literacy Rank*	*Female Literacy*	*Sex Ratio*		
			Overall	*0-6 Years*	*Sex Ratio Rank*
Kota	1	61.25	895	902	23
Jhunjhunu	2	60.10	946	867	12
Sikar	3	56.70	951	882	10
Jaipur	4	56.18	897	897	21
Churu	5	53.87	948	913	11
Tonk	27	32.30	936	922	14
Jaisalmer	28	32.25	821	867	32
Bhilwara	29	31.47	964	951	8
Dungarpur	30	31.22	1027	963	1
Jalore	31	27.53	968	924	6
Banswara	32	27.46	978	972	4

Source: DPEP, Jaipur.

Literacy and Health Indicators

Literacy also has a positive effect on the number of institutional deliveries. While only 13 per cent illiterate women in Rajasthan seek institutional delivery, more than 70 per cent of women who have completed high school are attended to by a doctor or a nurse during delivery.

TABLE 13.15

Female Literacy and Other Development Indicators for Rajasthan

Indicators	*Literate*	*Illiterate*
TFR	2.64	3.47
IMR	52.8	94.6
Under 5 mortality	65.43	136.5

Source: RCH Situation in Rajasthan, *IIPS, Mumbai.*

According to *RCH Situation in Rajasthan,* only 18 per cent of illiterate women in Rajasthan were aware of HIV/AIDS as compared to 54 per cent in the case of literate women and 92 per cent of women who have completed high school or higher level of education.

Health and Nutrition

The levels and distribution of income, social and cultural practices and technology are all factors that influence and are, in turn, influenced by the health indicators of a society. The subordinate status accorded to women in a society raises questions about how they perceive their own health, their access to health care and control over their own bodies.

Given the predominantly patriarchal pattern of society, women get a smaller share in the intra-household distribution of health goods and services. However, they bear the major share of economic, procreative and family responsibilities. As a result, their health suffers. According to the NCAER's *India Human Development Report,* there are significant gender differentials in morbidity, with male morbidity in rural India at 108 per thousand against 116.6 in the case of rural females. In the case of urban males, the morbidity rate was 99.7 per thousand against 118 in the case of urban females.

Maternal mortality is higher in Rajasthan than most other states (Table 13.16). Between 15 and 20 per cent of deaths among women the in reproductive age group are related to pregnancy and childbirth. Women's illnesses are usually treated lightly and often attributed to female biology. This leads to women's health problems being concealed and this prevents effective intervention.

In all the programmes, be it child survival and safe motherhood or maternal and child health, only the reproductive role of women was considered. There was no mention of her reproductive health needs, apart from child bearing.

TABLE 13.16

Maternal Mortality Ratio in Selected States

	(1998)
Andhra Pradesh	159
Assam	409
Bihar	452
Gujarat	28
Haryana	103
Karnataka	195
Madhya Pradesh	498
Orissa	367
Rajasthan	**670**

Note: Maternal mortality ratio is a number of maternal deaths per 1,00,000 live births.

Source: National Human Development Report 2001, Planning Commission, GoI, 2002.

The Reproductive and Child Health (RCH) programme, initiated in 1996-97, has tried to make amends by addressing women in a holistic manner and ensuring male participation in family planning. The programme is, however, too centralised.

TABLE 13.17

Health Facilities in Rajasthan at the Grassroot Level, 1995

Facility	*No.*	*Population Served*
Sub-centre	9400	3611
PHC	1616	21002
CHC	261	1,30,000

Source: DGHS, 1997.

The majority of home deliveries in Rajasthan, especially in rural and tribal areas, are attended by *dais* or traditional birth attendants (TBA). Recognising the role of the TBAs, a Dai Training Scheme has been operational for more than a decade. However, even after this training, the TBA qualifies as a trained attendant and not 'skilled' attendant at delivery. The auxiliary nurse midwife (ANM) is a skilled attendant who, unfortunately, is still at the fringes of obstetric care, despite the role being envisaged at the core of obstetric service delivery in the rural areas. This is partly due to improper training which makes the ANMs less confident and partly due to the service charge they take, which people in the rural areas find to be on the higher side. The unpredictability of the ANM's visit is also a major hurdle. Strengthening the role of ANMs and female health assistants in the health system is also important.

Rajasthan has an extensive network of sub-centres, primary health centres (PHCs) and community health centres (CHCs) to provide primary health care, including maternal and child health care and family planning services. The system has not been able to match up to the goals with which it was planned. The lack of female medical officers in the peripheral health institutions is a deterrent to women seeking early treatment for reproductive tract infections and sexually transmitted diseases.

Such facilities for safe family planning methods are widespread in the context of Rajasthan. As the rural settlements are far flung, the population-based norms for setting up of various tiers of health centres may result in health centres being located far away from settlements. Hence, in these areas the criteria for setting up a health facility should be on the basis of distance from the facility rather than the population served.

In spite of abortion being legalised, 10 per cent of all maternal deaths and 13 per cent in rural areas are due to unsafe abortions. Nine out of 10 abortions are performed illegally.

Women are more vulnerable to chronic illnesses such as general weakness, dizziness and anaemia, especially in rural areas.

Health Systems

Male domination is evident in the medical profession, with male doctors cornering most of the prestigious posts in the profession.

Public health financing is characterised by an emphasis on tertiary rather than primary care, urban rather than rural populations, medical officers rather than paramedics; services that have larger private rather than social return; and family planning and child health to the exclusion of wider aspects of women's health. There are several women-specific health problems and hence there is a need for a gender-focussed understanding of health issues.

Nutritional Discrimination Against Women

Gender disparities in breast feeding and feeding patterns of infants reflect deep-rooted gender biases. Inadequate diet also results in poor adolescent weight. It is estimated that 47 per cent of 15-year-old girls in India have body weight less than 38 kg and 39 per cent have height less than 145 cm., which is recognised as a obstetric risk factor. Between 40 and 50 per cent urban women and 50-70 per cent of rural women suffer from anaemia. Malnourishment among girls and women are observed in all economic classes and thus cannot be attributed to poverty. Anaemia not only reduces resistance to disease, but also results in failure to achieve genetic potential in physical growth and development. This has serious implications on work performance and reproductive health, resulting in underweight and undernourished babies. Such children perform poorly in academics and this affects their participation in economic life in adulthood. All this has implications for future generations.

Teenage pregnancies are a rule rather than the exception in Rajasthan. Large number of girls in the 14-18 years age group are forced to bear children even before they have had a chance to complete their own physical growth and development, and attain adulthood, because of early marriage.

Violence Against Women

Violence against women starts even before they are born in the form of pre-natal sex determination tests and female foeticide. The Central government enacted the Pre-Natal Diagnostic Technique (Regulation and Prevention of Misuse) Act in 1994. However, it has not been very effective.

TABLE 13.18

Women's Autonomy and Domestic Violence in Rajasthan

	Illiterate	*Literate< Middle*	*Middle School Complete*	*High School Complete*
Domestic violence victims	12.7	15.8	16.6	12.6
% involved in decision making	39.0	42.2	43.7	52.2
Decision on own health care	50.4	571.2	35.6	—

Source: NFHS - 2.

TABLE 13.19

Relative Situation of Violence against Women in Rajasthan

Title	*Cases on Record*			*Increase/Decrease*		*Percentage*	
	1999	*2000*	*2001*	*1999-2000*	*2000-01*	*1999-2000*	*2000-01*
Dowry death	423	412	352	-71	-60	-16.78	-14.56
Dowry suicide	85	98	88	+3	-10	+3.52	-10.20
Atrocities against women	5122	5162	5291	+169	+129	+3.29	+2.49
Rape	1127	1161	1001	-126	-160	-11.18	-13.78
Eve-teasing	2923	2913	2766	-157	-147	-5.37	-5.04
Abduction	2433	2560	2060	-373	-500	-15.33	-19.53
Miscellaneous	119	170	349	+230	+179	+193.27	+105.29
Total	**12232**	**12476**	**11907**	**-325**	**-569**	**-2.65**	**-4.56**

Source: Annual Report, Department of Home Affairs, Government of Rajasthan.

TABLE 13.20

Relative Situation of Violence against Women belonging to Schedule Tribe

Title	*Cases on Record*			*Increase/Decrease*		*Percentage*	
	1999	*2000*	*2001*	*1999-00*	*2000-01*	*1999-00*	*2000-01*
Death	13	11	12	-1	+1	-7.69	+9.09
Grievous injury	46	22	21	-25	-1	-54.34	-4.54
Rape	33	39	42	+9	+3	+27.27	+7.69
Grievous damage	12	9	11	-1	+2	-8.33	+22.22
Protection of Civil Rights Act	—	—	—	—	—	—	—
Other Crimes under IPC	826	860	776	-50	-84	-6.05	-9.76
Prevention of Crime Against SC/ST Act	189	213	108	-81	-105	-42.85	- 49.29
Total	**1119**	**1154**	**970**	**-149**	**-184**	**-13.31**	**-15.94**

Source: Annual Report, Department of Home Affairs, Government of Rajasthan.

TABLE 13.21

Relative Situation of Violence against Women belonging to Schedule Caste

Title	*Cases on Record*			*Increase/Decrease*		*Percentage*	
	1999	*2000*	*2001*	*1999-00*	*2000-01*	*1999-00*	*2000-01*
Death	49	43	47	-2	+4	-4.08	+9.30
Grievous injury	106	95	77	-29	-18	-27.35	-18.94
Rape	138	119	146	+8	+27	+5.79	+22.68
Grievous damage	61	50	44	-17	-6	-27.86	-12.00
Protection of Civil Rights Act	2	3	—	-2	-3	-200	-300
Other crimes under Indian Penal Code	4027	3921	3756	-271	-165	-6.72	-4.20
Prevention of Crime Against SC/ST Act	912	875	601	-311	-274	-34.10	-31.31
Total	**5295**	**5106**	**4671**	**-624**	**-435**	**-11.78**	**-8.51**

Source: Police Records published in Rajasthan Patrika (28 December 2001).

If a female child is born, there is always the fear of infanticide. During childhood and adolescence, they are vulnerable to sexual abuse, sometimes from close relatives and friends.

After marriage, women are subjected to domestic violence for various reasons. Sometimes, such violence results in their death. This violence cuts across all classes of society and affects literate and illiterate women alike.

A disturbing fact recorded by the Second National Family Health Survey (NFHS-2) is that almost 50 per cent women who are subjected to domestic violence actually justify the violence. The instances of dowry deaths, rape and sexual harassment have increased over the years in Rajasthan.

Women's Political Participation

Of the 200-member Legislative Assembly there are only 12 women members. In December 2003, Rajasthan got its first woman Chief Minister. However, there is no woman minister in the Council of Ministers as of May 2004. There were only four women in the 30-member Council of Ministers of the Gehlot government. Rajasthan has only one woman member of Parliament (MP) out of the 25 MPs the state has. The percentage of women elected to *gram sabhas* in Rajasthan is 32.48 per cent.

The compulsory reservation of 33 per cent seats in local bodies for women in the 73rd and 74th Constitutional Amendment Acts have opened up several opportunities for women, a large number of whom have been elected to *panchayats* as *sarpanchs*. These elected women representatives have been drawn from a wide cross section of society and many of them are rural animators who had the opportunity to work with NGOs in the women's empowerment programme and various development campaigns. The need for effective training as a means to address centuries of powerlessness among women has been recognised as a precondition for active participation in local self-governance. There is also some scepticism about the opportunities offered by the PRIs, especially the effective devolution of decision-making powers to them.

TABLE 13.22

Women's Representation in the PRIs (1998) (%)

India	31.37
Haryana	33.10
Uttar Pradesh	25.55
Gujarat	33.35
Andhra Pradesh	33.84
Kerala	37.81
Karnataka	43.79
Rajasthan	33.63

Source: National Profile on Women, Health and Development - VHAI, WHO, 2000.

Women have begun to occupy important positions in local bodies but they are not able to fully exercise their powers for various reasons. In many cases, they are often proxy representatives while their male relatives wield the real power. Yet there are also examples of determined elected women leaders who are doing exemplary work, despite being illiterate.

Women and the Voluntary Sector

The non-governmental sector has a wide network in Rajasthan, working in various sectors, and each of them focuses on women. The voluntary sector is involved in the implementation of various state government-run programmes like IRDP, ICDS, WDP etc. They have the advantage of having a strong field presence and are aware of the issues on the ground and the relevance of various interventions. However, they do not have the capability of dealing with in-depth issues which influence policy matters. Besides, they are generally not very well organised and they need to take concrete efforts towards the cause of women. In fact, there are instances where the voluntary organisations have done more harm than good for the cause of women.

Conclusions and Recommendations

Gender equality is a distant dream for Rajasthani women. They lag behind men in various health and educational indicators. Women's WPR is lower than men by only a small margin in the rural areas. The majority of women are engaged in agriculture and other underpaid work. Though they bear a double burden of domestic chores and work outside the home, nearly 80 per cent of them are registered as non-workers in the Census, raising serious questions about the validity of the definition of workers.

This situation exists despite half a century of planned development in the state. Most of the programmes in the spheres of health, education and rural employment have failed to have the desired impact on the status of women.

The present poverty alleviation programmes are primarily meant for the those in abject poverty, but are not able to reach them. Women are more vulnerable than men. In addition to self-employment programmes, women must be given higher share in wage employment programmes. The focus of training under various programmes should on helping them upgrade their skills. Other forms of public support like health care, education, protection from harassment and violence are equally important.

In order to assist in the empowerment of women, it will be necessary to provide support services like crèches, maternity benefits and working women's hostels. Appropriate technologies and mechanisms to reduce drudgery in domestic chores should be explored.

With women constituting the single largest category of the BPL population, their economic empowerment is vital and for this they should be provided with adequate credit, skill development and managerial training. Appropriate backward and forward linkages should be ensured to help women rise above poverty.

Till recently, health care for women in India has been synonymous with only maternal and child health services. A perceptible shift came with the RCH programme. The training of a single *dai* per village needs to be reviewed. All *dais* should be properly trained so that everyone can benefit and the prevalence of caste considerations should be eliminated.

The poor working conditions in the rural areas discourage doctors, especially women, from working there. There should be sufficient incentives and motivation for doctors to work in the rural areas.

Lack of accountability, weak supervision and difficult field conditions result in health workers not being regularly available to women. Women should be able to depend on the availability of ANMs. The monthly roster of the ANM and outreach staff must be approved by a Panchayat Health Committee and publicised.

Annual social audits of maternal, infant and child deaths should be done by the *gram panchayat*. Public hearings could be held annually in the *panchayat* at which information on health performance, social audit and resources is placed before the community.

Education is the key to women realising their rights and achieving their aspirations. The momentum for women's education has been created, but needs to be kept up. Apart from enrolment in schools, retention of girls should be top priority. The government should increase the reach of primary and secondary education to under-served areas. More female teachers should be recruited, school infrastructure and physical facilities should be improved, separate schools should be constructed for girls and the quality of education should be improved to make it more practical and employment oriented.

The needs of adolescent girls call for special attention through special programmes which should be implemented effectively.

The problem of growing violence against women needs to be addressed through a multi-pronged approach. Though there are several laws to safeguard the rights of women, they are poorly enforced, and women rarely exercise their rights. The government should work out strategies to ensure the strict enforcement of laws.

Awareness of legal rights is an absolute necessity. The government should set up legal aid cells and NGOs should be involved in imparting legal literacy to women.

For any women's programme to have an impact, it must address men. There should be a strategy aimed at changing their perceptions of and behaviour towards women. Without such sensitisation, no matter how effectively women's issues are addressed the desired results will not be forthcoming.

NGOs should be involved in the process of gender empowerment as partners, in planning for specific projects. They can work with PRIs, impart community education about available health services, identify problems and educate people on access to services.

The DWCD and the Women's Commission should be strengthened, as they will have an important coordinating role in women's development. They should have appropriate linkages with the Departments of Health and Family Welfare, Labour, Rural Development, Agriculture etc., for an integrated approach to women's development. These sectors have a gender dimension. Necessary amendments in the existing laws relating to these departments should be made with their cooperation.

Gender-based data on various development indicators for women should be available with the DWCD. The creation of a gender databank will go a long way in addressing gender issues and formulating appropriate policies. The Women's Commission should make good use of the powers entrusted to it and the Gender Cell could be developed as a pool for all data related to women. The Women's Resource Centre should be provided adequate funds and be more involved in research and documentation, instead of being restricted to training.

Awareness generation is a pre-requisite for the process of gender empowerment. This need not wait till women get educated and there should be programmes for illiterate and semi-literate women as well. Such awareness of their rights and duties will encourage them to demand quality services.

For empowering women for sustainable development, there is need for a radical change in social attitudes and values relating to women's roles and rights. Interventions at all levels – social cultural, political, economic – are required for enhancing women's status, and this is possible only if changes take place in the existing social systems and structures.

This change cannot be brought about overnight because women have been subjected to exploitation for ages, and cannot break the shackles of illiteracy, poverty and tradition in one stroke.

Chapter 14

Status of Environment

Rajasthan is the eighth most populated state in India. In 1901, the population numbered 10.29 million. In the last 100 years, this number has grown more than five times to the present 56.47 million, and it is still growing at a decadal growth rate of 28.3 per cent. This huge growth in population has taken a massive toll of the state's meagre natural resources.

Rajasthan's population of 56.47 million is spread over 41,538 villages. The growing population needs more food. Modernisation of agriculture and massive industrial development through the adoption of new technology have been the means to serve this purpose. But modernisation of agriculture leads to increased use of fertilisers, agro-chemicals and pesticides, changes in land-use systems and accelerated urbanisation, while rapid industrial development leads to the production of more industrial goods, increased use of machinery, enhanced mining activities, and increased facilities in the means of transport. All these tend to raise the standard of living of the people and improve their quality of life. But they also lead to an ecological imbalance that bears catastrophic consequences for the land. The physical environment in Rajasthan now exhibits signs of land degradation, desertification, constant droughts, deforestation, depletion of water resources, heavy air and water pollution, and roads choked with vehicles. Large-scale deforestation has been observed in the Aravalli mountain ranges, which has led to soil erosion, intensifying the process of desertification and the emergence of ravines and gullies.

If many of these effects are attended to in time, their severity can be brought under permissible limits in order to avoid ecological disaster in the state. It is, therefore, very necessary to find ways of lessening the environmental damage and safeguarding the ecology to achieve sustainable development.

Rainfall and Drought

An analysis of Rajasthan's rainfall data indicates that 40 out of the last 50 years have been drought years. The analysis further reveals that the climate of Rajasthan has exhibited a continuing trend towards desiccation, particularly after the severe drought of 1987. Rainfall has been substantially lower in the last three decades of the twentieth century than it was in the first seven decades. Individual years such as 1987 and 1998, 1999 and 2000 witnessed an almost 50 per cent drop in the level of precipitation.

Climatic changes have already set in within Rajasthan, resulting in changes in rainfall and temperature. An analysis of the temperature data of the last 100 years indicates a rise of 0.60C in Rajasthan's temperature. The changes in rainfall and temperature are largely human induced, caused by emission of greenhouse gases such as carbon dioxide, which prevent heat from dissipating into space.

After very low precipitation in 1999 and 2000, 2001 and 2002 also brought severe drought to the state. The drought affected 31 districts out of the 32 in the state, 32 million people and 40 million cattle. It accelerated the process of desertification. The year 2001 was the third successive year of drought and, by then, the capacity of the people to cope and their economic potential had been largely eroded. In Rajasthan, 70 per cent of the population is dependent upon ground water for both drinking and irrigation purposes. Ground water levels have dropped by an average 15 metres over the last 10 years.

The analysis of data from 1981 to 2000 clearly indicates the fragile nature of the rural economy in the state. Constant droughts during the last 30 years have ravaged it almost systematically. The state has had to bear the brunt of drought and famine, severely affecting its gross domestic product and its overall economy, as stated in Chapter 3.

Droughts in Rajasthan

According to the National Commission on Agriculture (1976), arid regions in India are those that are chronically drought-prone, facing droughts in more than 40 per cent of the years. Analysis of rainfall data (1901-1999) reveals that out of 99 years, the Rajasthan region has experienced serious droughts in one part or the other in the last 33-46 years. There is a general belief that irregular and uncertain rainfall followed by drought and famine is inevitable, and comes in a three-year cycle to Rajasthan. The droughts put tremendous pressure on natural resources and lead to severe scarcity of water, food and fodder. The major causes of drought are a region's geographic location not favouring abundant monsoon rainfall, poor quality and deep ground water limiting its use for irrigation, absence of perennial rivers and forests, the poor water holding capacity of the soil, and huge withdrawal of limited ground water resources. The increased pressure of both human and livestock population during the last decade has also affected the land, vegetation, and surface/ ground water resources.

Causes of Drought

In Rajasthan, droughts are caused mainly by the failure of rainfall from the southwest monsoon. Recent studies on global circulations show that the El Nino phase of the Southern Oscillations (ENSO) has the largest impact on India by way of droughts. Besides, climatic changes as a result of increased concentration of the atmospheric carbon dioxide, methane and nitrous oxide also influence the frequency of droughts in the region.[1]

Nearly two-thirds of arid Rajasthan is made up of dunes and sandy plains with a disorganised drainage network over a major part, deep and often saline ground water and high rates of evapo-transpiration. Spatially, the rainfall is erratic and meagre with decreasing gradient from 500 mm in the eastern margin along the Aravalli hills to less than 100 mm in the west in Jaisalmer district; the increasing year-to-year variability increases from 40 per cent in the east to 70 per cent in the west. Besides, the region supports a high human and livestock population, the livestock outnumbering the humans. As a result, there is an annual fodder shortage of 28.2 million tonnes. Also, in about 75 per cent of the area, the water table is declining at a rate of 0.20-0.40 m annually due to overexploitation. A sharp increase in human population by 400 per cent and livestock population by 127 per cent during the twentieth century, resulting in a major shift in land use patterns and tremendous pressure on surface and ground water resources, were the main causal factors for drought and desertification in the state.

Impact of Drought

Irrigation through surface water storage was never a significant input for farming in Rajasthan. The duration of water availability in surface water storage has declined from 3-12 months in a year to 1-9 months in a year over the past decade, and this supply, too, dries up quickly before the onset of summer in drought years. The ground water table has declined by 12-15 metres so that shallow wells have dried up, deep wells have got further deepened, and the quality of water in the deep wells has deteriorated from saline to brackish. The concentration of undesirable elements such as fluoride and nitrate has increased to harmful/toxic levels from 15 to 20 and from 800 ppm to 1400 ppm as against the permissible limits of 1.5 and 20-100 parts per million (ppm), respectively. Poor people suffer the most since the wells owned by them are shallow and they cannot afford to deepen them.

More than 600 plant species have been recorded in the Indian arid zone and these are fairly well adapted to the harsh climatic conditions of this region. But continuous drought has had an adverse effect on these desert plants, too. Many xerophytes fail to germinate in the meagre precipitation occurring during drought. In many cases, the germinated material fails to cross the vegetative stage.

The drought situation may continue in Rajasthan. Proper planning is needed to combat the situation. The impact of drought is generally more severe on livestock than on human beings. Some of the measures that can be taken up to fight drought are discussed below:

Short-term Measures

- Drought monitoring and early warning should be carried out on the basis of long, medium, and short-term forecasts.
- Task forces should be constituted in each district to initiate relief measures as soon as drought strikes.

1. Houghton, J.T.; Jenkins, G.J.; Ephracums J.J. (1990) *Climate Change*, DIPCC Scientific Assessment WMO/UNEP, Cambridge Press, Cambridge UK.

- Good quality drinking water should be supplied to people and livestock in severely affected areas.
- Fodder banks should be established in the region. Low quality fodder/alternate fodder resources should be enriched to meet the protein requirement.
- Cattle camps should be opened and fodder should be provided at a subsidised rate.
- Contingency crop plans should be prepared in advance to meet aberrant weather conditions such as early/late setting in of monsoon and/or early/late withdrawal of monsoon.
- Crop and livestock insurance schemes should be implemented.
- Timely credit should be made available, and arrangements made for the postponement of revenue collection and repayment of short-term agricultural loans.
- Personnel involved in drought relief measures on a short-term basis should be given proper training.

Long-term Measures

- Rainwater harvesting should be undertaken for both drinking and *in situ* cropping purposes; traditional rainwater harvesting systems and rainwater conservation and efficient utilisation techniques should be improved and popularised.
- Traditional rainwater harvesting systems such as *bawaries, nadis, tankas,* and *khadins* should be rejuvenated.
- The use, artificial recharge and augmentation of ground water aquifers should be studied systematically.
- Human and livestock populations should be managed to reduce the pressure on the fragile, arid ecosystem.
- Improved agronomic practices should be popularised to maximise the crop yield per raindrop.
- Integrated watershed management for efficient management of land and water resources should be given top priority. Appropriate land use planning, discouraging water intensive crops, encouraging sprinkler and drip irrigation methods, and practising alternate land-use strategies such as agro-forestry, agro-horticulture and silviculture would have a long-term drought proofing effect on the region.

Water Environment

Rajasthan has 1.2 per cent of India's water resources in the form of annual rainfall, against a more than 10.4 per cent share in geographical area. This means that water is the single most scarce resource in the state, and a critical input for all developmental activities. The drinking water supplies in the rural and urban areas and for irrigation are based on ground water, surface water and water from inter-state river systems.

The scarcity of water in Rajasthan has become increasingly acute in the last two decades. The use of water for irrigation and industries has increased manifold, though this is essential for providing food and employment. The basic need for water to fulfil metabolic demands is also increasing every day. In view of the erratic and untimely rainfall in the state, the surface water resources are exhausted before the commencement of the next rainy season and so ground water remains the only source for fulfilling people's requirements.

Ground Water Potential

On the recommendation of the Ground Water Resource Estimation Committee, the Central Ground Water Board has provisionally estimated ground water resources in Rajasthan in 1998 as:

• Assessed replenishable ground water resource (provisional)	12,602 mcm (million cubic metres)
• Total assessed draft (pumpage)	8,708 mcm
• Drinking and domestic, industrial use	983 mcm
• Irrigation	7,725 mcm
• Ground water balance	3,894 mcm
• Stage of development	69 per cent

Rajasthan has 32 districts and 237 blocks. In 2001, 49 blocks were classified in the 'safe' category, 21 in 'semi-critical', 80 in 'critical', 86 in 'over-exploited' and one in the saline category. The block with saline ground water is Taranagar in Churu district. Quite a large number of the over-exploited blocks fall in the Alwar, Jaipur, Jalore, Jhunjhunu and Nagaur districts. (Table 14.1). The people of these villages are not assured of having safe drinking water supply.

TABLE 14.1

Status of Ground Water (number of blocks)

Category	*1984*	*1998*	*2001*	*2002*
Safe	203	135	54	49
Semi-critical	10	34	32	21
Critical	11	26	65	80
Over-exploited	12	41	85	86
Saline	1	1	1	1

Category of Block	*Percentage of Development of Ground Water*	*No. of Blocks*
Over-exploited	Areas with declining trends in ground water levels (>100)	41
Critical	> 90	26
Semi-Critical	70-90	34
Safe	<70	135
Saline	—	1
Total		237

Note: One block, Taranagar in Churu district, has saline ground water at all levels and, therefore, resource assessment has not been done here.

Status of Rural Drinking Water Supplies

From the perspective of developing the entire water resource potential by the turn of this century, the government is committed to providing potable and safe drinking water to all urban agglomerates, cities, towns, and villages.

As per the 1991 census report, there are 37,889 major habitations in Rajasthan. Of these, 37,477 have purportedly been catered to for drinking and domestic water supplies. In fact, however, in many villages, water supply is not available as per the norms. This is partly due to the increase in the population and partly due to the inadequacy of the water source(s). Also, in many villages, the water is not of acceptable drinking water standards as per quality considerations. The minor habitations (*dhanis*) have not been covered so far.

Drinking Water Requirements

The demand on ground water for drinking and domestic purposes was assessed as 983 mcm as on January 1, 2001. Keeping in view the projected population scenario, the urbanisation and the upgradation of socio-economic status in urban and rural areas, this requirement is estimated to increase nearly three times to 2,600 mcm by 2025. To meet this requirement, irrigation water supply will have to be cut down by nearly 1,600 mcm. In fact, the state government must encourage farmers to grow water saving crops, which may, *inter alia*, warrant a substantial reduction in the irrigation subsidy.

Areas of Concern

Areas of Depletion of Ground Water in 2001

The over-exploited blocks are the principal area of concern and adequate attention needs to be devoted to regulating the development and management of ground water resources here. In addition, some parts of 80 blocks in the critical and 21 blocks semi-critical categories, where water levels show some decline, also merit priority attention.

Areas with Poor Quality Ground Water

Urban agglomerates	Jaipur, Jodhpur, Udaipur
Industrial pollution	Bhilwara, Udaipur, Jaipur, (Sanganer), Kota, Pali, Barmer (Balotra), Jodhpur, Pali, etc.
Base metal mining and processing	Zawar, Agucha, Rajpura, Khetri, Bichri
Thermal power generation	Kota, Suratgarh
Marble mining & polishing	Makrana, Rajsamand, Andhi, Suket, Jhiri, Kishangarh

Managing Scarce Water Resources

- Estimate regional water carrying capacities via some cost-effective technique and introduce a regional water auditing system.
- Initiate a comprehensive characterisation of ground and surface water, not in terms of their chemical properties, but also for recording trace water contents.
- Promote membrane technology and solar stills to redress this problem. It must, however, be ensured that such technology is cost-effective. Such costs should be eventually recovered from users.

Besides the short- and long-term measures mentioned above, other additional measures may also be considered.

The Fluoride Problem

Another dimension of meeting the demand for water is the availability of potable water. Estimates show that more than 6,000 villages of Rajasthan are suffering from the scourge of fluorosis, caused by excessive fluoride in drinking water which leads to degeneration of the teeth and humped backs. Fluorosis is both widespread and acute in Rajasthan. All the 32 districts in the state have been declared fluorosis prone (Table 14.2).

Nearly 3.5 lakh inhabitants of the desert belt of Rajasthan suffer from fluorosis and are victims of the neglect of the concerned government officials. The Siwana block of Barmer district is a glaring example of this. When the Barmer Lions Club organised a dental check-up in 2001, it discovered that as many as 76 per cent of the children there were already in the first stage of fluorosis. An entire sub-region called Banka Patti (humpback strip) in Nagaur, most of the villagers suffer from fluorosis.

TABLE 14.2

No. of Problematic Villages/Other Habitations in Rajasthan (1991 & 2001)

Parameters	*Survey Year*	*No. of Affected Villages*	*No. of Affected Habitations*	*Total Affected Villages/ Habitations*
Fluoride>1.5mg./l	1991	9,741	6,819	1,65,650
	2001	11,052	7,557	18,609
Nitrate >100 mg./l	1991	—	—	7,305
	2001	4,249	2,239	6,488
TDS>1,500 mg./l	1999	9,508	4,907	14,415
	2001	10,489	5,855	16,344

Source: PHED, 2002, Government of Rajasthan.

TABLE 14.3

Number of Districts Affected by Fluorosis in Rajasthan

District	*No. of Villages with Fluoride Content of more than 3.00mg/l of Water*	*District*	*No. of Villages with Fluoride Content of more than 3.00mg/l of Water*
Ajmer	584	Jaisalmer	161
Alwar	223	Jalore	160
Banswara	95	Jhalawar	18
Bharatpur	163	Jhunjhunu	16
Barmer	249	Jodhpur	67
Bhilwara	619	Kota-Baran	17
Bikaner	7	Nagaur	364
Bundi	3	Pali	103
Chittorgarh	23	Sawai Madhopur -Karuali	190
Churu	28	Sikar	269
Dholpur	40	Sirohi	44
Dungarpur	85	Tonk	270
Ganga Nagar -Hanumangarh	278	Udaipur -Rajsamand	155
Jaipur-Dausa	1230		

Note: The newly-formed districts are mentioned along with the districts of which they were earlier a part.

Source: PHED, 2002, Government of Rajasthan.

As shown in Table 14.3, the worst fluoride affected districts of the state are Nagaur, Jaipur, Sikar, Jodhpur, Barmer, Ajmer, Sirohi, Jhunjhunu, Churu, Ganganagar and Tonk.

Water and Air Pollution

Water pollution has also become a serious threat in Rajasthan. In Pali district, 916 units of textile industries have been identified as water polluting units. Similarly, in Sanganer and Bagru in Jaipur district, 400 small, medium and large-scale textile units, blue pottery units, paper and pulp units, and domestic sewage have been identified as responsible for water pollution. Balotra in Barmer district has 222 water polluting textile units. In Kota, chemicals, alkali and rayon industries, a thermal power project, 212 textile units, and 101 rolling mills are the culprits. The pollution of water in Udaipur is mainly because of the 200 small and large-scale zinc smelters and fertiliser, chemicals and pesticide industries there. In Alwar, nearly 400 industries like breweries, chemicals and distilleries are reckoned to be polluting the water.

Bhilwara, which is famous for its large-scale textile printing, weaving and dyeing houses, also has its ground water polluted to a great extent. However, Bhilwara is in a better condition because the units here have installed treatment plants to treat their waste water and to use it for plantations within their premises.

Thus, the major air and water polluting industries in Rajasthan are smelters, thermal power plants (five) major brick/lime kilns (1,000), stone crushers (10,000) and mines (40,000). Some of these units have recently undertaken adequate pollution control measures, but the majority continue with their age-old practice of emitting hazardous dust and gases into the air. The mining units at Makrana, Rajsamand, Modak, Aandhi (Jaipur) and Dholpur are also responsible for air pollution because they generate hazardous dust and marble/stone slurry, which cause respiratory diseases.

In urban centres like Jaipur, Udaipur, Jodhpur, Kota, Alwar, Bhilwara and Chittorgarh, heavy traffic is also leading to air pollution. Air pollution due to heavy traffic has crossed the permissible limit in Jaipur, especially in the walled city, which accommodates around five lakh people and an equal number of vehicles.

The major pollutants in the air and water are suspended particulate matter, oxides of nitrogen, oxides of sulphur, acid mist, fluorine, hydrocarbons, lead, oxides of carbon, carbon monoxide and chlorofluorocarbons. The sewage that is still being permitted to flow into the Chambal river is also a problem.

Floods

Rajasthan, for the most part, has shallow streams that flow in the rainy season for a few days. A strong spell of rain for a day or two causes these streams to flood their surrounding areas and displace the population there. Jhalawar and the western districts, in particular, face this problem. One reason for frequent floods in these districts is that human habitations have cropped up along the banks of the river channels. Another reason is that the vegetation along the river embankments has been depleted by grazing and tree felling.

Forest Environment

Forests and grasslands are important components of the environment. But despite the efforts to restore forest ecosystems, the problem continues to grow. Plants regulate the environment of terrestrial and aquatic life. But in Rajasthan, the stress of human and cattle populations upon the land has devastated this natural ecosystem. The vegetation cover is falling prey to over-grazing, tree felling for fuel, gaseous pollutants from the atmosphere and chemical pollution of water and soil.

Natural vegetation not only provides clean, oxygenated air, it also controls floods and prevents the abnormal rise and fall of temperature. Rajasthan can boast of only a few patches of tree plantations on the embankments of the Indira Gandhi Canal; the overall view of the state reflects a general trend of forest depletion.

Only 9.32 per cent of the geographical area of Rajasthan is recorded as forest, and only 3.18 per cent of the area is actually forested. This is the lowest percentage in India. (Table 14.4)

TABLE 14.4

Forest Cover in Rajasthan

Rajasthan	*Area*
Total geographical area	3.422 crore hectares
Total forest area	31.9 lakh hectares
Dense forest	3.6 lakh hectares
Open forest	9.5 lakh hectares
Barren forest	18.8 lakh hectares
Per capita forest	0.07 hectares

Rajasthan has two national parks and 23 wildlife sanctuaries, spread over 9,282 square kilometres and constituting nearly 2.8 per cent of the state's geographical area. There are 32 closed areas spreading over 14.8 lakh hectares, constituting 4.38 per cent of the state's geographical area (Table 14.5).

TABLE 14.5

National Parks & Sanctuaries in Rajasthan

National Parks	*Area in Sq.km*
1. Keoladeo Ghana (Bharatpur)	28.73
2. Ranthambhore (Sawai-Madhopur)	392.00
Sanctuaries	
1. Band Baretha (Bharatpur)	192.76
2. Bassi (Chittorgarh)	152.90
3. Bhansrorgarh (Chittorgarh)	229.14
4. Darrah (Kota)	265.80
5. Desert N.P. (Jaisalmer, Barmer)	3,162.00
6. Fulwari Ki Nal (Udaipur)	511.41
7. Jaisamand (Udaipur)	52.00
8. Jamwa Ramgarh (Jaipur)	300.00
9. Kaladevi (Sawai Madhopur)	100.00
10. Kaladevi (Sawai Madhopur)	676.30
11. Kumbalgarh (Pali-Udaipur)	578.25
12. Mount Abu (Sirohi)	288.84
13. Mahargarh (Jaipur)	50.00
14. Chambal Sanctuary (Kota) (548sq.km total including in M.P.).	280.00
15. Ramgarh Vishdhari (Bundi)	307.00
16. Sajjangarh (Udaipur)	5.19
17. Sariska (Alwar)	492.00
18. Sitamata (Chittorgarh)	422.94
19. Sawai Mansingh (Sawai Madhopur)	103.25
20. Shergarh (Baran)	98.71
21. Tal Chappar (Churu)	7.90
22. Tatagarh (Ajmer)	495.27
23. Van Vihar (Dholpur)	89.93

Source: Department of Forest, Government of Rajasthan.

Efforts have been made in the past to ensure people's participation in forestry by promoting social forestry, agro-forestry and silviculture, but these efforts failed to develop the ecology of the state to any meaningful extent. Social forestry had its initial impact about a decade ago, but is now largely forgotten. Agro-forestry was not acceptable to farmers with small parcels of land, who were scared of birds perching on the trees and eating away their farm produce. Silviculture is practised, but in a minuscule way in the southern hilly and tribal districts of Banswara and

Dungarpur. Nonetheless, augmenting the forest produce of the southern plateau region of the state has given a fillip to the attempts to protect forests, if not augment the area under forests.

Biodiversity and Wildlife

The dilemma of conserving wildlife to enthuse biodiversity and create independent natural ecosystems has been lost in the din of overcrowded cities and villages. Most of the endangered species of birds and mammals in Rajasthan are on the brink of extinction. The population of eagles, storks, pochards, tigers, great Indian bustard and many other species has shrunk to remote habitats in the state. The constant onslaught on them by humans, coupled with their inbreeding tendencies, may wipe them out totally.

Fortunately, both the people and the government have now come to realise this. Serious attempts are now being made to restore these delicate ecosystems and start working on the conservation projects of Rajiv Gandhi National Park and the Keoladeo wetlands with technical and financial support from World Wildlife Fund and other agencies.

In Rajasthan, where, for centuries, religious rituals have included worshipping trees and idols of tigers, elephants, eagles and kites, there is now a struggle between humans and animals to occupy more and more land for agriculture and dwellings. The foothills and slopes of the Aravallis, which were formerly covered with dense vegetation, housing several kinds of wildlife, have now become agricultural fields booming with human activity. The staggering decline in forest cover and wildlife is greatly detrimental to these fragile ecosystems. Even the decimation of a minor snake or uprooting a wild grass may lead to a chain reaction that leads to the extinction of some species and the proliferation of others. Development of national parks and sanctuaries appears to be obviously aimed at creating holiday sites and picnic spots, with scant regard for the animals and birds these are meant to protect.

The history of wildlife inhabiting the desert is fascinating. The Asiatic lion, now found only in the Gir forest, was found in a fair number of areas in the plains of Rajasthan till 1870. Leopards were common in the Siwana hills of Barmer district. Over 60 species of mammals are still reported in the desert, which is also rich in several species of snakes. In addition, there are as many as 200 species of plants of minor medicinal use in Rajasthan.

The biodiversity of Rajasthan, especially the desert ecosystem, is intimately associated with the habitat diversity. Each of the various habitats and land forms in the desert support distinctive types of plants.

However, increased land use has meant that numerous plant species are disappearing from Rajasthan at an unprecedented rate. Around a million species are estimated to have been lost in the last century alone. This amounts to an irreversible loss of a unique natural resource. While many forms of environmental degradation can be reversed, the extinction of a species is irreversible.

The plants most at risk of extinction in Rajasthan are *Phog, Rohida, Khejri, Babool Kumat, Jal, Sevan, Ker, Nagori, Ashgandh* and *Guggal*. Among the animals, the *Chinkara*, bustard and black buck have already been declared endangered species.

Biological impoverishment is not usually caused by the deliberate over-exploitation of a species. In virtually all cases, it results from the degradation of a species habitat by some human activity such as agriculture and deforestation. Indeed, biological diversity contributes to such vital human activity as the production of food, fibre and fuel. These activities, along with population growth, are the principal causes of depletion of biological diversity. In Rajasthan, biological diversity is subject to biotic interference. The human and livestock populations are rising beyond the land's carrying capacity. Thus, the depletion of biological diversity is due to increasing pressure on land from both human beings and livestock.

The degree of endemism and danger to plant and animal species in the desert of Rajasthan is comparatively higher than in other deserts of the world. In Rajasthan, 6.4 per cent of the total plant species in the desert are endemic, as opposed to 3 per cent in the Sahara Desert in Africa. Endemic species require immediate attention for conservation in order to save them from extinction.

Biodiversity Conservation Efforts

The conservation of biological diversity requires a major shift in thinking at all levels of decision-making. It involves a commitment to step up levels of human and financial support towards capacity building in a country like India. For the conservation of biological diversity, it is imperative to understand the status and role of species and ecosystems, as well as the distribution, adaptation patterns, economic uses, biology and genetics of priority species. Research activities need to be opened up to public scrutiny, and the results need to be widely disseminated. Comprehensive and reliable information is especially important to enable biodiversity to be fully integrated into all levels of decision-making, from individuals and local communities to governments and multinational industries.

Despite efforts made over the last 20 years, the world continues to lose its biological diversity. The most effective way to conserve biological diversity is through *in situ* conservation of ecosystems, which respects the eco-systemic interactions within and between wildlife populations as well as among different species.

The Convention on Biological Diversity was presented at the United Nations Conference on Environment and Development held in June 1992 at Rio de Janeiro, Brazil. By December 1993, a total of 167 countries had signed the document, and 36 had formally ratified it.

India has over 1,15,000 species of plants and animals. It is one of the world's 'mega diversity' centres. It has contributed nearly 167 economic plants such as rice, sugarcane, millets, lentils, brinjal, cucumber and a number of medicinal and ornamental plants, too.

The Biodiversity Convention became a reality on 29 December 1993. But a bigger reality is that the repositories of India's genetic wealth, the 410 sanctuaries and 69 national parks that constitute 3 per cent of the country's total land, are dwindling day by day. Many of the 1.15 lakh plant and animal species in these national parks and sanctuaries have become endangered because of the shrinking forest cover. Population pressure has led to encroachment and illegal exploitation of forest resources. Immense pressure is mounted on protected areas by the increasing demand for fodder, fuel wood and other plant produce. Nearly 72 per cent of the sanctuaries and 56 per cent of the national parks are housing people within their boundaries. Roughly, 250 million tonnes of fuel wood is chopped every year. If the human population increases at this rate, there will be no forest cover left by the middle of the twenty-first century. Major economic, social and political reforms need to be reinforced to tackle the population-poverty cycle.

The spread of industrial activity into protected areas has also caused major havoc. For example, all the political parties in Rajasthan are pushing marble, dolomite, barytes, soapstone, feldspar, quartozite, fireclay and granite mining in the Sariska Tiger Project area in Rajasthan, to serve their respective political goals. The announcement by the Union Ministry of Forests and Environment regarding an umbrella legislation for biodiversity, the formation of a 'cats' crisis cell and the setting up of a strike force in all Project Tiger areas is welcome. But it is more important to implement and tighten the legal system. There are no environmental courts, and the introduction of the National Environmental Tribunal Bill has been delayed. The first crucial act is to make a directory of all plant and animal species. Only then can the loss rate of species be evaluated.

Suggested Measures for Biodiversity Conservation

In the Thar Desert, around 10 per cent of the existing biological diversity is endangered due to the demand for agricultural land, fodder, fuel wood, industries, medicines and grazing lands. To protect the biological diversity, it is recommended that:

- A regular environmental impact assessment should be conducted to check ecological refuge, deforestation and loss of biological diversity.
- People should be made aware of the importance of the local fauna and flora.
- Environmental education should be imparted to 'ecosystem people' and to those who are directly dependent upon biomass for their basic needs.
- Environmental ethics and religious means should be used for *in situ* conservation of biological diversity. Village grazing lands (*orans*), permanent pastures (*jhors*), long fallows and land in the name of gods and goddesses should be given importance for protection, development and expansion. *Orans* are of religious and ceremonial significance and provide protection to native species. They now function as centres for the dispersal of genetic material,
- The practice of replacing indigenous species with exotic species should be discouraged.
- Merely declaring an area to be a sanctuary, Tiger Project area or national park will not do; we should believe in people's participation and make the 'ecosystem people' free from their dependence on biomass.
- There is a very strong need for motivating the people in the Thar Desert for *in situ* conservation. India lacks awareness (among village people) of biodiversity and the political will to prepare its people for *in situ* conservation.

- Denotification in the areas of existing sanctuaries, Tiger Project areas and national parks should be stopped immediately.
- To make this approach more effective and widely acceptable, it also seems plausible to constitute Green Brigades in all schools, as has been done in many states. Effective awareness campaigns for adults can be organised in each *mohalla*/ward.

Urban Environment

Rapid growth of human population and its concentration in cities and towns all over the world are affecting the long-term outlook for humanity. Now, at the beginning of the twenty-first century, city systems have become a dominant factor in Rajasthan's social, economic, cultural and political matrix. Burdened with all the problems of economic growth, the state's cities are increasingly subject to dramatic crises, such as unemployment, environmental degradation, lack of urban civic services, deterioration of existing infrastructure and lack of access to land, finance and adequate shelter. The cities will increasingly become test beds for the adequacy of political institutions, the better performance of government agencies, and the effectiveness of programmes to combat social exclusion, protect and repair the environment and promote human development in a meaningful manner.

Like most other states, Rajasthan also faces the problem of unchecked urbanisation. Out of the 222 towns and cities in the state, 22 cities have attained populations of more than 100,000 each. Urban population data from the 2001 Census reveal that Jaipur and Kota districts have reported the highest percentage of urban population (more than 42.50 per cent), followed by Bikaner, Churu, Jodhpur and Ajmer districts, where the urban population ranges between 27.51 and 42.50 per cent. It is interesting to note that the percentage decadal growth of the urban population in Rajasthan has shown a declining trend from 39.62 per cent recorded during 1981-91 to 31.17 per cent in 1991-2001. During 1991-2001, Jaipur has registered the highest growth of urban population (59.37 per cent), followed by Hanumangarh (56.71 per cent). On the other hand, Beawar has recorded the lowest growth of 17.99 per cent during 1991-2001.

Lack of Sanitation Facilities

One glaring problem that cities and towns in Rajasthan confront today is lack of sanitation. The prevailing conditions in the cities of the state are indicative of gross neglect of sanitation services, not just over the last few years, but over several decades. Many cities do not have sewerage systems, and even where these systems do exist, their capacities are not enough to cope with the increasing pressure being put on them.

The International Drinking Water Supply and Sanitation Decade (1981-90) recommended almost 100 per cent population coverage with proper sewerage and sewerage treatment facilities in the Class I urban centres of India, but a number of cities in Rajasthan, including the developed ones, have only partial coverage under sewerage services.

Of the total population of Rajasthan, 4 million people living in urban areas and 30.6 million in rural areas did not have access to any sanitation facilities in 1991. In the urban areas, this number rose to 4.8 million people in 1996 and 5.8 million people in 2001, and it is expected to rise further to 7.1 million people in 2006 and 8.8 million people in 2011.

The main reason for insufficient toilet facilities is the poverty of the people and the resultant prioritising of other items by them.

A similar situation exists with waste water disposal systems in housing units. More than 50 per cent of urban houses have a system of direct pipes to the roadside drain. The rest dispose their waste water either onto open land or streets without drains. A number of problems arise due to this, not the least of them being unhygienic environment around the houses.

BOX 14.1

Growth of an Elite Slum

A glaring example of lack of civic infrastructure is Jawahar Nagar Colony of the Rajasthan Housing Board in Jaipur, where the owners of houses have started to use them for various non-residential purposes. Schools rub shoulders with buffalo dairies and small shops. Drain water keeps flooding the roads, and cars are parked all over without any regard for the proper flow of traffic. Temples have cropped up in the small parks causing shrinking of open space and the government remains a mute spectator. In the wake of urbanisation, quality of life has been lost and it is feared that such residential colonies will soon turn to elite slums. This trend can be witnessed in other big cities of Rajasthan, too.

In overcrowded cities, vertical expansion has started for want of horizontal space and the roads are thronged with cars and buses. Much remains to be done to channel sewage and to provide water supplies. Open spaces exist only in the form of small parks, which are also overcrowded now. The root cause of the urban malady lies in the fact that the owner of a piece of land is allowed to do what he wants with it, irrespective of public interest.

Jaipur City: A Tale of Urban Waste

Increase in the volume of urban waste is due principally to increasingly affluent lifestyles, rather than urban growth. Municipal solid waste production continues to grow both in per capita and overall terms. As per rough estimates, 400 tonnes of solid waste is generated per day in Jaipur city – around 3.8 kg per day per person. As per another estimate, the generation of liquid wastes in Jaipur per day is about 283 kilolitres.

In Jaipur city, there are nine hospitals with provision for more than 200 beds, 16 hospitals with 50-199 beds, 145 hospitals with 50 beds, 292 clinics and diagnostic centres and 18 laboratories. This excludes the number of beds in major government hospitals. There are no authentic figures available for hospital waste in Jaipur, but Table 14.6 may provide a rough idea of the rate of generation of such waste in a month.

TABLE 14.6

Estimated Hospital Waste in Jaipur

Hospital	*Hospital Waste (Kg/Month)*
SMS Hospital	60,000
Janana Hospital	32,000
SDMH	10,117
Soni	2,159
Jaipuria	11,700
Monilake	9,500

The amount of hazardous household waste and waste from small industries and medical clinics also continues to increase. Therefore, there is an urgent need to increase awareness about the importance of solid waste management and its contribution to a healthy living environment. Central and state governments should stimulate public awareness and compel waste producers to take full responsibility for its treatment and disposal. An efficient urban solid waste management service should comprise of an appropriate combination of public, private and community involvement, while focussing on simple management information systems that allow the waste management sector to engage a range of local service providers.

There are two key principles of environmental management. One, the environment is not an end in itself; it is not something to be protected from development, but a resource to be carefully managed on a sustainable basis. Two, urban development necessarily depends upon the natural resource base available to a city, which, in turn, has an impact on the state of those resources. It is, therefore, crucial to improve understanding of the two-way relationship between environment and development.

Urban Air and Noise Pollution

Jaipur is one of the fastest growing metropolitan cities of Rajasthan. In the last decade, there has been a tremendous growth of motorised vehicles in Jaipur from 3,31,693 in 1993 to more than 600,000 in 2001, causing several problems like noise pollution, air pollution, parking problems, traffic congestion and increase in accidents.

Road traffic is the main source of noise pollution, which contributes about 55-60 per cent of the total noise pollution in the city. In every locality in Jaipur, noise pollution levels exceed (at 78-87 decibels) the permissible level of 70 decibels.

Air pollution is increasing because of heavy traffic contributing hydrocarbons, carbon monoxide, suspended particulate matter (SPM) and sulphur dioxide. As of 2001, the level of SPM in heavy traffic regions was about 700-800 mg per metre cube, which is much higher than the permissible level of 500 mg per metre cube. Sulphur dioxide levels are also very high at 60-70 mg per metre cube against the permissible limit of 40 mg per metre cube.

For Rajasthan as a whole, the vehicular air pollution load has been estimated to the tune of 2,99,260 tonnes a year. Redressal of the problem obviously requires a pollution control action plan at least for the major cities of the state.

There is also a need to check the urban sprawl in Rajasthan, especially in Jaipur, Jodhpur, Kota, Ajmer and Alwar. Non-agrarian secondary and tertiary occupations should be started in nodal villages or satellite towns, so that the rural population does not crowd urban centres and deplete the environment.

Mahatma Gandhi's views on urbanisation are most apt in this context. According to him, "Urbanisation is a product of machinery and industrialisation. The cities thrive on exploitation of villages by replacing traditional cottage industries and handicrafts. The blood of the villages is the cement and mortar by which the edifice of the cities is built. All this means that cities cease to sponge upon the villages to resuscitate their ruined economy. Even in cities, people should live in harmony with nature and not to exploit it to the verge of extinction."

Agriculture, Irrigation and Livestock

Motivated by the pressing need to increase agricultural production for its incessantly growing population, Rajasthan has been striving hard to cultivate fallow land and even barren land. Increasing productivity through the extensive use of fertilisers, pesticides and mechanised methods is not sustainable and will only lead to land degradation. Wilderness absorbs more cosmic radiations and reduces surface temperatures, which decelerates the greenhouse effects. In a similar way, marshy lands and wetlands are highly useful for absorbing solar radiations and enriching flora and fauna. So, they need to be conserved and not used for cultivation. The conservation of the wetlands of the Sambhar Lake has been a welcome development in the recent past, and this scheme needs to be replicated in other parts of the state, particularly in the desert ecosystem areas, which already suffer from lack of biota. Low productivity, tiny stock holdings and shrinking of common grazing lands over a period of time have widened the gap between demand and supply of fodder. The situation is further aggravated by the increasing population of cattle that is no longer reproductive.

Salinity Hazards and Waterlogging

Improper canal water management leads to water logging and salinity. Salinity of soil affects the agricultural productivity of land in a big way. Earlier, it was believed that the soil salinity in the Rajasthan desert was linked to marine regression and the wind-borne particles travelling from the Rann of Kutch. Scientists at the Central Arid Zone Research Institute (CAZRI) in Jodhpur, however, have proved that the origin and distribution of the salt lakes are linked with the courses of earlier drainage channels.

There are two types of salinity. One is natural salinity, comprising of *ranns* and other saline depressions. The other is man-induced salinity, and occurs in the alluvial plains. Both types of salinity hazards are linked with the courses of earlier drainage channels

Natural Salinity

It has now been established that the salt basins are nothing but relics of earlier well-integrated drainage systems. Along with different kinds of sediment, mineral salts detached themselves in soluble form from the parent material and were carried downstream along the channels and precipitated according to their solubility. For example, the calcium and sodium chloride deposited at Thob, Pachbhadra, Sanwala and Bhethada are relics of the Luni-Jawai drainage system.

In general, these saline depressions consist of silt, clay and sand, the whole mixture overlaid with a thin layer of blown sand and underlaid again by sand. Below the land, a thick layer of silt and clay with *kankar* nodules occurs above the basement rocks. These depressions are affected by severe to very severe salinity, while the palaeochannels are afflicted by severe salinity.

Man-induced Salinity

Man-induced salinity has resulted in recent times because of the construction of tanks and canals along the courses of the earlier drainage channels. Such constructions along or across earlier drainage channels result in surface and sub-surface water logging. In the Luni basin, the total area affected by natural and man-induced salinity is about 452 square km.

Plants and trees that help in solving the problem of salinity and are suitable for Rajasthan should be grown here. Some species of salt-tolerant plants are:

- *Zygophyllum simplex*
- *Cressa cretica*
- *Euphorbia granulata*
- *Portulaca oleracea*
- *Sagonia baryosma*
- *Trianthema postulacastrum*
- *Echinochloa colonum*
- *Chloris virgata*
- *Schoenfeldia gracilis*
- *Eleusine compressa*
- *Dactyloctenium aegyptum*
- *Sporobolus helvolus*
- *Peganum harmala*
- *Suaeda fruticosa*
- *Haloxylon salicornicum*

Waterlogging

Waterlogging conditions usually occur in areas where the ground water recharge is in excess of ground water discharge. In such areas, the ground water storage level starts rising, and this is reflected in the use of ground water canals. As the water table reaches within two metres of the land surface, the water table starts losing excess water through evapo-transpiration, either through direct contact with the atmosphere via a capillary zone, or through perennial vegetation and crops. The National Commission on Agriculture (1976) has defined an area as waterlogged when the water table rises to the extent that the soil pores in the root zone of a crop become saturated, resulting in restriction of the normal circulation of air, decline in oxygen levels and increase in the level of carbon dioxide.

In Rajasthan, the behaviour of the water table is being monitored through 549 observation wells spread all over the state. The water table to the west of the Aravalli hills is usually deeper than that to its eastern side. The depth of the water table varies in general from less than 10 metres below ground level (bgl) to more than 20 metres bgl. The water table in Rajasthan varies from less than two metres bgl in the western parts to more than 10 metres bgl in parts of Ganganagar, Jaipur, Bundi and the other eastern districts.

Waterlogging conditions are evident in parts of Kota and Bundi districts because of the surface irrigation in the Chambal command area. In the areas around Suratgarh, Anupgarh, Sripuriwala, Baropal and Rangmahal, too, waterlogging conditions have been observed. These can be attributed to the compounding of the Ghaggar flood water in the natural depression in the east and south-east of Suratgarh, and also due to surface irrigation from the Indira Gandhi Canal, and the Bhakra and Gang canals. Depth of water within two metres bgl has also been observed in some of the wells, located in the hard-rock terrain around Naradora (Dungarpur district), Kenna (Chittorgarh district), Diwains, Thikrawas Brar (Udaipur district) and Toda (Sikar district).

The Indira Gandhi Canal Project has developed a widespread problem of waterlogging and soil salinity in the Stage 1 area, where irrigation has been introduced. Out of the total 7,000 square km of the project, 7.33 per cent (513 square km) is already waterlogged. About 24 per cent (14.33 per cent and 9.67 per cent) of the project area is liable to be waterlogged if the use of water continues at the present rate. In the Indira Gandhi Canal Stage II area also, there are scattered stretches of waterlogged and marshy lands, and standing water in depressions along the running portion of the main canal, the construction of the water supply channel, and surplus water saddle tanks.

In the Indira Gandhi Canal Stage II area, about 34 per cent of the gross command area (3,34,034 hectares) has a shallow hard pan or barrier (depth ranging from five to 10 metres below ground) and is likely to develop a high, perched water table on intensive irrigation.

In waterlogged fields, such as in the command areas of the Chambal and Indira Gandhi projects, which have shallow water, pilot projects for fisheries and cultivation of crops may be initiated at least initially. This will not only give the farmers additional income, but also help in ensuring optimum use of water resources. Gradually, the results obtained from such pilot projects can be replicated in other command areas. However, it is necessary to assess the technical feasibility of such initiatives before beginning work on them.

Land Degradation and Desertification

Ravine erosion

The problem of ravine and gully erosion is a major menace to agriculture in Rajasthan. Kota, Bundi and Sawai Madhopur account for 77 per cent of the total land affected by ravines in Rajasthan.

Efforts have been made in the recent past to reclaim ravines, but the success rate has been low. One of the major reasons for the low rate of success in ravine reclamation is inadequate understanding of the causes of ravine formation. In India, enough attention has not been paid to this problem, though it is estimated that three million hectares of agricultural land are affected by ravines, out of which 0.4 million hectares alone are found along the Chambal river and its tributaries.

Ravines along the Yamuna, Chambal, Mahi and other rivers are estimated to have damaged 36.96 lakh hectares of land in the states of Uttar Pradesh (12.36 lakh hectares), Madhya Pradesh (6.83 lakh hectares), Rajasthan (4.52 lakh hectares), Gujarat (4.0 lakh hectares) and Maharashtra, Punjab, Bihar, Tamil Nadu and West Bengal (9.04 lakh hectares).

In Rajasthan, ravines can be found along the Chambal, Kali-Sind, Banas, Banganga, Sahibi and Mahi rivers in the districts of Kota, Bundi, Jhalawar, Tonk, Sawai Madhopur, Alwar, Banswara and Dungarpur.

Policy of Ravine Reclamation

The Central government drew up a seven-year plan (1972-1979) for ravine reclamation, which aimed at tackling 3.3 lakh hectares of the total problem area of 15.58 lakh hectares in Rajasthan, Madhya Pradesh and

Uttar Pradesh. The plan was carried out satisfactorily and its targets were met.

It is pertinent to mention that most of the strategies followed by the government during last two decades have been flexible and influenced by pseudo-economic indicators. Now it is felt that there is a need for change in the basic thinking of such strategies. Such a vast area with all its complex problems cannot be taken up by the government alone. A long-felt need has been to start a mass movement on ravine area development by including the community as the key focal point and all other institutions (Central, state and local governments, NGOs and the private sector) as support structures.

Ravine topography is a product of the erosive force of water. In alluvial soil, it becomes necessary to follow the geographic unit of a catchment and to integrate its various aspects to produce economically viable returns for community.

Environmental Status of the Aravalli Hills

The Aravalli hills intersect Rajasthan into two major geographical units. The western part, which occupies about two-thirds of the state, is almost arid, while the eastern part is comparatively well drained and fertile.

The Aravallis are spread across 12.65 per cent of Rajasthan, influencing the ecological equilibrium in 29.72 per cent of the state and directly influencing the climate and hydrology of a much larger area there. A remote sensing data analysis indicates that only 1.7 per cent of the Aravalli area is under actual forest cover. This critical situation of fast-depleting forest resources requires special efforts at regeneration and sustainable development.

The national significance of the Aravallis lies in the fact that these hills block the march of the Indian desert and that they separate the Indus and the Ganga basins. This region is believed to be the cradle of civilisation, a source of rich mineral wealth, a significant resource base, a rich habitat for wildlife and a congenial habitat for tribals. The hills also check the occurrence of droughts.

But today, the Aravallis are under serious ecological stress because of deforestation and overuse of natural resources. In the last decade, the environmental status of the region has changed alarmingly, thanks to accelerated soil erosion, sediment transportation, siltation, drying up of lakes, dams and surface water sources, and lowering of the water table (by 15-20 metres). The region has become a critical zone from the point of view of ground water resources.

Regeneration of the Aravalli hills is an urgent need if the local biodiversity, mineral wealth and tribal habitat are to be sustained. These hills, therefore, need to be considered under the Hill Area Development Programme, with sufficient funds allocated to it in the next plan. The hills of Rajasthan must be protected, and efforts made to make them green in order to bring about favourable aerodynamic effects.

It is evident from the information provided so far that a policy must be made to reclaim the ravines, wasteland and the slopes of the Aravalli hills. Once reclaimed, this land can be allotted to landless persons or marginal farmers after ascertaining the area-specific economic viability of each piece of land.

Mining Activities and Forest Degradation

In an effort to accelerate the pace of economic development, mining activities have increased in Rajasthan. Surface mines and quarries cover about 1 per cent of the area in the Aravallis and the desert zone, both of which have extremely fragile environments. Large areas of plateaux and hills have been defaced and seared by stone and slab quarrying. In addition, mineral deposits of limestone, gypsum, rock phosphate, copper and zinc are being extracted from several spots, resulting in land dereliction of astounding proportions. Even though the impact of these operations is at present a local phenomenon, numerous local occurrences will eventually constitute a more serious problem. Environmental degradation tends to extend beyond the excavation and surface plant areas of both surface and sub-surface mines.

Large areas around Makrana, Rajnagar and Kishangarh have now become useless because of the marble slurry being dumped here. The dust emanating from drilling and blasting in the mines eventually pollutes the air and causes respiratory problems among the people living in the area. Water resources, both surface and subterranean, are particularly vulnerable to degradation. Surface drainage is often polluted and altered at mine sites and mineral benefaction areas as has happened in Udaipur and its surrounding areas. Collection of waste minerals in the tail dam of the Khetri Copper Project has caused the infiltration of trace elements in the underground water; these trace elements include copper, lead molybdinum and other compounds that are dangerous for human beings and animals.

Rajasthan is rich in mineral wealth. Many important and valuable minerals are located in the forest areas here and, in some cases, the mineral potential zone is in the middle of dense natural forests. In other cases, mineral exploitation has virtually eliminated the other natural resources that are crucial for sustaining the life support system as they provide security of livelihood to the poor. There are many long-term mining leases that cover large areas of the forests, some even more than 200 hectares.

Because the demand for mineral resources is likely to increase in the future, efforts have to be made to solve both on-site and off-site problems by controlling sediment, water and air pollution through good engineering and conservation practices.

Energy Resources

"There is nothing more valuable than energy. Energy is the heart of present lifestyles and we all are totally dependent on it," former prime minister Indira Gandhi said at the Third World Energy Conference in 1983. Energy policies and plans in the past have provided the urban population with reasonable access to practically all forms of commercial activities, but have left out the vast majority of the rural population, which forms 65 per cent of India's total population. As a result, the rural people have had to depend on non-commercial fuel such as fire, wood and cattle dung.

Energy resources are meagre in Rajasthan, although startling progress has been achieved in the recent past by generating thermal power at Kota, Antah and Suratgarh. More thermal power projects are in the pipeline at Dholpur, Jaipur and Jodhpur. Fossil fuels like coal, petroleum and natural gas, which are being used to generate energy today, are incomplete parts of the biological decomposition of dead organic matter. When they are burnt to create energy, it causes heavy pollution in the air because they contain carbon, sulphur and nitrogen, which, upon oxidation, forms gases that are hazardous to the health of human beings, animals and plants alike.

During the last decade, it has become evident that the power crisis in Rajasthan is a major obstacle in its development. The state is located far away from the conventional energy sources of coal, oil, etc., and has to pay high transportation costs for obtaining energy. However, there are great possibilities of harnessing oil and natural gas in the western part of the state. There is also need to harness renewable energy sources such as solar radiation, wind power and bio-energy in order to achieve sustainable development.

Conclusion

The above analysis of the geo-environmental status of Rajasthan makes it clear that the environment in the state is currently under great stress. Some of the environmental hazards that the state faces include:

- Drinking water scarcity
- Occurrence of brackish water, largely in western Rajasthan
- Presence of fluoride in the ground water in most districts
- Salinity, waterlogging and a rising water table in the vicinity of canal irrigated areas and high prospects of floods
- Sand reactivation, wind erosion and deposition leading to the acceleration of the process of desertification
- Destruction of natural vegetation by deforestation for fuel and fodder and mining activities
- Creation of a scarred and derelict landscape due to the open-cast mining of minerals and raw material resources
- Air, water and noise pollution in the urban and industrial centres.
- Inefficient management of urban solid wastes
- Depletion of biodiversity and stress on wildlife habitats

The environment of Rajasthan has become degraded largely due to human activities aimed at accelerating the economy. The visible environmental impacts make it clear that scarce and exhaustible resources have been used incessantly.

Ecological security is as desirable as economic development. So, conservation and management of the state's water resources should be the first priority in planning. An analysis of the water resources of Rajasthan shows that the increase in population, urbanisation, growth process and expansion of developmental activities have led and will continue to lead to increasing demand for water use for various purposes. It has been estimated that the requirement of water will be fulfilled by the available utilisable water only till 2025. After that, demand will exceed the available utilisable limit of water. Water resources, therefore, have to be treated as a national asset and their development and management have to be planned in an optimal manner by adopting different techniques of water conservation and appropriate water management techniques. Efforts need to be made to increase available fresh water by harnessing the surplus monsoon run-off, and recharging it underground and recycling and reusing water. Special attention will need to be paid to the conjunctive use of water resources and the use of the saline/brackish water in the state's western parts.

It has been agreed that the water crisis today is more about water management than water itself. Injudicious management, lack of political will, improper incentives and disparity in allocation of resources are threatening available water resources. The real solution, therefore, requires an integrated approach towards water resources management. Ground water augmentation, conservation and protection should be the state policy, in which there is an urgent need to adopt a conservationist approach rather than an exploitative one. An expert group may examine the implications of using organic farming and bio-control devices since dissemination of such technology warrants a cost-effective and all-purposive use of media.

Rainwater conservation is the best method of deriving adequate supplies of water. Rainwater harvesting was practised for many centuries in western Rajasthan, where people used to conserve water in *tankas*, *nadis* and *khadins*. But over a period of time, these age-old methods were abandoned. They must be brought back into practice.

Rajasthan is in the take-off stage for industrialisation and economic progress, which cannot be brought to a halt because of the need for environmental conservation. So, both the environment and the economy must be brought into a state of happy coexistence. Methods and techniques to reconstruct the environment may be expensive, yet these methods are the dire need today. The task may be difficult, but it is not impossible.

APPENDIX A-14.1

List of Critical and Overexploited Blocks (as on January 1, 2001)

S. No.	District	Total No. of Blocks	Name of Blocks in the Critical Category	Name of Blocks Falling in the Overexploited Category
1.	AJMER	8	1. Arain	1. Bhinai
			2. Jawaja	2. Pisangan
			3. Masuda	3. Srinagar
			4. Silora	
2.	ALWAR	14	1. Ramgarh	1. Behror
			2. Umrain	2. Bansur
			3. Srinagar	
			4. Kishangarh	
			5. Kotkasim	
			6. Laxmangarh	
			7. Mardawar	
			8. Rajgarh	
			9. Neemrana	
			10. Reni	
			11. Tijara	
3.	BARAN	7	1. Baran	
			2. Chippabarod	
4.	BARMER	8	1. Sindhri	1. Baetu
			2. Sheo	2. Balotra
				3. Chotan
				4. Dhorimanna
				5. Siwana
5.	BHARATPUR	9	1. Sewar	1. Nadbai
				2. Weir
6.	BHILWARA	11	1. Asind	1. Hurda
			2. Banera	2. Raipur
			3. Jahajpur	3. Suwana
			4. Kotri	
			5. Mandal	
			6. Mandalgarh	
			7. Sahada	
			8. Shahpura	
7.	BIKANER	4	1. Bikaner	
			2. Nokaha	
8.	BUNDI	4	1. Hindoli	
			2. Nainwa	
9.	CHITTORGARH	14	1. Bari Sadri	1. Arnod
			2. Bhopalsagar	2. Begon
			3. Dungla	3. Bhadesar
			4. Rashmi	4. Chhoti Sadri
				5. Chittoregarh
				6. Gangrar
				7. Kapasan
				8. Nimbahera
				9. Pratapgarh
10.	CHURU	7	1. Churu	1. Rajgarh
			2. Sujangarh	
11.	DAUSA	5	1. Dausa	1. Bandikui
			2. Sikraj	2. Mahua
				3. Lalsot
12.	DHOLPUR	4	1. Dholpur	
			2. Baseri	
13.	DUNGARPUR	5	1. Bichhiwara	
			2. Dungarpur	
			3. Sagwara	
			4. Simalwara	
14.	JAIPUR	13	1. Bairath	1. Amer
				2. Bassi
				3. Govindgarh
				4. Jhotwara
				5. Kotputli
				6. Sambher
				7. Sanganer
				8. Shahpura
				9. Chaksu
				10. Jamwa Ramgarh
15.	JALORE	7	1. Jaswantpura	1. Ahore
				2. Bhinmal
				3. Jalore
				4. Raniwara
				5. Sanchore
				6. Sayla
16.	JAISALMER	3	1. Jaisalmer	
17.	JHUNJHUNU	8	1. Alsisar	1. Udaipurwali
				2. Buhana
				3. Chirawa
				4. Jhunjhunu
				5. Nawalgarh
				6. Surajgarh
				7. Khetri
18.	JODHPUR	9	1. Luni	1. Balesar
			2. Phalodi	2. Bhopalgarh
			3. Shergarh	3. Bilara
				4. Osian
				5. Mandor
19.	JHALAWAR	6	1. Jhalrapatan	
			2. Bakani	
			3. Dag	
			4. Manohar Thana	
			5. Pirawa	

Contd...

...Contd...

S. No.	District	Total No. of Blocks	Name of Blocks in the in the Critical Category	Name of Blocks Falling in the Overexploited Category
20.	KARAULI	5	1. Hindaun	
			2. Todabhim	
21.	KOTA	5	1. Khairbad	
22.	NAGAUR	11	1. Degana	1. Kuchaman
			2. Jayal	2. Merta
			3. Makrana	3. Mundwa
			4. Nagaur	4. Parbatsar
			5. Riyan	
			6. Didwana	
23.	PALI	10	1. Desuri	1. Jaitaran
			2. Sojat	2. Karachi
			3. Bali	
			4. Rani	
			5. Rohit	
			6. Sumerpur	
24.	RAJSAMAND	7	1. Amet	1. Deogarh
			2. Bhim	
			3. Khamnor	
			4. Kumbalgarh	
			5. Railmagra	
			6. Rajsamand	
27.	SAWAIMADHOPUR	5	1. Gangapur	
28.	SIKAR	8	1. Lachhmangarh	1. Danta Ramgarh
				2. Dhod
				3. Sri Madhopur
				4. Khandella
				5. Piprli
29.	SIROHI	5	1. Abu Road	1. Sheoganj
			2. Pindwara	2. Reodar
			3. Sirohi	
30.	UDAIPUR	11	1. Dhariawad	1. Badgaon
			2. Gogunda	2. Bhinder
			3. Jhadol	3. Girwa
			4. Kherwara	4. Mavli
			5. Kotra	
			6. Salumber	
			7. Sarada	
	TOTAL		80	86

APPENDIX A–14.2

List of Semi-Critical Blocks (as on January 1, 2001)

S. No.	District	Total No. of Blocks	Name of Blocks falling in Semi-Critical Category
1.	AJMER	8	1. Kekri
2.	ALWAR	14	1. Thanagazi
3.	BANSWARA	8	1. Kushalgarh
			2. Sajjangarh
4.	BARAN	7	1. Chhabra
			2. Atru
			3. Shahbad
5.	BARMER	8	1. Barmer
6.	CHITTORGARH	14	1. Bhainsrorgarh
7.	DUNGARPUR	5	1. Aspur
8.	JAISALMER	3	1. Sankra
9.	JHALAWAR	6	1. Khanpur
10.	KARULI	5	1. Karuli
11.	KOTA	5	1. Ladpura
			2. Sangod
12.	NAGAUR	11	1. Ladnu
13.	PALI	10	1. Raipur
14.	SAWAI MAHDOPUR	5	1. Sawai Madhopur
15.	SIKAR	8	1. Neem Ka Thana
16.	TONK	6	1. Malpura
			2. Tonk
TOTAL		237	21

Chapter 15

Human Resource Development

In a broader sense, development implies not only increasing the production of goods and services, but also, *inter alia,* increasing the capabilities of people to lead more productive and satisfying lives. The term, 'human development', includes an assessment of parameters like increase in national or per capita income, expectation of life at birth, infant mortality, level of nutrition, level of education, ratio of people living below the poverty line, gender-related indicators, environmental sustainability, protection of human rights, etc. Thus, it encompasses all the parameters that indicate the performance of a society on the economic, social and political fronts. Based on such parameters, an attempt is made to prepare a Human Development Index (HDI), which helps in ranking a country among the 162 member countries of the United Nations. India at present stands 127th on the HDI, which is an improvement over its status a few years ago.

Human Development Index of Rajasthan

In 1991-92, A.K. Shiv Kumar prepared an HDI for 15 Indian states and observed that Rajasthan stood twelfth on the list. It was followed by Bihar, Madhya Pradesh and Uttar Pradesh.

Recent data show that the human development scenario has not changed in the decade that followed. It is interesting to note that whereas Rajasthan has more than 10 per cent of India's total geographical area, its population is about 5.9 per cent of the country's total population. Further, the rate of growth of population in Rajasthan during the past two decades has been significantly higher than that recorded for India as a whole. In short, its high population growth has been responsible for Rajasthan's lagging behind on the human development front.

Human Development Indicators

Health

Under the global mandate for 'Health for All', pronounced in the Alma Ata Declaration (1978), the governments of different countries committed themselves to achieving the goal of providing health to all their citizens by 2000. It was resolved in the declaration that stress would be laid on policies and programmes that would help in expanding health facilities and the infrastructure required for attaining health for all.

Yet, despite the satisfactory progress made on this front since 1949, the status of health in Rajasthan has remained poor.

Infant Mortality Rate: Table 15.1 shows that notwithstanding a significant decline in the infant mortality rate (IMR) during the 15 years beginning 1985, the level of IMR in Rajasthan is still extremely high.

TABLE 15.1

Infant Mortality Rate: Rajasthan and National Average

Year	*Rajasthan*	*India*
1985	108	97
1990	184	80
1995	86	74
1999	80.4	68

Note: Even in 2001, Rajasthan's IMR was as high as 79.

The latest data on IMR shows that in 2001, the IMR in Uttar Pradesh was 84, in Orissa 97 and in Madhya Pradesh 91. Yet, in Rajasthan, the attempt at reducing the IMR has not been quite satisfactory. It is interesting to observe that between 1991 and 1999, the IMR in rural areas has fallen from 84 to 80, and in urban areas, from 65 to 59.

State-wise data for 1998-99 show that only three states have IMR levels higher than Rajasthan: Uttar Pradesh (87), Madhya Pradesh (86) and Orissa (81). Kerala has an IMR of just 16.3, while in some other states, the IMR levels are as follows (IMR in terms of deaths per 1,000 births)

Bihar	73
Assam	70
Andhra Pradesh	66
Punjab	57
Delhi	49
Maharashtra	44

Source: NFHS-2

In short, the efforts of the state government in reducing IMR have not yielded the desired results.

Crude Birth Rate and Crude Death Rate: Data about the Crude Birth Rate (CBR) and Crude Death Rate (CDR) across Rajasthan are available for up to 1999 from the state government's Sample Registration Scheme (SRS), 1999. However, the state's demographers have estimated numerous parameters like CBR, CDR, IMR and TFR (Total Fertility Rate) for the years beyond 1997. (See Table 15.2)

Fertility Rate: The Total Fertility Rate (TFR) in Rajasthan was 5.2 in 1981, but is likely to be slightly lower than 4 in recent years (Table 15.2). The TFR in rural and urban areas was estimated at 4.1 and 3, respectively, by the Second National Family Health Survey (NFHS-2). Thus, attempts made in the past few decades to reduce TFR, especially in rural areas, have not yielded much success.

Table 15.2 shows that the CBR in the state fell from 37.1 per 1,000 to 31.1 per 1,000 (and is likely to be 29.7 per 1,000 in 2001). According to SRS 1999, while the CBR for Rajasthan was 31.1 in 1999, the respective CBR levels for rural and urban areas in 1999 was 32.5 and 24.9. These levels are significantly higher than the all-India levels. However, as the table shows, over the period under review, CBR has registered a significant decline.

According to the Population Census of 2001, the literacy rate of women in Rajasthan has risen from 20.44 per cent to 44.34 per cent between 1991 and 2001. NFHS-2 shows that there is an inverse relationship between the level of literacy/education and the TFR. Obviously, the TFR in Rajasthan can be brought down significantly by raising the level of educational attainment.

TABLE 15.2

Demographic Indicators of Rajasthan

Year	*CBR*	*CDR*	*TFR*	*IMR*
1981	37.1	14.3	5.2	108
1991	35.0	10.1	4.6	79
1992	34.9	10.5	4.5	90
1993	34.0	9.1	4.5	82
1994	33.7	9.0	4.5	84
1995	33.2	9.1	4.4	85
1996	32.3	9.1	4.3	85
1997	32.1	8.9	4.2	85
1998	31.6	8.8	4.1	83
1999	31.1	8.4	4.1	81
2000*	30.6	8.0	4.0	80
2001*	29.7	7.8	4.0	79

Note: Projeced by the demographers in Kothari, D.K., 'Population Projections for Rajasthan: 2002-2011', (2002)

It is very interesting to observe that in urban areas, 51 per cent of women having two living children do not want any more children. Even in rural areas, 24 per cent of women having two living children, and 30 per cent of women having three living children, showed no desire for another child. In short, awareness about the benefits of smaller families is taking root even in rural areas, and it has to be ensured that over the next decade or so, such awareness is translated into reality.

Immunisation: Vaccination of children against six serious, but preventable, diseases (tuberculosis, diphtheria, pertussis, tetanus, poliomyelitis and measles) has been a cornerstone of the child healthcare system in India. The National Immunisation Programme is being implemented in all Indian states. Mothers are required to obtain a vaccination card for each child born since January 1995.

However, NFHS-2 shows that in Rajasthan, only 15 per cent of children in the age group of 12-23 months had received vaccinations for all the six diseases; the percentage of children of the same age group who had received polio vaccinations was higher at about 40 per cent. The percentage of children who had been vaccinated was 33 per cent in rural areas and 53.1 per cent in urban areas. Interestingly, the percentage of children receiving the first polio vaccine remains around 70 per cent, but the figure declines drastically for subsequent vaccinations. Thus, it appears that even against a disease like polio, the government has failed to motivate parents to adopt vaccination on a universal basis.

The indifference among parents to get their children immunised against measles, DPT and BCG is evident in both the rural and urban areas of Rajasthan. Further, while immunisation coverage in other states has increased, it has declined drastically in Madhya Pradesh and Rajasthan. (Table 15.3)

TABLE 15.3

Change in the Level of Immunisation Coverage (%)

State	*1992-93*	*1998-99*
Madhya Pradesh	29	22
Rajasthan	**21**	**17**
Bihar	11	11
Uttar Pradesh	20	21
Orissa	36	44
All India Average	**35**	**42**

Sources: NFHS-1 & NFHS-2.

Notwithstanding the variations in different reports, it is evident that concerted efforts need to be made in immunisation coverage by the medical and health departments of the government of Rajasthan so as to achieve the goal of universal immunisation in the shortest possible time. The NFHS-2 estimates on total immunisation put this level at 64.8 per cent for Delhi, 58.7 per cent for Andhra Pradesh, 72 per cent for Punjab, about 78 per cent for Maharashtra and 80 per cent for Kerala. Interestingly, Kerala also had 85 per cent literacy among women in 1998-99, thus showing that a high level of female literacy implies a higher level of immunisation[1] for their children.

Health and Nutrition: The health status of a child depends largely on the nutritional status of its mother initially and, later, on the composition of the food consumed by both the mother and her child. It is surprising to observe that whereas the proportion of families living below the poverty line in Rajasthan has declined from 27 per cent in 1993-94 to 15 per cent in 1999-2000, there has not been a corresponding improvement in the diet of both women and children.

It is estimated that about 48.5 per cent women of child-bearing age (15-49 years) had anaemia (based on haemoglobin tests), and 82.3 per cent of the children in the age group of 6-35 months had some form of anaemia or the other, largely due to under-nourishment. Table 15.4 shows that the status of health among children and women in Rajasthan was quite low in 1998-99, the year of NHFS-2.

TABLE 15.4

Anaemia Among Women and Children and Underweight Children in Rajasthan and Selected States (1998-99)

State	*Anaemia Among*		*Underweight Children Aged below 3 Years*
	Women (15-49 yrs)	*Children (6-35 months)*	
Rajasthan	**48.5**	**82.3**	**50.6**
Bihar	63.4	81.3	54.4
Punjab	41.4	80.0	47.0
Maharashtra	39.7	76.0	49.6
Uttar Pradesh	48.7	73.9	51.7
Andhra Pradesh	49.8	72.3	37.7
Delhi	40.5	69.0	34.7
Assam	69.7	63.2	36.0
Kerala	42.4	43.9	26.9
All India Average	**51.8**	**74.3**	**47.0**

Table 15.4 shows that even though the percentage of children having anaemia in Rajasthan is the highest in India, the occurrence of anaemia among women is higher in Assam and Bihar than in Rajasthan. Bihar and Uttar Pradesh have a higher incidence of underweight children than Rajasthan. Yet, as noted earlier, with a drastic reduction in the level of poverty in Rajsthan, one can certainly expect a distinct improvement in the health status of women and children.[2]

Malnutrition among Children: Between 1992-93 and 1998-99, malnutrition among children increased significantly. During 1992-93, about 42 per cent of children under three years were suffering from malnutrition, but this percentage rose to 51 per cent by 1998-99. In contrast, in all the other states, the level of malnutrition among children declined during the period under review. Thus, on this frontier, Rajasthan's performance has been the worst among all the Indian states.

1. The statistics published in 1999 by the Union Ministry of Health and Family Welfare, however, suggest that in Rajasthan, 63 per cent of children in the age group of 12-23 months are fully vaccinated. The coverage for BCG and measles was reported as 81 per cent and 71 per cent, respectively. For the third doses of polio vaccine and DPT, the coverage was reported at 73 per cent each. However, explanations of the methodology used for these data is not available to compare these data with the figures reported under NFHS-2

2. According to a UNICEF study conducted in 2000, Rajasthan has the highest proportion of low birth weight babies in the country. In Rajasthan, about 30 per cent of babies weighed below 2,500 grams at birth, while the corresponding percentage even in economically poor states such as Orissa, Bihar and Madhya Pradesh ranged from 20 to 24 per cent.

Health Cover and Access to Health Facilities

Health Cover: On the eve of Independence, Rajasthan had just 418 medical institutions, consisting of 390 hospitals and dispensaries and 28 mother and child welfare centres. By 1999, the total number of hospitals, primary health centres (PHCs), sub-centres, and dispensaries rose to about 12,150. Of these agencies, about 80 per cent were sub-centres and 13.5 per cent were PHCs. Thus, over the past 50 years, the state government seems to have made concerted efforts to provide adequate health cover to the rural population. Yet, an analysis of health facilities across the districts shows that there is still a wide inter-district variation in the coverage of the population by any medical institution (Appendix A–15.1).

It is evident that the state government has created more medical institutions in sparsely populated districts like Jaisalmer and Barmer and tribal districts like Banswara and Dungarpur than in districts that are relatively advanced. However, the cost of delivering medical services is very high in districts with a low density of population.

Access to Health Facilities: The NFHS-2 showed that in 1998-99, out of the 38,000 villages in Rajasthan, 52.8 per cent had some health facility within the village, while 35.7 per cent had a health facility within 5 km distance. Thus, one may deduce that the villages of Rajasthan have fairly good access to health facilities. What seems to be missing is quality in the services available to villagers at these institutions. It is a widely known fact that dispensaries and PHCs set up in rural areas by the state government have so far failed to address the problem of poor availability of doctors, nursing staff and medicines.

Delivery Care: Depending on the age of the mothers, 56-79 per cent of child deliveries in Rajasthan take place within homes; less than 20 per cent mothers give birth to their children in hospitals. The percentage of women delivering children with the assistance of *dais* (local midwives) is very high. Thus, the majority of child deliveries in Rajasthan are done without ensuring proper hygienic conditions and without seeking help from trained health professionals. In the majority of cases, mothers receive no postpartum check-ups or advice about caring for or feeding their infants.

Life Expectancy: Rajasthan's life expectancy rate has been amongst the lowest in India. It was 59 years in 1991. Over the past five decades, only Orissa, Assam, Uttar Pradesh and Madhya Pradesh have had lower life expectancy rates than Rajasthan. However, the rate of increase in life expectancy has been higher in Assam and Uttar Pradesh than in Rajasthan, which has reduced the gap in this indicator between Rajasthan and the other states. Further, as compared to Rajasthan, life expectancy in Andhra Pradesh, Gujarat and Tamil Nadu was considerably low in 1951, but due to a phenomenal decrease in the IMR in these states, they now stand far ahead of Rajasthan. It is interesting to note that in 1991, the life expectancy rate in the western districts such as Ganganagar (70 years), Jhunjhunu (69 years), Bikaner (67 years), Sikar (68.4 years) and Churu (67 years), was higher than the corresponding rates recorded for the eastern districts.

Community Health Centres: In 1985, the Rajasthan government began setting up Community Health Centres (CHCs) with the objective of providing specialist medical, paediatric, obstetric and surgical services with a minimum number of medical officers and paramedical staff. Each CHC is expected to serve about one lakh people. By the end of 2001, there were 263 CHCs located in different parts of the state.

Family Welfare Programme: The Family Welfare Programme was introduced in India during 1952, but in Rajasthan, the progress on this front has been very slow. For example, during 2001-02, against the targets of 3.26 lakh sterilisations and 2.56 lakh IUD insertions, only 1.37 lakh and 1.73 lakh procedures, respectively, had been achieved till the end of December 2001. Oral contraceptives have become popular of late all over the state. Against a target of 2.92 lakh oral contraceptives kept aside for 2001-02, 3 lakh pills had been distributed by December 2001. Yet, despite all these efforts, the level of couple protection rate (CPR) in Rajasthan has remained low at 45 per cent.

Chief Minister Jeevan Raksha Kosh: This is a novel scheme introduced in Rajasthan in 1999-2000. Under it, families living below the poverty line are given financial assistance for surgery relating to cardiac problems, cancer or renal failure. Till January 2002, a sum of Rs 310 lakh had been disbursed to 562 patients under this scheme. For 2002-03, a budget of Rs 500 lakh has been kept aside for this scheme.

Medical Facility Card: This facility was introduced in 1999 with the goal of providing free medical facilities to BPL families in villages and towns. Such families will be given cards for availing of these facilities. Until August 2001, 2.23 lakh BPL families had been given the cards all over Rajasthan.

Problems of the Health Sector

- Low accessibility of health facilities,
- Lack of trained medical and paramedical staff,
- Reluctance of doctors and paramedical staff to work in rural areas,
- Lack of resources with the state government, and
- Lack of effective monitoring of non-qualified doctors and nursing staff.

Recommendations

Considering that the resources of the state government are grossly inadequate to provide health for all, it appears imperative to encourage the private sector and philanthropic organisations to come forward and provide health cover to those sections of the community that have no or very little access to these services.

Medical graduates and nursing personnel who have joined the Rajasthan Medical Services must be forced to stay in rural areas and work there. At the same time, they must be ensured proper residential facilities and provided with adequate supplies of medicines at all PHCs and sub-centres. At the same time, subsidised payments must be taken from non-BPL families for investigations, consultancy and medical/surgical treatment provided in government hospitals. In select hospitals, this practice has already been introduced under the Rajasthan Medicare Relief Societies Scheme.

Effective monitoring is required to check the operation of non-qualified doctors. It seems appropriate to involve people's representatives in the management of all medical institutions. Finally, systematic revival and restoration of Indian systems of treatment must be envisaged without any duplication of such services.

LITERACY

The levels of literacy in Rajasthan on the eve of Independence were extremely low, both in urban and rural areas. Over the years, the state government seems to have done a commendable job in creating a vast network of primary schools so as to ensure that every village in the state has at least one primary school. By the end of March 2001, Rajasthan had more than 65,000 government schools and over 17,000 Rajiv Gandhi Pathshalas imparting primary education to all eligible boys and girls. Besides, there are schools run by charitable trusts and societies, though most of them are located in urban areas.

Table 15.5 shows the progress achieved by Rajasthan on the literacy front since 1951.

TABLE 15.5

Literacy in Rajasthan

(Per cent)

	Rajasthan			*India*		
Year	*Male*	*Female*	*Total*	*Male*	*Female*	*Total*
1951	13.09	2.51	8.02	24.68	7.88	16.67
1961	23.71	5.84	15.21	34.45	12.95	24.02
1971	28.74	8.46	19.07	39.45	18.72	29.46
1981	36.30	11.42	24.38	46.89	24.82	36.17
1991	54.99	20.44	38.55	63.86	39.42	52.11
2001	76.46	44.34	61.03	75.85	54.16	65.38

Thus, there has been a fairly good increase in the level of literacy in Rajasthan, with respect to both males and females. Literacy in the state has increased to the level where the variation in male and female literacy rates between Rajasthan and the rest of India has narrowed considerably over the past 50 years.

Yet, a closer analysis of literacy levels in Rajasthan and the other states of India, as also among different districts in Rajasthan, reveal that all is not well on this front.

Table 15.6 shows the distribution of districts by literacy rate in Rajasthan according to the 2001 Census. It is evident that notwithstanding a phenomenal increase in the literacy levels during 1991-2001, 18 out of 32 districts have less than 60 per cent literates, while four districts have more than 70 per cent literacy.

TABLE 15.6

Literacy Rate in Different Districts of Rajasthan

(2001)

Literacy Rate Range	*Level of Literacy in Districts*	*Number of Districts*
70+	Jaipur (70.63), Sikar (71.19), Jhunjhunu (73.61), Kota (74.45)	4
60-70	Baran (60.37), Dholpur (60.77), Alwar (62.48), Dausa (62.75), Bharatpur (64.24), Karauli (64.59), Ganganagar (64.84), Ajmer (65.06), Hanumangarh (65.72), Churu (66.97)	10
50-60	Bhilwara (51.09), Jaisalmer (51.40), Tonk (52.39), Chittorgarh (54.37), Sirohi (54.39), Pali (54.92), Bundi (55.80), Rajsamand (55.82), Sawai Madhopur (57.34), Jodhpur (57.38), Bikaner (57.54), Jhalawar (57.98), Nagaur (58.26), Udaipur (59.26), Barmer (59.65)	15
40-50	Banswara (44.52), Jalore (46.51), Dungarpur (48.32)	3
	Total	**32**

If the level of literacy recorded for 2001 is compared with the corresponding level in 1991, Bundi, Jhalawar, Banswara and Bikaner have performed better than Hanumangarh, Ajmer and Jodhpur. However, the literacy level across the state has shown a distinct improvement in 2001 as compared to 1991.

Female Literacy

The average literacy level among females in Rajasthan was estimated at 44.34 per cent in 2001. However, available data shows that Jalore and Banswara have less than 28 per cent female literacy. In the tribal district of Dungarpur and the arid district of Jaisalmer, female literacy rates were estimated at 31.2 per cent and 32.2 per cent, respectively. The total number of districts where the female literacy level is below the state average was 23 out of the total 32 districts. On the other hand, in Jhunjhunu and Kota districts, the female literacy level was estimated at more than 60 per cent.

Enrolment and Drop-out Rates

In 1998-99, the state government introduced a novel scheme for providing primary education to every eligible boy and girl. Numerous agencies such as the Directorate of Primary Education, Directorate of Literacy and Continuing Education, Directorate of Panchayati Raj, District Primary Education Project, Lok Jumbish Council and Shiksha Karmi Board are currently engaged in the task of attaining the coveted goals of universal primary education and adult literacy. Greater emphasis is being laid, however, on the universalisation of primary education all over the state. It is envisaged that within the next five years, all the children in the age group 6-14 years will be enrolled in schools. All the aforementioned agencies responsible for primary education have been directed to work with this mission.

According to an estimate made by the Lok Jumbish Council, currently, there are about 54.9 lakh boys and 44.3 lakh girls in the age group 6-14 years. Obviously, to impart primary and upper primary education to so large a number of boys and girls is a Herculean task. It is estimated that 10.3 per cent boys and 28.1 per cent girls have never been enrolled in any school so far. In 10 districts (Bikaner, Jodhpur, Jaisalmer, Barmer, Jalore, Sirohi, Ajmer, Udaipur, Dungarpur and Banswara), between 35 and 25 per cent of the children in the age group of 6-14 years have thus far remained deprived of schooling.

Further, in nine districts, more than 40 per cent girls have never been enrolled in any school. These districts are: Bikaner (40.2 per cent), Sawai Madhopur (40.0 per cent), Jodhpur (41.4 per cent), Jaisalmer (49.0 per cent), Barmer (43.6 per cent), Jalore (41.7 per cent), Sirohi (41.0 per cent), Tonk (41.0 per cent) and Banswara (42.5 per cent).

Thus, the goal of achieving universal primary education, especially for female children, appears to be still far from reality.

Enrolment Rates

The net enrolment rate (NER) of children in the age group of 6-14 years has been estimated at 81.7 per cent. The NER for boys and girls is 89.7 and 71.8 per cent respectively. The performance on the NER front, especially for girls, has been highly satisfactory in districts like Ganganagar, Hanumangarh, Kota, Dholpur, Jaipur, Sikar and Jhunjhunu, where more than 80 per cent of girls in the age group of 6-14 years have been enrolled in schools. In Jhunjhunu and Sikar, the total percentage of enrolment was estimated at 94.7 per cent and 97.8 per cent, respectively, and the percentage of girls enrolled in schools was 91.3 per cent and 96.8 per cent, respectively.

According to the data published by the government of Rajasthan, 76.61 lakh children in the age group of 6-11 years were enrolled in primary schools during 2000-01, of which 49.29 lakh (64.3 per cent) were boys, while the rest were girls. In the upper primary classes (age group 11-14 years), the total enrolment was estimated at 23.53 lakh of which only 6.46 lakh (only 27.4 per cent) were girls. Thus, girls constituted less than 35 per cent of both groups. In a state where girls constitute about 44.5 per cent of the total number of children in the age group 6-14 years, this low enrolment really raises serious questions about the success of universal primary education.

Among the boys and girls enrolled in primary schools (age group 6-11 years), district-wise distribution had a very high concentration in Jaipur, Alwar, Jodhpur, Sikar and Jhunjhunu. The district-wise distribution of girls in primary school enrolment was also heavily concentrated here. In short, attempts to enrol all eligible boys and girls in primary schools are yet to yield the expected results (See Appendix A–15.2).

Drop-out Rates

Studies conducted by the State Institute of Educational Research & Training (SIERT) in 1998 show that notwithstanding the "more or less satisfactory macro-level educational attainment" depicted by the enrolment rate, the retention rates of children in schools have been dismally low, especially for those who are enrolled in primary schools, in the age group of 6-11 years. Recent data on such drop-outs have not been published. In fact, optimum use of the infrastructure created for primary schools as well as that of the teaching faculty warrants that children stay in schools and complete their education. The mission for universal primary education can be accomplished only via universal retention.

It appears that parents in the rural areas prefer to enrol their children in the Rajiv Gandhi Swarna Jayanti Pathshalas than in government schools. According to statistics published by the Directorate of Education, 60 per cent of the children drop out before completing class V.

According to the SIERT study, the aggregated drop-out rate among the children enrolled in primary schools (age group 6-11 years and classes one to five) in the 1996-97 academic session was 56.6 per cent. Surprisingly, the corresponding rates for boys and girls were not significantly different – for boys, the drop-out rate was estimated at 54.7 per cent, while for girls, it was slightly higher at 60 per cent.

A district-wise analysis of drop-out rates has been presented in Table 15.7.

TABLE 15.7

Drop-out Rates Among Primary School Boys and Girls for Select Districts (1996-97)

(Percentage of Enrolment)

District	*Boys*	*Girls*	*Total*
Jaisalmer	67.1	78.8	71.2
Banswara	73.4	77.0	74.6
Ganganagar	67.6	67.8	67.7
Chittorgarh	64.9	70.6	67.9
Nagaur	64.3	70.7	66.6
Jhalawar	61.8	71.5	65.3
Rajsamand	62.1	67.6	64.0
Jaipur	41.7	40.2	41.1
Jhunjhunu	47.4	31.3	41.3
Kota	48.4	54.1	51.1

In Karauli, Sirohi and Jhalawar, more than 70 per cent girls dropped out of schools in 1998-99, while only 35 per cent and 44 per cent girls dropped out in Nagaur and Jhunjhunu, respectively. The drop-out rates among boys was not documented. It is thus evident that on the front of enrolment as well as retention rates for children in the age group 6-11 years, Jaipur, Jhunjhunu, Dausa and Sikar present a better scenario as compared to the tribal and arid-zone districts. Serious measures are required to retain children in primary schools. Special attention is, however, needed to retain girls in schools after they have been enrolled. The state government faces a two-fold challenge:

- Enrolling all eligible boys and girls in schools, and
- minimising the drop-out rate, especially that of girls.

Causes of High Drop-out Rates

A study conducted by an official of the Rajasthan Lok Jumbish Council[3] in 2000 shows that 65.5 per cent of the children dropping out of primary schools or never getting enrolled in schools in Rajasthan do so because they are involved in household activities such as farming, baby sitting, caring for livestock, etc. About 9 per cent children drop out due to the poor economic conditions of their guardians. Only 7.74 per cent girls drop out on account of the resistance of their parents to female education or lack of basic facilities in schools such as toilets and urinals. This implies that children who drop out of primary schools support their parents in one way or the other and, as such, their retention in the school receives low priority. Even where children stay on in a primary school, 52.75 per cent children in Classes I to III repeat their enrolment; in tribal areas, this percentage is 64.1 per cent. This repetition rate gradually declines as the child moves to higher classes. However, 30 per cent of children enrolled in primary classes take eight to nine years to pass class V.

Repetition Rate

The Rajasthan government has introduced mid-day meal programmes for school going children. Notwithstanding the high dropout rate, many children re-enrol themselves in the same class, presumably to take advantage of this nutrition programme.

Literacy Among Adults

According to *Shiksha Darpan*, 2000, there are 33 lakh people in the age-group of 15-35 years in Rajasthan, of which 55.6 per cent are men. While 84.8 per cent of the men are reported to be literate, less than 50 per cent of the women are literate. The overall percentage of literates was estimated at 69. This means that with 48 per cent of girls getting married by the time they are 15 years of age, almost half of them remain illiterate even after marriage.

---

3. Ganesh K. Nigam, *Shiksha Darpan*, 2000.

A district-wise analysis of adult literacy shows that in Churu, Jhunjhunu and Jaipur, 80 per cent persons in the age group of 15-35 years are literate, while only 48.4 per cent of this group are literate in Banswara. In Banswara, Dungarpur, Jaisalmer, Sirohi, Jodhpur and Ajmer, the female adult literacy rate was estimated at between 28 per cent and 36 per cent. It seems that the focus of the Adult Literacy Programme has been largely on men because it is convenient to both the clients as well as the persons who run the programme.

Education At Your Door (Shiksha Aapke Dwar)

In November 2001, the government of Rajasthan initiated a novel mission to reiterate its commitment to achieve the goal of universal primary education. The objectives of the mission were as follows

- Integrating various programmes related to primary education.
- Transforming elementary education and the social-cultural situations prevalent in the state via such a social mission.
- Initiating the following steps for the universalisation of education in the age-group of 6-14 years by 2003:
  - Improving the access of children to school, by ensuring that one school exists within a distance of one km from their village.
  - Raising the enrolment of children to 100 per cent and the rate of retention to 90 per cent.
  - Ensuring that despite repetition, 80 per cent children complete their primary education.
  - Making primary education obligatory for every child in the age group of six years and above.
  - Raising the adult (15-35 years) literacy rate for men and women to 100 per cent.
  - Focussing on the education of girls and thus removing discrimination, if any, against girls in schools.

It is hoped that these goals will be attained by 2005. The results of such novel initiatives have been satisfactory thus far, though the progress on the front of minimising drop-out rates and universalisation of primary education among girls will be known only after some time.

The Rajasthan Primary Education Council has been designated as the nodal agency for the implementation of *Shiksha Aapke Dwar* (SAD). District collectors will be required to report the progress of SAD in their annual reports.

Population Growth and Required Enrolment of Children

The current TFR in Rajasthan is around four, whereas the CBR and CDR are 29.7 per 1,000 and 7.8 per 1,000, respectively. Even if TFR and CBR are reduced to 3.32 and 28.0, respectively, (and CDR reduced to 7.1) by 2011, the population of Rajasthan is expected to be 69.4 million by 2011. Obviously, the increased population is likely to increase the stress on the state's resources. It will also increase the need to provide wider health cover and educational facilities.

Demographers, however, feel that reduction in the TFR and CBR will have a slightly positive effect on the resources required for enrolling children in primary schools. In fact, favourable changes in the determinants of population growth such as TFR and CBR would imply narrowing the base of the population pyramid, so that by 2011, the state would have fewer children in the age group of 6-11 years, but many more in the age group of 11-18 years. Thus, on the education front, more resources will have to be provided for secondary and senior secondary school education, while in primary and upper primary schools, the focus has to be largely on improving the quality of education. This may include construction of school buildings (fully equipped with toilets and other facilities) and better monitoring of the performance of teachers.

HIGHER AND TECHNICAL EDUCATION

Higher Education

At the time of Rajasthan's formation, it had 24 colleges imparting liberal education and five colleges offering professional education. There was only one university that granted affiliation to these colleges. The total number of students enrolled in various courses was 12,440.

By 1998-99, the state had four conventional universities with 257 affiliated colleges. That year, these 257 non-technical colleges had 2.62 lakh students enrolled with them. Besides, the state had one open university at Kota and three deemed universities/ autonomous technical institutes at Banasthali Vidyapeeth, Pilani (BITS) and Udaipur.

By 1998-99, there were 101 government colleges, 75 aided colleges (with private management) and 81 unaided colleges. Thus, it is clear that the state is getting enough support from private and philanthropic educational societies for the promotion of higher education. Such traditions have persisted in Rajputana for more than a century.

Between 2000 and 2002, three more universities have been set up in Rajasthan. These are the Sanskrit University in Jaipur, the National Law University in Jodhpur and the Agricultural University in Udaipur, which is the second university there. In April 2002, the state government also decided to set up Hadoti University at Kota.

Thus, by the end of 2001-02, Rajasthan had nine universities and four deemed universities (including BITS, Pilani). The total number of government colleges and private aided and un-aided institutions of higher education were 111 and 180, respectively, in March 2002. The total enrolment in all these colleges was about three lakh, while students appearing as private candidates numbered another four lakh.

According to the population of the different Indian states estimated in 1991 and the enrolment of students in the colleges of Rajasthan measured per one lakh of population, the state requires 311 more general education colleges to attain the national average. As a matter of fact, the enrolment of students in Rajasthan per one lakh of population has been significantly lower than that in Kerala, Karnataka, Uttar Pradesh, Bihar, Andhra Pradesh, Tamil Nadu and Gujarat.

Likewise, Rajasthan lags behind many other states in teachers' education, engineering and medical education. According to a recently conducted study[4], in view of the population, area and NSDP of Rajasthan, if the state wants to attain the national average of enrolment, it needs another 19 engineering colleges, 30 medical colleges and 32 teachers' training colleges. This implies that to attain the national average in number of colleges (general as well as professional), Rajasthan has to mobilise huge resources, or raise tuition fees in order to meet the rising costs. Alternatively, the private sector may be encouraged to fill this gap.

Technical Education

Engineering Colleges

Rajasthan has taken numerous initiatives in the last few decades to build the professional capacity of its young boys and girls. Besides offering technical education (degree or diploma courses) in engineering colleges, the state has created two other types of institutions, polytechnic colleges and industrial training institutes (ITIs).

Since the total number of entry-level seats in the existing engineering colleges has been less than 1,500 for many years, the Rajasthan government recently decided to involve the private sector in the promotion of technical education. There are six engineering colleges at present in the state in the public sector, and 24 private engineering colleges. The total induction capacity of these colleges is 5,704 students. Letters of Intent have been issued to 10 agencies to start new engineering colleges over the next five years with an additional induction capacity of 2,180 students. By 2007, the total number of seats in all the 34 engineering colleges of Rajasthan will be about 8,000 students. There are also proposals to introduce new courses in these colleges, which would be more relevant in the changing corporate scenario, and would offer good job opportunities.

Polytechnics

Unlike the Bachelor's and Master's degrees offered by engineering colleges, polytechnics provide engineering diplomas in technical education. Currently, there are 15 public sector polytechnic colleges, six women's polytechnic colleges and three privately-run polytechnic colleges in Rajasthan. All these institutes offer 18 engineering and six non-engineering diploma courses. However, due to lack of vision and absence of proper manpower planning, the majority of these diploma holders are unable to find jobs. The present capacity of all polytechnic colleges is 2,380 students.

In order to provide employment to the new diploma holders, the government polytechnic colleges at Jodhpur and Kota have introduced diploma courses in computer science and engineering. In addition to these, diploma courses in information technology have been started at BITS, Pilani, and the Vidya Bhawan Polytechnic College at Udaipur. The state government does not seem to have any plans to increase the number of polytechnic colleges or even the induction capacity of existing institutions at present.

Industrial Training Institutes

Across Rajasthan, there are 106 Industrial Training Institutes (ITIs) in the government sector and 39 ITIs in the private sector. Their induction capacities are 10,164 and 2,496 students, respectively. The state

4. M.L. Sisodia, *Higher Education: Growth and Future Options*, 2000, University Book House, Jaipur.

government has recently decided to start ITIs at each panchayat samiti headquarters. All these institutions will be set up by private sector agencies. They will offer short-term courses for small-scale industries and handicrafts and run job-oriented training programmes.

However, for a meaningful programme of technical education, proper manpower planning is as necessary as is designing the courses to suit the long-term market conditions. The mismatch between supply and demand must be avoided at all costs.

Problems Confronting Higher Education

It is thus evident that as far as the number of universities and colleges for liberal and professional education is concerned, Rajasthan has achieved the targets set under different Plans and policies. Yet, these institutions are under heavy financial stress because very meagre funds are allocated for setting up or upgrading laboratories and procuring books, all of which are necessary for imparting quality higher education.

Secondly, the curricula for liberal education (in arts, commerce and science) are outdated in most of the state's universities. Unless the pattern of examinations is changed to match the standards already attained by universities in the more advanced states, the graduates of Rajasthan will not be able to compete with their counterparts at all-India level competitive examinations.

Thirdly, the teachers at the state's universities, as also those working in government and private colleges, need to be made more accountable. The system of monitoring their performance in the area of teaching and research warrants streamlining.

Need for a Master Plan for Human Development

Considering all the points mentioned above, it becomes evident that unlike irrigation and infrastructure development, there is no vision for manpower development in Rajasthan. Therefore, it seems desirable to develop a holistic and all-pervasive master plan for, say, the next 20 years, which will include strategies for health, education, drinking water and nutrition and facilitate the achievement of the given targets. In fact, there is no manpower planning at all and the state government has permitted a large number of private educational institutes to impart training in medical sciences, engineering, management, information technology, etc., without estimating the demand for such professional services. A task force needs to be set up to assess the situation in manpower planning and submit its report to the state government at the earliest.

HOUSING AND HOUSING POLICY

The demand for houses in Rajasthan has been rising at an annual rate of 2 per cent. However, apart from meeting this demand, the state needs a policy of upgrading rural houses and improving the living conditions of the weaker sections and slum dwellers in towns and cities.

At the time of the 1991 Census, the number of persons having no house (rented or owned) in Rajasthan was estimated at 1.16 lakh, implying that less than 0.3 per cent of the population had no house at all. In 1991, there were 70.9 lakh residential units across the state, of which the number of urban houses was 16.49 lakh or slightly less than 24 per cent. Of the total 1.16 lakh people without houses, 72.5 per cent were located in rural areas.

The state has no long-term policy for providing houses to people of different categories, though the Rajasthan Housing Board has been constructing houses for households of different income groups in urban areas, and in the rural areas, houses are being built for underprivileged people under the Indira Awas Yojana. It seems the state government is constrained by financial resources, and that the construction of houses in both rural and urban areas via public sector allocation receives very low priority.

District-wise Analysis of Condition of Houses[5]

According to the 1991 Census, the majority of households in the different districts (except in Barmer, Ganganagar, Hanumangarh and Churu) lived either in *pucca* or semi-*pucca* houses. In Barmer, Ganganagar and Hanumangarh, more than 66 per cent households lived in *kachcha* houses, and in Churu, 54.6 per cent households lived in *kachcha* houses. However, even the *pucca* and semi-*pucca* houses in rural areas were generally found to have no direct source of drinking water and no toilets. (Appendix A–15.3)

According to NFHS-2, the status of houses in the rural and urban areas of Rajasthan was as follows:

5. Rajasthan Human Development Report (2002), Planning Department, Government of Rajasthan.

Types of Houses in Rajasthan

(Per cent)

	Urban	*Rural*
Kachcha	8.1	39.1
Semi-*pucca*	16.8	30.5
Pucca	75.1	30.1
Missing	0.0	0.3
Total	**100.0**	**100.0**

Thus, the majority of households in Rajasthan – even those living in rural areas – live in *pucca* and semi-*pucca* houses. It is also evident that even in urban areas, only 25 per cent of the houses are *kachcha* dwelling units.

Housing conditions in Rajasthan generally do not depict congestion. NFHS-2 shows that while the mean number of persons occupying urban houses is 2.6 per room, the corresponding average in rural areas is 3.1. Further, NFHS-2 shows that for 66.4 per cent urban population and 53.1 per cent rural population in Rajasthan, the mean number of persons occupying one room is less than three. In short, houses in both urban and rural Rajasthan are not congested.

But the state still needs a housing policy for the following reasons:

- A quarter of its urban population lives in *kachcha* houses or *kuchchee bastees*, and these people need to be provided houses equipped with basic amenities like toilets.
- Almost 40 per cent of the rural population of Rajasthan lives in *kachcha* houses with walls made of mud and thatched roofs, which make their living hazardous in winter and the rains.
- Most of the people who live in inhuman conditions belong to the scheduled castes, scheduled tribes and other such underprivileged classes. They must get support from the state for improved housing conditions.

Policies for Urban and Rural Housing

A. Urban Housing

The Rajasthan Housing Board (RHB) was formed in 1970 to redress the problem of the rising demand for houses in cities. RHB's main function was to construct houses for people in various income categories. During the last three decades, it has constructed about 1.56 lakh houses. However, only 28.5 per cent and 30.7 per cent of these houses were built for Lower Income Group (LIG) and economically weaker section (EWS) households, respectively. Interestingly, 10.6 per cent of the houses intended for EWS households and 15.2 per cent[6] of the houses intended for LIG households remained unallotted.

The Nirwan Committee clearly stated in its report that "the Rajasthan Housing Board has played a limited role in providing housing for people in various income categories and other economically weaker sections". The committee further stated that the RHB had failed to meet the requirements of the downtrodden and weaker sections of society. The committee urged that the RHB regain the confidence and trust of its clients. It also suggested that the board be converted into a corporation and part of its shares be allotted to private companies.

One complaint that allottees of houses built by the RHB generally have is that the houses are not complete and worth living in, as only basic structures are handed over to them. An allottee is thus required to invest a lot of money prior to occupying the house. Secondly, the instalments that the RHB requires an allottee to pay is not commensurate with his income.

Regularisation of Land Allotted by Cooperative Housing Societies

Over the past four years, the state government has taken numerous steps to regularise the allotment of agricultural land by registered cooperative housing societies to people living in cities. However, those who have encroached on land owned by the government have not been given any relief under this campaign.

Such steps by the government have led to the conferment of ownership rights of residential plots on almost 90,000 citizens across the state. Construction of houses in cities like Kota, Udaipur, Jaipur, Jodhpur and Alwar has received a boost as a result of these initiatives. Besides, the government has also regularised the colonies in which houses were constructed in the last three decades without the approval of the JDA and the UITs of these cities. Residents who had built houses in these colonies as per the rules enforced by the state town planning department got relief after paying the development charges, conversion charges and periphery charges prescribed by the state government for such colonies.

---

6. Even during 2000-01 and 2001-02, the RHB had targets of constructing 2,042 and 5,110 houses, respectively, but could construct only 1,426 (70 per cent) houses.

B. Rural Housing

In rural areas, the state government has formed its policy with a view to upgrading the living conditions of underprivileged households and bridging the gap between demand and supply of houses in villages. Houses are being constructed for people belonging to the weaker sections in rural areas under the Indira Awas Yojana.

Over the last 25 years, until January 2003, a sum of Rs 95 crore has been spent on construction of houses in rural areas under the Indira Awas Yojana. Under the Tenth Five-Year Plan, a sum of Rs 45.10 crore has been allocated to the scheme. The Yojana was started in 1985-86 with a view to providing shelter to the people of weaker sections. It is proposed to construct 64,000 new houses in villages and upgrade another 32,000 in the Tenth Plan period. During the Ninth Plan period, about 78,000 new houses were built under this programme, and 26,787 rural dwellings upgraded. In addition, 64,770 latrines were constructed in rural areas for the use of villagers. The target for rural latrines under the 10th Plan is 60,000.

In the first four years after its inception (1985-89), the progress of houses constructed under the Indira Awas Yojana was rather slow. During the last few years also, especially since 1997-98, the rural houses actually built under this programme have fallen short of targets. Against a target of constructing 1,22,172 houses during 1997-2002 (the ninth Plan period) the number of houses actually built was only 77,082. The progress of upgrading rural houses has also been rather unsatisfactory during the period under review. During 1999-2002, the target was to upgrade 29,772 houses, but only 7,498 houses were upgraded. During 2001-02, it was proposed to build 30,182 houses under the Indira Awas Yojana, but actual achievement that year was 117 per cent of the target.

What is actually required is to provide sanitation, drinking water and other basic amenities in the houses in rural areas. More than 39 per cent houses in the villages of Rajasthan are *kachcha* houses devoid of such facilities. A long-term programme for upgrading these houses needs to be prepared and area-specific priorities determined to make the living conditions of people in the rural areas a little more comfortable. PRIs should be involved in selecting the sites for such houses and allotment of land. As far as possible, the private sector must be encouraged to build houses in villages with support from financial institutions so that the allottees benefit from a long-term repayment schedule. Already, banks and other financial institutions have scaled down interest rates on house construction, so the benefits of such concessions should trickle down to the people of weaker sections as well.

Tenth Five-year Plan

During the Tenth Plan, a sum of Rs 744.8 crore has been allocated for housing in the public sector. Of this amount, Rs 1.90 crore is allotted for LIG houses, Rs. 15.68 crore for middle income groups (MIGs), Rs. 23.76 crore for rental housing and Rs. 18.22 crore for judicial housing. Two important changes are, however, noteworthy. Firstly, under the Pradhan Mantri Gramodaya Yojana (PMGY), a sum of Rs. 65.28 crore has been allocated for village housing. Secondly, more responsibility has been given to PRIs for acquisition and development of suitable land for allotment of plots for house construction.

For the development of urban housing, the RHB has been allotted a sum of Rs 620 crore in the Tenth Plan. To sum up, one can visualise a paradigm shift in the housing strategies of the Rajasthan government during the Tenth Plan. Yet, its housing strategies need a more holistic approach.

APPENDIX A–15.1

Medical Institutions per Lakh of Population in Rajasthan (1997-98)

District	*Number of Medical Institutions*	*Rank*	
		1980	*1998*
Ajmer	20	5	14
Alwar	24	6	11
Banswara	34	5	3
Baran	22	4	4
Barmer	33	7	4
Bharatpur	26	3	10
Bhilwara	29	5	7
Bikaner	23	6	12
Bundi	28	6	8
Chittorgarh	31	4	5
Churu	27	5	9
Dausa	19	5	15
Dholpur	26	3	10
Dungarpur	39	7	2
Ganganagar	27	7	9
Hanumangarh	27	7	9
Jaipur	19	5	15
Jaisalmer	42	1	1
Jalore	31	4	5
Jhalawar	28	3	8
Jhunjhunu	27	4	9
Jodhpur	26	6	10
Karauli	27	6	9
Kota	22	4	13
Nagaur	30	5	6
Pali	34	3	3
Rajsamand	30	5	6
Sawai Madhopur	27	6	9
Sikar	27	5	9
Sirohi	34	2	3
Tonk	31	3	5
Udaipur	30	5	6
Rajasthan	**27**		

APPENDIX A–15.2

District-wise Enrolment in Rajasthan (2000-2001)

(in thousands)

No.	*Name of the District*	*Age Group 6-11 Years*			*Age Group 11-14 Years*		
		Boy	*Girl*	*Total*	*Boy*	*Girl*	*Total*
1.	Churu	183	101	284	57.46	27.28	84.74
2.	Bikaner	120	71	191	34.40	17.65	52.05
3.	Jhunjhunu	201	125	326	69.81	26.37	96.18
4.	Sri Ganganagar	129	86	215	58.17	25.76	83.93
5.	Hanumangarh	99	54	153	43.71	19.52	63.23
6.	Jaipur	368	222	590	223.18	87.52	310.70
7.	Bharatpur	195	143	338	51.10	26.57	77.67
8.	Alwar	261	156	417	113.31	44.72	158.03
9.	Dholpur	92	42	134	19.74	7.12	26.86
10.	Dausa	154	83	237	57.57	22.51	80.08
11.	Sikar	227	119	346	74.97	19.37	94.34
12.	Jodhpur	228	166	394	100.97	43.30	144.27
13.	Pali	177	80	257	50.79	14.90	65.69
14.	Jaisalmer	47	17	64	9.30	3.65	12.95
15.	Jalore	115	39	154	39.20	10.53	49.73
16.	Sirohi	91	39	130	20.23	7.20	27.43
17.	Barmer	163	71	234	44.37	8.49	52.86
18.	Udaipur	203	104	307	61.62	25.46	87.08
19.	Banswara	137	75	212	36.18	14.86	51.04
20.	Dungarpur	113	57	170	26.30	9.13	35.43
21.	Rajsamand	100	43	143	34.40	13.29	47.69
22.	Chittorgarh	150	79	229	42.39	15.42	57.81
23.	Ajmer	212	135	347	72.84	36.51	109.35
24.	Bhilwara	166	62	228	43.28	17.87	61.15
25.	Tonk	121	66	187	37.60	11.43	49.03
26.	Nagaur	233	109	342	68.69	17.44	89.13
27.	Kota	158	115	273	55.95	24.44	80.39
28.	Jhalawar	106	60	166	28.23	10.50	38.73
29.	Sawai Madhopur	100	50	150	43.91	11.25	55.16
30.	Bundi	80	44	124	15.58	5.95	21.53
31.	Bara	100	56	156	28.69	6.70	35.39
32.	Karauli	100	53	153	45.32	13.79	56.11
	Total	**4929**	**2722**	**7651**	**1708.48**	**646.50**	**2354.98**

APPENDIX A–15.3

Household Status in Rajasthan
(As per 1991 Census)

(% of Houses)

S. No.	*District*	*Households in Pucca Houses*	*Households in Semi-Pucca Houses*	*Households in Kachcha Houses*
1.	Ajmer	75.8	9.5	14.7
2.	Alwar	67.7	7.0	25.3
3.	Banswara	20.5	69.2	10.3
4.	Baran	60.4	35.0	4.6
5.	Barmer	16.8	17.1	66.1
6.	Bharatpur	66.2	6.1	27.8
7.	Bhilwara	54.6	32.7	12.7
8.	Bikaner	52.7	3.9	43.4
9.	Bundi	52.2	4.21	5.7
10.	Chittorgarh	47.9	46.3	5.9
11.	Churu	69.6	5.9	54.6
12.	Dausa	70.3	7.2	22.5
13.	Dholpur	63.0	3.7	33.3
14.	Dungarpur	26.6	68.1	5.4
15.	Ganganagar	26.7	4.9	68.5
16.	Hanumangarh	26.7	4.9	68.5
17.	Jaipur	70.3	7.2	22.5
18.	Jaisalmer	32.5	14.3	53.3
19.	Jalore	22.8	54.7	22.5
20.	Jhalawar	41.8	55.1	3.2
21.	Jhunjhunun	83.0	6.1	10.9
22.	Jodhpur	65.1	9.8	25.2
23.	Karauli	62.4	29.3	8.3
24.	Kota	60.4	35.0	4.6
25.	Nagaur	71.4	6.5	22.0
26.	Pali	56.4	34.5	9.2
27.	Rajsamand	58.5	37.3	4.3
28.	Sawai Madhopur	62.4	29.3	8.3
29.	Sikar	81.7	4.6	13.7
30.	Sirohi	46.3	48.2	5.5
31.	Tonk	35.2	39.6	25.3
32.	Udaipur	58.5	37.3	4.3

Source: Rajasthan Human Development Report, 2002, Govt. of Rajasthan.

References

Acharya, S.S. (1998). *Irrigation in Rajasthan; Prospects and Issues*, ACRPU, Planning Commission, Ahmedabad.

Ahluwalia, M.S. (2001). "States Under Reforms: Uneven Growth Momentum," *Survey of Indian Industry*.

Anand Mukesh, Amaresh Bagchi and Tapas K. Sen (2000). "Fiscal Discipline at the State Level: Perverse Incentives and Paths to Reform," *Discussion Paper No.1*, NIPFP, New Delhi, January.

Anant, T.C.A., K.L. Krishna and Uma Datta Roy Choudhary (1999). "Measuring Inter-State Differentials in Infrastructure," *EFC Report*, June, 2000.

Asian Development Bank (2001). *Asian Development Outlook 2000*, Oxford University Press.

Bhusnurmath, Mythili (2002). "Revisiting State Finance," *The Economic Times*, 25 February.

Bokil, Milind (2000). "Drought in Rajasthan," *Economic and Political Weekly*, 25th November.

CMIE (2000). *Report on Profiles of Districts*, October.

Dainik Bhaskar (2001). *Press Report*, December 3.

Department of Tourism (2000). *Tourist Statistics*, Government of India.

———. (1999). *Tourist Statistics*, Government of India.

Directorate of Census Operations (2001). *Distribution of Workers & Non-workers, Paper-3 of 2001*, Jaipur.

———. (2001). *Distribution of Rural-urban Population, Paper-2 of 2001*, Jaipur.

———. (2001). *Provisional Population Totals, Paper-1 of 2001, Series 9*, Jaipur.

———. (1991). *District Census Handbook, Series 21 for all Districts*, Jaipur.

———. (1991). *Provisional Population Totals, Paper-1*, Jaipur.

Ministry of Finance (2000). *Eleventh Finance Commission Report*, June, Government of India.

EPW Research Foundation (2003). *Domestic Product of States of India – 1960-61 to 2000-01*.

Government of Madhya Pradesh (1998). *Human Development Report*.

Government of Rajasthan (1954-55 to 1998-99). Directorate of Economics and Statistics.

———. (2003). *Budget at a Glance: 2002-2003*.

———. (2003). *Economic Review: 2002-03*.

———. (2002). *Vital Agriculture Statistics*, Directorate of Agriculture, Jaipur.

———. (2002). *Economic Review: 2001-02*.

———. (2002). *Rajasthan Human Development Report*, Planning Department.

———. (2002). *Budget at a Glance: 2001-2002*.

———. (2002). *Fifty Years of Agriculture Development in Rajasthan*, Directorate of Agriculture, Jaipur.

———. (2001). *Budget at a Glance: 2000-2001*.

———. (2001). *Annual Plan: 2000-01*, Directorate of Local Bodies, Rajasthan.

———. (2001). *Report of Watershed Development and Soil Conservation Department, Activities and Achievements*.

———. (2001). *Report of PHED*.

———. (2001). *Administrative Reforms Commission*, Volume II, March.

———. (2000). *Draft Master Plan*, Town Planning Department.

———. (2000). *Budget at a Glance: 1999-2000*.

———. (2000). *Statistical Abstract of Rajasthan*, Directorate of Economics & Statistics, Jaipur.

———. (2000). *'Vision 2045' : State Water Resource Plan*, Department of Irrigation.

———. (2000). *Database Management Information*, PHED.

———. (2000). *Some Facts About Rajasthan*, Directorate of Economic & Statistics, Jaipur.

———. (1999). *Budget at a Glance: 1998-1999*.

———. (1999). *Annual Survey of Industries: 1998-99*, Volume I.

———. (1999). *The White Paper on the Status of Economy of Rajasthan*, Jaipur.

———. (1998). *Budget at a Glance: 1997-1998*.

———. (1998). *Rajasthan Forest Statistics*, Forest Department.

———. (1998). *Water Resources Planning for the State of Rajasthan*, Tahal & WAPCOS.

———. (1998). *Public Enterprise Profile: 1997-98*, Bureau of Public Enterprise, State Enterprise Department, Jaipur.

———. (1997). *Annual Progress Report*, Directorate of Local Bodies, Jaipur.

———. (1997). *Ninth Five Year Plan: 1997-02*, Planning Department, Jaipur.

———. (1997). *PAHAL: Phase II Reference Document*, PAHAL, Dungarpur.

———. (1994). *Resource Atlas of Rajasthan*, Department of Science & Technology.

———. (1985). *Draft Master Plan*, Town Planning Department.

———. *Various Reports*, Directorate of Horticulture.

———. *Five Year Plans of Rajasthan: First to Ninth Plan*, Planning Department.

———. *Raj Darpan* (http/www.rajgovt.org/itwork/mineral policy.htm).

Gupta, L.C. and Vinod K. Sharma, *Drought in Rajasthan: 2000-01*, IDS, Jaipur.

———. *Drought in Rajasthan: 1999-2000*, IDS, Jaipur.

Hemlata Joshi (2003). *Educational Development Index – Rajasthan*, Institute of Development Studies, Jaipur.

Hindu (2001). *Survey of Indian Industry*.

IBM, *Indian Minerals Year Book, 1999*.

———. *Indian Minerals Year Book, 1998*.

———. (1997) Report No. 409, March.

International Institute of Population Sciences, *National Family Health Survey–II* 1998-99, Mumbai.

Kavoori S. Purnendu (1999). *Pastoralism in Expansion: The Trashuming Herders of Western Rajasthan*, Oxford University Press, New Delhi.

Kirti S. Parikh (2000). *India Development Report 1999-2000*, IGIDR, Mumbai.

Kothari Devendra (2002). *Population Projections for Rajasthan and Districts – 2002-2011*, IIHMR, Jaipur.

Kurian, N.J. (1999). "State Government Finances – A Survey of Recent Trends," *Economic and Political Weekly*, May 8, 1999.

Malhotra S.P. (1983). *Socio Economic Structure of Population in Western Rajasthan*, ICAR/CZARI, Jodhpur.

NSSO (2001). *Employment and Unemployment in India 1999-2000*, 55th Round (July1999-June 2000) Report No. 458, May (Part I).

Nigam, G.K. (2000). "Shiksha Darpan," *Lok Jumbish*, Jaipur.

Planning Commission of India, (2003). *Successful Governance Initiatives & Best Practices*, Academic Foundation, New Delhi.

———. (2002). *National Human Development Report*, New Delhi.

———. (1998). "Agro-climatic Regional Planning – Recent Development ARPU", *Working Paper No. 10*, New Delhi.

———. (1997). *Report of the 25 Years Perspective Plan for the Development of Rainfed Areas*, New Delhi.

Rajasthan Chamber of Commerce & Industry (2002). quoted from *Hindustan Times*, Jaipur Live, March 8.

Rangarajan, C. (2001). "Saga of Paradigm Shifts," in *Survey of Indian Industry*.

Registrar General of India (1999). *Sample Registration Bulletin*, No. I Vol. 33, April.

———. (1998). *Child Mortality Estimates of India*, Occasional Paper No. 5, Demographic Division.

———. (1997). *Sample Registration Bulletin*, No. I Volume 31, January.

———. (1997). *District Level Estimates of Fertility and Child Mortality for 1991 and their Inter-relationship with Other Variables*, Occasional Paper No. 1 of 1997.

———. (1995). *Sample Registration System Statistical Report*.

———. (1995). *SRS Based Abridged Life Tables 1988-92*, Occasional Paper No. 4.

———. (1995). *Sample Registration Bulletin*, No. I Volume 31, January.

———. (1994). *Medical Certifications of Cause of Death*, Ministry of Home Affairs, New Delhi.

———. (1994). *Indirect Estimates of Fertility and Mortality at the District Level 1981*, Occasional Paper No. 4.

———. (1993). *Medical Certifications of Cause of Death*, Ministry of Home Affairs, New Delhi.

———. (1992). *Medical Certifications of Cause of Death*, Ministry of Home Affairs, New Delhi.

Reserve Bank of India (1998). *Reports on Currency & Finance*.

———. (2000). *Report of Development Banking in India*.

Srivastava, D.K. and Tapas K. Sen (1997). *Government Subsidies in India*, NIPEP, New Delhi.

Sisodia, M.L. (2000). *Higher Education: Growth and Future Options*, University Books House, Jaipur.

UNDP (2001). *Human Development Report, 2001*, Oxford University Press, New York.

Wali, M.M.K. (2001). *Decentralised Planning – Proposed Plan of Action*.

World Bank (2001). *World Development Report – 2000-2001 – Attacking Poverty*.